D1106457

BEATING THE ODDS

To Mannie Hess,
To a very
Special lady who has given
much to Alberta. Regards,
Fondest Regards,
[signature]

© 1998 by Loram Corporation
All rights reserved. Published 1998
Printed in Canada

No part of this book, including any text, illustration or cover design,
may be reproduced or transmitted in any form, by any means
(electronic, photocopying, recording or otherwise) without the prior
written permission from Loram Corporation.

BEATING THE ODDS

A History of the Mannix Family in Business

1898 – 1998

Loram Corporation
Calgary, Alberta

December 1998

This book chronicles the achievements of the many wonderful and talented people with whom we have had the privilege to be associated and who contributed to the success of "the outfit." It has been commissioned with the greatest respect and appreciation for the many different opportunities and challenges of business and life presented to our family, employees, associates and customers during the last century.

We have faith in the future and in the people who live, love, learn and are leaving a legacy in this great experiment and country called Canada. We believe that as a nation we are providing a good example of peaceful coexistence, entrepreneurial spirit and freedom. We have hope for the future, as we try in our own individual ways to apply the principles, values and lessons learned from the past. By publishing our story, it is our intention to give to our family and community a perspective of the history of Canada and our business enterprise, which helped build our country and a few other parts of the world.

We wish to recognize and thank most sincerely the thousands of exceptional people who have contributed their efforts to building the different businesses with which we are or have been associated. We also want to thank the hundreds of devoted people who helped preserve our history by very generously sharing their recollections of earlier days. In many cases they also contributed pieces of memorabilia that, together with official company records and outside sources, made it possible for us to capture the spirit of our endeavours. We hope that within these pages you will learn about the incredibly fortunate, exciting, interesting and unique past that we share and that you will recognize your own family history within the context of our nation's growth and worldwide development.

We appreciate just how fortunate we have been and will try never to take for granted the numerous blessings provided by our Maker. Please enjoy reviewing this book and learning about the 100 years of the Mannix family business enterprise. We wish every reader good luck and may God bless you as He has our family, our associates and our land.

Sincerely,

F.P. Mannix   M.G. Eberts   R.N. Mannix

Loram
COMPANIES

Table of Contents

PROLOGUE: CHOOSING OUR DESTINY i

CHOOSING OUR DESTINY

What has been must go.

What has gone will rise again....

Get ready to live.

— Gustav Mahler, Austrian composer and conductor

There is an evolutionary flow to history. One stage builds on another; each creates precedence for the next. Yet change does not always evolve as a smooth continuum. History has shown us several periods characterized by sharp breaks with the past and entirely new sets of realities and demands. For the survivor, historical breaks require a leap from the conventional into the untried. The entrepreneur realizes that while one can do a good many things with an informed sense of history, one cannot usefully deny that the past is just that — gone. True leaders realize that what may have been premises for success in the past may not be viable for the future.

Private ownership is a hallmark of a free society. Private, personal ownership of an enterprise is the most resolute expression of freedom and responsibility a person can make. More than 85 per cent of the companies in the world — including one-third of Fortune 500 companies — are either owned or controlled by a family. Two-thirds of the jobs in the world are created by family-owned companies. Yet for all its strengths, a family business is not unlike a bumblebee. Some years ago a group of scientists studied the bumblebee and concluded that, according to all known principles of aerodynamics, it could not possibly fly. Seven out of ten family businesses crash shortly after takeoff and do not survive transfer to the second generation; only one in ten will make it to the third. To build a large successful business is an equally rare phenomenon; less than one per cent of all businesses employ more than 500 people.

For a family business to successfully survive successive generations, it must have a driving central belief. This vision is partly a product of the family's environment and upbringing. If one follows the path woven by the Mannix family for over a century, from the Old World to the New, from one generation to the next, from one business to the next, one will see how the Mannixes are not only survivors and entrepreneurs, but leaders. Throughout famine, wars, world financial crises and periods of great epochal change, they remain true to a belief that is as fundamental to their core as breathing. For the Mannixes, that driving central belief is that the past is not something to cling to, but a springboard into the future. They are not, nor have they ever been, afraid. Passionate people who care greatly about the fate of their lives and the lives of others, they seize opportunities for change. The test of a century has proven that they are in the business of business.

As with all family companies, it is difficult to know where the family starts and where the business ends, but this is not a business history. It is not a history of a construction company, or a coal company, or an energy company, or a railway maintenance company, although it speaks to all these things. It is a story about human beings, about gambling on the unknown, about beating the odds. It is a history of survivors, of entrepreneurs, of leaders, of the literally thousands of individuals who helped the Mannixes build their family business.

History is something that happens while ordinary people go about their daily lives; all great historical events carry within them a multitude of human destinies. It obviously was not easy in the "good old days." For that matter, it is not easy now. Only a fool would claim that throughout history, security and tranquillity were ever guaranteed. Yet throughout the ages, like a pebble thrown upon the water, the actions of a single human who chooses his own destiny can ripple through time.

THE MATERIAL
CALLED MAN

1845 – 1862

Ireland is not a manufacturing nation, says the political economist. Indeed, my good sir,
you are wholly mistaken. She is not only a manufacturing nation, but she manufactures nations.

There is no nation under the sun which manufactures
the material called man so readily as does that grass-covered island.
— William Francis Butler, Irish soldier-adventurer

Left: Irish countryside.

Ireland is a land of triumphs and tragedies, of passions and brilliant hues. The Irish culture is fervent, the Gaelic language rolls freely and poetically off the tongue, and the land is enchanting. Centuries-old stone walls grace the landscape. Verdant fields shimmer with more than 40 shades of green. The piping of bagpipes can be heard wafting over the mist. Above all is the dominating presence of the sea — crashing at the base of the towering Cliffs of Moher, meeting the mighty Shannon River, or washing amongst the boulders along the Kerry shore. Throughout the centuries she has eaten into Ireland's coastline, shaping it into wild and beautiful headlands.

Irish history is as epic as the isle itself. It is a saga full of tales of heroes and villains, of wise men and fools, of God and superstition, of poverty and greed, of love and hate. It is said that in Ireland there is no future, only the past happening over and over again. It is also said that Ireland's most valuable export is not fine wool or linen, but a material far richer than any cloth — the material called man. The history of the Loram Companies begins with one of them.

Right: The Cliffs of Moher, County Claire.

"And that was the beginning of the great trouble and famine that destroyed Ireland."

George Charles Mannix was born May 12, 1845, at County Cork, Ireland. That summer the fungus *Phytophthora infestans* struck Ireland causing potato blight. Since the beginning of the 18th century when the two main sources of food were pastoral products and grain, the potato had been the mainstay of the diet of at least one-third of the population. The loss of the potato crop caused mass starvation on a scale not witnessed in Western Europe in more than 100 years. Repeated failures of the crop led to the deaths of one million people in the five years after the first blight and two million more fled the country in the following 10 years. The Great Famine caused a startling redistribution of Ireland's population. Ireland's highest recorded population was 8,175,000 in 1841. A decade later, there were scarcely six and a half million people left on the island. Nearly a million fled to the United States, three-quarters of a million emigrated to Britain, a quarter million went to Canada (then known as British North America) and about 70,000 sailed to the Australian colonies.

"The discovery of the potato blight in Ireland." A painting by Daniel McDonald.

The Great Famine was a watershed in Irish history and the last major European famine. The whole face of the country changed. On June 29, 1846, *The Times* reported, "from the Giant's Causeway to Cape Clear, from Limerick to Dublin, not a green field is to be seen." Violent thunderstorms occurred and lightning played over the blackened fields. Torrential rain fell. An extraordinary dense fog descended over blighted areas, cold and damp without any wind. It was, declared *The Times* on September 2, "total annihilation." At this moment of suffering, unprecedented weather added greatly to the misery of the people. The climate of Ireland is famous for its mildness; years pass without a fall of snow. Yet in 1846, at the end of October, it became cold, and in early November snow began to fall. Frost was continuous. Icy gales blew snow, hail and sleet. Roads were impassable and transport was brought to a standstill. It was as if Nature herself had become an enemy.

Unable to pay their rents, more than half a million Irish men, women and children were evicted from their cottages. Thousands starved to death by their cabins or crawled into towns, seeking shelter in the government poorhouses, which were soon overflowing with the dead and dying. Others wandered about, looking for food or work, spreading typhus and cholera throughout the land. By the middle of 1847, one-third of the population of County Cork consisted of people who had fled from other parts of the country since the previous October, individuals described as "shadows and spectres, the impersonation of disease and famine." One priest lamented that during the period of the Great Famine, 1845 to 1850, "the angel of death and desolation reigned supreme in Ireland."

1837 ▶

Map prepared by Canada's premier map maker, J. Arrowsmith, showing British, American and Russian claims to North America.

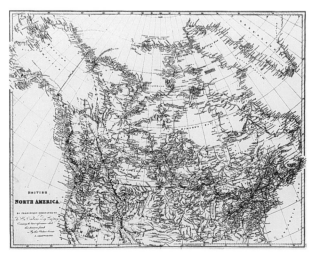

1845 ▶

Sir John Franklin and crew sail from England in search of the Northwest Passage. They disappear.

On a very real, human level, it is impossible to grasp a tragedy that wiped out one million people in half a decade. Fortunately, the Irish have a long tradition of, and infinite respect for, the oral tradition. The following are the words of the men and women who grew up surrounded by the physical and psychological legacy of the Famine; their voices echo the memories and images passed on to them. One hundred and fifty years is just a blink of an eye in a country like Ireland, and things echo for a long, long time.

"A mist rose out of the sea, and you could hear a voice talking near a mile off across the stillness of the earth. It was the same for three days or more, and then when the fog lifted, you could begin to see the tops of the potato stalks lying over as if the life was gone out of them. And that was the beginning of the great trouble and famine that destroyed Ireland." — Unnamed farmer.

"Next morning when they awoke and went out, to their consternation their lovely potato plants, which were in such bloom and showed such a promise of beautiful crops the day before, were all covered over with black spots and the leaves and stalks hanging down as if dead. The potato blight had appeared for the first time in Ireland. The awful smell and stench of the blight was everywhere." — P. Foley, a farmer of Knockananna, County Wicklow.

Ballinskelligs, County Kerry. Sunrise over the ruins of St. Michael's Abbey.

"The Parish Priest, Fr. Kenny, who died in 1896 aged close to ninety years and who had charge of the parish long before the Famine, told me that on a certain Saturday on his way to church to hear confessions he anointed nineteen on the roadside dying of starvation. On another occasion he pointed out to me a spot on the road just outside the church gate where he found a poor man sitting one Sunday morning. The man had a small loaf clutched in his hand and was making attempts to raise it to his mouth. He was so weakened from hunger and exhaustion that he had not sufficient strength to lift the bread to his mouth. Then he used to bend his head down, holding the loaf between his knees, to try and get a bite in that way, but the result was that he simply toppled over. The priest then anointed him and he died there tearing the dough with his nails." — Pádraig Sabhaois, Moycullen, County Galway.

"There were so many deaths that they opened big trenches through the graveyards and when they were full of dead they filled them in. No one was allowed into the graveyards except the men hired to cover the graves. Two guards were always on to keep the people out and there were many rows with people trying to get in. They dug graves twelve foot deep and put seven or eight bodies into each grave. They never put coffins on them at all." — John Doyle, Craffle, Ballyteigue, Aughrim, County Wicklow.

1847 ▶

Irish emigrants travel to the New World in makeshift accommodations in the holds of cargo vessels and mostly unregulated passenger ships.

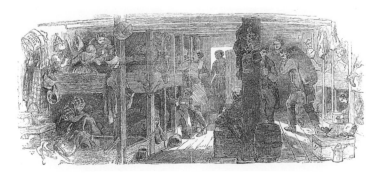

1848 ▶

Contrasted with the cramped confines of emigrant ships, Aboriginal Peoples of the Pacific Coast live in established communities and comparative luxury.

where some turf was still smouldering on the hearth, brought them out on a shovel and placed them among the thatch of the roof. In a few moments it was ablaze, fanned by a strong south-westerly breeze and in a short time his home was gone. His neighbours were so amazed that they could say nothing, and they made no effort to prevent him when he climbed onto the roof, scooped out a hole, and in a short time had reduced what was once the home of himself, his father and grandfather, to nothing but a few fire-scarred walls. When the landlord tendered Diver the money he had thus so strangely earned, he coolly put it in his pocket, turned on his heel, nodded to the neighbours and disappeared from the scene."
— Michael Gildea, Dromore, Ballintra, County Donegal.

Left: An early morning mist enshrouds the ruins of Hore Abbey.

Below: This 1859 photograph by William England shows the quay at Cork, Ireland. It is likely that George Charles and Henry Arthur Mannix embarked from this quay in 1862.

"Nothing but a few fire-scarred walls"

It is impossible to be certain about how many people were evicted during the years of the Famine and its aftermath. The police, who began keeping an official tally in 1849, recorded a total of nearly 250,000 people as formally and permanently evicted from their holdings between 1849 and 1854, a figure which is considered to be an under-estimate of the harsh reality. If one were to guess at the equivalent number for 1846 to 1848 and to include the countless thousands pressured into involuntary surrenders during the whole period (1846 to 1854), the resulting figure would probably exceed half a million people.

"The usual procedure after an eviction was to burn the thatched roof to prevent the tenant from entering the house again after the bailiff and his assistants had left the scene. A man named Diver who lived in this townland was among those who were evicted out of their homes. The landlord himself was present on this occasion and he offered the sum of one pound to anybody who would set fire to the house. Diver, who was standing out on the street with a number of neighbours, stepped forward and said he would earn the money. He thereupon stepped into the kitchen

1849 ▶

British North America in 1849. The Province of Canada is formed by uniting Upper and Lower Canada (1840). The international boundary to the Pacific Ocean is settled by the Oregon Treaty (1846). The British government leases Vancouver Island to the Hudson's Bay Company to form a colony.

British
American
Danish
Russian

"If crosses and tombs could be erected on the water"

Getting out of famine-stricken Ireland was a matter of life or death for many of those who emigrated and the scale of that flight was unprecedented in the history of international migration. Emigration during the early 1840s was 50,000 to 100,000 people a year. Between 1846 and 1850, about a million people left the country and emigration was still greater over the following five years. The majority of pre-Famine emigrants settled in Britain, although increasing numbers chose the more expensive and dangerous option of the New World. The subsequent redirection of most emigration from Britain to North America was largely an accident of timing. A serious recession between 1847 and 1851 made Britain unattractive as a place of settlement. The Australian colonies were also in economic crisis, and did not regain their popularity until the discovery of gold in 1850.

"The depopulation of this district during 1845-1855 or so, according to what I can gather, is almost unbelievable. The depopulation was caused far more by emigration than by deaths caused by hunger, although hunger took its toll in every district here, and indeed in every townland. I was told that most people who could muster sufficient money to pay the passage to America went, father, mother, children, young and old. All sailed from Sligo and the voyage, I was told, took sixteen weeks. One voyage to Quebec was given to me very accurately in one instance as sixteen weeks and three days." — Unnamed, Dromore West, County Sligo.

In the absence of extensive assistance from either public or philanthropic sources, the removal of more than two million people in a decade, from an impoverished country, represents a miracle of private ingenuity and determination. But for those lucky enough to escape by emigrating, the horrors of an Atlantic crossing lay ahead. The Famine exodus placed unprecedented pressure on the rickety and under-regulated passenger trade. Many steerage passengers endured dangerous conditions on crudely converted cargo vessels. Sailing ships, some of which came to be known as coffin ships, often put to sea without adequate water, provisions, medical assistance or cooking or sanitary facilities. During the year of Black '47, mortality rates of Irish travelling on coffin ships were as high as 40 per cent.

A LEGACY OF BUILDERS

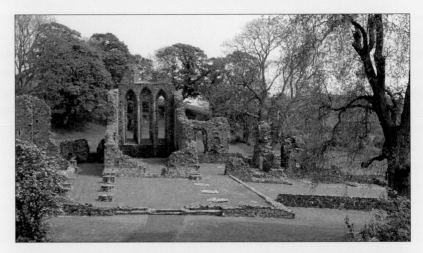

Mannix family genealogies claim two distant ancestors — John de Courcy and Cormac McCarthy. In 1166, John de Courcy, a Norman invader, conquered Ulster, located in what is now Northern Ireland. To strengthen his hold on the territory, de Courcy erected huge fortifications, improved prehistoric hilltop raths and built numerous abbeys. In 1185, de Courcy was appointed justiciar of Ireland. He was later deposed when he refused to submit to the authority of King John.

Cormac McCarthy, the Baron of Blarney, constructed Blarney Castle in 1446. Kissing a stone within the walls of the castle is said to give one the gift of eloquence.

Above: Inch Abbey, County Down, built by John de Courcy.

Left: Blarney Castle, County Cork, built by Cormac McCarthy.

◀ 1853

This famous painting by Frederic Remington shows Radisson (standing) and Groseilliers canoeing north in search of the "Bay of the North" in the 1600s. Two hundred years later, canoes are still used to explore and settle the land that becomes Canada.

◀ 1855

First train crosses Niagara suspension bridge linking the Great Western with American railways.

An emigrant ship battles the North Atlantic during its voyage to the New World.

Conditions in steerage were atrocious. Passengers remained on deck as much as possible, but when the fierce North Atlantic gales struck, immense spume-swept waves forced them back into steerage. Sometimes, as they lay listening to the howling wind, feeling their fragile vessel reverberate with each crashing wave, watching in horror as the planks gave way to the torrent of the onrushing sea, their quest for a new life ended in a watery grave.

Of the more than 100,000 emigrants who sailed for British North America in 1847, it is estimated that 8,000 were buried at sea. Crossing the Atlantic exacted such a fearful toll that one of the commissioners for emigration wrote, "If crosses and tombs could be erected on the water, the whole route of the emigrant vessels from Europe to America would long since have assumed the appearance of a crowded cemetery."

"MY WISH"
by William McCarthy Mannix

Peace and content — a pig a cow

My wishes humble — cottage low

My garden stocked with apple trees

And in it placed a hive of bees

A little man to use the spade

To milk my cow a little maid

Some ducks and chickens hens & cock

And on my wall a cuckoo-clock

A spring of water sparkling clear

And just a thousand pounds a year!

"Bandy Legs"
George Charles Mannix as drawn
by his father, William McCarthy Mannix.

"Buoyancy and cheerfulness, and hope"

Every Irish emigrant's story is unique and intensely personal. Each emigrant is a citizen of two nations, torn between the opportunities of the New World and their memories of the Old. In the Irish, or Gaelic, language, the act of leaving Ireland was most often described by the word *deorai*. Deorai translates into English not as "emigration" but as "exile." These sentiments inspired many tragic songs, perhaps the most famous of which is *Old Skibbereen*. Skibbereen, which had always been a great potato-growing district, was a town in County Cork.

> *Oh, father dear, I oftentimes hear you speak*
> *of Erin's isles,*
> *Her lofty scenes, her valley green, her*
> *mountains rude and wild.*
> *They say it is a princely place wherein*
> *a king might dwell.*
> *So why did you abandon it, the reason*
> *to me tell.*
>
> *Oh son, I loved my native land with*
> *energy and pride,*
> *Until a blight came on the crops, the sheep*
> *and the cattle died,*
> *The rent and taxes were to pay, I could*
> *not them redeem,*
> *And that's the cruel reason why I left old*
> *Skibbereen.*

Few contemporaries imagined that the expatriate population would continue to grow after the Great Famine. However, there was a widespread recognition that emigration was becoming an expected and even a desired episode in the Irish life cycle.

1857 ▶

December 31, Queen Victoria chooses Ottawa as the capital of the new Province of Canada.

1858 ▶

The first successful oil well in North America is hand-dug at Oil Springs, Ontario. Successful well drilling follows in the 1860s.

The transition from a panic-driven expulsion to a calculated pursuit of economic improvement began as emigrants wrote home reporting their success in finding opportunities overseas. Neither Irish poverty nor North American opportunity was alone sufficient to stimulate mass migration across the Atlantic Ocean, however. The most important reasons for post-Famine emigration were changes within Ireland — the commercialization of agriculture, the decline of rural industry and the Anglicization of Irish cultures. Given the changes in Ireland's economy and social structure, and given the consequent dearth of available land and employment, from a purely economic standpoint, it became natural for young people to emigrate.

Most prominent among these consciously voluntary emigrants were Irish Protestants and Anglicized Catholics, particularly those of upper- and middle-class status. These were people who had never been, or were no longer, bound to the traditional, communalistic constraints of Gaelic culture. In outlook, such emigrants were modern, often entrepreneurial, imbued with the spirit of improvement and acquisitive individualism. Reflecting such positive attitudes, contemporary ballads often described emigration as opportunity, not exile. One County Cork clergyman, Patrick Sheehan, lamented that many embarking Irish no longer displayed "sad weeping and melancholy farewell, but buoyancy and cheerfulness, and hope," while "the crowds on the shore look with envy at the more fortunate friends who are escaping."

Descendants of these Irish immigrants helped define the word "Canadian." They brought to bear on Canadian life many values that were Irish in origin. Education, law and politics all felt the impact of the Irish mind. Well-known pioneering Irish in Canada include Edward Blake, Guy Carleton, John Joseph Lynch, D'Alton McCarthy, Thomas D'Arcy McGee and Eugene O'Keefe.

Another Irish immigrant whose legacy would indelibly mark the Canadian landscape was George Charles Mannix. In 1862, at the age of 17, George Charles left the isle of his birth. Accompanied by his older brother, Henry Arthur, he set sail across the thundering Atlantic that had surrounded him all his life. On such beginnings — one man's spirit lifting him above seemingly insurmountable challenges and leading him into the unknown — hangs the future of the world.

McCarthy-Mannix Heritage

In the 1800s, William Mannix married Sarah Barter. They had one daughter, Elizabeth, who married William Justin McCarthy of Batview, County Cork. Elizabeth and William had three sons: William, Thomas and Allan. About 1849, it is believed that William and Elizabeth McCarthy were killed in an accident involving a cart and a runaway horse. The fates of two of their sons, Thomas and Allan, are unknown. William was adopted by Elizabeth's cousin and his wife, Thomas and Charlotte Mannix. Thomas and Charlotte, who were childless, wished William to take their name, Mannix, also William's mother's maiden name. Thereafter he was known as William McCarthy Mannix.

William McCarthy Mannix married Mary Eleanor King Hamilton-Rowan. They had seven children, three boys and four girls. All three sons — William Henry, Henry Arthur and George Charles Mannix — emigrated to Canada. William and Mary's youngest daughter, Henrietta, died in Ireland in 1850 at the age of 10. The two oldest daughters, Emma and Adelaide de Courcey, lived in Ireland until their deaths at age 62 and 81, respectively. Charlotte Elizabeth, the fourth daughter, emigrated to Australia where she died in 1917 at the age of 79.

Top: William McCarthy Mannix.

Above: Mary Eleanor King Hamilton-Rowan, wife of William McCarthy Mannix.

1858 ▶

Canadian government sends Henry Hind and S.J. Dawson to explore the West and North-West. Travelling by canoe and foot, they are to report on conditions for settlement and search for a feasible east to west transport route that does not enter the United States.

1862 ▶

Lighthouse on cliffs at Baltimore, County Cork. Possibly the last view of Ireland seen by George Charles and Henry Arthur Mannix as, together, they sail to North America.

THE JOLLY BOYS
AND THE GREAT LONE LAND

1863 – 1880

There is no other portion of the globe in which travel is possible where loneliness
can be said to live so thoroughly. One may wander 500 miles in a direct line
without seeing a human being, or an animal larger than a wolf.

If vastness of plain, and magnitude of lake, mountain, and river can mark
a land as great, then no region possesses higher claims to that distinction.

— William Francis Butler, *The Great Lone Land*

Left: Members of the Red River Expeditionary Force begin a portage en route to Fort Garry.

After months at sea, George Charles and Henry Arthur Mannix reached British North America where they were joined by their eldest brother, William Henry, who also emigrated from Ireland. Regulations required that all ships with passengers coming up the St. Lawrence River stop at the quarantine station on Grosse Île, located downstream from Quebec. A beautiful little island, Grosse Île's coastline is enhanced by tiny, rocky bays. In the interior, large trees grow from green turf and there exists a remarkable variety of wild flowers. Trees and shrubs grow down to the water's edge where they are mirrored in the St. Lawrence, so that the island seems to float. The quarantine buildings are low and white and do not detract from the beauty of the landscape. On the rising ground above them, a small white church nestles in green trees. "A fairy scene," exclaimed one emigrant as he first caught sight of the island, "exquisite glades, groves, wild flowers and glimpses of the St. Lawrence."

Right: Quarantine station at Grosse Île.

Thousands of emigrants entered British North America via Grosse Île; thousands died there. In one of the most beautiful of the miniature valleys of the island, once the site of the emigrant cemetery, a monument commemorates those who crossed the Atlantic, only to perish upon reaching shore. The inscription reads:

In this secluded spot lie the mortal remains
of 5,294 persons, who, flying from pestilence
and famine in Ireland in 1847,
found in America but a grave.

Among those believed to have died on Grosse Île was the wife of John Ford, a small farmer from County Cork. John Ford escaped fever and went on, by one of the customary emigrant routes, through the Great Lakes to Detroit, where he carved himself a farm out of the wilderness. He was the grandfather of Henry Ford — inventor and maker of the Ford motor car, and founder of the automobile industry. George Charles Mannix, also from County Cork, chose to stay and make his home in British North America, settling in Bury, Quebec. He was the grandfather of Frederick Charles Mannix — a man of exceptional talent and vision, and one of the great builders of modern Canada.

The Fenian Raids

For several years George Charles Mannix lived peacefully, working as a farmer. But troublesome times prevailed and George, along with his brothers Henry Arthur and William Henry, elected to play a crucial role in the early development of Canada. They answered their first call to arms in 1866, helping to defend their new country against invading Fenians.

Desperate charge of Fenian rebels near Ridgeway Station, 1866.

Fenians were members of a movement initiated in 1857 by Irish-Americans to secure Irish independence from Britain. Its titular chief, James Stephens, organized an underground movement in Ireland with the aid of funds collected by his American deputy, John O'Mahony. At the end of 1865, the Fenians had nearly $500,000 and about 10,000 American Civil War veterans organized in military clubs. At this time they split into two factions, one led by O'Mahony, favouring an uprising in Ireland, and another led by William Roberts, intent on British North America. When it became obvious that there was to be no immediate uprising in Ireland, O'Mahony launched a raid against the New Brunswick frontier in April 1866. The raid collapsed; its only lasting consequence was to turn opinion in the Maritimes in favour of Confederation. The Roberts wing crossed the Niagara frontier on June 1, defeating Canadian

1863

Rugged fur traders continue to penetrate Western Canada. They trade with Aboriginal Peoples and provide transportation for settlers and supplies.

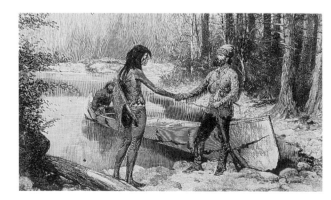

militiamen at Ridgeway, and withdrew. A second group crossed the Quebec frontier at Baie Mississquoi on June 7, and remained 48 hours. Active fighting ensued at many points and George Charles, William Henry and Henry Arthur joined the volunteer forces that repelled the invaders.

The Drive Toward Continentalism

Fenians added a page to Irish folklore and helped to unite Canadians by providing an external threat during the period of Confederation. A little more than a year later, on July 1, 1867, the British North America Act united the Province of Canada (divided into Ontario and Quebec) with Nova Scotia and New Brunswick to form "One Dominion under the Name of Canada." One of the dominant creative minds that produced the British North America Act was Sir John A. Macdonald. Macdonald, a lawyer who had emigrated from Scotland with his parents at the age of five, was named Canada's first prime minister. A shrewd and ingenious politician who had great faith in the future of the Dominion, he championed the new nation's expansion from sea to sea, proclaiming: "One people, great in territory, great in resources, great in enterprise, great in credit, great in capital."

The British North America Act was only the first stage in the building of the new nation. The far greater task of territorial expansion lay ahead. There are many theories concerning the origin of the name Canada, but the most popular one comes from Jesuit Pierre-François-Xavier de Charlevoix, the great early historian of New France. He says the name Canada is derived from the word "kanata," a Huron-Iroquois term meaning village or settlement. It is a fitting choice, as these first "Canadians" in the new sense of the word — citizens no longer of disjointed colonies, but of a potential nation — were a very small village, totalling only three million people. The two central provinces, Ontario and Quebec, made up the great majority of this total, while residents of Nova Scotia and New Brunswick numbered less than a fifth of the whole.

Beyond the restricted boundaries of the Dominion stretched the immense, vulnerable and largely uninhabited rest of British North America. In the East were Newfoundland and Prince Edward Island. Newfoundland had fewer than 150,000 settlers, and Prince Edward Island, with a population of approximately 94,000, was less populated than Montreal, Canada's largest city. The colony of British Columbia, which was separated from Canada by Rupert's Land and the North-West Territories, had a non-Indian population of about 10,000. The Red River community at the junction of the Red and Assiniboine rivers numbered slightly fewer than 12,000 inhabitants, mostly mixed bloods.

Welcome address to returning volunteers from the Fenian Raids, Montreal, 1866.

1864 ▶

Architects of Confederation include, from left to right, Sir George-Étienne Cartier, George Brown, Sir John A. Macdonald and Thomas D'Arcy McGee.

Canada's drive toward continentalism was strengthened by two external forces: Great Britain and the United States. Since 1861, Great Britain had been moving toward honourable withdrawal from British North America. Eager to recall her isolated military garrisons and escape her remaining territorial obligation in North America — the ultimate responsibility for the future of the Hudson's Bay Company lands — she wholeheartedly supported Canada's expansion. If Canada acquired Rupert's Land and the North-West Territories, England would be relieved of an unwanted burden. If Canada remained a fragment of a disunited British North America, she would be vulnerable. Only by acquiring all remaining British territory and reaching her continental limits, would she have the best chance to survive.

Even as Great Britain was encouraging Canada to hasten her national expansion, a predatory and resentful United States was nipping at her borders. In the mid-19th century, the United States regarded their expansion to the Pacific as their manifest destiny — an inevitable and ostensibly benevolent policy of imperialistic expansion. Following the end of the American Civil War in 1865, the triumphant republic used its resentment of the sympathy that both the British and the colonials had shown the Southern cause as an excuse to further expand its territory. The American government demanded reparations for the losses inflicted by the Alabama (a Southern blockade runner built in a British shipyard) on American shipping during the war, going so far as to suggest that the whole of Rupert's Land and the North-West Territories be ceded to the United States in satisfaction of the Alabama claims. Two years later, the United States purchased Alaska from Russia, effectively

View of Quebec City, mid-1800s.

surrounding Canadian territory on the Pacific Ocean and sparking a smouldering territorial dispute. Not long after, in 1869, Ulysses S. Grant, commanding general of the Union Army in the Civil War, was elected president of the United States. It was no secret that Grant was an expansionist prepared to use almost any method to acquire all or part of British North America. Newspaper articles such as the following only served to further inflame concerns of American intervention:

1865 ▶

The U.S. Civil War ends. Slavery is abolished throughout North America.

1865 ▶

Transportation in pre-Canadian Pacific Railway British Columbia. The Cariboo Road, 18 feet (six metres) wide and almost 400 miles (645 kilometres) long, connects the interior gold fields with Fort Yale on the Fraser River.

That the U.S. are bound finally to absorb all the world and the rest of mankind, every well-regulated American mind is prepared to admit. When fever is on our people do not seem to know when and where to stop, but keep on swallowing, so long as there is anything to reach. To use a popular Californianism, we 'go for everything that is in sight.' — The Daily Alta California of San Francisco, February 3, 1869.

In the East, where there were established colonies, the danger of American intervention was less of a threat, but as long as Nova Scotia was dissatisfied and Newfoundland remained outside the Dominion, there was still a danger. The likelihood of American intervention was greater in the West where Americans were casting covetous glances upon a vast and almost empty territory that seemed as if it might be theirs for the taking — American settlers had already taken the territories of Oregon and Washington from the British. Obviously, if Canada wanted to protect what she saw as her territorial rights, the new government had to act quickly.

Since the 1850s, the movement to annex Rupert's Land had been gaining momentum, and provision had been made in the British North America Act for its admission into Canada. Recognizing that speed was of the essence, the first parliamentary session of the Dominion of Canada moved swiftly to negotiate its purchase.

The Purchase of Rupert's Land

Back in 1670, King Charles II of England granted to the Hudson's Bay Company a large portion of North America, named Rupert's Land in honour of Prince Rupert, the King's cousin and the company's first governor. This grant comprised the entire Hudson Bay drainage system, which in modern geographical terms included northern Quebec and Ontario north of the Laurentian watershed, all of Manitoba, most of Saskatchewan, southern Alberta and a portion of the North-West Territories. The company was to have a monopoly and complete control of the territory. However, by the mid-1850s, the age of the great trading monopolies was on the wane in Britain and many British were hostile to an extension of the company's monopolistic licence to trade. There was

HUDSON'S BAY COMPANY

The oldest incorporated joint-stock merchandising company in the English-speaking world

A Hudson's Bay Company York boat en route to Oxford House.

Médard Chouart Des Groseilliers and Pierre-Esprit Radisson were the first to propose a trading company to reach Canada's interior via Hudson Bay. Failing to obtain French support, they went to England in 1665 and sold the idea to Prince Rupert, cousin of King Charles II. Rupert then persuaded the King, some merchants and noblemen to back the venture.

The first ships, the *Eaglet* and the *Non-Such*, were dispatched in 1669. The royal charter was proclaimed on May 2, 1670. The "Governor and Company of Adventurers" were granted wide powers, including exclusive trading rights in the territory comprising the Hudson Bay watershed. This vast region was named Rupert's Land. When Hudson's Bay Company sold Canada its rights to Rupert's Land, the company retained title to the land surrounding the 97 trading establishments it had built over the centuries. By retaining large irrigable landholdings on the Prairies and the parcels adjacent to its posts, the Hudson's Bay Company became one of the most important developers in Western Canada.

1866 ▶

Parliament Building completed for the last legislative session of the Province of Canada. Upon Confederation, this building becomes the centre of federal Canadian government.

1866 ▶

On his fourth attempt, Cyrus Field succeeds in connecting Newfoundland and Europe with a transatlantic telegraph cable.

THE NORTH WEST COMPANY
Hard-Driving, Ruthless and Rowdy

La Compagnie du Nord, the French-backed, Montreal-based competitor to the fur empire of Hudson's Bay Company, failed. By 1779, the remaining French trappers and Scottish merchants began to join together in a loose confederation of common interests called the North West Company. After serving an apprenticeship in "Indian country," a man graduated to full partnership and a share in the profits. Having cut their teeth on the western trade, the men knew every aspect of the business.

The Old Trapper, François Gros Louis, 1866

The contrast with its rival, the Hudson's Bay Company, could scarcely have been more pronounced. Cautious and monolithic, the Hudson's Bay Company was directed from London by men who had no first-hand knowledge of the fur trade. The North West Company — never more than a restive, loosely organized partnership — was flexible and aggressive. At the North West Company's centre was a circle of closely related Scottish merchants. The ties of race and family created a degree of enthusiasm and enterprise that, for a time, completely dominated the western fur trade. It also created a company with a rather fractious, independent spirit.

What began as a vigorous competition between the two rivals ended in bloodshed. On March 26, 1821, the North West Company agreed to amalgamation. Later that year British Parliament granted the new Hudson's Bay Company a trading monopoly over the entirety of British North America west of the Ontario border.

also a growing suspicion that the Hudson's Bay Company was promoting the image of the North-West as a wasteland in order to discourage settlement, thereby protecting its fur trade. The company's rule was under attack from Britain, Canada and the United States.

In 1863, the International Financial Society bought controlling interest in the Hudson's Bay Company, signalling a shift in the company's outlook. Most of the new shareholders were less interested in the fur trade than in real estate speculation and economic development in the West — in particular, the possibility of a transcontinental railway. After lengthy negotiations, the controlling shareholders of the Hudson's Bay Company agreed to surrender its monopoly over the North-West, and arrangements were negotiated to transfer sovereignty to Canada. In exchange for its rights to the territory, the Hudson's Bay Company would receive £300,000, certain land around its posts and some 2.8 million acres (1.13 million hectares) of farmland in what today comprises the Prairie provinces. The deal was a coup for the already profitable financiers as not only did they receive the substantial cash payment, but they retained their fur-trading operations and land worth more than their 1863 purchase price. For Canada, the purchase of Rupert's Land extended her boundaries to the Rocky Mountains and the Arctic Ocean. She also assumed control of natural resources, in particular, unallocated land that would be sold to support the building of a Pacific railway — the magnet for a vast immigration across the Prairies.

Had the country bordering on Red River been an unoccupied wilderness, the plan carried out in effecting the transfer of land from Hudson's Bay Company to the Crown, and from the Crown to the Dominion of Canada, would have been an eminently wise one. Unfortunately, there were some 12,000 people living in possession of the soil thus transferred, and those 12,000 people — nearly all the people of Rupert's Land had some sort of informal claim to the land; hundreds held legal deeds from the Hudson's Bay Company — quite naturally objected to having themselves and their possessions signed away without negotiation or consent. During the lengthy bargaining period, which took place in London, no one thought to consult the people living on the land, negotiating the transfer of Rupert's Land as if it were uninhabited.

1867 ▶

The Dominion of Canada is created uniting Ontario, Quebec, New Brunswick and Nova Scotia as a single country. Queen Victoria receives, and knights, Sir John A. Macdonald, the first prime minister.

1868 ▶

Citizens of Barkerville, British Columbia, watch a cattle drive on the main street. A surveyor's error led to the narrow street and closely set buildings. A drunken miner's error in knocking over a stove while chasing a buffalo gal caused the fire that levelled the city.

The Red River Rebellion

In 1869, the federal government, anticipating the transfer of Red River and the North-West from the Hudson's Bay Company to Canadian jurisdiction, appointed William McDougall as lieutenant-governor of the new territory. When the government sent survey crews to Red River, the Métis — people of mixed Indian and European blood, predominately French-speaking Catholics — feared for the preservation of their land rights and culture. Wary of the Anglo-Protestant immigrants from Ontario, and still suffering economically from the grasshopper plagues of 1867 and 1868, they organized a National Committee. Louis Riel was named secretary. Riel did not begin the Red River Rebellion — also known as the Red River Resistance — but his political and oratorical skills quickly led him to become the leader of it. In a remarkably short period of time, Riel transformed himself from an obscure young man teaching school at a Jesuit mission in Montana, to one of the most controversial characters in Canadian history.

The committee halted the surveys and prevented McDougall from entering Red River, repelling him at Pembina on the U.S. border. On November 2, 1869, Riel and his supporters seized Fort Garry, the Hudson's Bay officials offering no resistance. The committee then invited the people of Red River, both English- and French-speaking, to send delegates to Fort Garry. While they were discussing a "List of Rights" prepared by Riel, a group

Pembina settlement, where Red River rebels turned back Lieutenant-Governor William McDougall.

LOUIS RIEL

The Potentate of Red River Valley

Perhaps more words have been written about Louis Riel than about any other person in Canadian history. Yet from his sudden appearance resisting Canadian authority at Red River to his death in 1885, Riel remained an enigma. In Ontario, he was denounced as a traitor. In Quebec, he was regarded as a hero. He became a symbol of the uneasy alliance created by Confederation, a test of the dual nature of the new nation.

Louis Riel, leader of the Red River Rebellion.

of Canadians, led by John Christian Schultz and John Stoughton Dennis, organized an armed resistance. Because of the Métis uprising, the federal government postponed the transfer planned for December 1 and Dennis and McDougall returned to Canada. When Schultz and his men surrendered to Riel, he imprisoned them in Fort Garry. Riel then issued a "Declaration of the People of Rupert's Land and the Northwest," and on December 23 became head of the provisional government of Red River. Fearing the United States would take advantage of the political crisis and seize control of the region, Sir John A. Macdonald reluctantly agreed to negotiate with the 25-year-old Riel.

The Canadian government sent special commissioners Abbé J.B. Thibault, Colonel Charles de Salaberry and Donald A. Smith, chief representative of the Hudson's Bay Company in Canada, to Red River. On January 19, 1870, more than 1,000 men and scores of women assembled in a large field — there was no building large enough to hold them — to hear Donald Smith present his case for Canada. While they stood stamping their feet in a vain effort to keep warm, Riel called the meeting to order, his voice reverberating loudly in the thin, cold air. His first act was to propose Thomas Bunn, a respected member of the English community, for chairman. Bunn was dutifully elected. Following a rousing speech given by Smith the next day — during which he claimed

1868 ▶

Fenian unrest continues with the assassination of D'Arcy McGee, longtime Fenian opponent and popular federal politician. Thousands mourn at his Montreal funeral.

1869 ▶

A church and mission school at the Red River Settlement.

that he would resign from the Hudson's Bay Company "at this moment" if that would help Rupert's Land — Riel moved that a Convention of Forty be held, starting January 25, to consider Smith's commission and what would be best for the welfare of the country. Twenty delegates would be elected by the Scots and English, the same number by the French. The motion carried.

On March 22, 1870, selected delegates of the provisional government received a commission from Thomas Bunn, secretary of state of the Riel government, authorizing them to present to the federal government the list of conditions upon which Assiniboia would consent to enter into Confederation. Not too long after, negotiations were concluded with an agreement that, on the surface, met Métis demands. The Manitoba Act, which received royal assent on May 12, 1870, safeguarded French-language rights and Roman Catholic educational rights. It also provided for the entry of Red River into Confederation, not as a colony, but as a small province in the heart of Rupert's Land to be named Manitoba. An Indian word, Manitoba was taken from a lake near Winnipeg. Addressing Parliament on the Manitoba Act, Sir George Cartier proclaimed: "The name of the new Province will be Manitoba, a very euphonious word meaning 'the God that speaks.' Well, let Canada's latest addition always speak to the inhabitants of the North-

West the language of reason, truth and justice." In addition, the federal government agreed to a land grant of 1.4 million acres (566,580 hectares) for the Métis. From the Métis point of view, their movement appeared a huge success and Riel a hero.

One tragic error ensured that Riel's downfall was as swift as his rise. On March 4, 1870, he allowed a Métis firing squad to execute Thomas Scott, a prisoner in Fort Garry, who had participated in two abortive revolts against Riel's regime. Riel decided to make an example of this obstreperous Orangeman, apparently feeling that an act of capital punishment would accredit his government in the eyes of the world and forestall future opposition. He grossly miscalculated. Scott's death caused great indignation in English Canada and such hatred of Riel that he would never again play a legitimate role in the politics of the Dominion.

Even as the Canadian government was negotiating with the insurgent Métis, a military expedition in the East was being readied to take possession of Red River. They had no trouble getting volunteers. One man eager to join the expedition was a young British officer named William Francis Butler. Learning from a newspaper dispatch that the Canadian government was sending a military expedition to the district of Assiniboia to suppress an insurrection, he immediately dashed off a telegraph, "To Winnipeg

Top: Garnet Joseph Wolseley, Commander of the Red River Expeditionary Force.

Above: The route of Red River Expedition, which followed the ancient fur trading route from Lake Superior to the West.

1869 ▶

Edward Desbarats' Illustrated Canadian News is the first periodical to use half-tone photographs, not artists' engravings, in print.

1870 ▶

Grasshopper swarms that wipe out crops are a recurring problem in the newly acquired Hudson's Bay Company lands. Manitoba is created from a portion of these lands and is admitted as the fifth province of the Dominion.

George Charles Mannix, at the time
he enlisted for the Red River Rebellion,
Second Battalion, Quebec Rifles.

Acheson G. Irvine, George Charles
Mannix's commander at Fort Garry
during the winter of 1870-1871.

WILLIAM FRANCIS BUTLER

*The Great Lone Land:
A Narrative of Travel and Adventure in the North-West of America*

Sir William Francis Butler was one of the great soldier-adventurers of the 19th century. An Irishman and a Catholic, he rose in the British army to the rank of lieutenant-general. After serving as an intelligence officer during the Red River Rebellion, Butler chose to remain in the West. His reason was a poetic one. Butler had fallen in love with "the great lone land."

"I had seen a sunset over the prairies," he wrote, "and the dream of it was ever in my mind — a great golden mist, a big river flowing from it, a dark herd of buffaloes slowly moving across the prairie distance to drink at the river, and the sun himself seeming to linger above the horizon as though he wanted to have a longer look at the glory he had made below."

Butler's extensive journeys throughout Western Canada provided him with material for *The Great Lone Land*. Published in 1872, the book's haunting descriptions of "that great, boundless, solitary waste of verdure" caught the imagination of the Canadian public and the title entered the language of the day.

*Captain William F. Butler
and Cerf-Vola.*

Expedition. Please remember me." He then caught the first boat leaving Ireland for Canada. He arrived too late.

"When I reached the city of Toronto, capital of the province of Ontario," Butler wrote in *The Great Lone Land*, "I found that the Red River Expeditionary Force had already been mustered. Making my way to the quarters of the commander of the Expedition, I was greeted every now and again with a 'You should have been here last week; every soul wants to get on the Expedition, and you haven't a chance. The whole thing is complete; we start tomorrow.' At last I met the commander himself. 'My good fellow, there's not a vacant berth for you,' he said; 'I got your telegram, but the whole army in Canada wanted to get in on the Expedition.'"

1870 ▶

Charles de Volpi engraving of Red River
Expedition members hauling a Red River cart
during a portage en route to Fort Garry.

1870 ▶

Winnipeg, shown in this early drawing,
becomes the capital of Manitoba.

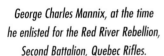

Even though the staff vacancies were filled by the time Butler reached headquarters, Colonel Wolseley commissioned Butler to go alone by way of the United States to Assiniboia and gather all available information about conditions prevailing in the district. He was then to travel up the Winnipeg River by canoe to rendezvous with Wolseley and the expedition in the vicinity of Lake of the Woods. Though Butler faced a lone, dangerous trek, it paled in comparison to the hardships Wolseley's forces would endure on their expedition west. It is doubtful that a man among them understood how gruelling a task they had undertaken.

"Hurrah for the boats and the roads, jolly boys!"

By an order-in-council on April 16, 1870, selected Canadian militiamen were enrolled for a period of one year, commencing on the 1st of May 1870. The City of Toronto raised the First Battalion of Rifles. In Quebec, two of the men to enroll in the Second Battalion, Quebec Rifles under Colonel Casault, were Sergeant George Charles Mannix and Corporal Henry Arthur Mannix. In addition to these two Canadian militia units there was the Fourth Battalion, Sixtieth Regiment, of the Imperial Forces. When the force mobilized at Toronto, they were joined by a detachment of artillery, sappers and miners. The force totalled 1,100 men, not including the 100 or so teamsters and 400 voyageurs and guides. The expedition was under the command of Deputy Quartermaster General Garnet Joseph Wolseley, who, at the age of 37, was already a veteran of the wars in Burma, India, the Crimea and China.

The traditional route from Eastern Canada to the Red River Settlement lay through the United States, but as it was out of the question to send the troops through a foreign country, an alternate route within Canada had to be found. The one chosen was an old canoe route which had been discovered by the fur traders of the North West and Hudson's Bay companies nearly a century earlier. The expedition's circuitous route through inhospitable country is still regarded as a small marvel in military movement. Even for the soldiers of today with their modern equipment, it would likely be a most difficult undertaking, and yet not a single man was lost to accident or sickness. This is not to say, however, they did not suffer mightily.

Wolseley claimed that he could move his army from Toronto to Fort Garry via the Dawson Road and Lake of the Woods in 72 days. He was wrong; it took 96. Nevertheless, it was a remarkable feat. The most gruelling part of the 1,280-mile (2,060-kilometre) journey from Toronto to Fort Garry was the 50-mile (80-kilometre) uphill stretch between Fort William and Shebandowan Lake that took eight long weeks to negotiate.

The expedition left Toronto on May 14, 1870, travelling by train to Collingwood, and then by steamship to Fort William on Lake Superior. From Fort William to the Red River Settlement, the forces crossed inhospitable land by foot and canoe. The 650-mile

WHISKY FORTS

After the sale of Rupert's Land to the Dominion government in 1869, fur traders from Fort Benton, Montana, journeyed into present-day southern Alberta and built Fort Whoop-Up, near modern Lethbridge. That same year, Dave Akers and Liver-Eating Johnston built the Spitzee Post on the Highwood River. Other so-called whisky forts were added during the next year or so, including a fort built within the present limits of Calgary.

Traders supplied the forts with wagonloads of whisky and rifles. These were traded to the Natives for buffalo hides, wolf and fox skins. The forts were well fortified with loopholes in the walls for rifles and bars blocking the chimney tops. There were small wickets in the wall through which the Native pushed his skins. In return the traders presented him with a cup of "Whoop-Up bug juice," or whisky. And such whisky!

Fort Whoop-Up.

Tobacco, old tea leaves and molasses brought to a full rolling boil, then cooled, seasoned to taste with Perry's painkiller, Tabasco, red pepper, ginger, molasses, tea and sulphuric acid. This fiery concoction was then dolled up to a dubious pink with red ink. There were many formulas, but all were deadly. The notoriety of the forts was one of the reasons behind the formation of the North-West Mounted Police.

1871 ▶

British Columbia joins the Dominion of Canada following the promise of the federal government to build a transcontinental railway within 10 years.

1871 ▶

Government survey party members relax in their camp along the Saskatchewan River on the western Canadian plains.

"In God We Trust; All Others Pay Cash"

Some of the men who operated the whisky forts established legitimate businesses after the arrival of the North-West Mounted Police. One of these men was Harry (Kamoose) Taylor, who set up a hotel in Fort Macleod. Due to the rather unpredictable and volatile nature of some of his guests, Mr. Taylor posted the following:

1. Guests will be provided with breakfast and dinner, but must rustle their own lunch.

2. Spiked boots and spurs must be removed at night before retiring.

3. Dogs are not allowed in the bunks, but may sleep underneath.

4. Towels are changed weekly; insect powder is for sale at the bar.

5. Special rates for the Gospel Grinders and the gambling profession.

6. The bar will be open day and night. Every known fluid, except water, for sale. No mixed drinks will be served except in case of a death in the family. Only registered guests allowed the privileges of sleeping on the bar room floor.

7. No kicking regarding the food. Those who do not like the provender will be put out. When guests find themselves or their baggage thrown over the fence, they may consider they have received notice to leave.

8. Baths furnished free down at the river, but bathers must provide their own soap and towels.

9. Valuables will not be locked in the hotel safe, as the hotel possesses no such ornament.

10. Guests are expected to rise at 6:00 a.m., as the sheets are needed for tablecloths.

11. To attract the attention of waiters, shoot through the door panel. Two shots for ice water, three for a new deck of cards.

No Jawbone. In God We Trust; all others Pay Cash.

(1,046-kilometre) journey from Fort William to Fort Garry was particularly hazardous. The troops moved along poorly charted waterways, through untrodden forests and swampland, and over rocky terrain. Because the country was totally lacking in useful supplies, the men had to carry, or "portage," the boats, guns, ammunition, food and other provisions over 47 portages, some more than one mile (1.6 kilometres) in length.

Many of the volunteers were inexperienced and unaccustomed to military discipline. Even the regulars were ignorant of the exigencies of wilderness travel. Few of the soldiers could handle boats and they knew little about woods or prairie trails. For this they had to take along, and feed, a company of Iroquois, French-Canadian "voyageurs" and Métis guides. Food was the major concern. Between Lake Superior and the Red River there

Fort Garry and ferry on which Louis Riel may have escaped.

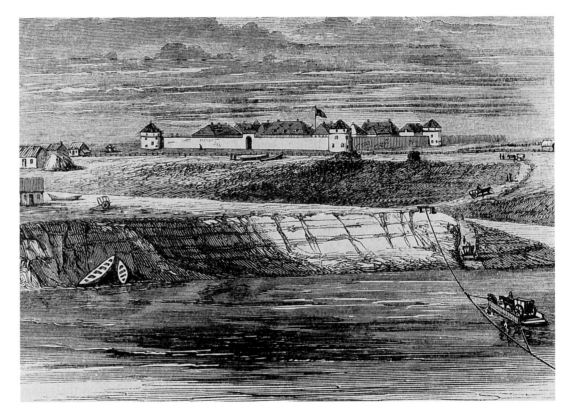

1871 ▶

The Treaty of Washington is signed. The United States recognizes the southern border of Canada. England promises funds for Canada's transcontinental railway and the last British troops leave North America.

1872 ▶

Parliament passes the Married Women's Property Act that decrees a woman's earnings are her separate property (the husband must consent to allow her to work). "You are complaining my poor husband, about your 10-hour work day. I've already been working for 14 hours and I haven't yet finished my day's work."

"A Bully Good Horse to Ride Upon"

Constable William F. Parker, North-West Mounted Police.

William McDougall, the first Canadian lieutenant-governor of the North-West Territories, was instructed to organize a police force in 1869. As half the force was to be local Métis, the plans were shelved as a result of the Red River Rebellion. It was not until 1873 that a force was established. Many of the recruits were young farm boys, blacksmiths and carpenters who hailed from Ontario, Quebec and the Maritimes. One recruit, William Parker, wrote that "everybody around here thinks it is a splendid thing for a young man to go into." Pay would be 75 cents a day, "travelling expenses paid, a bully good horse to ride upon, and if I serve three years, I shall get a grant of 160 acres of land."

In the summer of 1874, the force headed west. Sub-Constable Joseph J. Carscadden complained in his diary that "they content themselves with a snail's pace for they have not yet learned to ride." Available grass and water were insufficient; 40 of the horses died. "Had nothing to eat all day but oatmeal made into porridge," wrote Carscadden on August 5. A few weeks later he noted: "it looks very much like starvation, so much so that we must keep moving ahead or sure death awaits us." On September 11, the forces reached their destination. They were the founders of what would gradually become known as the North-West Mounted Police; the finest wilderness police force in the world.

Dead Horse Valley. Sketch made by journalist Henri Julien during march west.

Were few settlements. Wild game was so scarce that it was rumoured that small Indian bands who wandered into this area often perished from starvation.

Undoubtedly there were a few glorious days when the sails filled with an exhilarating breeze and the boats glided effortlessly across the sparkling blue lakes, but for the most part, the expedition was pure drudgery. Even when the men were able to put the boats in the water, it was often necessary to drag them upstream and through river rapids. At these points, the men had to partially remove the load from the boats, toss tow lines ashore and pull the boats upstream or through the rapids to calmer water. Then they unloaded the boats and went back for another haul. Butler was awed by the endurance of the two regiments of Canadian militia, extolling: "Let us not forget the men who, following in the footsteps of the regular troops, were now only a few marches behind their more fortunate comrades. To the lot of these regiments of Canadian Volunteers fell the hard toil of oar and portage. The men composing these regiments were stout athletic fellows, eager for service, tired of civilian life, and only needing the toil of a campaign to weld them into as tough and resolute a body of men as ever a leader could desire."

The forces sweltered under a blistering sun on a high rock carry only to plunge moments later into damp, cold, sunless trails deep in the woods. They sank to their knees in muskeg and were hauled half-drowned from icy waters. They fought cramped muscles, sore backs, insects, dysentery and exhaustion. The days were unpleasantly hot and the nights were intolerable due to mosquitoes and black flies. But they sang. One of their favourite songs was *Tenting on the Old Camp Ground,* which they renamed *Tenting on the Old Damp Ground.* Another was *Jolly Boys:*

1873 ▶

Prince Edward Island joins Canada as the seventh province. Charlottetown, shown in this early painting, becomes its capital.

1873 ▶

Steamship Atlantic *sinks off Nova Scotia after running aground; 547 drown, 300 are saved. The rescued captain wailed, "Would to God even one woman had been saved."*

Come boys, cheer up! We'll have a song in spite of our position.
To help us in our labours on this glorious Expedition!
We'll keep our spirits up, my boys; and don't look sad or sober
Nor grumble at our hardships on our way to Manitoba!

Jolly boys, jolly boys,
Hurrah for the boats and the roads, jolly boys!

Some grumble, loudly exclaiming, 'Tis not as I expected;
I did not know that great stockade would have to be erected;
It was only as a volunteer that I left my abode —
I never thought of coming here to work upon the road!

We have talked about our going home, but now it don't appear
That we shall see our homes again in quite another year;
For if the girls of Manitoba are as kind as they are charming,
The half of us will stay behind, and settle down to farming!

The expedition reached Fort Garry on the 24th of August 1870, to be met not by Riel and his forces, but by mud. "To march upon Fort Garry was out of the question or at least it would have been folly to have attempted it," wrote a frustrated Colonel Wolseley, "when we had the means of going there by water as the face of the country was changed into a sea of mud. This necessary change of plan was annoying, as we had looked forward to advancing upon the Fort in all the pride, pomp and circumstance of war."

The troops were met not only by mud, but by an unnatural, unsettling quiet. "Everything remaining silent," Wolseley wrote. "Some staff officers were sent galloping round to see if the southern gate was open, and what was going on in the rear of the Fort. They soon returned, bringing word that it was evacuated and the gates left open. This was at first a sad disappointment to the soldiers,

MANNIX MILITARY DECORATIONS

The medal awarded by the British government in recognition of a man's participation in the Red River Expedition of 1870 was the Canada General Service (C.G.S.) Medal bearing the 1870 clasp. This medal has always been a popular but rather elusive item, as relatively few were awarded; only 502 recipients of the C.G.S. Medal with the Red River clasp have been traced. Fewer than half of the men who participated in the Red River Expedition ever actually received a medal. For a medal buff, any C.G.S. Medal with a verified Red River clasp is in the rare-to-extremely-rare category. Only 120 Red River medals with the clasp combination of 66-RR (66 = Fenian Raid 1866; RR = Red River Expedition 1870) were awarded. Two of the recipients were Sergeant George Charles Mannix and his brother, Corporal Henry Arthur Mannix.

For service rendered in the Red River Expedition, this warrant gave George Charles Mannix the right to choose a quarter section — 160 acres (65 hectares) — of land.

1876 ▶

August 10, Bradford, Ontario — Alexander Graham Bell makes first telephone call to Paris, Ontario.

1876 ▶

North-West Mounted Police pattern full dress uniform of William D. Antrobus, one of the original members of the force.

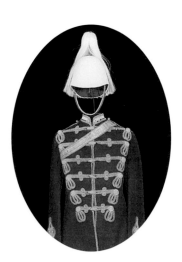

TO THE SOLDIERS OF THE CANADIAN MILITIA

Colonel Wolseley's Valedictory Address to the Soldiers of the Canadian Militia

"I congratulate you upon the success of our expedition, which has secured to this country a peaceable solution of its late troubles. The credit of this success is due to the gallant soldiers I had at my back; upon you fell the labour of carrying the boats and heavy loads, a labour in which officers and men vied with each other as to who should do the most…. From Fort William to Fort Garry is over 600 miles through a wilderness of forest and water, where no supplies of any description are obtainable. You had to carry on your backs a vast amount of supplies over no fewer than 47 portages, making a total distance of seven miles, a feat unparalleled in our military annals. You have descended a great river esteemed so dangerous from its rapids, falls and whirlpools, that none but experienced voyageurs attempt its navigation. Your cheerful obedience to orders has enabled you, under the blessing of Divine Providence, to accomplish your task without any incident.

"Although the banditti who had been oppressing the people fled at your approach, without giving you an opportunity of proving how men capable of such labour could fight, you have deserved as well of your country as if you had won a battle…. I can say without flattery that although I have served with many armies in the field, I have never been associated with a better set of men."

G.J. Wolseley,
Commander, Red River Expeditionary Force.
Dated at Fort Garry, 9 September 1870.

Memorabilia of Lord and Lady Wolseley.

who, having gone through so much toil to put down the rebellion, longed to be avenged upon its authors."

Abbé Dugas, who also wrote about the taking of Fort Garry, explained the quiet. "On the morning of the 24th," he said, "an English settler arrived at full gallop to say to Riel, 'For the love of God clear out, the troops are only two miles from the city and you are going to be lynched.' He had only just time to cross to St. Boniface; to avoid being pursued closely, he cut the cable which held the ferry boat." So, what began in rhetoric, ended bloodlessly. Even though not a single shot was fired, the arrival of the troops ensured order was restored and a permanent garrison was established at Fort Garry. After a few days of rest, the British army regulars began their homeward journey, arriving back in Montreal in October. The two militia battalions spent the ensuing winter at Fort Garry. In the spring of 1871, George Charles Mannix took his discharge.

One of the Pioneering Families in Western Canada

The story of Canada is the story of a nation unique in the world. Politically young, Canada is rich with a multitude of languages and religions, races and cultures, ideologies and legends. Canada is a country of immigrants with a long tradition of welcoming people from all over the world. Perhaps nowhere can this heritage of cultural tolerance be seen more clearly than in looking at the lives of individual

1878 ▶

April 26, first shipment of John Deere plows reaches Manitoba. They are expected to help conquer the heavy, root-massed prairie soil making it suitable for cultivation.

1880 ▶

Fort Calgary, the name given the North-West Mounted Police fort at the confluence of the Bow and Elbow rivers in what will become Alberta.

people such as George Charles Mannix and Frances Bunn, the niece of the secretary of state of Riel's provisional government.

Not long after arriving in Manitoba, George Charles discovered that, just as the song *Jolly Boys* predicted, the girls of Manitoba were as kind as they were charming, and he began courting a young lady by the name of Frances Bunn. A descendant of pioneering North West Company and Hudson's Bay Company families, Frances' Scottish, English and Cree heritage mirrored the cultural depth and diversity characteristic of the early settlers of Manitoba.

It was typical of the rich promise and cultural tolerance of the New World that Frances should meet and fall in love with a young man from County Cork, Ireland, who journeyed to Red River to claim the land for Canada. And it was typical of the hope and sense of renewal implicit in that world that they should pledge their allegiance to each other. On November 25, 1872, George Charles Mannix and Frances Bunn were married at St. Paul's Middlechurch by Bishop Robert Machray, who later became archbishop and first primate of Canada.

That same year, the Canadian government granted land to the officers and men of the Ontario and the Quebec Rifles in recognition of their service as members of the Red River Expeditionary Force. These men of the Canadian militia were eligible for a grant of 160 acres (65 hectares) of Dominion land situated in the Province of Manitoba or the North-West Territories. Many of the expedition participants took this opportunity to become pioneering settlers in Western Canada. George Charles Mannix was one of them. Having emigrated from a country where land was parcelled out in tiny plots, where the sight of families being evicted from their homes was commonplace, George Charles Mannix was now the owner of property in the Great Lone Land.

A MARRIAGE OF PIONEERS

When Frances Bunn married G.C. Mannix, she brought a unique, and distinctly Canadian bloodline to the union. Frances' ancestors included Nahovway, a full-blooded Cree, and three early Canadian families: the Sinclairs, the Bunns and the Campbells.

William Sinclair arrived in Canada in 1792. A graduate of the University of Edinburgh, he became a factor for the Hudson's Bay Company, developing Oxford House, a major trading post. Sinclair married Nahovway of the Cree Nation. They grew hay and grains at Oxford House and imported Orkney dairy cattle. Nahovway cared for their

many children long after William's death. One son, Colin, a sea captain, established a monument in her honour outside Winnipeg. Another son, James, became a famous traveller throughout Western Canada and the northwestern United States. A daughter, Phoebe, married Thomas Bunn, a native of southern England. Bunn was the contemporary, friend and confidant of her father and also a factor and bookkeeper for the Hudson's Bay Company with a post some miles from Oxford House.

The Campbell family came to the New World with Lord Selkirk and settled in the wilds of Manitoba in about 1812. By the early 1820s, Colin Campbell was far to the west at Fort Dunvegan on the Peace River in northern Alberta. He wed Elizabeth McGillivray, the daughter of a North West Company employee. To educate their children, the Campbells journeyed by canoe and portage to the Red River Settlement where their four daughters entered Miss McCallum's School for Girls. One of their daughters married James Sinclair and, accompanied by two of her sisters, travelled to the Oregon Territory where James was killed by hostile Indians. The fourth daughter, Magdalan, remained in Manitoba and married William Bunn, the son of Thomas and Phoebe Bunn, in about 1845. Magdalan and William Bunn had some 12 children. Frances, the second born, married G.C. Mannix on November 25, 1872.

1880 ▶

St. Paul's Middlechurch, parsonage and school, the church where George Charles Mannix and Frances Bunn were married.

BORN WITH THE RAILWAY

1881 – 1919

*On my journey through the country of white savages, I came to a big trail,
which was made of iron…I stooped down and felt it with my hands.
The iron trail was so heavy that I could not lift it, and the savages had fastened
it to the prairie, lest some thieves come along and steal it.*

*Whilst I was examining it, I heard a terrible noise like thunder, and…
looked to see what had made such a hideous sound, and as I stood in amazement,
there came another peal of thunder…down the iron trail came a fire-horse,
roaring like a demon, and blowing great clouds of smoke out of his mouth.*

— Apokena, Blackfoot chief

Left: The Canadian Pacific Railway plays a major role in the development of Western Canada.

Charles de Volpi engraving which appeared in Harper's Monthly in 1860. It shows horses being purchased at St. Paul, Minnesota, for Red River carts bound for the Red River Settlement.

Within a decade of leaving Ireland, George Charles Mannix, now 27, was a pioneering settler in the middle of the Great Lone Land. Known as the "Bull's Eye of the Pacific," the Red River Settlement was located at the confluence of the Red and Assiniboine rivers, midway between the Atlantic and Pacific oceans. While George Charles may have chosen this land as home, this land was not necessarily hospitable to settlers. When the Red River Settlement was incorporated as a city in 1873, it adopted the name of Winnipeg. The community numbered only 3,700 and was little more than a collection of shacks. Floods were a problem. This is perhaps understandable when one learns the word Winnipeg is derived from the Cree name *win-nipi,* meaning muddy or murky water. A chronicler of one early flood wrote: "Dwelling houses and barns were floating in all directions like a sloop under sail, with cats, dogs and poultry in them…the very mice, snakes and squirrels could not find a hiding place above or below ground."

In the spring the chomping of grasshoppers made a noise like a giant cutting machine; the grasshopper plague of 1867-1868 devastated the economy. One settler, James Ashdown, having walked beside his ox cart from St. Cloud to the Red River Settlement — a 19-day trek — was not exactly thrilled at the sight of his new home, writing: "The season for reaching the Fort was not an auspicious one. The Grasshopper Plague had visited the Settlement the year previous and again was within it, and the Grasshoppers themselves coming down in their flight were found piled up against the south wall of the Fort in such numbers as necessitated their dead bodies being carted to and dumped into the Assiniboine River and within three days there was scarce a blade of grain anywhere to be seen."

Grasshoppers were not the only insects to plague the settlers. In the spring, the very air reverberated with the whine of mosquitoes. John West, a Protestant missionary, noted in his journal: "The trees are breaking into leaves… but this sudden and pleasing change has brought with it unceasing torment. Night and day you are perpetually persecuted with the mosquitoes that afford you no rest but in the annoying respiration of a smoky room."

And then there was the weather. Where else could you find diary entries such as these?

"*Oct. 30*   *Crossed Red River on ice.*
Nov. 3   *Crossed ice with a train of horses, loaded.*
Nov. 11   *Ice gave way. Down I went… almost got drowned.*
Nov. 19   *Plowed & harrowed 2 acres & sowed it with garden seed.*
Nov. 23   *Snow fell.*"

"My father thought he would like to try his hand at growing some grain."

Despite the mud, grasshoppers, mosquitoes and climate, each settler had wood, water and land. This rich Red River gumbo inspired Charles Muir to wax lyrical in *The Globe:* "The man must be corrupt as death who, unaccustomed, can look unmoved upon this August material presence, this calm, unutterable vastness. Man is a mere grasshopper here — a mere insect… and yet man is the master of all this. Hither will he come and plough, and plant and reap. Many things he will grumble about, doubtless, for man is an habitual grumbler: but he will not complain much over his land."

It was in this land, situated where the Canadian Shield gives way to the prairie, that George and Frances Mannix made their home. It was here, in what was known as the "Gateway to the West," that they would raise their seven children: Mary Madeline, born 1873; William Alfred Victor, born 1875; George Arthur de Courcey, born 1877; Frederick Stephen, born 1881; Francis Clements, born 1884; Leonard Nial, born 1887; and Frances Alicia, born 1891.

Red River Settlements Cottage in 1872.

On the occasion of her 105th birthday, George and Frances' oldest daughter, Mary Madeline Mannix Procter, recorded her memories of life in the newly created province of Manitoba. If you listen carefully, you can hear not only one of the early western pioneers speak, but the sound of the Indians' oars dipping in the water as their canoes glide

1881 ▶

A sketch drawn by the Governor General of Canada, the Marquis of Lorne, while he and his wife, Louise, the fourth daughter of Queen Victoria, visit Calgary.

1883 ▶

Canadian Pacific Railway trains stretch across the Prairies and reach Calgary. In one passenger car travels Sarah Toyi Costello. In November, she gives birth to John Calgary Costello, the first white child born in Calgary.

along the river. "My father, George Charles Mannix from Quebec, was a County Cork Irishman," Mary Madeline recalled. "He came west with Colonel Wolseley's Expedition in 1870 to help quell the Riel Rebellion. The troops were garrisoned at the Lower Fort. My father was among the young men who chose to remain in Manitoba after the Rebellion. The fact that my parents were married on November 25, 1872, by Anglican Archbishop Machray and I arrived one year and two weeks later, speaks loudly that my father lost no time in looking around and finding my mother Frances Bunn.

"I was born in the home of my grandparents, Mr. and Mrs. William Bunn. William Bunn was a carpenter and half-brother of Doctor John Bunn, the first surgeon and doctor at Red River, now Winnipeg. My grandparents lived on the bank of the Red River at Middlechurch quite near Lower Fort Garry. When my parents moved to a little house, one of several, in the Victoria District, north of Stonewall in the mid 1870s, I was left behind and began school in the company of my young aunts and uncles. We loved to watch the traffic on the Red River, the Indians and settlers in their canoes and boats, and the York boats freighting back and forth; the dog teams and sleds on the ice in the winter. Christmas was a great time. The Indians called regularly in those days, never asking but always receiving, tea, tobacco, sugar and cakes which they stowed away in the pouch of the blanket robe they wore tied with a thong at the waist. When the Indian mother came, she slung the papoose from her back and stood the whole thing, baby, board and all, up against the banking of the house, on the sunny side or out of the wind."

"My father's soldier friend, John Cavers, homesteaded near the Vincent's farm in the Victoria District," said Mary Madeline. "Father, too, looked for a homestead

THE PASSING OF AN ERA

"Mother told of her older sisters driving down to St. Paul, Minnesota, to get dress-making supplies," recalled George and Frances Mannix's oldest daughter, Mary Madeline (Minnie) Mannix Procter. "The buffalo herds were feeding at a distance, but when the sisters turned and the sun shone on the little glass on the back of the buggy top, the glitter attracted and annoyed the old bull who threw up his head and came charging across the prairie. The girls sensed their danger and quickly unhitched the pony and betook it and themselves to the shelter of trees nearby. The enraged buffalo never stopped snorting and stamping until the buggy was in matchwood."

"By the time I was born, the prairie herds had been driven further and further away or slaughtered," Minnie said. "Only the herd Colonel Bedson, warden of Stony Mountain Penitentiary, had acquired caused us excitement from time to time." One day Minnie took her younger sister for a walk "down the path west of our house and stopped short in our tracks. There, passing a few yards in front of us was a buffalo cow and calf. At a short distance behind walked Joe Daniels, Colonel Bedson's half-Indian herder, armed only with a short stick. The cow had strayed up to Monkman's Point on Shoal Lake, a hark back to ancestor roaming days."

The population of prairie bison, or buffalo, is estimated to have been 50 to 60 million in 1800. By 1885, they were virtually extinct.

and found one across the line north from his ex-sailor brother, William Mannix, up in Erinview. I had joined my parents by this time and we lived close to Shoal Lake. My brothers, Alf and Fred, and I had happy times sliding down the snow banks and in the spring seeing who could have the biggest fire burning the long reeds along the shore. We also enjoyed playing with our cousins in the daytime and the sing songs the grown ups enjoyed together in the evening with gentle Aunt Mary at the piano. From our home, we could see the Fred Robertsons' 18 x 30-foot steam launch

1885 ▶

Jumbo, the star elephant of P.T. Barnum's "Greatest Show on Earth," is killed when struck by a Grand Trunk locomotive. Tom Thumb, the miniature elephant, is also injured.

1886 ▶

On her first trans-Canada rail trip, Sir John A. Macdonald's wife rides the train's "cow catcher" through the Alberta and British Columbia mountains. Many later adopt this unusual method of sightseeing.

Climbing the Rockies.

taking their guests for boat rides on the lake. Uncle Will's sailor experience fitted him well to be the engineer. The *Lady of the Lake* was painted white; she gleamed in the sun as the flag from the tall staff fluttered and the veils of the ladies floated out on the lake breeze. My family were regular attendants at All Saints Church which was built with money sent out to the Robertsons from Fred's sister in Lincolnshire, England. Later a driving shed was added and used as a school, which I attended at one time. It was over four miles distance, so I did not get there very often.

"After some years at Erinview, my father thought he would like to try his hand at growing some grain. He had advanced Julie Morrisette $600 as a mortgage on her property deeded to her by the Crown as a scrip in 1878; father purchased this land. I remember very well the day we drove down from Erinview to begin building our log house. The wild strawberries were very thick so mother gave Alf and I a cup each to pick some for dessert, while she made a camp fire to boil water for tea. After my parents established this home, west and north of Stonewall, we moved there each spring to farm the land. We returned to Erinview to put up hay in season and returned there to winter the cattle near the feed. As autumn approached each year, the cattle herd would become restless and disappear. Unfailingly, the old cows in the lead, they headed north. My brother Fred and I were then packed up to follow the herd and care for them until my family would finish up the harvest. Fred and I milked the cows, set the milk in the shallow pans, skimmed the cream each day for churning into butter and carried on alone for a month or two each year."

Mannix family portrait, circa 1878. Front row, left to right: Alfred Bunn, Magdalan (Campbell) Bunn, Alfred Mannix on knee, Mary Madeline Mannix. Back row: George Charles Mannix and his wife, Frances (Bunn) Mannix.

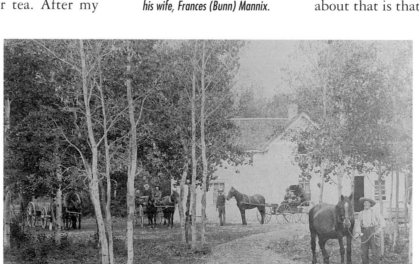

George Charles Mannix, centre, at his Stonewall, Manitoba, farm in 1890. Frederick Stephen Mannix, age nine, far right.

An Apprenticeship in Toil and Sweat

It may have been a simple life, but it was a rough one. As William Butler recorded: "The early settlers in any country are not by any means persons given to the study of abstract justice, still less to its practice; and it is as well, perhaps that they should not be. They have rough work to do, and they generally do it roughly. The very fact of their coming out so far into the wilderness implies the other fact of their not being able to dwell quietly and peaceably at home. They are, as it were, the advanced pioneers of civilization who make smooth the way of the coming race. Obstacles of any kind are their peculiar detestation. That is about their creed, and it must be said they act up to their convictions." For the Mannixes, their particular obstacle was rock.

"At the end of the Manitoba Uprising, grandfather was given the opportunity to pick land to use as his farm on the understanding that he would settle in Red River Valley," explained George Mannix. "The interesting thing about that is that he stood on a rock and picked out what land he wanted. It was only after he picked his land that they named it Stonewall — the land was apparently all covered with rock." George Charles' wife, Frances Bunn, was also entitled to land. When Manitoba became a province in 1870, the Manitoba Act set aside 1.4 million acres (566,580 hectares) of land for distribution to "the children of the half-breed heads of families." Each child got 240 acres (97 hectares). Subsequent legislation gave the Métis adults in Manitoba scrip worth $160, with which they could buy Dominion lands at a dollar an acre. "So after he married Frances Bunn, grandfather stood on another rock and chose the rest of the rocks,"

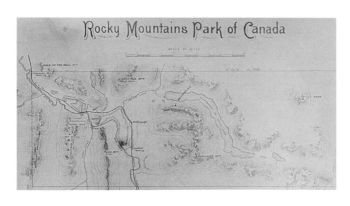

1887 ▶

Rocky Mountains Park, centred around Banff, in the District of Alberta, is established by the Canadian government. Hunting, logging and mining are allowed within the park boundaries.

1888 ▶

The plains buffalo population in Alberta dwindles; only six are sighted during the year. The largest, most devastating animal killing spree is over.

George Mannix said. "Apparently, they spent most of their life just picking up stones from the farm. To this day, you will never find a Mannix that is afraid of a stone."

While they may not have been afraid of stones, there is no denying that farming in a rocky land was rough work. Frederick Stephen drove a team of horses 35 miles (56 kilometres) to Winnipeg to sell wood he had chopped to buy his own shoes. "I can't remember if it was Dad or Uncle Alf who said that they stuck around long enough until they could walk far enough, and then they walked away," related George Mannix. Frederick Stephen left his Manitoba farm to support himself at age 14. "Grandfather had taken him to the shed," said Kathy Mannix Parry, "and, at 14 years old, he wasn't going to be taken to the shed anymore." So he set off to make his own way in the world.

Companies, like countries, have a great many mythologies, and there are many stories about how F.S. Mannix spent his teens. His daughter, Alice Mannix Kramer, recalled that "he hauled logs in the wintertime and made enough money to buy a horse. He didn't start in the construction business, but he hauled logs to help pay for his first team of horses." It is said that he worked for the Government of Manitoba on rural roads, digging ditches and filling holes. It is told that he worked for a smelting company in Trail, British Columbia, where he contracted lead poisoning. It is said that he spent time in the United States, moving dirt in Peterson, Iowa, and picking apples for a childless couple on a farm in Washington. It is related that young Fred so impressed the Washington couple by his hard work and diligence that they said they would leave the farm to him, if only he would stay. He declined and moved on. Perhaps F.S. Mannix did all these things. Perhaps he did none. In many ways, it does not really matter. What does matter is that he worked hard, pulled his own weight and was an independent man.

CALGARY POWER LTD.
Helping to Build a Better Alberta

According to the story, one dark night in 1887, the sober and business-like Peter Anthony Prince of Eau Claire Lumber Company fell off a plank sidewalk, severely injuring his pride. His vow to bring electrification to Calgary was the first step in a complex series of events which led to the creation of Calgary Power — the name under which TransAlta Utilities Corporation operated for more than 70 years.

The first "hydro" developments in the Calgary area were small water-wheel plants designed to serve single mills and individual operations. One of these was the Calgary Water Power Company plant on the Bow River just west of the present Centre Street Bridge. In 1898, the Calgary Water Power Company, which was later taken over by Calgary Power Ltd., was granted the Dominion Government Water Power Licence Number 6. A 280-horsepower plant was built, using water that flowed over the mill dam of the Eau Claire sawmill. By 1909 the need for, and acceptance of, electricity had grown a great deal. That year the Calgary Power & Transmission Company began construction of the Horseshoe Falls project on the Bow River 55 miles (85 kilometres) west of Calgary. The job was finished two years later and provided 20,000 horsepower for the growing needs of the city. The Calgary Power & Transmission Company later became Calgary Power Co. Ltd., Calgary Power Ltd. and, finally, TransAlta Utilities Corporation.

1890 ▶

Chief Crowfoot, the proud and great Blackfoot, dies after a long illness. As a young warrior he was wounded six times and went to war 19 times. As chief, he welcomed the abolition of the whisky forts and made peace with the Canadian government. He died disillusioned by Canada's refusal to abide by Treaty No. 7.

1891 ▶

Sir John A. Macdonald, Canada's first and current prime minister, dies.

By today's standards, F.S. Mannix was an uneducated man. Yet, like most entrepreneurs, he taught himself what he needed to learn to succeed in his world. During his apprenticeship, he learned the ways of men, money, horses and machinery. Opportunities abounded in Western Canada for those who knew how to seize them. By the time F.S. Mannix was 17, he was ready to grab the reins. Like his father, George Charles, before him, Frederick Stephen's birth coincided with an event that heralded great change in his country. Yet, unlike his father, who was born in the year of Ireland's Great Famine, F.S. was born in a year that heralded explosive growth for his country, not its death knell. F.S. Mannix was born on February 3, 1881. On February 15, the Canadian Pacific Railway was incorporated. Linked by birth, F.S. Mannix hitched his fortunes to the iron rail.

Above: Frederick Stephen Mannix.

"One of the most foolish things that could be imagined"

The basic rule of railway economics is this: the fewer towns along a railway line the less money the line will make. For Canada it posed a dilemma. Canada had to either connect East to West through American territory or defy the economics of the railway industry. The government of Sir John A. Macdonald chose the latter. In 1870, Macdonald argued conclusively for building a transcontinental railway. This railway not only would bind together the far-flung provinces, colonies and territories, but also join them as partners in nationhood. When Macdonald promised a railway in just ten years, the Liberal leader, Alexander Mackenzie, declared that the promise was "an insane act of recklessness." That to attempt to build a railway across Canada was "one of the most foolish things that could be imagined." Here was a country of only three and a half million people, not yet four years old, pledging to construct the greatest of all railways, longer than any line yet built.

Left: The Canadian Pacific Railway in the British Columbia mountains.

The task was immense: to locate a viable route through 2,500 miles (4,000 kilometres) of rock and muskeg in the Canadian Shield, across virtually unoccupied prairie, through the forbidding mountain ranges and the narrow canyons of British Columbia. Yet it was the promise of the completion of a transcontinental railway that encouraged British Columbia to join Confederation in 1871, thereby extending the political reality of Canada from sea to sea. "One of the conditions of British Columbia entering the Confederation was that the Canadian government commit to building a road from the East Coast to the West Coast, right across Canada," said Norris Roy (Buck) Crump. Crump, who began as a labourer on the Canadian Pacific

1892 ▶

Calgary, shown, is incorporated as Alberta's first city. Edmonton is incorporated as a town.

1893 ▶

The Stanley Cup is donated by Governor General Lord Stanley for presentation to the amateur hockey champions of Canada. First awarded to the Montreal Amateur Athletic Association, it becomes the oldest trophy competed for by professional athletes in North America.

Railway, rose to become its president, senior executive officer and chairman before his retirement in 1972. "Before the agreement was signed, the road was quickly changed to a railway."

Competition for the lucrative railway contract was fierce and dirty. The solicitation by Prime Minister Sir John A. Macdonald, Sir George-Étienne Cartier and Hector Langevin of some $260,000 in campaign funds for the August 1872 general election, from promoters including Sir Hugh Allan, resulted in what was known as the Pacific Scandal. Macdonald and his Conservative colleagues needed money to fight the elections in Ontario and Quebec, where a number of seats were in jeopardy. Notwithstanding his bribery of electors, Macdonald did badly, his 1867 majority being substantially reduced. After the election, Allan was rewarded with the contract to build the Pacific Railway, on the assumption that he would divest himself of American control on his board of directors. Since Allan, unbeknownst to Macdonald, had used American money to bribe the government, this proved difficult, and ultimately resulted in blackmail. The Liberals broke the story on April 2, 1873. Shortly thereafter, the Macdonald government was obliged to resign. Allan's company never did get started. When Macdonald returned to power in 1878, the construction of a transcontinental railway once again became a priority.

There was little hope of attracting any foreign capital to help offset the enormous cost of this venture. Attempts to raise funds in the financial capital of the time, the London money market, amounted to little or nothing. For British investors, the memory of the failure of the Grand Trunk Railway — constructed largely with funds from England in the late 1850s, the Grand Trunk Railway went bankrupt in 1861 with debts exceeding $13 million — was too fresh to hazard any more funds on grandiose Canadian schemes. "So a group of entrepreneurs in Montreal formed a private syndicate and took on the contract in 1881," said Crump. "Very few Canadians understand that from 1870 to 1881, the Canadian Pacific Railway was government-owned. It wasn't until 1881 that the Canadian Pacific Railway became a company. The Syndicate, as it was called, completed the railway in five years." Donald A. Smith, James Jerome Hill and George Stephen headed the Syndicate.

SOME ENCHANTED EVENING

Donald Alexander Smith, Lord Strathcona.

Far from Red River, in distant Labrador, a story unfolded that would play a key role in the next chapter of the West's history. George Simpson, the Hudson's Bay Company's "little emperor," married his cousin, Frances Ramsey Simpson. Frances, 20 years her husband's junior, became captivated with a young Scottish clerk at the Hudson's Bay Company's Montreal office. The extent of their relationship is entirely speculative, but Simpson dispatched the young man to Tadoussac, Quebec, and later to the Labrador department.

The young man displayed an irrepressible talent, converting both departments into high-profit centres. He then worked out an ingenious investment scheme. His colleagues, who saved about £750 a year, invested it at a two per cent return. Simpson promised he could get them three per cent. Working with his cousin, who was in the textile business in Montreal, he invested their money at rates up to 16 per cent. After giving his cohorts their promised three per cent, he pocketed the rest. The young man was Donald Alexander Smith. His cousin was the Montreal financier, George Stephen.

In 1869, Smith returned to Montreal a rich man. Working with his cousin, they took over the faltering Bank of Montreal. Smith then bought so heavily into the Hudson's Bay Company that he became in effect its chief officer in Canada. In this role, the government of Sir John A. Macdonald sent him west to resolve the Riel insurrection. Returning from Red River, Smith was dog-sledding through a blizzard when he spied another lone team. The two men met and camped together. While the wind howled around them, they developed a scheme that would eventually change, even more than the Hudson's Bay Company, the course of the West's history. The other dog-sledder was the great American railway builder James Jerome Hill. The business enterprise they conceived during that long, cold night was the Canadian Pacific Railway.

1894 ▶

A campaign for better roads throughout the province is initiated by the Ontario Good Roads Association.

The difficulties of construction and demand for early completion of the line ensured generous provisions to the Canadian Pacific Railway, including $25 million in cash, 25 million acres (10 million hectares) of land in a belt along the railway and the cost of surveys totalling $37 million. The CPR also received all the completed railway track, tax-free status on its railway property and a monopoly on all railway traffic in Western Canada for 20 years; a two-decade head start before any competition. Opposing interests loudly denounced these terms. However, in the face of westward American expansion, Macdonald and the federal Conservatives considered completion of the railway a national imperative.

The railway was completed in three phases. First, the line crossed the Canadian Shield. Although the section of the line hugging the northern border of Lake Superior would not be completed until 1885, the majority of the line successfully traversed a treacherous landscape of rocky bluffs and bottomless muskeg. Next, William Cornelius Van Horne, who was appointed general manager of the CPR in 1882, used his excellent managerial skills to improve the organization of prairie section construction. With a work force of more than 5,000 men, the railway made comparatively good progress across the plains. By October 1882, trains were running on a regular schedule from Winnipeg to Regina. In August of 1883, the CPR reached a small Canadian frontier town called Calgary. The settlement was little more than a police fort and a collection of trading posts. Under the influence

Laying track on the plains.

Calgary, mid-1880s, looking southwest from the north bank of the Bow River. Centre left are the North-West Mounted Police barracks. The CPR bridge over the Elbow River is on the extreme left.

of the CPR, Calgary was quickly organized and incorporated as a town by the end of 1884.

With the CPR's arrival in Calgary, the second phase was completed. Now the CPR faced the last great hurdle: crossing the Pacific mountain ranges. In 1882, exploratory teams had found a suitable pass through this immense natural barrier. But it was still tough sledding. As the building crews made slow progress through some of the most rugged terrain in the world, the CPR found its financial situation growing steadily more desperate. Reminding the government in Ottawa that "the day the Canadian Pacific busts, the Conservative party busts the day after," it begged for additional Dominion funds to complete the job. Soon, satirists, political wits, and Liberal politicians were wondering what would prove more bottomless: the great muskeg swamps of the Canadian Shield or the CPR's demands for more government money.

Just at this moment of crisis, the enigmatic figure of Louis Riel made his second, and final, appearance on the national stage. Ironically, Riel's presence again had a lasting impact on the destiny of the Mannix family. It was Louis Riel's leadership of the first Rebellion in 1870 that drew George C. Mannix to Manitoba. The aftermath of the second Riel Rebellion of 1885 ensured the successful completion of the CPR and guaranteed a future in railway construction for G.C. Mannix's son, Frederick Stephen.

1896 ▶

After a hiatus of 1,500 years, the Olympic Games are revived in Athens, Greece.

1897 ▶

The federal government and the CPR sign the Crow's Nest Pass Agreement. Following the grant of a $3.3-million cash subsidy in return for reduced rates for goods shipped east and some personal possessions shipped west, the CPR begins construction of its line over the pass in July.

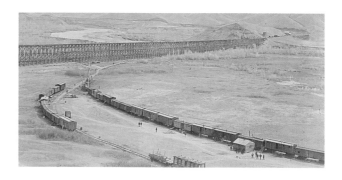

The North-West Rebellion and the Driving of the Last Spike

Just as the CPR seemed to be drowning in a sea of red ink, trouble once again erupted among the Métis. There had long been unrest in the North-West, arising from the federal government's indifference to the grievances of the population since the Red River Rebellion. Of greatest concern was recognition of the legal rights to land occupied for up to 15 years but not yet surveyed. Petitions regarding redress of grievances had been presented to Ottawa as early as 1878. When the discontented voices went unheeded, many people spoke of violence. The Métis called Louis Riel back from exile in Montana in June 1884. As tensions mounted during the severe winter of 1885, the possibility of peaceful settlement waned; after Duck Lake, negotiation was impossible.

On March 26, 1885, a skirmish between the Métis and the North-West Mounted Police occurred at Duck Lake, located some 30 miles (50 kilometres) southwest of Prince Albert, North-West Territories, now Saskatchewan. When a small party of North-West Mounted Police rode from Fort Carlton toward Duck Lake for supplies, they were fired upon and turned back. To assert police authority, 56 Mounties and 43 Prince Albert settlers, led by Superintendent L.N.F. Crozier, set off for Duck Lake. They, too, were intercepted by Métis and Indians. When Crozier attempted to negotiate with their commander, Gabriel Dumont, a shot was heard. The police fired. Well-hidden snipers

Forces of the Canadian Militia overrun the rebel stronghold at Batoche, North-West Territories, effectively ending the North-West Rebellion of 1885.

Chief Poundmaker, a Cree adopted into the Blackfoot Nation, surrenders to Major-General Middleton at Battleford, Saskatchewan.

fired back. Dumont lost five men, while Crozier lost 12, with another 11 wounded. Duck Lake gave Riel an important victory. It was also the scene of the outbreak of the 1885 North-West Rebellion.

The Canadian government reacted with all possible speed, considering that the Pacific Railway north of Lake Superior was incomplete. CPR general manager William Van Horne quickly arranged for Canadian troops to be transported across the gaps, enabling them to reach the North-West Mounted Police post at Fort Qu'Appelle by April 10. Indians under Cree Chief Big Bear had already killed or captured nine people at Frog Lake. Major-General Frederick Middleton, commander of the Canadian Militia, intended to send a three-pronged attack from the CPR line north toward the settlements. Major-General T.B. Strange was dispatched to Calgary, and was to progress north toward Edmonton. Lieutenant-Colonel William Otter was to move north from Swift Current toward Battleford, where NWMP officers warned of the threat presented to the white population by the area's Cree. Middletown himself was to move north from Qu'Appelle toward Batoche.

On April 24 at Fish Creek, the Métis and Middleton's forces fought an indecisive battle. On May 2 at Cut Knife Hill, Otter withdrew in the face of stiff resistance from Chief Poundmaker's Cree forces. Only during the days of May 9 through 12, at Batoche, were government forces able to

1898 ▶

Dawson City becomes the largest city west of Winnipeg after the discovery of gold in the Klondike area of the Yukon. Territorial status is awarded to the surrounding area. One-fourth of the Canadian Army arrives to assist the NWMP in maintaining the peace.

1899 ▶

Treaty No. 8 between Indians and the Canadian government is signed. It covers the huge area north of Treaty No. 6.

1901 ▶

Queen Victoria dies. Many in Ottawa attend her memorial service.

THE LAST SPIKE

On November 7, 1885, the last spike was driven on the Canadian Pacific Railway. The spike marking this incredible feat of human vision and perseverance was not made of gold, silver or other precious metal, but of iron. Driven during a simple ceremony, it stands in testament to the many thousands of people whose lives and labour created the railway.

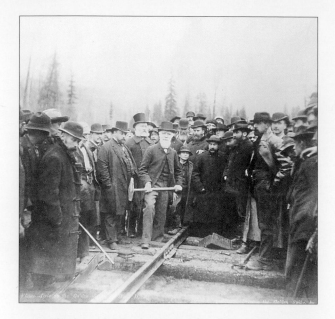

The choice of spike also signalled that, despite the fact that the railway was conceived in the lofty realm of men's dreams, it was a working railway. William Cornelius Van Horne, the brilliant railway general manager whose drive and determination were largely responsible for the rapid completion of the CPR, is reported to have proclaimed, "The last spike will be just as good an iron one as there is between Montreal and Vancouver, and anyone who wants to see it driven will have to pay full fare."

win decisively. The battle at Batoche broke Métis resistance. Riel was taken into custody May 15. Métis leader, Gabriel Dumont, escaped to the United States. Big Bear remained at large until July 2, after encountering and retreating from government forces on May 28 at Frenchman's Butte. Most of the Indian and Métis leaders were imprisoned and later granted amnesty. Riel was hanged in Regina on November 16, 1885. The North-West Rebellion cost the Canadian government some $5 million; 38 government troops and 72 Métis and Indians were dead.

While the rebellion focused national attention on western grievances — and some concessions were subsequently granted to the white population — it was also a marvellous piece of advertising for the CPR. The sight of Canadian troops quickly moving from one part of the Dominion to another was a thoroughly persuasive argument for the capacities of the new railway. Public opinion shifted in favour of additional financing for the CPR. With money no longer a problem, the railway was quickly brought to completion. On November 7, 1885, at Craigellachie in the mountains of British Columbia, Donald Smith drove the fabled last spike. The first transcontinental train left Montreal on June 28, 1886, and arrived at Port Moody, British Columbia, July 4, 1886.

After the trainload of dignitaries who posed for the official last spike photograph rolled off toward the Pacific, CPR workers pose for their own last spike ceremony at Craigellachie, British Columbia.

1902 ▶

The first gasoline-powered automobile arrives in Alberta.

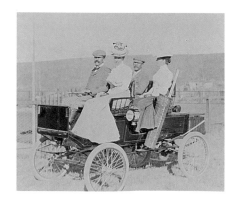

"One Fresno and one horse paid for, one not"

One cannot help but be awed by the prodigious feats performed in the construction of the Canadian Pacific Railway across the top of the North American continent. It was a tremendous triumph of will, of courage, of human tenacity. The work was slow, done mainly by hand labour and horses. Even so, track was laid across the prairie at a rate of three to five miles (five to eight kilometres) a day. Perhaps the most gut-busting job was building grade. Literally thousands of privately owned horse outfits — dirt movers of the time who had horses and equipment were known as "outfits" — performed this work. Very few of these outfits survived past the building of the railway and its feeder lines. A few did. One such outfit was owned by F.S. Mannix.

In 1898, longtime rail grade contractors, the Keith brothers, contracted with the CPR to extend the line north of Stonewall, Manitoba. That same year, at the age of 17 — the same age his father set sail from Ireland — F.S. Mannix returned to Manitoba, bought a slip and a team of horses for $150 and went to work on the railway. His first earth-moving jobs were for branch lines the CPR constructed in Manitoba and Saskatchewan. After some time, his younger brother, Len, expressed an interest in working for him. However, when F.S. went to an auction to buy a team for Len, he discovered he did not have enough money to make a

Railway contractor and builder, J.D. McArthur.

Alf Mannix uses a Mormon board and a four-horse team to level dirt in the early 1900s.

successful bid. Fortunately, his youthful gumption so impressed a perfect stranger that he was lent the money. According to Alice Mannix Kramer, daughter of F.S., the stranger was none other than J.D. McArthur, a successful and influential contractor. "That was the beginning," she said. "J.D. McArthur helped my dad when he first started with one Fresno and one horse paid for, one not."

From that humble beginning, F.S. Mannix began to expand his outfit. "All he wanted to do was get a team of horses and a Fresno and drive those horses on the job of building that railroad," recalled William (Bill) Hamilton, a longtime Mannix employee. "That was his ambition. He worked hard, and pretty soon he had two horses, two teams, three teams, four teams. Pretty soon he was doing his own contracting with about 60 teams."

Dirt movers start from scratch; they literally scratch a living from the soil. There are few obstacles they do not confront: obstreperous men and mercurial weather, ornery horses and difficult equipment, raw whisky and tricky cards, the very earth itself. F.S. Mannix started contracting in an era where rugged independent men carried their business in their heads and hip pockets. Life itself was a gamble; business was no different. A man's only security was confidence in his own ability. The tools of his trade were horses, a slip and a Fresno.

A slip, also known as a drag scraper, was a flat metal plate with attached sideboards. At the base in

◀ **1903**

A huge rock slide partially destroys the Alberta town of Frank.

1904

Canada first competes in the Olympic Games. Gold medals are won by Étienne Desmarteau in the hammer throw and George Lyon in golf.

front was a strip of iron that served as the cutting edge. The side extended into a pair of handles at the rear; two or more heavy work horses or mules were harnessed to its double-trees and the outfit scraped up loose earth as it slipped or dragged along on its belly. Aside from the wagon and cart, this amazingly simple device appears to be man's first practical mule- or horse-powered tool. A slip could excavate 30 to 40 cubic yards (23 to 31 cubic metres) of dirt every 12 hours.

In 1885, Abijah McCall, a blacksmith and earthmoving canal builder of Fresno, California, patented a new type of scraper. The Fresno scraper, as it was called, proved to be the best earthmoving mule- or horse-powered tool ever devised. As the horses or mules pulled the Fresno along, the driver stood on a tailboard hinged to the front board. The handle of the Fresno was an iron bar, which could be as long as eight feet (a little over two metres). Using the pressure of his weight, the driver lifted up the handle. This tilted the blade forward, forcing the cutting edge into the ground. On a nine-hour work day, a good muleskinner could move 100 cubic yards (76 cubic metres) of dirt.

Following the Iron Rail West

In 1904, F.S. Mannix moved farther west to Edmonton, in the portion of the North-West Territories that was to become the province of Alberta in 1905. The reason for this move was the opportunity to work on the construction of the Canadian Northern Railway and the Grand

William Alfred Victor (Alf) Mannix.

Leonard Nial (Len) Mannix.

Below: Jasper Avenue, Edmonton, Alberta, circa 1906.

Bottom: A mile north of Morinville, construction continues on the Canadian Northern Railway grade toward Athabasca Landing, June 1909.

Trunk Pacific, the two transcontinental lines that would eventually become the main lines of the Canadian National Railways. The Canadian Northern Railway and Grand Trunk Pacific followed a more northerly route across the Prairies of Western Canada and converged at Edmonton. They crossed the Rockies via the Yellowhead Pass. Winning work with the Canadian Northern Railway for grade construction in Saskatchewan and Alberta in 1904, F.S. Mannix subsequently established headquarters in Edmonton in 1905.

Though F.S. Mannix established his headquarters in Edmonton, he still had to travel to Winnipeg to bid for work. Winnipeg, known as the "Gateway to the West," was the great distributing and railway centre of the North-West. For 100 years, as a trading post and business centre, Winnipeg was a tollgate on the only practical access route into and out of Western Canada. A million settlers moved westward through Winnipeg in a single decade. The freight trains that brought all the consumer goods and production machinery into the West were broken up in Winnipeg. Their contents were distributed throughout the huge complex of wholesale ware-houses in the centre of the city. From there they moved out again in the wake of a small army of travelling salesmen who carried their order books as far afield as the Peace River.

The wheat from the West found its way to world export mar-kets over the same railway system, while the wheat merchants of the Grain Exchange siphoned off their

1904 ▶

Rail is laid on Mannix-built railway grade near Turtleford, Saskatchewan.

1905 ▶

Alberta is named a province.

1905 ▶

The Canadian Northern Railway line from Winnipeg reaches Edmonton on November 24, inaugurating the first rail service to Edmonton that does not go through Calgary.

Left: Winnipeg stockyards.

commissions. Winnipeg's slaughterhouses rivalled those of Toronto and St. Paul, and cattle from the West moved through the city's stockyards to southern, eastern, and United Kingdom markets. All this required several thousand skilled craftsmen in three mammoth railway shops to keep the trains moving. Many more thousands manhandled the merchandise in and out of numerous warehouses. In the centre of it all, within a four-block stretch of Main Street, was the financial heart of Western Canada. The western head offices of the chartered banks, trust companies and insurance companies were located in this small section of the city. Decisions made in these offices would fuel the many western booms.

Below: Byryid Helen Fitzpatrick Mannix and Frederick Stephen Mannix after their January 9, 1907, wedding in Edmonton, Alberta.

"A very happy household"

Two years after moving to Edmonton, F.S. Mannix married Byryid Helen Fitzpatrick, a young woman he met through her brother, Tom Fitzpatrick, who also worked as a railway grade contractor. Born in Ontario, Byryid moved with her parents to a homestead near Stony Plain, Alberta, when she was three years old. On the Fitzpatrick family farm, Byryid experienced all the difficulties and discomforts of any frontier family. Land had to be cleared. Wood had to be cut. Washing and baking were constant features of daily life. Byryid married Frederick Stephen when she was just 16 years old. By the time she was 23, she was already the mother of four children. She was to have six children in all, five girls and one boy: Eleanor Mannix, born 1908; Byryid Alicia, born 1909; Margaret Helen, born 1911; Frederick Charles, born 1913; Florence Dora Evelyne, born 1915; and Luella, born in 1918.

Fred Mannix could not have made a better choice for a lifelong companion and friend. His wife provided a sense of stability and strength in the nomadic world of a dirt mover. With her husband travelling extensively to both bid and supervise jobs, Byryid Mannix shouldered most of the burdens at home. "She was really almost a mother and father to all of us," said Alice Mannix Kramer. "In those days, the construction business was far different than it is now," added Margaret Mannix Walsh. "There was only the train to take to get anywhere. You didn't have the transportation you do now, so everything took a long time. Father had to do all his bidding for work in Winnipeg so he would be away for quite some time, probably two or three weeks. No sooner would he get back, then he'd be off to one of the camps, so we didn't see him until the fall. Do you know the expression, 'When the work will be all done this fall?' Well, it was really true in his case because when the work got all done each fall, he would come home. So we had him home during the wintertime. That was a big deal."

1905 ▶

Canadian curling, 1905.

"We used to have great races when Dad came home," recalled Florence Mannix Pallesen. "Dad would come to the front door and we used to have a race to see who would kiss him first. It was great fun. We were quite a sentimental family that way. We used to push poor Luella out of the way. She was kind of little. It used to be sort of a family ritual to see who could kiss Dad first when he came home. If you got up in the morning when my father was home and came down with a long face, he would say, 'You had better go up and get out of the other side of the bed.' There was no way you could come down in the morning without a smile on your face. So, you see, my reminiscences of childhood are nice and sweet. It was a very happy household."

Both Byryid and Frederick Stephen were firm believers in education. "Father went back to school after he was married," said Mrs. Pallesen. "He went back to night school because he didn't think his multi-plication and division and all that were sharp enough. He went back so that he could estimate jobs and keep track of things. My father could go over a job and he wouldn't need a pencil. He wasn't an engineer or anything like that, but he could walk over a job and practically tell how much he was going to charge a yard for dirt hauling, as he called it."

If F.S. Mannix felt the lack of a good education — he only completed schooling through the fourth grade — he was determined to make sure his children had a better start in life. "My father's number-one principle was for us all to get a good education," said Luella Mannix Wilson. "He only had a very sparse education himself. His dad

Left to right: Byryid Alicia (Alice),
Margaret Helen (Margie), Eleanor and
Frederick Charles Mannix, circa 1914.

The F.S. Mannix family about 1920. Left to right: Margie,
Byryid, Eleanor, Luella on knee, Frederick Stephen,
Frederick Charles, Alice and Florence Dora Evelyne Mannix.

wouldn't let him go to school. He made him work. Dad thought that was the worst thing that ever happened to him. Dad was really proud of Margie and me, just because we graduated from the university. He was just really, really sold on education. He was very farsighted. The thing he thought best was to have your education and do some travelling. He gave that to all of us. We all could have had as much education as we ever wanted. My dad was a fantas-tically kind man and very generous. He always said it's much nicer to be able to give than to receive, and to remember that for the rest of your life."

"That was the key to why F.S. Mannix was a successful contractor."

In 1907, F.S. Mannix contracted to build railway grade between Unity, Saskatchewan, and Hardisty, Alberta. The job went well until 1909, when the Mannix outfit encountered the curse of all construction work: bad weather. The skies opened, the rain came down and the soil turned to muck. Vapour shooting out their nostrils, their coats glistening with sweat, the horses struggled to keep their footing. Yet no matter how hard they struggled, the Fresnoes and slips remained mired in the mud.

Week after week it rained. Production fell and swamp fever struck the horses. Things were bleak — losing the horses meant losing your shirt. Despite the difficulties, Mannix crews continued to work as best they could and by the end of the year the job was completed. The horses were on their last legs, the job had made no money, but F.S. Mannix made sure that the work

1905 ▶

Canoeing provides summer recreation
throughout Canada.

1906 ▶

Tommy Burns, the first and only
Canadian to win the world heavyweight
championship, defeats Marvin Hart
in 20 rounds.

was finished and done properly. It was the start of the Mannix tradition that continues to this day: "Do the job. Do it right. Do it on time."

Two years later, the Mannix outfit contracted to build the stretch of the Grand Trunk Pacific Railway from Balcarres to Fort Qu'Appelle, Saskatchewan. R.A. (Bob) Kramer, who would later become a partner, recalled F.S. Mannix talking about the job. "Fred Mannix was working west because the railroads were being built west. He kept getting the odd job now and then, mainly from the Canadian Pacific Railway. I remember him telling me that he had this job with Bill Dutton, Red Dutton's father. Fred Mannix had the stretch from Balcarres to Fort Qu'Appelle. He told me how he used to walk into Fort Qu'Appelle. He would carry out a full sack of potatoes on his back to keep his crew going. It was that tough."

"You could judge by the food that was served in the dining room whether the man was a good contractor or not," said Merv (Red) Dutton, who apprenticed under his dad, Bill Dutton. "That was one of my dad's strictest rules: you feed and bed your men; feed them as much as they can eat, and good food, too. That was a ritual. It had to be. Mannix was the same. Mr. Mannix and my dad did a lot of work together in joint ventures. He and my dad were close friends. I got into contracting with my brother and then we split and he went with somebody and I stayed alone. I worked all year for Mr. Mannix but I never had a contract with him. His word was as good as his bond. If you were in trouble, you could call Fred, and if it was warranted, you got help. Everybody respected him. He was a good father. He was good to his family. I knew his family so well, it was just like our own family.

"My father and Mr. Mannix were the top men in bidding or securing work. There is quite an art to bidding on work. There's a price for dirt, a price for hard pan, a price for loose rock, a price for solid rock. Your price for dirt would be 25, 26 cents. Your hard pan would maybe be 30 cents. Your loose rock would be 45 to 50 cents. Solid rock would be $2 or $2.50. You wouldn't get much solid rock, but loose rock used to get you out of the hole sometimes. There were a lot of prices, a lot of different materials you had to move. That was the key to why F.S. Mannix was a successful contractor — he could size up work so quickly. Mr. Mannix was a man who didn't waste money. He worked hard for it."

An elevating grader cutting grade on the Hoadley to Lacombe, Alberta, job. Big Steve, standing, controls the cutting depth of the grader while Jim Procter, the high skinner, drives the pulling horses. The low skinner, Hugh Procter, drives the team pushing the grader from behind.

"Mannix gathered a lot of good subcontractors," continued Dutton. "He maybe had four or five contracts and he was always out on the work site from one job to another. It was quite a day when F.S. would come out to the work site. He was always welcome; he always made some kind of contribution. When we were working for him, he had the right to say what he wanted, but he could size whether you were doing a good job or whether you needed help or more equipment. It was amazing to me how quickly he could size up a job. I've seen him do it three or four times. I remember

1906 ▶

In the 1880s, Michel Pablo rounded up buffalo to live with him on the Flathead Reserve in Montana. The reserve is lost to settlers in 1906, but Pablo possesses the largest buffalo herd in the world. They are herded toward northern Alberta, to what becomes Wood Buffalo National Park. Their descendants will constitute one-half of all buffalo in the world.

1907 ▶

John J. McLaughlin, Toronto pharmacist and bottler, creates Canada Dry Ginger Ale.

one time I was up at northern Saskatchewan. It was a tough piece of work — there was a lot of rock in it, a lot of boulders that you had to break up to get loose so that you could move them. I was down on what we called the adobe shot, where you take the powder and put some dynamite on it and put a cap on it and blow it so you break the rock. I didn't see Fred arrive. I was down getting this all fixed up and there was Fred. He said, 'Move that over just a little bit. Just move the whole shot about like this, powder and dynamite on top.' He wanted me to move the dynamite over a little bit to get a fair break on the rock. He was right."

While F.S. Mannix was known for his ability to size up a job quickly, he was also known for his faith in his men and their decisions, going so far as to back them against the wisdom of greenhorn railway engineers. "There was an incident where an engineer had just come out of college," recalled Dutton. "He had the theory, but he didn't have the practice. I was pretty near going nuts over him. I knew he was wrong in what he was doing. I tried to tell him he was wrong, but he said, 'This book and one per cent of my own knowledge tell me everything.'" So the next time F.S. Mannix visited the

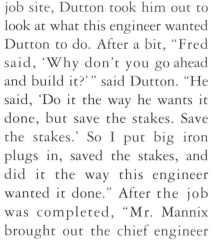

A Mannix elevating grader shown with three dump wagons. Each wagon is pulled by a three-horse team. When filled by the buckets of the grader, each wagon pulls away to allow the next wagon to be filled. This allows constant operation of the grader outfit.

Two elevating grader outfits and their accompanying dump wagons pause and illustrate the entire grading operation in this photograph, circa 1910.

job site, Dutton took him out to look at what this engineer wanted Dutton to do. After a bit, "Fred said, 'Why don't you go ahead and build it?'" said Dutton. "He said, 'Do it the way he wants it done, but save the stakes. Save the stakes.' So I put big iron plugs in, saved the stakes, and did it the way this engineer wanted it done." After the job was completed, "Mr. Mannix brought out the chief engineer of the CNR, a fellow by the name of J.L. Charles, who was a great friend of Mr. Mannix's," Dutton said. "I took him down to where this piece of work was. I just let him have a look. I didn't say anything. Mr. Mannix was with him, and he didn't say anything but Charles, being an engineer, saw it right away. He didn't say anything to me then, but he said something to the engineer afterwards.

"F.S. Mannix was a great man. I loved the old fellow. We subbed on several jobs for Mr. Mannix, then Mr. Mannix kind of worked the west and my dad worked the east. Fred worked on the irrigation ditches. My family, or the Dutton outfit, W.A. Dutton, didn't do any of that work at all. My father died in 1934, but Fred Sr. was the man."

1907 ▶

F.S. Mannix crews begin a multi-year project building rail grade between Unity, Saskatchewan, and Hardisty, Alberta.

1909 ▶

The giant dam and irrigation project near Bassano, Alberta, begins. It will run until 1914, with secondary facilities built in the surrounding counties.

Branching out into Irrigation

In 1909, F.S. Mannix used the skills acquired in railway construction to branch out into a new field — irrigation. The West had opened, the Canadian Pacific Railway had arrived, but the expected land rush did not happen. It took a railway hungry for people and freight to get things moving.

Long before the turn of the century, the federal government was anxious over the Palliser's Triangle in Western Canada. This enormous stretch of Canadian prairie covered much of southern Alberta and Saskatchewan and a corner of southwestern Manitoba. Both the Palliser and the Dawson expeditions had declared the land unfit for agriculture. As much of the land was dry, Ottawa began drafting a western water policy. One plan, the North Saskatchewan Diversion Scheme, would have carried water into dry southern Alberta through a network of great canals. It also would have cost $100 million. Perhaps because of the price, politicians decided drought was just a passing annoyance and Alberta's soil could withstand an occasional dry year. Unfortunately, drought was a reality that withstood the optimism of politicians.

This was not acceptable to the Canadian Pacific Railway, which needed settlers to survive. In taking up its remaining land grants in the West, the CPR accepted certain blocks on the understanding that they would be improved through irrigation. The subsequent irrigation work undertaken by the CPR required massive amounts of capital and the permission to radically change the geography of southern Alberta. It also created a new area of profitable work for the Mannix outfit. And it was excellent timing. In less than a decade since Mannix followed the iron rail to Alberta, railway construction projects were becoming far less frequent.

In 1909, contracts were awarded to Noehren & Mannix to build irrigation ditches and structures for the Southern Alberta Land Company, Limited. This company was part of the giant British-sponsored irrigation project. Noehren & Mannix was to help build a connecting canal

PROMOTING THE GREAT LONE LAND

With a steel backbone uniting the Dominion from sea to sea, Prime Minister Sir John A. Macdonald had accomplished one of the main objectives of his national policy. With the railway in place, the next step in that program could begin. Macdonald envisioned that the railway would be a prime factor behind the expansion and settlement of the Canadian West. It was his dream that the Canadian Pacific Railway would carry new settlers into the broad emptiness that stretched between the Great Lakes and British Columbia.

When Canada acquired Rupert's Land from the Hudson's Bay Company, the region was little known and virtually unsettled. The CPR had to find some way to lure people to these vast, empty lands. "One of our prominent historians, Sir William Francis Butler, called Western Canada the Great Lone Land," said Norris (Buck) Crump, former president and chairman of the Canadian Pacific Railway. "I have always liked that phrase because there was nothing here. There was nobody for 500, 800, almost 1,000 miles except a few Indians."

"Because this was the Great Lone Land, when the Canadian Pacific was built across to Calgary in 1883, they had to provide all the services," Crump said. "They not only built the railway, but they also built the telegraph line because that was the only form of communication. The CPR had their own colonization service in Europe — the government didn't have a colonization department, so we had to do it. We had to have settlers and farms and industry to feed freight traffic to the railways. We had to establish agricultural schools and farms to teach immigrants how to farm, because if there were no people, the railway would go broke. It was a matter of survival."

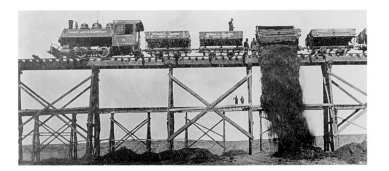

1909 ▶

Mannix crews help build the 40-mile (64-kilometre) connecting canal from the Bow River to the newly planned reservoir, Lake McGregor.

THE ORIGINS OF IRRIGATION IN SOUTHERN ALBERTA

Irrigation is a relatively recent phenomenon in Canada. Before the 1890s, private individuals developed all irrigation systems. In 1877, 40 Mormons, under the leadership of Ora Card, emigrated from the United States to present-day Cardston. Skilled irrigation farmers, they built a small irrigation system using water from the Milk River.

The Northwest Irrigation Act passed in 1894, allowing those who improved a parcel of land by irrigation to claim it. Not long after, the Mormons reached an agreement with the Galt family, who owned coal properties near Lethbridge. The Galts would put up the money to establish a method of saturating the arid land. The Mormons, through their church in Utah, would supply the labour. This was the beginning of an irrigation system that would soon crisscross southern Alberta.

In the very dry country between Medicine Hat and Calgary, the Canadian Pacific Railway developed a massive irrigation system to transform the area from a marginal to a productive agricultural zone. It began in 1894 when the CPR agreed to accept a large block of land as fit for settlement because of its location next to the main line and irrigation potential. The government turned over this block of 2.9 million acres (1.2 million hectares) in 1903 and by the following year irrigation work started on the section closest to Calgary. By 1909, 1,600 miles (2,600 kilometres) of canals and ditches were dug. In April 1914, the dam across the Bow River near Bassano, Alberta, was opened. Connected to it were another 2,500 miles (4,000 kilometres) of waterways to serve the eastern section of the Irrigation Block.

from the Bow River to flow more than 40 miles (64 kilometres) to a newly planned reservoir, Lake McGregor. The next year, while still working on the Bow River/Lake McGregor project, J.D. McArthur — the same man who had loaned F.S. Mannix money to buy his brother, Len, a team of horses — sent his brother, D.F. McArthur, to meet F.S. Mannix to discuss a contract for the excavation of a large CPR irrigation canal in Gleichen, Alberta. Noehren & Mannix did not have the equipment for both the Southern Alberta Land Company work and such a large contract, so J.D. McArthur Company Limited bankrolled additional equipment. "In the spring of 1910," recalled F.S. Mannix's son, Frederick Charles, "J.D. McArthur sent his brother to F.S. with a contract for irrigation work at Gleichen. He went in with six new dump wagons to haul dirt and an elevating grader pulled by 14 horses. That job had good horses, good equipment and good men. The next year, the Mannix outfit was awarded the biggest dirt moving job let in Canada — the irrigation canal at Brooks, Alberta." The proposed irrigation system would provide water for 200,000 acres (81,000 hectares) by a combination of 2,000 miles (3,200 kilometres) of canals and ditches. Lake Newell Reservoir would provide the water for canals to Rosemary, Gem and the Brooks area.

Byryid Mannix, standing left, with longtime Mannix helper and cook, Pearl Lawler, standing centre, with their children. The building is the Mannix family's construction shack during the summer of 1912.

1909 ▶

Douglas McCurdy inaugurates the first airplane flight in Canada when he becomes airborne in a Silver Dart built by Alexander Graham Bell.

1910 ▶

Near Alliance, Alberta, Mannix crews build rail grade using wheeled Fresnoes.

J.D. McArthur Company lent the Mannix outfit a little more than $7,000. The goods and chattel listed as collateral show the growth of the Mannix outfit: 27 horses and a brown mule named Jean; 11 tents varying in size from 10' x 12' to 30' x 20'; "8 Stroud little red waggons for grader; 1 Stroud grader; 1 disc for grader; 1 Mormon scraper; 5 Fysh waggons; 2 Moline Waggons; 1 Adams waggon; 7 National wheelers; 10 slip scrapers; 1 John Deere scrub plow; 1 John Deere road plow; 2 Western grubber plows; 1 Dosh plow; 1 Blacksmith's outfit; 11 sets double harness; 1 buggy; 1 cooking outfit including stoves, dishes, all cooking utensils, etc., having a capacity for 25 men; 14 sets of whiffle trees and neck yokes; 14 shovels and crow-bars."

By 1912, Noehren & Mannix was so well established in irrigation work that they subcontracted some dirt moving to others. One such sub, Craig & Hiss, out of Nebraska, performed part of the Tilley spillway work, moving, as C.A. Hiss claimed, more than one million cubic yards (763,000 cubic metres) of dirt in 1912 and 1913. This huge CPR irrigation project featured one of the early uses of the elevating grader in Western Canada. The elevating grader was a simple, but ingenious, design — a four-wheeled scraper with an elevated conveyer belt rising from the front to the back wheels, or off to the side. Depending upon the type of terrain, the grader was pulled by teams of between 18 and 24 horses. At the front of the machine, an angled blade, or plow, extended down between the front wheels. As this blade broke the ground, it guided the loose dirt into a number of boxes or "elevators." A belt mechanism linked these elevators together to form an endless band of boxes that revolved as the wagon was pulled forward. When a box of earth reached the top of the belt, it emptied into a trailing dump wagon. As each dump wagon was

Top: Listed are some of the Mannix animals used by Frederick Stephen Mannix to secure a mortgage from the J.D. McArthur Company Limited during irrigation work near Tilley, Alberta. Each animal is identified by type, sex, name, weight and age.

Above: Some of the Mannix equipment during the construction of irrigation structures near Tilley, Alberta.

filled, it would move out of the way and let an empty dump wagon take its place. An experienced operator could move 80 to 90 cubic yards (61 to 69 cubic metres) of dirt per hour. For this job, Noehren & Mannix also purchased new Athey wagons. Athey wagons were tracked, not wheeled, wagons that were pulled alongside an elevating grader. The elevating grader dumped the dirt it scooped up from the ground into the Athey wagon, which then hauled the dirt to the dump areas. This job also used huge, for the time, steam draglines. Often two worked side by side within a canal, excavating both banks simultaneously.

"That was one thing about them, boy, they had real good horses."

Horses were crucial to operations and a good contractor took great pride in his teams. "My step dad was a partner with Mannix and I drove dump wagons with horses when I was going to high school," recalled Earl Dunn. "In the summer, I'd go out and work. It was all horses when I first started. They had about ten dump wagons, three horses on each dump wagon, an elevating grader. You drove under it and the dirt came up. The thing was not to get dirt on the seat because you sat there. You got to be pretty good because you didn't want to get dirt on your seat. You kept the horses moving, oh yes.

"They had good horses, too. That was one thing about them, boy, they had real good horses. They always were proud of the horses. Something like nowadays you see these big horses in the beer ads? Well, the horses were in that category. I remember they had one horse, they called him 'Old Bill,' he weighed over a ton. He was a big horse and a lot of them weighed very close to that. They took good care of their horses. They had what they call a Barn Boss who looked after them. Of course everybody had to

1910 ▶

The Mannix outfit begins building the irrigation structures around Gleichen, Alberta.

1911 ▶

Described as the largest dirt-moving contract ever let in Alberta, the irrigation system at Brooks, east of Bassano, includes the spillway and adjacent structures at Tilley. F.S. Mannix and his crews tackle this project.

look after their own team, the horses they were driving, but when you'd come in from work they watered them and cleaned them, curried them and brushed them down."

"When I was out at Drumheller working, there were a lot of horses," Dunn said. "You know, when you got horses, you got flies. I maintain that you had to run to the cookhouse and get in because when they rang the bell for a meal, why, the flies ran too. They knew that things were on the table and bi gosh, it was crowded in there. Why, those flies were just as thick as they could be. But camp life wasn't bad. Mostly you were so tired, getting up early in the morning, that you went to bed and slept. They had breakfast at a quarter to six in the morning. We worked 10 hours a day. They used to take two hours off at noon though, to rest the horses. There was no lunch break, although I used to take something and put it in my pocket to have something to eat after a while, because I used to get hungry.

"One time Cecil McCormick was on a grader and I was pulling these wagons. We were working overtime and the cook sent us out a couple of sandwiches to eat. We opened our sandwiches and there were about five dead flies in them. There was a house on the top of the hill and I went up there and there was a girl there about my age and I says, 'You wouldn't have a drink of nice, cold milk?' A German family it was and they had a lovely home and farm. She says, 'Come on in,' so I went in. She got me a cold glass of milk and she brought out a great, big chocolate cake and gave me a great big piece. I should have stayed around longer but I left; I was young. But I will always remember eating that piece of cake and then going back and telling Cecil what I had."

F.S. Mannix stands next to one of his many draft horses.

"A gentle yet somehow determined kindness"

The very nature of the Canadian landscape, coupled with working with horses and primitive equipment, produced more than a few men who could have inspired the phrase, "They sure don't make them like that anymore." Two of the more colourful characters associated with the Mannix outfit during this time were Gus Enarson and Ora Burggren. Both hard workers, they could not have been more different. Gus Enarson was a deeply religious man who was not known to drink, smoke or swear. Ora Burggren was, well, Ora Burggren.

Gus Enarson began work with F.S. Mannix in 1912. He was newly arrived from Denmark, filled with the confidence and skill that only a builder's hands can know, and he used those hands and that skill with single-minded intensity for the next 42 years. F.S. Mannix's son, F.C. Mannix, credited Enarson with teaching him much of the ways of dirt moving. "I think of the word kindness when I think of Gus Enarson," F.C. Mannix once reflected. "A gentle yet somehow determined kindness — with the workhorses of those early days, with the men under him, and especially with a rather willful boy who had to be taught the ways of construction and the things he would have to know."

Bob Kramer could not agree more with that assessment. "If it wasn't for old Gus, I don't think Freddie and I would be where we are today," he said. "Gus started us off on the right foot and showed us how to do this work and make sure we did it properly. Old Gus didn't say a heck of a lot, really, but if there was a job to do, boy, you did it. He had the ability to get all these fellows to work for him without very much coercing or instructions."

1911 ▶

While the huge CPR irrigation system is being built, workers' families often live in makeshift camps during the construction season.

1912 ▶

After striking an iceberg off the Newfoundland banks, the White Star liner Titanic sinks. One of the more than 1,500 drowned is Charles M. Hays, president of the Grand Trunk Railway.

"Dad worked on small subcontracts," said Gus Enarson's son, Ernie, who also worked with the Mannix outfit for many years. "The fellows who did that were called gyppos. They would take just a small section of road and then, with their horses and Fresnoes, they'd build a section of road for the main contractor. Mannix was the main contractor, and he would sublet little portions to different people; Dad was one of those subcontractors.

"My dad grew up with horses. He knew what it was to have horses, how to handle them and get the work out of them. Also, the men who worked under Dad liked him as a superintendent. They really worked for him but he respected them as well. I remember one time he told me, 'If you've got 60 men working for you and if you lose one minute, you've lost an hour.' So he wanted to start on time, but then, at the other end of the day, he also quit on time. I think that both Mannix and the fellows who worked for him respected him for that — for working it right at both ends."

"Gus Enarson was a foreman for Mannix for 45 years," recalled Blondie Garbutt. "I liked old Gus. Old Gus was quite religious. He didn't know how to tell a lie. One morning I had to start a machine to do some little job, I forgot what it was, and the atmosphere was just absolutely loaded with moisture — water was dripping off everything. I went to start the little starting motor, which was gas. I was at the front cranking it over and it wasn't firing at all because everything was so wet. So I said to Gus, 'Gus, you sit on the track and hold that wire a little bit from the spark plug and see if there's a spark coming through.' He was holding it, and I said, 'Are you ready?' And he said 'Yep,' so I cranked it over and I saw Gus give a little jump.

Top: The Ora Burggren outfit about 1912.

Above: The Enarson brothers' outfit in 1910.

Like I said, he was quite religious and he stammered a little bit, too. I knew he'd got a jolt, so I said, 'Spark there, Gus?' and he said, 'Yes, a bitch of a spark!' Golly, I just doubled over and started laughing, oh, I couldn't help myself. Gus was looking at me and said, 'What are you laughing at?' and I said, 'Gus, I think that's the first time I ever heard you swear!'"

"At one point, my dad's health wasn't very good," added Ernie Enarson. "He was the foreman in a camp. He was bothered with rheumatism so bad that he couldn't unlace his boots. He couldn't take his boots off at night, so he just slept with his boots on. He did that for about a week, but it got to the point where he had to get help to take his boots off. Mannix arranged to send him to the Mayo Clinic in Rochester for medical attention. He paid his room and whatever he needed. When Dad came back, he stopped by the Calgary office and walked in and thanked Mannix kindly for that. Then he said, 'Here, I didn't spend this,' and he gave Mannix the money he hadn't used. That's the kind of guy he was."

"I had two horses, two mules and my foot gear."

Ora Burggren was born in Innsbruck, Illinois, in 1888. His father had emigrated alone, from Stockholm, Sweden, to the United States at the age of 12. After completing schooling through grade eight, Ora took a job as a farm hand in Iowa. His pay was $7 a month. With his first two months' pay, Ora bought a $7 suit and a pair of patent leather shoes from the Sears Roebuck catalogue.

Ora early on developed contracting fever. He hired out to grease the sky end of Iowa windmills and he was in great demand for stacking straw. He drove stagecoaches

1912 ▶

F.S. Mannix subcontracts Alberta Central Railway Company work west of Red Deer to his brother, Alf Mannix.

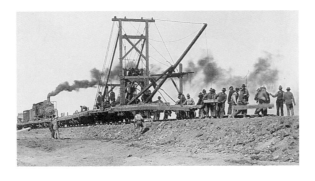

1912 ▶

With his partner, Chris Noehren, F.S. Mannix acquires the Thumb Hill Ranch. The ranch is located about six miles (10 kilometres) north of Dorothy, Alberta.

SELLING THE WEST

To populate the Great Lone Land, the CPR mounted a massive advertising campaign. With the aid of promotional maps, posters and advertisements, they sold the West. Agents travelled far and wide in exhibition cars, extolling the agricultural potential of the land. Two people who would become associated with the Mannix outfit as a result of this promotion were Ora Burggren and Bob Kramer.

Ora Burggren came to Canada in 1909 at the direction of his boss, Dr. Henderson of Oregon. Dr. Henderson was one of many in Oregon who succumbed to advertisements about wheat fortunes to be made in Western Canada. After he bought farmland near Strathmore, Alberta, he sent his office boy, Ora, to run it.

Kramer's family, too, was lured by the CPR's aggressive promotion of the Canadian West. "My dad had a chicken ranch in Petaluma, California," Bob Kramer said. "He went to the world's fair in San Francisco in 1915. The CPR had a big exhibit showing the land where he bought the farm. It showed how they were raising strawberries and watermelon. It was such a good exhibit that it influenced 27 families from Petaluma and the Suisun Valley to move to Alberta to that irrigation district."

"My two brothers and I went from Frisco to Lethbridge, Alberta, and Coaldale in a boxcar with four head of horses in the other," Kramer recalled. "We were allowed one man to go along with the boxcar to look after the horses. We arranged the furniture in the boxcar so that it formed a tunnel about two feet square. Whenever the train stopped, my oldest brother and I had to scoot back in that tunnel and hide because we weren't supposed to be on the train. The train stopped every once in a while because my other brother had to take the horses out and water them."

from Devils Lake to Fort Totten, North Dakota, making the 32-mile (52-kilometre) round trip each day, alternating two four-horse teams. It was after this job that Ora got into the dirt-moving business, using wheelers — scrapers with wheels — and slips to build streets in the town of Devils Lake. He was 16 years old.

Ora next served as an office boy for a Dr. Henderson in Oregon. Dr. Henderson, like many people at the turn of the century, succumbed to glorious advertisements telling about wheat fortunes to be made in Western Canada. He bought a farm 16 miles (26 kilometres) out of Strathmore, Alberta, and on February 28, 1909, Ora Burggren came to Canada to run it. He had a carload of horses and farm equipment, nine years of making his own way and very little else. Down the road from Dr. Henderson's homestead, some early contractors had set up a construction camp. Among the contracting partners was a man named McIntosh. His daughter, Muriel Genevieve, did the camp cooking. Ora, living a bachelor's life in the farm shack he built, soon discovered Muriel. "Oh, she was a dandy," he recalled. With an eye for the ladies, and no doubt a desire to improve his bachelor's fare, Ora married Muriel on August 10, 1910.

In 1912, Ora went contracting on the Eastern Irrigation District, building ditches on the Bow River slopes south of Brooks. "I started digging ditches on what they called the bull slope," Ora recalled. "I had two horses, two mules and my foot gear. I had a beautiful pair of red button shoes and that's what I wore to dig dirt because I didn't have anything else." On the spread next to Ora was a joint venture job headed by F.S. Mannix and Chris Noehren. "Mr. Mannix and Chris Noehren were doing a main canal near Castle, Alberta, just west of Brooks. They also worked there the next year, the year that Freddie [F.C. Mannix] was born. That called for a celebration which was quite a 'do.'

"I didn't see much of Mr. Mannix after that until 1918. He had a big farm near Rockyford and he ran it like he did everything else — always a going concern, and ready to chance doing anything. My next meeting was in the summer of 1927. During the interval I had done some highway building in Colorado and picked up a good deal of know-how that I was very proud of. I had taken six miles of municipal road near Strathmore, Alberta, and was on the finishing. I had eight horses on a blade machine and I saw a Packard car pull up alongside and follow me at a distance. The car then drove ahead and a man got out and walked back. Here it was Mr. Mannix after all these years! I got off and shook hands with him and the first thing he said was, 'It looks like you

1913 ▶

Discovering gas seeping from a fissure on the banks of Sheep Creek, Okotoks area rancher William Stewart Herron convinces A.W. Dingman and William Elder to join him and form the Calgary Petroleum Products Company. The next year, their well, Dingman Number 1, comes in with oil. The Turner Valley boom is on.

1914 ▶

A steam tractor and elevating grader outfit during the final stages of the Bassano Dam construction.

could finish a road for a man.'" F.S. Mannix invited Ora over to his Packard to have a drink and discuss the possibility of future employment. When they got to the car, Mannix opened the back door and the owner's engineer fell out. He was passed out cold, an empty whisky bottle at his feet. For years, Ora figured Mannix owed him a drink.

Ora Burggren would serve under three generations of Mannixes, working as a superintendent into his eighties. Over the years, he quite naturally inspired a number of legends. The following story was unfailingly told to newcomers in camp. An early riser, Ora was the first to stumble to the cookhouse for that all-important first cup of coffee. When somebody else came in and sat down, the coffee pot would always be by Ora, so the newcomer had to hold his cup out to Ora to be filled. Ora, who often had a bad case of shakes in the morning, would pick up the coffee pot, shaking like mad. Finally, he would look the guy straight in the eye and yell, 'Damn it, can't you shake in time?'"

Booms and Busts

Backed by good horses and good men, by the early 1900s, F.S. Mannix had become a successful contractor. "He had made a good deal of money in construction, so he decided he was going to branch out," said Margaret Mannix Walsh. After buying a large diamond ring, he looked around for other investments. "He bought some apartment buildings and a ranch in Drumheller," said Walsh. "He said he was going to be a big tycoon." He could not have had worse timing.

Largely due to advertising in Europe by the emigrant-hungry Canadian Pacific Railway and by Clifford Sifton, Canada's minister of the interior, the tide of immigration to Canada had become a torrent. In 1913, 20,000 people poured into Edmonton. At the height of the boom, more than 2,500 people were camped in tents on the city fringes and river flats. More than half the businesses registered in the city catered to land speculation.

Top: Settlers from the United States arrive in Alberta by the thousands during the first decade of the twentieth century. Many were given free land and charged only a $10 entry fee.

Above: A young Ora Burggren and friend in 1909, shortly after Ora's arrival in Canada.

No fewer than 32 real estate brokers, 336 real estate agents and 135 financial agencies lined the city streets. Land speculation was at a fever pitch. Like many other Edmontonians, F.S. Mannix invested heavily in the city's exploding real estate market.

In 1912, in partnership with Noehren, Mannix bought the lease to the Thumb Hill Ranch, located southeast of Drumheller. The purchase included about 35 head of cattle and some horses. Times were hard and hired help was easy to get. Unemployed railway men worked on the ranch for as little as $5 a month. Hay was hauled with six teams. One winter the stacks were completely drifted over with snow. During these years the first land to be broken on the ranch was seeded to oats and yielded 100 bushels per acre (3,524 litres per hectare). Old-timers recall seeing Mannix and Noehren coming down the steep Campbell hill in their Model T Ford with a stone boat hitched on behind to slow their descent.

For F.C. Mannix, the ranch held several vivid memories for a young child. "When I was a kid out on the ranch," he recalled, "we used to have these broncs. Lee Clapsaddle was foreman at that time. We had some particularly ornery horses and they found me wandering around in with all these horses that the men wouldn't even go in with. I was about three years old, but I didn't come to any harm. The horses didn't want to hurt me, but they would run off any men coming into the corral. Then we had these big Russian wolfhounds that used to stay in the back of the democrat when travelling into town. When they would see a coyote, they would jump out, kill the coyote, then jump back into the democrat."

Mannix and Noehren ran about 200 cattle, 60 mares and two Belgian stallions. Later they brought in 1,400 sheep. These were brought in during a snowstorm and corralled in the dipping vat overnight. The next morning the men hauled out hundreds of dead sheep. But even bleaker events in 1913 caused dead sheep to be

1914 ▶

In August, World War I erupts. It engulfs most of Europe and the Middle East in a four-year conflict.

1915 ▶

In June, a severe tornado and rainstorm washes out the Centre Street Bridge and virtually isolates Calgary.

the least of F.S. Mannix's worries. Following a rash of mysterious fires, the Edmonton real estate boom crashed and he lost heavily. "Dad decided that from then on, he was not going to be any tycoon," said Mrs. Walsh. "He was going to stay in the construction business, which he knew about."

In 1914, Noehren & Mannix secured a contract near Calgary — the excavation of the canal from the outlet structure of the Little Bow Reservoir to its junction with the old main canal and the Little Bow Reservoir Outlet Dam. This work was let in three schedules, all to Noehren & Mannix. The excavation contract paid 12 cents for Class 1 material, 30 cents for Class 2 and one and a half cents for overhaul.

That same year, the Mannix family moved to Calgary. Like Edmonton, Calgary had undergone a period of rapid expansion. In 1901 there were only 1,689 homes in the city; by 1912, that figure had grown to more than 11,000. Assessed property values rose from $2.3 million to more than $133 million. Because of the tremendous growth in the value of real estate, Calgary also experienced a boom-and-bust cycle of land speculation in 1912 and 1913. But, like Edmonton, by 1913 the boom was clearly over. Building permits fell from a value of $20 million in 1912 to less than $9 million in 1913. Would-be millionaires found themselves struggling to survive. As the autumn winds blew cold, men searched for work amid the 400 boarded up real estate offices lining the city streets. Scores of half-finished buildings made the once-booming city look like a ghost town.

Left: In 1914, F.S. Mannix and Chris Noehren dabble in the oil business — to the tune of $1 million.

Above: The dipping vat at the Thumb Hill Ranch.

The War to End All Wars

Events in Europe in 1914 made the relative booms and busts of Edmonton and Calgary fade into insignificance. In August of that year, German troops wheeled into Belgium, setting off a worldwide conflagration that would cost millions of lives and alter forever the social fabric of the western world. Within three weeks of the outbreak of hostilities, the first group of Albertans left for training in Quebec. By the end of 1914, the first contingent of the Canadian Expeditionary Force set sail for England. Within two years, Canada had more than four divisions serving on the Western Front. Over the long course of fighting, they distinguished themselves in a number of battles, including the second and third battles of Ypres, the Somme offensive, the capture of Vimy Ridge, the campaign of Passchendaele, and the final breakthrough at the second battle of Mons. While their countrymen struggled in the mud of northern France and Belgium, other Canadians took to the sky, serving in the Royal Flying Corps. Among them was a small-town Ontario boy, Billy Bishop, who shot down 72 German planes and became the leading Allied air ace. But the cost of service was high. All in all, about 425,000 Canadians served overseas, and more than 60,000 died — not far from the deaths incurred by a ten-times more populous United States, after it entered the war in 1917.

1915 ▶

Alberta voters ban the sale, but not importation, of alcohol into the province.

1917 ▶

The Canadian Corps wins abiding fame at Vimy Ridge, France. It is the first time the Canadians attack together. They achieve a magnificent victory, sweeping the Germans off the ridge. The price in blood is high, however. They suffer 3,598 deaths with 7,004 injured.

In 1910, the Canadian Navy is established. The Niobe, one of Canada's early warships, serves in World War I.

Captain W.A. (Billy) Bishop, V.C., Royal Flying Corps. During World War I, Billy, who hails from Ontario, is credited with downing 72 enemy aircraft.

At first the war hurt a troubled economy, increasing unemployment and making it hard for Canada's new, debt-ridden transcontinental railways, the Canadian Northern and the Grand Trunk Pacific, to find credit. By 1915, military spending equalled the entire government expenditure of 1913. Minister of Finance Thomas White opposed raising taxes. Since Britain could not afford to lend to Canada, White turned to the United States. Also, despite the belief that Canadians would never lend to their own government, in 1915, White asked Canadian citizens for $50 million; they gave $100 million. In 1917 the government's Victory Loan Campaign began raising huge sums from ordinary citizens for the first time. Canada's war effort was financed mainly by borrowing. Between 1913 and 1918 the national debt rose from $463 million to $2.46 billion. Canada's economic burden would have been unbearable without enormous exports of wheat, timber and munitions.

Canadian agriculture and industry went into high gear to meet the needs of the war effort. During the war years, more land in Western Canada was brought under cultivation than in her entire prior history. Some estimates put the total rise in wheat acreage alone as high as

THE FAMOUS FIVE
A Fight for Women's Rights

In 1915, suffragettes led by Emily Murphy, a self-taught legal expert, persuaded the Alberta government to give women the vote. The approval was granted in April 1916. That year, Murphy became the first

woman magistrate in the British Empire. On her first day in court, Judge Murphy faced an antagonistic defence lawyer who asserted that, as a woman, she had no status under British law. "You're not even a person," shouted lawyer Eardley Jackson. "You have no right to be holding court." The hapless Jackson never knew what he was starting. Murphy spent the next dozen years leading a determined fight to have Canadian women legally recognized as "persons," and thus entitled to such privileges as Senate appointments.

Her crusading companions were four well-known Alberta women of the period: Nellie McClung, Henrietta Edwards, Louise McKinney and Irene Parlby. Together, they became known as the Famous Five.

1917 ▶

Mont Blanc, a French munitions ship, explodes in Halifax harbour killing 1,600 and virtually flattens the city. The Halifax explosion is the biggest man-made explosion until the atom bomb.

THE BIGGEST RANGELAND EXTRAVAGANZA EVER

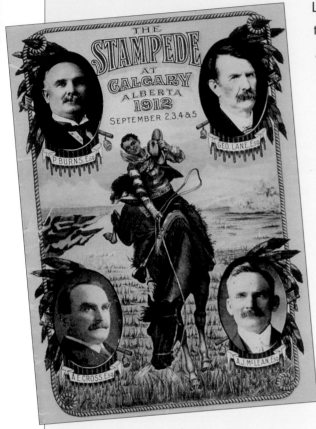

Long before the Calgary Stampede was conceived in 1912, the local Agricultural Society held an annual fair. The Agricultural Society, formed in 1884, bought Victoria Park for $235 in 1889, and consequently went broke. The site was far out of town, south along the Elbow River, and nobody thought it was worth much. Calgary later paid a $7,000 debt of the society and assumed ownership of the property. From then on, the annual exhibition was genuinely a community affair.

The show might have remained a county fair, except for Guy Weadick, the legendary long, lean cowboy who came to Calgary with a Wild West Show. Weadick, a good rider and roper, was an even better promoter and public relations man. What he envisioned for Calgary was the biggest rangeland extravaganza ever held anywhere. He called it Stampede, a name designed to distinguish it from all the various rodeos, roundups and frontier days held elsewhere in Western Canada and the United States.

In 1912, the district's "Big Four" ranchers — George Lane, Pat Burns, A.E. Cross and Archie McLean — underwrote the project for the then astronomical sum of $100,000. As it turned out, the $100,000 guarantee wasn't needed. Despite inclement weather, the first Stampede broke even. The show was acclaimed as "the most colossal and graphic portrayal of pioneer and range existence that has ever been started in all the world." World War I delayed the second event until 1919, when a "Victory Stampede" was held. The Calgary Stampede then became an annual event.

In 1919, F.S. Mannix, shown here with Nellie, begins farming operations near Rockyford, Alberta.

80 per cent. Western Canadian meat exports increased from $6 million to $85 million. The growth in Canadian industry was equally extraordinary. Mineral production increased from $129 million to $211.3 million. The rich nickel deposits at Sudbury, Ontario, provided the nickel necessary for producing armour plate and armour-piercing shells; Canadian industries turned out more than one-third of the shells required for the Allied artillery. In response to the call for more efficient transportation, Canada rescued the bankrupt Canadian Northern Railway and the equally troubled Grand Trunk Pacific-National Transcontinental, assuming management responsibility for both in 1917.

Although Canadian agriculture and industry were inflated by the outside stimulus of war, the construction business had neither the capital, nor the men, required to carry on business. F.S. Mannix had been moving his crew to a new job when news of the war reached them. After all his young and able-bodied men rushed to join up, he pastured his horses at the Thumb Hill Ranch. There, he provided work for those who were too old or unfit for service, and supported the war effort by producing grain and beef.

1918 ▶

World War I ends with an Allied victory over Germany, Austria-Hungary, Turkey and Bulgaria.

1918 ▶

First airmail service between Calgary and Edmonton occurs when Katherine Stinson stops in Calgary for mail on her way to the Edmonton Exhibition.

Peace Overseas, Discontent at Home

The cessation of hostilities in 1918 brought an end to the War to End All Wars. With the artificial stimulus of the war removed, the economy foundered. During the war, with agricultural production in Europe disrupted, Canadian exports of wheat and grain to its western European allies soared. With the resumption of peace, this demand quickly declined and the price of wheat and other farm products plummeted. Western Canada was particularly hard hit by the depression of 1919.

A pervasive feeling of discontent took hold of Western Canada. Many westerners felt that the politicians in Ottawa were insensitive to their needs. Some felt the railways abused their powers by charging western farmers exorbitant rates to move their produce to the markets in the East. Many also believed that the policy of high tariffs and protectionism — which favoured the development of eastern Canadian industry — was detrimental to the consumers of Manitoba, Saskatchewan, Alberta and British Columbia. For many western Canadians, the years following the war strained their resources and reserves to the breaking point.

Prior to the war, Winnipeg — the city where F.S. Mannix bid and networked with other contractors — was in the throes of the biggest real-estate boom of them all. Although the war brought the boom to a full stop, everybody assumed that when the war ended, the boom would start up where it had left off. Everybody was wrong. Winnipeg became a storm centre for the rising anger of discontent. As unemployment spread, the cost of living soared and tempers flared.

On May 15, 1919, more than 25,000 workers including firemen, postmen, railway shopmen, utility employees, streetcar operators and metal workers walked off the job. Within three days, the entire city of Winnipeg was virtually paralysed. On Sunday, June 21, a group of war veterans marched through Winnipeg to show their sympathy with the strikers. Charging on horseback, the North-West Mounted Police broke up the march. When the violence was over, two people were killed and 30 injured. Within four days of "Bloody Sunday," the Winnipeg General Strike of 1919 was over.

Crowd during the Winnipeg Strike outside the Union Bank Building on Main Street.

No strike so large and comprehensive had ever before gripped Canada. It severely damaged Winnipeg's economy and tarnished the city's image to the point where the inflow of investment capital was seriously reduced. Coupled with the passage of the first ship through the Panama Canal, thus enabling Vancouver to service western markets previously supplied by Winnipeg, the city was caught in the grip of the doldrums. The fighting may have ended overseas, but peace and prosperity at home had yet to return.

1919 ▶

After engine failure, World War I ace, Freddie McCall, stacks up his biplane atop the Stampede carousel. No one is injured.

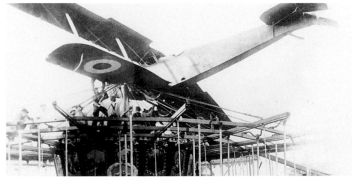

GAMBLING
ON THE TIMES
1920 – 1934

*What really impressed me was the way he made his money. He said, 'When I was working
my first gigs, I was broke; I didn't have money. I had enough to pay the fellows who were working for me,
but I'm a good gambler.' He said the fellows couldn't get away because it was too far to go home.
They all enjoyed gambling and he used to win all his money back. He said that's the only way he made it,
that if he couldn't win the money back from the men, he wouldn't have had enough to pay them the next time.*

*He'd win all the time. He had the know-how in construction, and what to do,
and who to do it with and he had good ideas. He stuck with them and put them together. Perseverance and luck
and a good gambler. Some people are just born winners. I think Mr. Mannix was a born winner.*

— Peggy Stack, nurse to F.S. Mannix in his later years

Left: A cyclone strikes Vulcan, Alberta, causing much destruction.

Right: The Wall Street stock market crash on October 29, 1929, in part begins the economic slide into the Great Depression.

Ushered in on the heels of the war, the 1920s was a fleeting golden age. The Roaring Twenties was a considerably misunderstood decade, made up of equal parts of fact and fancy. The fancy of the era was perhaps best symbolized by the introduction of neon lights, which first appeared in Calgary in 1928, along Eighth Avenue. It was the age of jazz, flight, radio and the automobile. It was also the age of gangsters, bootleggers and bathtub gin. Cars brought Alberta into fleeting contact with the world of Dillinger, Capone and Bonnie and Clyde. Occasionally robbers rode north across the American border to crack safes in small town banks. More often, cars loaded with booze roared south across the border into a thirsty United States, which had opted for Prohibition in 1919.

The fact was that the Roaring Twenties began slowly for Calgary. The 1921 population was 63,000; in five years it grew by scarcely 2,000. Farm prices had

dropped after the war, and Calgary's prosperity depended on farming. Alberta crops were poor the first two years of the decade. Dry weather forced many farmers to sell out and look for literally greener fields. Calgary's oil business was still tiny and uncertain, and it had trouble finding investors. The upturn was gradual, fuelled largely by better crops and better prices. In 1927, Alberta farmers' wheat income reached a peak that remained unequalled until 1945. The oil business, too, began to look more promising. In October 1924, the spectacularly productive well, Royalite No. 4, blew in. The trade in oil stocks became brisk again. Speculators also shared in the huge profits to be made on the American exchanges. The atmosphere was confident, yet speculative. On October 29, 1929, it collapsed.

The era that began with the 1929 Wall Street crash and ended with the invasion of Poland in 1939, affected the people of Western Canada more profoundly than any decade in peacetime history. However, to ascribe the origins of Western Canada's Depression simply to "Black Thursday" would be to misdate it. The Depression in Western Canada was actually three different depressions, separate in time and space, and different in cause and effect.

The farm-drought depression began in 1929 and grew progressively worse until the complete disaster of 1937. The prices-debts-interest depression — which was worst in Alberta, where it gave rise to the Social Credit revolution of 1935 — was only partly the product of the Canadian collapse in prices that followed the Wall Street crash. Equally important contributing factors were postwar inflation, the high cost of mechanization, exorbitant interest rates, and boom-bust-boom grain prices that kept the rural West in a turmoil throughout the 1920s. The third depression was caused by unemployment which reached crisis proportions in late autumn 1930.

In less than a decade, Albertans moved through a cycle of postwar depression, renewed hope, prosperity and collapse. It was a trying time. For the outfit to survive, F.S. Mannix would have to pull a few aces out of his sleeve. But all this came naturally to F.S. Mannix who, if not a born gambler, would not have started a business in Western Canada in the first place. He would have stayed with that nice family in the state of Washington, someday inheriting their farm, or continued to work for any number of other people. But F.S. Mannix was a determined and successful gambler who loved any game of chance. He gambled on wheat, horses, cards and the fickle fortunes of Lady Luck. Above all else, he gambled that he had what it took to survive. So with a what-the-hell optimism that kept his attention permanently focused on the bright side, he dove right into the turbulence of the times, trusting his instincts to keep himself, his family, and his business afloat.

Early contracting families.
Left to right: the Timothys,
the Mannixes and the Noehrens.

Gambling on the Wheat Market

Members of the Mannix family relate that F.S. Mannix got clipped in the oil business in about 1914. Accordingly, he was none too eager to repeat the experience. "There were lots of people running around then asking Dad if he would like oil leases on this and oil leases on that," recalled Luella Mannix Wilson. "Heavens, they'd phone him every day. Either the lease people or the jockeys phoning about the horses. He didn't do too badly down in the oil business in Montana for a while, but he didn't get into it, really, too much up here."

One area where F.S. Mannix did speculate was the grain exchange futures market. In this he was not alone. Although they loathed the futures market as a mechanism for selling their wheat, western farmers by the thousands could not resist taking an annual fling at the market.

1920 ▶

The Winnipeg Falcons win the gold medal at the
Olympic Games in Antwerp, Belgium.

1920 ▶

Radio CNRW broadcasts from the Fort Garry Hotel in
Winnipeg, Manitoba.

After Noehren & Mannix sold the Thumb Hill Ranch to Alex Nesbitt of Bassano in 1918, F.S. Mannix purchased a 2,000-acre (809-hectare) farm near Rockyford, Alberta, about 40 miles (64 kilometres) east of Calgary. "It was more of a wheat farm than a ranch," stated Florence Mannix Pallesen, "though they had some cattle out there, too. Dad started plowing it and getting it into shape so he could grow some grain, and sometimes my brother Freddie would work out there in the summers."

"My experience in farming wasn't very good," admitted F.C. Mannix. "I hauled grain from the farm to Rockyford, which was seven miles. I took a team down there and one time there was a hailstorm. The hail hit so hard, I got a concussion. It was all right for me to drive a horse taking grain to town, or in the summers following seeding, but in the fall of the year, when there was heavy work like trying to pitch bundles, it didn't work out. I tried that at 13 and 14 and pretty near killed myself. Trying to pitch bundles in those days was a hard job. You needed to be stronger than I was, but I liked the work."

Another young man who helped on the farm was Hugh Procter, F.S. Mannix's nephew. In 1920, Hugh left his Manitoba home to make his way in the world. Learning that his Aunt Byryid and Uncle Fred were staying at the Royal Alexander Hotel in Winnipeg, he arrived, unannounced, for a visit. "I cleaned up as best I could," he said, "as my clothes were anything but what you'd expect to wear in such a ritzy place. After a little disagreement with the desk clerk he allowed me to go to their apartment. I knocked on the door and when it opened my aunt gave

Threshing on the Mannix farm at Rockyford. Whisky Jim heads for the granary.

me such a nice embrace. She did not care about my clothes — just so glad to see me. She told me Uncle Fred was over at the Fort Garry Hotel, playing poker with his friends. There was always a prearranged game when he came to Winnipeg. She wanted to know why I was in Winnipeg and what I was doing. When I told her my story she said, 'Now you have no ties, you have got to come back to Calgary with us.' I ventured off to Calgary by train with my uncle and aunt, when arriving there we went to their home. I could not believe the luxury I was to stay in! The address was 529-19th Avenue West, located near the banks of the Elbow River. That summer they had won first prize for the best landscaping and best maintained grounds for the city of Calgary. They had five girls and only one boy. They were very kind to me and accepted me right into the family."

"Uncle Fred and his poker buddies pretty much lived at the Empire Hotel downtown, yet there was harmony in the marriage," Procter said. "He followed the horse-racing circuits and he had gone to Santa Anita, California, to a meet just after the New Year. One afternoon a long distance phone call came for Auntie. Wheat had gone up quite a little and I guess even though Uncle Fred was playing the horses, he was still watching the market. He told Auntie to get in touch with Roy Coffman and get the wheat out. Uncle had a farm nine miles northwest of Rockyford, in the Drumheller area, northeast of Calgary. He kept it to have a place to winter the horses from the railroad. They ran out there at the straw stacks all winter. There must have been 150 head. This is where the wheat was.

1920 ▶

The CPR continues to promote immigration. British youth is one group actively recruited for the development of agriculture in Canada.

1920 ▶

This poster suggests that hard work will bring prosperity in the Canadian West.

"Roy came to the Mannix house and plans were made for the big haul. Wheat was between four and five dollars a bushel and had gone up a few cents, so Uncle sold the wheat and immediate delivery was on the contract. I was to go with Roy and other fellows who had worked under him the previous summer, for the big haul. They knew the machine stock from the dump wagon stock. The whole lot of horses was running loose. When we got them corralled up, the ones we wanted were cut out, the rest were just let go again. The machine horses and the wagon horses were trained differently. Machine stock were trained to the demands that 'Hi' meant stop, and 'Yea' was to go, whereas the wagon stock was 'Whoa' to stop and 'Giddup' to go. There is a very good reason for this, as when the dump wagon was loaded from the elevator of the machine, the high skinner yelled 'Hi' and the machine stopped. The wagon teams would keep on going to make way for the next wagon to get under the belt. When the high skinner would yell 'Yea' they went ahead, the horses hitting the collars for all they were worth."

"It was all machine stock that had been caught, all bigger horses," continued Procter. "It took a bit of getting used to with the 'Yea' and 'Hi' but those horses knew nothing else. Six outfits were readied to go, each consisted of four horses hooked two and two, tandem style, and with a 125-bushel grain tank with an eight-inch extension board added to the sides all the way around, we could haul 160 bushels. We hauled for 31 days steady, Sunday no exception, as arrangements had been made at the elevator to take the wheat any day at any time. Because of the price increase, the farmers were trying to get it all in and you had to wait your turn and stay in line. We could only make one trip a day as it was nine miles each way, then you had to get your next load ready for the morning, as we were on the road long before the sun came up. We hauled nearly 30,000 bushels without a break. That was my initiation to the West."

Long-time Mannix bookkeeper Jimmy Nairn.

Jimmy Nairn's office in Calgary.

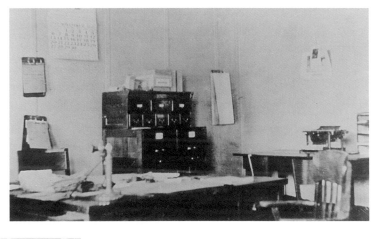

"Phew, for a minute, I thought I was going to get fired." During the 1920s, F.S. Mannix operated his business through limited partnerships created for specific jobs. This policy allowed Mannix to take on additional work, acquire more complex and expensive machinery, garner experience in new areas of construction, and share the financial risk involved in each venture. Some of the partnerships during this period were Mannix & Walgren, Noehren & Mannix, Mannix & Lawler, Mannix & Owens, Mannix & Foley, Mannix & Hill, Mannix & Coffman, Mannix & Davidson, Mannix & Grant, Mannix & Tredway, Mannix & Henderson, Dutton & Mannix and Dutton, Mannix & Foley. Of all the partnerships, the most significant was Mannix & Kramer, formed in 1927 with Bob Kramer, who was married to Alice, the second of Byryid and F.S. Mannix's daughters.

Concurrent with extending the scope of his operations, F.S. Mannix continued to modernize his fleet of earthmoving equipment. To help keep track of his expanding operations, he hired James (Jimmy) Nairn in 1920. Nairn, who was born in Scotland, came to Canada in 1905. He previously worked on the railway from Edmonton to Prince Rupert and on the Pacific Great Eastern Railway from Vancouver to Prince George. After joining Mannix, his duties included keeping the books, acting as timekeeper and paymaster, driving a wagon for supplies, even pitching in as camp cook.

Nairn was a confirmed bachelor with a wry sense of humour. "We lived in tents," he recalled, "which was fine except for the flies." On one bush job Nairn "built an office of rough sawn lumber and bunked in there. It was built on a kind of side hill and it was frozen; we couldn't get any dirt to do the banking. We used horse manure, and that was all right as long as it was frozen. But in the spring this thing started to heat and I woke up with tears streaming down my cheeks. It would have been real good for sweet peas."

1920 ▶

Settlers head west in immigrant railway cars.

1920 ▶

The Royal North-West Mounted Police and Dominion Police join to form the Royal Canadian Mounted Police. The RCMP enforces federal law.

1920 ▶

F.S. Mannix reaps a bountiful wheat crop at the Rockyford farm. Proceeds from the sale of the crop provide capital following the nearly disastrous rail job at Cochrane, Ontario.

As Nairn took on more responsibility for the Mannix outfit, he left an indelible impression on F.S. Mannix's associates and members of the Mannix family. Stories abound concerning Nairn's capacity for hard work, his diligence and his legendary frugality. "Jimmy Nairn operated a small office in the Mackie Block which was located at Eighth Avenue and Second Street West," said Bob Kramer. "Jim did all of the bookkeeping. He typed out all of our financial statements with his two index fingers and, boy, he could rattle that thing to beat the band." Deeply loyal, Nairn took care of F.S. Mannix's money as if it were his own. "One year Mr. Mannix gave Jimmy a holiday to Scotland and told him to get his

tickets and gave him some money," Kramer said. "When Jim came back he gave Mr. Mannix back $200 or $300. Fred questioned how he travelled and Jimmy said he just bought a tourist ticket. When Mr. Mannix asked why he didn't buy the other class — meaning first — Jimmy said, 'Because there was no third.'"

"Jimmy was tighter than you wouldn't believe," said Florence Mannix Pallesen. "One Saturday morning, I told Dad I really needed some money, a little bit of money. He said, 'All right, you go down and ask Jimmy.' I went down to the Mackie Block and Jimmy was sitting there with his glasses on his nose. I said, 'I really need some money, Mr. Nairn.' We didn't call him 'Jimmy,' not

Above: Looking west down Eighth Avenue from First Street West, Calgary, early 1920s.

Left: Mackie Block, Eighth Avenue and Second Street West. The home of the Mannix Calgary office from 1926 to 1938.

1921 ▶

F.S. Mannix, in partnership with Clarence E. Walgren, purchases a two-yard steam dragline from D. Tredway & Son.

THE PITCH POT

During the 1920s and 1930s, the dirt-moving fraternity was a close-knit group. In addition to his numerous business partners, F.S. Mannix had many gambling friends among his fellow contractors. Among them were Don Grant, W. A. Dutton, Jimmy Spears and Charlie Rowe.

F.S. Mannix had rummy friends and pitch friends and racetrack friends. They met at the Palliser Hotel in Calgary and at the Fort Garry and the Royal Alex in Winnipeg. He would meet with his friends in the cattle and ranching business — people like Alec Gillespie, Charlie Hillebright and Ott Hamel — down by the stockyards for a game of cards. According to Luella Mannix Wilson, "Dad used to have card games with these men. He used to play pitch, and they used to have a pitch cup." Sometimes they would play all night, for weeks on end. "This pitch cup was a little pot they had," said Mrs. Wilson, "and they used to pack it around. Quite a little bit of money used to pass around in the cup, you know."

for a long time. He said, 'All right,' and he took out a dollar and handed it to me and said, 'That should do you for a long time.' I said, 'Thank you, Mr. Nairn.' A dollar he gave me! Jimmy Nairn would not part with any money."

Nairn also kept a tight rein on the operational side of the business. "Jimmy was supposed to keep track of everything that went on in the office," said Ernie Enarson. "One day, F.S. Mannix went and hired some trucks and truck drivers to do a job. He didn't tell Jimmy about this. That made Jimmy pretty mad. When Mr. Mannix came into the office, Jimmy Nairn really gave him a scolding about this. He really raked him about not telling him. When Fred walked out of the office, there were some fellows sitting there, waiting to go in and get their cheques. F.S. Mannix just shook his head and said, 'Phew, for a minute, I thought I was going to get fired.' "

"He sure looked after his men. That was his reputation."

Although Jimmy Nairn was known for his frugality, neither he nor F.S. Mannix ever scrimped on the men. As no construction work was done during the winter, the farm at Rockyford was offered as a safe haven for Mannix crews until spring and the resumption of work. Many of these men were new Canadians from foreign lands with nowhere else to go.

"Fred Mannix bought this farm out at Rockyford," said Bob Kramer, "and he fixed up a big bunkhouse for his help to live in. In those days, we had the horses and dump wagons, so we had a lot of old-timers whom we could depend upon to come back every year to work for us in the spring. We generally finished the jobs about the middle of November when freeze-up came." Since there were no paycheques in those days, the men were paid in one lump sum at the end of the season. "After these fellows

Frederick Stephen Mannix, circa 1922.

1921 ▶

F.S. Mannix subcontracts CNR rail work to his brother Alf, in the Battle River area of Alberta.

1921 ▶

United Farmers of Alberta sweep to election victory, although the party has selected no formal leader to be premier.

The farm at Rockyford. Many of the men lived in the bunkhouse during the winter and F.S. Mannix wintered his horses and stored his construction equipment in the fields until the next construction season.

were given the money they had accumulated since spring, they headed into town," Kramer said. "What with seeing the ladies and getting drunk and gambling, they would lose all their money in no time. When they ran out of money, Mr. Mannix would come up to the office and have Jimmy Nairn give them $10 or $15 and a railroad ticket. Then they went out to Rockyford where they spent the rest of winter, until the spring thaws came.

"We had one old gentleman who worked for the company, for Mr. Mannix even prior to my association, who was called Whisky Jim. He was an educated man. At one stage of his life he was a track engineer on the Southern Pacific Railroad. He got to drinking whisky and got fired. Mr. Mannix hired him to drive a team of horses. Old Jim worked for us for so long that Gus and I used to hitch his horses up and help him get up on the dump wagon and he drove all day. It got to the stage where old Jim figured he owned the ranch because Mr. Mannix used to give him his old suits. I would see him talking to his old cronies, pulling his vest down, and tightening his buttons. He would say, 'That Fred Mannix is getting too fat. I can hardly keep these clothes on any more.' Jim drove a team of horses for us as long as I can remember. He died sometime during the Depression and we buried him here in Calgary. The funny thing about it is, he was really a very well educated man."

RISKY BUSINESS

Every year, F.S. Mannix would go away for a month in the winter, usually to Los Angeles, California. However, one year, he and his friend, Don Grant, took a boat to Cuba. "They both got seasick," said Luella Mannix Wilson. "Dad said it was so terrible. He said to Don Grant, 'Here's a couple of life jackets. Put them on.' Don Grant said, 'Give them to me. I'll tie them on my feet so I'll sink faster.' Oh, they were sick."

F.S. Mannix and Don Grant had many adventures together. Not long after buying identical multi-carat diamond rings, they discovered that the rings attracted some of the more unsavoury characters of the times. Don Grant nearly lost his ring, and his finger, in Chicago. "He had won a whole bunch of money," recalled Mrs. Wilson. "Dillinger's gang was in Chicago at the time, and they followed Don Grant back from the racetrack to the hotel. You should have heard Don Grant telling about it. He said, 'There I was in bed and these guys came in with a gun.' He said he couldn't say another word except, 'Take everything.' They said, 'What about that ring you've got on?' Don said, 'I can't get it off.' So one of them said to the other one, 'Here's my knife. Cut his finger off.' Don said, 'God, that ring just dropped off right there.' "

According to the story, F.S. Mannix was also robbed after a visit to the racetrack. In one day at Santa Anita, California, he won what was then a princely sum of money — $40,000. Observant gangsters followed him back to his hotel. He had barely entered the room when they pulled a stocking over his head. The gangsters then relieved him of his winnings and his diamond ring. Not long after, F.S. Mannix tracked the gangsters down and bought his ring back.

Don Grant (second from left) and Fred S. Mannix (far right) in Cuba.

1921 ▶

Special logging railways help logging operations expand.

1921 ▶

The Bluenose fishing schooner, built at Lunenburg, Nova Scotia, defeats her American challenger, winning the coveted International Schooner Championship. Her continued success becomes so great that her image will grace the modern Canadian dime.

"One thing about F.S. Mannix, he took care of all his crew who worked for him," recalled Bill Hamilton. "A lot of the fellows could hardly speak English. In the fall of the year, they'd go into one of the hotels where they stayed. Around about Christmas, they were all broke. They would come up to the Mannix office and see Jimmy Nairn. Nairn would contact Mannix. They were all staying at the Empire Hotel, so F.S. would trot down to the hotel and tell them to send the bills to his office. Then he would go next door to Cristy's Cafe and tell them to forward their bills to his office. Of course, as soon as the work started again, they were all working again.

"I've heard the stories about F.S. Mannix being broke at different times. He had a great big diamond ring, and he'd take that diamond ring and hock it to get enough money to pay his men off. Those fellows stuck with him, year in and year out. You can replace a machine, but you can't replace men; that's the way old man Mannix looked at it."

"One day they said they thought Joe Polaski died and they wanted me to go to the Empire Hotel and identify the body," Hamilton said. "So I went up and said yes, that was Joe. F.S. Mannix said, 'Okay, Jimmy' — Jimmy Nairn — 'arrange for a funeral. Bill, you go out and get five or six of the old boys so that you have a few pallbearers.' F.S. gave me $30, saying, 'This is for whisky so you can have a drink at his funeral. Go up in the hotel and have a wake.' He did things like that. He sure looked after his men. That was his reputation. His word was better than his bank account. As a contractor, if he said something, that was it, period, whether he won or lost."

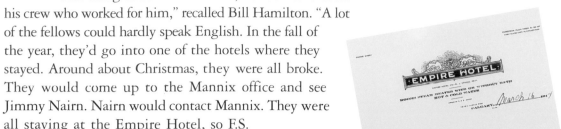

Top: The Empire Hotel, where many of the outfit spent the off season.

Above: The Mannix construction camp during rail grade construction in the Battle River Valley, Alberta.

The cookhouse on the Battle River rail grade job. Sam the baker, shown at right, made batches of fresh doughnuts each morning.

Another person impressed by F.S. Mannix's dedication to his men was a young neighbour boy named Vince Allen. "I only saw Frederick Stephen in his home," recalled Allen. "He was a very cheerful, well-dressed, well-turned-out man, considering he was the boss of the outfit. He dressed meticulously. I never saw him wear anything but a blue suit and a wide-brimmed, semi-Stetson hat; not the pinched crown sombrero, but the rolled crown. He would roll in after spending the whole day down in a hotel where he used to hang out with other contractors. People used to visit and consult there.

"When he arrived home, the younger children would sit on his knee and he would ask, 'What have you done today?' Sometimes he would be called to the phone because somebody had some hard luck. In those days, you had no social security; you had nothing. In the summer, workers were expected to make a grubstake in a seasonal job, which would carry them through the winter. Some of these people ran into hard luck, like medical bills. They would go in to see Jimmy Nairn, who ran the books of the company. Jimmy would phone Fred and say, 'You know, so and so has had a bit of hard luck.' Fred would listen and say, 'Well, Jim, I guess we have to fix him up.' I was very impressed by this as a young fellow. Here was a man who in his leisure time looked after his employees, no matter what. They were not on his payroll, but he would expect them to come on the payroll next summer when there was work, so he assisted them."

To F.S. Mannix, it wasn't just good business to take care of his men, they were part of his family.

1922 ▶

Noehren & Mannix subcontract Lethbridge Northern Irrigation work to Mannix & Walgren.

1922 ▶

Insulin, a treatment for diabetes, is discovered by four doctors at the University of Toronto. Two of the doctors, Dr. Frederick G. Banting and Dr. Charles H. Best, are awarded the Nobel Prize for their work. Dr. Best (left) and Dr. Banting are shown here with a diabetic dog saved from death with insulin treatments.

"When we were very young," said Margaret Mannix Walsh, "one of our summer vacations would be going out to the construction camp for a few weeks, so we got to know some of the old retainers. These were the men who came every summer and worked for Dad and drove the dump wagons. When the day was over, and it was quitting time, we would walk out to the site where they were working. Each one of us would get on one of these wagons — on Bohunk Steve's or Little Joe's or Whisky Jim's — and then we would race to the horse tent. These men were so good to us."

An Era of Innovation

The year Jimmy Nairn joined F.S. Mannix, 1920, was nearly his last, as the company just about went under. That year, Noehren & Mannix took on a large railway job at Cochrane, Ontario. Chris Noehren was to run the Ontario job, while F.S. Mannix looked after other contracts. According to Nairn, they underestimated the difficulty of the Ontario job and overestimated the capacity of the equipment. When the partners held an interim meeting, they realized that they would lose $90,000. They made the decision to finish the job on time, even though the capital drain would nearly bankrupt them. F.S. Mannix pawned his diamond ring and bought seed for Rockyford. "Father went broke about this time," said F.C. Mannix, "largely through losses on a railroad job in Ontario. But a good crop in 1921 — with no income taxes in those days — put the family back on its feet."

Although the Ontario job nearly ruined the Mannix outfit, Nairn recalled that F.S. Mannix never broke his stride. He continued to take on new partners,

Blacksmiths and the blacksmith shop, Battle River rail grade job. Bill Waters on far right.

Top: Horse-drawn Fresno teams dig a deep cut on the Lethbridge Northern Irrigation project, circa 1922.

Above: Curly Pridmore operating a Mannix steam dragline cutting a drainage ditch in Kinistino, Saskatchewan, in 1921.

new work, and to expand and modernize his equipment whenever possible. "In 1921," Nairn recalled, "Noehren & Mannix had a subcontract for the eastern section of the Lethbridge Northern Irrigation project. The job consisted of excavating the main canal and laterals from Kehoe Lake east. The main contractors were Grant Smith & Company and McDonnell Ltd. Jack and Herbert Campbell were the moving spirits with that company in those days — and later with the Campbell Construction Company Ltd. Noehren & Mannix subcontracted their dragline work to Mannix & Walgren, owners of one of D. Tredway's two-yard draglines. The outlet of the canal was quite heavy work and there were two draglines on that end — Mannix & Walgren and D. Tredway. Both draglines were steam machines. They were moved on timbers and hardwood rollers, as there were no crawlers in those days. All the work was subbed out, and next to the draglines was Martin Fogarty with an elevating grader outfit. We used Fresnoes for completing the bottom of the canals. Fresno outfits were used on all the smaller laterals."

In 1922, Mannix & Walgren took on a grading project for the Lacombe & Northwestern Railway, providing grade from Hoadley to Breton, Alberta. The job featured one of the first uses of a gasoline-powered shovel in Canada. That same year, Mannix & Lawler contracted work for the Canadian National Railways near Turtleford, Saskatchewan. Mannix's partner on this job was Pearl Lawler's husband, J.W. Lawler. Pearl had long been associated with the Mannixes. "Pearl was with us for several years," said Alice Mannix Kramer. "She was a great, great help to Mother when we were young. Then she

1923 ▶

Railway grade construction near Wadena, Saskatchewan. A joint venture of Dutton, Mannix & Foley.

1923 ▶

Prohibition inspires creative smuggling techniques. Seven seized carcasses of dressed hogs containing contraband liquor.

Above: Horse-pulled equipment cutting new highway grade above Drumheller, Alberta, in 1928.

Right: An early Mannix Northwest shovel building railway grade near Nipawin, Saskatchewan.

married one of Dad's business contemporaries and they had their own camp and she cooked in camp. She could cook for those crews for half the price that a male cook would. She always said that sugar was much cheaper than meat, so she'd fill the men up on cookies and cakes and pastries and pie. The men wouldn't take any second helpings of the meat. They just wanted to eat all the pastries."

"Pearl Lawler was an exception in those days," concurred Bob Kramer. "She was a pro. She said if I bought her all the sugar and flour she needed, she would feed our crew — anywhere from 300 to 400 men — for a dollar a day. And she did it, too. Pearl's baked goods were so stupendous that when the dinner bell rang, the men dropped whatever they were doing and raced for the mess tent. Stragglers usually found themselves out of luck, for the men consumed generous portions of Pearl's pastry before the main course was ever touched. I think Freddie came to our camps just because of Pearl's famous pies, and the crews, well, they were spoiled rotten. Inevitably, when we had some run-of-the-mill bull cook filling in for Pearl, we had a rough time persuading the men to stay with us. The fellas would simply walk out in the middle of a project, hoping to secure a job where Pearl was stationed."

Although there is no denying that Pearl Lawler was a great cook, perhaps the way meat was stored in those early days had a bit to do with her popularity. "In those days we had no refrigeration," Bob Kramer said. "The only way we could keep a quarter or a half of beef would be to use a block and line and a hook and haul it up to the top of a 30-foot pole. That way the meat would keep for one week or longer — it was high enough that the flies couldn't get at it. The sun made a crust on the out-

side of the carcass. When the cook needed some meat, he'd take the pulley and let it down to the ground, cut off what he needed, and string it back again."

While the construction crews of the '20s were fuelled by meat and pastries, the roar of the '20s was fuelled partly by gasoline. By 1925, Alberta had 65,000 cars, and the number was rising quickly. The *Calgary Herald* devoted two or three pages a week to advice and advertisements intended for would-be motorists. (One local dealer warned against buying little-known makes that would soon vanish from the market. He had a Studebaker franchise.) Most of the roads were terrible. A drive to Banff and back was a long day's adventure, enlivened by mud holes and flat tires. The combination of bad roads and the demand for even more automobiles led to a boom in highway construction. F.S. Mannix aggressively pursued this line of work. As early as 1924, the outfit performed a survey for Highway No. 2 from the U.S. border to Cardston, Alberta.

As F.S. Mannix pursued new areas of work, he continued to modernize the outfit's earthmoving equipment. "My father used to go down to the States and watch the big jobs and also the small ones," said F.C. Mannix. "He'd see

1923 ▶

F.S. Mannix enters into a partnership with F.A. Owens. They begin building CNR railway grade between Duhamel and Camrose, Alberta.

1923 ▶

Fifteen teams of horses pull six wagonloads of grain to an elevator in Vulcan, Alberta.

Horses and automobiles share a street in Cardston, Alberta, circa 1926.

the new equipment they had at each one. And he'd adapt the equipment he saw down there and bring it up here. My father had draglines in 1924. He took them up and kept them in Canada. He was dredging out swamps with them and fixing up irrigation districts."

In 1924, Mannix purchased the outfit's first Northwest dragline for use on drainage work in Manitoba. Although innovative equipment such as the Northwest dragline would ultimately be quite cost-effective, the initial cash outlay for such equipment could be a bit of a stretch. However, while F.S. Mannix may not have always had cash, he was always willing to give credit. "I never will forget a young fellow by the name of Fred Walgren who worked with Mr. Mannix on different dragline operations," Bob Kramer recalled. "Walgren's dad had a half interest with Mannix in the jobs they did and he used to get credit. One time, we were sitting around talking and trying to settle up, Walgren said to Fred, 'Oh, Fred, how about a little cash instead of that damn credit?' "

Although innovative equipment no doubt improved production, it could also prove a bit shocking to the crews who had to master the new technology. "The first Northwest shovel with both dragline and shovel boom was Serial No. 1019," Nairn recalled. "The operators on it were not any too familiar with the working of the gasoline engines, having been formerly on steam machines, and we had some magneto trouble with this machine. The boys undertook to repair it on the job. 'Poker' Pete Johnson was dump man, and they got him to hold the wires of the magneto when they were testing it. They said if his ears flapped it was okay!"

THE BENJAMIN HOLT LEGACY

Benjamin Holt and his machines have literally changed the face of the earth. As president of the Holt manufacturing enterprises from 1883 to 1920, Holt fashioned a career that influenced the lives of millions of people. He was largely responsible for two significant technological advances in engineering — the development and refinement of the combine harvester and the invention of the Caterpillar track-laying tractor.

Imbued with a love of machinery, Holt spent most of his working hours in his experimental shop at the factory. There he donned old clothes and worked with the materials at hand. Holt's intense mental concentration was a standing joke among his employees. As he worked, he had the habit of picking up rags used for wiping grease from machinery and sticking them in his pocket. When he needed a handkerchief, he would absentmindedly wipe his face with these oily scraps, prompting one visitor to ask a worker how long "that man" with the dirty face had been working in the plant. "Fifteen or twenty years," replied the foreman, who did not explain who that man was. "Is that all," the visitor replied, "I didn't think a man could get that dirty in 20 years."

Holt's inventiveness revolutionized farming and earthmoving practices in most countries of the world. He was known as a friend of the common man, one who used his genius to invent machines that lightened the burdens of man and beast.

1924 ▶

F.S. Mannix purchases his first gas-powered shovel, a Model 104 Northwest, with a dragline boom. The shovel is used on the Lacombe and Northwestern rail work with the Mannix & Walgren steam dragline.

1924 ▶

The Red Ensign, showing the Canadian crest on a red flag with the Union Jack in the upper corner, is chosen by the government as Canada's official flag.

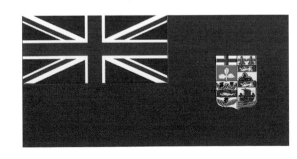

From Hundreds of Horses to 60 Cats

Clearly, the era of mechanized equipment was nipping at the horses' heels. As the 19th century drew to a close, animal power still reigned supreme on the farm and with earthmoving equipment. Yet, as power sources, horses, mules and oxen had decided limitations. They had to be fed, housed and cared for throughout the year, not just when working. In the field, heat took a heavy toll as animals laboured in the sun. Because Fresnoes were drawn by multiple horses, the slightest provocation — even a bee sting — could cause a stampede.

In a process that spanned decades, mobile steam traction engines began to replace animal power on farms. Manufacturers of steam traction engines sprang up across the United States and Europe. Most products were small — generally under 50 horsepower. One of the problems with these early machines was that their wheels, which were usually made of metal, added greatly to the weight of the heavy steam engine. In addition, the wheels only partially improved flotation; a low spot could easily mire the machine, and freeing it from a bog could take days. The metal wheels also made it difficult to steer and turn.

In 1904, a man named Benjamin Holt combined known concepts and new theories when he hit upon the idea of replacing wheels with tracks to increase the engine's area of contact with the ground. Holt ingeniously mounted a pair of crude wooden tracks on a steam engine from which the wheels had been removed. Tracks were not a new idea. By the turn of the century, well more than 100 patents

A 60 Cat attached to an elevating grader. One Caterpillar pulls the grader, replacing more than 20 horses.

CATERPILLAR TRACTOR COMPANY

In 1925, Holt Manufacturing Company and the C.L. Best Tractor Company merged, ending protracted legal struggles over patent rights. Both names were removed from the masthead. The resulting corporation was named the Caterpillar Tractor Company.

The decision to merge proved economically sound. Total sales of the Caterpillar Tractor Company grew from $14 million in 1925 to $21 million in 1926. By 1929, sales reached $53 million.

had been granted in the United States, England and France for track-type mechanisms. The difference was that as president of the Holt manufacturing enterprises in Stockton, California, Holt could afford to build and test prototypes under working conditions. The result was the world's first practical track-laying tractor. The 40-horsepower tracked machine could pull four gangs of plows two inches (five centimetres) deeper than the 60-horsepower wheeled steam tractor.

When the first Holt track-type tractor was tested on November 24, 1904, one of the men present was Charles Clements, the Holt company photographer. As the machine worked its way along the street, Clements viewed the test through his focusing ground glass. Seeing the whole thing upside down — the image being inverted by the camera lens — he was mesmerized by the motion of the track undulating between the drive gear and the front idler wheel. When he emerged from beneath his black focusing cloth, Clements exclaimed, "It crawls just like a caterpillar!" The Holt Manufacturing Company registered the trademark "Caterpillar" with the United States Patent Office in 1910. Caterpillars soon became known as "Cats" and the nickname spread throughout the world.

According to F.C. Mannix, his father bought his first Model 60 Caterpillar tractor to pull an elevating grader. "Dad brought them down at the railroad job he had for the CNR and the CPR from Drumheller to Rosemary, which was about 60 to 100 miles of railroad," he said. "We started out there, and

1924 ▶

Mannix crews continue to extend the railway known as the Cut Knife line near Artland, Saskatchewan. Two elevating graders work with 10 dump wagons each.

1924 ▶

Montreal Canadiens defeat the Calgary Tigers, including Red Dutton, for the Stanley Cup.

we had one tractor pulling an elevating grader — the one that takes and lifts the dirt up into the wagons. That was the first one we had. That was about 1928 or 1929."

"I can still remember taking the old elevator down to the blacksmith's shop for a little reconstructive surgery," recalled Kramer. "We had the blacksmith cut off the pole, remove the horse hitch, weld on a drawbar and then hook the revamped elevator onto the new 60 Cat. Our plow shaker and high skinner, the two men who drove the elevator's 20 head of horses, shook their heads in disbelief, arguing the contraption would never work."

"When they brought the Caterpillars in to pull the grader, it was quite a deal," said Earl Dunn, "because it took a lot of horses on those machines. When they brought the machine in, it made a lot of difference. They didn't need the horses and crew." Indeed, it was not long before the Cats were soon put to work hauling Euclids. "The first Euclids were bottom dumps on crawler tracks purchased for the work from Acme to Sunnyslope branch line in 1929," Nairn noted. "A 60 Caterpillar hauled two of them. For the Acme to Sunnyslope branch of the CPR, four Euclid crawler wagons were purchased. That was a Mannix & Kramer contract."

"When Mannix & Kramer purchased Caterpillar 60 gas Cats, there was much comment by old-time muleskinners," said Cecil (Cec) McCormick. "For the first year there was considerable trouble with them and anyone owning a cap with a visor on it wanted to become a gas

Top: Euclid bottom dump wagons on Athey crawler tracks were first used in 1929. In this image, two Euclid wagons filled with camp supplies are pulled by a Cat to the next campsite.

Above: Tom Kramer and Spottie, the Mannix dog, with a 60 Cat and elevating grader in southern Alberta.

engineer! A few things seemed pretty funny at the time, except to Gus Enarson, the foreman."

Bob Kramer was not amused, either. "I will never forget the first year we got the 60 Caterpillar to pull a grader," he said. "There was one old guy we used to call B.S. Brown. He was an old muleskinner and he drove the 20 head of horses on the grader. He just about died the day when I pulled the grader down to the blacksmith shop and cut the pull off and hooked the Cat on. He couldn't believe it. He kept saying, 'It will never work. It will never work.'

"In those days, we had 20 head of horses on the front of the grader and there were six at the back pushing. Those fellows just couldn't believe it could actually do it. I was a little doubtful myself, as a matter of fact. None of us had ever seen a Cat and we didn't know anything about it. To drive the Cat, Mr. Mannix hired an expert out of Calgary, whom we paid an exorbitant wage of $1.25 an hour. Granted, none of us had ever seen a Cat before, much less operated one, but this guy wouldn't let us near the thing. He wouldn't even let us see how he started it!"

"The first thing we had to do on the CPR project was move the Cat down the Red Deer River," Kramer said. "We packed lunches and travelled all day, sleeping under a wagon on the way down the trail. When we finally reached our destination four days later, we set up camp, housed the horses and got cranking on the job. Old Gus and the engineers staked the first cut with the

1924 ▶

Expanding further into highway work, a Mannix crew takes its 1923 Overland automobile and surveys the route for Highway No. 2 from the U.S. border to Cardston, Alberta.

1924 ▶

Squadron leader Basil Hobbes begins an aerial survey of water routes in northern Manitoba and northern Saskatchewan. He and three crewmen will photograph from a new Vickers Viking flying boat. With more than half of Canada unmapped, Hobbes and his colleagues have a lot of work to do.

R.A. (BOB) KRAMER

Of all the partnerships formed by F.S. Mannix during the 1920s, the most significant was the one formed with R.A. (Bob) Kramer. "We were introduced to the Mannix family by Bill Dilly, a close associate of F.S. Mannix," Kramer recalled. "We knew Bill as the high-powered CPR salesman through whom Dad had purchased our property in Coaldale. My sister Margaret eventually married Bill and she helped establish a strong friendship between the Mannix and the Kramer families.

"Byryid Mannix, her son Freddie, and her five daughters, all came to visit us on the farm. Freddie and I became longtime friends. As much as I liked Freddie, I surely liked his sister, Alice. I eventually left my parents' farm to finish high school in Calgary. I boarded with the Mannix family for almost a year while studying at Calgary Normal School. My career plans were to become a teacher and as I pursued my academics, I also courted Alice. By 1925, Alice and I were married. Alice was 16. I was 19. The two years that followed passed quickly and after standing in front of a classroom in rural Alberta for $80 a month, I realized that teaching was not meant to be my lifelong profession. I wanted a far greater challenge and I got it, as my natural interest in construction led me to Alice's father.

"In 1927, I was given a job by F.S. Mannix to go work on a railroad job on the Cut Knife line. I served as timekeeper and general roustabout. Gus Enarson was the foreman. Toward the middle of the job, F.S. came over to our office tent and said he'd like to talk to us. He asked Gus and me whether we'd like an interest in the company instead of wages. Gus said, 'I think I'll take the wages.' I said, 'Sure Fred, I'll be glad to.' I was about 22 years old at the time. Those were some of the best years of my life. We'd put those horses to bed in the tents at night. Then young Freddie and I would go over and play poker with the fellows all night. We'd then get up at six or seven o'clock in the morning, hitch the horses, and away we'd go."

Cat pulling the grader. Everything ran smoothly until late one afternoon when the Cat operator walked into my tent. 'Mr. Kramer,' he said, 'we won't be able to start in the morning. Some guy has lost the plugs to the oil pans on the tractor. I won't be able to drive it until I get ten gallons of transmission oil.'"

"My dad told me about that," said Ernie Enarson. "I don't know who the Catskinner was, but they were having trouble with the steering clutch slipping. So this fellow looked underneath the tractor and he saw oil dripping out. He was so proud. He was telling Mannix how he found the trouble. He whittled a stick and he used it to plug this drain hole underneath."

"Losing the Cat would put us behind schedule, so I jumped in my car, an old Chrysler, and drove ten miles down the river valley, a really bad trail, to our main campsite," Kramer said. "Fortunately, the guys there were using a steam engine and a steam shovel, so they had plenty of transmission oil on hand. I loaded up the car, then spent the whole night driving back to camp. When I returned, the Cat driver filled the tractor with oil, hooked it back up to the elevating grader. Once again we were ready to start moving dirt, or so we thought. Only two rounds were made before the Cat operator found himself stuck at the bottom of the hill. 'Well, I can't see what's the matter,' the Cat operator said, 'I can't turn the tractor.'"

"It wasn't many days before they couldn't drive the Cat at all," said Ernie Enarson. "Because it filled up with oil. Finally, the clutch just slipped, so he couldn't move. And there he was bragging about how he had found the trouble."

Two Mannix & Kramer gas 60 Cats in 1930 on the Estevan rail job. Left to right: Bob Kramer, Alan Dryden, Earl Adams and Tom Kramer.

1925 ▶

Hoadley to Breton extension of the Northern Alberta Railway.

1925 ▶

F.S. Mannix joint ventures with longtime dirt mover W.A. Dutton. Together they form Dutton-Mannix Companies Limited. An early job is the CPR branch line on the Alberta-Saskatchewan border.

"By this time, Old Gus was steaming mad," Kramer said. "I took off again and drove all the way into Calgary, without getting any sleep in 24 hours. I finally arrived in town the following afternoon and located a fella by the name of Jimmy Costello, the service manager for Union Tractor. Since we had bought the Cat from Union, I figured our problems were their problems. I told Costello how I spent the entire day and night driving around because of that darned Cat. I also told him about the transmission oil. 'Where'd you put the oil?' Costello asked. I explained, as best I could, where I saw the driver pour the transmission oil. Costello knew right away what was wrong. That overpaid Cat driver dumped the oil into the wrong system — the steering clutches! Costello asked if I had any fuel at the site. I told him we had barrels, since the Cat burned a ton of it. He rode back to camp with me, took the plugs out of the steering clutch compartment, drained the oil and fixed the Cat himself. Once the Cat was running, he taught me how to drive it. I kept on driving it for the next month, until Nairn found a replacement for the operator we fired."

"We cast until breakfast."

While the men were learning the ways of Cats, horses still laboured alongside. James Alexander (Jim) Lang, who first started work in 1924 with the Alberta government in the Department of Public Works, and who would later work for the Mannix outfit for a number of years, recalled working with horses and Caterpillar 60 gas-driven tractors to build a highway between the towns of Rosedale and Wayne in the Rosebud Valley in Alberta. "We used a 60 Cat tractor with a mechanical Fresno attached," he said. "The Fresno had no wheels and had a capacity of about three cubic yards. It would dump either forward or backward but was none too perfect in either. This Cat was the first I had ever seen on highway work. We constructed the Rosedale-Wayne Highway up the Rosebud Creek; it was mostly adjacent to the CNR rail right-of-way. The distance from each town up the valley

THE SIXTY CAT

When Holt Manufacturing Company and C.L. Best Tractor Company merged to create the Caterpillar Tractor Company, each company brought an existing line of track-laying tractors to the union. Holt, who built its first such machine in 1904, contributed the 2 Ton, 5 Ton, and 10 Ton. Best, who built its first track-laying tractor in 1913, contributed the Thirty and Sixty.

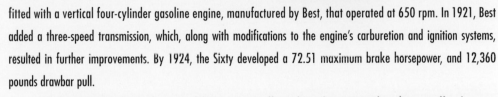

Best introduced the Sixty in 1919. The company rated its performance at 60 belt and 35 drawbar horsepower. The Sixty was fitted with a vertical four-cylinder gasoline engine, manufactured by Best, that operated at 650 rpm. In 1921, Best added a three-speed transmission, which, along with modifications to the engine's carburetion and ignition systems, resulted in further improvements. By 1924, the Sixty developed a 72.51 maximum brake horsepower, and 12,360 pounds drawbar pull.

The Sixty's greatest strength was its ability to operate effectively in almost any soil condition. It offered greater traction and flotation than wheeled tractors. Consequently, the track-equipped Sixty was widely adopted for agricultural, logging, mining, earthmoving, road building and other construction applications.

In 1931, after years of research and an investment of $1 million, Caterpillar introduced its first diesel engine, a four-cylinder design with 6.125 x 9.25 inch bore and stroke. The earliest production diesel tractors were constructed on the Sixty chassis, and were designated the Diesel Sixty. The performance characteristics of the Diesel Sixty were decidedly impressive: 77.08 maximum brake horsepower; 65.11 maximum drawbar horsepower; 11,991 pounds drawbar pull; and a record-setting horsepower-to-fuel efficiency ratio of 13.87 horsepower hours per gallon of fuel. In spite of the economic downturn of the Depression years, the new tractor was an immediate success.

1925 ▶

The League of Nations unanimously elects Canadian Senator Raoul Dandurand president. Senator Dandurand is shown at the League to the right of Prime Minister King. On King's left is Ernest Lapointe, minister of fisheries.

1926 ▶

The British Commonwealth of Nations is adopted. Canada and other former colonies are granted equal status with Britain. They are now free to exercise their own domestic and foreign policies, ending more than a decade of effort by Canadian Prime Minister William Lyon Mackenzie King (centre) and others.

was only four miles, while to get there overland was some 16 miles. We crossed the creek nine times in that four miles. The bridges were 100 feet long, so it was an expensive road as far as structures were concerned. The steel was mostly salvaged material from other sites that had been replaced. Several of them were from a bridge in Calgary which had been constructed to carry streetcars."

"On that project, we used a horse bulldozer," Lang recalled. "It was constructed on the job using the front wheels and pole of a wagon. The pole was made solid to the front axle. At the point of the pole in front of the neck yoke, a blade was fixed hard solid to the pole with timbers. The blade was constructed out of rough two-inch material and was

some five feet long and two and one half feet high. The horses were harnessed to this in full regalia. The blade ran on the ground when moving ahead and was half lifted and half dragged when the horses moved back. This was the hardest work I ever saw a horse do. It was not the pushing of the dirt over the edge of the fill so much as backing the outfit up. A horse was never made to back up and work. Those poor horses were lathered in sweat near all the time."

A horse bulldozer. Perhaps the hardest work performed by a team of horses.

DEFINITION OF A CATSKINNER

In the early days of the Old West, goods and materials were frequently hauled by wagons drawn by up to ten pairs of mules. Expert drivers were able to handle the often balky animals. They were also adept in wielding the long, black, snakelike whips with devastating accuracy. It is said that a top driver could use his whip to skin a mule at 20 paces. Hence, drivers became known as muleskinners.

When the Caterpillar company pioneered the use of tracked machines, Caterpillar became shortened to Cat. The term Cat was soon adopted as the generic name, regardless of the manufacturer. As mules gave way to mechanization, the term muleskinner evolved to its modern equivalent — Catskinner.

To understand how hard not only the horses, but also the men and equipment, worked during these pioneering construction days, simply listen to Cec McCormick reminisce about a few of the early jobs. "In those days, a great deal of company work was on railroad contracts," recalled McCormick. "In 1923 I went to Ontario. There, Dutton, Mannix and Foley had a contract putting in double track near Kaministiquia. The Kaministiquia job showed a typical layout of equipment for railroad jobs in those days. The spread consisted of a Marion steam shovel — track cars and dinkies — one steam shovel on crawler tracks, and a number of loading dump wagons pulled by three horses. Today, equipment can break down, but we had our difficulty in those days, too. I remember on this job we had a good deal of trouble through a hoof rot infection contracted by horses, caused, I believe, by the wet clay in which they were working. There were about 100 men on the project who were housed in large wooden bunkhouses, and the food was of the best.

"The following year, 1924, I went down with Mr. Mannix Sr. to Artland, Saskatchewan, to work on a

1926 ▶

F.S. Mannix is an original investor in Calgary-based Home Oil. The well Home No. 1 comes in with natural gas and naphtha at a depth of one mile (1.6 kilometres).

1926 ▶

Northern Alberta Railway construction continues near Hoadley and Leduc, Alberta.

continuation of the Cut Knife line. Mr. Mannix purchased a bunch of broncos which were really wild. They hitched one or two broncs with a similar number of steady horses, with the result that after they were hooked up there was quite a bit of excitement. The broncs were trying to take off across the prairie and the steady ones were trying to get on with the job. Equipment consisted of two elevating grader spreads, with 16 head of horses pulling each machine and loading into dump wagons pulled by two or three horses, with about ten dump wagons to each elevating machine. They organized the work so that one machine would be on the long haul and the other on the short haul, using the greater number of wagons on the long haul to get away from any lost time."

"In 1925, I worked for Mackay & Dempster who were subbing for Mannix out of Hoadley," continued McCormick. " That was the CPR spur line of Lacombe, Breton, Leduc, and it never stopped raining. In 1926, I was back at Hoadley with a gas dragline, loading dump wagons under a hopper. In the spring of 1927, I went down to Islay, Alberta, on the Cut Knife line to load horses and equipment for the Foley brothers. In the fall of 1927, I moved to Sunnynook to begin work on the CPR railroad, East Coulee and Dorothy. Work in the spring of 1928 got under way about April 15th. That spring

Left: Approaching Mile 23 along the Red Deer River southeast of Rosemary, on the way toward Gem, Alberta. Mannix crews build rail grade for the joint CPR/CNR project along the line drawn on the cliffs above the river.

Below: Preparing rock and soil for blasting and later excavation. The CPR/CNR project is shown along the Red Deer River near Dorothy, Alberta.

Above: To blast out the railway bed along a steep section of cliff, coyote holes are dug, filled with explosives and set off to loosen the hillside for excavation.

Left: At Mile 14 along the Red Deer River, after exploding the coyote holes and laying new rail, a steam shovel excavates material for crib ballast.

1926 ▶

Canada achieves a new level of political independence with the appointment to Washington of Canada's first foreign diplomat. The prestigious post is awarded to Vincent Massey, former Liberal cabinet minister. Massey essentially becomes Canada's ambassador to the United States.

1926 ▶

This steam dragline is used for several years on the drainage project in Morris, Manitoba.

Mannix-Kramer purchased Caterpillar 60 gas Cats to pull elevating graders.

"In the spring of 1929, back on the Hoadley branch at Warburg for Mannix & Owens, I was holding plow and Blackie Sayce was foreman. In the fall we moved down to Youngstown to put in sidings and also the top of high fills which had to be placed with horse Fresnoes. In 1930 we moved to Drumheller, this time in highway construction. The roads were 20-foot top, and where the terrain was flat, we rounded. We cast with elevating graders until dark and, as there were no dozers, the material that was cast had to be levelled and widened with pull graders. The fills were then brought up to grade in the daytime with the dump wagons and horses. The finishing was done with horse-drawn Fresnoes and a pull grader. When there was a great deal of casting which could not be completed after dark, the foreman set his alarm for 2:30 a.m. and we cast until breakfast. Freddie [F.C. Mannix] working during school holidays, was hauling culverts, hay and camp supplies with a one-ton Ford truck and drove the Cat, casting, on early morning shift.

"We drove that fall to Netterhill, Saskatchewan, on more road work. We had just moved and got nicely started when on October 14th a blizzard struck — blew down horse tents, dining tent, and tore sleeping tents. As soon as the storm abated, we closed camp and put the horses out with farmers to winter. We left for West Saunders when the rock contract on the railroad was under way. Charlie Alexander was foreman on this work. It was a mild winter and we completed the work and moved back to Netterhill — Charlie, the mechanic Homer Graham, and myself, to repair the Cat 60 tractors."

A McLaughlin Buick touring car, often the vehicle of choice for hauling bootleg booze.

Charlie Alexander, Curly Pridmore and Johnny Lynch, lying down, take a day off in their camp shack.

"We could hear these big, high-powered cars roaring by our camp."

In many ways, the Roaring Twenties was a time of transition and Prohibition was responsible for some of the more interesting times. In 1918, in part as a wartime measure, the federal government stopped the manufacture of liquor and its importation into provinces where purchase was illegal. In the early 1920s, importation was again cut off by provincial plebiscites. Though originally seen as a patriotic duty and a sacrifice to help win the war, Prohibition was also the culmination of efforts by generations of temperance workers to close the bars and saloons. Bootlegging — the illegal sale of alcoholic beverages — rose dramatically. Rum-running flourished.

By constitutional amendment, the United States was under even stricter prohibition than was Canada from 1920 to 1933; liquor legally produced in or imported into Canada was exported legally under Canadian law to its "dry" neighbour. The Bronfman family — descendants of a prosperous Russian immigrant — had purchased the Anglo-American Hotel in Emerson, Manitoba. Business boomed with the construction of the CPR and by the middle of World War I, the family was running three profitable hotels in Winnipeg, much of the profit coming from the hotel bar. It was Harry Bronfman's imagination and momentum that carried the family into the liquor trade. His credit allowed the family to purchase large stocks of liquor. This liquor was sold at a good profit in the interprovincial package trade during Prohibition in Canada. A similar move prior to Prohibition in the United States gave the family a large stock for export into that country. One result of Harry

1926 ▶

Just as the rail did more than half a century ago, the car is changing the Canadian way of life. The car craze creates jobs and an unprecedented boom in tourism. Shown here are proud new car owners washing their automobiles in the Humber River, near Lampton, Ontario.

1927 ▶

Canadian amateur swimming champion, George Young, is the first person to swim the 22 miles (35 kilometres) from Santa Catalina Island to the California mainland. Of the 95 swimmers from around the world who vie for the $25,000 prize, 17-year-old Young is the only swimmer to finish the race.

Bronfman's vision was that the Bronfman family got very rich; another was that the Mannix outfit lost a cook.

"The Bronfman brothers were big bootleggers in those days," recalled Bob Kramer. "They were running touring cars from their warehouse in Saskatchewan through to Montana. In 1929, we were building the railroad for the CPR down from Cardston to Woolford. The highway was parallel to where we were going to build the railroad, and we could hear these big, high-powered cars roaring by our camp. They had these McLaughlin Buicks with the big, yellow wheels. Occasionally one of them would stop and sell booze to the crew."

"We had an old elevating grader disc hung up for a bell," continued Kramer. "Every morning at five o'clock the cook would ring the bell to wake us up. One morning I didn't hear the bell. I lay in bed for about five or ten minutes, but I finally couldn't take it anymore. So I hollered at old Gus. We were both sleeping in what we called our office tent: a 16-by-16 tent with no floor. Gus and I went over to the cookhouse and there the cook and the two flunkies were, dead drunk, stretched out on the floor. There was a little bit of snow on the ground, but not too much, so I dragged these guys out in the snow. Mr. Mannix's brothers, Alf and Len, were working with me on that job. I went back to the bunkhouse and got Alf up. I said, 'You've got to come in here now, we got to get breakfast for these guys.' Alf pitched in and we made coffee, bacon and eggs for the crew and got them working." Then Kramer headed to the nearest town. "I called the office and said to Jimmy Nairn, 'You've got to get another cook for

FREDDY McCALL
Flying Ace

Frederick Robert Gordon McCall was Canada's fourth-ranked air ace in World War I. Serving with the Royal Flying Corps, he accounted for 37 enemy planes. Some of McCall's home-front exploits were equally hair-raising.

Freddy McCall founded the first Calgary-based aircraft company, McCall Aero Corporation Limited, in 1919, and the Calgary Aero Club in 1927. In 1928, he flew 200 deadly quarts (190 litres) of nitroglycerine from Montana to Calgary to explode in the Turner Valley oil wells.

McCall, who also served in the Second World War, died in 1949. Calgary's International Airport, McCall Field, is named in his honour.

me right away. This guy is dead drunk and I canned him.' But a new cook never arrived. Alf and I cooked for that whole crew — 150 men — for weeks until we finished the job."

"It was a joyous household."

Throughout the turbulent 1920s, Byryid and F.S. Mannix served as a stable and supportive influence for many young people. One person helped by the Mannixes during this time was Vince Allen. "We were neighbours of Alfred Mannix's family in Calgary," said Allen. "Their son Beverly and I were school pals. Alfred was a brother of Frederick Stephen. He was a subcontractor on some of the big jobs that Frederick Stephen used to take on. I wasn't conscious of the Fred Mannixes in those days but in 1924, some of Fred Mannix's children came to visit the Alf Mannixes.

"Later I accompanied Alf's children on the return visit to 529-19th Avenue in Calgary, and from then on, I became a regular invitee. It was an open house. There would always be something to eat at the Mannix home. It was marvellous. Alice Kramer was the great housekeeper and cook in the family, and everybody used to go to her if they needed a birthday cake or something special made. Eleanor ran the business side of things and did office chores for her dad. The Mannix home became a second home to me in 1924-25, while my mother was dying. I was 17. There was another connection, as well. I was a saxophone player in a small combo orchestra and the Mannixes used to have parties. The pianist, the drummer, and one or two others with whom I played used to be

1927 ▶

George Lyons running shovel and Earl Dunn on iron mule near Paradise Hill, Saskatchewan.

1927 ▶

This three-cent stamp commemorates the 60th anniversary of Confederation.

hired — alone or together — for the dances at the house. And over the weekends, I'm not joking, 25 or 30 young people would show up at any time."

"It was a joyous household," Allen said. "I had the wonderful feeling that I was always welcome in this family. There was a lot of respect and love amongst them that you felt completely at home with, and presiding over this was Mother Byryid. You had the feeling that whatever her husband did was the right thing, and that she ensured that it was the right thing. Mother Byryid was always cheerful, in spite of the economic ups and downs that the Mannix family had in business from year to year, and some health problems. Byryid was a very direct, impressive lady. She always seemed to have a firm hand on the family tiller, whichever way it was going. All the boys came there. We would go and talk to her just like she was our mother. And these young men not only respected her and listened to her, but they received a lot of encouragement from her. She was interested in whatever they were doing. It was just incredible. I think her basic philosophy about young people was that all you had to do was master something well and work hard at it and you would get to the top."

Above: The Mannix family home at 529-19th Avenue West, Calgary, Alberta.

Left: F.S. and Byryid Mannix's children. Left to right: Alice, Margie, Luella, Florence, Frederick Charles and Eleanor.

1928 ▶

Continuing to help develop northern Alberta, Mannix crews lay rail bed near Slave Lake — an area known for muskeg.

1928 ▶

At the IX Olympic Summer Games held in Amsterdam, the six-member Canadian women's team, in the first year women are allowed to compete, outscores all other teams. Canadians Ethel Smith, left, and Fanny Rosenfeld, second from left, compete in the 100-metre race.

"I received moral support and confidence from Byryid Mannix at a time when I had no hope whatsoever," said Allen. "My father had lost his business; he was a very weak reed to lean on. I had very little hope of going beyond high school, but thanks to the Mannixes, I was able to go to university and then choose a profession I love. They gave me the opportunity to earn money by their teaching me to drive a car. It sounds so insipid, really, to say that, but in those days it was terribly important. And my family didn't own a car. When I told Mrs. Mannix this, she said, 'Well, you will learn to drive a car.' They had this Studebaker Commander, a beautiful eight-cylinder car. She got Bob Kramer to take me out on the road to Bowness for a couple of Sundays to learn how to drive. As a result of that, I was able to pick up more lucrative jobs."

"I am indebted to the Mannixes in a practical way, apart from some wonderful memories of things that happened," continued Allen. "For example, financial assistance. Frederick S. lent me $200 on two occasions. Perhaps it doesn't seem like a large amount in these days, but then, a $200 loan without security required a great deal of faith in a person, unless you were prepared to write it off at once." Upon graduation from university, Vince Allen joined the Foreign Service. After he was posted to Hamburg, Germany, as assistant Canadian trade commissioner, he was able to pay off his debts. "At that time, I was told in a letter written by Frederick's eldest daughter Eleanor that, 'Dad was very pleased to help you and

A summer outing of the Mannix family in 1925. Byryid is fifth from left with a young F.C. Mannix second from right.

TEN CENTS A DANCE

"My mother's sister, Olive, was married to Alf Mannix, F.S. Mannix's brother," Earl Dunn said. "We were no relation whatsoever, and yet we figured they were our cousins when we were kids growing up. Auntie Byryid used to have jitney dances — ten cents a dance. They used to have them out at Bowness Park. The sides were all open in the summertime, and there was a fresh breeze going through. There were tables all around and in the centre they had the dance floor.

"I was about 18. You had to buy a ticket to dance with the girls. I remember Alice [Mannix] asking me if I had ten cents to buy me a ticket so I could dance. Ten cents was a lot of money though."

will not consider interest on either loan,' which is really fantastic," he said. "The letter went on to say that, 'He did not believe that he has a note, nor can he find one.' I think the real truth is that he just never kept the note. I think he tore it up. I suspect he helped many other young men of my generation in a similar way."

"An enemy which man could neither trap nor tame"

To Albertans in the late 1920s, the possibility that a financial crisis in far off New York would alter their way of life was remote indeed. Although increasingly dependent upon American markets and industrial goods, Alberta's economic forecasts were based upon fluctuations in national and world wheat prices, not the vagaries of New York market brokers. However, when the New York stock market crashed on October 29, 1929, Albertans quickly felt the reverberations.

Few countries were affected as severely as Canada by the worldwide Depression of the 1930s. It is estimated that between 1929 and 1933, gross national expenditure declined 42 per cent, 30 per cent of the labour force was unemployed — until World War II, the unemployment rate was never below 12 per cent — and one in five Canadians became dependent upon government relief for survival. Because 33 per cent of Canada's gross national income derived from exports, the collapse in world trade particularly affected Canada. The four western provinces, dependent almost exclusively on primary-product exports,

1928 ▶

Calgary, Edmonton and Regina are connected with regular passenger, mail and express service. This service is provided by Western Canada Airways.

1928 ▶

After several years, the drainage work performed near Morris, Manitoba, concludes. The original Mannix & Walgren two-yard dragline, purchased in 1921, is sold at the site.

A dust storm approaches Pearce, Alberta.

were the most affected. In Saskatchewan, plagued by crop failures and the lowest wheat price in recorded history, total provincial income plummeted by 90 per cent within two years, forcing 66 per cent of the rural population onto relief. The other western provinces were technically bankrupt from 1932 onward.

The worst Depression years in Calgary were between 1932 and 1936. Farmers brought in a decent crop in 1932, but the bottom fell out of grain prices — at $9 a ton, the price of wheat was a dollar less than a ton of sawdust. Money became so scarce that farmers were unable to get adequate payment for their crops. Many farmers defaulted on their mortgages and thousands deserted their farms.

9-9-9

"During the height of the Depression, F.S. Mannix searched far and wide, looking for work," recalled Ora Burggren. "In 1934, he called me one day and took me with him for about ten days' driving and looking. In those days, what few contracts could be found were let at the famous Dirty Thirties price of 9-9-9 — nine cents for common, nine cents for loose rock, nine cents for solid rock."

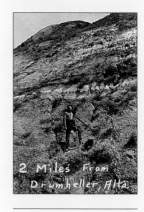

To add to these hardships came a period of drought. Drought was followed by a destructive grasshopper plague. Then came sheets of hail and blizzards. Hail and blizzards were followed by hot winds which blew away the topsoil of millions of acres of cultivated fields. Fences and farm boundaries disappeared under windblown soil drifts. The railway snowplows cleared the tracks of soil drifts 10 feet (three metres) high. Conditions led to the general use of strip farming. Farmers plowed strips at right angles to the prevailing winds to lessen the exposure of the loose topsoil to wind erosion.

For *Calgary Herald* columnist Ken Liddell, the Depression had a sound — it was the wind. "The memory is not so much the sight of the land, but the symphony of the wind, an orchestration that cursed each day, day after day, for weeks on end. It would die, occasionally, toward sundown to make night a blessed relief from the agonizing moans of some unseen and powerful monster that literally tore the guts out of the land and its people, an enemy which man could neither trap nor tame. You couldn't breathe without choking. You couldn't talk without screaming. You couldn't see without blinking to protect the eyes from pellets of dust. They could do nothing but listen to the weird,

1929 ▶

Revolutionary Caterpillar gas 60 Cats are used to pull elevating graders on the CPR job from Drumheller to Rosemary. One Cat replaces up to 26 horses per grader.

1929 ▶

First use of crawler-track-equipped Euclid bottom dump wagons on the Acme CPR project near the Mannix farm at Rockyford.

mind-numbing song of the wind, a sound that could be neither duplicated nor forgotten, once heard."

For Bob Kramer, the Dirty Thirties was simply that — dirty. "Fred and I used to eat our lunch in construction camps," he recalled. "When the dinner bell rang, we ran in there and flipped our dishes over, knocked the dirt out, and had our dinner. In all the dining halls, we had to turn the dishes upside down to keep the dust and dirt out of them. That was the Dirty Thirties, the start of the bad Depression."

There were few jobs, little money, and no demand for goods or services. Wages plummeted and prices dropped even faster. In Calgary, a can of pork and beans cost five cents. Steak dinners could be had in restaurants for 25 cents. Men's suits of wool, tweed and serge were advertised for $9.95, extra pants $3. Ladies' spring hats sold for 98 cents. Hotel rooms averaged $1 to $2 a night. Regular airmail service between Calgary and Winnipeg, inaugurated in 1930, was abandoned in 1931 because it was too costly.

Some fared comparatively well during the Depression. Anyone who had saved $500 during the 1920s was well off, as was anyone who could hold onto a job paying $25 a week. But the farmers, the unemployed, people coming onto the job market and finding no jobs, and investors who went broke in 1929 had no way of fending for themselves. "We were one of the few who were fortunate," said Margaret Mannix Walsh. "Dad was in good shape when the Depression came."

Although in good shape financially, the family faced far greater troubles, as Byryid had been fighting cancer since 1926. "Dad often said, 'Thank goodness, I had enough money to take care of Mother,'" said Walsh. "When Mother got sick, Dad had just got to the stage where he was just about on Easy Street and had enough savings." With the start of the Great Depression, however, F.S. Mannix was hard-pressed to take care of his wife, look after their children, and keep his construction business going.

In 1930, Mannix & Kramer was awarded a railway contract to build 39 miles (63 kilometres) of track from Vanguard to Mayronne, Saskatchewan, for 10 cents a cubic yard. "We got the contract on the condition that we would employ all the local people," said Kramer, "so we employed everybody who wanted to work. We were hoping to finish the job and park our equipment for the winter, but a very severe snowstorm hit the first week of October. The ground froze and we

BYRYID MANNIX

In 1926, F.S. Mannix's wife, Byryid, was diagnosed with cancer. "The day after she was told that there was no hope, Dad and Mother left for the Mayo Clinic in Rochester, New York, where Mother had radium treatments," recalled Alice Mannix Kramer. "Anything that she thought would help her, Dad would give her," added Florence Mannix Pallesen. "He said, 'I can find the money for anything for your health,' and he did."

In another attempt at a cure, Byryid, accompanied by her eldest daughter, Eleanor, went to a doctor in Los Angeles. Not too long after, Eleanor phoned her father and said, "You better come right away because Mother is not going to last." F.S. Mannix arranged for a private plane — no easy feat in those days — to fly him to his wife's side. The plane he hired was one of Freddy McCall's. It had an open cockpit. "It was the mail plane," said Margaret Mannix Walsh. "Dad said there weren't any seats so he had to sit on a bucket."

"I remember being at the airport with him," added Luella Mannix Wilson. "He had a parachute on his back, and he climbed into that airplane. Dad was very brave to go in that little thing. He told me later that he was sitting in the Salt Lake City Airport waiting to fly the next day because they couldn't fly at night. A man pointed to his parachute and asked, 'What is that for?' Dad said, 'God, I don't know because if the plane crashes, it is not going to do me a damn bit of good.'"

"Dad left on the Friday," said Mrs. Pallesen. "Mother died at noon on Saturday. Dad didn't get there until Saturday night. But she knew he was coming." Byryid Mannix died October 3, 1931, at Los Angeles, California. She was 42 years old.

1929 ▶

Massive destruction is caused by a tsunami (tidal wave) that strikes the Burin Peninsula in St. John's, Newfoundland. The tidal wave lifted this house from its foundation and floated it into the harbour.

1929 ▶

Mannix & Owens and Mannix & Walgren work in Saskatchewan on rail and road projects.

HOME SWEET HOME

When Alice Mannix married Bob Kramer, as with most new brides, her mother took her aside for a private chat. Byryid Mannix had a few simple words to say. "Mother said, 'Don't you ever live in a tent,'" recalled Alice. "Mother had lived in camp, and she said, 'You insist on a shack.' So I did. My mother taught me that."

Despite Alice's insistence, a few years went by before tents gave way to shacks. "Early in our marriage, Alice joined me at our campsites," Bob Kramer recalled. "Since there were no hotels or cabins where we worked, we lived in tents with dirt floors. I laid a gunny sack on the ground so Alice could stand on it while getting dressed, hoping to make her more comfortable. I couldn't do much more until I climbed a little higher on the company ladder. Once I did, I built a shack for us out of shiplap, two-by-fours and tarpaper. I transported it along with me from one camp to another.

"I remember getting Alice settled into the shack, which was on skids instead of wheels. Each morning, I hooked it up to a Caterpillar tractor and towed Alice away with me, before she even awoke. Nonetheless, staying at the work camps was rough on Alice, and she really hated our dingy blankets. I couldn't blame her though, because while everyone was allotted three covers each, our bedding was laundered only once a year."

couldn't plow. The groceries ran out, the supplies ran down — even the coal used for the coal stoves. The storm howled for over a week. There were cattle frozen on the range. The sleet and snow and ice fell on them. We had to come back in the spring and finish the job, which was a lot of extra expense. Gus Enarson and I herded that bunch of horses across 100 miles of prairie roads to winter pastures and we had to drive them back that spring."

Almost as if the weather was in cahoots with the economy, the snowstorm was followed by a tornado. "The CPR had abandoned an old high-level bridge and we were building the header banks for the

The CPR trestle near Estevan, Saskatchewan, destroyed by the 1931 cyclone.

1929 ▶

Mannix & Henderson crews work in Magrath, Alberta, installing a sewer and water system for Calgary Power. F.S. Mannix purchases a ditch cleaner for this project.

1930 ▶

Poverty spreads as the Depression hits. Cots are set up in offices to provide overnight accommodations for the homeless.

One of the Mannix & Kramer Graham trucks.

new bridge, which was going to be a small framed-in bridge," explained Kramer. "Curly Pridmore was doing the dragline work. One night just about dinner time, a big black cloud came down the valley. Curly thought he was going crazy. He had been swinging the dragline around and bringing up a bucket of dirt and throwing it over; then he was facing this big, high-level bridge. This bridge was the highest and the longest frame-bent bridge in the whole world and he said the next swing he made he looked around and it was all clear sky. The cyclone had leaned the bridge right over on its side. That bridge was over a mile and a half long.

"Then the cyclone came on down to the camp from the valley. Our camp was about three miles from the bridge. They were just going into dinner and it cleaned our camp right out. Mr. Mannix had sent a fellow by the name of Henderson down to build the bridge. We had this little 16-by-16 tent that we used as an office tent. Gus Enarson and Mr. Henderson were in this tent. They were standing on each corner trying to hold it down with a two-by-six. I had gone into town that afternoon to buy some hay and oats for the horses. I was heading back down the valley from Estevan when the storm hit. I got out of town just at the top of the hill. The wind was so strong it backed the car against a big telephone post. I couldn't move."

"I was getting a little higher in society," Kramer said, "and I built a shack of shiplap and two-by-fours and tarpaper for Alice when she came to visit. The cyclone took my shack out. I never saw a piece of that shack to this day. It just broke it up like a box of matches. Part of it went through the top of the office tent and cut Henderson's head off. Gus Enarson was a little shorter than Henderson and it missed him."

"Dad told me that he was in the office tent that day," said Ernie Enarson, "and the wind was really lifting. So some of the guys just grabbed hold of the inside of the tent and hung on to try and hold it down. One fellow, right alongside Dad, got killed. Something came and hit him and killed him. It knocked Dad over, too, but the other guy got killed. Then they sort of picked up the pieces. After that, Mannix had the job of rebuilding the bridge in a hurry."

Other events in the Estevan area dramatized the abysmal economic conditions during the 1930s almost as convincingly as the weather. At the start of the Great Depression, coal production in Canada dropped from 17.6 million tons (16 million tonnes) in 1928 to 12.2 million tons (11 million tonnes) in 1931. The coal mining industry in Western Canada was particularly hard hit. As the amount of manufactured and agricultural goods produced in Canada plummeted, railway freight orders dwindled and railway

A DOLLAR A DAY

"In the old days, going back to the 1930s, the camps were tents," recalled Art O'Hanlon. "All you got was a mattress and a pillow and blanket, and you slept in the tent. When we were at Sheerness stripping the mine, we had horses and wagons and the elevating grader. The bunkhouse was a big tent with metal beds in it with a mattress and a pillow, no sheets or anything, and a blanket. That was it.

"The fellows driving the horses were getting 10 cents an hour and their board for 10 hours a day. A dollar a day and their board. Virg Kramer was driving the Cat, and he was getting 20 cents an hour and his board. If anybody didn't like those wages, there were fellows waiting to take their place. It was during the Depression — $30 a month and your board. Of course the dollar went a lot further in those days, but I don't think anybody saved any money, no. You were just lucky to have a job that was all."

1930 ▶

Eastern Canada, though suffering from unemployment, sends shipments of relief food to Western Canada, where the effects of the Depression are most severe.

orders for steam coal fell accordingly. In Saskatchewan, provincial coal production actually increased during the first years of the Depression, rising from 472,000 tons (428,000 tonnes) in 1928 to 663,000 tons (601,000 tonnes) in 1931. But that increase was almost entirely due to the start-up of the Truax-Traer Mine, which in 1931 produced 247,000 tons (224,000 tonnes). At the underground mines in the Estevan area, production declined. As the price of lignite fell, the underground mine owners cut the miners' wages to around 25 cents per ton of coal. Some mine workers blamed Truax-Traer for these wage cuts, and there was at least one attempt to sabotage the company's big earthmoving equipment. "During the time we were building the railroad there, they were having a lot of labour troubles," Kramer recalled. "In fact, they tried to blow that shovel up. They found dynamite set under it one day."

On September 29, 1931, miners and their families marched to Estevan in protest. They were met by the Royal Canadian Mounted Police. Bob Kramer happened to be in town. "I was in the machine shop, getting some repairs done for one of our tractors," he said. "When the police started shooting, I went down into the basement and watched out the basement windows. I can still hear those bullets ricocheting off buildings and see all those people running.

THE ORIGINS OF SASKPOWER

In 1929, the Saskatchewan Power Commission was created. One of the commission's first projects was to construct a small coal-fired generating station in Saskatoon. During the 1930s, the commission began to take over municipal generating stations in the province, developing a provincial system of transmission lines. In the 1940s, the commission bought the two privately owned generating stations in the province — Dominion Electric Ltd. in 1945 and Canadian Utilities Ltd. in 1947. In 1949, the commission was reorganized as a Crown corporation and renamed Saskatchewan Power Corporation (SaskPower).

I tell you, I won't forget that for a long time." The riot at Estevan left three young miners dead and an estimated 50 people injured.

The next day, the Mannix & Kramer operation became the target of a group of protesters. "Our camp was only two miles out of Estevan, down in the river valley," Kramer said. "The cook was just going to ring the dinner bell and here we saw all these people coming down the road. They surrounded my little office, which was a little tent where I slept, and they milled around the camp. One of these fellows came into my tent and said, 'Who's boss around here?' I said I was, and he said, 'You're not allowed to operate this equipment another day. We're here to see that you don't.'"

"The police had told me the day before that if I had any trouble to come in and get them," Kramer said. "So I crawled under the back of the tent, lifted the canvas up, and got through the crowd to get into my car. The police came out, but they still shut us down for four days. It was a very dangerous situation. These guys were out of work, they had no means of support, they had nothing to eat. It looked pretty bad."

1930 ▶

The Depression places the fates of an ever-growing number of people in the hands of charity. Food kitchens are established across the country.

1930 ▶

In spite of the worsening Depression, a Mannix & Walgren highway crew surveys from Nipawin to Prince Albert, Saskatchewan.

"It would have broken anybody's heart. It sure broke mine."

Although some people in the Estevan area seemed to regard Mannix & Kramer, with its dragline and Caterpillar tractors, as a big company, the truth was that the Mannix outfit had more in common with the Estevan underground miners than companies like Truax-Traer. Following the completion of the Vanguard railway job, Mannix & Kramer found itself with just one job on its books, a small earth-filled dam at Val Marie, Saskatchewan. "When we finished that dam, we parked all the wagons and camp equipment in a farmer's yard, thinking we would use it again," Kramer recalled. "But then the CPR and all the people we had contracts with cancelled out everything. So we drove the horses cross-country out to Buffalo Hills Ranch, 90 miles east of Calgary. For three winters, we wintered them there for $1 a head a month. Once in a while, Mr. Mannix or I would make a trip in the wintertime in the old cars we had — they had no heaters — to see how the horses were doing. Every trip Mr. Mannix made, he'd come back and tell me that one of mine had died!

"It got so expensive that Mr. Mannix decided to sell the whole bunch. There were no prospects of working, so in 1933 Mr. Mannix sold them to a meat-packing plant in Montreal. Some of those teams we paid

as high as $2,000 a pair for. But we sold the whole bunch for $1,800, about $20 a head. I imagine they all went into the slaughterhouse for dog food. It would have broken anybody's heart. It sure broke mine."

From 1931 to 1934, Mannix & Kramer shut down operations as construction work across Canada ground to a halt. "Dad reserved his capital because he knew it would not last forever," said Margaret Mannix Walsh. "He had been through the Depression of 1919, and he knew what to do. He said, 'I held back then, so I'll hold back now.' So he just held back and waited for better times. He was very wise when he did that."

"Bob Kramer and F.S. Mannix were in the construction business, but they had no business," recalled Bill Hamilton. "Everything was tied up. There were no contracts; it was dead. Bob was at loose ends and didn't know what to do. F.S. Mannix decided to give him some money to get into a service station here in Calgary, at Fourth Street West and 24th Avenue, the old Imperial Oil service station. He bankrolled Bob into a service station — tools, gas, oil, and so forth. His partner was a chap by the name of Mickey Menzies. It was in the summer of 1933 that I first met Bob Kramer and started to purchase my gas there. As I was also out of a job, I spent the odd hour around the service station. They managed to keep really busy and their business kept expanding. For customers they had F.S. Mannix, Red Dutton,

TOM BAINES

And the Beginnings of the Calgary Zoo

The Calgary Zoo on St. George's Island, began in a modest way. In 1922, a black-tailed deer from a travelling circus was presented to the Calgary Street Railway System, which had no place to keep the animal. It was sent to the 42-acre (17-hectare) island. After it was decided to turn the island into a zoological park, various people contributed a miscellaneous collection of pigeons, hawks and owls. A person with a bear cub in his backyard was told to get rid of it. He gave it to the zoo. Others chipped in with a goat, a swan and a kangaroo.

In 1928, the Calgary Zoological Society was organized. In 1929, a severe setback occurred when the Bow River flooded and washed away the bear and the goat. That year, the society hired Tom Baines, an English immigrant, as curator. During the next 40 years, Baines built the zoo into what it is today. Living in his bachelor home on St. George's Island, he was available 24 hours a day.

1930 ▶

On February 5, Prime Minister William Lyon Mackenzie King announces the appointment of Canada's first female senator, Cairine Wilson of Ottawa.

1930 ▶

Draglines are ferried across the Saskatchewan River to construct the Nipawin Highway.

Paul and Tiny Thompson, and a few more NHL hockey players. Wherever these people went they had a following, and naturally Fred Jr. was hanging around, in between his university tours.

"I bought into the gas station in the spring of 1934 for $350, which was enough money to fill one underground tank. Old Fred had asked Jimmy Nairn to keep the books as it was his money that started Bob in this service station, so our accountant was the same Jim who ran F.S.'s office. Young Fred was always broke, so while we were working on the pumps, he would help himself to money out of our cash register — maybe $5 or $10. He always left his IOU and we included these with our daily cash receipts in our safe. When Jim came around to do our books, he would blow his cork and immediately issue a cheque to cover it. We never knew if this came out of Jim's pocket or if he collected from old Fred."

"Somewhere about this time, Fred's dad purchased a new Ford sedan for the company business from Maclin Motors," continued Hamilton. "The cost then was about $1,900. One evening young Fred got his hands on the new car. He and a buddy picked up a couple of girls and drove out to the Bowness Dance Hall. On the way back, on a perfectly straight stretch of road, young Fred rolled the car over and they had to thumb their way home. The next morning, his dad asked where the car was and Freddie said he had a small accident and left the car on the Bowness Road. The old man phoned for a tow truck to bring it in and advise him when it would be ready. A few hours later, Maclin phoned and advised that they would allow Mannix $500 toward a new car."

Everett Costello (far right), F.C. Mannix (middle right), and two friends on a cattle boat en route to England.

It was about this time that young F.C. decided to go to Europe. "Father didn't have a job for me in order to keep others working," he said. "Besides, I had flunked out a year at school and figured it would be a good time to be out of town. I had an opportunity to go with my friends with the cattle from Hays' cattle farm. I went down there with Harry Hays and got aboard a ship with some of the cattle. I went over to England with the cattle and with Everett Costello. I got about $50 from my father and that is as much as we had." That is, until young Freddie rolled the dice.

"Before Freddie Jr. and Ev Costello left, Fred had started to frequent one of Calgary's major gambling clubs," said Hamilton. "It was operated by Jack Baxter, and Jack had specific instructions from Fred's dad to keep him out. However, the night before they left Calgary, Fred somehow managed to sneak into the club and he made himself a bundle. He neglected to tell his dad the next day when he was collecting money as promised for the trip from his dad. A couple of days after he left for Europe, Baxter advised the old man of Fred's club visit."

"I was rolling dice," F.C. Mannix recalled, "and I won about $2,000 or $3,000." This unexpected windfall did not last long, however. "It apparently went fine on the cattle train, until they hit Montreal," Hamilton said. "Then the money in Fred's pocket was burning a hole in it, so they went on a big party. We heard via the grapevine that they had gone broke, but they, nevertheless, continued on to England on the cattle boat, so at least they had bed

1930 ▶

After a decade of nearly continuous Liberal rule, Richard Bedford Bennett replaces William Lyon Mackenzie King as prime minister of Canada.

1931 ▶

A search in the Arctic for remains of the Franklin expedition uncovers a number of fragmented skeletons scattered about the southern shore of King William Island. Sir John Franklin, naval officer and Arctic explorer, set out from England in 1845 to discover the Northwest Passage. Neither he nor his crew ever returned. It is believed the discovered skeletal fragments belong to the crew of the ill-fated Franklin party.

and food." To pay for their keep, "we cleaned the cattle stalls and walked the cattle around the decks for exercise," said F.C. Mannix. "Once we got to Europe, we stayed for a couple days in port. Then we went in and got a bus and went on to London. In London, we stayed at a boarding house for a while. We just rattled around and saw the country. We went to all the pubs and to shows. Then we went up north through Birkenhead, near the Tyne River. We shipped out of there with the boat coming back to Canada. We got a ride back with some other cattle coming back from England."

"The next we heard of them they were back in Canada and beating their way from Montreal to Sudbury, Ontario, via the 'rodes' — that is, empty freight cars," Hamilton said. "We got into Toronto, but we didn't have any money at all," said F.C. Mannix. "I wired my sister, Florence, in Sudbury and she sent me $20."

"Fred had a sister living there, so they holed up for a few days to recuperate and sleep, eat and get their clothes washed," Hamilton said. "Then, on starting out for Calgary again, they hit the rodes, but Everett fell off a boxcar, and so they returned to Sudbury for another couple of days before continuing on for home." According to F.C. Mannix, "I jumped on and he tried to get on. He couldn't make it, so I got off." Said Hamilton, "To this day, Everett Costello still shakes his head every time he hears a freight roll by."

In 1934, Mannix crews begin stripping prairie overburden at Claude Gallinger's coal mine near Sheerness, Alberta.

The Move into Contract Coal Mining

Just a year after the horses were shipped off to the meat-packing plant in Montreal, the fortunes of Mannix & Kramer revived. "In the spring of 1934, Bob Kramer advised his partner that he was pulling out, as F.S. Mannix was beginning to get the odd contract," said Hamilton. "All of a sudden it broke. Mannix got a job, so Bob said, 'Goodbye, Bill, she's yours,' and walked out, just like that."

The event that brought the company back to life was a contract to strip overburden at a new surface coal mine being developed at Sheerness, Alberta. It was still the Dirty Thirties, and coal stripping was dirty work, but Mannix & Kramer was back in business. Early in 1934, Mannix & Kramer reactivated their company and headed off for Sheerness with some new teams of horses, an elevating grader, several Cats, and some new Euclid crawler wagons outfitted with tracks.

Interestingly enough, the coal stripping contract came about because of cattle. The Sheerness mine was owned by Claude Gallinger, a rancher and a businessman, nationally known as a breeder of purebred Scottish Shorthorn cattle. "It meant that he always went down to the bull sale," said Gallinger's mine manager, R.L. (Woody) Wood, who would later join the Mannix organization. "We would have a week's holiday at the bull sale where we'd meet Fred Mannix Sr. We'd sit down at the Palliser Hotel and talk about coal and cattle. I'd sit there for

1931 ▶

F.S. Mannix contracts with the City of Calgary to help build the Glenmore Dam and water supply system.

1931 ▶

As the Depression deepens, Mannix & Kramer see many contracts revoked. With no work in sight, they pasture their horses at Buffalo Hills Ranch, 90 miles (145 kilometres) east of Calgary.

George Charles Mannix

Patriot, Pioneer and Politician

George Charles Mannix served in the Fenian Raids of 1866 and the Red River Rebellion of 1869-70. He was one of the few people awarded medals for both services. After the Red River Expedition brought him west, G.C. Mannix settled in Manitoba. In 1904, he moved his family to Victoria, settling in the municipality of Saanich. He was a member of the Saanich Council during the years 1907-1909.

Like many men of his time, G.C. Mannix was a complex character — tough and tender. His grandson, George Mannix, said that when he went up for reelection to the Saanich Council, he was defeated by only a few votes. "The fellow who beat him out only lasted less than a month, so they asked George Charles Mannix if he would resume his seat. He said, 'No. They once had their chance to get me and they didn't take it.' He never went back to politics. He had a cussed streak."

George Charles Mannix, second from left.

Johnny Lynch winding Euclid belly dump wagons in the Sheerness dust.

hours while they visited back and forth. Mr. Gallinger was always telling Fred that he had to get into the cattle business and Fred, of course, was getting on. I don't know whether Mr. Gallinger influenced him, but F.C., Freddie — he was still a kid — went into cattle. So they talked cattle. They didn't argue; they made a deal and set a price. I wanted Mannix to strip because they worked well with us and we worked well with them. We'd set the price, shake hands on it, and that was it. Somebody would say, 'You'd better write a letter,' and Fred would say, 'Whoever says it first.' That was our contract. We confirmed with a letter, but the letter was incidental. In fact, it may have gone a year or two without the letter. A handshake was as good as the best lawyer could have drawn up."

As it turned out, that contract was not only a turning point in the history of the Mannix organization, it also marked a major turning point in the history of the western Canadian coal mining industry.

1931 ▶

Cramped dormitories in relief camps lead to unrest. On May 8, Inspector L.J. Sampson of the RCMP is killed and three other Mounties are injured when Mounties and city police clash with about 300 unemployed protesters in Saskatoon.

1932 ▶

Small earthmoving projects are still performed by Mannix & Owens, including railway bridge fill in Saskatchewan.

Gallinger, who also owned the Tofield Mine, an underground mine near Tofield, Alberta, felt that strip mines were the only viable way to mine coal with low Depression era coal prices. As he did not know how to develop a mine of this type, he hired Mannix & Kramer not only because he worked well with them, but because of the outfit's reputation in moving earth for railway and highway construction. This stripping contract, which lasted from March to September of 1934, was the first of a series that continued until the late 1940s. "We paid them 10 cents a cubic yard," recalled Wood. "And that went on for years. I think later we paid 12 cents, maybe up to 15 cents, but in those early days it was 10 cents a yard."

One of Wood's jobs was to measure the number of yards stripped each day and to confirm them with the Mannix & Kramer crew. "They took my measurements," Wood recalled. "I'm not naive enough to know that they didn't have the measurements themselves because they knew what yards they were moving. They followed it very closely each day, how many yards they should have had. On the job, this bone, the rock in the coal seam, was a headache to get off. They grumbled about the bone, but they'd do it. That's one thing I liked about them. They did a job. They never complained. I think they made money on it. If they didn't make money, you wouldn't know it. They never cried. They were a bunch of working fools."

One of the Mannix & Kramer crew was Johnny Lynch, the husband of Eleanor, the oldest of Byryid and F.S. Mannix's children. Lynch went to work for Mannix & Kramer in 1934 at Sheerness. "I started out winding wagons," he said. "After they loaded those wagons with the elevating grader, they would haul out the dirt and dump it. When they dumped the wagon and the dirt fell out, the bottom had to be cranked up again. I was the one who used to have to run to that wagon, close it up, and catch the next one. They would say, 'Come on, Lynch, what's the matter with you? You're too damn slow there.' Of course, I was slow, after doing that for 10 hours a day!"

"Boy, oh boy, I remember at Sheerness we used to take out the horses and take a rag and wet it and put it over their faces so they wouldn't choke from the dust that was coming," Lynch continued. "They would tie the horses up to the wagon wheels so the horses couldn't break away. Those storms that used to come in and blow the dust were terrible. Everything was always turned over, never right side up. There might be pretty near an eighth of an inch of coal dust around that area. A lot of it was just plain dust, too, but on account of the coal that had been taken out and the earth being all loose — there wasn't any grass — everything was dirty and dusty."

While the work the Mannix & Kramer crew did was tough, so was the work of the coal loading done by local mine employees. This

"HE ALWAYS GAVE ME A ROSE"

Blanche Mannix Hilborne recalled a gentler part of George Charles Mannix's character. "One very nice thing about Grandfather was that he always had an eye for the ladies," she said. "After his wife had passed away, he lived with his daughter, Alice, and her husband, Fred Toms, and they had a garden with many roses. You know those straight pins that used to come in sheets? Well, there was a little story that went around about the number of sheets of pins used where Grandfather pinned the roses onto the ladies as they were passing the front gate. People who lived in Victoria for a long time say, 'There was an old gentleman on Douglas Street and he always gave me a rose,' and it was Grandfather."

G.C. Mannix died in Victoria in 1934 at the age of 89. With his passing, Western Canada lost one of its last, true pioneers.

1932 ▶

The railway bridge fill at Kerrobert, Saskatchewan, uses dump wagons pulled by 60 Cats to cover the existing rail trestle with soil.

1932 ▶

The prairie drought and windstorms continue. Average wheat prices plummet to 34 cents a bushel, with some prices in the Calgary area hovering around 27 cents a bushel. These prices bring financial disaster to farmers and wheat pools.

labour-intensive mining operation led Wood to develop an incentive type of pay system. The wage scale Wood voluntarily put into place was considerably more lucrative than the one the miners in Estevan and Bienfait had struck to get. "Back in those years, Sheerness coal was selling for $1.50 a ton, and the wage rate in the field was 25 and 30 cents an hour," recalled Wood. "So we put our boys on contract at 40 cents a ton." Wood also increased production through the use of new technology. "The men had these wheelbarrows with iron wheels, which used to dig in, so they were hard to push," Wood said. "I was in Calgary one time and I saw that they'd come out with a rubber-tired wheelbarrow. I looked it over, and I think I took a dozen of those tires. Did that ever speed up production! The men thought that was the greatest invention there ever was."

In the Business of Business

While the Mannix & Kramer crew stripped coal at Sheerness, F.S. Mannix continued to aggressively seek highway projects. Between 1934 and 1935, Mannix tendered on no less than 18 highway projects. He won four contracts totalling more than $120,000. Each job required a bond of approximately $10,000. One banker will never forget how F.S. Mannix tucked those bonds into his inside pocket.

"I joined the Royal Bank of Canada in 1918 and was transferred to Calgary in 1926," recalled Robert H. Mawhinney, a retired officer of the Royal Bank of Canada. "I came to know F.S. Mannix through his business activities, mainly road building. We had every confidence in him; the bank had great respect for him. He was never known as Fred to us. He was known as Mr. Mannix. Mr. Mannix could have asked for anything, and he would have received it on his own word. He was that kind of gentleman. But he would never ask you for anything, he would never presume. Mr. Mannix was a man of his word. His word was his bond, and everyone knew him as that. If he said he was going to do something, he did it. No need to worry about it. You didn't have to write it out. The bank didn't need any bond from Mr. Mannix. His word was gilt-edged."

"I was very fond of Mr. Mannix because he was such a gentlemanly man," continued Mawhinney. "He was always nicely dressed, always neat in his person; he always wore a blue serge suit. He was very full-chested, spoke quite low, and was a very nice gentleman — one that appealed to you at once. Those that knew him thought highly of him. He would only speak when he had something worthwhile to say. That seemed to be his motto. He had a number of friends in the business and he used to help them out occasionally. He was generous to his friends, almost to a fault, but he never exceeded the limits of good, sound judgment. He would never fling money around; he never extended himself beyond a certain limit. He was careful."

As Mawhinney relates, banking was a bit different in the 1930s. "Very rarely did Mr. Mannix come to the bank to transact business," Mawhinney recalled. "He had a room in the Palliser Hotel. The manager of the bank, the assistant manager of the branch, and myself in my capacity as head accountant, would go to his room. The manager would always say, 'Well now, you know what Mr. Mannix likes.' The favourite drink in Calgary, in those days, was Johnny Walker Black Label Scotch Whisky. We would get one of our messengers to pick up one or two bottles. Mr. Mannix was abstemious; he never overdid it. For a gentleman in his position, something else was very noticeable, and we used to mention it at the bank. He would never swear. Oftentimes, a contractor would get a little bit out of bounds and express himself, but not Mr. Mannix. So we would have a drink and have a little chat about business, and then return to the bank office."

"Mr. Mannix kept $50,000 in bonds in his safety deposit box, which was quite a bit of money in those days," said Mawhinney. "When he was going to make a bid, he would come to the bank to get the bonds. He would take them from the safety deposit box in the bank, which was downstairs. One of our commissioners was delegated to look after that kind of business, and he would hand the bonds over and ask, 'Would you like them in an envelope, Mr. Mannix?' 'No, thank you,' he would say. He'd put those bonds in his inside pocket and upstairs he would come. He'd always have the bonds in his inside pocket. I can see him now. Always the same amount."

When the Social Credit government came to power in 1935, it saw highway construction as a way of alleviating the labour surplus in the province. The policy of competitive tenders was abolished in favour of government-directed grading projects using day labour and rented equipment. On June 9, 1936, F.S. Mannix wrote to the newly appointed minister of public works, William A. Fallow. F.S. Mannix offered to do grading work on Highway No. 2 from Crossfield to Red Deer, Alberta, stating that he would take three per cent government bonds payable in 1940 as payment. Mannix also offered to move the earth on a unit basis

1932 ▶

Two RCMP members with a seized still.

1933 ▶

Bennett buggies — automobiles propelled by animal power because of lack of funds to buy gasoline — provide transportation throughout Alberta. The buggies are named in honour of Canada's prime minister and his Depression policies.

1933 ▶

The Banff School of Fine Arts is created.

of 15 cents a cubic yard for all material except solid rock, a good price since the rate for earth alone was expected to be 15 cents. His offer was rejected.

On August 16, 1937, a Public Highways Energy Commission proceeding, before Justice Lunney, met to detect acts of incompetence on undue expense in government-run highway construction. The commission used two Mannix jobs, the Lethbridge-Iron Springs and the Calgary-Strathmore highways, contrasted with two government jobs under inquiry. Mannix was shown to work equally or more efficiently than the government for less cost. In their conclusions, the commission castigated the government for not taking the 1936 Mannix proposal seriously and further for not considering him for equipment rental since he owned two LeTourneaus, the most cost-effective machines in the province.

Fallow defended his actions, telling the commission that he considered the letter at the time to be "propaganda." It is difficult to conceive of propaganda entering into a straightforward business letter in which a man offers to do work at a price, but Fallow stated that F.S. Mannix offered a proposal that "couldn't be considered," adding, "I made it plain that the policy of the government would be to build their own highways, I know they [the private contractors] would not be very happy about it. I knew they would do anything to discourage that way of building roads. I knew I had crossed swords with an organization that was 100 per cent hostile."

The roadblock set up by Fallow did not slow F.S. Mannix; he simply continued to pursue other avenues of work. One could label F.S. Mannix many things — a gambler, a dirt mover, a contractor — but to use any or all of these terms would be to underestimate the man. Above all else, F.S. Mannix was an operator. He knew the outfit's success depended not on railway work, or irrigation work, or highway work, or any other narrowly defined area of work, but on his ability to be flexible and adapt to the market conditions of the time. F.S. Mannix understood that to succeed in the long term, he had to be in the business of business.

F.S. Mannix in the Rocky Mountains with his new Packard car.

1934 ▶

Mannix & Kramer begins coal stripping operations at Sheerness, Alberta. They strip 115,113 short tons (104,648 tonnes) in the first year of operation.

1934 ▶

A "black blizzard" sweeps across the Prairie provinces, leaving farmers in trouble and city dwellers covered with dust. The storm's fierce winds pick up the parched topsoil to such an extent that it blocks out the sunlight. Along with the topsoil goes grain seeds planted only a few days before.

FRED MANNIX & CO. LTD.

FM CO.

FRED MANNIX
& COMPANY, LTD.
1935 – 1942

"At that time there was Mannix & Son. There was also Mannix & Kramer.
Freddie would make money and Bob would lose money, or Bob would make money and Freddie would
lose on some of his jobs. So finally, Dad said, 'Let's have one company. I'll take half and Freddie can have
one-quarter and Bob will have the other quarter. Then, no matter which job we're doing, we'll pool the money.'

So whether Freddie lost money and Bob made some, or vice versa, at least in the fall we'd have something.
Freddie would eat, and Bob and I would eat. That way one of us wouldn't starve while the other
lived high off the hog. In those times, the jobs were pretty unpredictable. If you had a terribly,
terribly rainy season, you'd lose money, sure as God made little green apples."

— Alice Mannix Kramer, daughter of F.S. Mannix and wife of R.A. Kramer

Since its beginnings, the Mannix outfit was very much a family business. Two of F.S. Mannix's first employees were his brothers, Alf and Len. They worked alongside F.S. until the mid-1930s, when they took off on ventures of their own. "They had an entirely different attitude toward the business than Dad did," recalled Luella Mannix Wilson. "Dad used to say, 'God, if they only knew how much I owe the banks.' They didn't worry about things. As Dad used to say, he would get in the elevator and see them going down to the beer parlour to have a drink while he was going up to worry about how he was going to get the next payroll ready. They were just having a good time. They had an entirely different attitude toward life, really." According to Mrs. Wilson, the split came when Alf and Len "headed up the union and unionized against my dad. I don't know which union it was, but Dad had sure had enough."

Right: The inner office of Ferguson Supply in Calgary, circa 1912. Left to right are Ed Foley, Tom Callison, Steve Ferguson, Malcolm Grant, Alex Lou and Ira Ferguson.

"Dad never said anything about a problem to our immediate family," recalled Florence Mannix Pallesen, "because I was a good friend with my cousin and we used to visit and go skating and that sort of thing. So he didn't make it known in our own personal home life. If there was a problem in construction or the business end of it, he didn't bring it home with him, which made it easier on us."

While F.S. Mannix did not mix business with his home life, he did try to facilitate opportunities for his children and their mates to get ahead in the world. Accordingly, he gave Alice's husband, Bob Kramer, and Eleanor's husband, Johnny Lynch, their start in the business world. He also gave Florence's husband, Norman, the backing for a new venture. "Norman was in the creamery business, the milk business," recalled Mrs. Pallesen. "His father was quite well-known here. At one time, the Pallesens had about 28 creameries in Alberta. He was really quite successful, so my husband stayed in it. Gradually, he worked up a bit and was managing the largest creamery in Alberta; it wasn't just milk, it was eggs and poultry and everything like that. Then this opportunity came up with the Ferguson Supply. He'd known the Fergusons for years — they were a Calgary company — and he knew it was coming up for sale because they were moving to Vancouver. He thought he knew how to manage a creamery and how to handle men and whatnot, so he phoned them to come down to see about it."

"I remember one remark when my husband mentioned this," continued Mrs. Pallesen. "He said, 'Your father said if I can manage a creamery, I can manage nuts and bolts. It doesn't matter what business you're in; if you know how to manage it, you'll be successful.' So he backed him up. He could see Norman could run a business; it didn't matter what kind. He said, 'We'll have to do this in a businesslike fashion,' which was better for me, for Norman, and for my father, too. It was all legally drawn up, a certain amount a year, so it made it much easier. Bob [Kramer] and my brother [F.C. Mannix], too, he got them both started very well. I imagine there were quite a few other people that I don't know about; he lent them money or backed them."

While F.S. Mannix was particularly keen to give his only son a start in the business, F.C. Mannix had a few wild oats to sow. "Freddie was the apple of Dad's eye," recalled Alice Mannix Kramer. "But sometimes he didn't behave too well. As long as Mother was living at home, it wasn't too bad. Mother managed fine. It was after Mother got sick and he had nobody to help him. Dad was so busy trying to make a living and take care of us all. It would take so much of his time to travel from one job to another, so it meant that much less time at home. I think Dad used to lean very heavily on Eleanor.

"Freddie spent money like water and was always broke. Dad had a terrible time. Every once in a while Freddie would get in a scrap and Dad would have to get him out. That would be pretty discouraging for Dad, but then he'd start all over. I think Dad's greatest ambition was that Freddie would take over."

A Chip off the Old Block

Known as "Sunshine" to his mother and "Moonshine" to his father, from early childhood, Frederick Charles Mannix showed the personality traits that would later help shape his exceptional career as a businessman. Among these qualities were tremendous energy, a love of adventure, and fearlessness when it came to taking risks. According to Bob Kramer, these qualities sometimes made little Fred C. a bit of a terror. "Each summer, the Mannix family came to visit my mom and dad at Coaldale," Kramer recalled. "I think Freddie was about seven or eight years old the first time. Although we always looked forward to seeing the Mannix family arrive for these visits, sometimes I wasn't too sure whether Freddie was welcome or not because he used to be somewhat of a mischief-maker and was always upsetting my dad's plans. Freddie always used to leave the gates open and let the cows and the pigs out of their pens. One day someone happened to snap a picture of Freddie with four or five large Yorkshire boars, one of which he was riding!"

"He was dreadful, dreadful!" laughed Mrs. Kramer. "He was happy-go-lucky and he played tricks and giggled and laughed until we could have just killed him. Being the only boy, he had to be treated

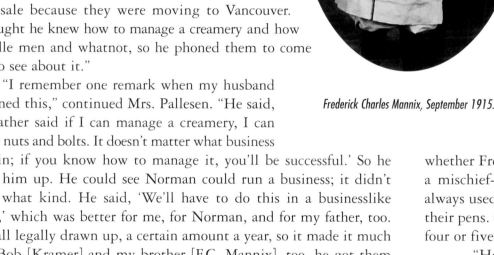

Frederick Charles Mannix, September 1915.

1935 ▶

F.S. Mannix brings his son, F.C. Mannix, into the business as a partner. They finance a 75E Cat and LeTourneau scraper for earthmoving projects in southern Alberta.

1935 ▶

The airport for the Royal Canadian Air Force at Currie Barracks in Calgary, a Mannix & Owens project, is completed. The diesel Caterpillars prove a valuable addition to the company's machinery.

differently, of course. Oh, we used to get so mad at him sometimes. He was just a tease, a dreadful tease, and he was untidy. If someone said, 'Freddie, your clothes don't match,' he didn't care. He didn't care about clothes. That was the least of his worries, as long as he was able to giggle and laugh and play tricks."

Young Fred spent his childhood with the construction people in the field. Thrust early into a man's life, he started doing a man's work at a very young age. "From five or six and on up until I was about ten years old, my father took me out to the camps," he recalled. "I used to go out to the camps all by myself with a bunch of the guys looking after me. At the age of eight, I used to go with Mrs. Lawler, whose husband was a partner with Father. I was 13 when I took my first construction job during the summer vacation. I worked as a bull-cook, chore-boy, drove a dump wagon and helped the blacksmith shrink tires on wagon wheels."

When Fred C. was just 15, he worked on a project to construct railway grade for the CPR/CNR branch line between Drumheller and Rosemary. Young Fred drove trucks, even though he was not old enough for a driver's licence. "The big thing that happened to me there was that I backed into a car one time with the truck, and I was under-age," he said. "But it got straightened out and I was able to continue driving the truck. I hauled oil and gas, oats and hay for the horses, and food for the men. That was about a 50-man camp, with 100 head of horses. I worked with Blackie Sayce who had been shell-shocked and lost an arm in the first war. He was a real good teacher and we got to be good friends. We drove 100 head of horses from Rockyford to Drumheller — one guy with a democrat and two on horseback. It was a long day in the saddle from 3:00 a.m. until arrival in Drumheller about 9:00 p.m."

An incident from that job provides a revealing insight into F.C. Mannix's character. One day, Bob Kramer, the project manager, sent young Fred into town with a truckload of empty 45-gallon (170-litre)

A young F.C. Mannix on the farm near Lomond, Alberta, where he works for Joe Lawler during the summer.

barrels to get gasoline for the two Caterpillar tractors. After several hours the boy had not returned, so Kramer drove off to see what had happened. "Fred had gotten stuck on the way home," Kramer said. "So, he unloaded all the barrels of gas, got the truck out of the mud hole, and loaded the barrels back on. He took one of the sideboards off the truck, rolled the barrels down and then rolled them back up again. How in hell, at his age, he ever did that I could never understand. Those barrels weighed 200 or 300 pounds apiece filled up, and he got all of them off and back on again." F.C. Mannix's own recollection of that day was typically matter-of-fact. "The barrels were easy to get off," he said. "It was getting them back on that was the trouble."

During this period, young Fred was also learning the financial side of the business. "F.S. Mannix had a first-class accountant, a Scotsman by the name of Jimmy Nairn," recalled Robert Mawhinney. "Nairn used to make up bids for the contracts. Other contractors would probably have to go to chartered accountants, but Nairn was able. He had been reared with a Scot's background and was very careful and canny. Jimmy Nairn expressed himself freely about Mr. Mannix's son, whom we knew as Freddie in those days. Freddie used to follow Nairn around. He wanted to become familiar with the business while he was in the office and also in the bank. I recall very vividly how Nairn was transacting some particular business with our bank. I was sitting at my desk, and he leaned over the counter and said, 'I don't know what I am going to do with this kid.' It was a typical comment."

While young Fred was learning the business, he knew that success is not always attributable to perseverance and hard work — sometimes Lady Luck lends a winning hand. F.S. taught his son that there are times when a man has to take a gamble, be willing to lose in order to win. Young Fred took to this rather unorthodox business skill like a duck to water. "When Freddie was about 15 years old, he used to

1935 ▶

Italy, led by the Fascist Benito Mussolini, invades Ethiopia.

1935 ▶

Work in Calgary includes driving piles for the west retaining wall of the Louise Bridge.

come out to the camp as a roustabout when we had the horses and dump wagons," Bob Kramer recalled. "The guys would put the horses away after supper and clean the sweat pads and then they'd go to the bunkhouse and start to play poker. Freddie would go over and play poker with them and he'd take them to the cleaners. Guys were coming back to the office for more money every night. In those days, we never had a payroll, the fellows would work for us for the whole season and they drew cash as they needed it. They kept coming over and getting more money until they were getting in the hole on me.

"It got to the stage where these guys were raising cane about it. Mannix working in the camp and taking all their money! I had guys who would want to get transferred to another camp so they wouldn't have to play poker with him and get beaten. Freddie was a good poker player. If I had all the money he'd taken from me in poker games, I wouldn't have to work anymore. Freddie was a born gambler. He was always able to throw aces."

Hollis O'Hanlon, F.C. Mannix and Mickey Rooney in Southern California.

While young Fred was lucky at cards, his luck with automobiles was another matter. This, too, was a trait he inherited from his father. "Dad used to drive out to the farm," F.C. Mannix recalled. "He had old touring cars, 1921 and 1922. I used to go out with him. One time, he tipped the car over twice with me in it." Undaunted, father and son simply got out of the car, rolled it back up on its wheels, and continued on home. "Freddie and Dad came home, and Dad was combing his hair and whatnot," recalled Luella Mannix Pallesen. "He was sitting there and his shoelaces all fell apart. Mother asked him what happened, and he said that the acid from the battery had gone all over them. He hadn't really told her that it was that bad, I don't think."

Perhaps because of his own exploits with cars, F.S. Mannix was tolerant of his son's. One story tells of Fred C. taking his father's brand-new, three-day-old Packard for a spin. Soon after taking off in the gleaming V-12 with beautiful yellow wooden spokes, young Fred had the car up on a street island, ignominiously dropped on its belly pan, the broken spokes strewn like fancy-coloured toothpicks about the street. "During my last year at university, I met F.S. for dinner in Edmonton," Vince Allen recalled. "He was chortling about how Frederick Charles had wrecked a car the night before by straddling a street island and shearing the wheels off. There were no regrets at all in his voice. He seemed to be proud that Frederick Charles was exhibiting some of his father's traits!"

F.C. Mannix, left, hauling rocks in the mud at Sedgewick, Alberta, in 1931.

Although F.S. Mannix may have been proud of his son's youthful antics, sometimes he used his sense of humour to put young Fred in his place. The story goes that one day F.S. Mannix took his son for lunch at the Club Cafe in Edmonton. After ordering them each a dozen oysters, F.S. liberally poured Tabasco sauce all over his. Eager to emulate his dad, and never having experienced oysters before, young Fred followed his father's lead. What he did not know was that, "Dad had his thumb over the bottle when he put it on, but Freddie didn't see it," recalled Luella Mannix Wilson with a chuckle. "Oh, I remember Dad came home, laughing so hard — 'That kid, acting so smart. He thinks he can do everything I can do,' Dad said. 'I showed him today!'"

There was one area where F.S. Mannix and his son diverged, however. Perhaps because he was denied an education by his father, F.S. Mannix was quite sold on the benefits of a formal education, backing

1935 ▶

Coal stripping continues around Sheerness with a total of 122,348 short tons (110,992 tonnes) mined.

1935 ▶

Laplander Andrew Bahr and his crew succeed in delivering 2,200 reindeer to the eastern Mackenzie River Delta from Alaska. The reindeer drive spans five years and is hoped to successfully introduce this species to the Far North.

numerous young people in university. "Dad never spoke about anyone; we didn't know whom he was helping at all," recalled Mrs. Pallesen. "But I know he lent money to a variety of different men who needed to go to university. He never told us about this, but they did. I can remember two, in particular, saying, 'Didn't you know your father lent me the money to go to the university? He said I could pay it back when I could.' Dad didn't want people to think he was going to be a sucker or anything like that, but even if they hadn't paid it back, I imagine it would have been all right with him. He gave them the responsibility of saying, 'Fine, but I'll get busy and pay it back someday.' These two different gentlemen both said, 'We made sure we paid it back, but if it hadn't been for your father, we would never have gone to the university.'"

While F.S. Mannix's encouragement and generosity enabled many young people to get the education they might otherwise have been denied, his son displayed little interest in continuing his formal education. "It was fun, a pretty nice place, but I had other things to do," he remarked. After graduating from Brentwood College in 1931, he attended the University of Alberta in Edmonton and the University of British Columbia in Vancouver. According to Mrs. Kramer, the family joke was that whatever university Fred C. attended, he always graduated at Christmas. "If anybody asked my dad about Fred's education," she said, "he would say, 'He's been through many universities — in one door and out the other!' University was too slow for Freddie. He was anxious to get going and make some money."

One of F.C. Mannix's classmates at the University of Alberta was Robert J. Burns. "We hit the university at about the same time," Burns recalled. "We were freshmen in the same year, along with Everett Costello, who became one of Fred's lifelong associates. We lived in the same residence. F.C. was given to partying with some of the other boys and got into a fair amount of trouble, to the point where he was not invited back after Christmas. They had a habit in those days of weeding out the freshmen fairly strenuously. I don't know how it worked, but it wasn't unusual to not be invited back after the Christmas break, and I think that happened to Fred. So his father put him to work in one of their construction outfits and he got his education that way."

The first Mannix LeTourneau scraper is pulled by a diesel Cat near Rycroft, Alberta, 1936.

Showdown at Picture Butte

In 1935, F.C. Mannix's life reached a turning point. That year, his father won a small contract to construct a highway and an earth-filled dam for a sugar refinery near Picture Butte, Alberta. The senior Fred Mannix purchased a new 75E Caterpillar and LeTourneau scraper for the job. Then he made an offer to his son, who was to be the project manager. F.S. Mannix explained that if the job ran smoothly, the company would make the cost of the new machinery and young Fred could earn a half interest in this equipment. "Father bankrolled the job for $20,000 and me for $10,000," said F.C. Mannix. "I worked seven days a week and received $100 a month for my keep."

"That job was really a trial run for F.C. Mannix," recalled Frank O'Sullivan, who had emigrated from England to Canada to work on a farm. "A few years later I had a chance to acquire a truck, and soon I had 12 trucks and I went into the contracting business. They were going to build a sugar factory at Picture Butte — that's about 20 miles north of Lethbridge — and Mannix bid on building the dam to store the water for use in the sugar factory. Fred S. had bought this 75 diesel Cat and scraper, and he had a crew in there running the Cats. One of them was Blondie Garbutt and the other

1935 ▶

After 10 years of evangelistic radio broadcasting, William Aberhart and his Social Credit party sweep the United Farmers of Alberta from office.

1935 ▶

Up to 2,000 unemployed men from British Columbia and Alberta commandeer CPR boxcars in an attempt to ride them to Ottawa to present their grievances to Prime Minister Bennett. The RCMP, acting on orders from Ottawa, stop the trains in Regina. Clashes occur.

THE BIGGEST, BEST EARTHMOVING EQUIPMENT

F.S. Mannix acquired his first LeTourneau scraper in 1935. This machine, one of the first of its kind in Canada, was put to work at Sheerness mine. Woody Wood recalls that F.S. Mannix was regarded as an innovator in the construction business for bringing mechanized earthmoving equipment to Western Canada. "Fred S. Mannix wasn't afraid to go to the gas Cats," Wood said, "and he wasn't afraid to go to LeTourneaus. He would be first. If it was good and he thought it would work, he'd be in there. He was progressive in this business. He kept the equipment in good shape, too. He believed in maintenance. He kept it clean on the job, no fooling around. They weren't sloppy housekeepers at all, which gives the operators pride in their equipment. They soon learned this was important and they looked after their equipment better. It's a good philosophy."

"LeTourneaus were much bigger scrapers than what we were using," added Ernie Enarson. "They could take 12 cubic yards in one load. The other little scrapers they had then could haul maybe two or three yards. The LeTourneaus were also cable-controlled from the tractor, so one operator could drive the tractor and control the scraper as well. It was a prestigious thing at the time, because that was the biggest, best earthmoving equipment around. If you were a LeTourneau skinner, that was really something."

one was Cec McCormick. Fred C. ran one shift by himself. They had rag houses; those were tents. They lived in tents — the night shift had one and the day shift had the other.

"I had a contract from the Lethbridge Northern Irrigation District to supply the rock, big boulders and gravel, for the riprapping of this dam. F.S. Mannix hoped that F.C. would go in and cut it. Well, there was no question about cutting it. He did a good job. They broke records moving dirt with one Caterpillar and one scraper. Fred C. had his whole heart and soul in it, and he would rather have died than let his dad down. He did a tremendous job and I admire him for it."

"Then they had a contract to build the road from Lethbridge to Iron Springs," continued O'Sullivan. "This was supplied by the government so they could work in the sugar factory and haul the beets in. Fred S. Mannix had the contract which was subbed out to Mannix & Son, Mannix & Kramer, and Mannix & Mannix. Alf Mannix was a brother of Fred Mannix and he had one of the contracts. It was subbed out to several outfits, and I had the contract for crushed gravel. We got it done by August 31, 1935, as the sugar factory had to be finished by that time. We worked until almost midnight that night to have it finished on time. But we always said, when you want a job done on time, call Mannix."

"Dad was superintendent on the job," recalled Gus Enarson's son, Ernie. "It was a hot, blistering sun out there on that bald prairie. The first job they gave me was to help a fellow assemble creosote culverts. They told me, 'Now, be careful. Don't get this creosote on your skin because it will blister your skin. So I started working and helping this fellow. I started to sweat. I had gloves on to keep the creosote off, but then I'd wipe my forehead with the back of my hand. No one had told me that you shouldn't rub your skin, because the fumes from the creosote will blister your skin. This was on a Saturday; I came Friday night and Saturday I worked this way. Sunday morning, my one eye was swollen half shut and the other was completely shut because of this creosote.

1935 ▶

The fall of the year sees F.C. Mannix running three road construction jobs on Highway No. 95 along the Columbia River between Golden and Radium, British Columbia.

1935 ▶

Other highway projects include work near Jasper National Park and between Calgary and Strathmore.

"Right at this time, the fellow who was driving the 60 Caterpillar tractor got drunk and got into a real row and Dad fired him. So Monday, they wanted a Catskinner, and Dad says, 'Now, you go and drive this tractor.' That's how I got started driving a Caterpillar tractor. I remember when I was sitting on the tractor, I was really feeling good. I said to myself, 'Every minute I sit here, I make one penny,' because I was getting 62 and a half cents an hour. I really felt I was raking in the money."

Another whose financial situation and status improved considerably after the Picture Butte job was young Fred C. Mannix. "Freddie came back after he finished the job and went to the office to settle up the books," recalled Mrs. Kramer. "Dad handed him a cheque for $4,000, and Freddie looked at it and said, 'Is this mine?' Dad said, 'Yes, you made that money on the job.' Well, it was a real shock to Freddie that he'd done so well and made so much money. I think at that time Dad figured, 'At last Freddie realizes that if he would put his nose to the grindstone, he could be very successful. Now, I hope this is the beginning.' Freddie had got into so much trouble, caused so many headaches, had such a good time, and here he

FRESH FRUIT FOR SALE

"We crossed Thompson River with Cats in the wintertime," recalled Blondie Garbutt. "This was in the fall, the ice was just forming, and the ferry couldn't run because the ice was a couple of inches thick.

"This is a picture of a load of fruit that a driver brought down from Amos. He was on his way to Val-d'Or, about five miles away. It was about 50 miles back to Amos. He was afraid of the ice, but thought that if he turned around and went back to Amos, maybe the fruit would freeze before he got back. He finally decided he'd try and get across. And the darn fool, he didn't ride in the cab, he ran along beside it, steering in through the window. He was going too slow and the truck broke through the ice. It hung suspended for about an hour and then finally it let go and went down in 18 feet of water.

"They waited for about a month until the ice got strong enough to support a derrick. And by golly, the first hook they sent down grabbed the frame of the truck and they hauled it up. The fruit wouldn't freeze down in the bottom of the water, but it stayed cold so they dashed that truck into Val-d'Or and they sold the fruit. Apples and bananas and oranges. We crossed that river with D-8 Cats later on when the ice got thick. Those D-8 Cats weighed something like 18 tons."

had finally done something that was really successful. He almost surprised himself." While the Mannix family regarded Picture Butte as the place where young Fred came of age, F.C. Mannix himself regarded Picture Butte in a less dramatic fashion. "It was just that I had work to do, and I did it," he said. "That's all. I bought a half interest in the scraper and Cat, which was $7,500. I borrowed some of the money from my father and paid him interest on it."

F.C. Mannix may have proven his worth on the Picture Butte job, but he did not let his new emerging maturity spoil his innate love of fun and good times. "One time down at Picture Butte it was raining and we couldn't work, so we got into a poker game," recalled Blondie Garbutt. "Freddie's luck was bad, and my luck was bad, so he gave me a poke in the ribs and said, 'Let's get out of here.' We went into Lethbridge and drank beer all afternoon. Then we hooked up with three other guys. I didn't know them very well, but we were each supposed to pay our own way. Freddie didn't have much money in those days. He'd maybe get five bucks from the old man and then he'd borrow five or ten bucks from me. Anyway, we threw in a dollar apiece to buy a bottle

1935 ▶

In national elections held in October, W.L.M. King ousts Richard B. Bennett in an overwhelming repudiation of Bennett's Depression era policies.

1936 ▶

Montreal thoracic surgeon, Norman Bethune, a volunteer for the Republican forces in Spain, creates the first mobile blood transfusion unit. He saves lives and changes trauma treatment for all time.

KEEPING CLEAN IN THE FIELD

"Bob Kramer is the type of fellow who is very immaculate, and everything had to be just clean and spotless and nice for him," Ernie Enarson recalled. "I remember when we were in around Val-d'Or on that job, there was another fellow and myself, and we had a new Caterpillar RD-7 tractor. It was muddy and wet, but it wasn't dusty, so every Sunday, we would go out there and clean this tractor and keep it clean. Bob Kramer came by one time and saw this, and he went back to the other camp where my father was superintendent. He told my dad, 'Ernie and this Bob Parks, they sure keep their Cat nice.' He was really proud of that.

"When we were at Lake Minnewanka, Bob Kramer would dress up very nice, and then he would have his light cream-coloured, leather boots laced up to here. Bob was polished, nice, you know. He was helping us fuel up one time, and when he pulled the hose out of the tank of the tractor, it sloshed around and splashed fuel oil on these boots. He started to rub, but he couldn't get it off, and he cursed and swore around there for a long time. About three, four days later, he came by again with a new pair of boots. He just would not have boots that were stained. That's the way he always was. He was always dressed very immaculately. He really took care of himself that way."

of Scotch. So we went on down into the States and Freddie got into a poker game and lost every nickel he had, which wouldn't be very much. He came back about breakfast time and we went up to Lethbridge to have breakfast. And the young waitress came around to take our order. Freddie said, 'Bring me three raw eggs and a bowl.' She brought these eggs and he cracked them into this bowl. He added Worcestershire sauce and salt and pepper to no end and tipped the bowl up and drank it down. It pretty near made me sick, as I was sober by that time. And when the waitress came around again, he said, 'Better bring me three more eggs.' What a character!"

Another trait F.C. Mannix retained was his total lack of concern regarding clothes. "Freddie had come back from Gilcrest Ranch, out at Manyberries, and had finished the job down there," recalled Hans Olesen, who began work for the Mannix outfit driving trucks and Cats in 1935. "Then they had a job at Golden and Spillimacheen and Radium; three little road jobs. Ben Coleman was the foreman and Mrs. Coleman was running the kitchen. Freddie was the big shot; he was supposed to run the three jobs. Anyhow, Fred Mannix Sr. came up there this day and he said, 'For heaven's sake, can't you get Fred to dress up a little bit?' He was just wearing a pair of overalls and high-top boots and all, and walked around like that. Mr. Mannix said, 'Get him to dress up when he goes to see the engineers.' So we talked to him and got him to put on clean clothes once in a while."

A Sign of the Times

When the Depression hit, at first it was said that prosperity was just around the corner. The reassurances went on even as the news got worse. Eventually it became clear that nobody knew when or how the Depression would end. By the mid-1930s, people, tired of outwaiting the drought and Depression, began to look for economic solutions to the times. Technocracy attracted some attention and Communism won a few converts. But the real Alberta story was social credit.

The man who brought social credit to Alberta was William Aberhart, radio evangelist and principal of Crescent Heights High School in Calgary. In 1932, Aberhart thought he found the answer to the Depression in the principles formulated by an English engineer, Major C.H. Douglas. Douglas, who argued that economic hardships resulted from an inefficient capitalist economy which failed to provide people with sufficient purchasing power for them to enjoy the fruit of a

1936 ▶

Both the Val Marie, Saskatchewan, and Brooks, Alberta, dams are built, increasing the irrigation potential of the Palliser Triangle.

1936 ▶

Highway construction between Lethbridge and Iron Springs during the summer.

well-developed production capacity, advocated the distribution of money, or "social credit," so that people might purchase the goods and services readily produced by capitalist enterprise. Aberhart launched the Alberta social credit movement into politics at a meeting in the Prophetic Bible Institute in Calgary. In 1935, Aberhart, who was the first to use radio effectively in Alberta politics, became premier of Alberta.

In the midst of the uproar over social credit in Alberta, dictators were on the march in distant parts of the world. Adolf Hitler, who had taken over as chancellor of Germany in 1933, brought in compulsory military training in 1935. The German army, dismantled after the First World War, was rebuilt and on the march. That same year, Fascist Italy attacked Ethiopia. It was a disturbing sign of things to come.

Perhaps as a reflection of the times, the year 1935 saw the Mannix & Kramer operation under attack. "One of the projects we secured was another contract under the relief plan to build the Currie Barracks in Calgary," explained Bob Kramer. "Since employment opportunities were still scarce, my brother, Tom, joined me on the project. To help build the barracks, we purchased four state-of-the-art machines from Union Tractor — two 75E diesel Caterpillar tractors and two Model J LeTourneau scrapers. These were the first diesel-powered tractors that I know of that were used in Canada in construction work."

"Those tractors and scrapers were said to handle an enormous workload and we were eager to start moving dirt," continued Kramer. "There were those, however, who opposed our use of machinery. At that time, the whole world was in a very bad economic condition. There was tremendous unemployment. The government was building projects with the relief plan and trying to give people jobs, but unemployment was still out of control. When we unloaded our machinery in Calgary, we were followed by about 5,000 people. I don't think they were armed, but some were carrying sticks and pieces of wood. They came out and told us that we weren't going to build the airport with those machines. They thought we should build the airport by hand labour, with wheelbarrows, and hire all the people who were unemployed in Calgary. I didn't know what to do. I certainly wasn't going to try and stop all those people. Most of the protesters were members of the labour union, angry and ready to fight, along with their families and friends. I wasn't about to test their word, nor did I think we were any match for their collective might. They shut us down for about a week, until officials from the federal government and the City of Calgary finally talked the union leaders out of it and we went on with the job."

Building the Currie Airport in Calgary mixes old and new construction methods.

Once they were allowed to continue work, Mannix & Kramer got their first exposure to diesel Caterpillars. "They ran quite well until we had operated them approximately a month," recalled Kramer, "and then they began to lose power. We decided to take them apart and find out what was the matter. We found that the piston rings were carboned up and seized. So every Sunday, we had to take the pistons out and clean the carbon out of the rings and have them ready again for the night shift. This went on for a long time. F.S. Mannix and everybody else concerned was after the Caterpillar Tractor

1936 ▶

The reservoir at Mirror, Alberta, is excavated using Cats, scrapers, wagons and draglines.

1936 ▶

Work for the Canadian National Railways includes a reservoir constructed near Rycroft in northwestern Alberta and stripping near Kinsella in southeastern Alberta.

PUTTING THE BEARS IN THEIR PLACE

"Mother would take us to the camp at Minnewanka and we would go into the cookhouse," Marilyn Kramer Acteson said. "Pearl Lawler was the cook and she made these huge cookies for us. They were real big cookies and we would each get one.

"There was a bear that used to come down to the cookhouse. His name was Tony and he even knew how to open the latch on the screen door. He would come in and go up and down the aisles where the men ate. We were all very excited about seeing him in the kitchen. There was a shelf underneath the counter that had a cake the size of a coffee table and it had pink icing. This bear took a swipe at it and just cleaned off a third of the cake. Pearl got so mad at the bear that she slapped him on the nose, gave him a kick in the rear end, and sent him yelling out the screen door. And this was a wild bear!"

Pearl Lawler was not the only one who stood up to the bears. "There was an Indian who was like a camp maintenance man," said Ernie Enarson. "They called him a bullcook. He tended the fires and so forth in the bunkhouses. In the spring, bears came around and upset the garbage and that really annoyed this fellow. Many Guns was his name. It really annoyed him because it was his job. He had to shovel all this garbage back into the barrel. One time he came around the corner of the bunkhouse, and here was the bear, halfway into the barrel, digging the stuff out. Many Guns got so mad he walked up behind the bear and kicked him right in the pants. The bear just got out of the barrel and took off up the mountainside."

Company and the oil companies to find out what was causing the carboning up of these engines. It wasn't settled until a little later when the oil companies came up with the detergent oil that they use today. That oil dissolved all the carbon in the diesel engines. Actually, we were the guinea pigs in showing how to correct the faults in the first diesel engines."

The Way to Lance Brown's Place

In addition to airport work, the Mannix outfit put its new LeTourneau scrapers to work on smaller jobs. One of these jobs included building a dam for a farmer named Lance Brown. While the job itself was not particularly challenging, finding the actual job site turned out to be something of an ordeal. "We were building two little dams down at Manyberries," recalled Blondie Garbutt. "We were running three shifts and there was hardly any camp at all. I doubt we had a washbasin to wash in. I think we had to go out and wash a bit in the puddles.

"Anyway, we built two small dams for the ranchers and then we were going to move over into Cypress Hills and build another dam there for a rancher named Lance Brown. They let the other two guys go and I was to take the machine over to Cypress Hills, which is a little town in the hills about 35 or 40 miles away. Freddie came to me and said, 'I know the way into town, so I'll go mark the trail. At every turn you've got to make, I'll hang a white flag. If you've got to make a turn to the left, there will be a little white flag hanging on the left-hand side of the tree.'

"Then he said, 'I don't know how to get from there out to this Lance Brown's place, but I do know the storekeeper at Cypress Hills. I'll have him make a map and leave it on the table with a coal oil lamp. You call in there and this map will be on the table. Get that map as it will tell you how to get from there out to Lance Brown's place.'"

"The town was about five miles away," said Garbutt. "The Cat could travel seven miles an hour, so I had no

R.A. Brown Sr., shown seated next to his son Bobby, strikes oil in Turner Valley, Alberta, igniting a major oil boom.

Canadians receiving government relief drop from almost 1.5 million in 1935 to 1.2 million. However, the Prairie provinces add more than 8,000 people to their relief roll as the Depression worsens for the West.

trouble getting to this little store. And sure enough, here's the coal oil lamp and the map. So I started out and, by gosh, I came to a hole, a kind of a creek, I'd guess you'd call it. This creek was pretty deep, maybe about 20 feet. There was this rickety old bridge across it and I got off the machine and looked at it. By that time it was three o'clock in the morning and I was all alone. All I had with me was this big LeTourneau scraper and some mattresses in the scraper. I don't know how the mattresses came to be there, but that's all I had. And I wasn't absolutely sure that I was on the right road. I thought, 'Ye gods, if I happen to be on the wrong road and go through the bridge, then I'm in trouble.'

"So I thought this over. Then I spotted a light way down to the southwest and I thought, 'By golly, I'll go down there to the light and ask whoever's there if I'm on the right road to this Lance Brown's place. So I left the Cat running and I walked way down there; it was three-quarters of a mile away. It was three o'clock in the morning and I went up to the house and knocked on the door. There was no

answer, so I finally went in. It was just a small house, a couple of rooms, and here was the light burning, a coal oil lamp, and an alarm clock was ticking away. I shouted and shouted, but no sir, I couldn't rise anybody. I looked and looked and there was nobody there. It was odd."

"So, finally, I decided I had to go back," said Garbutt. "I was still afraid of this bridge, so I thought, 'The heck with this. I'm not going to take a chance on that bridge.' It was kind of cold, so I got some mattresses out and laid them down and I crawled in between the mattresses and went to sleep. I woke up, oh, maybe 5:00 or 5:30. It was getting daylight and I heard a rooster crow back behind me so I thought, 'Gosh, where there's

a rooster, there must be people living there and I can find where this Lance Brown lives.' So I walked back and then the fog rolled in. Gosh, you could hardly see 10 feet in front of you. But this rooster kept crowing so I followed him. God, what an experience!

"I walked in this house and they were just having breakfast. I asked them if I was on the right road and they said, 'Yep, you go on up there and you'll find a swing gate made of poles.' So I went back to the machine and thought, 'Well, I'll have to take a chance on that bridge.' And it held. I found this gate and went in. Then I walked over to Lance Brown's place, which was a good three-quarters of a mile from the gate.

He was just getting up. He showed me the place where I was to build this dam and it was a pasture field. It had been surveyed two years before that. The cattle had been running in there and had knocked down quite a few of the stakes, but I found enough so that I was able to start work. I think I built that dam in three days — it was just across a little coulee — and then I was on my way out."

Mannix veterans at the Thompson River grading project near Val-d'Or, Quebec, 1937. From left to right, Hans Olesen, Cec McCormick, Alan Dryden, Ernie Harrison, two unknown men and Blondie Garbutt.

Breaking into the East: A Mixed Blessing

As Canada slowly emerged from the worst of the Great Depression, work began to open up. Late in 1935, in Alberta, Mannix & Kramer worked on the Hardisty Highway and on a pile-driving project on the Bow River. The following year, the company took on the Brooks Dam project in Alberta and the Val Marie Dam in Saskatchewan. The latter was under the auspices of the Prairie Farm Rehabilitation Agency (PFRA).

In late 1936, Mannix & Kramer was awarded the contract for the construction of the Val-d'Or Railway, a 100-mile (160-kilometre) branch line for Canadian National Railways. "The Quebec job running from

1936 ▶

The Canadian Broadcasting Corporation is created.

1936 ▶

Although Alberta faces continuing and often worsening drought, the number of farmers in the province reaches 99,732, an all-time high.

Senneterre to Rouyn was a significant project for us," recalled Kramer. "It marked the first and only time the Mannix & Kramer company broke into Eastern Canada. The job came at a high cost, however, with Quebec's under-the-rug tax laws, whereby every government official we encountered expected a payoff. Such bureaucracy didn't sit well with Mr. Mannix, for he was a very honest man, but we shipped 22 railroad carloads of machinery out of Calgary."

"In one way, that job from Senneterre to Rouyn was a big, big plus for the Mannix construction company," Luella Mannix Wilson said. "They had never broken into the East before and they got that job in Quebec. That was a really big thing, but it was also a big lesson to Dad. They had very unusual tax laws down there. In a way, it was a disaster because Dad had to pay out so much money."

F.S. Mannix also had his hands full with the crew. "That was his first big job," recalled Hans Olesen. "Old Fred, Mr. Mannix, came down this day. We were sitting in the cookhouse. Mr. Coleman and Mrs. Coleman were there and he says, 'By golly, I got a job now and I'll be able to turn over in bed before we are finished.' This was in 1936. On Boxing Day we left Calgary by train to Senneterre, Blondie Garbutt and myself. Cecil McCormick and Dunc McDonald went down ahead of us to get ready to set up camp. They got to Senneterre on New Year's Eve, had a party, and were sitting out back of the hotel drinking quart bottles of beer and having a good time. But the next morning, they went to work. Mr. Mannix was there himself to see if they were out there working. He stayed for maybe a week or so. Then he went back to Calgary and then

he came back again. As soon as things went a little haywire, Mr. Mannix would drop in and then things would be squared up in no time."

"When Mr. Mannix came out to Senneterre the first time, Freddie was running the job," continued Olesen. "Mr. Mannix would come out on the job and say, 'Where's Freddie?' Maybe Freddie would be uptown some nights playing a little poker. But he would always get to the job ahead of his dad. He was always one step ahead of his dad, every time. It seemed like he could smell him coming. But they always stuck up for Freddie. Even old Gus Enarson always stuck up for Freddie. He would say, 'Don't forget, you didn't have the same chances that your son has, you know.'"

Val-d'Or would test the patience of just about everyone involved. To begin with, there was the country itself. "It was beautiful," said Blondie Garbutt, "but it's a wonder we didn't get eaten alive by the mosquitoes and flies! Harry and Art O'Hanlon were down with us in Quebec. One night we were sleeping in this old log cabin and, oh God, the mosquitoes were bad. We had no spray to protect us. There was no screen door or anything. Some of the boys had a screen netting up around their cot to keep the mosquitoes out, but I didn't have one because they cost $3.00 or $4.00 and that was a lot of money then. Anyway, the next morning Harry was telling us that they woke up during the night and there were two mosquitoes down at the foot of the cot. They were arguing and one said, 'Will we eat him here or take him down to the swamp?' and the other one said, 'No, we better eat him here because if we take him down to the swamp, some of the big buggers will take him away from us!'"

Top: Some of the men relax off shift in their tent during the Quebec summer.

Above: At the Val-d'Or project, workmen cross the temporary bridge on the Bourlemac River.

1936 ▶

Mannix crews work in Claude Gallinger's coal mine near Sheerness, Alberta.

1936 ▶

Fred Mannix & Company, Ltd. is awarded the contract to build a Canadian National rail line from Senneterre to Rouyn, Quebec. This 100-mile (160-kilometre) project, more than 1,200 miles (2,000 kilometres) from Calgary, represents a significant expansion of the outfit.

"The mosquitoes were just terrible in that part of the country," concurred Ernie Enarson. "You had to put some fat on your face to make them go away — cooking fat, anything like that. You had to, or the mosquitoes would be biting your face all the time. One time the mosquitoes were biting Cec McCormick so bad that he took alamite grease and pasted it over his face. Then the mosquitoes got into that, and they couldn't even lift their feet. So they'd drag and crawl. That was almost as bad as mosquitoes biting."

"To compensate ourselves for working under such miserable conditions, we began carousing in town, well aware that, sooner or later, Mr. Mannix would hear about our slacking off," explained Kramer. "And, sure enough, he arrived one day, unbeknownst to us. After checking into a hotel, Mr. Mannix conducted a short investigation in town and learned that Cec, Freddie and I, as well as the rest of the crew, were raising hell and partying nearly every night. Senneterre was simply too small a community — it was a small town of about 300 people — for us to get away with anything.

"Mr. Mannix wasted no time in seeking us out. Cec was collared first. He was on the job and had just scooped up a yard of dirt and swung it over when he saw Mr. Mannix coming down the finished grade about 100 yards off. Cec wasn't going to talk with Mr. Mannix, knowing he'd catch hell for boozing, so he tried to ignore Mr. Mannix, who stood behind his dragline, waving and shouting, trying to get his attention. Cec just kept on swinging. He wouldn't turn or stop. Then he started going the other way. Mr. Mannix became so pissed off, he started throwing rocks at Cec's cab, which got Cec so rattled, he ran the bloody dragline right off the pass. Then when Cec tried to move the

Top: The bunkhouse at the Val-d'Or job. Winter temperatures reached lows of -40° F inside the bunkhouse.

Above: Railway grade extends out into the muskeg of northern Quebec during the Val-d'Or project, 1937.

dragline forward, he drove it right into the swamp. Mr. Mannix had a few choice words for Cec after that, and it took us several days to get the machine back onto dry ground."

"Although Cec was the first one to get nailed, Freddie and I were right behind him," continued Kramer. "Initially, we thought we had gotten off easy, since Mr. Mannix had returned to Calgary without confronting us, but the job was running behind schedule and he came back to collect our dues. In the office, or should I say our portable shack, Mr. Mannix told us that from then on, the job had to go smoothly and we had to meet our goals. To ensure no misunderstanding, Mr. Mannix spelled out every point on the map and each milestone date we were expected to meet. 'Bob,' Mr. Mannix commanded, 'you're to run the day shift and Freddie's going to run the night shift, since he's such a hoot owl.' Of course, that was Mr. Mannix's way of keeping both of us out of trouble, especially Freddie.

"A few months later, Alice came down to visit and she wanted to know where Freddie was. He was working at night and she never got to see him hardly at all. She said, 'Dad, I don't think you're very nice, making Freddie work all night,' and he said, 'No, heck, he likes the nightlife.'"

It was a good plan, but it was not a flawless one. Not long after his dad's visit, young Fred got his nose broken. The story goes that after Fred fired someone, the man walked outside, then called Fred C. to a window. When Fred stuck his head out, the man hit him in the face with a two-by-four. According to Kramer, although young Fred did not start the fight, "Freddie went to jail, and it took me until four o'clock the next morning to get him out. After that last brawl,

1936 ▶

Armand Bombardier is granted a patent on his track-equipped snowmobile.

1937 ▶

The last will of Toronto sportsman and financier, Charles V. Millar, at his death in 1926, promised a small fortune to the woman who produced the most offspring in the decade after his death. The "stork derby" concludes with four women tied, each with nine children, and each more than $100,000 richer.

Freddie got tired of having his nose broken — it had been broken about five times prior to that — and quit fighting altogether."

Some days it must have seemed to F.S. Mannix that nothing could go right at Val-d'Or. "Cec McCormick had the job of running the dragline," recalled Ernie Enarson. "One night, F.S. Mannix went to a movie in the theatre, and all of a sudden, it went black in there. Mr. Mannix said, 'Damn that Cec McCormick. He must have swung the dragline into the power line.' And that's exactly what had happened! That old man Mannix was just about right every time. He was darn good."

Despite the trials and tribulations of the outfit's first job in the East, F.S. Mannix personally saw to it that the job was completed. "When we were in Quebec, we were working at a cut at Pascalis," recalled Art O'Hanlon. "You could see about five miles down the right-of-way. Every once in a while, you would see something white way down there coming closer and closer. A couple of hours later, it would arrive. It would be old Fred, walking the right-of-way. You know, just checking it out."

Following the Val-d'Or job, F.S. Mannix decided to consolidate his family business dealings. While he had spent the bulk of his business career in a series of partnerships, in reality he was not overly fond of this form of business. According to family members he was known to say, "Partners are always easy to get, but hard to get rid of" and "The only ship that never sailed was a partnership." Yet F.S. Mannix was determined to make at least one partnership, the family partnership, sail. Accordingly, in 1936, he incorporated Fred Mannix & Company, Ltd., the first incorporated Mannix company. "That was after he had gotten it all straightened out," said F.C. Mannix. "He had one big job in Quebec and he gave Bob 25 per cent and me 25 per cent."

Margaret Ruth Boughton, 1938.

A Most Remarkable Love Story

Two years after Fred Mannix & Company, Ltd. was incorporated, Fred C. Mannix met a young woman who would have a dramatic impact on the future of the Mannix outfit. That woman was a beautiful young lady from Hull, Quebec, named Margaret (Margie) Ruth Boughton. Although Margie would deeply touch the heart and soul of the Mannix organization for the next 40 years, her first meeting with Fred was not an auspicious one.

"My mother was engaged to a man in Ottawa," recalled Maureen Mannix Eberts, "and her older sister, Evelyn, wanted her to think twice before she settled down. So Evelyn went with Mom on an extended tour. They went to Florida by train, then across the United States to California. Evelyn, recently married, was missed by her husband, so he flew to California to take her home. Mom continued on to Washington alone.

"After visiting friends in Spokane, Mom got up at four in the morning to catch the train to Seattle and the plane to go up to Vancouver. At that time, there was wonderful service between the trains and planes as there was an airline limousine that would pick you up at the train station. But it didn't come and it didn't come and she's getting quite anxious. She was just about to hire a cab, when the limo comes rushing up. There's four people in the limo, including a really scruffy man. They get to the airport and

1937 ▶

Producing wells west of Longview Hill in southern Alberta.

Mom checks in to go to Vancouver and this scruffy thing also checks in to go to Vancouver. This guy is unshaven, he is unclean, he is as completely ruffled as you can get. What happened is that the limo had called to his hotel and he wasn't ready. The limo had waited for him and he got up, threw himself together, checked out of the hotel and jumped into the limo, which made the whole limousine full of people late."

"But they do get to the airport, they do get on the plane, and be damned if this scruffy thing doesn't sit down beside my mother," continued Mrs. Eberts. "He smells badly and he's rough. He is slightly shaky. He's very hung over; you could still smell the booze. After the plane takes off, he gets up and takes off down the aisle. A little while later, a young man comes and goes to sit down in the seat beside her, but Mom says, 'I'm sorry but I don't think this is your seat.' And he says, 'Yes, it is my seat.' This guy has gone to the washroom. He has put on a tie. He has straightened up. He has shaved. He has brushed his teeth. He has washed his face. He has combed his hair. And he doesn't smell quite so badly."

After chatting for a while, Fred asked Margie where she was staying in Vancouver. Learning that she was staying at the Hotel Vancouver, he promptly responded, "That's where I'm staying! I'll drive you into town." But Fred C. was not on his way to Vancouver. "In actual fact," said Mrs. Eberts, "he was supposed to be on the next plane to Calgary. His father was very angry with him for not returning to the job."

For the next two days, Fred C. inundated Margie with phone calls. He insisted on taking her around town and showing her the sights during the day. During this time, Margie's male friend, a dentist whom she was visiting in Vancouver, was also showing her the sights in the evening. "So she had a very good comparison of tours," laughed Mrs. Eberts. After two days of sightseeing, the dentist takes her to the train to Calgary. As he is loading her on the train, Fred Mannix is getting on the next car," said Mrs. Eberts. "Mom waves goodbye to this

MARGIE MANNIX

Born in Ottawa in 1916, Margaret (Margie) Ruth Boughton was the daughter of Mr. and Mrs. Frederick Herbert Boughton. According to family records, Margie's mother, Elsie May Cushman Boughton, was a descendant of Robert Cushman. Cushman is said to have been a gentleman in the court of King James. He sailed to America in 1620 on the Pilgrim vessel *Speedwell*, which accompanied the *Mayflower*. Margie's grandfather was Sturgis Salmon Cushman, vice president and director of the E.B. Eddy Company Limited of Hull, Quebec.

May Queen, Margie Mannix, centre, with her May Court.

Margie graduated from Ottawa Ladies College in 1933. During her last year, she was elected Queen of the May Court, a student philanthropic organization. Money raised by the May Court was given to various worthy causes, including the Welfare Bureau, the Protestant Children's Hospital, the Salvation Army, the United Children's Campaign and the Emergency Relief Fund. In her acceptance speech, Margie said, "The May Court stands for the highest ideals and endeavours of our school life, and, in this way, helps not only those with whom we come in contact, but ourselves also, as it offers us the opportunity to cultivate daily the spirit of unselfishness, kindness, and sympathy for those less fortunate than ourselves."

Before her marriage to F.C. Mannix, Margie received an honours certificate of merit from the Canadian College of Music in pianoforte playing in 1930. She also completed a one-year course of stenography and typewriting at Branksome Hall, Toronto, in 1935, and graduated from a course in dental nursing from the University of Toronto in 1936.

MISSION ACCOMPLISHED

One of Fred C. Mannix's strengths as a businessman was his tenacious persistence. When he wanted something, he went after it until he got it. Perhaps nowhere was this persistence seen more clearly than in his courtship of Margaret Ruth Boughton.

The fact that Margie turned down Fred's initial proposal of marriage did not daunt the ardent young suitor. "All summer long, every week-end, there would be a dozen long-stemmed red roses and phone calls," recalled Margie's sister, Ev Wilkinson. "The summer went into fall, and the phone calls continued. In November, Fred said to his father — they always took their holi-days in California and played the horses at Santa Anita — 'I'm going to Ottawa to persuade a girl to marry me and I'm not going to leave until I get an answer.' So his father said, 'Well, good luck, son. I'll meet you at Santa Anita.'

"Fred went to Ottawa and, sure enough, won Margie's hand. Not long after, Fred sent a telegram to his father. It read: 'Mission Accomplished.'"

fellow who has taken her to the train, and zappo! Fred Mannix is right beside her. She says, 'Oh, no! Not you again!' And he says, 'Come on, Margie. This is a beautiful train ride. Let's go to the dining car and we'll have dinner.'

"They've finished dinner. Everybody else is leaving the dining car. She says, 'Fred, I am really tired. I'm going to bed.' And he says, 'No, no, Margie you can't go to bed.' She says, 'What do you mean I can't go to bed?' He says, 'You cannot go to bed. Tomorrow's your birthday and I want to be the first person to wish you happy birthday.' She says, 'Fred, I don't know a single soul on this train except for you. It's 10:30 at night, not anybody is awake, and I think that these nice people who are serving here would like to clear off the tables and go to bed them-selves.' Well, to hear Mom tell this story she is sitting there asleep in her chair because he won't let her go to bed. The train is rumbling along and he's just talking away. She's got her eyes closed and her head supported by her hands and she's rocking with the train — sleepy, sleepy, sleepy. Finally it's a little bit quiet and then she hears, 'Four, three, two, one. Margie! Give me your hand. Margie? Happy birthday! Will you marry me?'

"Startled, she said, 'What do you mean get married? You don't even know me. I don't know you. We only met two days ago. No! I won't marry you. I'm engaged.' Dad said, 'It doesn't matter. You'll marry me.' They talked until four in the morning about philosophy, feelings and the meaning of marriage. Then he made her get up at sunrise to watch the view all the way into Calgary. So she gets to Calgary. Of course, my father being the only boy with five sisters was totally indulged by these five sisters and their mother having been deceased, the five sisters all felt that they had to look out after their rogue brother. As he gets off the train, he takes Mom's bags and hands them to her. When he turns around, there's three of his sisters, totally scrutinizing this female whose bags he's picking up. They grab him and he's gone."

"On the other hand, Margie is being met by her friend Kay Hooper," continued Mrs. Eberts. "Kay sees her get off the train, sees Fred help her with her bags and says, 'Margie! Do you know who that guy is?' And my mother says, 'Yes, it's Fred Mannix. He's a nut case.' And Kay says, 'He's the town rogue. He's notorious. You can't go out

1937 ▶

Coping with winter conditions while working on the CNR Val-d'Or project results in innovations such as equipping a Ford car with tracks to allow snow and ice operation.

1938 ▶

The airport construction at Penhold introduces the first hydraulic grader to the earth-moving machinery of Fred Mannix & Company, Ltd.

with him. You shouldn't even be talking to him.' So Kay becomes exceedingly protective of Margie. My mother goes to stay with Kay and her husband, Paul. Of course, Fred Mannix has already weaselled out the name and where Mother is staying. That afternoon Margie gets a phone call saying, 'Come on. I'm taking you out to dinner.' And Kay says, 'Like hell you're taking her out to dinner. I'm coming, too.' So Kay and Paul go out to dinner with Fred and Margie. Mother was only in Calgary for four or five days, but every day Fred made sure he saw her, and every day Kay made sure she was with them.

"On the weekend, Daddy breaks loose from his job. He's got a car and he takes off to show Margie around. Well, Kay's not letting Margie out of her sight. Therefore Fred has two women in the car — Margie in the front seat and Kay in the back seat. They go driving through Kananaskis and down to Spray Lakes. When they're coming back across to Fort Macleod, they pass this guy and Daddy waves. Then this man passes Dad and he waves. So these two guys start playing leap-frog. And Daddy says, 'That's a friend of mine.' After getting the guy to pull into a service station, Daddy jumps out of his car, runs over to him and says, 'Hi, my name's Fred. What's your name?' And he says, 'My name's John Doe.' So Dad says, 'Where are you going?' And the guy says, 'I'm going to Calgary.' And Dad says, 'Great!' This is a travelling salesman going to Calgary, whom Dad had never before met in his life. But Dad passed himself off as being a friend of this man, gave him a great big hug and said, 'Come on out! Meet these two girls! And will you take this bloody Kay Hooper with you?' So he passes off Kay Hooper on this absolute total stranger. Kay Hooper gets practically

An early flyer showing E.B. Eddy's establishments in Hull, Quebec.

F.C. and Margie Mannix arrive in Hawaii during their honeymoon.

bodily picked up and dropped in this guy's car. They fill up with gas. I think Daddy paid for the guy's gas so that he'd take Kay and off they drive to Calgary. That was the only private time that Kay allowed Fred to have with Margie. And then Mother left for Ottawa. That was in April. From the first week that she came home she got a dozen red roses every Friday. Fred phoned her constantly, wrote to her, saw her every chance he got to go to the East."

Finally, his persistence paid off. On November 25, 1939, exactly 67 years to the day when two other improbable lovers — George Charles Mannix, an Irish-Canadian soldier from Eastern Canada, and Frances Bunn, a pioneering western Canadian — were married, Frederick Charles Mannix took Margaret Ruth Boughton's hand in marriage. Having won his bride, Fred C. took steps to ensure they might finally be alone. He hired two cars for the wedding. One car was covered with flowers and marked, "Just Married." The other car was unadorned. After the ceremony, which took place in Ottawa, Fred C. and Margie hurried to the unmarked car. The ruse was soon discovered, however, and the wedding guests followed in hot pursuit. Undaunted, Fred C. told the driver, "There's $20 in it for you, if you lose them," and he did.

Fred C.'s new bride was an enormous hit with the family. "I remember Freddie bringing Margie over to our house for us to meet," said Bob and Alice Kramer's oldest daughter, Marilyn Kramer Acteson. "We all thought she was gorgeous with this gorgeous red hair. She was elegant. She sat down and played the piano for us with delight."

"When Margie arrived in Calgary, she had a nice little green convertible Buick coup," added Alice Mannix Kramer. "She was

1938 ▶

Legendary Canadian conservationist, Grey Owl, dies. It is discovered that he was not an Apache after all, but Archibald Stansfeld Belaney, an Englishman, who came to Canada at the age of 17.

1938 ▶

Work begins on an international airport near Patricia Bay on the Saanich Peninsula on Vancouver Island. The airport is completed within the year. This airport is today's Victoria International Airport.

LIFE ON THE ROAD

"Our first home was a 16-foot trailer," recalled Margie Mannix with fondness. "We were very comfortable and cozy in our close quarters and enjoyed being out on the jobs. For nearly two years this was home as we moved from one construction job to the next.

"Camp moving days were always exciting. We could look back on a job well done and look ahead to a new location and a new challenge." Moving days were also exciting because when it came time to move, Margie hauled the trailer herself.

very glamorous. But Margie was nice to us all. She won us over. It took some managing, of course, and I give Margie a lot of credit walking into a family with all the sisters looking her up and down."

"Margie had been brought up much different to how we had been brought up," continued Mrs. Kramer. "She had a considerable amount of money and a guardian and a house-keeper because her mother was gone, too. She was very, very strictly supervised and that wasn't our lifestyle at all. We were brought up in an ordinary household where every-body did the dishes and had their chores, but Margie didn't have that kind of upbringing. She must have been in love with Freddie because she sure had to adjust. She was made of good stuff."

Although Mrs. Mannix was from an established eastern Canadian family, she adapted to the rough-and-tumble style of construction life in the West with great spirit. Her first accommodations on the job site ruffled a few feathers, however. According to the story, she came by train to the town nearest the campsite. Her husband then went out for her from the campsite by taxi. When the taxi delivered them to the job, she said, "Where am I going to stay?" And Fred C. said, "In that building over there." She went over, looked at the building, came back and said to him, "That's a chicken house. There are chicken feathers right inside of it." She then said to the taxi, "Don't you leave." After negotiation, Fred and Margie spent the night in town. Not long after, Margie got a trailer. "She was happy to be out there," said Maureen Mannix Eberts. "I think she was challenged by it all. She was very proud of her little trailer."

The young couple's first trailer was bought in Regina during the summer of 1940 when F.C. was building the highway between Regina and Pence. "While they were there they had a grasshopper plague," Bob Kramer said. "The grasshoppers were so

Top: The last campsite of the Regina road job, 1940. F.C. and Margie Mannix's trailer is on far right. The wooden shacks are pulled from camp to camp by a Cat.

Above: Margie Mannix inside the couple's trailer at camp, 1940.

"She hauled a house trailer from Calgary down to Macleod," recalled F.C. Mannix with obvious pride, "and it was quite a feat. It was very hard for her, because she'd never driven a trailer before. She learned all by herself going down there."

1938 ▶

Highway construction includes the road from Penhold to Red Deer, Alberta, one of the last jobs where Cats and horses work together.

1938 ▶

August 29, the Comoil No. 2 well blows in.

thick you could walk on them. When you drove your car down the highway, you had to be careful of putting your brakes on because you'd slide. Freddie and Margie had this little trailer out on the construction camp and the grasshoppers nearly ran her out. That was her first experience in the West. I'm surprised she stayed."

Even though Margie readily adapted to camp life, she found one skill just a bit daunting. "Mother had never really learned how to cook because she hardly ever had to do any cooking," said Mrs. Eberts. "It was especially a challenge when she was out in a trailer on the job site, because you don't have the availability of supplies so easily. One time Dad fired the cook and said, 'Margie, you can cook.' Well, she had hardly ever cooked before and it did not work out too well. I don't think she made it one meal before she took herself out of the running. My father always said the lesson he learned from that is that you don't fire the cook until you have a replacement!"

"And, strangely enough, we became good friends."

It was in 1938 that F.S. Mannix met a young man by the name of Leroy Allan (Chick) Thorssen. "I first met F.S. Mannix on an airport project in 1938," Thorssen recalled. "I was a third-year engineering student when I went to work for what was then the Civil Aviation Department of Transport. That spring, I worked on initial surveys of land that was later developed as the Calgary International Airport. Then I was sent up to Penhold to do surveys for an emergency landing strip. Trans-Canada Airlines started in 1938, but at that time they were flying through Lethbridge and couldn't have the Lethbridge-Edmonton run until they had an emergency landing strip halfway between Edmonton and Calgary. These emergency fields were simply one landing strip of grass. They let the contract for the Penhold field in early summer of '38 and Mannix got the contract.

"I was a 21-year-old kid when I was sent up to Penhold. I was told that I was going to have a lot of problems with Mannix. They were one of the old railway builders and contractors, and they were a rough, tough bunch and really hard on engineers. Let's face it, back then it was a pretty cutthroat business with some pretty hard drivers."

Equipment innovation includes fabricating a wooden dozer blade for a 60 gas Cat at the Penhold Airport job, 1938.

"I really didn't know what to expect but there I was," continued Thorssen. "I had a little tarpaper shack, a one-room shack office. One afternoon some equipment arrived, along with old Mr. Mannix and Bob Kramer, his son-in-law who was going to be a superintendent, and Tom Kramer, Bob's brother, who was going to be the mechanic. I chatted with them for a bit and asked Mr. Mannix if he'd come into my office. He came in and I sat down with him and I said, 'Well Mr. Mannix, something you should know is I've never been on a construction job. I'm an excellent surveyor and I've got the work all laid out. I can guarantee that you will get every quantity measurement for every yard of dirt you move, and I can assure you that you will have your estimates at noon of the day following the end of the month.'

"He sat and looked at me for a bit and he said, 'What do they call you?' I said, 'They all call me Chick.' He said, 'All right, Chick, I'll make you a deal. You guarantee that I'll get all the quantities and that you can have my progress estimate the day after the end of the month, and I'll see if I can't help you.' He gave me two or three tips as to what I should and shouldn't do and off he went. I said, 'Great,' and finished the job. Over the years I've realized that he didn't give me one single bum steer. He was right on everything. And, strangely enough, we became good friends. I will always appreciate what he did to help me get going. In some ways, he almost treated me as though I were a son. He seemed to really want to help you, and was always interested in what you were doing."

1938 ▶

Anti-Semite rioters in Berlin, Germany, kill up to 90 Jews, burn and loot homes and break thousands of windows. So many windows are broken throughout the capital that the night is known as "crystal night."

1939 ▶

Royal Winnipeg Ballet presents its first public performance in June.

A World Again at War

By the mid-'30s, the shadow of another European war darkened the international horizon. Seen by many Germans as the salvation of their country's dignity and fortunes, Adolf Hitler's Third Reich was on the march. In 1936, Hitler sent troops into the Rhineland, a demilitarized zone since the First World War. This act was in defiance of the Versailles Treaty, which had been intended to bring peace to Europe by crippling Germany's power to make war.

In 1938, Hitler annexed Austria. Later the same year he demanded that the Sudetenland area of Czechoslovakia be turned over to Germany. At a conference in Munich, the democracies, France and Britain, agreed to let Hitler absorb the Sudetenland. British Prime Minister Neville Chamberlain returned to London proclaiming, "Peace for our time."

Peace turned out to be worth not much more than the piece of paper on which it was signed, however. Six months later, in March 1939, Hitler's army marched into what remained of Czechoslovakia.

Hitler's next target was Poland. Britain and France warned that they would come to Poland's aid if Germany attacked. In August 1939, Hitler signed a non-aggression treaty with Germany's supposedly deadliest enemy, Russia. His eastern flank thus protected, Hitler attacked Poland on September 1, 1939. Keeping their pledge to Poland, on September 3, Britain and France declared war.

Canada came into the war a week later, declaring war on Germany on September 10, 1939. In 1914, as part of the British Empire, Canada had automatically — and enthusiastically — joined in the First World War by Britain's decision. This time, Canada declared war as an independent nation, by an act of her own Parliament. In stark contrast to the First World War, however, there was no boasting or cheering; this was just a grim job that had to be done. And there was much to be done. When Hitler took over the Sudetenland, General A.G.L. McNaughton, Canada's chief of staff, was asked to report on the state of the military stockpile. His report said: "Except as regards rifles and rifle ammunition, partial stocks of which were inherited from the Great War — there are none."

May 1940, a departing soldier kisses his daughter goodbye on his way to training at Camp Shilo.

The Second World War was immensely complicated, with events occurring almost simultaneously in widely separated fields of conflict. More than a million Canadians would serve in the army, navy and air force in the Second World War — of these, nearly 50,000 were women. Under the British Commonwealth Air Training Plan, 97 flying schools across Canada produced more than 130,000 aircrew for the Commonwealth air forces. The Canadian Army fought primarily in Europe, except for about 2,000 who were sent to Hong Kong shortly before it fell to the Japanese. The Royal Canadian Air Force served in almost every field, from southeast Asia to Europe and the Mediterranean. The navy's biggest role was in the North Atlantic, where it convoyed shipments of food and war material to Britain through the German submarine wolf packs.

1939 ▶

King George VI and Queen Elizabeth (now the Queen Mother) visit Canada for almost a month. They are the first ruling sovereigns to visit Canada since Confederation.

1939 ▶

Coal stripping near Sheerness uncovers 168,354 short tons (152,727 tonnes) of coal.

The Second World War had a tremendous impact on Canada's economy, providing the economic stimulus that lifted the nation out of the Great Depression. Between 1939 and 1944, steel production increased 120 per cent and aluminum production rose by almost 500 per cent. Mining, shipbuilding, automobile production and tank and truck manufacturing all leapt forward. With the increase in national wealth and production, Canadians provided more than $12 billion in victory loans and war taxes.

It was a total war, and no one at home was allowed to forget it. Meat was rationed. Sugar was rationed. Gasoline was rationed. There were no new cars, and no new tires to replace old ones. Civilians were barraged with reminders to do without — don't hoard, don't waste, turn in your aluminum pots to make bombers, buy victory bonds. There was very little grumbling; the war came first.

To support the war effort, Fred Mannix & Company, Ltd. worked at a breakneck pace. Mannix crews were seen throughout Western Canada building airports, hydroelectric dams and major highway projects. The company also moved heavily into coal stripping. "The war came along in '39 and put a new perspective on everything," recalled former Alberta premier, Ernest C. Manning. "The whole idea was to get it built. Anything goes. No public hearings or anything else. It was a whole new ball game. Everything was geared to getting it done as quickly as you could. And if anyone had the expertise and the equipment, you wanted to get them involved and get them to work. The Mannix group had a tremendous reputation in coal mining. They were in that in a big way right from the start — a great record."

BUY **VICTORY BONDS**

Top: Canadians of all ages enthusiastically support the war effort through the purchase of victory bonds.

Above: To help build the main highway between Austin and MacGregor, Manitoba, F.S. Mannix purchases this LeTourneau scraper and D-8 Cat for $18,000.

Getting the Boys in the Air

Soon after Canada entered World War II, the Commonwealth decided the country would be an ideal air training centre. Chosen for her unlimited airspace, far beyond the reach of enemy aircraft, Canada also had the largest aviation industry of any in the Dominion. When the British prime minister sent Mackenzie King the proposal to use Canada as an air training centre for the Commonwealth, the Canadian Cabinet readily accepted the challenge. The first school was opened April 29, 1940. The training of navigators, wireless operators, air gunners and pilots was officially designated the British Commonwealth Air Training Plan. A total of 131,553 aircrew would graduate under this plan. They were found in the skies above every battlefield, from the Atlantic to the Far East.

The Wartime Bureau of Technical Personnel directed F.S. Mannix's young friend from Penhold, Chick Thorssen, then a civil engineering graduate, to teach engineering at the University of Alberta and work on wartime construction. "After France fell, they couldn't continue to train aircrew in England, so it was decided to set up what was called the British Commonwealth Air Training Plan in Canada," explained Thorssen. "Canada then took the responsibility for training aircrew from Australia, New Zealand, England, Canada; we even had Polish over here. So we had to go into major airport construction in the spring of 1940."

"The first airport to be built under the British Commonwealth Air Training Plan was the Currie Barracks field here in Calgary," Thorssen said. "I was the resident engineer. I still have a stack of correspondence about that thick as to why I couldn't be resident engineer, because in

1939 ▶

Six days after declaring war on Germany, the first Canadian convoy leaves Halifax harbour for the European theatre. Popular support for the war is so great that more than 60,000 Canadians volunteer for overseas duty during September.

1939 ▶

Following the German invasion of Poland, Canada joins Britain and France and declares war on Germany on September 10. The Calgary Highlanders are ordered by telegram to mobilize.

FLYING OFF THE RUNWAY

During the early years of the war, Fred Mannix & Company, Ltd. was awarded contracts for the Patricia Bay Airport, the Williams Lake Airport, the Dog Creek Airport and the Comox Airport in British Columbia. In Alberta, the outfit helped construct the Fort Macleod Airport and the Calgary Municipal Airport.

"I did every job that old Fred could get until the war came on," said Bob Kramer. "Then we started getting more than we could do. We built airports for the fighter pilots and bomber pilots,

to train them. They were flying these airplanes off the runway before we finished. They had airplanes going to beat hell while we were trying to build the airports. I just about wore the highway out going between Edmonton and Macleod, way south. I kept moving this machinery back and forth between one job and another, to get the airports finished for the airplanes."

those days you weren't supposed to be a resident engineer unless you were at least 50. I was 23. It was decided that I could be resident to get the field laid out and the construction started, as they were going to have a whole bunch of fields coming in, and I was the only one that could get Currie started in a rush. And it was a rush."

"I arrived on the job on a Sunday from university, and equipment had started arriving on Saturday," continued Thorssen. "I had one old surveyor and engineering students. We went to work on surveying and laying out. We were in the field from six in the morning 'til six at night, and two of the fellows and I would plot notes until midnight. Then we'd be out in the field again at six in the morning. We did that for 18 straight days, got everything laid out. We never held up a machine for an hour.

"I mention it because this was a $300,000 job. It would be a few million now, but to take on a $300,000 job, there were five contractors in a joint venture. There were the old Dutton brothers, who were old railway builders with some dirt-moving equipment. The second company was J.R. Pagett from Winnipeg, which was another railway builder with some equipment. The third one was Oliver Machine here in Calgary, which was owned by Reg Jennings and had a gravel-crushing plant. The fourth was old Fred Owens, who was a partner of Mannix; it was Mannix & Owens who had a big dragline. The fifth one was Columbia Bithiolitic from Vancouver, who had an asphalt plant and some paving equipment. All five of them had to go together to do one job that size."

Competition for the airport work was intense. "I drove Dad up to Williams Lake to bid on the Williams Lake Airport job," said Luella Mannix Wilson, who often drove her father during this time. "We had to drive up at night through Fraser Canyon from Vancouver because Dad knew all the contractors from Vancouver were going up there. He didn't want them to see that he was going up there to look it over. So we drove up at night and came back early in the morning."

While work for the British Commonwealth Air Training Plan attracted new talent to the Mannix outfit — including James Welch and Ray Vennard — the airport jobs also gave some old-timers a chance to show off their skills. "I did the finishing out on the Pat Bay Airport," Blondie Garbutt recalled with pride. "The strip was 500 feet wide and

This letter of introduction shows the assistance given to members of the construction industry to help speed the war effort.

1939 ▶

Two Canadian veterans of the Mackinzie-Papineau Battalion return from the Spanish Civil War after the fascist victory over Spanish Republican and international volunteer forces.

1940 ▶

Quebec grants women the right to vote in provincial elections. It is the last province to do so.

Quebec Women Given Provincial Franchise

Bill Grants Them Right to Become Candidates in Legislative Assembly

Quebec, April 26 (CP)

Quebec women, who have gone since 1834 without an official vote in the affairs of their province, gained that right yesterday when a law granting them the vote in provincial elections and opening to them legislative assembly seats was entered in the provincial statutes.

The lieutenant-governor, Sir Eugene Fiset, accorded the measure Royal assent shortly after it had been ratified in third reading by the legislative council, Quebec's Upper House. The bill, sponsored by Premier Adelard Godbout, was approved April 18 by a 67-9 vote in the assembly.

The 24-seat council voted 13-5 in

maybe a mile long. We'd got a piece done but it wasn't finished, it was kind of rough, so old Gus Enarson said, 'Blondie, we want you to go back and level that off.' The engineers staked it out and it was fill and cut all the way from five- or six-tenths, seven- or eight-tenths at the most, either fill or cut. I got quite a stretch done, then I saw the engineer, Ray Byers, and I said, 'Ray, would you give me some second stakes on that if you're not too busy?' When he asked why I said, 'Well, I'd like to know if I've got to do a little trimming up.' He said, 'We've already checked it. We went over all that and we didn't find a piece that was over half a tenth out and that's good enough for us.' That made me feel pretty good, to think that I was that close."

Providing Power to Manufacture Explosives

The Second World War brought an unprecedented intensity to the development of Canada's natural resources, not the least of which was power generation. The war caused the electrical load in the province to grow rapidly and Calgary Power Company, Limited, the predecessor of TransAlta Utilities Corporation, expanded to meet this need. A.W. (Bert) Howard, who went to work with Calgary Power as an apprentice engineer in 1935, and rose to become the company's chairman and president, explained how Fred Mannix & Company, Ltd. came to be involved in this work. "In those earlier times, there was a very close connection between Montreal Engineering Company and Calgary Power Company, Limited," he related. "In the late '30s, I went to Montreal and worked for Montreal Engineering, to a large extent on Calgary Power activities.

Top: Building the Patricia Bay Airport in 1939. A D-8 Cat pulls two dump wagons while a 60 Cat pulls an elevating grader. Harry Keppel, Al Dryden and Charlie Alexander, left to right.

Above: Charlie Alexander, on the grader, pauses while Gus Enarson measures the depth of the cut during the construction of the Patricia Bay Airport, 1939.

"At the beginning of World War II, Montreal Engineering got involved in the design and construction of the Cascade plant, for which the Mannix company, in due course, became contractors. It was considered to be an important war project because its main purpose was to supply the electric power requirement for the manufacture of explosives needed for the war effort. There was a lot of detail work in getting the Cascade plant constructed, mainly because it was located in a national park, which was rather unique in itself."

"We utilized the Mannix organization on the project and they built the main dam and several of the other structures," continued Howard. "The project was difficult because, since it was being built in a national park, the government was very sensitive about the effect on the environment and possible damage to park property. The plant was completed very successfully. That was one of our early large projects with the Mannix company."

When Fred Mannix & Company, Ltd. was awarded the $2 million contract to build the Lake Minnewanka Dam for Calgary Power's Cascade generating station in Banff National Park in 1941, it was the largest job in the company's history. Howard explained why the Mannix organization was chosen for the project. "Most of our projects then involved earth-filled dams, and though they might seem rather simple to build, they actually are very complicated works," he said. "They're very specialized engineering structures. The Mannix company was highly experienced in constructing such projects, so the tendency was to go where the know-how was, and that's what the Mannix people provided. They had a good reputation and in fact were probably the best in the business at that time."

1940 ▶

Montreal Mayor Camillien Houde is arrested and sent to an internment camp when he protests the new law requiring registration for military service and suggests others boycott the act. Ottawa considers him "a citizen against public safety."

1940 ▶

The British Commonwealth Air Training Plan causes airport construction to boom in Alberta. Mannix crews work on extending the runways at the Currie Barracks field in Calgary and help build the Fort Macleod Airport.

ROBERT G. LETOURNEAU

Robert G. LeTourneau was born in 1888 in Richmond, Vermont. Traditional education held little interest for him and, at the age of 14, he left school. After apprenticing at a variety of trades where he learned the foundry and machinist trades, he learned welding skills and became familiar with the application of electricity. In 1920, LeTourneau purchased a used Holt tractor and, with a hired scraper, commenced business as a land-levelling contractor. One year later, he purchased a plot of land in Stockton, California, and established a small engineering workshop. In 1929, R.G. LeTourneau, Inc. was incorporated.

LeTourneau's inventive genius — LeTourneau holds hundreds of patents in the United States alone — propelled him into the spotlight of modern earthmoving. LeTourneau was the first to develop a power control unit with cable that could pull from virtually any direction. He was the first to put pneumatic tires on earthmoving off-road equipment, and the first to weld (rather than rivet) his structures together for less weight and more strength. He was the first to build a two-wheeled tractor coupled with a scraper for high-speed earthmoving. And he was the first to develop all-wheel electric drive machines for use in heavy construction work. During World War II, LeTourneau is reputed to have produced more than 70 per cent of the earthmoving equipment for the Allies.

R.G. LeTourneau is considered one of the greatest inventors of earthmoving and material-handling equipment in the world. Few manufacturers of that era had such a profound effect on the art of earthmoving as did R.G. LeTourneau. He died in 1969, at the age of 80.

"Calgary Power was going to build a Minnewanka power development in Banff Park in order to supply power to the Cominco plant here in Calgary for manufacturing explosives," added Chick Thorssen. "It was a high priority rush project. F.S. Mannix had the contract, and although he couldn't stay in Banff, he was up every day. His daughter would chauffeur him to Banff every morning and back every night. F.C. was in charge of the work on the job and, again, son-in-law Bob Kramer was in charge of the maintenance and shop and all of the equipment. I was resident on part of the work. Every so often they'd run into problems, and F.S. Mannix would come by the office and I'd go out with him for a while. We'd go out and sit on the side of a hill or whatever, look down at the work and talk about the problem. He'd say, 'How would it be if we do this? You can't do that because of this and this, technically,' and I'd say, 'Can you do such and so?' He'd think for a bit. Then we'd talk back and forth for half an hour, sometimes two hours, and we'd almost always come up with an answer.

"F.S. Mannix had an excellent mind and knew a tremendous amount about organization and organizing people. He was very creative in terms of how to go about

Above: F.S. Mannix, standing on the bank, supervises a Cat pushing a LeTourneau Tournapull smoothing the canal to the penstock at the Lake Minnewanka Dam construction site, 1941.

Below: Tournapulls, at times, proved quite challenging to operate.

1940 ▶

German prisoners of war arrive in Canada from internment camps in England. Fearing an invasion of the British Isles, the Germans are transported to North America to remove the possibility of their assisting the invading Nazis.

1940 ▶

May 10, the Germans begin their offensive against Belgium and Holland. By June 4, the thoroughly routed British, French and Belgian troops are evacuated from Dunkirk.

work, especially with things he hadn't encountered before — he could come up with all kinds of ideas to discuss and shift and sort. I thought he was a tremendous person. Where a lot of those old-time contractors like F.S. were considered rough, tough and unscrupulous characters, from my point of view he was anything but; I couldn't have met a finer person. He was a polite, quiet-spoken person. I certainly never saw any rough side, and I doubt if he had one. I know Mr. Gaherty of Calgary Power Company was out a lot and he and old Mr. Mannix were very good friends. If Mannix hadn't been a very topnotch person, he wouldn't have been a good friend of Gaherty's. Gaherty was a tremendous man who didn't have time to spend with people that he didn't think were worth it."

"One of the reasons for their success, particularly in heavy construction and mine stripping," continued Thorssen, "is that they were so far ahead of the pack in terms of exploring the further potential of new equipment. For example, at Penhold they had the first two scrapers in Western Canada. It was a scraper pulled by a Caterpillar tractor. When we did the Minnewanka job, they had four of these new rubber-tired scrapers — again, a first. They were willing to put the money up, and in a lot of cases they were willing to gamble, but they seemed to be able to assess the extent of any risk. I don't know of a single case where they really botched it."

Lake Minnewanka Dam was a prime example of the Mannix willingness to take risks when it came to bringing in new equipment. "I used to drive Dad to the dam at Minnewanka in the summer," recalled Luella Mannix Wilson. "We used to get up every morning, drive to

Below: A Tournapull at Lake Minnewanka Dam, early 1942.

Above: Ernie Enarson improves dam facing. He drives a Cat down, not across, the sloping face of Lake Minnewanka Dam.

Minnewanka, have lunch at the camp, and come back to Calgary because he didn't like to sleep in Banff. He said the altitude was too high. After we came home, I used to make Dad shell the peas while I got the dinner. I knew nothing about cooking and neither did he. I can remember him sitting there shelling peas and he'd say, 'God, if I had time, I'd certainly find a machine that would get these peas out of here.'" Although Mr. Mannix never invented a pea-shelling machine, he was responsible for bringing in the first self-propelled scrapers, known as Tournapulls, in Western Canada.

In 1937, R.G. LeTourneau, president of the LeTourneau company, designed a heavy-duty, rubber-tired prime mover specifically for use with earthmoving equipment. The mechanical design of the new machine was very similar to a track-type tractor, but two large rubber tires replaced the crawler tracks. Despite numerous difficulties, a prototype was built. The first machines were not very successful; they sold despite their mechanical difficulties because they moved dirt cheaply.

"At Lake Minnewanka they brought in some crazy machines called Tournapulls," Ray Vennard recalled. "They were terrible things to run. They took the old Catskinners, who had been with them quite a while, and put them on those machines. They found out that those people had been running Caterpillar tractors, but they couldn't think fast enough for those machines because they were rubber-tired, so they took us truck drivers and put us on the Tournapulls. I pretty near lost my life a couple of times. Once they pretty near put me in the lake while I was breaking a fellow in. Another time, I was

1940 ▶

A program is instituted between Britain and Canada allowing British children to be evacuated to Canada for the duration of the war to avoid the air war being fought over the British Isles.

1940 ▶

Ottawa orders 64 corvettes and 24 minesweepers built for the war effort.

breaking a fellow in and he rolled us over. When we landed, I was standing on the ground with my feet on one side and my head out through the cab on the other side. The Tournapull was laying on its side. They were hectic things to drive."

One reason Tournapulls were difficult to drive is that they "didn't have a steering wheel," explained Vennard. "They drove similar to a Caterpillar tractor, except when you pulled out the steering clutch, you had to put it back in again. With a Caterpillar, after you pulled out the steering clutch, you just let it go and it engaged itself a lot of times. But when you put the clutch back in on the Tournapull, it wouldn't engage. It would slip and you just didn't know where the thing was going to steer. It was a real crazy thing."

LOOKING FOR A TRUCK IN ALL THE WRONG PLACES

"In 1941, they were building the dam at Lake Minnewanka," Ray Vennard recalled. "I went up there in February to drive a truck. We were driving on two shifts. As I was on the day shift, I was sleeping in bed one night when the fellow on the night shift came in. He woke me up at about two o'clock in the morning. I said, 'What are you doing?' He said, 'I'm looking for a flashlight so I can find my truck.' I said, 'Where is it?' He said, 'In the bottom of the lake.' They were hauling across the ice and it had broken through. There is the truck on its side with the name Fred Mannix & Company right on it. You could read the name right through the water."

Lake Minnewanka served as yet another example of Mannix crews using existing equipment in new and innovative ways. "We got the dam built up to a certain level, then we needed to trim the slopes on the dam," said Ernie Enarson. "At that time, whenever they trimmed any slopes, they would travel back and forth along the length of the dam. My dad told me to trim a portion of the dam that way, and then he left the job because he had to go some place. I got to thinking there must be a better way of trimming the slopes. When you're doing it that way, it's hard to control the Cat. I decided to try driving straight down the slope; I'd be going downhill and it would be easier to push the dirt. That way I could take a big load with me and I could just lay it down smooth. And then I'd drive up a little farther over and get another load and I could use my path as a guide.

"When my dad came back to see how I was doing, he was surprised that I had accomplished so much. At first, he didn't like the fact that I was going downhill. But he could see that my way was better. So, after that, on Mannix jobs, they would do the slopes that way — going up and down, rather than lengthwise on the dam. When you worked for my dad or for Mr. Mannix, they tried to get the fellows to think on the job. It was never a matter of having a boss bellowing the orders and the others jumping to attention. They had us working together and they used all the brains that were around."

Two of those brains were Fred C. and Margie Mannix. "The first major project that F.C. ran was the Minnewanka power job," said Thorssen. "There was no doubt that he went to work there. He was right on the job, period.

1941 ▶

In January, F.S. Mannix contracts with Calgary Power to construct the Cascade hydroelectric project, including the Minnewanka Dam, by the spring of 1942. This job is the first use of Tournapulls by the outfit.

1941 ▶

The Mannix camp for the construction of the airport at Dog Creek, British Columbia.

No fooling around about whether the job was going to get done or not. I think from that point on F.S. didn't have any concerns about what his son could do." While there is no doubt that Fred C. continued his maturation process on the Lake Minnewanka Dam, there also is no doubt that he was greatly helped in his efforts by his new wife and partner, Margie.

"When Fred came to Minnewanka, he moved into a trailer," said Thorssen. "His wife Margie also moved onto the job. She was a real lady, very capable, and she knew a tremendous amount of what was going on. They had a little trailer right in the middle of the job site. I was up there for about five months and Margie was up there for most of that time. I think she probably spent most of the day keeping Fred sorted out. F.C. was more dynamic than his dad. F.C. can dart off in so many directions in a heck of a hurry, whereas I never saw F.S. that way, he was much cooler. But F.C. had lots of energy, lots of ideas, and he always wanted everything done yesterday.

"I think she did a lot to keep Fred slowed down a little. I think without her influence he would keep going and going until he killed himself, because he was a doer, there are just no two ways about it. Margie was a tremendous influence on him. She also served as a sounding board, particularly about people. She had a very good feeling for what people were like."

Grace Horspool (left) and Margie Mannix (right) share lunch during Banff Carnival week, 1941.

"THEY ALSO SERVE WHO ONLY STAND AND WAIT"

Christine Vennard stands in front of her tent at the construction site.

One of the most famous statements in English poetry is Milton's line, "They also serve who only stand and wait." Obviously, Milton was not thinking about the wives of Mannix men, yet his line is a very apt description of them. The nature of construction work meant that most of the men working for Mannix had to move around a great deal. Wives had to put up with living in tents or trailers, with midterm school changes for the youngsters, or with husbands away from home for most of the year. Without their self-reliance, loyalty, helpfulness, humour, patience and encouragement, in many cases — indeed, in most cases — the Mannix outfit would not have done so well, or so much.

"We roughed it. I tell you, we really roughed it," recalled Ray Vennard's wife, Christine, whose husband was a 40-year man with the company. "We didn't have the conveniences that we do now. You had the children, you had the babies, and you had to wash diapers and you had to wash them on the board, too." At one point, Ray went seven years without taking a holiday. "My kids used to say, 'Where's Dad? Does he ever come home anymore?'" said Mrs. Vennard. "They were in bed at night when he came home and in the morning he was gone when they got up.

"We had five children. When they got to school age, it always seemed we moved just before Christmas. It got to be pretty rough sometimes. But it was good for them in a sense, because it made them realize what it was all about and they didn't ever fail; mine never did. I remember my daughter came home from school one day and she said, 'Mom, you know this girl has lived in the same house all her life?' She just couldn't believe it."

1941 ▶

Under the War Exchange Conservation Act of 1940, certain nonessential items are banned, including comic books from the United States. Filling the need of Canadian kids for heroes, Cy and Gene Bell create a comic starring "Johnny Canuck." He promptly attacks the evils of the Axis powers and becomes an instant success.

1941 ▶

Women are allowed into the Canadian Armed Forces to serve in a variety of noncombatant roles. This will make hundreds of otherwise occupied men available for combat.

Another who thought highly of Margie Mannix was James Welch. "When Lake Minnewanka came into being, I was asked to go there," he said. "At the time, I was getting promoted from pickup driving to grease monkey to Catskinner. That was the ultimate thing at that time. But it was also the people you met there. There's not too many of them around anymore. They're either retired or passed away, so I think that's what was really important; it's the people you meet that is the most memorable thing. F.C. Mannix ran that job. My impression of him there was of the best. He and Margie had not been married too long at that point. At Minnewanka, they had their own trailer. It was just below the campsite. I got to know them fairly well. I think it was because I was the youngest fellow employed there and they took it upon themselves to make sure that I was okay. Margie was a real lady. I thought a lot of her. She was always pleasant. Just a real nice person."

While F.C. Mannix handled the day-to-day supervision of the project, the elder Mannix still walked the job, just like always. "I first met F.S. Mannix at Lake Minnewanka," recalled Ray Vennard. "I was working down in this canyon cleaning up some rocks. We had little rails and little cars that we loaded the stuff into, because we had to clean up the bottom of this canyon real good in order to put the clay core in. I said to one of the guys, 'Who is that old fellow that comes up and stands there at the top and looks down on us?' And he said, 'Oh, that's Mr. Mannix. Has he not talked to you?' And I said, 'No, he never has.' And the other guy said, 'Well, you must be doing all right then.' But he was a very nice man and he never spoke harshly to me. I had lots of respect for him."

Hand-cleaning the bedrock before the clay core is placed at Lake Minnewanka Dam, 1941.

The isolation of the Mannix camp at the Kananaskis Dam project.

"We worked day and night. We never had any rest."
As work neared completion on the Lake Minnewanka project, Mannix crews transferred over to the Kananaskis power project. "The first of the major earth dams involving the Mannix organization was the second stage of the Upper Kananaskis Lake storage project," explained Bert Howard of Calgary Power. "That was started in '42, about the same time as the Cascade project. It was relatively large in terms of earth dams at that time. The Mannix companies also worked on other projects we had. The company was growing very fast and needed additional power plants to meeting the rapid growth of electric loads in Alberta."

Situated at the upper Kananaskis Lakes, the job for Calgary Power involved building a series of small storage dams which had been designed to control the waters feeding the Kananaskis drainage basin. The dams would also feed the Barrier, Horse Shoe and Ghost power plants.

"Kananaskis was just around the corner from Minnewanka, really," recalled James Welch. "Bob Kramer was the boss at Kananaskis while Freddie was still running Minnewanka. It stands out in my mind as a more difficult job than Lake Minnewanka. There wasn't any road to speak of."

The inaccessible and sometimes dangerous terrain surrounding Kananaskis quickly became evident. "Freddie, Howard McLean of Calgary Power and I decided to go in and look at this job site on skis," said Bob Kramer. "There was no road in there or anything else. So we got skis and we skied in the 40-odd miles to the site of the proposed Kananaskis Dam. This was even though we didn't have any experience on skis before. At that time, the power company had a little log cabin up at a place called Pocaterra

1941 ▶

December, Japan attacks Hawaii, Hong Kong, the Malay Peninsula, the Philippines, Singapore, Thailand and several South Pacific islands. Canada, the United States and Britain declare war on Japan.

1942 ▶

The Lake Minnewanka Dam, canal system and control dams for the Cascade hydroelectric project are completed. The main dam is 2,025 feet (617 metres) long at the crest.

LIFE WITHOUT DAD

"My first memory is of 1941 at Minnewanka Dam," Marilyn Kramer Acteson recalled. "Mother moved us up to Banff and we stayed up there for that summer. We were all out on the job site quite a lot. I can remember Freddie working out there. Dad and Mother used to see Grandpa a lot because he would be coming back and forth. Mother rented a little house in the town of Banff. She had the four of us and Dad there and she functioned and maintained a family.

"Right after Minnewanka was the Kananaskis Dam. We lived in Calgary at the time. My memory of the construction company is that Dad was away all the time, always away. And when he came home, it was practically a holiday. I can remember staying home from school when he was home. When he was in Quebec with Freddie, they were gone a year. When I turned five, Dad sent me a bicycle. Oh, to this day, I have never forgotten that bicycle."

Falls. They maintained it and kept it supplied for the men who went up to check the water levels in the lake. We hit this little cabin just about sundown. We got within a half mile of it and we were just about dead. We saw there was a light in the window of the cabin. Howard said, 'There isn't supposed to be anybody in there.' So we slid up to the cabin and got off our skis and found a man inside. He had been poaching and making a living off the Banff National Park. He was supporting his mother and two sisters during the Depression. He assumed we were game wardens. He figured we had finally caught him.

"He had a fire on in this cabin and it was real warm. As soon as Freddie and I got in the door, we headed for the double-deck bunks. Freddie flopped on one and I flopped on the other. When we finally woke up, this poacher had some kind of mulligan stew for us. So we woke up and had lunch. We told him what we were doing and he was pretty happy about that. When we told him we had to go another nine miles to the lake, he said he would go with us. So we looked all around the job. Anyway, after we had seen the site, the poacher came back to Banff with us and he worked for the Mannix company as a cook for seven or eight years. His name was Johnny Muska."

"In 1941, they were surveying that job in Kananaskis," added Bob's daughter, Marilyn Kramer Acteson. "Dad and Freddie went in to do a lot of the survey. Three men went in the survey — Professor Webb from the university in Edmonton, Alistair Ross, and Bruce Broderick, the mountain forest ranger. While they were surveying, they slipped in the shale rock and went over the edge. Bruce Broderick was killed. Dad bought Bruce's horse, Toby, and used him to ride to and from Kananaskis. When the road was built, they no longer needed the horse, so I inherited him. I thought I had the world by the tail with Toby. I was ten years old. Toby didn't have a bridle, a halter or a saddle."

After the survey, it was necessary to transfer equipment from one job site to the next. "F.C. Mannix was with us in a pickup, and we had these four Tournapulls and a Cat coming behind us," recalled Ray Vennard. "They've got a nice paved road now, but in those days, the road was just real narrow and it came along to this side hill cut. It was real icy and we stopped and looked at it. Fred said to me, 'Do you think we can take the Tournapulls

The skis worn by F.C. Mannix when he surveyed the Kananaskis job.

1942 ▶

Airport development for the British Commonwealth Air Training Plan continues with the construction of the Williams Lake Airport in British Columbia.

1942 ▶

Mannix coal strip mining, begun in 1934, intensifies due to war demands. The circuit of strip mines includes those in the Sheerness area and several near Taber and Grassy Lake in southern Alberta.

down there?' I said, 'I don't think we should, Fred. I don't think it'll make it. I think we'll go over the side with it.' The ice was built up and it was all over and then you dropped way off. Fred said, 'Okay, we'll leave them for the night.' We went back and stayed in a line cabin. We hoped there would be some food in there but there was nothing. There were six or seven of us in that party and we just covered up with some old canvas and stayed the night. We didn't move the equipment the next day either. We just left it until they fixed up the road better. Then we went back and took them in."

"Kananaskis Dam was kind of hectic," continued Vennard. "It was an exceptionally wet year and the lake rose faster than they had anticipated. They didn't make provision for the rising water, so they had to build the dam fast enough to beat the water as the lake rose. We worked night and day. We never had any rest. There was gravel on both sides of the dam and then a clay core. We left the gravel behind and the water came up over the gravel. We kept the clay ahead of it, as the water wouldn't go over. If it had started over, it would have washed the dam out and we would have lost a year's work. But we made it. The dam is still there."

Gus Vissac and the Emergency Coal Production Board

As World War II assumed global proportions, Canada responded by increasing agricultural and industrial production to aid her allies. These home front efforts supporting the war led to a tremendous increase in rail traffic, which in turn revitalized the railway steam

coal market. The United States and other countries restricted exports of petroleum into Canada to meet their own wartime energy demands which also increased the demand for coal. In the face of this national energy shortage, western Canadian coal suddenly became a resource of vast importance. Unfortunately, the coal mining industry, which had lost most of its work force during the Depression, was unable to meet the huge increase in demand for coal.

By 1942, Canada's wartime energy shortage reached a critical stage. It was clear that the coal mining industry had to greatly increase production. That year, the government formed the Emergency Coal Production Board to increase national coal production, control wages, and freeze coal prices. That same year, coal miners were placed under the Selective Service Act, through a legislative act that forbade anyone with two years' coal mining experience from taking any job other than in a coal mine.

The person selected to head the Emergency Coal Production Board was G.A. (Gus) Vissac. A highly respected consulting engineer, Vissac formerly was the chief engineer for West Canadian Collieries, one of the largest coal mining companies in the Crowsnest Pass. Well-known for his knowledge of coal geology, Vissac was also famous as the inventor of the Vissac jig, a device which allowed coal-washing plants to lower the mineral content (or "ash") of metallurgical coals. The Vissac jig, adopted in the 1930s by the coking coal mines in the pass, was crucial in helping these companies remain competitive in the metallurgical coal marketplace.

MOVING DAY

Supplies were not the only thing difficult to get to the Kananaskis job site; wives were another. "We could only drive as far as Ribbon Creek," recalled Ray Vennard. "Then we had to leave the car there and use what they called a Cat wagon, which was pulled behind a Cat. They had filled the bottom of the wagon with drums of diesel fuel, with lumber on top of them, and groceries on top of the lumber. On top of that was where we sat going in, with our tent, the tent sides, and some lumber to build a platform.

"The Cat got stuck several times, but we finally arrived in the camp around two o'clock in the morning, in the rain, soaking wet. Alfie Wright, an engineer, and his wife, had a cabin up there. Another chap, Ross Gainer, and his wife, Nora, were on that same road going in and they were doing the same thing we were, taking in a tent and building it to live in. The next day, we all got together and built one place for the women to stay, and then we built the other one. Then we were in business."

1942 ▶

Another Calgary Power project to develop the hydroelectric potential of the Bow River watershed is the Mannix-built Kananaskis Dam and the Interlakes storage development.

1942 ▶

A Mannix crew on packhorse surveys the valley next to the Three Sisters range for the Spray Lakes development. Shown is one of the dams under construction.

Although Vissac's background was primarily in underground mining, he realized that surface mining was the only way to boost national coal production rapidly. As head of the Emergency Coal Production Board, Vissac planned to open new prairie strip mines in Alberta on abandoned coal properties formerly mined underground. As these mines were to be operated on contract to the government, and because there was virtually no surface mining expertise among Western Canada's leading coal mining companies, Vissac sought out construction companies with earthmoving equipment to do the mining. One of these companies was the Mannix outfit.

Vissac was familiar with Mannix because of their work at Claude Gallinger's Sheerness mine. "Vissac was working for the Dominion government and he came in and asked us if we wanted to work," F.C. Mannix recalled. "My father took an interest in him and listened to him. Vissac saw other contractors, but he couldn't speak very good English, so they never listened to him. When he started to talk, they just forgot him, whereas my father paid attention to him and got the work."

Turning Over the Table

F.S. Mannix was so busy supporting his country's needs during the war, he seldom took a break. His daughters, who used to drive him to the job sites, vividly recall how hard he worked, rushing from one project to another. "There was one circuit we took which was 1,100 miles," said Alice Mannix Kramer. One day, Alice asked her dad if they could please stop for a Coke. "I was drinking the

The operations at Coal Valley, Alberta, 1941.

Prairie strip mining and waste piles before reclamation, Grassy Lake, Alberta, early 1940s.

Coke and he looked at me and said, 'Couldn't you drink that out of two straws?' I thought, here I was up early in the morning, up to the airport, drive like the devil, then he couldn't even give me the time to drink my Coke. Suddenly he realized he was being a little bit demanding and he started to laugh. After that, every time he was in a hurry, he'd say, 'Listen, drink it out of two straws and get going!'"

"Dad had a shirt he called his 10,000-mile shirt," added Luella Mannix Wilson. "He said that it didn't have to be laundered for 10,000 miles. He could just put it back on if we didn't come back to the hotel. The summer Dad was building the Fort Macleod Airport, I used to drive him down there every morning. It was a 107-mile round trip. We could do it in two hours and back."

"I remember going to church with Dad on Easter Sunday," continued Mrs. Wilson. "The sermon was on 'Six days only shall thou work and on the seventh day thou shall rest.' Dad was doing the Currie Barracks at the time and he had shifts on night and day. He turned to me and said, 'Six days only shall thou work and on the seventh day thou shall labour.' He said, 'That's the Bible I read.' When we left church, he said, 'I don't know if it's a good thing to sit in church and think about the work, or if you're better off to sit at work and think about the church.'"

The Second World War was so vastly different from the First World War that perhaps the only common denominators were the loss of liberty, wounds and death. The United States had exploded into the war on December 7, 1941, when Japan launched an attack on

1942 ▶

Allied forces attempt a raid of the European town of Dieppe. Canadians comprise the bulk of the attackers. Of the almost 5,000 soldiers, more than 50 per cent are killed or captured during the eight-hour raid.

1942 ▶

Estevan Point lighthouse and wireless station on the west coast of Vancouver Island is shelled by a Japanese submarine.

HIRING THE FIRST ENGINEER

Alf Wright, hired in 1938, was, according to most accounts, the first engineer hired by the Mannix outfit. "F.S. Mannix said he wanted to hire an engineer so that an engineer could talk to an engineer when they were discussing the job, rather than having the owners represented by an engineer, and no engineer to represent him," explained Ernie Enarson. "That's why he hired Alfie."

While Alf Wright brought to Fred Mannix & Company, Ltd. his engineering expertise, in typical Mannix style, some in the outfit decided to share their expertise with him. At the Lake Minnewanka job, for example, they decided to teach Alfie how to ski — indoors. After fitting him with a pair of skis, they sent him down a flight of stairs at the Mount Royal Hotel in Banff. Not unlike many first-time skiers, Alf Wright's training run ended in a fall. "I scooted around the corner and smashed," he said. "Oh, my."

Undaunted, Alfie simply took on further adventures. For instance, there was the time he took on the Royal Canadian Mounted Police. The story goes that there was a Mountie who used to come around to the Mannix company barbecues and parties. After these events, several bottles of booze would always be missing. It was obvious to the Mannix people that the Mountie took them. So this one day, after Alfie saw the Mountie carry out a box, he had one of the men distract him while he jimmied the trunk of the Mountie's car. Alf then took all the booze out of the Mountie's car, closed the trunk, and returned the ill-gotten spoils to camp, never hearing one word from the Mountie.

Left to right: Jim Stephenson, George Roberts, Johnnie Lynch, Alf Wright, Fred C. Mannix and Cliff Blackall.

Pearl Harbor, Hawaii. The surprise attack by 360 planes was hugely successful. In all, 18 ships were hit, 177 aircraft were destroyed, and the dead or missing numbered 3,219. The fleet was incapacitated and could not defend its interests in the Pacific Rim and in Asia.

Only eight hours later, Japan launched an aerial attack on the Philippines. With a garrison of 19,000 U.S. troops, 12,000 Philippine Scouts, and about 100,000 of the newly raised and partially equipped Philippine army, the soldiers were ordered to "lay down a bunt." Their mission was to stall the Japanese advancement for as long as possible, thereby buying the critical time needed to rebuild the American Pacific fleet. Despite a shortage of food, medicine and ammunition, the Bataan Peninsula held out until April 9, 1942, when they surrendered to the Japanese. Although buses were available to transport the prisoners, the Japanese decided to march the "Defenders of Bataan" to their destinations. This 55-mile (88-kilometre) march, which became known as the "Death March," cost the lives of hundreds of men.

Heroic loss of life was not confined to the Pacific, however. On August 19, 1942, Operation Jubilee — the raid across the English Channel on Dieppe, a small port on the French coast between Le Havre and Boulogne — took place. Planned as a "reconnaissance in force" to test the defences of Hitler's continental fortress and the capability of the Western Allies to launch large-scale amphibious assaults against Hitler's *Festung Europa* (Fortress Europe), it exacted an enormous toll in human lives. Of the total force of 6,100 men who assaulted the heavy fortifications on the Dieppe beach, nearly 5,000 were Canadians. Of these, 3,367 were casualties, of whom 900 were killed and 1,300 taken prisoner. In nine hours, Canadians lost more prisoners than the army would lose in the 11 months of the 1944-1945 northwestern Europe campaign.

Yet, as so often happens in war, the human spirit rises above inconceivable horror to perform unbelievable selfless acts of heroism. Following Dieppe, two Canadians

1942 ▶

Also on the West Coast, more than 22,000 people of Japanese ancestry are moved to work and detention camps in the interior. Most are Canadian-born. Many who protest are placed in internment camps.

1942 ▶

In a rare surface engagement, the Canadian destroyer, HMCS Assiniboine, sinks a German submarine 400 miles (645 kilometres) off Newfoundland.

received the Victoria Cross, awarded in recognition of the most exceptional bravery displayed in the presence of the enemy.

By 1942, the war had exacted its grisly price not only from those who served their country on foreign soil; it had taken its toll on those who served on the home front. Among these people was F.S. Mannix.

In 1942, F.S. Mannix was 61 years old. He was tired and in ill health, suffering from adult-onset diabetes. At this crucial juncture in the outfit's history, he decided to take perhaps the biggest gamble yet. Ready to retire, the elder Mr. Mannix searched for some way to finish the educational process he began for his son. He achieved this when he sold his controlling interest in Fred Mannix & Company, Ltd. to one of the "big six" contracting firms in the United States — Morrison-Knudsen, then one of the largest heavy construction companies in the world.

"I think that Fred S. was looking for an outfit that he could connect up with, get some more expertise and get Fred C. going," said Frank O'Sullivan. "He felt that the Morrison-Knudsen association was one way of doing it as long as the deal had some provision for a buyback. He felt that the deal should allow Fred C. to buy back controlling interest when he was in good enough shape financially."

It was a tremendous move. "Fred Mannix quits as a big contractor," announced a local newspaper. "Fred Mannix of Calgary, one of Canada's biggest contractors, is taking it easy in Victoria today after disposing of his business…. 'My health convinced me it was time to quit,' said Mr. Mannix at the Empress Hotel. He has been in the business for 40 years and his name is associated with some of the largest highway and building construction jobs in the country. Fred Mannix Jr. is still carrying on with the firm under the new management, the veteran contractor said."

According to F.C. Mannix, poor health was not the only reason his dad wanted to retire. "He sold because he wanted to get out," he said. "That's all. Because it was too tough to keep gambling all his money all the time." Instead, F.S. gambled that Harry Morrison would serve as a mentor to his son. In this, as in most of the gambles of his life, F.S. Mannix pulled up aces.

Above: F.S. Mannix (left) with R.A. Kramer at Fort Macleod Airport.

Left: Margie Mannix with the proud grandfather, Frederick Stephen Mannix. He holds the first-born of the third generation, Frederick Philip Mannix.

1942 ▶

In only the second plebiscite in Canadian history, Canadians are asked to release the government from Prime Minister King's 1940 reelection pledge not to impose conscription. Overall, 63 per cent of the voters approve; Quebec votes 70 per cent to reject.

1942 ▶

Originally proposed in 1938, the Alcan Military Highway becomes the first highway between Dawson Creek, British Columbia, and Fairbanks, Alaska. Military engineers complete the 1,600-mile (2,575-kilometre) road in eight months.

ertificate
Shares
SUED TO
Morrison,
Idaho.
H. W. Morrison
ANSFERRED
Incorporated
SHARES
ONE

MEETING THE TEST
THE MORRISON-KNUDSEN YEARS
1943 – 1950

*When F.S. Mannix decided that he was going to get out of things,
he said something to the effect, 'If he [F.C. Mannix] works hard enough,
maybe he can buy it back someday.' The real credit, in my mind, was that
F.S. gave him a challenge. I think F.S. was just putting him to that test —
that if he could make it, then he'd really make it go.*

*I'm sure that this is what F.S. wanted, or could see in it. That M-K brought in
a lot of knowledge and where-for-all. F.S. recognized that if you were going to have
a really big outfit, you had to have M-K's knowledge and their capability.*
— Rod McDaniel, Mannix family friend

*Left: Harry W. Morrison and
Fred C. Mannix in Calgary, Alberta.*

*Right: The Second Canadian Infantry
Division liberates Dieppe, France,
two years and two weeks after the
same division sustained terrible losses
in the notorious Dieppe Raid of 1942.*

In 1943, Hitler's fortunes and the Second World War reached a turning point. In preparation for the Allies' second front, the United States air force dropped the first of 1,500,000 tons (1,360,770 tonnes) of bombs on Hitler's *Festung Europa* (Fortress Europe). In February, the German Sixth Army surrendered at Stalingrad. In July, the Canadian First Division joined Allied forces in the attack on Italy. The First Division was heavily engaged in the Sicilian campaign as part of the British Eighth Army, and subsequently took part in the December advance up the mainland of Italy. In the spring of 1944, Canadians under Lieutenant-General E.L.M. Burns played a leading role in breaking the Hitler Line barring the Liri Valley. At the end of August, the corps broke the Gothic Line in the Adriatic sector and pushed on through the German positions covering Rimini, which fell in September. These battles cost Canada its heaviest casualties of the Italian campaign.

While the tide of the war was turning in favour of the Allies, the war had a direct impact on the fortunes of the Mannix outfit. In 1943, the giant heavy construction firm, Morrison-Knudsen (M-K), of Boise, Idaho, went looking for Canadian partners. What the firm found was Vancouver-based Marwell Construction Company, Ltd. Marwell then led M-K to Fred Mannix & Company, Ltd.

Harry Morrison — A Most Perfect Mentor

Harry Morrison, the president of M-K, was born in central Illinois near Kenney (population 409), where his father worked in a gristmill. When Harry Morrison was four, his mother died. After that, Morrison remembered his early life "as one of those things where the children get passed around among the various relatives."

When he was 14, Morrison got a vacation job as a water boy for the Chicago construction firm of Bates & Rogers in Idaho. Five years later, after two years of high school and a business school course, he went to work full-time for Bates & Rogers, building a dam and powerhouse on the Snake River. He hustled so hard that other men called him "that damn kid."

The story goes that on a Boise River project in 1908, when Morrison learned that one of the contractors would make $100,000, he said, "If that fellow can make $100,000, I can make $1 million." With that, he marched up to a small contractor

Harry W. Morrison, president of Morrison-Knudsen Company, Inc.

named Morris Knudsen, who owned a few horses and was building a road to the dam. Introducing himself, Morrison said, "I'd like to go into business with you." Somewhat taken aback, Knudsen responded, "What do you have?"

"Plenty of guts," replied Morrison.

"I mean how much money?" asked Knudsen.

"No money, just guts," replied Morrison.

Those Were the Days

Diary of ANN MORRISON

Since her marriage to Harry Morrison in 1914, Ann Morrison never missed a trip with her husband — who regularly logged more than 150,000 air miles (240,000 kilometres) per year — whether it be whirling over the Canadian mountains in helicopters or jouncing over Afghan trails on a camel. No matter how long her day, each night she worked at her diary, *Those Were the Days.*

September 14, 1947. "Harry and I left Boise 10:00 a.m. via M-K Beechcraft for Calgary, Canada. Landed at Spokane to clear customs. Ray Shinn joined us there.... Landed at Calgary airport 3:00 p.m. Fred Mannix Jr. met us there. Delighted to see Freddie. A pleasant drive to town in Freddie's car. Weather bright, clear, a little crimpy, too. Checked into Palliser Hotel. Harry, Ray and Freddie off immediately for Mannix office for conference. At 5:30 p.m. returned to hotel for me and then to Mannix home where we were served a most delicious home-cooked Sunday dinner — a real treat. Margaret and the children well. Freddie III and little Maureen have grown a little since we last saw them. Lovely children. We enjoyed the evening visiting and Freddie returned us to the hotel at 11:00 p.m."

September 15, 1947. "Harry and I having a dinner party this evening for Mannix organization men and wives.... We are very pleased to have Mr. Mannix Sr., who has been confined to his home the past few days with the flu, with us tonight. The gathering without the daddy of the Mannix company would indeed had been incomplete and we sincerely trust Mr. Mannix will suffer no ill effects.... Freddie's organization is tops! We very much appreciate having them as our guests and are especially happy to have the opportunity of meeting the wives."

1943 ▶

Mannix crews complete the Kananaskis Dam in May. The dam is located in the rugged western Alberta Rocky Mountains.

1943 ▶

In Quebec City, Prime Minister W.L.M. King hosts an Allied conference with British Prime Minister Winston Churchill and United States President Franklin D. Roosevelt to formulate the strategy to end the war.

In March 1912, Morrison-Knudsen was formed as a partnership. At 23, young Morrison had youth, ability and irrepressible ambition. Knudsen, at 50, had maturity and a know-how about horses, then the standby of all heavy construction. M-K's first capital consisted of $600 in cash, a dozen wheelbarrows, a few horses, some picks and shovels. The company's first job — a $14,000 subcontract to build a pumping station on the Snake River — brought only a small profit. For the next few years, M-K crawled, and after that, said Morrison, "it walked." In 1914, M-K made $14,000 on a $120,000 contract for the Three-Mile Falls Dam on Oregon's Umatilla River. "Up to then," said Morrison, "I really had no idea that you could make money on a dam. But when we came out with more than 10 per cent, what a lift!"

The other big event of that year was Harry Morrison's marriage to Anna (Ann) Daly, who lived next door to Morrison's sister in Boise. After their marriage, Harry and Ann were a team, travelling the world together. In all their time together, she never missed a trip. When her husband's work took him to Wake Island to build an airport during the war, she accompanied him. She was one of the last women to leave Wake Island before the Japanese attack.

Ann Morrison ordered supplies for camps, kept accounts, even filled in at the cookhouse when the cook was drunk. At the work sites, she talked to the wives of M-K's men, asked after their children, gave them news of the latest fashions and whatever else she thought they might want to hear about life back home. At the end of each day — which could easily run 12 to 14 hours — she wrote in her diary, *Those Were the Days.* These warm, chatty entries, which were later reprinted in the company magazine, *The EM-Kayan,* were read by thousands of M-K people around the world.

Ann Morrison (in plane) with her husband Harry Morrison (third from right) at a construction site in Saudi Arabia.

While Ann Morrison came to embrace her life on the road, at first she wondered "why any girl would cast her lot with the big, romantic outdoor type." Her first home was a dirt-floor tent in the Utah wilderness. The mess hall was crawling with ants. To top it off, M-K lost $17,000 on the job. What made it worse was that few banks were willing to risk money on a young, untried company. It took years of savings before M-K got its first big steam shovel. For young Harry Morrison, the machines opened up a new era. For his partner, Knudsen, they closed one. As machinery gradually took over, the horses disappeared. Lost in the new technology, Knudsen turned over M-K to Morrison in 1939. Four years later he died.

In 1925, Morrison took his new equipment and joined the big Utah Construction Company on a joint bid for the $2.3-million Guernsey Dam in Wyoming. He followed it up with another bid for Deadwood Dam in the mountains in central Idaho. On Deadwood, M-K used some of the first bulldozers, began testing diesel trucks and gas-powered revolving shovels and learned to haul equipment on log roads over mountains as high as 7,400 feet (2,256 metres). Even more important, M-K's idea for joint ventures was a solution to the dam builders' growing financial problem: projects so huge that few companies possessed the means or courage to tackle them because a single mistake could wipe them out. But in joint ventures, with many companies sharing costs and profits, or losses, construction men could aim for the moon.

1943 ▶

Fred Mannix & Company, Ltd. continues to strip coal, but now often works with its new affiliated company, Marwell Construction Company, Ltd.

1943 ▶

Alberta Premier William Aberhart (standing) dies. He is succeeded by Ernest C. Manning (shown seated, centre right).

This experience gave M-K the know-how to tackle the biggest of them all in 1931 — the Arizona-Nevada giant Hoover Dam. Rising 726 feet (221 metres) above the Colorado River, the Hoover Dam generated power at the rate of four billion kilowatts a year. "It's the glamour dam," Morrison once reflected. "I still can't go down in the elevator and step out on the intake and look up without being inspired."

For Hoover Dam, Harry Morrison put together the famed Six Companies, Inc. While named Six Companies, Inc., in actuality, there were eight companies: Morrison-Knudsen; Henry J. Kaiser Co. (Oakland, California); W.A. Bechtel (San Francisco, California); Utah Construction Co.; MacDonald & Kahn Inc. (San Francisco); J.F. Shea Co. Inc. (Los Angeles); Pacific Bridge Co. (Portland, Oregon); and General Construction Co. (Seattle, Washington). Harry Morrison contributed $500,000 as his share of the $5-million capital. When Hoover was finished five years later, M-K's share of the $10.4-million profit was about $1 million.

Throughout the 1930s, M-K worked on large dams, including the Bonneville Dam on the Washington-Oregon border and the Imperial and Grand Coulee dams in Washington — a total construction effort of more than $300 million. The company built the San Francisco side of the 4,620-foot (1,317-metre) Bay Bridge and increased its railway work to a steady $10 million a year. Despite the Depression, M-K showed a profit in every year except 1932 and 1937.

During the Second World War, M-K, with seven other firms, helped build the Pacific air base program for the United States navy. This program spread runways and revetments in 28 different locations on a $1.16-billion contract, the largest by any government up to that time. In 1943, the company's gross revenue shot to a whopping $87 million, from just under $9 million in 1939.

A man who thought of nothing but work, Harry Morrison had a simple adage to explain his passionate absorption. "A man's worth," he said, "is counted in the things he creates for the betterment of his fellow men." In all his endeavours, Harry Morrison never forgot that he was a hardheaded American businessman working to make a profit. But that was not his only objective. "We're not missionaries," he once said. "We're represented abroad by some of the ruggedest, two-fisted construction men in the business. But from the dams and the roads and canals that we build come new hopes. What we do is often taken to be representative of what all America does. We like to think we leave the impression around the world that all America is interested, earnestly and hopefully, in economic and social progress for all men."

At M-K's one-storey Boise headquarters, Harry Morrison was known to point his finger at a wall map studded with pins marking M-K's jobs. "On that map," he would say, "is summarized part of our basic philosophy. It's the philosophy of spread the risk. If you're losing on one job, take your loss, finish it on schedule and make it up on others, making damn sure you have others." Harry Morrison always made sure he had others.

Harry Morrison ran his company like a football coach with a four-platoon team. Known to buy entire companies to get a few top hands, he paid his men well and tacked on bonuses for jobs well done. He knew the business inside out and could operate efficiently thousands of miles away from his Boise headquarters. His number one commandment was to get the job done on

HARRY MORRISON

"What man in history has done most to change the face of the earth? Politicians might name Augustus Caesar or Adolf Hitler. Military men might name Napoleon Bonaparte, or perhaps General 'Tooey' Spaatz, whose U.S. bomber fleets levelled Nazi cities in World War II. But among builders, there is no disagreement. The man who has done more than anyone else to change the face of the earth, lives in a one-story frame house in Boise, Idaho. He is Harry Winford Morrison, 69, white-haired boss of Morrison-Knudsen Co., the world's biggest heavy construction firm. In his 50 years as a builder, Harry Morrison and his men have moved mountains, tamed rivers, built scores of dams, tunnels, power plants, railroads, highways, bridges and airfields around the world." — *TIME*, May 3, 1954.

BUILDERS ABROAD
Ambassadors with Bulldozers

BUILDER HARRY MORRISON
To tame rivers and move mountains.

1943 ▶

In July, Canadian troops, with other Allied forces, invade and capture Sicily. On July 25, Benito Mussolini and his cabinet are forced to resign.

1943 ▶

Princess Juliana of the Netherlands lives in Canada while her country is occupied. Margriet, her third daughter, is born in Ottawa.

time, even at the expense of the 10 per cent profit he tried to make on the big ones. When his estimators made a mistake, Morrison never tried to squirm out from under. When the boss of a job wanted help, the boss did not go to Boise; Morrison or one of his lieutenants went out to the job. Otherwise, Morrison gave his project managers all the elbow room they needed.

While an astute businessman, Morrison seemed to care little about personal wealth. Though he and his wife owned 22 per cent of M-K's stock, he drew a very modest salary. The Morrisons, who had no children, had little social life. Once in a while, among friends, Morrison was known to take a sociable bourbon and ginger ale and plunk a guitar. When one friend remarked that he had "never heard Harry Morrison crack a joke," another friend replied, "And I've never heard anybody crack a joke about Harry Morrison."

Besides the high devotion to his job, Morrison had the knack of handling men. "Guys walk into his office swearing they'll never go back to Brazil or Afghanistan," recalled an old M-K hand. "They come out treading air and acting as if they wouldn't trade places with God Almighty." In short, Harry Morrison was the perfect man to complete the apprenticeship that F.S. Mannix had begun for his son, F.C. Mannix.

"I think I can find you a buyer."

Hugh Martin, who, in partnership with Doug Welch, owned Marwell Construction Company, Ltd., was a friend of F.C. Mannix's from school days. He explained how Morrison-Knudsen came to buy controlling interest in Fred Mannix & Company, Ltd. "When the war came along, we graduated into the construction of wartime facilities on a very extensive basis," he said. "By 1943, we had some $15 million worth of work for the federal government. This enormous expansion of our workload put terrible financial strains on the company to meet its payrolls and its payables, because we virtually had no working capital. The federal government assisted us with a special loan approved by order-in-council, but they told us we had to seek more capital to be injected into the company.

"I was directed by a friend to discuss our problem with a large American construction company, Morrison-Knudsen. I met with their vice president in Seattle. This vice president talked with the president of the company, Mr. Harry Morrison, who invited me to come to Boise, Idaho. I proceeded to Boise and had prolonged meetings with Mr. Morrison, outlining the prospects for construction work in Western Canada and acquainting him with the company's activities. He indicated a strong interest in purchasing controlling interest in our company and he sent some of his financial people to Vancouver to examine the company's financial condition. He pointed out to me that one of the principal difficulties we had was the excess profits tax, which did not permit the company to retain any earnings. He said that this did not make it extremely attractive for Morrison-Knudsen to come in, unless something could be done to find a way to retain some profits."

"It was at this juncture that I visited with Fred C. Mannix at the Hotel Vancouver," continued Martin. "I remember he had a drawer full of pint bottles of rye whisky, which was just like gold in those days. We had a good visit and polished off some of the rye. When F.C. mentioned that his father was not well and that it had been decided that they should sell the company, I said, 'Well, Fred, what sort of a tax base has your company got?' In answer to my question, Fred said, 'I think it would be about $105,000 or thereabouts. Make it about $100,000.' I said, 'Fred, I think I can find you a buyer.' I immediately recounted to Mr. Morrison that I had found a company which had this fortunate tax base. I then asked Fred if he would confer with his father and his brother-in-law, Bob Kramer. I told Fred to let me know as soon as he could if there was some interest."

"I phoned my father and asked him how much he wanted for it," recalled F.C. Mannix. "Mr. Martin then phoned Morrison." Martin concurred adding, "F.C. Mannix got back to me within two or three days and said they would be prepared to sell for $200,000. I relayed this information to Mr. Morrison and he said, 'Well, I think we'd be prepared to talk business.' So then Fred C. came to Vancouver, and we joined with our counsel, Alan Russell, and proceeded to Boise, Idaho, to talk with Mr. Morrison. Originally, the deal was that Morrison-Knudsen was going to buy all of the Mannix organization, and we were going to get 49 per cent of the combined two companies. We were going to owe our portion of the purchase of the Mannix company, which would be about 15 per cent of 49 per cent, to Morrison-Knudsen because they were putting up the money to buy the whole thing."

"Fred called me a day or two later and said that he would like to know if he could remain as one of the partners in the combined companies," continued Martin. "I said, 'It sounds all right by me, Fred, but let me call Mr. Morrison to see what he says.' So I asked Mr. Morrison if he would like to have Fred along with us as a partner. He said, 'Maybe we had better all go up to Calgary and talk to everybody and see the lay of

1943 ▶

Trans-Canada Airlines modifies a British Lancaster bomber for use in their new transatlantic air service. The first TCA flight cuts 25 minutes from the previous speed record.

1943 ▶

Canada takes another step toward full nationhood by naming her own ambassadors. The prior minister to the United States, Leighton McCarthy, becomes Canada's first ambassador.

M-K "Joins Up" in Canada — Mannix Knows the Dirt

"Taking a new and possibly an epochal stride in its Western Hemisphere expansion, Morrison-Knudsen Company, Inc., has recently added two Canadian affiliates to its family of associated corporations. One is Fred Mannix & Company, Ltd. with headquarters at Calgary, Alberta, and the other, Marwell Construction Company, Ltd. of Vancouver, British Columbia.

"Between the Western United States, where M-K projects have dotted the map during the last 30 years, and the Territory of Alaska, where in the past two years, M-K built military installations have sprouted at strategic points over a many-thousand-square-mile area, stretches a tremendous field for structural development. Mannix and Marwell, situated on opposite sides of the Canadian Rockies, have had wide and successful experience which apparently could be enlarged in scope when combined with the broader resources of Morrison-Knudsen Company, Inc. President H.W. Morrison with Vice President C. Ray Shinn, boss of M-K Alaskan and northwestern states operations, effected a three-way merger."

— *The Em-Kayan,* October 1943.

the land.' So I chartered a Trans-Canada twin-engine Lockheed Lodestar, probably the first one that was ever chartered, and we went down and picked up Mr. Morrison and a couple of his vice presidents. We proceeded to Calgary and there we had a luncheon with Mr. Mannix Sr. and Fred and Bob Kramer. A deal was made to buy the Mannix company for $200,000. Kramer was paid $50,000, and Mr. Mannix Sr. got $100,000. Fred C. put his $50,000 back in. So Fred had one-third of 49 per cent, I had one-third of 49, and Welch had one-third of 49. We then proceeded to put together all the legal work and the incorporation and that sort of thing. The two companies continued to operate as separate operating entities, but the ownership was vested 51 per cent to Morrison-Knudsen and 49 per cent to the three Canadian partners."

Bob Kramer explained why he opted to take his money out. "When Mr. Mannix sold out, he offered Freddie and me our share," he said. "Either way I decided I would just be working for a large corporation, so I decided to take my money out of it. Freddie was smarter than I was and left his in. I was just a little stupid is all. When I heard about Morrison-Knudsen, I didn't know anything about them and I said, God damned, if I was going to work for the rest of my life, I was going to work for myself. I didn't do too badly, though. I didn't have to work near as hard as Freddie did because I didn't have to live in those construction camps anymore." Shortly after selling out, Bob Kramer purchased the Caterpillar dealership in Regina, Saskatchewan. "It was on June 1, 1944, a date I'll never forget, that I opened the doors to my Cat dealership in Regina, which came to be known as the Kramer Tractor Company," he recalled. "I ran my business very successfully, due in large part to the shortage of machinery. Freddie also contributed to my prosperity, as he bought a hell of a lot of yellow paint from us."

Under the Morrison-Knudsen umbrella, the Mannix and Marwell operations were to be run in tandem as one company, with F.C. Mannix, Hugh Martin and Doug Welch each having an equal interest in the 49 per cent of the two companies. Morrison-Knudsen vice president, C.R. Shinn, was president of Fred Mannix & Company, Ltd.; Fred C. Mannix was vice president and general manager; Hugh A. Martin and R.D. Welch were vice presidents. After a year, this arrangement came to an end. "There was some difference of opinion of how things were to be run," explained F.C. Mannix. "I wasn't running the whole thing at the time. Since the building business was foreign to me, I let Marwell run the building business. But Morrison-Knudsen didn't get along very well with them. They wanted to buy out Hugh Martin and Doug Welch. I told them I didn't figure that was right. I said, 'Let me buy them out.' We had a big argument about that, so I said, 'Hell, you might as well take mine, too, then.' Mr. Morrison didn't want to do that, so he let me get the 49 per cent."

In 1944, F.C. Mannix bought out the interests of Marwell and Welch in the partnership with Morrison-Knudsen, thereby becoming the owner of 49 per cent of Fred Mannix & Company, Ltd. In March 1945, he was named president and general manager of Fred Mannix & Company, Ltd.

1944 ▶

Coal stripping for the war effort continues in much of Alberta and at Roche Percee, Saskatchewan.

1944 ▶

Canadians make up 25 per cent of Britain's Royal Air Force.

Morrison-Knudsen: The Foundation for Success

During the association with Morrison-Knudsen, Fred Mannix & Company, Ltd. grew into one of Canada's largest heavy construction firms. "I think it is fair to say that the education and the broad horizons and the access to heavy construction technology that was given to the Mannix group by their association with Morrison-Knudsen was the foundation of the Mannix company becoming the enormous organization it eventually became," Hugh Martin reflected. "The involvement with Morrison-Knudsen was the proving ground and the educational process that brought the Mannix organization into very big business. Fred C. was a protégé of Harry Morrison. Harry had no children, and he took a great liking to Fred C. He became almost a surrogate son to Harry Morrison."

F.C. Mannix, for his part, placed great value on his relationship with Harry Morrison. "He used to take me around and show me all of his jobs," he said. "He was always constructive and objective about the business. He helped me get organized to run the big jobs. That was the main thing." As Harry Morrison took Fred C. Mannix under his wing, Ann Morrison, who took a great liking to Margie Mannix, was also serving as an excellent role model.

While exposure to the Morrison-Knudsen operations proved crucial in the growth of Fred Mannix & Company, Ltd., so were the people F.C. Mannix recruited for "the outfit," as he always referred to his company. F.C. Mannix proved to be an extraordinary judge of talent, assembling what would grow into a first-rate management team, whose key members included his old friend Everett Costello, Eric Connelly, Karl Collett (who came from Morrison-Knudsen), Si Fraser and Brock Montgomery.

F.C. Mannix, as chief, and fellow members of Fred Mannix & Company, Ltd. celebrate the 1948 Christmas season at the Flying Club of Calgary. This is the outfit's first Christmas party.

MAN OF THE MONTH

Fred Mannix Jr.
President and General Manager
Fred Mannix & Company, Ltd.

"The story of Fred Mannix Jr.,

is the closely interwoven history of a father and son who by dint of their combined efforts and knowledge have made the earthmoving business which bears their name one of Canada's leading construction firms. During his association with his dad's company, Fred has worked on almost all types of heavy earthmoving construction plus innumerable railroad jobs of sizable magnitude, coal stripping contracts, and several hydroelectric operations. The Mannix firm, though at one time confined to earthmoving operations, has expanded throughout the years and earned a name for itself in many widely different types of construction." — *The Em-Kayan,* September 1945.

1944 ▶

Supporting the Allied invasion of Normandy, Canadian troops attack Juno and Nan White beaches. More than 150 Canadians captured by German forces in the early hours of the invasion are bayoneted or killed by firing squad.

1944 ▶

June 4, Rome falls to the advancing Allied troops, including Sherman tanks of Calgary's Fourteenth Armoured Regiment.

EVERETT COSTELLO

The Costellos were one of the first families to settle in the newly established town site of Calgary. E.W. (Everett) Costello was born November 25, 1909, in Calgary. He received his law degree from the University of Alberta in 1935. According to George Eckenfelder, who lived in the same residence as Costello at university, "Ev was known as 'Sleepy,' and he looked sleepy. He always looked as though he was half asleep. But he was one of the brightest people. He never seemed to do any work. He was a quiet chap, but he was always at the top of the class. He was really quite brilliant. He and Fred C. were always very close friends."

After being admitted to the Calgary bar in 1936, Costello joined the firm of Sanford & Costello. Not long after, World War II interrupted his legal career. Costello joined the Canadian Armed Forces, serving with the Canadian Armoured Corps and the staff of the Judge Advocate General. Following the war, he joined the Mannix organization.

"In the Mannix organization, they had the idea that they had to have three people in any facet of the operation," said R.J. Burns, who served as a legal advisor to the Mannix family at the time. "One should be an operating man; that is, an engineer or a practical operator of some kind. There should then be an accountant on one side of him and a legal person on the other side of him."

Costello joined Fred Mannix & Company, Ltd. as secretary and general counsel in 1946. He brought to the organization a shrewd analytical mind, formal and practical training in law, and a great deal of that rather uncommon commodity, common sense.

ERIC CONNELLY

Eric Connelly was born in Northumberland, England, in 1910. He was brought to Calgary the next year by his parents. Educated at Crescent Heights High School, his principal was William S. Aberhart, who later became premier of the province. "He told me at the time that I would never succeed because I was too radical," recalled Connelly. After working one summer as a lifeguard at the Banff Springs Hotel, one year in a public library, and taking a correspondence course from Queen's University, Connelly articled to become a chartered accountant with Harvey & Morrison, a senior accounting firm in Calgary.

In 1935, Connelly joined Alberta's provincial audit staff; he lasted nine months. "On my own time, I worked out a plan that would have saved them about $800,000," Connelly said. "The whole province's budget was only $50 million, and this was in the middle of the Depression. But the report was destroyed and I was told that within the government, it was impossible to reduce expenses." Offered the opportunity to go to Toronto with Touche Ross, a large accounting firm, Connelly gladly accepted.

Connelly did postgraduate work at the University of Toronto, but within a year he moved to Port Arthur, Ontario, to work with the Purdy family's wood-preserving business. Connelly then suffered a grave, personal setback. In the late 1930s, he was diagnosed with tuberculosis. He spent the next four years at Keith Sanitarium in Calgary. The time at the sanitarium was hardly wasted, however. Connelly studied the Canadian tax code at length, virtually committing it to memory. That knowledge would eventually earn him the reputation as one of the best tax men in Canada. But that was in the future. In the present, "people didn't like to hire people with a health record like mine," Connelly said. However, impressed by this young man's abilities, Fred Mannix & Company, Ltd. hired Eric Connelly as controller and assistant treasurer in 1947.

1944 ▶

Airport construction activity continues with the construction of a satellite airport at Edmonton, Alberta.

1944 ▶

The federal government passes an allowance program for families with school children under 16. Each child will be issued a monthly payment for the necessities of life. This baby bonus costs $250 million in the first year alone.

Will Register Children For Allowances

Provincial Offices To Be Set Up; Bill Is Passed

BROCK MONTGOMERY

B.L. (Brock) Montgomery was born in 1910 in New-Richmond, Quebec. After earning a degree in mining engineering at McGill University in 1934, he took an engineering position with Cominco Ltd. at the Kimberley Mine in British Columbia. In 1939, Montgomery left Cominco to take a job as an exploration engineer for a mine in Cuba. When financing for the project collapsed, he returned to British Columbia and joined Crow's Nest Pass Coal. Montgomery joined the Canadian Army in 1940. He served four years with the Tenth Field Squadron of the Royal Canadian Engineers, serving in England and Italy, where he was wounded in combat. After his discharge from the army with the rank of major, Brock rejoined Crow's Nest Pass Coal.

In 1946, Montgomery was given the task of selecting a site for Crow's Nest Pass Coal's first surface mine. Upon completion of his work, the company called in Gus Vissac of the Emergency Coal Production Board to confirm the exploration results. Vissac also made a recommendation on a contractor to handle the work. "He said, 'The company to hire is Mannix,'" Montgomery recalled. "'Nobody else is capable of doing it, so you had better go and hire them.'"

Not long after, Montgomery met F.C. Mannix. "We were renegotiating the contract," he said. "The general manager's strategy at Crow's Nest Pass Coal was that he was going to keep quiet and let Fred do all of the talking. Then he was really going to come back tough. He was right, but he didn't have much chance coming back. It ended up that there was five cents difference a yard. Fred said, 'I'll toss you for it,' and he tossed and won. That was a pretty fair hunk of money we were talking about."

Brock Montgomery joined Fred Mannix & Company, Ltd. as superintendent at the Blackbear Coal Mine near Princeton, British Columbia, in 1948.

These men were all exceptionally bright, strong-willed people, with talent and drive to function at the highest executive levels in business.

It would be nearly impossible to overestimate the importance of the M-K years for the future growth and development of the Mannix outfit. "During those years we couldn't have been associated with finer people than Morrison-Knudsen," Connelly stated. "I knew very little about the construction business. I went down to Boise and all branches of their organization were opened to me, including the great encouragement of Mr. Morrison himself. I was able to find out their pattern of operation, how they bid, how they negotiated, how they banked, and all these sort of things — which was tremendous because they had worldwide experience. So I was able to come in and set up cash, budget and purchasing controls, and also to complete graded files on personnel so that we were always able to have a pool of top personnel at our fingertips. At first, equipment was all over the lot — nobody knew where it was. But we were able to get all that functioning, and we were also able to set up proper cost and operational controls so that we were able to get the organization tied in and functioning."

"Because of our association with Morrison-Knudsen, our reputation just flowed out," Connelly continued. "Our banking associations became very much better. We were able to get to know the top people in the head offices of banks both in Montreal and in New York. We got to know them personally at a very high level. Naturally, that kind of connection works two ways. Being close to them, there was no way we would want to abuse their friendship. So we learned to be very factual, honest, and so on in all our dealings with them. Likewise, with the bankers themselves, the more trust they gave us, the more leeway we would have. Not only that, but at that time, the Americans were placing a great deal of money in Canada and also stimulating a great deal of the development that was taking place in Canada. Consequently, engineering and so on was being done in the United States. Because of our association with Morrison-Knudsen, we were able to get work. That's how we got into the pipeline business. Also, we were able to build earth dams. So we were getting jobs from the States."

The relationship with Morrison-Knudsen also enabled Fred Mannix & Company, Ltd. to get much-needed equipment. "It was during the war years that Morrison-Knudsen bought into the Mannix Group of Companies," recalled Ray Vennard. "From that time, we could get equipment from the United States by the trainload. That was when there were many jobs begging to be done in Canada that we didn't have the equipment for. You couldn't even get repair parts. Everything was on a priority basis.

1944 ▶

When the RCMP patrol vessel, St. Roch, completes the Northwest Passage east to west, she becomes the first ship to successfully transit the passage in both directions. Previously, she was the only ship to complete the passage west to east. These record-setting feats help solidify Canada's claim to the Far North.

1944 ▶

Jet fighters are designed to fly faster and higher than propeller craft. To ensure the new jet engines will work in the extreme cold of high altitude, Canada's National Research Council tests the engines during the winter in Winnipeg, Manitoba.

"BECAUSE I WAS RUNNING!"

Pansy Strange was recruited to Fred Mannix & Company, Ltd.'s Edmonton office in 1947. Her capacity to absorb an ever-increasing and extraordinarily diverse workload made her a legend in her own time. Key among

her duties was tracking down men who were available for work. Sometimes Pansy found people even when they were least expecting it. "My wife and I were sitting in some cafe in northeast Edmonton eating supper at about nine o'clock," recalled Blondie Garbutt. "And, by gosh, somebody came in and said, 'You're to phone Mannix's office, phone Pansy Strange right away.' I said, 'You're full of hogs! Pansy won't be there at this time of night. It's after nine o'clock.' He said, 'Yes, she is. She's standing there waiting for a call from you.' He was really serious so finally I called and, sure enough, Pansy answered. 'You're to go back out and put the batteries in the machine, load it and ship it down to Camrose,' she said. I thought my wife was going to jump out of her skin."

In addition to her other duties, Pansy Strange pitched in as a hotelier. "This was when they first discovered oil, near Edmonton, and there were no places to sleep," she explained. "They'd phone me up and say, 'Get us a reservation,' and I'd feel absolutely sunk. I'd phone and phone but you couldn't get rooms. So I got these two cots and put them up in the spare room we had at the office and got bedding and pillows and things like that. I charged them 50 cents a night for sleeping in there, but that was for the laundry. I told them I was a hot and cold running chambermaid, because I was running!"

If you had a high enough priority, you could get parts, but not if you were way down the ladder. But the equipment really came down the line when Morrison-Knudsen bought into the company. They had a lot of used equipment which was almost new. And because they had a 51 per cent interest in the company, they would send it up here. So that period from 1943 to 1951 turned out to be big years for the Mannix company. They had the equipment where other people didn't."

Morrison-Knudsen also introduced the outfit to many corporate traditions that Fred Mannix & Company, Ltd. adopted as its own. In addition to the origins of *The Loram Story* and film and the annual eastern bank visits, where the outfit shared its financial outlook for the coming year, three other Loram traditions have their roots in the M-K years. They are the Christmas parties, the Superintendents' Conferences and the Presidents' Conferences. A far cry from today's elaborate affairs, initially these events were quite simple. In fact, one woman, Pansy Strange, baked or took notes for many of them.

Pansy Strange was recruited in 1947. "Si Fraser kept chasing me until I finally gave up and joined the outfit," Strange recalled. "I resisted at first because I didn't think there could be anything for a girl in construction. But I finally decided to take it temporarily while I looked for something else. Well, I took it temporarily for 30 years. At that time, Si was the only man in Edmonton for Mannix. At first, it seemed an easy job without too much to do. But it just grew and grew until I was working Saturdays and Sundays. A lot of the work was rounding up construction men for the various projects.

The Fred Mannix & Company, Ltd. management team at the 1948 Christmas party.

1944 ▶

Amsterdam Jew Otto Frank and his family, including daughter Anne, are betrayed to the Gestapo after two years of hiding. They are deported in the last convoy to Auschwitz. Anne's diaries are found after the family is deported.

1944 ▶

Ex-Montreal mayor, Camillien Houde is released after almost four years of internment for inciting opposition to compulsory military registration. In December, he is reelected mayor of Montreal for the fifth time.

Elect Houde Montreal Mayor In Close Vote

Canadians Took Part in Great U-Boat Massacre

Teamed with British Navy to Set Stage

I kept track of the men. I used to spend my weekends hunting them up."

"Pansy was the mainspring of everything that went on up there," said Reg Pinchbeck, who supervised the Edmonton office in the early 1950s. "She hired men for every job there was. She kept track of every operator, Catskinner, and dragline operator there was in the country. She kept a book on all these guys. She could tell you where anyone was at any given time. She was just incredible." Brock Montgomery concurred, adding, "Pansy Strange became the greatest person to find all the best operators that were in the country. I checked one year and found that Pansy had done more hiring than the personnel department in Calgary, which had three people down there. The operators kept in touch with her. They'd write her a Christmas card or a note and say, 'I'll be ready when you get a job, and this is where you can find me.'"

In addition to her other duties, Strange helped inaugurate the company's annual Christmas party, perhaps the most significant of all the traditions adopted from M-K. "Fred C. and Karl Collett and I planned the first Mannix party up in our Edmonton office one day when they had come in from a job and were waiting for a chance to take me out to lunch," recalled Strange. "The restaurants were so full in those days, you had to line up — it was the beginning of the oil strike. While we were waiting, Karl Collett said, 'I think we should have a Christmas party.' I thought it was just talk, but sure enough, the time came for the Christmas party, and we were all sent invitations. This was held in the Flying Club at Calgary, and through the years the annual party went from the Flying Club to Penley's Dancing Academy and from Penley's to the Palliser Hotel. It got too big for the Palliser, so it went to the Calgary Inn. And when it got too big for the Calgary Inn, it went to the Convention Centre. People would come into Calgary on the company planes from the West in Nechako and from down in the East. When the planes came in, we used to go down and meet them to see who was coming to the party. The hotels were just full of Mannix people. I loved it because I'd go down there and meet people that I hadn't seen for two or three years. It was great."

Margie Mannix with her children, Frederick Philip (standing), Maureen Gail (on lap) in 1945, and Ronald Neil Mannix, born 1948.

"The Christmas party was the highlight of the year for most of us," agreed Frenchy Hamilton. "You were treated like a king. You got a beautiful hotel room, nice meals, dancing, and then the big get-together, where you'd meet people you'd known for years. Fred and Margie and the family, all of them would be there, and they just treated you like you were part of the family, coming home for Christmas dinner."

The strong family feeling during this stage of the organization's development was a reflection of F.C. Mannix's own life during these years, which saw the births of his three children, Frederick Philip in 1942, Maureen Gail in 1944, and Ronald Neil in 1948. A key to building the outfit's remarkable esprit de corps was his wife, Margie. "Margie supported me in all my work," F.C. Mannix said. "She knew all about the jobs we were bidding on and the work we were doing, so she helped me in ways that a good partner would. She'd have the fellows in and entertain them. She'd make them feel at home."

"This was an exciting period when everyone in the company was working together and operating as a family," added Eric Connelly. "The company didn't have much money. But money, somehow, didn't make very much difference. We went all out to make the company really go. There were no office politics. It was rewarding just to be there."

The End of World War II and the Beginning of an Emotional Disquiet
On June 6, 1944, the final great campaign of World War II in northwestern Europe began with the Normandy invasion (code name *Operation Overlord*). The Canadian First Army took part in the pincers movement that closed the Falaise Gap and cut off thousands of Germany's best remaining troops. Marching north from France, the corps helped liberate Dieppe, Ostend, Boulogne and Calais. Pushing on into Belgium, they triumphed at the Battle of Scheldt. Moving still further north, Canadian forces marched into the Netherlands.

Canadian forces helped in the massive Allied effort to pierce the Rhineland and carry the war into the very heart of the German fatherland. In the spring of 1945, they aided in breaking through the "invincible"

1944 ▶

The United Fruit Company introduces the Chiquita banana brand in the attempt to make bananas a brand-name item and not a generic commodity. Radio advertising plays the snappily sung lyrics backed up by an orchestra.

1945 ▶

Work begins on the John Hart Highway. The highway crosses rugged northern British Columbia wilderness.

PILOT RED RODGERS ASKS FOR A RAISE

"The company was involved in a joint venture on the Pine Pass Highway," recalled Mannix chief pilot, Hal O'Keefe. "The project had been using a small amphibian aircraft called a Sea Bee. The pilot was an ex-air force chap named Red Rodgers. He was so proud of himself and the little airplane that he even had his name 'Pilot Red Rodgers' painted on the side of the aircraft.

"During the summer that I was up there, and flying the Cessna Crane on the project, I was able to teach the project manager, Jim Pickard, the basic fundamentals of flying. It proved to be a very good system because Jim was then able to fly the aircraft and position it when he was looking down at the site of the roadbed instead of always having to tell me what he wanted to see. But Red Rodgers didn't know that Jim was being so ably trained.

"One day, when they were up with the Sea Bee, Red Rodgers thought that this would be a good chance for him to suggest a raise in his salary. On the way back into Prince George, he folded his arms back and said to Jim Pickard, 'Well, I guess this is a good time to ask for a raise.' Jim Pickard reached over and took hold of the control column. He quietly flew the airplane right into just about the point of touchdown, when Rodgers couldn't stand it any longer and took over the controls, did the touchdown and landed the airplane. As soon as they landed, Jim Pickard, being a very slow-spoken fellow, got out of the airplane and without a word, got on the ground. Red got out of the airplane behind him. Jim said quietly, 'You better go down and pick up your time. That's enough.' So, that was the end of Red Rodgers and his career there."

Siegfried Line in the Reichswald. As American and Russian troops linked up in central Germany, the Canadian forces in the Netherlands accepted the unconditional surrender of their German opponents. On May 1, 1945, Adolf Hitler committed suicide in his bunker beneath the streets of the German capital. On May 8, the last survivors of the Führer's crumbling empire formally acknowledged the end of the "thousand-year Reich." The war in the Pacific raged on.

On August 6, a B-29 dropped an atomic bomb on Hiroshima. The city was devastated. Three days later a second bomb levelled Nagasaki. Five days later, the greatest war in history ended. In its battles, 80 million people had fought and 14 million died. The war cost a trillion dollars and destroyed inestimable stores of natural wealth. The cost of the Canadian war effort was astronomical. Expenditure for the fiscal year 1939-1940 was a modest $118 million. The next year, it rose to $752 million; in the peak year, 1943-1944, it was $4.6 billion. During the war, 1,086,343 Canadian men and women performed full-time duty in the three services. The cost in blood was smaller than in World War I, but still tragic: about 42,000 people lost their lives.

Modern war brought frontline hazards to civilians, too. Mass bombing almost made the term "noncombatants" obsolete. Another term, "genocide," was coined to describe mass extermination, a crime so unthinkable that the language previously had no name for it. At war's end the atomic cloud spread an emotional disquiet throughout the social climate of the world.

One of the First Canadian Companies to Start an Aviation Division

The war made a new world, yet not altogether a better one. However, one great fear about the postwar world proved unfounded; there was no relapse into the Depression of the Thirties. Work left undone since 1929 was finally completed, and goods that people had gone without for 16 years were in demand. Returning soldiers started new lives. One of those people was a young man by the name of Hal O'Keefe.

After his discharge from the Royal Canadian Air Force in the fall of 1945, O'Keefe started Rocky Mountain Air Service Ltd., a flight training school at the Calgary Airport. He explains how he came to work for Fred Mannix & Company, Ltd. "I knew Virgil Kramer [Bob Kramer's brother], who had been employed with the company, or outfit, prior to the war," he said. "Virgil and I had gone through the war and flight training in the Commonwealth Air Training Plan. After the war, Virgil came back and joined the outfit again. They purchased a Cessna Crane from war assets

1945 ▶

The Hart Highway introduces innovations in road construction including the use of prefabricated bridges. These bridges were a wartime development integrated into civilian construction by Mannix crews.

1945 ▶

Painter and writer Emily Carr dies. Northwest Coast art strongly influenced her work.

for the big sum of $700 and he flew that for a while. I was with my little aviation company and took care of the servicing of their aircraft. Next they acquired an Anson 5, which was a modified military version as well, from an outfit by the name of McDonalds Aviation in Winnipeg."

According to O'Keefe, Fred Mannix & Company, Ltd. was one of the first Canadian organizations to start an aviation division. "In my memory, Imperial Oil were the only people that had an airplane based here at the Calgary Airport, a corporate business aircraft," he said. "Shortly after, Red Dutton also acquired a business aircraft, probably trying to keep up with Fred. All aircraft, which were used by corporations at that time, were just those that had been disposed of by the military. They were mainly aircraft that had been used for training in the Commonwealth Air Training Plan."

On February 14, 1947, Virgil Kramer and three senior Mannix employees — Stanley G. Moseson, assistant general manager of Fred Mannix & Company, Ltd., who had been with the company for four years; Alan G. Dryden, project superintendent who was a 15-year Mannix veteran; and Leo Spohn, a superintendent who had also been with the firm for about 15 years — "took the Anson down to Coleman, Alberta, on a business trip relative to coal mining in the area," recalled O'Keefe. "The west wind was blowing very strongly as it can do in that particular valley. It was a grass field, of which there were a lot in those days, that we made use of for airports. This was a designated airport, but a herd of cows was allowed to graze on the airport; it was really just a grass field. The cows were on the airport that morning and Virgil made a couple of low passes over the airport to scare the cows off of his landing path. Then, feeling that the cattle were free, he went back around and began his approach from east to west and, unfortunately, came in contact with some trees right at the approach end of the runway and crashed the aircraft. All of them were killed. That was a very sorry thing that happened in the outfit."

"After some considerable delay, from that time on, whenever the Cessna Crane was to be used, Fred would call me to get it ready for the specific trip," continued O'Keefe. "One day, he called me from Vancouver and said he wanted me to go up to Prince George with the Cessna Crane. Then he said, 'Well, why the hell don't you come and work for the outfit?' It didn't take me long to decide. I went with the Mannix firm, set up their aviation division and stayed with them until 1963."

Above: Hal O'Keefe, Lou Pozzi and Pansy Strange toast the 1950 Christmas season and the conclusion of a successful year.

Left: The outfit's Anson 5 in the Crowsnest Pass area.

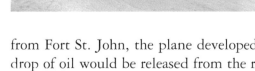

Initially, "we carried on and made several trips using the little Cessna Crane," O'Keefe continued. "It wasn't very practical for the job, but we made the best of it. On one occasion, I did lose a passenger, however. In the very early days, Fred C. Mannix and I were coming back from Fort St. John to Calgary. Our plan was to overfly Edmonton right into Calgary, but about halfway back from Fort St. John, the plane developed an oil leak through a rocker box cover on the starboard engine. Every time a drop of oil would be released from the rocker box cover, it dropped right on the hot exhaust stack and a puff of smoke would entail. Fred was sitting alongside of me at the time. I used the story on him that I would like to change seats with him and fly the airplane from that side so I could watch the oil leak a bit more closely. We did change seats, but

1945 ▶

Calgary Power turns to the outfit to construct Barrier Dam in the continued effort to harness the Bow River for hydroelectric development.

1945 ▶

Although the war in Europe is drawing to a close, Mannix coal stripping volumes increase almost 400 per cent.

MINTO THE BEAR

"The last year we were at Minto," recalled Charlie Thalheimer, a 40-year construction veteran with the outfit, "the people who owned the trading post had a garden about a mile from the trading post. The mother was working in the garden and a grizzly bear came down the hill off the mountainside. The people that they had bought the trading post from, the man who owned it before, had been killed by that same grizzly. She ran home and her sons went down and shot this grizzly bear. That night they came over to our place and wanted to know if I'd come help them get the bear out. When we got to where the bear was, why, we discovered two cubs. So we brought them in. One of them died that night, but my wife raised the other one. We named him Minto after the settlement. My wife used to take him on a leash when she went down to the trading post. She had to walk through the Indian camp to get there, so she would take this little grizzly bear."

Noni Thalheimer feeding Minto.

"The little fellow got just a little bit mean so we made arrangements through the curator, Tom Baines, of the Calgary Zoo to bring this grizzly cub back down to Calgary," added Mannix chief pilot, Hal O'Keefe. "Bob Hunter, my copilot, and I had the shop build a very strong wooden cage. We put the bear cub in this cage and loaded him into the nose compartment of the Lockheed Lodestar which sits between two piston-powered Pratt and Whitney engines."

"Minto had quite a life," continued O'Keefe. "After a considerable time at the Calgary Zoo, he went to the Winnipeg Zoo after a trade. He then became the mascot of the Air Force 402 Squadron that was based in Winnipeg." Finding Minto a bit too frisky for a mascot, the squadron traded Minto to the zoo in Chicago, where he fathered three little cubs. Minto died in 1969 at the Chicago Zoo.

I don't think the story went over too good with Fred. We landed at Edmonton instead of continuing on to Calgary, because I wanted to make sure of the problem. When we got inside the terminal, Fred said, 'I don't know about you, Hal, but I'm taking the Trans-Canada from here.' So, that's one passenger I did lose and it happened to be the top man."

In June 1948, Fred Mannix & Company, Ltd. purchased a Lockheed Lodestar from Air Canada, then called Trans-Canada Airlines. "Just after the war there was very little money around," said O'Keefe. "So it was foresight on Fred Mannix's part to see the value of the aircraft and to have purchased it for $20,000, which was a lot of money in those days. It was a very useful tool. Whereas a lot of corporate airplanes were restricted for the use of just the top executive people, we did not. We made it a workhorse and used it everywhere we could — hauling equipment or personnel. The majority of our jobs were all located in remote areas. Building roads, building dams, building airports, working on railways, all required considerable travel and the use of the aircraft. We built landing strips at several of the job sites in order to facilitate contact with the management of the job."

The Mannix Lockheed Lodestar, shown in Boise, Idaho. From left to right, Hal O'Keefe, Edith O'Keefe, Leah Collett, Bob Hunter (copilot), Margie Mannix, Fred C. Mannix, Ann Morrison, Barbara Connelly and Eric Connelly.

1945 ▶

Allied armies cross the Rhine River on March 24 and move into Germany. The first Canadian troops across are members of the Highland Light Infantry who cross at 4:25 a.m.

1945 ▶

Canada is one of the 50 original nations that pledge to support the fledgling United Nations by signing the World Security Charter. Canadian officials arrive in San Francisco for the signing.

Although Fred Mannix & Company, Ltd.'s airplanes were workhorses that saved the company a considerable amount of time and money, some of the old-timers had rather strong opinions about this newest addition to the Mannix outfit. "One day Freddie came to the job," Ora Burggren said. "The car I was driving was an English, right-hand drive. Freddie rode around with me and afterwards I drove him to the airport. When we got to the airport, he asked me to take a look at his new plane. I looked it over inside and out, and said, 'That yours?' Fred said that, yes, it was his airplane. 'Well,' I said, 'By God, you ride around in a thing like that and you tell me to walk a mile and a half around the project, there's something wrong with your head!' I never heard another word about it, but two days later I had a brand-new Chevy truck."

The John Hart Highway
A Long and Rugged Road

While Fred Mannix & Company, Ltd. was taking to the air, the outfit continued to build highways, an avenue of work F.S. pioneered back in the 1920s. During the mid-Forties, Fred Mannix & Company, Ltd. won three significant highway contracts: the John Hart Highway, the Mackenzie Highway and the Minto to Mayo Highway. It was the John Hart Highway — the last link in the Vancouver-Prince George-Fairbanks highway system — that nearly broke the outfit. It did, in fact, bankrupt the old and respected Campbell Construction Company Limited.

In July 1945, the Province of British Columbia awarded Fred Mannix & Company, Ltd. a contract to construct part of the Peace River Highway at a bid price of $1.3 million. The Mannix outfit contracted to build Section "B," the 57 miles (92 kilometres) from Azouzetta Lake to Commotion Lake. The Province simultaneously let Section "A" to the Campbell Construction Company

F.C. Mannix with R.H. Campbell, at the Hart Highway office at Commotion Creek.

Top: The Commotion Creek base camp, built by Ora Burggren, for the Hart Highway project.

Above: Late fall Hart Highway construction in the northern British Columbia wilderness.

Limited of Toronto. Campbell contracted to build the 94 miles (151 kilometres) from Summit Lake to Azouzetta Lake. The two contracts together, which aggregated $3.1 million, constituted the biggest public works road job awarded in many years. After the contracts were awarded, Mannix and Campbell decided to make the project a joint effort. Mannix took charge of production while Campbell took over the planning and administration of office and camp organization, financial and accounting work.

Upon completion, the highway was to be named the John Hart Highway. In retrospect, a more appropriate name might have been the Heartbreak Highway. "The Pine Pass or Hart Highway was one of the first jobs I took on after my father's retirement," said F.C. Mannix. "We bid on that in '45. We based our bid on the prices of labour going down, but the prices went up. We also had some very wet years up there. And the government had trouble locating the road. So we were losing a lot of money on it. We were pretty near broke when it was finished."

"That was a hell of a big job," agreed Everett Costello. "It was so much bloody trouble and took so much money that it was hard to get any other big jobs going on in those years. One problem was that the government never had the road properly located. They used to wait for us to go in and make what they called a tote road. Then they would go ahead and locate the main highway. So nobody knew where the bloody road went. The location of the Pine Pass Highway was just a line on a map."

"I first got started with the outfit on the Hart Highway job," recalled George Goodine, a 20-year Mannix veteran. "It was rough work. Especially the muskeg. And it rained all the time. The mud would cut the brakes out as fast as they could fix them. So they quit putting brakes on. You had to turn the key off if you wanted to stop. We sure

1945 ▶

Maurice (Rocket) Richard scores an amazing 50 goals in 50 games. His two closest rivals are tied with 39 goals each.

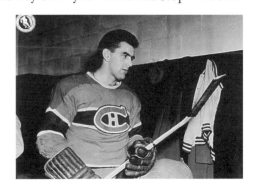

"I SURE BUSTED UP THAT CRAP GAME!"

"In 1946, I started the Calgary warehouse and shop," Bill Hamilton recalled. "Fred C. Mannix had come to me and said, 'We have parts scattered all over the country.' He said he wanted all the parts gathered up and brought back to a place in Calgary. I found this place way down in east Calgary; it had been a cement plant. I opened with one room and ran it for three years by myself. Gradually it grew into a big operation, with a large office staff and shops with mechanics and large yards to store equipment. Perhaps all told there would be more than 100 men working during the winter months.

"Fred C. was a frequent visitor. I remember one particular winter day. It was a Saturday and bitterly cold, about 30 degrees below. There was a crew of about eight of us and we took turns going back into the shop to get warm. About 6:00 p.m. we were all sitting around at the rear of the warehouse, having a drink and shooting dice, when in walked

Calgary warehouse and shop.

Fred C. with Ev Costello, Si Fraser, and three of Fred's friends from Eastern Canada. Fred was quite proud of his outfit and was showing his shop to his eastern friends.

"When Fred found us shooting dice he was just as surprised as we were. 'Well,' he said, 'this won't take long.' He picked up our dice saying, 'All right you so-and-sos, turn your pockets inside out and put your money in front of you!' We counted about $140. Fred started to throw the dice, but we stopped him — where was his money? He didn't have a cent on him, so he had to borrow from either Si or Ev. He threw a ten spot and after several tries came up with a seven spot. So we all picked up our winnings. Fred threw the dice out the window, saying to his friends, 'I sure busted up that crap game!'"

didn't make any money on that job. I know we had to put in a big claim after it was done. I heard that we got some money out of that. But, after what we had been through, it wasn't nearly enough."

"I remember when my brother Freddie was on that Pine Pass job," recalled Margie Mannix Walsh. "It was really a difficult contract. It was a disaster. But my dad said to him, 'Do it anyway. Do it right. That way, you'll always have a good name. If it's a bad job, finish it anyway. Keep your good reputation.' I think that was really brave advice because the company was losing money, and plenty of it, on that job."

As work neared completion, the Mannix outfit began to prepare a claim for additional funds to recover its losses. Jack Bruce, then a young man working in the project field office, remembers the start of that claim effort. "I started with the Mannix Group in Prince George in 1948 as a sort of timekeeper and cost clerk," he said. "They were finishing their work and moving their equipment out at the time. We ended up having a warehouse of equipment along the track there in Prince George. We almost had a flea market there. We were selling off commissary and camp canned goods, and shipping the equipment off to other projects. Some of it went as far north as the Yukon. After the job, the company was in a claim position with the British Columbia government, the Department of Highways. We anticipated a claim because it was a tough job done under changed conditions. In a remote, dirt-moving type of project, the conditions that you bid on are set out in the specifications. If they change drastically, you have to negotiate or get a revised price for your work."

Winning this claim became paramount to winning the company's future. "When I went to Mannix in 1947, the company was virtually bankrupt," said Eric Connelly. "They had a joint venture with Campbell Construction building the Pine Pass Highway. They were losing a great deal of money up there. And so there were demands all the time from the Mannix organization to Morrison-Knudsen for money to keep operating. Naturally, the person who gets

1945 ▶

In May, western Canadians discover small bomb-carrying balloons launched from Japan. Each carries a small explosive device. They drift across the Pacific and land as far inland as the Prairies.

1945 ▶

On August 6, the United States drops an atomic bomb on Hiroshima, Japan. The explosion destroys over two-thirds of the city and kills 80,000.

caught in a situation like that is the finance man. I remember a fellow named Charlie Wilbanks, who represented M-K, came into my office, and asked me what I thought about what was happening. I said, 'Well, in my estimate, we're going to have a $3-million loss.' Wilbanks trotted back to M-K with this news and everything broke loose."

"We spent the next four or five months arranging for a claim, arranging a position where we would be able to be bailed out," Connelly said. "You must remember that this contract was bid during the end of the war. After that time, certain restraints were off. Inflation, which had been held in check during the war, just took off. Consequently, there was really room for argument that the people in British Columbia had gotten something at a discounted value through no fault of the people who were performing the work. Because we got a good settlement there, we actually saved the organization." In 1949, after a two-week review by a special committee of the British Columbia legislature, Fred Mannix & Company, Ltd. was unanimously awarded a settlement of $1.2 million. The Campbell Construction Company was awarded $515,042.

The John Hart Highway was a symptom of a much greater malaise — the Canadian government's sluggish response to her populace's demand for new and improved roads. The Alberta government spent just $10 million on highway development in 1946, a figure considered below the national average. By 1947, 77 per cent of Canadian highways remained unsurfaced. In Saskatchewan, out of the 205,000 miles (330,000 kilometres) of highway, 95 per cent were unsurfaced. Some people held a pessimistic view of the need for development of new roads in the Prairie provinces, based on a comparison of the influx of settlers in the early part of the century with the current stable population. Others were more optimistic. "I suggest

F.C. Mannix, the retiring executive chairman of the Prairie Road Builders Association, at the 1948 annual convention.

Once completed, the Hart Highway provides opportunity for commerce and scenic enjoyment.

to you that this view overlooks the increase in prairie population which is bound to be felt with more complete development of the northern mining areas and as the effects of the Prairie Farm Rehabilitation Act projects become more generally recognized," stated Robert Drummond, then Ontario vice president of the Canadian Construction Association. In a speech given in Saskatoon in 1947 at the annual meeting of the Prairie Road Builders Association, Drummond urged Prairie Road Builders to press for further development.

That same year, F.C. Mannix was elected executive chairman of the Prairie Road Builders Section of the Canadian Construction Association. In his role as executive chairman, he attended a two-day convention in Saskatoon. At a banquet held in the delegates' honour, the guest speaker was none other than his father's old nemesis, W.A. Fallow, minister of public works of Alberta. During his speech Fallow allowed that good highways were absolutely indispensable in a properly organized society and could be made one of the most lucrative, self-liquidating utilities in any branch of the government. He then went on to acknowledge that, "We have been very slow to recognize that principle in Canada and blindly stumble along 25 years behind the times."

What is notable about Fallow's speech is that Fallow had denounced F.S. Mannix's 1935 proposal to perform grading work on the Alberta Highway No. 2 from Crossfield to Red Deer for government bonds as "propaganda" which "couldn't be considered," adding, "I made it plain that the policy of the government would be to build their own highways." One would hope that as F.C. Mannix listened to Fallow's speech, he allowed himself a discreet smile. Perhaps if the government had granted his father more highway contracts in the Thirties, highway progress in Alberta might have motored just a bit further along.

1945 ▶

On August 8, the United States drops a second atomic bomb on Japan. Much of Nagasaki is left in ruins.

1945 ▶

The last Canadian to die in action in World War II is Lieutenant Robert Hampton Gray, a Royal Canadian Navy pilot. He is awarded the Victoria Cross for a valiant dive-bombing attack on a Japanese destroyer. Though wounded and his Corsair in flames, he sank the ship with a direct hit.

THE ANATOMY OF A COAL BRANCH

The Coal Branch is located approximately 130 miles (210 kilometres) west of the city of Edmonton on the eastern slopes of the Rocky Mountains. The name is derived from the branch shape of an inverted Y which was formed by the railways constructed to serve the many mines in the area. The stem of the inverted Y starts at the rail town of Bickerdike, west of the city of Edson on the main rail line. The stem heads south across the McLeod River, to the towns of Embarras, Robb, and finally to Coalspur where it branches to the southeast to include Sterco, Coal Valley and Lovettville, and to the southwest to include Mercoal, Leyland, Cadomin and Mountain Park. From Leyland a short spur reaches out to the northwest to include Luscar.

The dominant rivers in the Coal Branch played a major role in the development of the area, as flooding was a critical problem in the early history of the mines. The Coal Branch is drained by two major river systems, the McLeod River and the Pembina River. The McLeod River has its origin south of Mountain Park, flows past Cadomin and leaves the area slightly southwest of Mercoal in a northerly direction. Two of the McLeod's major tributaries are the Gregg River, which has its origin just west of Luscar, and the Embarras River, which flows past Coalspur and Robb. The Lovett (Little Pembina) River has its origin west of Coal Valley and flows southeast to join the Pembina River.

The Development of Surface and Open-Pit Coal Mining

From the first small stripping contract at the Sheerness mine in 1934, the Mannix organization played a leading role in the development of surface and open-pit coal mining in Western Canada. In the 1940s, Fred Mannix & Company, Ltd.'s contracts for stripping spread from the small prairie mines in Alberta and Saskatchewan into the two large coal-producing areas in the mountains of Alberta and British Columbia. For Fred Mannix & Company, Ltd., the 1937 contract at Coal Valley Mine was the first in a series of ongoing contracts with the Coal Valley Mining Company and other mining companies in the Coal Branch.

Karl Collett (left) and Harry Morrison, standing in the mud and blowing drizzle of the Crowsnest, examine coal pit excavation operations.

Through this early work at Coal Valley, Fred Mannix & Company, Ltd. gained a reputation in the Coal Branch. During the Forties, the large mining companies increasingly began to develop open-pit mines. Fred Mannix & Company, Ltd. was awarded stripping contracts with Cadomin Coal Company Ltd. for an open-pit mine near Cadomin, and with Sterling Collieries Ltd. for a mine near Sterco. In the mid-1940s, the Mannix organization also began working at the Gregg River Mine, a new mine being developed by Cadomin Coal Company, and at a new Luscar Collieries Ltd. strip mine near the Gregg River Mine.

In 1946, the Mannix organization set up headquarters for the Coal Branch in Cadomin. Alan Dryden was named area manager. Late that year, Ray Vennard went to Cadomin to manage the stripping operations at the Coal Valley Mine. Vennard was promoted to area manager following Dryden's death in the plane crash that also claimed the lives of Stan Moseson and Leo Spohn. To replace Moseson as general manager, Morrison-Knudsen assigned one of their top managers from the United States. This was Karl Collett, a man with extensive experience in large earthmoving and hydroelectric projects. Collett, one of the great construction men in North America, embodied dynamic, aggressive building at its best.

1945 ▶

The S.S. Pasteur arrives at Halifax, Nova Scotia, with repatriated Canadian soldiers.

1945 ▶

On August 14, following devastating air raids, two atomic bomb attacks in four days and Russian entry into the conflict, Japan surrenders aboard the U.S.S. Missouri. Japan first attacked Manchuria in 1931, beginning the conflict in the Pacific.

Born on March 29, 1898, in the town of Vernal, Utah, Collett was educated at Brigham Young University in Provo, Utah. Collett was only 20 when he started in construction — ballasting railway bed with a crew of Mexicans. He then joined Utah Construction Company. Over the years, both with Utah Construction, and later with Morrison-Knudsen, Collett was associated with many of the legendary construction projects of this century. He was a superintendent on such famous structures as Hoover Dam, Shasta Dam and Red Butte Dam. He built highways in California, Idaho and Washington, C-4 wartime ships at Richmond, California, a giant rock-filled dam at Nantahala, North Carolina, and many dams in Mexico. It was from Mexico that Karl Collett received a call to come to Canada on February 24, 1947. The job was to last three months, but F.C. Mannix was quick to recognize Collett's talents and tremendous vitality and recruited him into the Mannix company.

Collett's first days on the job were typical of his style. Arriving from the heat of Mexico into Calgary's below-zero weather, Collett was out on the job site before the welcomes had a chance to die away. "He started buying equipment and got things moving pretty fast in the coal area," recalled Karl's wife, Leah, with a chuckle. "They were all scared to death that he was going to bankrupt them before he'd been there 24 hours. But they realized how right he was about the decisions he was making, and went along with him."

During World War II, coal mining in the Crowsnest Pass had boomed. Coal sales had reached

Top: A tracked steam dragline loads a Caterpillar DW10 tractor pulling a Caterpillar W10 wagon at Coal Valley, Alberta.

Centre: The pit at the mine located at Eyremore, southwest of Brooks, Alberta.

Bottom: A D-8 Cat and scraper strip at the Alberta Collieries in 1946.

record levels of production for both thermal coal, sold to the Canadian railways, and metallurgical coal, mostly exported to the United States. Following the war, when demand for coal dropped and prices fell, the coal companies in the Crowsnest Pass began to shift from expensive underground mining to surface mining. They turned to Fred Mannix & Company, Ltd. to put their new open-pit mines into production. Fred Mannix & Company, Ltd. was awarded the contract to develop the first large open-pit mine in the pass for West Canadian Collieries on its properties near Blairmore in 1945. This first major contract quickly led to more work. Between 1946 and 1949, the company put four more new open-pit mines into operation: the Corbin Mine, near Coal Mountain, British Columbia; Hillcrest Mohawk Collieries' Tent Mountain Mine, a new open-pit mine near Blairmore; Crow's Nest Pass Coal's first surface mine, located to the north of Michel, British Columbia; and a second West Canadian open-pit operation, the Adanac Mine near Bellevue.

Former Morrison-Knudsen engineer, Dick Stein, joined Fred Mannix & Company, Ltd. in 1948. He assumed overall supervisory responsibility for all Mannix contract coal mining work in both the Coal Branch and the Crowsnest Pass. Although Stein remained in this position for only a year before becoming a special assistant to F.C. Mannix on heavy construction projects, he left his mark on the coal mining operations through equipment innovations. One of his most famous inventions was christened the Steinmobile. "Dick got the brainstorm of putting this

1945 ▶

December 29, the federal government releases World War II casualty numbers: 41,371 Canadians are killed, 53,178 wounded, 10,044 taken prisoner and 332 are missing. Deaths number about 20,000 fewer than World War I.

Canada's War Casualties Total 104,925
41,371 Were Killed, More Than Half Army Losses
OTTAWA, Dec. 29 (CP) — Canadian service casualties in the six years of the Second Great war totalled 104,925, including 41,371 dead, compared with casualties of 190,092, including 62,817 dead, in the four years of the First Great

1946 ▶

The Mackenzie Highway development begins in the northern reaches of Alberta and the Northwest Territories. The construction is between 56 degrees and 62 degrees north.

big air compressor on the back of an old D-8 Caterpillar," Bill Hamilton explained. "The air compressor was operated by the diesel motor that ran the tractor. They built racks and they had two air drills, and they could put steel in there and drill 20-foot holes for blasting rock. In all those mountain coal strips, we had maybe 18 to 20 feet of hard rock on top of the coal. We always had to drill and blast out all the rock to get at the coal."

Phil Shirley, who joined Fred Mannix & Company, Ltd. in 1946, worked on Steinmobiles at the new strip mines at Blairmore and Michel. "Dick had a lot of good ideas, and some of the things that he worked on are now being manufactured by large firms," Shirley explained. "The idea of the Steinmobile was that the operator could go along and pull his own stuff with him and then they could just drill and everything was all in one place. They do make those nowadays. Another one Dick made was what we called the wagon drill, which was a drilling rig on tracks with its own air compressor. It would move itself on the tracks with the air from the air compressor, and you could drill and save time. It could never be patented because it was bits and pieces of other companies' equipment, but the air track is quite a popular piece of machinery today."

Fred Mannix & Company, Ltd.'s crews brought a much different attitude to the coal mining business while pioneering surface mining in the Coal Branch and the Crowsnest Pass regions. For Brock Montgomery, who had worked at Crow's Nest Pass Coal, the largest coal company in the pass, before joining the Mannix outfit, the difference was a highly visible esprit de corps. "With Crow's Nest Pass Coal and Mannix, the

Top: R.C. (Dick) Stein.

Above: One of Dick Stein's innovations is the Steinmobile, a portable drilling rig that dramatically increases drilling and blasting production at mountain coal mines.

big difference was that the people working for Mannix were proud that they were working for Mannix. This was the first thing they'd say when they went anywhere, into the beer parlours or anything. However, in the coal mines, all of the workers were certainly not proud of working in a mine. The workers may have admired the individual managers, but they certainly didn't admire the companies, and they weren't proud of working for the companies."

With Mannix there was none of the us-against-them attitude that typified management-labour relations in the big underground coal mining companies. "F.C. Mannix used to come out to the pits and just chase around with everybody," said Louis Carriere, who joined the Mannix organization in 1946 as a Cat operator on the Coal Branch jobs. "He was a very nice fellow to talk to. You wouldn't have believed that he owned as big a construction outfit as he did. He'd talk to everybody, and he never showed any indication that he was in the position he was in. He was a very common man. He was like the rest of us."

"F.C. Mannix and Karl Collett always had the facility of remembering who was on the project and taking the opportunity to speak to everybody they could," concurred Fred Fenwick, who started his 40-year career with Mannix in 1949 as an engineering student at the Adanac Mine. "We thought highly of F.C. He was always well informed on what was going on at the job, and he knew the people. Karl Collett was also a rather remarkable man. He had an incredible memory, particularly for names and faces. When he would come to visit us on a project, I would see him driving down and waving to each of the machine

1946 ▶

Continuing to expand their construction expertise in the Alberta mountains, Mannix crews build the world famous Banff to Windermere Highway.

1946 ▶

Fred Mannix & Company, Ltd. builds the Snare River hydroelectric power development. The project is northwest of Yellowknife, Northwest Territories.

operators as he went by and calling them by name. And his memory extended to everything else. He knew what each project was about, what it had done to date, and where it was going. He was a very good, intuitive construction man."

Rita Welch, Jimmy Welch's wife, recalled that everyone particularly looked forward to the times when F.C. Mannix would bring Margie along on visits to the mines. "Fred was great," Mrs. Welch said. "When he'd come in with the company plane, he'd bring us things like fruit and whatnot, and he'd get everybody together so we'd all be able to find out what was going on in Calgary. He was really affable, outgoing. He treated everyone so well and was so much fun. And Margie was charming. She was always involved with her children and was interested in yours. I think that was a bond among all of us. She was a great gal, good-looking, with red hair and a beautiful smile. She really was a great person and so full of life, always interested in what everybody was doing, and she would remember everybody. She wouldn't forget your name if she had only met you once. She made you feel like you were one of the family."

The End of the Contract Coal Mining Era and the Start of Mannix Mine Ownership

In Alberta, the Emergency Coal Production Board provided the financing to put six prairie strip mines into operation. These mines, all previously abandoned underground mines, started up in 1943 and 1944 and ran until 1946. Fred Mannix & Company, Ltd. was the contractor at four of them. Two were in the Taber area, on properties formerly owned by Majestic Mines Limited at Taber and Continental Coal Corp. Ltd. at Grassy Lake. The other two were also in central and southern Alberta, on properties formerly owned by Birnwel Coal Limited at Eyremore and Camrose Collieries Limited at Camrose. Between 1943 and 1946, the six Coal Board prairie strip mines produced 844,000 tons of coal. Fred Mannix & Company, Ltd. was responsible for the bulk of this production.

The Emergency Coal Production Board work was a significant part of a rapidly growing business. During the war years, Fred Mannix & Company, Ltd. saw its contract stripping work for prairie coal mines expand dramatically. This led to the development of a stripping circuit. Mannix earthmoving machinery moved around from the coal mines in central and southern Alberta, then east into the Estevan area of Saskatchewan. In the Tofield-Dodds area, Mannix did contract stripping

"THAT WAS THE STATUS SYMBOL"

Mannix crews working in the Coal Branch received premium pay, compared with what the mining companies were paying their employees. The heavy equipment operator jobs were also regarded as prestige jobs by the mine workers. "I was at Cadomin when I first started, then I moved over to Coal Valley and then back to Cadomin and from there over to Luscar," Louis Carriere said. "We just moved from camp to camp, going wherever we were required."

Being a Cat operator was a tough job. Since the machines in those days did not have enclosed cabs, there was only minimal protection from cold weather and from flying rock. "All we had on the Cats was a canopy in case of falling rock," Carriere explained. "We were also supplied with canvases that you could put on the edges of the Cat. With that, we could keep ourselves warm, except for the wind. But I recall many times that we had to wear goggles, and I had to keep my face just below the dashboard of the Cat because the stones and chunks of coal were big and would hurt. When I went on the shovel, the wage was 90 cents an hour and later went up to $1.10, $1.25. That was the highest paying job in the coal mines at that time. When you were a shovel operator, you were pretty much the kingpin of the mine. In those days, we didn't have to wear hardhats, and if you were a shovel operator, you wore an engineer's cap. That was your main marking. That was the status symbol."

1946 ▶

The royal family of Holland sends Ottawa 10,000 tulip bulbs in thanks for the generosity shown Princess Juliana during her exile in Canada.

1946 ▶

Arthur Covington of the National Research Council begins Canadian experiments in radio astronomy.

for Claude Gallinger's Tofield Coal Company, the Dodds Coal Company, the Black Nugget Coal Company and the Ryley Coal Company. Further south, the Mannix organization continued to work for Claude Gallinger at Sheerness. In southern Alberta, the company had stripping contracts at Eyremore for the Westgate Coal Syndicate Mine and for a small mine at Bow Island. In the Estevan area, Fred Mannix & Company, Ltd. stripped coal at Roche Percee Coal's Old Mac Mine and at a new strip mine developed by Manitoba & Saskatchewan Coal on its Bienfait Mine property.

One of the key coal mining people of Fred Mannix & Company, Ltd.'s wartime operations was Ray Vennard. Shortly after completing the Minnewanka Dam project, Vennard began supervising stripping operations at the Emergency Coal Production Board mines. "In October 1942, we came back to do coal stripping at Grassy Lake," Vennard said. "I think we were at Grassy Lake until the next spring, 1943. In 1944 we went to Eyremore. We stripped coal there for the government during the war. I remember the first year, we put out 250,000 tons of coal for the war effort. The coal was being shipped to the army camps for heating and making hot water."

Another key person in the coal mining operations was Jim Welch. Like Vennard, Welch started as an equipment operator, but quickly moved up into supervisory positions. "In 1943, I went on the coal stripping circuit, which was Sheerness, Dodds, Tofield and Estevan,"

Top: A front-end loader dumps coal into a truck at the Grassy Lake, Alberta, mine.

Above: The Dominion Coal Board visits the Kandev Mine. Shown left to right are Ray Vennard, G.A. (Gus) Vissac and Karl Collett with Mannix stripping equipment.

Welch recalled. "These were jobs that only lasted for a short period, a month or maybe two months. The same crew and equipment moved from one to the other. We just stripped enough coal to last the coal company until the same time next year." At the new strip mine on Claude Gallinger's Tofield property, Welch received an introduction to reclamation work, something that few North American coal mining companies were doing.

"Gallinger raised purebred cattle and he didn't want to lose any pastureland," Welch recalled. "So the overburden that you took off one year had to be used the next year. You put the loam in a separate area, and then you piled up the other material. You used that subsoil to backfill the old pit, and then you had to put the black loam on top again. Gallinger was way ahead of his time."

While the work at Tofield anticipated modern reclamation practices, most prairie strip mining remained as primitive and labour-intensive as it had been in the 1930s. Welch was amazed by the coal-loading operations at the Dodds Mine. "When you first saw this, you wondered what they were doing," Welch recalled. "They actually loaded these boxcars with wheelbarrows. They did not have an eight-hour shift or a ten-hour shift. It was done by the boxcar. They had so many cars to load. If they did it in four hours, they were finished and if they did it in eight hours, they were finished. It was quite something to see them loading these cars with wheelbarrows."

1946 ▶

Several Canadians, including Fred Rose, a member of Parliament for three years, are convicted of spying for the Soviet Union.

1946 ▶

An estimated 20 per cent of unmarried Canadian men serving in the European theatre during World War II marry European women. These brides, some with children, begin arriving and assimilating into Canada.

The postwar years brought massive structural change to the western Canadian coal industry. Two events precipitated these changes. The first was the discovery of enormous reserves of oil and gas at Leduc, Alberta, in 1947. The first well marked the start of Alberta's petroleum industry; oil and gas rapidly replaced coal as the domestic heating fuel. The second event occurred in 1948. That year, Canadian railways announced that they would replace their coal-fired steam locomotives with diesel electric locomotives by 1956. The elimination of the railway market for steam coal doomed the mines in the Coal Branch, which marketed their coal almost exclusively to the railways. Even for the Crowsnest Pass mining companies, which served a more diversified market with metallurgical coal, the news was a severe blow. By the late 1940s, it was clear that work in the Coal Branch and the Crowsnest Pass would soon be ending.

These events marked the start of a two-decade decline for Canada's coal mining industry. National production dropped to levels not seen since before the First World War, when the industry was in its infancy. Within one decade, the Coal Branch was transformed from an area of bustling communities to a collection of ghost towns. All across the province, estimated to contain 15 per cent of the world's known coal reserves and 87 per cent of all the reserves in Canada, the collieries shut down one by one.

It was precisely at this point, with coal mining companies throughout Canada going bankrupt, that F.C. Mannix decided that the western Canadian coal industry had a future. Mr. Mannix's decision to invest in coal at this time was an outstanding example of the boldness of his entrepreneurial approach and his uncanny ability to assess risks.

"The coal business was at its lowest ebb," explained W.W. (Wally) Lynd, who provided legal counsel for most of the coal mines and many individual miners in Saskatchewan since he first arrived in Estevan in 1919. "Oil was coming in, gas was coming in, and they were losing contract after contract to gas and oil in these industrial plants and the railroads. It's easy to make deals when you're prosperous, but it takes a lot of backbone and courage to take on something that's in the dumps, and that's what the Mannix people did. They took coal and they kept faith in it. When F.C. Mannix started picking up this coal business, coal was dirt. It emitted a lot of smoke and dirt and grime, and they were selling it for two dollars and something a ton. I think that F.C. Mannix had started in this stripping of coal and it got into his blood. He could see that in spite of these travails, it would come through. He was right, because when your oil and gas is gone, you'll still have coal. He had

"IT WAS A TERRIBLE WINDSTORM, JUST TERRIBLE"

Of all the harsh conditions that Mannix crews faced working outdoors in the Coal Branch with the open construction equipment of the times, the fierce winds were undoubtedly the hardest to cope with. In 1949, Cadomin was hit by the worst windstorm ever to hit the area in modern times. "I remember getting home about eleven o'clock that night and my wife Chris and I were just putting the little one to bed," recalled Ray Vennard. "I got into bed, too, and the wind got stronger and stronger. All of a sudden, there was a terrible bang on the side of the house. The wind was blowing rocks, and it drove rocks right into the wood. It blew a sawhorse through the air and left it with one of the legs sticking through the wall of the kitchen.

"At one house, further from us, all that was left was the kitchen floor with the cook stove sitting on it. The rest of the house was gone. At another place, the roof had been picked up, moved about a foot, and set down again. The only thing that saved our house from being blown away was that I had built a cribbing around the house and put in about a two-foot fill of earth around to make it warmer. The wind blew boxcars off the tracks and blew the wagon drills over on their sides. I remember there was a fairly new, red pickup sitting there, and when I looked at it the next day, the one side of it that was into the wind had no paint left. It had sandblasted the paint right off. It was a terrible windstorm, just terrible."

1947 ▶

For the first time in history, a Canadian parliamentary committee consults Indian leaders on possible changes to the Indian Act. Blackfoot councillor Teddy Yellow Fly is one who addresses the committee.

1947 ▶

W.O. Mitchell writes Who Has Seen the Wind, his novel of coming of age on the Saskatchewan prairie. It becomes a Canadian classic.

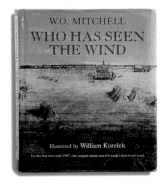

vision and foresight and courage and that's the whole gist of the story in a nutshell."

Fred C. Mannix's first wager on the future of coal mining in Western Canada was a small one. In 1946, when the work for the wartime Emergency Coal Production Board came to an end, Mannix acquired the leases for the Majestic Mine at Taber. Mannix then established a subsidiary to own the Majestic Mine, as Morrison-Knudsen had no interest in being directly involved in the acquisition of any coal properties. This new company, Southern Alberta Coal Company Ltd., was incorporated in 1946. That same year, F.C. Mannix also entered into a partnership to own and operate a second former Coal Board mine, the Camrose Collieries Mine. The arrangement here was a partnership with D. Twomey Jr., president of Stoney Creek Collieries Ltd. On May 30, 1946, a second Mannix coal mining subsidiary, Alberta Coal Company Limited, was incorporated. This company became the owner of the strip mine on the Camrose Collieries property.

Initially, operations at the Taber and Camrose mines were mixed in with the contract mining operations, under Stan Moseson's overall direction. Following Moseson's death in 1947, Karl Collett assumed responsibility for all contract mining work, including the newly purchased mines at Taber and Camrose. Then, in 1948, F.C. Mannix decided to establish a separate organization for the coal mining side of the company's operations. The person who would head the coal operations was Sheldon Alexander (Si) Fraser.

Born in 1902 in Knox, North Dakota, Fraser started his business career while still in high school, when he purchased ranch land in the Claresholm, Alberta area. Fraser operated his own ranching and farming operation until 1922, when he joined the Dominion

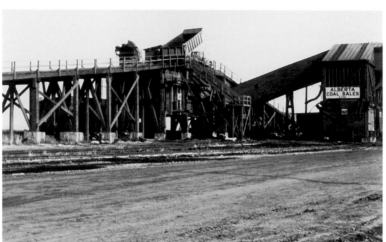

Top: S.A. (Si) Fraser, head of Mannix coal operations.

Above: The Alberta Coal Sales Ltd. tipple at the Majestic Mine at Taber, Alberta.

Trading and Export Company. By 1929, Fraser was active in several businesses — he owned part of a large ranch near Lethbridge, held a partnership with Frank O'Sullivan in a sugar beet trucking business near Picture Butte and was part owner of two sawmills in southern Alberta.

In the late 1930s, one of Fraser's customers for lumber was Marwell Construction. Marwell hired Fraser as manager for its Alberta operations. After Marwell and Fred Mannix & Company, Ltd. went into partnership in 1943, Fraser moved to Edmonton to work on special projects for the Mannix side of the business. When Mannix bought out Marwell's interest in the partnership with Morrison-Knudsen in 1944, Fraser decided to remain with the Mannix organization. Fraser was given no specific title, but functioned as a special assistant to F.C. Mannix. According to the story, Fraser pestered F.C. so much about the mining side of the operations that finally F.C. simply said, "Right. Now you're running it. Go fix it."

F.C. Mannix explained why he placed Fraser in charge of the coal operation. "We had so much other work that it was hard to tell who was where," he said. "Mr. Collett was the general superintendent for the company. He was running the mines and everything else at the time. Mr. Collett looked after the mines until one day I said, 'You don't look after the mines anymore. Mr. Fraser will look after the mines.' Mr. Collett was more oriented to contracting than he was to running a mine, so then he handled all the rest of the things that we were doing. Si Fraser organized the mines and kept them running. After it got going, he hired Chuck Doerr away from Western Dominion Coal Company. He also got Ed Panchysyn, who later headed exploration for us and found nearly all our coal."

1947 ▶

The St. Mary River head gates are built for the Prairie Farm Relief Administration in the St. Mary Irrigation District in southern Alberta.

1947 ▶

Yearly winter conditions stop construction of the Grimshaw to Hay River Highway in northwestern Alberta.

Fraser had no experience in the industry, nor did he have much knowledge of the operations side of mining. What Fraser possessed was a flair for the entrepreneurial, for finding business opportunities and making deals. He also had a capacity for handling an enormous amount of work. "I saw very little of him when he was with Mannix," recalled Si's wife, Katie Fraser. "One year he was only home about 15 days out of the whole year. My husband discovered Chuck Doerr and he was a great help to the coal companies. My husband always said that the coal division would be the most reliable division of the outfit. Sheldon was a fantastic businessman, I know that. He could make deals that no one else could."

One person who immediately recognized this ability was Eric Connelly. "Si Fraser was quite a guy," Connelly recalled. "Si was a wheeler-dealer, and he had a great deal to do with putting together the coal mining operation and the ultimate success of the coal business. Fred moved him into that division because it was sort of a lost child, as it were, and Fraser did an excellent job of it. He was always looking for the angle, and he had a nose for searching out where the strengths and weaknesses of somebody else's operation were."

The tipple at the Cordel-Vesta Mine near Halkirk, Alberta, one of four mines purchased in 1948.

Fraser negotiated two mine acquisitions of particular significance in 1948. The first was an underground mine near Lake Wabamun, in the Pembina coal field about 45 miles (72 kilometres) west of Edmonton. This mine, the Victory Mine, would eventually become part of the Whitewood Mine. The second mine Fraser helped purchase was the Cordel Mine. This small strip mine near Battle River, a few miles from the towns of Halkirk and Hanna, would be renamed Vesta Mine.

A map of the Calgary Power Ltd. Spray Lakes project, built by Fred Mannix & Company, Ltd.

The Continuing Relationship with Calgary Power

During the mid-1940s, Fred Mannix & Company, Ltd. continued to win significant contracts in hydroelectric development. These contracts included the Snare River hydroelectric project and the Spray Lakes and Three Sisters dams.

The Snare River hydroelectric power project was part of the postwar development of the Northwest Territories. Built for the Department of Mines and Resources, this development was to provide power for the mines of the Yellowknife District. The project was situated on the Snare River, some 160 miles (260 kilometres) northwest of the town of Yellowknife. Because the dam site was far from either rail or road supply, the project proved a formidable exercise in logistics. All equipment, men and materials had to be flown in or brought in by boat during the three brief months of summer weather. In addition, the presence of subarctic muskeg played havoc with the equipment. Despite these difficulties, the project, begun in the fall of 1946, was completed on schedule in the summer of 1948.

SPRAY PROJECT

Alberta's Great Spray Lakes Project To Produce First Power This Year

This $10,200,000 hydro electric project will provide additional power to meet Alberta's expanding needs.

CALGARY POWER LTD.
· SERVING ALBERTA ·

The Spray Lakes development was an ambitious extension of Calgary Power's plan to master the Bow River. "In 1948, after the war and after the discovery of oil, the electrical load in the province continued to grow rapidly and the company was in a continuous state of expansion," explained Bert Howard of Calgary Power. "So we proceeded to the Spray Lakes development. The Mannix companies were involved in many aspects of that, mainly with the dams and canals and the roadways."

Located in the Continental Divide region, south and east of Banff, the project called for four dams, three power plants and a major storage basin of water. After constructing an access road, Mannix crews went on

◄ 1947

The discovery of a major new oil field occurs when the Imperial Leduc No. 1 well comes in. Vernon (Dry Hole) Hunter discovered the field in November 1946.

◄ 1947

Gabrielle Roy is the first Canadian to win a major French literary award. Her 1945 novel, Bonheur d'occasion, or The Tin Flute, wins the Prix Fémina.

"I'll Shoot You, Not Them"

During the mid-Forties, there was much talk of "rural electrification" as a key factor in raising the convenience standards of country folks to those of town dwellers. Electric utility companies did a great deal of work to extend lines into rural areas, and at reasonable rates, despite the costs

Prisoners at the internment camp at Kananaskis.

of installing mains for widely scattered users. Exemplifying this trend in Canada, Calgary Power built the Barrier Dam in 1945, largely to supply electricity to the farmers of southern Alberta at rates comparable to prices in the city. Dam construction was done by Fred Mannix & Company, Ltd., with a little help from some rather unusual neighbours, who lived less than a mile away.

"They had a prisoner of war camp there for German officers," Ernie Enarson recalled. "When we were surveying there, they decided they were going to do some clearing. They got an agreement with the fellows who were looking after the prisoners. They put it to the German fellows that if they went out and did some clearing, they would get extra rations. So they came out and they cut trees.

"One time this Canadian guard came out with about 20 or more of these German prisoners. When he got to where we were surveying, he dropped his gun on the ground, peeled his shirt off, and laid down and started to get a suntan. I said to him, 'Aren't you afraid that the fellows are going to get away?' He said, 'Oh, no. They have signed that they will come back. If they don't that means they can be shot on sight.' The guard also told me that the officers had this kind of honour, that if they signed to work and come back, they would come back. Then the guard said to me, 'If you go up to one of those prisoners, and if any trouble comes up, I'll shoot you, not them. I'm here to protect them.'"

to build the Spray Lakes Dam at the mouth of the Spray Canyon, the Three Sisters Dam at the north end of the reservoir and a series of dikes and canals. The main dam, Spray Lakes, called for a 640-foot (197-metre) crest length and 1,117,000 cubic yards (854,000 cubic metres) of rolled glacial till core, earth fill and graded gravel embankments. The secondary dam, Three Sisters, called for an earth-filled construction, 2,200 feet (670 metres) long by 48 feet (15 metres) high. These two dams would form a reservoir of 190,000 acre-feet capacity.

For Ben Kessler, who would serve the outfit for more than four decades, the Spray Lakes project was his introduction to Fred Mannix & Company, Ltd. "After college, I worked in a flour mill for a while,

The Spray Lakes project is located in the rugged Rocky Mountains south of Canmore, Alberta. Shown here is construction of the Goat Valley Canal.

1947 ▶

Radical changes to Canadian immigration law double the immigration quota for European displaced persons, remove restrictions to Chinese immigration (in place since 1923) and rescind the deportation of Japanese Canadians.

1948 ▶

In April, Mannix crews tackle the Yukon wilderness between Whitehorse and Mayo. They build the Klondike Highway. Supplies are brought in by boat.

but I didn't like it," said Kessler. "I felt like I was in a rut. So I packed my bag and came to Calgary to look for a job. And I got one with Calgary Power. That was in April of 1950. At that time, Mannix was doing the majority of the work at the Spray Lakes project above Canmore. It was a difficult job. Construction-wise, it was quite difficult. They had a lot of engineering things they had to overcome. There was the main dam at Spray Lakes, the Three Sisters Dam and then there were an awful lot of canals. That was the first time in my life I had seen that much snow. Every month, we had snow up there. It was on that project that I first met Karl Collett. I remember that he used to really scream at some of those guys. Yes, he could really scream, but he was respected quite well."

"Spray Lakes was a very large project for its time," said 25-year construction veteran Jack Bruce. "It started initially with the construction of Spray Lakes Dam. That was the one where Karl Collett made a name for himself by setting some records in dirt moving. Spray Lakes was an ideal location for that. Karl had a Euclid loader there and he put it to good advantage."

"He had been away from getting out on the job for a while," explained Leah Collett, "because he was busy bidding jobs and travelling from place to place. When they decided to build those dams up in the Three Sisters area, he wanted to do the work so bad that they let him. It was just like going back out onto the construction job, which he loved. We had a little cottage at the back of a mountain, where we were kind of right at the foot of the third peak, and I would go up once in

The engineering and office crews at the Collett steak fry during the Spray Lakes project.

This aerial view of the recently completed Spray Lakes project shows the reservoir behind the upper dam filling, on the bottom right. The outlet canal to the lower dam stretches toward the cleared area in the left centre; this will become the lower dam reservoir. The Goat Valley Canal winds away from the lower dam in the upper centre before turning right, north, for the drop down to the Rundle power plant in Canmore, Alberta.

a while. He just wanted me to be up there with him and let the rest of the world go by. Of course, this was impossible because he was gone all the time. He worked from daylight to 11, 12 o'clock at night. I'd never see him, and it was rough and rugged. But he loved doing that work."

"Karl Collett seemed rough and tough, but he was really soft-hearted," added Graham Pollock who joined the Mannix organization in 1948 as a purchasing agent. "There was just something about him that's hard to describe. He was a diamond in the rough. He called a spade a spade. He was just a very unsophisticated construction guy that you couldn't help but like. I remember the first time I went up to the site. I met Karl and he asked me what I did. I said I worked in the purchasing department. He said, 'That's fine. You send up a grader and a D-8 tractor and a sheep's foot roller.' Well, I didn't even know what the hell those things were. I went back to Calgary and told my boss, John Crombie. By God, the next day, they were on their way up there. When Karl spoke, things started to move."

"Spray Lakes was for Calgary Power," continued Pollock. "The Mannix company had a very good rapport with Calgary Power. Calgary Power's people preferred to deal with people that they could trust to do a good job. With these contracts, the Mannix people could go out and get the bigger and bigger equipment that was coming out at that time. In those days, Caterpillar Tractor started coming out with the big D-7s and the D-8s and motor scrapers. We used to buy all of that equipment through Kramer Tractor in Regina. So Mannix started to buy that

1948 ▶

After a disastrous flood, the outfit is hired to build the Eau Claire Dam to support the sawmill.

1948 ▶

Samuel Bronfman agrees to underwrite life insurance policies for Canadian pilots who volunteer to fight for Israeli independence.

"DON'T LOOK AROUND NOW, THERE'S A BEAR BEHIND YOU"

"The bears were really a nuisance at Barrier Dam," recalled Doris Reilly, who married Al in 1942. "The homes were made out of two-by-fours, with the boards on the outside. But they were very comfortable. It was a home. The bears came frequently. They'd even scratch at the window screens and anything that was sitting on the counter was knocked over. I used to like to bake after supper and our windows pulled in, with a screen on them, and Al said, 'Don't look around now, there's a bear behind you.' But he was generally kidding about something, so I thought, 'Oh, well, it couldn't be,' and I turned around and yes, Al was right. A large bear was standing there smelling the cookies.

"Another night, my sister was up visiting and we had canned an enormous amount of fruit. We had a root cellar on the outside of the house. The bears were around so frequently that Al said, 'Why don't you put the washtub on top of the root cellar door, then if the bear goes down, you'll be able to hear him.' It wasn't long after the lights were out and, bang, you could hear the door flick back and away went the tub. I ran outside in my nightgown with a gun. My sister said, 'Don't go out there, foolish person, you're going to be killed.' I could see the bear down there and he looked at me as much as to say, 'You'll never hit me.' Anyway, I shot. It was enough to make him turn around and run up the steps. I shot at him again and he trundled off down into the bush."

equipment to bring the cost of construction down. That was good, because, more and more, the kinds of projects that were being awarded involved moving large volumes of earth. And Mannix was among the first to explore the opportunities of using very big equipment. So the experience Mannix got working for Calgary Power, in using big equipment and realizing how it could bring the cost of operations down, allowed them to bid larger and larger contracts and still be pretty confident of what they could do cost-wise."

A Matter of Attitude — The Half-Full Glass

Although the relationship with Calgary Power was vital to the success of the Mannix Group, as in the past, the most important relationships were with the extended family that made up the outfit. Not the least of this group were the wives of the construction men, who always managed to make the best of any given situation. "I met Fred when I was going to university," Mary Fenwick recalled. "That was in 1949. In 1950, Fred and I were married. We got married on a Saturday afternoon at three, and Fred went back to work Monday morning.

"Fred felt that we should live in the town closest to the job. He felt that if it was possible to live in the town, it was a better thing for the town to see the company as participating in town activities and being part of it, so that the construction company wasn't looked upon as 'those people up there.' So, as a bride, I went to Canmore. We lived in a tourist accommodation. Fred told me it was a little cabin by the creek. It was a cabin about 10 by 12, with a bed and a potbelly stove in the middle of it, and a place where you could put in some appliances. I was a city girl and I didn't know a thing about potbelly stoves, so I had to learn, which was just great.

"When we got married, we were given all sorts of electrical appliances. Mr. Anderson, who ran the tourist facility, used to have a really bad time with me because I used to get up in the morning, and from the bed we could throw a match in the stove and get it started. Then I'd plug in the coffee pot and make the coffee. Then I would plug in the waffle/toaster iron and blow the fuse. So, I became known as the fuse breaker. We didn't have a fridge. I had read in my Girl Scout books that if you wanted a fridge you dug a hole in the ground and then you covered it and you could keep stuff in it. So that's what I did. I went out to the side of the house and I dug this hole and I put down an orange box and then I covered it, and I had my fridge and it was marvellous."

1948 ▶

The RCMP revive their Musical Ride because of popular demand. Shown is the charge.

1948 ▶

Barbara Ann Scott of Ottawa, the first Canadian to win the women's world figure skating championship, becomes the first Canadian to win the Olympic figure skating gold medal.

"But the thing I remember most is the shower cabin, or hut," continued Mrs. Fenwick. "In the winter we used to have to go in and turn the hot water on to melt the ice on the walls when we had our shower. When you tell people about it, they think you must have been out of your minds to live like that. But if you wanted a shower, it was the place you went to get your shower. The other thing was, the outhouse was out away from the cabin. The first week I was there the door had blown off. I had said, 'Oh, Fred!' And he said, 'Married people travel miles to come to this beautiful country and when you go to the biff you can just look out and see the gorgeous mountains.' So, I think the whole thing is a matter of attitude. Like the optimist or the pessimist, you can have either a glass that's half full or a glass that's half empty."

"I was introduced to the job in the Spray Lakes development at Canmore," continued Mrs. Fenwick. "Alfie Wright and Bus Pickard organized all the people in the camp to shivaree us when we were there. And when they left — after they filled our little cabin and were toasting our marriage — there were so many cars, one backed up and backed into the house and another one backed up into the truck. We were sure they were going to turn our cabin over. I said to Fred, 'What do we do now?' He said, 'Turn out the lights and they won't know they're our friends.' But that was the right thing to do, come down and have a party at the newcomer's place. Sort of initiate you into the company.

"Vi Wagar, whose husband was a Catskinner, was my next door neighbour at Canmore and she was just a delight. She came over right away, saying, 'Your husband is with the company now. You're not a city girl any longer.' That's one thing about the company, you always felt that there were people around you who were saying, 'Let's make this a really good situation.' That was very positive, and I think it's one of the things the whole Mannix family tried to introduce into the company, that it's a family. And because of that, we cared about each other. The first seven years we were married, we had 17 moves and I had three children, so I really didn't have much time to get bored."

As a bride, Mary Fenwick discovers her new home to be a one-room shack complete with outdoor plumbing and a pot-belly stove for heating and cooking.

During the first few years of her marriage, Mrs. Fenwick also completed her nursing degree and became a public health nurse. "When we moved into Forestburg, they were building a dam," she said. "The men worked from sunup until sundown. We had three small children. I was brought up in a very close family, so the children knowing their father was very important in my life. So I used to, believe it or not, get the kids up at three o'clock in the morning so they could have breakfast with their father before he went to work. You know, it was ridiculous, but you did it."

The Quebec North Shore and Labrador Railway

The new decade of the Fifties dawned fraught with tension as the world teetered on the brink of nuclear war. On June 25, 1950, North Korean troops invaded South Korea, pushing back the poorly equipped and demoralized South Korean army. As it appeared that a Communist victory was inevitable, American President Harry Truman appealed to the United Nations to raise a multinational force to halt the North Koreans. Only because the Soviet Union was boycotting the Security Council at the time of Truman's request was the United Nations able to agree to the proposal and begin to raise troops. Louis St. Laurent pledged a Canadian brigade of 6,000 men and an air division of 12 squadrons of fighter aircraft.

With the arrival of the United Nations forces, the North Korean army was routed in the autumn of 1950. The government of the People's Republic of China, however, was reluctant to see the military destruction of its ally. The Chinese intervened and launched a massive counteroffensive of their own across the Manchurian border. As the U.N. troops reeled backwards in retreat, many powerful members of the American military establishment recommended using nuclear weapons against the Chinese. Although cooler heads eventually prevailed, throughout the autumn and winter of 1950, the possibility of a confrontation between the United States and China haunted the imagination of a fearful world. And, of course, if the Americans attacked this crucial

1948 ▶

The first STOL (short takeoff and landing) aircraft, the Beaver, is designed by de Havilland Canada.

1948 ▶

Britain requires a referendum over what system of government will control Newfoundland. Confederation forces, led by Joseph R. Smallwood, win the day with Newfoundland becoming the tenth province on March 31, 1949.

THE $50-MILLION COIN FLIP

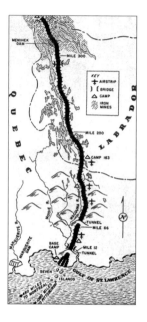

F.C. Mannix, Jim Pickard and Jim Scott (left to right) at the Quebec North Shore and Labrador Railway.

The Quebec North Shore and Labrador Railway was the kind of project that could make or break a company. Not surprisingly, there was some difference of opinion whether Fred Mannix & Company, Ltd. should bid on the job. Many old-timers recalled that the last big job in the East — Val-d'Or — was a mixed blessing. In addition, the company had recently just barely survived a bankruptcy situation on the Hart Highway job. For some, it may have seemed like a case of jumping from the frying pan of British Columbia into the fire of Eastern Canada.

Igors Silgailis, who headed the Mannix move into international construction projects in the late 1950s, remembers an anecdote that describes how the debate surrounding the Sept-Îles bid was resolved. "As the story goes," he said, "we had to decide if we would bid on the job on the Quebec and North Shore Railway. If we decided to go in, the bid would be about $50 million. That would make it the biggest bid the Mannix company ever put in. Normally, our procedure was to take a vote as to whether we would bid. On that particular job, three people voted for it and three against. It came Fred C. Mannix's turn to vote. Fred turned around to Phil Soukup, our general manager of construction. 'Phil,' he says, 'flip a coin for 50 million bucks. Let's see whether we go or not.' Phil flips the coin. It was tails. Fred says, 'Well, we bid.'

"Fred walked out of the room and said, 'I didn't give a damn whether it was heads or tails. We were going to go.' That was his character. He was going to bid. That was part of his quality of being able to inspire and lead. He was able to create a type of spirit and enthusiasm in a lot of people. He certainly inspired it in me."

ally of the Soviet Union, there was the high probability that the Russians would also enter the widening conflict.

As the Cold War loomed on the horizon, people went about their daily lives. At home, it was a time of pronounced economic growth for both Canada and the United States. The late 1940s and early 1950s marked America's predominance as the richest nation in the world. During these years, the United States produced over half of the world's manufactured goods, generated more than 40 per cent of the world's electricity, and pumped over 60 per cent of the world's oil. With a surplus of capital to invest in foreign nations, American investment in Canada rose dramatically. For example, net direct American investment in Canada rose from $84 million in 1949 to $200 million in 1950.

A sketch of the Quebec North Shore and Labrador Railway (QNS&L) project showing some of the camps, structures, dams and tunnels along the 360-mile (580-kilometre) right-of-way.

Alfie Wright, Jim Scott, Fred Mannix and Jim Pickard (from left) examine the cribbing during the early construction of the Menihek Dam in Labrador.

1948 ▶

Following the drought of the Depression years, the West practically drowns in rain and snow. Homeless total over 11,500.

1948 ▶

W.L.M. King, 74, on right, retires as Canada's longest-serving prime minister. Louis St. Laurent, left, is chosen to replace him at the Liberal party convention in Ottawa.

As a result of American investment in Canada, Fred Mannix & Company, Ltd. was awarded the largest contract, and perhaps the biggest challenge, in the history of the company to date — the development of a huge iron ore mining complex in Labrador for the Iron Ore Company of Canada.

The story of the fabled Quebec North Shore and Labrador Railway (QNS&L) began in the 1930s. At that time, Dr. J.A. Retty, a geologist employed by the Labrador Mining and Exploration Company, mapped a rich iron ore deposit in a 22,000-acre (8,900-hectare) area. This deposit, which was discovered near Knob Lake, on the border of Quebec and Labrador, was estimated to contain more than 441 million tons (400 million tonnes) of ore. It lay in desolate country, hundreds of miles from the faintest vestige of civilization. From the first, it was obvious that a railway was the only economical way to move in the equipment needed to build mining facilities and then to bring the iron ore out. This railway would run more than 300 miles (483 kilometres) from Knob Lake to a natural harbour on the St. Lawrence at Sept-Îles (or Seven Islands in English).

In 1942, Jules Timmins, head of Hollinger Consolidated Gold Mines acquired Labrador Mining, but lacked sufficient capital to fund development of the deposit. For the next seven years, Timmins sought to create a working partnership with the magnates of the American steel industry. In 1949, he achieved his goal. That year, the Iron Ore Company of Canada was formed to build, own and operate the mining facilities to work this enormous deposit. Joining the Hollinger

L.B. (Lou) Franco.

Winter conditions in camp, 1951, on the QNS&L Railway; bone-chilling cold with blowing snow.

Loading a Caterpillar scraper during the airlift of supplies for the QNS&L Railway. The partially deflated tires allow the machine to fit in the plane.

Consolidated Gold Mines were M.A. Hanna Company of Cleveland, Ohio, and five other American steel companies: Republic, National, Armco, Youngstown and Wheeling Steel. As these companies formed the backbone of the United States steel industry, the newly created Iron Ore Company of Canada could easily underwrite the project.

Fred Mannix & Company, Ltd. handled a considerable portion of this work, including the two main dams for the project's hydroelectric generating station, the ore loading and dock facilities on the St. Lawrence River, and the Quebec North Shore and Labrador Railway, the 360-mile (580-kilometre) line connecting the mines with the seaway.

Like many of the projects the Mannix company would undertake in the 1950s, this was a job of massive proportions. The new railway was not only the largest railway construction job in Canada in a decade; it was also part of what was by far the largest construction project of any kind in all of North America in the early 1950s, one that would involve the biggest airlift of men and machinery ever undertaken in the history of construction on this continent.

The entire construction project included several mines and related infrastructures, hydroelectric dams for power, a small town and the railway with docking and loading facilities for ships at Sept-Îles. Mannix sponsored the joint venture, which consisted of Cartier Construction, McNamara Construction, Morrison-Knudsen of Canada and Fred Mannix & Company, Ltd. The total project price tag was more than half a billion dollars. "That Quebec North Shore job was the biggest one in the history of the company,"

1948 ▶

Calgary Stampeders beat the Ottawa Rough Riders 12-7 to win the Grey Cup.

1949 ▶

The Mannix outfit builds the Spray Lakes project in an area previously surveyed by a Mannix crew in 1942. Two earth-filled dams are constructed.

FEAR OF FLYING

When F.C. Mannix talked to Lou Franco about joining the outfit as project director for the Quebec North Shore and Labrador Railway, although Mannix's enthusiasm was contagious, Franco still had some reservation about the project. "After a full day of discussion, I told Fred I'd go back home and let him know," Franco said. "But Fred said, 'No, you'll let me know now.' After dinner and a couple of drinks, I said, 'All right, I'll take the job, but I won't ride an airplane to Seven Islands.'

"'Oh,' Fred says, 'there are ships from Montreal to Seven Islands almost every day. You can get one of those.'" Reassured on that point, Franco went back to Kansas City to resign from his old job and tie up loose ends. Then he drove back north to Montreal to get the ship to Sept-Îles that F.C. Mannix had told him about. "I found out that was just sales talk," Franco said. "There were no ships to Seven Islands because the Gulf of St. Lawrence was frozen."

Franco, who absolutely loathed flying, had no choice but to take the plane. Before he boarded the Mannix company's Lodestar, however, he took certain precautionary measures. "When it got time to go to the airport, I got so nervous I didn't think I could even drive my car," Franco said. "So I went and bought a bottle of whisky, and I got about half lit up before I got on the plane." If whisky helped Franco get on the plane, it also helped get him off. "When we got to Seven Islands, there was a delegation there to meet us including Mr. Pickard and several people from Cartier Mining and Morrison-Knudsen," Franco recalled. "As I stepped out of the plane onto this little step, I fell flat on my face into a snowdrift. It was an embarrassing introduction to the group."

recalled Everett Costello. "It involved $56 million. We were partners with J.V. Cartier, McNamara and Morrison-Knudsen. Cartier and McNamara were kind of like blood brothers even though they were separate companies. Cartier was our French connection on that one. They enabled us to overcome the politics and get into that country."

Fred Mannix & Company, Ltd. began work on this historic railway in 1950. Karl Collett was the first project manager. As Collett's expertise was in the field of heavy earthmoving work, the company searched for a project manager with more railway construction experience. Dick Stein suggested a person he felt would be ideal for the job. This was Stein's brother-in-law, Lou Franco, who had extensive experience in both track maintenance and railway construction.

Lou Franco has been known to joke about being born in a boxcar, which is not far from the truth. Franco was born in a Great Northern Railroad section house in Kalispell, Montana, in 1914. The son of a railroad man, Franco did not wait long before getting into the business himself. At the age of 12, he quit school to work as a water boy for a 60-man Mexican railroad crew. Franco became so fluent in Spanish that during World War II he was sent to Mexico to recruit Mexican nationals for track labour in the United States. By that time, Franco was working for the Spokane Portland & Seattle Railroad (SP&S), where he rose through the ranks to become general road master for the entire system. After leaving SP&S, Franco worked as division road master for the Great Northern Railroad and then moved into the field of railroad construction. In 1947, as general superintendent with Brown & Root, the well-known engineering and construction firm, he managed a crew of hundreds rehabilitating the Alaska Railroad from Seward to Fairbanks. Franco then served as project manager on an SP&S line change at the McNary Dam in Washington. In 1950, Franco was in Kansas City, Missouri, supervising the building of a railway line into a new Ford plant.

Mannix asked Stein to call Franco in Kansas City to see if he might be interested in coming to Quebec to supervise the track laying for the QNS&L Railway. Following Stein's phone call, Franco, who liked his job, reluctantly agreed to meet F.C. Mannix and Jim Pickard, the Mannix project director in Sept-Îles. When Franco arrived for his all-day interview in Toronto, he had pretty much decided that he was not going to leave Kansas City for Sept-Îles. "The job was in cold country, it was isolated, and although there was a school for my daughter, there was none for my teenage son," Franco said. "As Fred was talking, I was thinking, 'What am I even doing sitting here?' But the longer Fred talked,

1949 ▶

Impounded Spray Lakes reservoir water runs through the Mannix-built Goat Valley Dam and Goat Valley dike system before entering penstocks for the drop down to the Canmore powerhouse.

1949 ▶

A Canadair North Star completes the first nonstop flight across Canada.

the more I liked him and the more he made the job sound like a big adventure. Fred was quite a salesman. He said that it was the biggest job at that time in North America, and that it would be quite an accomplishment to finish it in the allotted time. He made it sound challenging to make the 1954 deadline. I felt he was telling me, 'Gee, this is no piece of cake, but I think you can do it.' I thought so, too!"

Sept-Îles did, indeed, turn out to be quite an adventure. "Seven Islands ran for 365 miles over the toughest country in the world," recalled Dan (Frenchy) Hamilton, one of several supervisors Franco brought with him to Sept-Îles. "If it wasn't muskeg, it was rock. We had to build a lot of grade in the wintertime when it was 50 below and the muskeg was frozen. It was really tough to build."

"We also had problems with supplies," said Franco. "We had to have an air force to bring them in. We had DC-3's stationed at Mont-Joli. We also had a Flying Boxcar and a couple of helicopters. It was kind of amusing because people at that time were making such a big deal about the Berlin Airlift. The air force that Mannix had at the town of Mont-Joli was flying almost as much tonnage every day under a lot more trying conditions. They had no navigational aids or anything. They were just flying by the seat of their pants and not always in the best weather either. And they never lost an aircraft." By way of comparison, the Berlin Airlift, which airlifted supplies to an occupied Berlin at the end of the Second World War, flew in more than 2.3 million tons (2.1 million tonnes) of relief supplies.

"Of course, Mont-Joli was hardly a city," added Franco. "There were only two or three cars in the whole place. The chuckholes in the street were so deep that it

Top: Aerial view of the right-of-way near Mile 7, QNS&L Railway.

Above: Fuel drums are loaded for delivery along the QNS&L Railway.

was a wonder the cars could even get through. But there was no place to go anyway. You could go from the Sept-Îles hotel to the airport or to our camp. The hotel had a yacht club and quite a nice bar and dining room. So, if you were going out for a big night on the town, you went to the yacht club. And that was about it. But the company went to great lengths to make things as comfortable as possible for the people who worked there. They built a base camp. It had a monstrous kitchen that served about 800 men. They served six meals a day. They also had a 21-bed hospital. There was a separate barracks for the 80 women who worked in the office and a separate camp for all the married people. I think it had about 22 houses in it. Those houses had steam heat in them. They also built a little clubhouse at the married quarters. They called it the 'Rinkydink Club.' The women used to go there and wrap bandages for the hospital."

While the company went to great lengths to ensure that its workers were as comfortable as possible, Sept-Îles was not a very hospitable place. "On that job, you got more experience out of it than all the other ones combined," said James Welch. "The environment was really rough. It was cold in the wintertime; it got down to as much as 40 below. In the summertime, the moment it quit freezing, the black flies would be out and the mosquitoes were just terrible. You could see a crew working, and as you came toward them, you would see this black cloud over them. It would be black flies. They would just crawl out of the muskeg by the millions. Oh, they would bite."

Despite adverse conditions, within six months, Franco had the railway construction well organized and running smoothly. "All through that job, Fred Mannix was great, really great," said Franco. "That's what kept

1949 ▶

Avro Canada Ltd. is the first North American company to fly a four-engine jetliner. It is designed to carry 50 passengers.

1949 ▶

Alberta rural road construction continues with road grade built around Diamond City in southern Alberta and Stettler in central Alberta.

"No, You Haven't Quit"

After six months at Sept-Îles, Lou Franco decided to leave the Mannix organization. The problem was that when Franco tried to fire a man, it was quickly pointed out that Franco could not fire the man because he worked for Morrison-Knudsen. Franco's response was equally quick. "I said that if I couldn't fire the man, I couldn't work there," he said. "I left and went down to the dock where a ship with 3,500 tons of piling had come down from Montreal. I asked the captain, 'How are chances of getting a ride for my family, my car and myself back to Montreal?' He said it was fine if I could be packed and ready in less than two hours." Franco made the deadline. From Montreal, he returned to the United States, where he lined up a job in Pennsylvania.

Although Franco's association with the Mannix company appeared to have ended, F.C. Mannix had other ideas. A little over a week after his abrupt departure from Sept-Îles, Franco received a phone call. "I had just started my new job. We were staying in a hotel, when the phone rang and it was Fred Mannix," Franco related. "Fred said, 'What are you doing in Pennsylvania?' I said, 'I quit. I've got another job.' Fred said, 'No, you haven't quit. I'll be in Toronto next week, and I want you to come there.'"

At their meeting in Toronto, Mannix surprised Franco when he did not try to persuade Franco to return and finish the railroad in Quebec. Mannix wanted Franco to set up a separate railroad division for the Mannix company. Franco decided to take the offer. By persuading Franco to stay with the outfit, F.C. Mannix set into motion the chain of events that would ultimately lead to the formation of Loram Maintenance of Way, Inc.

me there. He was appreciative of anything you did. He was really wise about the work. He knew what you were doing, so it was easy to talk to him. And I enjoyed him as a person; it wasn't just because he was the boss."

When Franco left to set up the Mannix Railroad Division, Jim Pickard replaced him as project manager. The QNS&L Railway was completed by the Mannix company on schedule in 1954. Railway historians regard the line as precedent-setting, a unique railway compared to all others built previously. The design introduced a revolutionary concept to railroading. Built as common carriers, the majority of the world's railways carried whatever passenger or freight traffic was available, whenever offered. The QNS&L Railway was different. It was conceived as a single-purpose line, dedicated to a single captive market. It was like a 360-mile (580-kilometre) conveyer belt, part of a continuously operating production unit. While small single-purpose railways had been built in the past, nothing previously attempted was remotely close to the scale of the QNS&L Railway.

The tunnel through solid rock at Mile 12 of the QNS&L Railway.

Immediately after the tunnel at Mile 12, a bridge crossing the Moisie River is required.

◀ **1949**

Ballast, rail rehabilitation and tunnel projects for the CPR occur in Alberta, British Columbia and Saskatchewan.

◀ **1949**

The Mannix-O'Sullivan joint venture builds two airports and works on several highway projects in Alberta.

"And that's how Fred Mannix got started in the pipeline business."

By the 1950s, there was a growing demand for petroleum products by both Canadian and American industry and consumers. Never one to miss an opportunity to branch out into new areas of expertise, Fred Mannix & Company, Ltd. entered the burgeoning field of pipeline construction with both feet. In 1950, the company began work on the Montreal pipeline, the Winnipeg pipeline and the celebrated Interprovincial pipeline.

The Interprovincial pipeline was undertaken by a consortium of Canadian and American construction firms, under the sponsorship of the Bechtel Corporation. Fred Mannix & Company, Ltd. took the contract to build the 439-mile (706-kilometre) section from Edmonton to Regina. Although the route ran through comparatively flat sections of the Canadian Prairies, it necessitated more than 1,100 highway, railway and river crossings.

"After the war, one of our bigger jobs was the Interprovincial pipeline," recalled Brock Montgomery. "We had done a few pipeline jobs before that, but that was the first large-sized one." In building its portion of the pipeline, the Mannix organization had to face two major challenges. The first was the lack of Canadian expertise in the field of pipeline construction. Accordingly, the company recruited a number of American pipeliners to provide guidance and on-the-job training. The second was the weather. In June, the rains began and never seemed to stop. By fall, the early snows fell with unprecedented depth and severity. Neither of these obstacles proved insurmountable, however. For one thing, Mannix crews were used to battling the elements. For another, they were about to teach the Americans a thing or two.

Mannix pipeliners break into the pipelining business on the Interprovincial pipeline. Here a D-8 Cat with a side boom lowers pipe in the Prairies.

Pete Swityk joined Fred Mannix & Company, Ltd.'s accounting department in 1949. "I started out at $150 a month and I soon got a raise from Eric Connelly, who was then the controller, to $165," he recalled. "As far as head office was concerned, we worked 48 hours a week. That was the standard. We worked all day Saturday. Later on, we did get alternate Saturday afternoons off. Then we went down to a 44-hour week and that was really great. We thought we really had things good."

"In March 1950, Karl Collett told me I was going on the Interprovincial pipeline main line 'Big Inch' project," Swityk said. "Mannix had a joint venture with Sparling-Davis, which was owned by Joe Sparling and Eddie Davis. The project was a 16-inch pipeline from Edmonton over to Hughenden, the first leg of the pipeline to Superior, Wisconsin. The engineers were Bechtel, out of San Francisco. I went to Edmonton to help set up a project office. Jack Beaman was the construction superintendent. He was a real 'you-all' kind of guy from Oklahoma or Kansas. I reported to the office manager, Glenn Umbarger, who was from Bartlesville, Oklahoma.

"We moved out to the project site in Hardisty and rented an office. Prior to kickoff day the crews started coming in. Almost everybody came in from the States — Kansas, Oklahoma, New Mexico and Texas. There were people here who could have done some of this work, but the pipeliners already had their experienced crews together. We didn't have the type of experience required because no Canadian company had ever built a pipeline of that type and size before, so we had to bring these people in. They even brought in a utility welder, which is someone who just welds tracks, builds bucket teeth and normal steel things — not specific to pipelines only. But even he had to know what had to be done on that kind of job without being told and shown everything. Except for the labourers and clearing, grading and cleanup crews, they were pretty well all Americans.

1950 ►

The Korean War begins. Twenty-seven thousand Canadians will ultimately serve in this conflict. More than 1,600 are killed or wounded.

1950 ►

Canada agrees to pay $1,222,829 to Japanese and Canadians of Japanese ancestry forced from their West Coast homes during World War II.

Then we started bringing some Canadians into pipe-lining, like Charlie Broughton and Jim Cunningham. We picked them up right in Hardisty, and they became pipeliners in the truest sense. Some of them ended up in senior positions with different pipeline companies in Canada as a result."

The driving force behind giving Canadians experience in pipelining was Fred C. Mannix. "There were no large-scale pipelines being built in Canada at that time, but Mannix was determined that we were going to learn how to put in pipelines," said Frank O'Sullivan. "He formed a joint venture with Bechtel, called Bechtel-Mannix, to build the first 450 miles. Bechtel designed it and Mannix built it. Fred, always looking ahead, was determined that he would have Canadian people build it. We might have Americans to start, but we were certainly going to have Canadians do it the next time around. So he wanted to get me on the project and he wanted me to do the stringing."

"Bill Pyott was the chief engineer for Mannix at that time," continued O'Sullivan. "He was a big Texan. Fred said to him, 'I want Frank O'Sullivan to string the pipe on this pipeline.' Bill said, 'Fred, we can't afford to have a Canadian on that. They've got to be Americans because they know how to do it.' Fred said, 'There are three sections to this job. It's 160 miles from Edmonton to Hardisty. From Hardisty, it's another 160 miles to Rosetown. From there, it's about 160 more to Regina. Let's put Frank in the centre section. If he falls down, we'll have the other crews move in and take over.' So I went to Rosetown and picked up my crew.

"Rosetown is about in the centre of Saskatchewan. It was also in the centre of our 450-mile stretch of pipeline. When I got there, it was incredibly cold on the Prairies. If you weren't there, you couldn't possibly understand how cold it could get. In that area, four or five people froze to death. They had to leave their cars and try to find a deserted farmhouse or something and they just didn't make

Northwest of Rosetown, Saskatchewan, Mannix welders connect two sections of the Interprovincial pipeline.

When temperatures climb to 40 below, Frank O'Sullivan sends his crews out to complete their section of the Interprovincial pipeline.

it. I had roughly 200 railroad cars of pipe on the track there in Rosetown. We started to unload the pipe, but it was just too cold to work. One day it got down to 56 degrees below zero, and the cold wind was blowing from the Arctic. When you're on the prairie, there's just nothing to stop that wind. So I made a ruling that when it got up to 40 below and there was no wind, we'd start unloading. Every morning, I would go to the station agent at the railroad to find out what the temperature was — 56 below or 48 below or whatever it was. Then I'd go back to the hotel, have my break-fast, and let the boys sleep in. One day, I got a call from Bill Pyott. He said, 'Frank, you're not unloading any pipe.' I said, 'Bill, we can't do it. If it warms up to 40 below zero, we'll unload it. But right now, we just can't face it. We're all freezing.' As soon as it rose above 40 below, we started unloading pipe."

"People thought we would encounter prob-lems because this was our first time stringing pipeline," said O'Sullivan. "But as someone once said, 'I don't want educated men working for me because they spend their time telling you why a thing can't be done. I want fellows who don't know that the thing can't be done and then go ahead and do it.' So that's how we proceeded. We just used our common sense. For example, here's one thing that we changed. The pipe was 40 feet in length. It was tak-ing too many men to put a hook on each end of the pipe, so we made a set of pipe tongs. We had a welder in Rosetown make us a pair of tongs we could use to grab the pipe in the centre and pick it up with fewer men. Hauling pipe was another instance. Because we hadn't done it before, we didn't know any bad habits. We got trucks with dollies on them and we had pole trailers. We'd hook the trailers on behind. We also had one Lynn half-track. It was an American-made machine. It had wheels on the front and tracks on the back and it could go over practi-cally any terrain. We put an eight-wheel trailer

1950 ▶

In a joint venture known as Bechtel-Mannix, Mannix crews build the Interprovincial pipeline from Hardisty, Alberta, to Regina, Saskatchewan.

1950 ▶

The first heart pacemaker is developed. Dr. Jack Hopps of Canada's National Research Council designs a circuit that supplies a gentle electric stimulus to the heart muscle without causing injury.

The Lynn half-track pulling the dope pot, the coating used on the Interprovincial pipeline.

behind that. We found we could put a whole carload of pipe on that and it could go practically anywhere."

"Eventually, we ended up helping the Americans string pipe when they fell behind," O'Sullivan said. "We made a name for ourselves on that one. When we finished the job, Bill Pyott came down to me and said, 'Frank, when I'm right, I'm right, and when I'm wrong I'm the first person to admit it. You showed us how to string pipe. We've never strung pipeline like that before.' So we felt that we had won quite a victory. From then on, when the next contract came along, there were more and more Canadians on our crews until we didn't need the Americans anymore. And that's how Fred Mannix got started in the pipeline business."

Bringing The Outfit Home

With all the tremendous growth Fred Mannix & Company, Ltd. experienced during the Morrison-Knudsen years, as in the past, the bedrock of the organization continued to be the business principle that F.C. Mannix learned from his father. "Fred's father developed a philosophy that stood through my period in the organization," Eric Connelly said. "One thing that was a cornerstone was that even if you walked off the job with just a packsack on your back, you'd do good work. I was very proud of the way that Fred himself reacted to this philosophy because at no time did instructions ever go out that there were to be any shortcuts as far as the work was concerned." With characteristic simplicity, F.C. Mannix summed up the most important lesson he learned from his father in this way, "My father taught us that integrity in business was the way you did things."

His father could not have chosen a better organization than M-K to complete F.C. Mannix's apprenticeship. "Harry Morrison took Fred C. under his wing," said Allan Francis (Chip) Collins, who joined the Mannix outfit in 1950 as office manager in the head office. "Morrison didn't have any sons of his own and he more or less adopted F.C. as his son. I think he enjoyed teaching him the construction ropes. He taught him how to bid on the big jobs."

Despite the benefits of the Mannix outfit's ties to Morrison-Knudsen, Frederick Charles Mannix was very much his own man. "Fred Mannix would have no part of any outside control on a long-term basis," Collins said. "It just wasn't in his nature. He bought back his company at the very first moment he had 20 cents that he could use in that direction." By 1951, Fred Mannix was ready to bring full ownership of the outfit home to Canada.

"A FRONTIER OF ADVENTURE"

"I've always been amazed at the calibre of men that worked for Mannix, because they always developed this aura about them," reflected Mary Fenwick. "I think part of it was that construction was a frontier of adventure for men. And it was exciting. I remember in Spray Lakes when they wanted to build a road up. Everybody said, 'No, you can't do that. It's impossible.' And Alfie Wright said, 'I sure as hell can.' And the company encouraged that. If they saw men who had that pizzazz and that aura of adventure about them, they encouraged them, and that really does something to your psyche.

"Today we have computer challenges and outer space challenges and that, but I don't think they're quite as down-to-earth as some of the challenges that the pioneers had. How do you build a road, how do you invent road-building equipment? They'd say to the fellows, 'Well, you're the engineer, you do it.' I think the challenge was there."

When you drive south from Canmore, Alberta, up the steep twisting road to the Spray Lakes Dam and Reservoir, you travel up much of the road cut out of the cliffs by Mannix engineer, Alfie Wright, and his Cat.

1950 ▶

Rail work continues near Rosemary with the repair of the Rosemary trestle.

1950 ▶

Branching into hydroelectric development in Ontario, the outfit, in a joint venture with The Foundation Co. of Canada, builds the Fanshawe Dam for the Upper Thames River Conservation Authority, Ontario Hydroelectric Commission.

THE FLYING CIRCUS
AND THE
BUILDING OF MODERN CANADA
1951 – 1956

*F.C. Mannix was a remarkable person. He was very dynamic, very creative. He went after
a lot of good people and he had a lot of good people. If he didn't pick the right person, he had no qualms about
getting rid of him. Bang. If you worked for Mannix, you produced — there was no question about that.*

*F.C. had lots of energy, lots of ideas, and he always wanted everything done yesterday.
Back in the Fifties, the people with him called themselves "The Flying Circus" because they never knew where they
were going to be. That's the way Fred worked. You can criticize it, but he was successful. It's amazing how many
things you come across over the years and suddenly find that it either belongs to Mannix or he had a major say in it.
Because he was such a dynamic person, he accomplished so much. He did a lot for the community and the country.*

— L.A. (Chick) Thorssen, member, Order of Canada

*Left: The Mannix Lodestar, TDI,
over Mount Robson, British Columbia.*

*Right: Lester B. Pearson, left, is awarded
the Nobel Peace Prize for his continued
efforts for world peace.*

Often, the changing course of history is marked by a single symbolic act. For Canada, such an event occurred in the early years of the 1950s. In February 1952, Vincent Massey was named Governor General. As Canada's first native-born Governor General, Massey filled the role with distinction and in a manner that minimized the break with the past that the appointment of a Canadian represented.

Although mid-century brought great strides in politics, technology, medicine and engineering, it brought the world no peace. The Fifties was the time of Cold War. The Second World War, and the conflicts and coups that followed, had redrawn the maps of Europe and Asia. The result was that the eastern half of Europe and much of Asia was under Communist rule. Communism at mid-century dominated 850 million people, compared with

188 million before World War II. This central reality of mid-century world politics was in spite of the fact that Communists had not won a majority in any free election.

Again and again, events provided new grounds for fear of a world-conquering Communist movement. During this time of international strife, a generation of postwar Canadian statesmen worked as mediators of international disputes. From Korea to Vietnam to Egypt, Canada — not overwhelmed with the passion for confrontation and ideological conflict that characterized much of the Cold War — worked for peace in a spirit of negotiation and compromise.

In Korea — a nation divided in half at the 38th parallel since 1945, with U.S. interests controlling the south and Soviet interests controlling the north — the Canadian presence extended from the fighting fronts to the conference rooms of the armistice negotiations. In 1950, the Canadian government had decided to contribute a Canadian Army unit to assist the forces of the United Nations in that troubled land. In the government's view, Canada would fight not for Korea, but for the United Nations and the principle of collective security. During the war, Canadian diplomats sought to "constrain" the American decision-makers from risky actions. These diplomats worked with zeal and skill in both the United Nations corridors and Washington offices to advance arguments for a negotiated peace. In 1952, Canada's Lester B. Pearson was named president of the General Assembly of the United Nations, a post he used to further his quest for a peaceful resolution of the conflict.

Canada also worked for peace in strife-torn Indochina. When the French lost Vietnam in 1954, the one-time French colony was divided into a Communist north and a non-Communist independent south. Following the French defeat, Canada, along with India and Poland, was appointed to a three-member International Control Commission. This commission, which supervised the implementation of the armistice between the withdrawing French army and the forces of Ho Chi Minh, helped minimize further bloodshed.

Even as hostilities were ending in Indochina, the Suez Crisis threatened to escalate into another major East-West confrontation. In November 1956, a combined Anglo-French force landed in Egypt to prevent Gamal Nasser from nationalizing the Suez Canal, an action which immediately polarized the world community. As secretary of state for external affairs, Lester Pearson called for an international emergency unit to be sent to the Suez Canal to help find a peaceful solution among hostile British, French, Israeli and Egyptian forces in the area. Under the command of Canadian General Eedson L.M. Burns, the first United Nations peacekeeping force supervised the Middle East ceasefire. For his role in defusing the Suez Crisis, Lester Pearson became the first Canadian to win the Nobel Peace Prize.

But mid-century was not just about the Cold War, with its civil defence exercises and fallout shelters. The Fifties was about rock and roll, radio, television and tail fins on cars. For Alberta, the Fifties was the beginning of the oil and gas age. The first oil well at Leduc had started a boom that transformed Alberta into something far beyond the most lofty dreams of its pioneers. It was a time of change, of new beginnings, new opportunities. One of the biggest aspects of this change was the revolution in construction thinking. In the Fifties, there was almost no project too big to tackle and no reasonable limit to reshaping the earth to make it more productive. It was time for Fred C. Mannix to bring full ownership of his outfit home to Canada.

"An absolute turning point in the history of the company"

In many ways, and in many people's eyes, it was inevitable that F.C. Mannix would one day buy back M-K's controlling interest in Fred Mannix & Company, Ltd. "Fred could never have been happy staying under Morrison-Knudsen," Frank O'Sullivan said. "He had to run his own show. He had this bright star in his eye and he was going to go on his own, period. He decided to do it even though Harry Morrison thought the world of Fred. And we were all behind him."

George Eckenfelder also remembers F.C. Mannix's determination to be his own man. "After I was discharged from the army, I went directly to work for Calgary Power on the Barrier Dam," he recalled. "Mannix had the general contract on that one. At that time, Mannix was in the hands of Morrison-Knudsen. Fred C. Mannix was very active in the company. You could see that it was his ambition to recapture control. That was one of the first things that struck me about Fred — his determination to recapture control of his father's company."

"The big problem, what triggered the breakup between Mannix and M-K, was that M-K had a large interest in Northern Construction, another heavy equipment outfit, based in British Columbia," explained W.F. (Bill) Sharon, then chief engineer for Sparling-Davis Company Ltd. "The suspicion grew that they would both be bidding on the same jobs,

1951 ▶

The outfit begins Kenney Dam, the largest rock-filled dam in the British Commonwealth. It is constructed on British Columbia's Nechako River for the Aluminum Company of Canada, Limited.

1951 ▶

Because of the remote location, float planes are purchased to bring in personnel and material to the Kenney Dam construction site.

and Mannix wouldn't know it. Then Fred and a fellow by the name of Jack Bonny, who was the general manager, the chief operating honcho at M-K at that time, didn't like one another at all. Now, I think that old Mr. Morrison wanted Fred to move down to the States and take over M-K, and Jack Bonny wasn't happy about that. So there were some real hard feelings between those two."

"When M-K bought Northern Construction, they wanted me to go in and have 49 per cent of that, and I wouldn't do it," added F.C. Mannix. "So Morrison-Knudsen had the controlling interest in that company and the Mannix company. Then I told Mr. Morrison that I'd like to buy him out because of a contract in Ontario. We were supposed to have 10 per cent of the tunnels down at Niagara Falls, but they took five per cent and only gave me five per cent. I had a good financial man at that time, a fellow by the name of Connelly, who looked after the financial end of it. By 1951, they were all wound out, and I got the other 51 per cent. I think it was 10 years that we had to pay off, but, in any event, I paid it off as soon as I could."

Eric Connelly explained how he set up the deal. "At the time of the actual buyback, Morrison-Knudsen was also operating the Northern Construction Company in Canada," he said. "Northern was always trying to take our customers away from us. It was a slight irritation, perhaps not a serious one, but a slight irritation all the time. Fred wanted to stop this irritation. He wanted to get control of his own company again. He felt he could expand all over the world on his own — either in competition or association with M-K. Of course, there was no personal animosity there. Mr. Morrison was always trying to smooth the waters between the people in Boise and us. But still, this matter of Northern Construction would come up, one way or another, every time we went back to M-K headquarters."

"Finally, I hit upon a scheme," Connelly said. "In particular, the timing was absolutely right for my idea.

After 1949, capital profits were not taxable in Canada. After that date, depreciation was also calculated a different way on your equipment. So if you had taken depreciation and the equipment was sold at a higher price than was on the books, the difference had to be taken back into income. So here is what I suggested. Fred Mannix only owned 49 per cent of the old Mannix construction company. We then organized another company which was Fred's entirely. This was Mannix Ltd. Then we went ahead and sold all the equipment from the old construction company to Mannix Ltd. We actually reversed all the depreciation entries so that there was no recapturing depreciation. We had all the equipment valued at about three or four times what we paid for it and that was sold over to the new Mannix company. We could do this because Fred Mannix did not have control of the original company; Morrison-Knudsen did. But Fred did have the second company. So they sold it all over and that meant there was a capital profit, of substantial size, left on the books of the original Mannix construction company. Both Mannix and M-K shared on that capital profit on a 49 and 51 per cent basis."

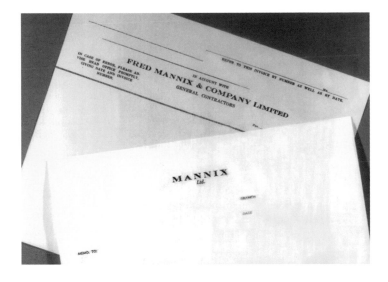

In March 1951, Fred C. Mannix begins to buy back Morrison-Knudsen's controlling interest in Fred Mannix & Company, Ltd. Mannix Ltd. becomes the new Canadian company.

"As a result of this, Mannix sold his share in the old company for his share of the marked-up price, which was all tax-free," continued Connelly. "The net result of this was that Mannix had the new company and all the equipment of the old company. Finally, what Mannix owed M-K, in effect, was just the amount for his share of the increased value of the equipment and the profit earned to date which wasn't very great. The net effect of

1951 ▶

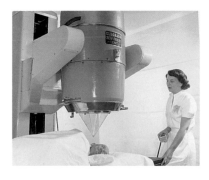

The world's first cancer-fighting Cobalt radiotherapy unit, developed in Canada, is installed at Victoria Hospital in London, Ontario.

1951 ▶

Mannix Ltd. begins the earth-filled, hydroelectric Chutes des Georges Dam located on the Shipshaw River north of Chicoutimi, Quebec.

this whole exercise was good for all the parties concerned. Morrison-Knudsen made a fairly substantial profit for those days. I think it was around $3 million. The federal government, through its depreciation, was able to pay for that full $3 million because we had set the equipment up to a higher price and then depreciated it against our profit. So that money flowed back into Mannix Ltd. without any tax and Fred Mannix had the cash available to pay off Morrison-Knudsen. In effect, Fred was able to regain control of his company for nothing. Oh, it did take another 10 years to totally pay off the debt. But we just settled up and paid it off at a very low rate of interest. M-K was very accommodating. So there was no problem about that."

The trust, respect and affection between Harry Morrison and F.C. Mannix is apparent in M-K's agreement to return the Mannix business to full Mannix family ownership. Solely on F.C. Mannix's promise to remain president of Mannix Ltd. until M-K was paid, was M-K satisfied they would receive full payment. M-K did not request any ownership interest in Mannix Ltd. while the debentures were being paid.

Mannix Ltd. was incorporated on March 7, 1951. On March 29, Mannix Ltd. agreed to purchase the property and assets of Fred Mannix & Company, Ltd. for $7,826,704. The total price was payable as follows: $3 million payable in cash upon execution of the agreement, $4.82 million payable in installments, and the balance of $6,704 in cash within

60 days of the agreement. Of promissory notes A, B and C issued to Fred Mannix & Company, Ltd., A was paid in full on May 1, 1956, while B had been previously paid on July 31, 1952. Promissory Note C was paid in full by the issuance of a Series B debenture to Fred Mannix & Company, Ltd. which was renamed Morrison-Knudsen of Alberta Limited. This latter company was subsequently wound up and its rights and interest under the debenture transferred to M-K. The unpaid balance of $2.2 million was paid in full by Mannix Ltd. with the issue of eight serial collateral Series B debentures. These were paid off as of March 1, 1962.

It was, quite simply, a rather dazzling financial transaction. "Eric Connelly was the person who set up the financial side of the deal," Bill Sharon said. "What Mannix basically did was buy M-K's share of the construction company for debentures. That was a brilliant financial manoeuvre; the tax savings resulting from it were pretty tremendous. Eric Connelly was one of the best financial minds Canada has seen."

Brock Montgomery concurred, adding, "Connelly was a guy who could change a company by a tax break, or tax loop. That's what he was excellent at; Connelly was quite a recognized tax expert. Ottawa used to get him down to discuss things with him."

While Eric Connelly is credited with setting up what was at the time a most innovative financial manoeuvre, he had nothing but respect for how F.C. Mannix backed his idea. Indeed, without

Fred C. and his father, Frederick S. Mannix.

1951 ▶

Margie Forsgren, Mannix comptometer operator, receptionist and Stampede Queen candidate. After her marriage to Ray Ellard, she will help set up the Mannix stables at Fish Creek.

1951 ▶

The Quebec North Shore and Labrador Railway project is in full swing. More than 140 dump trucks, 78 tractors, 25 shovels and draglines are unloaded from ships at Sept-Îles, then flown into work sites.

F.C. Mannix's backing, the deal may never have gone through. "There is one thing I really admire about Fred Mannix on that deal," Connelly said. "A deal like this, which is pretty important, goes to lawyers and accountants and everybody else to get opinions. Well, our accountants didn't back me, our consulting accountants didn't back me, and the lawyers didn't back me. The only lawyer who did was a fellow named Ross Tolmie, whom we were dealing with in Ottawa. He thought the scheme was not only feasible, but also could be supported in law.

"Fred weighed everything and backed me. The result, of course, was that he was able to get his company back for virtually nothing. It was an absolute turning point in the history of the company. Now I don't want to put down the association with M-K because without them we wouldn't have had the personnel, the know-how, or the backing to do all sorts of things. But still it was awfully good when control of the company came back to Canada."

"I think that of all the things F.C. did, that was probably the most remarkable," Chick Thorssen

THE END OF A CHAPTER

"Unlike many people, Fred S. Mannix saw his monuments long before he died. He was a builder of great magnitude and fine quality. There are no more worthwhile citizens than builders, and therefore Mr. Mannix must be ranked near the top for his citizenship. First in partnership and then with his own company, he played a major role in the building of the West. He was one of the first to demonstrate that the West can do its own building. Even for the biggest jobs it doesn't have to go to Ontario or the States, as long as construction firms like Mannix and Company exist here.

"Fred Mannix wasn't a one-line builder. He first made a name for himself in building roads and railroads, and his company is still foremost in that field. He tackled major jobs, huge military installations. He pioneered the wholesale mechanization of strip mining coal. There's hardly a chapter in the expansion of the West over the last 40 years that Fred Mannix didn't have a hand in writing." — *The Albertan*, July 20, 1951.

Frederick Stephen Mannix passed away on July 14, 1951.

said, "because he was able to get the wherewithal and his drive and energy into the thing in such a way that he was able to buy the company back. And F.C. did it. That was really quite an accomplishment."

Four months after the incorporation of Mannix Ltd., Frederick Stephen Mannix died at the age of 70 in Calgary on July 14, 1951. "Because of his diabetes and heart problems, my father had to have one of his legs amputated in 1948," said Margaret Mannix Walsh. "After that he wasn't able to get around to see very many of the jobs anymore. But he was always interested in what Freddie was doing. One time, Freddie came in and talked to Dad a while about the business. After Freddie left, Dad said to me, 'You know, it's nice to know about the business. But it's gotten so complicated and so much bigger that I just can't follow it anymore.' Of course, he didn't tell Freddie that. Dad wanted to hear all about things. And Freddie did try and tell him. But Dad couldn't quite follow it all. He said, 'Freddie has made it so big now.' So he knew about Freddie's success before he died."

1951 ▶

Mannix Ltd. sponsors a joint venture with McNamara Construction to construct the Toronto Subway. Working below busy downtown Toronto streets creates new challenges.

1951 ▶

F.C. Mannix forms Mannix-O'Sullivan Paving Company Limited with long-time associate, Frank O'Sullivan. The company is ideally situated to assist Edmonton development and Alberta-wide paving projects.

The Sky's the Limit

During the 1950s, Mannix Ltd. underwent a period of explosive growth, joint venturing in projects all across Canada. The relationship with Morrison-Knudsen had proved to be a valuable one, for it enabled Mannix Ltd. to enter the big league of construction projects. "The company was fairly small when I started in the late Forties," recalled Robert McNeill, who worked for Mannix as an aircraft and communications specialist. "We were not very big at all. Then we had the joint venture at Seven Islands with Morrison-Knudsen and it just kind of got started. Then we had the Kenney Dam job. Next, we got into the pipelines. That seemed to get the company stabilized. From then on, the sky was the limit. It just grew from there. We had a lot of jobs in those days. They were big jobs, too. We had hundreds and hundreds of men working for us. Things were busy. We had four, five, six big jobs going on all at once. We were spread out kind of thin, with people coming and going. But it was an exciting life. On the road, on the road, seemed to be the order of the day!"

"For me, the big era of the company was in the 1950s," concurred Fred Fenwick. One of the first engineers-in-training developed by the Mannix company job training plan, Fenwick worked for the outfit while he completed his civil engineering degree from the University of Alberta, School of Engineering. Upon graduation in 1951, he joined the company as a full-time employee. "At that time, the company was very aggressive, very modern, very innovative," he recalled. "It went after big work. That's when it built a lot of its size, expertise and reputation. During those days, we were working right across

Awaiting takeoff in the new Mannix Lodestar, CF-TDI.

Fred Mannix, third from left, during a flying inspection trip of the QNS&L Railway project. The always-open cockpit door is shown in the middle of the photograph.

Canada, from Quebec to the West Coast. That was a very exciting time."

"And standing over it all was F.C. Mannix," said Bob Bowhay, a partner of Peat, Marwick Mitchell & Co., who was associated with the Mannix companies as an auditor and tax advisor for more than 35 years. "He was a true entrepreneur and the right person at the right time. When he took over from his father, there was a great need for construction and building projects of all kinds. F.C. had a tremendous amount of drive and energy and vision; he had the foresight to move his company into many different areas. You name it, he was into it, anything involving heavy construction. There was very definitely a high energy and work attitude, or perhaps work ethic, in the group at that time. They enjoyed their work. It was nothing for people to work six or seven days a week at it. I think they had to force some of them to take holidays. They were all so involved in what was going on that they wanted to stay there at the office."

"It was a company that would dig into anything in order to make a dollar and make a name for itself," added R.A. (Dick) Peppin, who joined Mannix International in 1956. "I can remember walking with Fred C. Mannix down a railroad track. He was saying things like, 'Why don't you get this going? Why don't you get that going? Why don't you do this? And why don't you do that?' Well, I stepped in and said my piece. I said, 'It takes a little bit of time. We can only do so much in a day.' Mr. Mannix turned around to me and said, 'Do you know why Rome wasn't built in a day?' Of course, I had to say, 'No.' He said, 'Because we didn't have the contract.'"

1951 ▶

Campbell Construction Company Limited, a Mannix subsidiary, strips on Baldy Mountain near Natal, British Columbia, for Crow's Nest Pass Coal.

1951 ▶

During a visit to Calgary in October, young Princess Elizabeth and the Duke of Edinburgh are treated to a command performance of the Calgary Stampede. Wrapped in electric blankets to ward off an October snowstorm, the princess and duke are shown a fine Calgary time.

LONG DAY'S JOURNEY INTO FLIGHT

"Ev was away more than half the time," recalled his wife, Florence Costello. "I remember when Bill was a baby, just a year old, Ev had been away six months of the year. He'd come home at night and say, 'The plane's going off.'

"Ev came home one night and said, 'The plane's going to New York tomorrow morning, do you want to come?' I said, 'Sure.' But, heavens,

I didn't see much of New York because we got there and Ev was so busy. The next day we were supposed to do something and Ev said, 'We think we have to go to Toronto or Ottawa, so just wait, don't go anyplace.' So I packed our bags. Then they changed their minds. Ev said, 'Unpack, we're staying.' No sooner had I got unpacked than I had to pack again. That happened over and over again on trips."

"It was such a long trip east in the old planes," said Mrs. Costello. "He'd travel to Toronto and Montreal, spend the whole day travelling, and come back the next day. One time he went to Toronto and Montreal and then turned around and came back and went to Vancouver and back. From all the flying — the planes weren't pressurized in those days — he had such a buzzing in his ears that every time he sat down he couldn't stand it. So we'd go to a baseball game. He'd say, 'Come on, I've got to do something. I can't sit still.'"

The Changing Needs of the Nation

As Canadians worked for peace abroad, they enjoyed unprecedented prosperity at home. This trend can most clearly be seen in two developments: the growth of the Canadian natural resources industry and the expansion of Canadian cities.

In 1950, the Blair Report signalled the beginning of the development of Alberta's incredibly rich oil sands country. In 1951, for the first time in Canada's history, forest and mineral products both replaced farm products as Canada's leading exports. In 1952, iron ore production broke the five-million-ton (4.5-million-tonne) barrier. Between 1948 and 1959, uranium sales rose from a little more than $4 million to more than $331 million. Between 1945 and 1957, Canada's oil production increased 20 times.

At the beginning of World War II, 6.5 million Canadians lived in towns. By 1956, that number had grown to 10.7 million, an increase caused by both the rising tide of immigrants coming to Canada and by the postwar baby boom. Between 1948 and 1957, Canada became home for

Mannix Ltd. superintendents at the 1951 Superintendents' Conference.

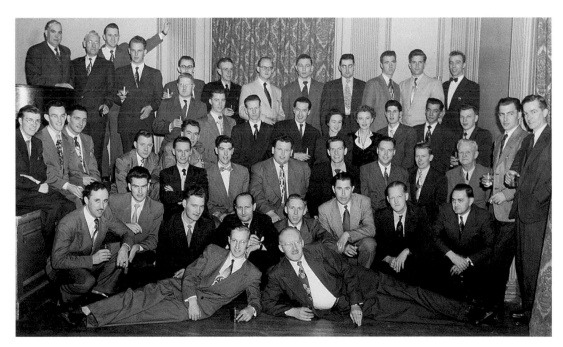

1952 ▶

Federal and provincial governments decide to build a major coast-to-coast highway. Mannix Ltd. begins work on one of many Trans-Canada Highway projects.

1952 ▶

Mannix Ltd. pipeliners build the Trans-Northern Pipe Line Co. spur line to Ottawa. This $4-million project involves 11 major crossings including the Rideau River and the Burlington Canal.

Oh, What a Beautiful Morning

Harry Duckett, founder and president of Ducketts Limited, Insurance Brokers, provided insurance for the Mannix organization for more than 30 years. He often accompanied Mannix executives on the company plane to inspect job sites. One flight in particular stands out in his mind. "We were on our way to New York," Duckett said. "This was in April and there was a blizzard blowing." After taking off from Regina, "it was blowing so hard that the airport was shut down immediately. There were six of us on the plane: a pilot and copilot, Lou Pozzi who was scared to death in an airplane anyway, Phil Soukup and Ben Goodman."

"We got about 50 miles from Regina, flying at about 7,000 feet, when all of a sudden, bango, everything started to go to pieces. The cockpit door was open, and we could see the instrument panel was just jumping, banging and cracking. They couldn't get the prop feathered because a piston was going through the engine and getting ground up. By the time they got the one engine settled down and got the prop feathered, we were down to about 2,000 feet."

"Fortunately, they had a really topnotch pilot, Hal O'Keefe, and a good copilot," Duckett said. "O'Keefe turned the plane around and headed back. There were a lot of white faces and no comments. Anyway, we landed. Nobody was scared of course, until we got on the ground, and then everybody started to shake hard. By nine o'clock that night, it cleared so that we could take off again.

"They flew the mate to the plane in from Cleveland and we took off for New York. My wife was in tears. We got into New York the next morning. The sun was just rising and hitting the buildings about halfway up. The Statue of Liberty was a beautiful sight. It was magnificent."

more than one million immigrants; during that same time period, more than four million babies were born in Canada.

The growth of urban Canada was a result of one other demographic trend. During the 1950s, many Canadians were leaving the family farm for urban areas. Despite an overall increase in the Canadian population from less than 13 million to more than 16 million between 1951 and 1961, the total number of farms in Canada decreased from 623,000 to 570,000.

As Canadians flocked to the cities, they demanded new and better homes to live in — wartime shortages of houses and building materials continued into the first years of peace, leading some Canadian families to live in "temporary" housing in air force huts left over from the war. Between 1948 and 1957, almost a million new houses were constructed across the country. In all provinces except Quebec, the vast majority of these homes were owner-occupied; most were single-family dwellings. One side effect of this trend was that many major Canadian cities began expanding into neighbouring suburban communities. In Toronto, in 1951 alone, the population of the surrounding suburbs rose from 242,500 to 441,700.

Canadians not only clamoured for new housing, they also demanded new and modern conveniences such as interior plumbing, central heating and electric ranges. In 1951, there were approximately 3.5 million Canadian homes. Of these, almost half depended upon wood stoves for cooking. More than one million homes had no refrigerator; 800,000 homes had neither hot nor cold running water. Almost one million homes had neither a flush nor chemical toilet.

The most primitive conditions existed primarily in Canada's rural areas. For example, in the predominantly rural province of Saskatchewan, more than 44 per cent of homes were without electricity in 1951. During the Depression and the Second World War, many Canadians tolerated such conditions, but by the 1950s a new consumer class was determined to live comfortably and well.

This desire for a better life at home led to a period of challenging and unprecedented nation-building projects in Canada. And while the very nature of these projects may have proved daunting to some heavy construction firms, Mannix Ltd. rose to the challenge. "We participated in all of the major jobs in Canada at that time," said F.C. Mannix with pride. "We did all the big jobs. We took a piece of them."

1952 ▶

Mannix Ltd., in a joint venture with the J.B. Gill Company of Long Beach, California, constructs three pumping stations for the Trans Mountain Oil Pipe Line Company.

1952 ▶

Britain's King George VI dies. Princess Elizabeth, touring East Africa, becomes Queen. She is the first monarch to ascend the throne while out of the country.

Meeting the Demand for Hydroelectric Power

The rapid expansion of Canadian industry and the mushrooming of Canadian cities caused the demand for hydroelectric power to escalate sharply in the early 1950s. To keep pace with the country's expanding appetite for electric power, Mannix Ltd. worked on several major dam-building projects in the first years of the decade. In 1951, the outfit took on the Chutes des Georges Dam in Quebec. In Alberta, the company tackled the Bearspaw Dam in 1952 and the Pocaterra and Ghost River dams in 1954. While each of these dams presented its own unique challenges, without a doubt the most challenging dam project undertaken by Mannix Ltd. during the early Fifties was Kenney Dam, located in the rugged northwestern coastal region of British Columbia.

Kenney Dam was part of the $500-million Nechako-Kitimat project of the Aluminum Company of Canada, probably the biggest construction job ever attempted by the private sector. Morrison-Knudsen, which had a $173-million share of this work, constructed the hydroelectric installation. To supply power for a new aluminum smelter, M-K dammed a river to form a 120-mile-long (193-kilometre) reservoir, hollowed out a mountain to enclose a huge powerhouse five city blocks long, and drilled a 10-mile (16-kilometre) tunnel to carry the water to the turbines. At ultimate capacity, Alcan's powerhouse would produce 1.2 million kilowatts, 34 per cent more than Hoover Dam — enough electricity to match the combined output of such U.S. giants as Shasta, Bonneville and Wilson dams.

Mannix Ltd.'s $21.5-million contract for Kenney Dam included a 1,430-foot (436-metre) diversion tunnel

Kenney Dam on the Nechako River in the B.C. mountains. Upon completion, Kenney Dam is the largest rock-filled dam in the British Commonwealth.

The Kenney Dam camp in 1951 is the home to some 1,300 people during the dam construction.

and approximately 60 miles (97 kilometres) of access road. "M-K had the overall contract at Kitimat to build the powerhouse," explained Graham Pollock, then assistant purchasing agent for Mannix Ltd. "Mannix got the project through their association with Morrison-Knudsen. Kenney Dam was just a huge rock and earthmoving job." Kenney Dam, which required no less than four million cubic yards (three million cubic metres) of heavy rock, core and fill, rose 324 feet (99 metres) above bedrock. It had a 1,550-foot (472-metre) crest length, a 40-foot (12-metre) crest width and an upstream slope of 1:2.5.

"After Sept-Îles, our next big job was the Kenney Dam in 1951," recalled Everett Costello. "It's hard to say which one of these projects was the largest in the history of the company to that point. They both were very large jobs, both from the physical and financial point of view. Of course, at Sept-Îles, we were in a joint venture. At Kenney, we did the work all by ourselves. There were no partners. Kenney Dam was a particularly challenging job. It was the biggest, rock-filled dam in North America at that time."

Kenney Dam was constructed on the Nechako River, some 200 miles (320 kilometres) east of the smelter site. Designed to create a huge impounded lake of water, the dam effectively reversed the flow of the Nechako River. M-K dug a tunnel west through the mountains, allowing the rising impounded water to flow toward the Pacific Ocean.

Kenney Dam was a tough job that extracted the best from all who worked on the project. "I went up to Vanderhoof in 1951," Charlie Thalheimer recalled.

1952 ▶

The Mannix Calgary office staff is flown to the Kenney Dam site for a weekend party celebrating the completion of the project.

1952 ▶

The Kenney Dam, originally scheduled for completion in 1954, is completed. The company motto, "When you want the job done, make it Mannix," is backed by performance.

FINDING TIME FOR A WEDDING

"I spent two years at Kenney Dam," recalled Ben Kessler. "I met my wife, Polly, there. We had in that camp what they called 'The Dollhouse' for the ladies — secretaries and bookkeeping machine operators — staying there.

"When that job started, it was a dry camp. There was no liquor allowed in there. That was a mistake because there was more liquor there than would have been had it been a wet camp. I always remember the day they were going to confiscate all the liquor. Two of us from the office went down to a shovel operator's room and he had all this liquor — it was rum — up in a back wall. He'd pull off a little panel and it was all stacked in there between the walls.

"That afternoon, the three of us drank five bottles of rum — two were twenty-sixers and three were mickies — because at five o'clock security was going to search every room for liquor. When I woke up, it was a wet camp. They decided not to confiscate the liquor because they were afraid all the men would go on strike. I don't think I've drank rum since."

"Anyway, my wife and I got engaged while we were there," said Kessler. "I had the cook make our wedding cake. They wanted to marry us there. We had a carpenter superintendent named Harry Christensen. He was going to build us a raft and Whitey, who had been a sea captain in the U.S. navy, was going to marry us on the raft. We were going to get married in September, but in those days, Eric Connelly didn't believe that you should take time off from the busy season. Well, since we worked all 12 months, I don't know what the busy season was." Ben and Polly were married after the job shut down, on December 17, 1952.

"That was on the Alcan project. We went into the Nechako riverbed where there was solid rock on both sides. We put in a diversion tunnel through the rock. We also put in a cofferdam which diverted the water through the tunnel. Then we built the dam. That was a rush job and a seven-day-a-week job. I cross-shifted with another guy; that meant we worked 12 hours apiece. I worked from six in the morning until six at night. He came out and worked until six the next morning. That way we could keep the equipment running. By the time we finished, we had built the highest earth-filled dam in North America."

While the actual building of the dam was a massive endeavour, so were the administrative tasks. In typical "Flying Circus" style, the paymaster at Kenney Dam, Pete Swityk, was flown into the project with virtually no notice. "Karl Collett had sent me out to a project in Watino," Swityk recalled. "While I was there, I had a call from him. I had just bought my first car and Karl said, 'I want you to drive up here to Edmonton and park your car at a garage. Pansy [Strange] will tell you where the best place is to go. We're going to have Hal O'Keefe pick you up at the airport in Edmonton and fly you out to Vanderhoof.' That was where the Kenney Dam project was. So that's exactly what I did.

"They told me that I'd only be out there for a few weeks to help get some cost reports out. I reported to the office manager. We had maybe 1,300 people who were hired under varying types of conditions: staff people, people working for subcontractors, your own people that were on your payroll, and people who were living in the married quarters or off-site in their own homes. You had to adjust to take care of all those things."

"My job initially was to assemble all the information on all the money we'd spent and put it together in a financial statement," continued Swityk. "God, we'd spent about $1 million at that time, which was a heck of a lot of money. Getting the first statement out was a little tough because we had to build our books up from

1952 ▶

Year two of the Quebec North Shore and Labrador Railway project finds tough going in the land called Ungava, which means faraway place.

1952 ▶

Mannix Ltd. crews are close to completing the Marguerite Dam west of Sept-Îles. They will work through the harsh Quebec winter to ensure the concrete spillway is ready for the 1953 runoff.

scratch. On one financial statement I worked virtually 72 hours straight. I just catnapped in the office. I had an accounting staff. Ben Kessler was part of it, and so was Don Webb, Titus Oates and a few other people. They worked on a shift basis, and I was coordinating everybody's work so that everything would come together. We put it out and got it done on time."

"That job had more employees and a bigger payroll than anything the company had ever seen," said Ben Kessler. "We worked an awful lot of hours trying to keep up with all the paperwork. I can think of a lot of times when I worked all day and all night without stopping. When you have over 1,000 men to deal with, there's quite a lot of that going on. We had about the biggest typewriter you could get. We had statements that were physically enormous, about two feet wide. It was an achievement in itself just putting one of those things together."

"Before the camp at the dam site was built, our office in Vanderhoof was on the main floor of an old liquor store," Kessler said. "We had four bedrooms upstairs. That's where we all slept and where we all played poker every night. Of course, we were all single then. I worked in accounts payable and then in purchasing. I did a lot of buying of the little purchases like socks, hammers, nails, screws and so on. It was an awful lot of work. That was the biggest job in the history of the company, so we were putting together a big camp. Vanderhoof only had a population of 1,500 people or so. Eventually, we moved over 1,000 people into our camp. We ended up buying everything there was in that town — every pair of work socks, every shovel and every pick."

Top: Both pride in their accomplishments and some camp humour are shown on the menu for the 1951 Joint Boards of Trade Prince George and Vanderhoof outing. Some dinner offerings include "Mannix pit-run potatoes," "impervious core cheese" and "blasted beverages."

Above: Drilling, blasting and excavating terraces on the hillsides above the Nechako River provide material for the rock-filled Kenney Dam. The 24-hour work schedule requires illumination towers, one shown on the extreme left of the photograph.

A few years into the project, a new office manager was assigned to the job — Ross P. Alger, who would become mayor of Calgary in 1977. "Ross and I used to spend a fair amount of time together because he was new to construction," recalled Swityk. "He was a chartered accountant. When Ross decided to leave, we both went out on the job site. We were watching the trucks in the quarries and hauling materials. They were pounding all this material into the clay core, which was the largest earth-filled dam in the British Commonwealth. It was quite an impressive undertaking. Ross said, 'You know, life is just too short for me to be out here. I just can't take it. I admire you for your tenacity, but I'm going.' Since the project was winding down anyway, I just took over the rest of the job and finished it off."

Near the end of the job, Mannix Ltd. hosted a grand party at the job site. "They loaded up the Lodestar with all kinds of people from the Calgary office and Hal O'Keefe flew them to Kenney Dam," said Swityk. "Everybody came out and we had barbecues and just had a real bang-up time. Of course, the cooks just outdid themselves with the pastries, and the meat was the best you could find — all the steaks and booze you wanted. Everybody who was there just thought it was great, both the people who were on the site and those who came to visit. That was the type of thing that helped morale and helped build the esprit de corps in the Mannix organization."

Mannix crews completed the dam in late 1952, several years ahead of schedule. It took many years before the Nechako River could fill the huge reservoir created by the dam.

1952 ▶

Far north in Labrador, Mannix crews begin the Menihek Dam that will provide power to the iron ore mine and provide a bridge for the QNS&L Railway across the Ashuanipi River.

1952 ▶

Most of the construction camps on the QNS&L Railway are supplied by air because of their remote wilderness locations. A veritable air force flies every day possible.

Helping to Build the Longest National Highway in the World

The Canada of the 1950s was a nation on the move. In 1951, 43 per cent of Canadian households owned a car. Between 1951 and 1957, auto registrations rose from less than three million to nearly four million. As the family car became a fixture of the Canadian lifestyle, a commensurate demand for better roads arose. This trend caused the celebrated Canadian social historian A.R.M. Lower to lament: "The god CAR has invaded every urban open space and threatened to destroy every urban blade of grass. They have knocked down houses. They have called imperiously for straight, wide roads to be carved out of our diminishing fertile fields. They are also ostentatious and vulgar to a degree."

Despite these lamentations, Canadians continued to demand "straight, wide roads" for their automobiles. And new highways were desperately needed in a country that, in 1948, could only claim some 10,000 miles (16,000 kilometres) of paved road. In response, both the federal government and various provincial authorities launched a period of intense highway construction.

Work on the ambitious Trans-Canada Highway began in the summer of 1950 with an infusion of $150 million of federal funds (half the estimated cost), provided for in the Trans-Canada Highway Act of 1949. Although Canada set 1956 as the year for completion, various provincial delays, some memorable routing arguments and the terrain itself made the job far lengthier, and far more costly, than anyone dreamed. When it was finally opened in 1970, the Trans-Canada Highway — the longest national highway in the world — cost more than $1 billion.

The 1955 De Soto, "motion-designed for the forward look," is poised to take Canadians wherever the new highways lead.

Building the Trans-Canada Highway will take a decade and require construction across most types of Canadian geography, including the Rocky Mountains.

The Trans-Canada Highway, which many believed would be as great a unifying force as the first transcontinental railway, was a job of staggering proportions. There are 3,772 rail miles (6,070 kilometres) from Halifax in the East to Vancouver in the West. Add to this the distance across Newfoundland and Vancouver Island and you have well over 4,000 miles (6,437 kilometres) of country. Trans-Canada specified up to a 200-foot (61-metre) right-of-way, a road that was to be 44 feet (13 metres) from shoulder to shoulder, and blacktop paving 24 feet (seven metres) wide. Conservatively expressed, Trans-Canada Highway would cover 97,000 acres (40,000 hectares) of right-of-way; 21,000 acres (9,000 hectares) of road; and a whopping 12,000 acres (5,000 hectares) of blacktop.

That is a lot of highway for any country, and certainly a giant undertaking for a nation with only 15 million people. Every family was theoretically responsible for about eight linear feet of the road, and in some parts of the Rockies, construction costs approached a million dollars a mile.

During the Fifties, Mannix Ltd. gained considerable Trans-Canada Highway experience, toiling in the granite hills north of Lake Superior, the semidesert area of southeastern Alberta, the rich farming and ranching country east of Calgary and in the Canadian Rockies. From 1952 to the beginning of the next decade, the eight years that Mannix Ltd. worked on the Trans-Canada Highway, Mannix crews laid sections near Calgary and Medicine Hat in Alberta and a section near Sudbury, Ontario. Crews also tackled difficult mountain sections in the Yoho and Glacier national parks, British Columbia, and in the Kicking Horse Pass which straddles the Alberta-B.C. border.

1952 ▶

Several times a day, the Menihek Dam site is supplied by a converted Lancaster Bomber. Weather permitting, the plane delivers a cargo of 190 sacks of cement.

1952 ▶

One of the first televised hockey games.

Creating Canada's First Subway System

While many Canadians were calling for a better way to drive across the country, the citizens of Toronto were calling for a better way to get across town. By the early 1950s, Greater Toronto found itself surrounded by an expanding cluster of suburban communities: four towns, 13 communities, three villages, and five townships.

To help ease traffic, the publicly owned Toronto Transit Commission was formed to develop and operate an integrated system of subway trains, street railways, trolley coaches, bus lines and intercity bus routes. In a rather bold move, the commission elected to create Canada's first subway system. The route, extending from Union Station in downtown Toronto to Eglinton Avenue, totalled 4.6 miles (7.4 kilometres) of track. Construction costs exceeded $50 million. The job required 1.5 million bags of cement, 11,000 tons (10,000 tonnes) of structural steel, 15,400 tons (14,000 tonnes) of reinforcing steel, 15 million board feet (6,400 cubic metres) of lumber and more than 1.5 million cubic yards (1.1 million cubic metres) of excavation. All work was performed right in the middle of one of the busiest urban areas in the country.

Not surprisingly, most construction companies shied away from the challenge. "On the Toronto Subway job there were very few bidders, but we decided to bid on it," recalled F.C. Mannix. "We had never done subway work before, but I thought we could make money on it, even though it was our first subway job. And we did."

Nevertheless, the logistics were daunting. "One of the most interesting jobs that we had in those days was the Toronto Subway," recalled Chip Collins. "In particular, the underground construction in downtown Toronto was very interesting. We actually dug out the whole tunnel for the subway. We put a steel surface on Yonge Street so the traffic could still run on the street. At the same time, we did all the construction that was going on underneath. That was a very exciting project." Mannix Ltd., which sponsored a joint venture agreement with McNamara Construction, began work on the subway in February 1951. This work was completed in March 1953.

Building the Toronto Subway, Canada's first, requires construction under the busy, operating streets of the city with as little disruption as possible.

The St. Lawrence Seaway — A Monumental Engineering and Construction Feat

During the 1950s, Mannix Ltd. seemed to relish the opportunity to put itself against the biggest and most difficult projects available. A large part of this driving force came from F.C. Mannix. "Let me tell you something about F.C. Mannix," said Gordon Walker, the director of the Mannix Petroleum and Pipeline Division in the 1950s. "Fred always wanted to get involved where the job was the toughest. He seemed to be more interested in taking a contract if it was a really rough job. He seemed to have more interest in the difficult projects than he did in the routine construction work." In the $1-billion international St. Lawrence Seaway, Fred C. Mannix found a challenge worthy of his interest.

The St. Lawrence Seaway-Great Lakes Waterway is the system of waterways linking the five Great Lakes and the St. Lawrence River with the Atlantic Ocean. The digging of shallow canals along the St. Lawrence River began as early as 1783. The first canal around Niagara was opened in 1829, and the first lock at Sault Sainte Marie in 1855. By 1900 there was a complete system of shallow canals from Lake Superior to Montreal. Between 1912 and 1932, the Welland Canal was gradually deepened, but the United States was a reluctant partner in a larger scheme, leaving a treaty signed in 1941 unratified by the Senate. It took a threat by the Canadian government in 1951 to build a seaway entirely in Canadian territory to bring about a final agreement in 1954.

1952 ▶

Coal stripping operations continue at Grassy Lake, Alberta.

1952 ▶

A Caterpillar DW20 tractor and scraper are push-loaded by a D-8 Cat with a dozer blade while widening the Edmonton to Jasper Highway between Styal and Chip Lake, Alberta.

On paper, the concept of the St. Lawrence Seaway was quite simple. From the open ocean to Montreal, the St. Lawrence River could accommodate all but the largest oceangoing vessels. From Ogdensburg, New York, to the head of Lake Ontario, the river could handle most deepwater traffic. Between Montreal and Ogdensburg, however, the river ran through 120 miles (193 kilometres) of non-navigable river, causing a severe bottleneck in trade. To remove this impasse, engineers envisioned a new system that would open the Great Lakes region to the oceangoing fleets of the entire world.

While the seaway appeared simple on paper, in reality, it was a monumental engineering and construction feat. Mannix Ltd. sponsored two joint ventures for the seaway: one with Raymond Concrete Pile Company for the Barnhart Cofferdam, the other with Miron & Frères Ltée. for the navigation channel and dike at Lachine Rapids. Neither was easy.

At the Barnhart Cofferdam, access was the first problem. The work area lay on an island between the canal and the river. Equipment and supplies were either tugged across the canal or taken upstream several miles to existing bridges and then hauled back down to the site. While the canal remained open in the fall, access was provided by tugs and barges. The roundabout road was also used until the entire area became a sea of mud. The mud posed a serious problem — thousands of yards of fill were unloaded in an attempt to provide better traction for vehicles and equipment, but in the glacial till the gravel soon sank out of sight. As work neared completion, the problem of keeping fill in place against the raging force of water became greater and greater. After what seemed like a never-ending struggle against

The Barnhart Cofferdam, an interlocking series of steel sheet piling cells, blocks the flow of the St. Lawrence River to allow the construction of a dam to stabilize water levels and produce energy for the St. Lawrence Seaway project.

This sign marks the location of the first Cardium oil well in Canada, the birthplace of the Pembina oil field.

the river and the weather, Mannix-Raymond successfully completed one of the largest construction jobs ever let in Canada.

The seaway, which was opened to commercial traffic in 1959, had a major economic impact on Canada, providing economical freight rates for bulk commodities. It made an important contribution to the basic industries of Canada; grain, newsprint, wood, industrial machinery and automobiles were shipped along the seaway to market. The seaway also made possible the exploitation of the vast iron ore deposits of Quebec and Labrador, turning Canada from an importer to an exporter of iron ore.

Making the Bid for Pembina
"We were actually laughed at."

Before 1953, the Indian word "Pembina" stood mainly for the dense highbush cranberries growing along the banks of the North Saskatchewan and Pembina rivers in west-central Alberta. When a consortium of companies concluded drilling that summer, however, Pembina also came to mean oil.

On June 20, 1953, Socony-Vacuum Exploration Company (a Mobil Oil subsidiary), Seaboard Oil Company, Honolulu Oil Corporation, Merrill Petroleum and Canadian Collieries completed "Socony-Seaboard Pembina No. 1." The Pembina well gave Canadian oil men the first indication that the Upper Cretaceous formation existed as an oil-bearing reservoir under the Alberta plains. So encouraged, Socony-Seaboard continued drilling, swiftly bringing in two more wells.

The following January, Pembina was recognized as an oil field of major importance when a number of companies bid millions of dollars for a shot at Pembina's

1952 ▶

The Railroad Division completes a 10-car string of new camp cars. This self-sufficient work train houses, feeds and supplies all equipment for a 60-person work crew. It is promptly dubbed the "Franco Freighter."

1952 ▶

Mannix Ltd. pipeliners build the last section of the Gulf-Stettler pipeline to Edmonton in a very fast 30 days.

hidden riches at a Crown lease and reservation sale. Within a mere two years, more than 380 exploration and development wells probed the earth's depths.

While this new field sat less than 100 miles (160 kilometres) from Edmonton, hauling the oil out by truck proved difficult and unreliable. Poor roads and the wide spacing of wells made the need for an extensive gathering system and pipeline urgent. At the time, the right to build a pipeline in Alberta was determined by competitive bidding. Major oil producers often had the inside edge. However, any company with the proper financial resources, expertise, a good plan and tariff structure could submit a plan to the province's Petroleum and Natural Gas Provincial Conservation Board. Mannix Ltd., an industry outsider, decided to submit a plan.

With the discovery of the Pembina field, F.C. Mannix had a solid reason for wanting to start a pipeline company. With a new Alberta oil boom poised to take off, building and operating the means to get the oil to market represented a profitable opportunity. In this, however, he was not fully supported internally. There were some who felt that Mannix Ltd. should not own a pipeline because it might interfere with construction work. However, Fred C. Mannix, a man of vision, was not to be deterred. But before Mannix could pull the deal off, three factors would have to fall into place: a little bit of luck, a lot more money, and a mistake by Eric Connelly.

A little bit of luck came about when Jim Scott, then assistant to the president of Mannix Ltd., found himself seated next to Jack Gallagher, chief officer of Dome Petroleum, on a commercial flight from Edmonton to Calgary. As Mannix was looking for partners, preferably Alberta partners that could help keep the new pipeline operating company a private operation, Jim Scott was serendipitously seated next to the right kind of guy.

Jack Patrick Edward Gallagher was known by at least two sobriquets: "Smiling Jack," and "a riverboat man in a gambler's industry." According to author Peter Foster's *The Blue-Eyed Sheiks,* an irreverent and controversial look at the Canadian oil establishment published in 1979, "Gallagher has perhaps the most influential teeth in Canadian business. A sighting of his smile on Bay or Wall streets is enough to send a frisson through the stock market. A flash of his dental work in Ottawa has been known to cause whole federal budgets to be reworked."

"WE STAYED UP ALL NIGHT LONG"

During the Fifties, Mannix Ltd. moved into the field of marine construction, building a number of wharves throughout Canada. These structures included the Burin Wharf in Newfoundland, the Port Maitland Wharf in Nova Scotia and the Baie-Comeau Wharf in Quebec. While these projects added a new area of expertise to the Mannix outfit, sometimes they added an element of heartbreak, as well.

"I went to Baie-Comeau because of my background in mining," explained Dan (Frenchy) Hamilton. "They were building a wharf there and I did the rock work. They had driven this 90-foot steel sheet piling. We were then filling it with rock. We had practically completed it all when they had the most terrible storm on the St. Lawrence River. I could see 40-foot waves come over the top of the structure. The water came over the steel sheet pilings. They went back and forth and then just broke off and fell into the river. Those pilings had come all the way from Belgium. It had taken a number of months to get them over here.

"Jock Sterling was the project manager on that one. I was with him on the wharf the night of the storm. We stayed up all night long and he was crying. I can't say that I felt very good either. It was a disaster." Despite the disaster, Mannix crews completed the Baie-Comeau Wharf on schedule in April 1954.

1952 ▶

Cats, scrapers and Tournapulls widen the main canal of the St. Mary Irrigation District.

1952 ▶

Track rehabilitation for the CPR begins near Morley, Alberta.

"Run Like Stink to the South"

While wharf construction could cause heartbreak, sometimes bridges proved no less trying. "We had the contract on the Groat Bridge in Edmonton across the North Saskatchewan River," Fred Fenwick recalled. "We had studied the river records going back 80 years, but no incidents had been recorded of anything untoward occurring in the flow of water. Very early in August, we were about a third of the way across with the construction and the deck. We then had a very bad rainstorm. It was so intense that it immediately raised the river above the level of the spring runoff. Of course with the very soggy riverbanks, the river at that height began to pull bushes and trees from its flow. They jammed up against this false work bridge and constructed a dam of debris, brush and old trees.

"One morning, one of the carpenters who was checking the posting underneath came up to me on the deck and said, 'The posts are leaning.' I said, 'You've got to be kidding.' I crawled underneath. Sure enough, the posts were leaning, which meant that our false work bridge had started to lean. I told the carpenter to get his crew off the bridge.

Fred Harvey, who was resident engineer for the Department of Highways ran out to me. He met me in the middle of the span and asked me what I was going to do. I said, 'I suggest you run like stink to the south and I'll run to the north.' We broke and ran and that middle section came out between us."

On August 26, 1954, the Groat Bridge collapsed. Following a period of heavy rainfall, the North Saskatchewan River had risen five feet (1.5 metres) in 24 hours. "And we were still able to finish the bridge according to the original timetable," said Fenwick.

Journalistic hyperbole, to be sure. But Gallagher, the son of an immigrant Irish railway worker, was an influential force in Canadian energy circles. Born in Winnipeg in 1916 and graduating from the University of Manitoba in 1937 — from the same class that produced Jack Armstrong, who would later head Imperial Oil — Gallagher became a visionary of Arctic oil exploration. He first grew intrigued with the region during the summer of 1936, when he headed into the subarctic Northwest Territories on a Canadian geological survey mapping expedition.

Gallagher began his practical petroleum education with Shell Oil Company in California, as field geologist in the Los Angeles Basin, the San Joaquin Valley and the Ventura-Santa Maria area, all sites of intense exploration and production activity during the 1930s. Then, "in January 1939, I went to Egypt for Shell as a geologist," Gallagher recalled. "When war broke out, I left Shell because they wanted me to go to the Dutch East Indies. I joined Standard Oil which is now Exxon, in Egypt, in December 1939. I spent a couple of more years with Exxon in Egypt working in Sinai and working in various parts of Egypt and Palestine. Then I went to South America for Standard Oil and worked in Equador and Guatemala, Honduras, Costa Rica, Panama and Peru and ended up in charge of exploration in the headwaters of the Amazon in Peru. I then returned to Canada, by choice, in 1949. I left Imperial here in Canada in 1950 to take on a private company that had just been formed known as Dome, Dome Petroleum."

"I was alone in Dome for two years," continued Gallagher, "because we had only a quarter of a million dollars in equity and some debt. This debt, in the form of bonds, was advanced by Dome Mines and the endowment funds of Harvard, Princeton and MIT. This group also put up the $250,000 for equity in the company at a cost for today's share of one-quarter cent per share. This was fair because they took the risk with their bond investment. We were fortunate in our search for oil and

1952 ▶

A joint venture of Mannix Ltd. and Wixson & Crowe clears the area that will become the reservoir behind the Cleveland Dam.

1952 ▶

The office staff of the Mannix-Wixson & Crowe joint venture, from left to right, Fred Fenwick, Jimmy Nairn, Lloyd Binkley and Emil Felstet.

gas in 1950 and 1951. We then went public in late 1951, and subsequently paid off the entire debt." The 1951 share offering, and another in 1955, raised a total of $10 million.

Interested in what Jim Scott told him of the Mannix plan for Pembina, Gallagher agreed to take on a share of the proposal. "Jim told me that Mannix wanted to bid on the ownership and construction of the Pembina pipeline from a new field that had been discovered by Mobil Oil southwest of Edmonton known as Pembina," Gallagher explained. "Jim indicated that Mannix was not able to handle the estimated $15-million cost on their own and was looking for a partner who, hopefully, was a producer in the province. After giving a little consideration to the proposal and meeting with the Mannix people, we at Dome committed to take on a share of the proposal prior to the hearing at the conservation board."

"Mannix indicated that they could handle roughly 25 per cent of the effort, and that they wanted to keep it a private company," Gallagher said. "We, at Dome, therefore, picked up 75 per cent. But behind Dome we brought in a company known as [Carl M.] Loeb, Rhoades and Company, investment brokers in New York, whose principals had a financial interest in Dome Petroleum."

Gallagher felt that the project might profit by offering 49 per cent of the total shares to Pembina's oil producers. "The reason we wanted to do that was if you have producer support and producer ownership, there was a better chance of getting the permit to build the pipeline," he explained. This plan would leave the Dome and Loeb group with a 26 per cent interest which, combined with the Mannix 25 per cent, would ensure control. But the plan never materialized. "The producers declined to participate since they would have to put up their share of the total cost," said Gallagher.

This meant that the group faced their hearing before the Alberta Petroleum and Natural Gas Provincial Conservation Board alone. Mannix Ltd. incorporated a new privately owned company, Pembina

Mannix Petroleum and Pipeline Division personnel plot the course of a proposed pipeline. From left to right, Joe Hlavay, Brock Montgomery, Phil Soukup, Dave Adams and Cal Baker.

Pipe Line Company Limited, to be the vehicle for the project. Pembina Pipe Line Company Limited then submitted the application to the board for the permit to build, own and operate the pipeline. Attorney Robert L. (Buz) Fenerty, a long-time counsellor to the Mannix family businesses, felt that the effort was a long shot. "Up to that time, pipelining was all a matter of producer-owned pipelines," he said.

Gordon Walker, who joined Mannix Ltd. in 1953 as manager, Pipeline Division, agreed, adding, "Traditionally, pipelining has been the preserve of the major oil companies. When a new field is discovered, they almost take turns, saying, 'It's your turn to run the pipeline system here.' The story I've heard is that it was Mobil's turn to build the line out of Pembina."

While pipelining may have been the preserve of the major oil companies in the past, the future was about to begin. "As a government, we were leaning strongly to the idea that we would like to see some competition in the pipeline field, other than just the oil companies," explained Ernest Manning, premier of Alberta from 1943 to 1968. "In a sense, this was an extension of the principle of not having the provincial gathering lines controlled by federal legislation. We didn't think it was too sound to have such lines controlled by the producers of the oil, which were mostly international companies. We thought as a general principle, it would be better to have a pipeline system that would be more independent from the producers as well as from the federal government. Our philosophy was that with the tremendous growth of the pipeline business, there were going to be a lot of pipelines built, and it would be a good thing to have some competition and not just have one industry controlling all of it."

"When Alberta Gas Trunk Line Company, which is now known as NOVA Corporation, was first formed as a special company by act of the legislature," continued Manning, "Alberta Gas Trunk Line was a gas-gathering system exclusively within the province. All gas that was being

1952 ▶

In an international joint venture, Mannix Ltd. helps build the Niagara Tunnels, a part of the Sir Adam Beck-Niagara Generating Station No. 2 project for Ontario Hydro.

1952 ▶

Mannix-O'Sullivan crews help build the Trans Mountain oil pipeline near Kamloops, British Columbia.

exported from the province was gathered from the various fields by the facilities of Alberta Gas Trunk Line and delivered to the export companies at the border of the province. Their facilities only came to the border and all the internal operation was within Alberta. One of the reasons for forming that company was that we wanted to develop a good provincial grid for gas gathering so that we could serve more local communities within the province."

"Anyway, it was within that context that the Pembina situation developed," Manning said. "We had two main oil pipelines that were under national regulation. One was the Interprovincial pipeline, which ran from Edmonton to Ontario, and the other was the Trans Mountain pipeline, which ran from Alberta to Vancouver in British Columbia. At the time the Pembina line was built, the Pembina oil field had been developed and was producing a substantial volume of oil. They wanted a pipeline to bring that oil into the tank farms in Edmonton, where it could be fed into the export pipelines. The oil companies that did the developing of the fields, and owned the oil, leaned strongly toward wanting to build their own pipeline, which was understandable. They had formed a separate pipeline company and apart from the fact that it gave them jurisdiction over their pipeline and its use, it also quite often had tax advantages. So the companies active in Pembina wanted to build the main oil pipeline to bring the oil into Edmonton."

"The Mannix group was becoming very active in getting into the pipeline business in a bigger way, and made an application to build the Pembina pipeline," continued Manning. "The Mannix application was very strongly opposed by the oil-producing companies for understandable

Suspended by cable from the winch on the heavy tractor on top, a small D-4 dozer cleans out the ditch for the Trans Mountain oil pipeline in the Coquihalla Canyon, British Columbia.

Trans Mountain pipeliners lower the final section of pipe to connect with pipe already laid at the bottom of one of the many river crossings in British Columbia.

reasons; it was to the companies' advantage to control their own lines. Again, as a government, we were leaning very strongly toward the idea that we wanted to see some competition in the pipeline field, other than just the oil companies."

Although the government favoured outside competition, the established oil companies strongly opposed Mannix Ltd.'s intrusion on their turf. "We were actually laughed at," recalled Brock Montgomery. "We were the first non-oil people to make an application for a pipeline. During intermissions at the hearing, men from the oil companies would come up to us say, 'Hell, you can't get anywhere. We're gonna beat you on your engineering.' " What the established oil companies did not count on, however, was that while Mannix Ltd. may have been newcomers to the field, they had plenty of what Montgomery aptly referred to as "raw brass."

Winning the Pembina Bid: "Nobody was dealing with us."

Among the main players opposing Mannix's Pembina consortium at the conservation board hearings were Texaco, Bailey Selburn and Socony-Vacuum, the Mobil subsidiary that discovered the field. "Mobil applied to build a pipeline directly north to a place called Edson," Jack Gallagher explained, "which was a pump station on the Trans Mountain pipeline that moved oil from Edmonton to Vancouver. Mobil would, therefore, be dedicating all of the Pembina oil to the Vancouver market or the West Coast, which could be a limiting factor on the amount of oil that could be taken by that area. Bailey Selburn was a Canadian independent with backing from Winnipeg and Toronto financial groups. They had some land and potential producing property in the Pembina area.

1952 ▶

Battle River Coal Company Limited, a partnership between Mannix Ltd., West Canadian Collieries and others, develops the Vesta Mine near Halkirk. Vesta is the Roman goddess of the hearth.

1952 ▶

A new receptionist and switchboard is cause for a group photograph of the Edmonton Mannix-O'Sullivan office staff.

1952 ▶

In February, Vincent Massey becomes the first native-born Canadian to be named Governor General of Canada.

"At the hearing, the Mannix/Dome group applied to build a pipeline directly from Pembina into Edmonton, which gave the flexibility of moving oil either east through the Interprovincial pipeline or west through the Trans Mountain pipeline. In hindsight, that was the right move, because it gave greater flexibility to the market. Bailey Selburn also applied to build a line from Pembina to Edmonton. Fairly early in the hearing, Mobil realized their proposal wasn't going to fly because of the limited market and they withdrew their application."

"Bailey fought the Mannix group very hard," continued Gallagher. "They had an outstanding lawyer by the name of Blackstock. I remember when Blackstock, on behalf of Bailey Selburn, challenged the Mannix/Dome group as to whether they could finance this sort of thing. Mannix was relatively small at the time. Their construction work on the Trans Mountain had not been very profitable. I think it was well-known they were not very affluent financially. But when Blackstock questioned the capability of our group to finance, Ian McKinnon, the conservation board chairman said, 'I have no questions.'"

Still, the Mannix team faced a fight from Bailey Selburn. A main objection to the Pembina proposal was Mannix Ltd.'s lack of experience in designing and building pipelines. "The oil companies, of course, argued before the commission that you shouldn't let an inexperienced new group

THE ROYAL BANK BUILDING

During the 1950s, Mannix Ltd. experimented with building construction. "We had a contract for the construction of the Royal Bank Building in Calgary," Chip Collins said. "That was the first building that the Mannix outfit had anything to do with. We hadn't been builders in the sense of building construction. We had been builders in the sense of dirt moving and dam construction and pipelines. So this was our first venture in a new field of construction."

Commissioned by the Royal Bank of Canada, the Royal Bank Building was built on the southeast corner of the intersection of Eighth Avenue and Fourth Street Southwest in downtown Calgary. Construction got under way in 1953 and was completed in the fall of 1955. Upon completion, the building replaced the bank's old headquarters at Eighth Avenue and Centre Street.

things that were much more difficult to do than the pipeline. But that was one of the strong arguments that was used against letting the newcomers into the field."

Another important element of the proposal rested with tariffs. As it turned out, Mannix controller Eric Connelly, who was also Pembina's first treasurer, came up with an innovation that pulled off the deal. "At the time, all pipelines wrote off their pipeline in 20 years," explained Brock Montgomery. "If we had done that, our initial prices would have been something like $2.00 to $2.50 per barrel to Edmonton. Connelly wrote up the tariff on the projected reserves of the Pembina field."

"The other pipelines that were run by other major companies charged much higher tariffs than we did," Connelly explained. "But you see, I made a mistake, because I used the gas formula instead of the oil formula. Now the United States has just changed the pattern of tariffs which makes the oil companies conform to the gas companies, but this is 30 years later. What I came up with sounded like a very good deal to me, to the company, the producers and the Province. And it was." Pembina Pipe Line's initial tariff was 25 cents per barrel. But by the end of 1955, the tariff was reduced to 12 cents, which included a seven-cent gathering charge and a five-cent transmission charge. "I admit I made a mistake in the deal," said Connelly, "but it worked out all right for the benefit of the company. In fact, if we

start in a project of this nature," Manning said. "They said it would be a hard line to build and they needed people with lots of experience. While the Mannix people hadn't built a lot of pipelines, they had built a lot of

had not done it that way we probably would never have had the pipeline."

Connelly's fortuitous mixup in gas and oil transmission formulas was a major factor in swaying the conservation board to award the permit

1952 ▶

Canadian Lester Pearson is named president of the General Assembly of the United Nations.

1952 ▶

The invitation and menu for the Christmas party.

"THE BUILDING BUSINESS WASN'T NEARLY AS EXCITING"

"The Royal Bank Building was relatively profitable and we found it was interesting work," explained Chip Collins. "So we decided to go into the building business on an ownership basis and develop an office building. That turned out to be the Financial Building in Edmonton."

Work on the Financial Building, an 11-storey reinforced concrete structure, began in the spring of 1956. The building was located at 100th Avenue and 107th Street. "We imported a German high crane that was the fore-runner of the tower cranes you see erecting buildings today," said Fred Fenwick. "It was certainly the first one in Western Canada. We set a building record at that time of a completion of a floor a week. That was the first time that had ever been done. After we erected the building, we managed it for a while with our partners. Subsequently, the building was sold by the partnership. After all, we were contractors, we weren't building owners."

Nor was the company interested in pursuing further building partnerships. With no sponsor and no mechanism for breaking a deadlock, the Financial Building experience proved a good lesson in how not to structure partnerships. Partly because of this experience, Mannix Ltd. decided to not pursue further work in this field of construction. Explained Collins, "It was Fred C. Mannix's decision that the building business wasn't nearly as exciting nor as profitable as heavy construction. It's just a totally different field of work. Fred saw that his main interests lay elsewhere. He said that we were just dirt movers in massive quantities."

to Pembina Pipe Line Company Limited. The low tariff, the flexibility of the plan to take oil into Edmonton and the makeup of the predominantly Canadian Mannix group won the deal. Winning the bid, however, did not make Pembina Pipe Line a popular company within the established Alberta oil industry. "Nobody was dealing with us," said Connelly. "We were like second-class citizens walking up and down the street because of our getting the line. The other oil companies thought that we were too aggressive or had too much association with the government in Edmonton, which we did not."

The Search for Outside Financing for Pembina
"The New Yorkers weren't interested in the idea, mainly because it had never been done."

Now that the group had won the deal, they needed to get their financing in place. "As a team we won the permit, the right to build the pipeline and were given a certain period of time to get started," said Gallagher. "Fred Mannix wanted the company to remain private, so we chose to see if we could finance this in the New York area, through the help of Loeb, Rhoades. We had a number of meetings with one group called EBASCO, which was a subsidiary of Electric Bond & Share."

Attorney Jack Saucier, whose law firm included Jack Gallagher as a client, participated in these negotiations. "When it came to Pembina pipeline," recalled Saucier, "there was great competition to get the permit to build it. Of course, everybody in the oil industry wanted the permit and the Mannixes were persona grata with the provincial government. So, with the Fenerty firm acting for the Mannix crowd, they got the permit to build the pipeline. At this point, Mannix got involved with Jack Gallagher of Dome Petroleum fame. Jack is an extremely clever fellow and he was to have an interest in the project. He had financial connections in New York with Loeb, Rhoades, so he persuaded Mannix that they should have separate counsel for Pembina. It shouldn't be just the regular Mannix solicitors. So that's how we got into the act."

"I didn't deal directly with Loeb, Rhoades," said Saucier. "I was acting for Mannix. I remember Jim Scott was at the airport. He was a graduate engineer and a graduate master of business administration from Harvard, and he wanted to know what I knew about pipelines. At this stage, it wasn't very much. But nobody in Calgary knew very much about pipelines either.

1952 ▶

During the Superintendents' Conference, Margie Mannix institutes the annual ladies luncheon for superintendents' wives.

1953 ▶

Long-timer Ora Burggren is in charge of work on the Spray Lakes pump stations near Canmore, Alberta.

"We went to New York and the heat was unbelievable. I had never been to New York during a heat wave, and I was afraid to walk across the street with all the masonry around for fear I'd collapse, the heat was so stifling. We stayed at an old hotel on Park Avenue. In the Mannix expedition was Fred Jr. [F.C.], and he had his young son, Freddie [F.P.], who was a little boy at this stage. He had him along for some reason and he had a spacious, beautiful suite. His right-hand men were Eric Connelly, chartered accountant, and Everett Costello, barrister and solicitor. Then he had an interesting private secretary, a fellow called Dave Leydon, a former professional boxer, who had once fought Sugar Ray Robinson to a draw."

"In addition," said Saucier, "there was a team of a dozen or more engineers. We were there a couple of weeks in this stifling heat. We met in various offices downtown. There was an outfit called EBASCO — they were originally Electric Bond & Share — a major consulting engineering outfit. We met there and also at Loeb, Rhoades and various other points downtown. We all had breakfast in Fred Mannix's suite every morning, everybody concerned including all these engineers, Costello, Mannix, and so on. We'd discuss various problems of common interest and we would make plans for the day. For some reason that I never understood, and still don't, Scott, who was the president of the company and had been hired by the Mannix people, chose to side with Jack Gallagher, who was competing with the Mannix company, trying to finagle control of the company because, obviously, it was a very valuable prospect. Since I was acting for the company, I refused to get involved in any of these competitions for control."

"Fred Mannix had a rather unusual habit," continued Saucier. "Instead of making an offer, he would negotiate like crazy with Loeb, Rhoades. Their representative was a very nice fellow called Cliff Michel, who later became a director of Dome. He and Jack Gallagher were trying to negotiate so that Loeb, Rhoades would get control of Pembina, but the Mannix boys were too smart for that. However, they tried and Fred Mannix had a peculiar system; instead of just making a counteroffer in simple terms, he always insisted on a draft agreement. So Costello and I and Connelly were madly drawing a new agreement every day. I would dictate it to Costello, Connelly would contribute to the discussion, and we'd wind up with something handwritten by Costello. We'd then get a typist to type it and we'd revise it and then we'd give this to Fred and he would present this to Cliff Michel and Jack Gallagher. And they would say, 'No way.'"

"We did this for a couple of weeks and they were getting nowhere," said Saucier. "Connelly and Costello would blow up at each other, particularly Connelly. Costello was a very quiet restrained fellow. He was a very bright fellow, usually very quiet and subdued. But he and Connelly would have the most terrific rows during the course of drafting these agreements. In the course of drafting one of these daily agreements — it was all very technical, who would be on the board and how the shares would be issued and how it would be financed, and all this sort of thing — Connelly, who was a very bright guy, came up with an original idea in financing a pipeline that was ultimately accepted. The custom up until that time was that when a group of oil companies promoted a pipeline, each of those companies would sign a throughput agreement. That meant the company would produce a certain volume of oil and put it into the pipeline per annum, failing which they would pay for it as if they had, even if they hadn't. Connelly came up with the bright idea of getting an engineering report of the reserves in the Pembina field, and using that as the basis on which the participating companies would make any contributions. But the New Yorkers weren't interested in the idea, mainly because it had never been done."

When this fell through, the group then had a number of meetings with Metropolitan Life. Gallagher met with the Metropolitan executives. "I remember I presented a map to Metropolitan Life showing the proven, probable and possible areas of the Pembina oil field in different colours," Gallagher said. "At the time, there were only 16 completed oil wells in the field. The remainder was just potential. I believe they were in favour of financing, but like all insurance companies, they went to an outside consultant for corroboration, in this case Degolyer McNaughton of Dallas. Degolyer McNaughton was much more conservative than I was, saying the field would produce a maximum of 55,000 barrels per day after five years of operation, and from then on it would decline."

The Dallas firm was, of course, dead wrong. "Actually, what happened was that by 1957, the Pembina field was producing over 100,000 barrels a day, with recoverable reserves approximately twice my estimate," said Gallagher. "I remember that the executive vice president of Metropolitan Life called me a few years after the line was built to tell me that the Met was embarrassed by the fact that their Degolyer McNaughton estimate had proved to be super-conservative. He said, 'Jack, I've got your rough map in front of me, and all the proven, probable and possible have now come in, and more.'"

1953 ▶

The Bearspaw Dam is built for Calgary Power Ltd. on the Bow River. This is one of six dams built by the outfit for Calgary Power on the Bow.

1953 ▶

Alec Guinness is a sensation in the Tyrone Guthrie production of Richard III at Stratford, Ontario.

Obtaining Financing From the Royal Bank of Canada
"And the banker went home and slept."

With the hope of private financing failing, the commitment was made with the Royal Bank to go public, even though Mannix initially wanted to keep the company private. Like the Alberta government, the Royal Bank had its reasons for wanting to see Mannix Ltd. break into the pipeline business. "As assistant manager of the main branch, you dealt with the major accounts along with the manager," explained Tom Dobson, then assistant manager of the Royal Bank's main branch in Calgary, "But it fell to the assistant manager's lot to do all the analytical work and the legwork of putting the proposition in banking form and submitting it to our head office in Montreal. It was because I had to do that detailed work that I became quite close with the Mannix organization.

"In those days, we had the bulk of the oil business and we had a tremendous construction business through Mannix. Mannix Ltd. was constantly expanding their construction activities, which was the dominant thing up until 1950. When oil was discovered in 1947, from then on, the whole province just boomed from an agrarian economy to oil, gas and construction. On the one side there was the oil industry with your large integrated giants, like Imperial Oil, Shell and Gulf, but in the non-oil exploration and production clients, my recollection would be that Mannix Ltd. was our major account."

"I'd never before been involved in an industry where you had such huge contracts and there were often the overruns because of

James Muir, president and chairman of the Royal Bank of Canada, 1954-1960.

unforeseen problems," continued Dobson. "They were quite legitimate overruns, but as a banker, I would see that the receivables no longer covered the loan. But Fred Mannix and his people had a tremendous ability to negotiate and renegotiate things. And they always ended up on the right side of things, and the banker went home and slept.

"The relationship with the Mannix family has been of paramount importance to me, not just as a banker, but as an individual. I say this because of their integrity, because they fully supplied the bank with all the information you could possibly want, and because you dealt with competent people. If you weren't competent, you were gone. There was just a tremendous respect I had for the whole organization."

"When you deal with a group like this, you develop a lot of confidence, so the fact that the company had no experience in running pipelines wasn't a concern," said Dobson. "So many of their construction jobs were totally different than any other ones they'd done. They had a broad range of capabilities for overcoming problems, and some of those were pretty major, in my view, compared to running a pipeline. But the Mannix group had people who knew how to do these things, or could learn, or they'd find the right people. But I think that was a major step in diversifying away from heavy construction as a high-risk business, certainly in bankers' eyes. We had no concerns about the capability of building that pipeline, and we liked the diversification — getting from the up-and-down heavy construction industry into something that's stable and a generator of cash."

1953 ▶

Mannix crews work with the Prairie Farm Relief Administration at the St. Mary Irrigation District and construct the Milk Ridge Dam, just southeast of Raymond, Alberta.

1953 ▶

The Toronto Subway is nearing completion. Mannix-McNamara crews finish the Davisville shops where the trains are stored and repaired.

1953 ▶

Near Golden, British Columbia, Railroad Division crews daylight the Palliser Tunnel. They remove the mountain through which the tunnel was cut, making the route an open cut.

The story of how F.C. Mannix got financing from James Muir, then head of the Royal Bank has become legend in Calgary circles. As the story goes, it took just 20 minutes with Muir to secure a $14-million loan for the construction. "You must remember, we'd had this close relationship with Mr. Muir over the years," explained Connelly, "and we were very friendly with the top people at the Royal Bank in Montreal. It wasn't like a bunch of strangers going in." It is said that James Muir asked Fred C. Mannix just three questions. The first was, "Fred, what are you here for?" F.C. Mannix is said to have responded, "We had made a promise to the Province of Alberta and we need help. We have this pipeline permit." Next, Muir asked, "How much do you need?" Mannix said, "We need $14 million." Muir then asked, "Will your construction company stand behind this?" When Mannix responded, "Yes," Muir said, "Well, you got it."

The Royal Bank's quick response would not have been possible without the clout of the legendary James Muir. Muir left high school at 1:00 p.m. in 1907 and joined the Bank of Scotland an hour later as a clerk. Fifty-three years later, he died, president of Canada's largest bank. "Muir is the reason the Royal Bank moved from third size to first size, the largest bank," said Dobson. "He got us all working and alert and alive to trying to develop new business, which was a new concept entirely. Where everything today is done by credit committees and policy committees, he made instant decisions. Lord knows, if Fred Mannix phoned through to James Muir and said, 'I've got a chance to build the Pembina pipeline. I think it's a really good deal and I need $14 million,' it wouldn't have surprised me if Mr. Muir said, 'You've got it. Go to the bank and get it and we'll work the details out later.'"

Following the Mannix group's brief, but fruitful, meeting with James Muir at the Royal Bank, "we were introduced to their pension fund and so forth, and we started setting up a pattern of sale," Connelly explained. "You see, Mannix didn't have any money to put into a deal like this, but we had the permit which was worth so much money, and then we had a contract for building the pipeline, which we could earn money out of in the construction business. So that's what formed our equity, that plus advances from the Treasury Branch which we were able to get to cover that situation through Sparling-Davis, a subsidiary of ours. Then we had promised Loeb, Rhoades and/or Dome 25 per cent of the equity if they would put up the cash. So they put up the cash."

Selling Pembina Stock
"The Province had never done anything like that before."

After the bank came in with their plan of financing, the Mannix group was referred over to Nesbitt Thompson. "That's when I first met Deane Nesbitt," said Connelly. "They would go ahead and put out convertible bonds and convertible preferred stock. I said, 'Well, for God's sake, where do we wind up with this?' It would be better for us, rather than having convertible shares and diluting our situation, to go ahead and bonus the bonds and bonus the preferred stock. Don't sell any stock out of our own pocket, then we're not diluted. So that is what we did, and we wound up with 85 per cent of the company, instead of being diluted down to practically nothing. Then, in order to maximize the tax advantage, it was necessary to reduce the share ownership of the Mannix corporation itself a bit."

"Jim Scott was Pembina's first president," explained Connelly. "He was the man who arranged for the getting together of the first staff, operating staff in the field, and also for getting the first construction under way. The construction work, of course, was left to the Mannix company, and they used the profit to purchase the equity in the company. That's how they got their equity, and I saw to it that the profit earned was sufficient for this purpose. I had some complaints from Scott, who wanted to do it differently, but I was looking at the whole Mannix picture, and it was necessary to protect the company.

Pembina Pipe Line Ltd., incorporated in Alberta, September 29, 1954.

1953 ▶

The camp at the Palliser Tunnel job is located between the rail right-of-way and the river flowing out of Emerald Lake. The idyllic noise of the river is shattered by the 22 trains a day that thunder by the site.

1953 ▶

Crossing the North Thompson River with a pipeline presents an interesting challenge.

PROTECTING THE PERIMETER

One of the outgrowths of the Cold War was that Mannix Ltd. branched out into a new and highly unprecedented line of construction work. In April 1955, Mannix Ltd. took on the Mid-Canada Warning Line, part of the program to erect a radar warning system on the 55th parallel which would warn Canada and the United States of air attacks. For Mannix Ltd. crews, the project meant more than two years of intense effort in an inhospitable climate. And yet, in true Mannix style, while they battled harsh weather, site access problems and rugged terrain, they always managed to fit in a game of pitch.

"When they started to build the radar system, Mannix got a job at Anzac, which is about 25 to 30 miles south of Fort McMurray," recalled Graham Pollock. "We opened a little office near the work site. I did the procurement and expediting for the job. The only way you could get up there was on a 'speeder.' That was a little railroad car that has a little gas engine on it. You would sit on it and it would just putt-putt along on the railroad track. It went about 20 miles an hour.

"On one trip, I went with Karl Collett. It was quite something for me to be riding with the general manager of the company. Karl just loved to play cards. So there we were under a tarp on this speeder playing pitch. We played pitch all the way up to the work site. I didn't have much money so Karl lowered the stakes, as we had to play for something. It rained the whole time we were playing but I thought it was really great."

"Most of the shares, of course, came to the Mannix company itself. Then a certain amount of the common shares were used as a bonus for bonusing the sale of the debentures and also the preferred stock to the underwriters — very little, 15 per cent altogether. Then we also had previous commitments to Jack Gallagher and Dome Petroleum. So he received in the company the option and the right to buy 25 per cent, which he exercised. That left 60 per cent. There was another 10 per cent which had to be distributed in order to bring the ownership of the company just down below 50 per cent. That was in order to make it possible, for tax purposes, to crystallize the value that we had placed on the permit itself. You see, the permit which we acquired, and paid for, had a certain value, so when it went into the company, it went in as a certain amount of money. But in order to get it to that value, there had to be a certain block of shares, around 10 per cent, which had to be distributed."

To comply with the bank's requirement of a public stock offering, a new company named Pembina Pipe Line Ltd. was incorporated on September 29, 1954. Pembina Pipe Line Ltd. would assume all property, assets and undertakings of Pembina Pipe Line Company Limited, its privately owned predecessor, when the pipeline was finished.

The sale of Pembina's stock stunned some in the financial community. "It was fun, because the financing houses, which were Dominion Securities and Tanner Brothers, insisted that the common stock had to be distributed across Canada because there wasn't enough market in Alberta to look after this common stock issue," said Connelly. "So we had a meeting between Mr. Manning, Mr. Tanner, Mr. Mannix and myself in a room in the Palliser Hotel. I took it upon myself to tell Mr. Manning that if there were any shares not sold in the province of Alberta, the Mannix corporation would pick them up. Well, that issue was oversubscribed five times. We didn't have the opportunity to pick up any shares."

"That was a cornerstone in the thinking and operation of development projects in the province," said Connelly. "The Province had never done anything like that before, but it was used as a basis for future development — Albertans first. What allowed me to make that statement was something that came out in the Pembina deal, because what I had learned in New York and Montreal was that lenders wouldn't finance without guarantees. But then we proved to them that we didn't need a guarantee because every bit of oil that is produced in the province had to have its proportional share. There's a built-in guarantee for the throughput

1953 ▶

Hupp & Elliott Construction Co. Ltd. is acquired and the name is changed to Hupp Ltd. Al Jones, left, with George Hupp supervise the Brock-Colville extension near Kindersley, Saskatchewan.

1953 ▶

Pete Krywy, Mike Bushuk, and Bill Parkinson, left to right, of Sparling Tank Limited, a newly acquired company, erect storage tanks at the Petrofina job in Hamilton, Ontario.

through your pipeline, so we used it in the gas pipeline developments, too. That came out of the Pembina situation, and out of that, of course, came the respect for the Mannix organization. Mannix was getting greater and greater respect in the general marketplace because of what was happening here.

"So we had the company in place, and at the same time, we were able to pay off the provincial government for its position in Sparling-Davis, which we had acquired. We were able to look after that responsibility out of this deal. So, really, the acquisition of that permit, the financing and the building of the pipeline, and the ownership of that pipeline, all those things constituted a major change in all the affairs of the Mannix organization and the Mannix family, especially as we were on our own now, after having bought out Morrison-Knudsen. Without that deal, I don't know what would have happened."

"I commend the efforts of Eric Connelly and the Mannix group in financing the project," Gallagher said. " Eric Connelly, on behalf of Mannix, was able to arrange that financing through the Royal Bank and Nesbitt Thompson. Under the new arrangement, Dome and Loeb, Rhoades dropped to 25 per cent. We — the Dome and Loeb, Rhoades group — held our shares for a number of years. Dome was in the need of cash and Loeb, Rhoades did not want to stay in the pipeline as long as we were stepping out. So after a number of years of enjoyable and profitable association, we sold our shares."

"Fred Mannix was dynamic and courageous," admired Gallagher. "People in the oil patch were anxious to be associated with people who were doing things. Mannix was one of the few companies in Western Canada that was willing to take on the major contracts that were available. It took a lot of courage to do so, because you can lose a lot of money. Fred was a hands-on operator, and he attracted doers around him. I was always impressed by the calibre of people that Fred Mannix assembled."

Designing the Pembina Pipeline
"Just remember, this looks like a goose."

One of the "doers" crucial to the early success of Pembina was Peter (P.G.) Clarke. A veteran of Mannix's pipeline construction jobs, Clarke earned his B.Sc. in civil engineering from the University of Saskatchewan in 1950. He joined Mannix as a superintendent/engineer of pipelines in 1953. "One of the important things about Pembina is the time frame when this was conceived," he said. "This was an idea, nothing more. Then we took it through the application, the hearing, the granting of the permit, the financing, ordering the material, building part of the line and having it in operation — all that was done very quickly. Connelly submitted the letter saying we'd like to be heard before the board on April 11, 1954. The pipeline had to be in operation by November 15, but they had one other string on that, which had never been put on before, and that was you had to start work by July 15. The board gave us a go-ahead at the end of May.

Peter (P.G.) Clarke.

"I was away on Easter holidays and Jim Scott sent me a telegram saying, 'Get down here right away.' They locked me up in a hotel room in the Wales Hotel. The only person that came around was Brock Montgomery, and I wasn't to be seen near the office. It was so secret, they didn't even tell me what I was there for. Brock said, 'Somebody will be coming over with a map.' I think it was Phil Buesnel who came over with this two-mile-to-an-inch map, and Brock said, 'This is going to be a gathering system out in the Pembina area.'"

"Then Brock said, 'Now, there will be another fellow along,'" said Clarke. "Sure enough, in about an hour, Bob Port, a geologist showed up. He asked me if I had the map, and I said, 'Yes, but I don't know what it's all about.'

1953 ▶

The reconstruction of the wharf at Burin, Newfoundland, results in a new concrete-topped, ballasted wharf prepared to handle large ships.

1953 ▶

The Mannix dredge Kananaskis at work in the St. Lawrence River, near Whitby, Ontario.

He got out his papers and said, 'Here's the three wells that are drilled. I'll draw you roughly the outline of the field. Just remember, this looks like a goose. There's another well called the Shell Peers well away from the main field, but there's a pinch out here and that's the neck of the goose. The Shell Peers well is the eye, and here is the rest of it, the body. I'll even make it look more like a goose because I don't know what's happening down at this end. So that's all the tail feathers.'"

"I had absolutely nothing except a pencil and a straightedge and Brock's location of the pump station," said Clarke. "So we started from there and I drew this map for the gathering system. It became an unbelievable thing, because there wasn't an oil field anywhere in the world that had that many wells. I thought I had better scale it down a little bit, so at the outer edge I scaled it down from four wells a section to something less. But it still came up to about 4,500 wells, which seemed far out of line with anything else. Then I'd been hearing from people that the viscosity would make the oil very hard to pump."

"I had worked with some pipelines as a contractor, but not as an engineer," continued Clarke. "So, without using slide rules or any design apparatus, I drew this gathering system. Now, they were all straight lines and they went from point to point. It was just a plain white sheet of paper with all the sections worked on it, but it didn't show roads or anything, and that was submitted at the hearing." When this seat-of-the-pants engineering was presented to the conservation board, it quickly became

The early gathering system planned, built and operated by Pembina Pipe Line Ltd.

apparent that Clarke's plan was much more suitable for Pembina's crude than what Texaco and at least one other pipeline bidder had planned. Texaco meant to use a gravity system like that employed at the Wizard Lake field. The system featured no pumps, trusting gravity to move the oil. For Pembina, it simply would not have worked. "Time has shown that they were dead wrong, and we were dead right," Clarke said.

"It only took P.G. about an hour and a half to do this," added Montgomery with amazement. "And if you go and look at that gathering system right now, you will find that it is exactly the same way."

Building a Gathering System and Pipeline for the Pembina Field — "It was the most God-awful country."
When Harry Booth joined the Pembina staff as controller in August 1954, the organization consisted of exactly two people: Jim Scott, the president, and Floyd Madill, an experienced oil man formerly with Imperial Oil, who had been hired as general manager.

"Jim Scott's background was in mechanical engineering, but he was also a Harvard Business School graduate," said Booth. "So his background was suited for new-project type things, and he was very good at heading up the company. We were starting with really just a paper company and the permit to build the pipeline. We had no people and no organization, so the staffing up of the company with competent people was the next challenge. From my own side of the thing, I knew absolutely nothing about oil pipelines. My accounting training and

1953 ▶

A view over the Miss Mannix in Port Maitland, Nova Scotia, in early work on the new steel sheet piling wharf that will replace the federal government's wooden wharf.

1953 ▶

Another steel sheet piling wharf is constructed for the federal government at Baie-Comeau, on the north shore of the St. Lawrence.

DRAYTON VALLEY

"Oh, it was a terrible place"

"In the summer they started the Pembina pipeline," recalled Robert S. (Bob) McNeill, who joined Mannix Ltd. in 1951 as a radio serviceman. "It rained. It was terrible. It affected everything. The only roads into Drayton Valley were dirt roads, and the only way to get in there was to go to the end of the paved highway and get a Cat to haul you the next 10 miles into the job. When you were finished, they'd haul you out again. There was just no way you could get around. In fact, they actually shut the job down for eight weeks, until the frost came along in the fall, so they could move around out there.

"Oh, that was a terrible place. We worked from five o'clock in the morning until God knows when at night. We were busy seven days a week. We never really stopped, other than days when it poured rain. Then you'd hang around a little bit, but most of the time we spent working."

"I remember Drayton Valley when we first went in there," said McNeill. "We were living in a tent and had a cookhouse in an old chicken coop. There were 10 of us, and we had a ticket to eat there. Other than that, there was no place except one little Chinese restaurant, and that had a line out the door, 24 hours a day. There was a store, a little garage, a service station, and half a dozen houses. That constituted Drayton Valley at that stage. There was just nothing there at all."

background, though, was really what was required for setting up the accounting and financial side of the business. There really wasn't a lot of precedent that I was aware of in Canada for the type of operation that we were going to set up. You had to be a little innovative, because we were breaking new ground."

While Mannix Ltd. had a solid background in pipeline construction through its work on the Interprovincial, Trans Mountain and several other Canadian pipeline projects, Pembina presented a different kind of animal. A small core of Mannix pipeliners were on their own, from the design to the completion of the system. They were not, by their own admission, oil and gas people. But throughout the summer and fall of 1954, they would learn the business from the mud up.

Two employees, a Dodge Power Wagon and the mud of the Pembina pipeline right-of-way, 1954.

1953 ▶

Construction of the Groat Bridge begins in Edmonton, Alberta. The project is a joint venture with Burns & Dutton.

1953 ▶

Mannix-O'Sullivan crews crush gravel and lay the surface of the new road at Valleyview, Alberta.

Specifications for the 16-inch (40-centimetre) pipe included that it be tested to withstand a fluid pressure of 1,400 pounds per square inch (9.65 million newtons per square metre). One particularly critical portion of the main line involved spanning the North Saskatchewan River. Here Pembina crews would secure two special 10-inch (25-centimetre) river-crossing pipes. Other specifications provided for the installation of four centrifugal-type pumps at the main station, and another packing 600 horsepower. Pembina crews also had to grade the ground for and erect three 80,000-barrel (9.5-million-litre) storage tanks, a warehouse, service garage and related structures. Meanwhile, as construction on the transmission line and other facilities started, work also began on the gathering lines and batteries.

This work would not have been particularly daunting, except for two things: the terrain and the weather. "It was the most God-awful country," said Clarke. "There was muskeg, bush and moose wallow." There was also rain. The summer of 1954 brought deluges of almost Biblical proportion. The average annual rainfall during the preceding 30 years at Edson was 14.07 inches (35.7 centimetres). However, during the three summer months of 1954 alone, a drenching 15.47 inches (39.3 centimetres) poured from the skies. Roads turned to mud and nearly all pipeline construction in Alberta was either slowed or stopped.

"One of the things that shut down the operations was that the government wouldn't allow us to use the roads," recalled Montgomery. "So we'd go out and grade the roads at our own expense, hoping they'd dry out. But then it would just rain again. We'd grade some more, and all that time the pipeline crews and all the equipment was just sitting there. We really didn't get good

weather until October, which was when the construction really got going."

But somehow, work continued through the soggy summer. "We worked every day that we could," Montgomery explained, "even if it meant working a day and stopping for a week." Crews were often cut off from supplies. "We had one camp at the North Saskatchewan River crossing," recalled Montgomery, "and it ran short of bread. A D-8 Cat was sent in from Alsike Corner, just north of Breton about 12 miles away, with a box of bread. Why they only brought one, I don't know." Added Gordon Walker, "The D-8 bulldozers were sometimes the only vehicles that could get through the muskeg. Even then, you quite often had to send out a second D-8 to bring the first one back in."

The vast expanse of the field also complicated the job of building gathering lines. Crews based in Drayton Valley frequently had to commute nearly 40 miles (64 kilometres) each way to get to a job site; once in the morning, and on the return each night. There was no bridge crossing the North Saskatchewan in the Drayton Valley area. In the dead of winter, traffic could cross on ice; during the summer, on a small ferry. However, the ferry was often unreliable, and could not operate when the ice was breaking up or flowing in chunks. On the days when the ferry was inoperable, to get from Drayton Valley to the south portion of the Pembina field, just across the river, one had to drive 90 miles (145 kilometres) to Edmonton, south to Leduc, west again to Breton and into the field. The detour totalled 230 miles (370 kilometres).

Communications were another problem. Drayton Valley was a toll office of Alberta Government Telephones, with only one circuit available. In April 1954, the

Top: Pembina employees (from left to right) Jack Barbeau, John Poloway, Al Horne, Larry Gano, John Carroll, Del Meads and R.H. (Spike) Brown, take a break in the dry, late fall of 1954.

Above: Pembina pipeline construction in the summer of 1954 faced rain, muskeg, rain, mud, rain, moose wallow and rain.

1953 ▶

The contract to grade and gravel the Sudbury Highway is the third section of the Trans-Canada Highway awarded to the outfit.

1954 ▶

Mannibec Ltd., a wholly owned Mannix subsidiary, is formed to pursue projects in Eastern Canada, particularly in Quebec and Labrador.

1954 ▶

One of the engineering marvels of the 1950s occurs with cooperation between Canada and the United States. The St. Lawrence Seaway requires several large construction projects, including the Barnhart Cofferdam, the largest steel sheet piling project on the St. Lawrence.

Alberta government approved Drayton Valley as an official town site, and a telephone system was installed. While there may have been telephones, for "the first couple of years, we didn't have any mobile communication," recalled Al Horne, who joined Pembina in 1954 as a field gauger. "It presented problems. If you got stuck out in the boondocks, you just walked merrily down the road until you found a ride home. If you found one."

Weather conditions in Alberta during the summer of 1954 put an end to any possibility of the Pembina job going at breakneck speed. For one thing, the muskeg could not support the weight of a backhoe. Consequently, the crew had to use what were called mats. "They were made out of timbers," explained P.G. Clarke. "They would be about four or five feet wide and, say, 10 to 12 feet long. You just kept moving them ahead of yourself."

"It was like a platform," added Montgomery, "and the backhoe sat on this square table. Only it was in pieces, and as you moved off one piece, it was picked up and placed in front again. But it really slowed things down. I don't think we made more than 1,000 feet in a day, or anything near that. If it had been winter, we could have used the trencher in the frozen ground. But, of course, we couldn't wait for winter."

The muskeg and boggy brush-covered ground — what P.G. Clarke called "moose wallow" — gave the pipeline builders little supportive ground. While trying to dig trenches that provided between 30 inches (76 centimetres) and three feet (0.9 metres) of covering atop the pipe, ditchers found that the set sides either caved in, or the trench kept filling with water.

But the biggest problem the crews faced was going through the oil fields adjacent to the Leduc area. The pipeline had to pass through a stretch of land that was laden with other lines. "Now, we had to get through there without breaking any," said A.M. (Sandy) Day, who came to Pembina after working with the Mannix company on the Interprovincial and Trans Mountain pipelines. "Because if we did, we could have set the place on fire, to start with, or we could have had a lot of trouble."

The Pembina crew had to research and discover the location of all the existing pipelines and flag the routes. "That's so the backhoe operator could see the flag and be more careful getting around them," said Day. "But we did get through the mass of lines and never broke one. It was quite an achievement, actually, because there were a lot of oil lines headed to storage tanks and gas lines, too."

"WE HAD TO EAT OUT ALL THE TIME"

"Pembina established an Edmonton office on 103rd Street, above Robertson Seed & Feed," recalled Al Horne. "When I showed up to work on November 22, 1954, I was introduced to Spike Brown, the area head gauger. He had started a week or two prior to that. He and I went across town to an army surplus store to pick up some surplus steel bunk beds. We took those to Drayton Valley and arrived to find the big metropolis of Pembina. It consisted of two 10-foot by 20-foot skid shacks. One served as the office and the other as the bunkhouse. Six of us lived in the bunkhouse. There were three bunk beds in there."

"That really was the sum total of our facilities," said Horne. "Mannix's camp was located behind Fuhr's garage in town. We used to go down there to use their washroom facilities in the morning. Then we'd tote off down the road a little bit to Ma's. It was run by an elderly couple who'd pulled together a couple of old farm granaries to make a restaurant. They had plank tables with plank benches to sit on. It was home-style cooking, with bowls of potatoes and meat on the table. We didn't have any facilities for cooking at camp, so we had to eat out all the time. There was an alternative. We could go downtown to a couple of restaurants, either the Drumstick or the Wildcat. They appeared about like they sound."

1954 ▶

Because of the commercial importance of the Baie-Comeau wharf, the vast majority of the reconstruction occurs during the freeze-up months of January, February and March.

"It Seemed Like You Were Going Across Forever"

For the Pembina field crews, crossing the river between the main pump station and the Buck Creek area required an act of faith. "One of the most exciting things I remember is driving across the ice when the river froze up," said John Poloway, who joined Pembina in 1954 as a field mechanic. "Maybe you'd get a warm night when you were coming back. We'd come to it and there was no track that you could see. I remember coming to it one time and it was all water. I thought, 'Gee, I don't know how deep that water is.' And I'm sitting there and I'm debating, 'If I'm going to go back to the pump station, back to Devon and on into Drayton Valley, it's going to take me all night.' I did get across, but I sure didn't feel very safe in doing it. It was an eerie feeling with all the water."

Another means of crossing the river was something called the cage. "That was the thing you got into and just pumped yourself across the river," explained Poloway. "That was quite an experience. We had production on the east side of the river; we had offices over there. Every day, we required the field tickets to see how much oil was shipped. Somebody would have to meet the ferry to get the mail."

"Whenever the ferry wasn't running, they had to go across and bring the mail back," said Poloway. "They used to ride across on this cage thing that held three people at the most. The cable came across the river, with the cable being high on each side of the river, but dropping down in the centre. So, you had to get in this thing, release the brake, and you'd go to beat the 60 down to the centre of the river. You're swaying in this cage, and once you reached the centre point, the little engine would take over and it barely moved at all. It seemed like you were going across forever."

All in all, managing the project proved a frustrating exercise. The contract was on a cost-plus-fee basis, rather than a fixed-price basis, which removed some of the financial pressures of the delays. "But F.C. Mannix recognized the importance in the oil industry of meeting deadlines, even though there were very few that gave him a chance to make it under the foul weather conditions," said Walker.

Drilling activity continued at a high level whenever weather and road conditions permitted. More than 50 rigs were often operating at one time in the Pembina field. This represents almost one-quarter of the drilling rigs active in all of Western Canada. Average completion, from spud to rig release, was less than three weeks.

In those early muddy, frustrating days, one man, W.F. (Slim) White, had a profound influence on Pembina's field personnel. A veteran with the Old Valley pipeline in Turner Valley, White joined Pembina Pipe Line as head gauger in 1954. "We called him the 'Great White Father,'" explained Reg Samis, who joined Pembina as a

From the Macdonald Hotel in Edmonton on November 15, 1954, Alberta Premier Ernest Manning telephones Pembina field employees and instructs them to start the flow of Pembina crude to the storage tanks in Edmonton.

1954 ▶

Mannix Gill Limited is formed. The J.B. Gill organization brings 31 years' experience with oil and gas engineering and construction, including new computer capabilities, to the Mannix Group.

1954 ▶

Mannix Ltd. wins the bid to re-grade the southern section of the Alaska Railroad, the main line from Seward to Portage, Alaska.

1954 ▶

The Soviet Union, appearing at the world hockey championships for the first time, defeats Canada 7-2 to win the championship.

gauger that same year. "When the company started there was a bunch of young people, and they didn't have much to do but raise hell. It wasn't easy to get people out here because the more stable people weren't quite as wild, or excited, or romantic about adventure. So Slim got all these young people and he had an awful handful.

"Slim was always able to get the best out of the men, though, and he didn't put up with any stuff. The main thing he didn't put up with was anybody that wasn't honest with him. Slim was a tremendously honest man. He was a completely fair man with anyone he dealt with, and always would be that way if they were fair with him. He was a man of great integrity. That's the way he ran the company and expected the people who worked for him to be. He was a hard worker and very efficient in his job. He expected the people who worked with him to perform to the best of their ability. He was a real cornerstone of what we have here now."

Al Horne wholeheartedly agreed, adding, "Slim was the one fellow at the field level, in my estimation, who came out here with a whole bunch of experience and a wealth of knowledge. Slim was probably 20 years older than virtually everybody else out there on the field crew. He inherited a bunch of green 20-year-olds, me being one of them. The people who were putting the Pembina organization together went looking for somebody with Slim's experience and found him in Turner Valley. There weren't that many pipelines in Canada, truthfully, so there weren't a bunch of experienced people around. How they coaxed Slim out from Turner Valley to that mud hole, I don't know, but it was a good move. Slim was really just like a father to that whole outfit in those early years. He literally kept it going. It was only to Slim's credit that this outfit ever got off the ground. He trained us on the

The "Great White Father" to many young Pembina employees, W.F. (Slim) White.

A GREAT, BIG RED TARGET

"All through those early years, while the producers didn't participate in the early formation or the ownership of the system, they did become militant about the way we operated the pipeline," recalled Larry Gano.

"They were watching us pretty closely and we had to provide some really outstanding service. We had to ship their oil at all times; that was central. We couldn't complain because there were lots of open threats about us. They said we should not even be in the pipeline business. There was a lot of jealousy because up to that time, and probably in North America, there wasn't any other pipeline gathering system such as this one. All of them were owned by the major oil companies, so we were interlopers in the business.

"We had some of the producers watch us with field glasses. One of the early managers, Ken McMillan, was the chap who chose the old Pembina sign with the big logo. It's a big red "P" for Pembina and it also denotes the inside of a pipeline. It's a great, big red target. Ken is the guy who chose that out of a number of suggestions. He said the reason he chose it was that he could see the Pembina trucks from a long ways away. Aesthetically, it's a very poor choice for a sign, but it was effective for that reason."

job. We were starting a lot of new systems up and Slim was everywhere and anywhere. Slim had a very, very high sense of good business ethics and honesty that laid the groundwork for the way we operate here. It's never been forgotten."

Due in large part to the Pembina crew's dedication, by November 1954, construction was completed on the three batteries, connecting 45 producing wells to the gathering system. Under a nearly impossible deadline, oil had entered the system. On November 15, Premier Ernest Manning opened the new field. "It was on November 15th, at about

1954 ▶

The old cribwork pier at Port Maitland, Nova Scotia, is shown at low tide. Newly installed steel sheet piling cells are visible at centre.

1954 ▶

Marilyn Bell, a 16-year-old from Toronto, is the first person to swim across Lake Ontario. Some 250,000 people cheer her finish.

VESTAL VIRGINS

And the birth of the company magazine

In 1950, the Cordel Mine at Halkirk was renamed Vesta Mine. In one of those strange twists of history, the challenge of marketing Vesta coal to the domestic market led to the creation of the Mannix outfit's company magazine.

In the spring of 1952, a young advertising man named David Wood talked to F.C. Mannix about doing an ad campaign for Vesta coal. "Being young and brash, I said we can come up with an advertising program that will help sell your coal," Wood said. "So I put together what I thought was a very good coal-selling scheme. The name Vesta had come from the Latin, from the goddess Vesta and the vestal virgins. That was a symbol of purity and cleanliness, so we decided to play on that theme in our proposal for advertising."

Although Mannix did not buy Wood's advertising campaign, he did offer him a job as Mannix Ltd.'s first public relations manager. "I didn't really know what a public relations manager did, but I pretended that I did," said Wood. After starting work in 1952, "it turned out that Fred didn't know what a public relations manager was any more than I did. But what he wanted was the kind of magazine that Morrison-Knudsen was putting out, which was called *The EM Kayan*. He wanted a public relations manager like theirs, only he wanted to be better." Wood immediately set to work producing a company magazine. In the early going, Wood handled all the writing, photography, editing and layout work for the magazine, which was called *The Mannix Story*.

three o'clock in the afternoon," recalled John Poloway, who joined Pembina in 1954 as a field mechanic. "It was a dark, grey day and the wind was blowing. I can remember this very plainly. I was envious of the people sitting in at the Macdonald Hotel in Edmonton enjoying the opening, while we were out here putting the first crude into the line. We knew the news was on that day at eight o'clock in the evening, so we rushed by car out to Fallis. We went into a cafe and asked them to turn the radio on so we could hear the replay of the official opening. We felt quite good about it."

In a remarkably short period of time, under some of the most adverse conditions possible, a small cadre of Pembina employees had conquered an inhospitable plain and added a new and significant chapter to the history of the Canadian oil industry. "At November 30, 1954, we employed 31 people," wrote Jim Scott in his letter to shareholders in Pembina's first annual report, for the year ending November 30, 1955. "At the end of the fiscal year, we employed 129. To the employees must go much of the credit for our successful growth. Their enthusiasm, cooperation and exceptional devotion to work, in spite of the fact that many had no previous experience in oil gathering, has made the phenomenal development of your company possible."

By November 30, 1955, the Pembina field had 725 producing wells, 98 batteries tied in and 241 miles (388 kilometres) of pipeline in place. Daily deliveries of crude oil had risen from about 12,000 barrels (1.4 million litres) per day in January 1955, to 60,000 barrels (7 million litres) per day by the end of November. At year-end 1955, Pembina's gross revenue from operations amounted to $2,031,511. The earnings attributed to common stock after allowing for income tax reserves were $319,428, equal to 80 cents per share.

Correctly Perceiving the Future of Coal Mining

While Fred C. Mannix was moving his organization into the oil and gas business, he was also laying the foundation for Canada's largest coal mining company. F.C. Mannix was an entrepreneur. One characteristic of an entrepreneur is the ability to see opportunities in situations where others see failure. Another is to move quickly. "Fred was a great gambler," once reflected Merv Dutton. "He had the power of his convictions, too. He didn't hesitate. If there was a move to be made, he made it. He was a driving force. He was a man to take advantage quickly of an opportunity. He saw there was something in that coal business that the rest of us never saw."

1954 ▶

Mannix International Inc., in a joint venture with Mannix Gill, constructs the water treatment plant at Blackwell, Oklahoma.

1954 ▶

The Mannix Ltd. Railroad Division employees prepare to lay rail for a switch on the British Columbia Electric Relay Railway project.

1954 ▶

Mannix Ltd. begins the Pocaterra Dam for Calgary Power Ltd. The dam is downstream from Lower Kananaskis Lake, Alberta. Shown is a dragline removing overburden from the core trench area.

To observers of the western Canadian coal mining industry, the obvious failure of the industry was due to the total collapse of the nation's two largest coal markets: coal-fired steam locomotives and consumer energy demands. The loss of these two markets, the base from which the industry grew, was traceable to one circumstance — the discovery of enormous reserves of oil and natural gas in Alberta. Starting in 1947 at Leduc, many large oil fields were brought in, culminating in 1953 with the discovery of the Pembina field. Pembina was not only the largest field in Alberta, but also the largest of its geologic type in North America.

The development of Alberta's petroleum industry immediately and drastically affected coal mining in Western Canada. Canadian railways scheduled the replacement of their fleets of coal-fired steam locomotives with diesel-driven locomotives by 1956. The effect of the railways' switch to diesel fuel was immediately felt in the Coal Branch. Starting in the early 1950s, the mines in this area began to shut down, one by one. By the end of the decade, Mercoal Mine, the last surviving mine in the Coal Branch, closed down. Meanwhile, plans were also being made to develop natural gas distribution systems throughout Canada. In 1956, the first huge gas pipeline, the TransCanada pipeline, was completed. Within a few years pipelines were delivering cheap natural gas to communities across Western Canada. By the early 1960s, the domestic market for coal would be virtually eliminated.

While the Coal Branch was hit hardest by the precipitous decline in demand for coal, all other major mining regions in Western Canada witnessed a similar string of mine closures. This rapid decline in the coal industry in Western Canada brought an end to the era of contract stripping by which the Mannix involvement in coal mining began. In the early 1950s, Mannix Ltd. crews continued to work in the Crowsnest Pass. Mannix Ltd. had contracts for open-pit mines at Grassy Mountain for West Canadian Collieries, at Baldy Mountain for Crow's Nest Pass Coal, and at Tent Mountain for Coleman Collieries. The last of these contracts, at Tent Mountain, was completed in 1956.

The petroleum industry also produced major changes in Western Canada's coal mining industry. The development of the Leduc field caused a tremendous surge in electrical consumption in Alberta, particularly in the Edmonton area, then the heart of the major oil fields. Oil refineries, pumping stations and pipelines all required enormous electrical energy to operate. The oil boom also created many new jobs, bringing a great influx of people to the province. This population

"To Knit All of Us a Little More Closely Together"

The Mannix Story, (renamed *The Loram Story* in 1975) premiered in November 1952, as the "No Name News and Safety Bulletin of Mannix Ltd." The magazine, which had no photos, was comprised of 20 mimeographed pages of safety announcements, accident reports, job updates and jokes. Plans for a full-fledged company magazine were announced and a contest was launched for a name. In February 1953, Muriel Fraser, a former secretary in Edmonton, won $25 for the winning entry of *The Mannix Story*.

"NO NAME"
NEWS AND SAFETY BULLETIN OF MANNIX LTD.
VOL.I - CALGARY, ALBERTA - NOVEMBER, 1952 - NO.1

Although the first issues of *The Mannix Story* were plain by today's standards, the magazine's intent was worth far more than any glossy, professional magazine. "It may be well, in the first issue of this publication to bear the new name, to tell you why it is being published," wrote F.C. Mannix in the February 1953 issue. "In it, we are not so concerned with the amount of machinery we own, but with the people who run it; we are not so concerned with the jobs we are doing as with the people who are doing them. Naturally we are proud of the work that has been entrusted to us, we are proud of our record of performance — but the primary purpose of this magazine is to knit all of us a little more closely together…. We want all of us to share in the magazine this way. *The Mannix Story* is published by Mannix Ltd. in the interests of its personnel and friends."

Correspondents included Joyce Hancock, Dolly Wells, Pansy Strange, Evelyn Koussaya, Jack Gearhart, Graham Pollock, Marnie Franco, and "Mannix personnel everywhere." For many years *The Mannix Story* continued as an employee newsletter announcing marriages, births and events of Mannix employees.

1954 ▶

The company picnic at the Pocaterra Dam construction site includes the Calgary staff.

1954 ▶

The remains of the rock-filled steel sheet piling cells at Mont-Louis, Quebec, after a vicious hurricane slashes the east coast of Canada.

growth would put even greater demand on Alberta's electrical generating system. Because of the prior hydro-electric construction performed by Mannix Ltd. in Alberta, F.C. Mannix knew the province's best hydroelectric sites were already developed. The prospects of future hydroelectric production in Alberta were extremely limited. Future hydro projects would be located in less accessible areas with greater construction costs and higher transmission line losses.

Mannix's familiarity with the electric utility business stemmed from the extensive hydroelectric construction work F.C. Mannix and his father, F.S. Mannix, performed for Calgary Power Ltd. during the 1940s. The success of these projects resulted in an excellent working relationship between the two organizations. "A relationship with a company like Mannix would be very different today than it was then," explained Marsh Williams, who joined Calgary Power as a young engineer in the 1940s, rose to president in 1973 and became chairman of the board of TransAlta Utilities Corporation (Calgary Power's successor) in 1984. "It was a different era. You didn't have to have the 100-page contract. Very often, you would simply sign a letter that we would go in and do the job. It would be on a cost-plus basis, because it was a relationship of trust. We both went in with the idea that we were going to build the best, least-cost facility on a particular site.

"The Mannix family were the prime [contractors]. If I could put just two elements on it, I'd say that the Mannix family had an inherent drive and pride. They also did not take very much truck with anybody who did not meet their standards. And they knew pretty quickly if they didn't meet their standards. So, as a consequence, from our side, from the client's side, there was a sense of trust and confidence that if they took on a job you could be pretty well assured that it was going to be done, it was going to be on time, and you were going to get your cost out of the other end of it. I think there was a realism that made this relationship work, despite the fact they were tough. Because they had that pride, we knew they weren't going to do a job that wasn't going to be successful."

"Back in the early days of hydro developments, it was such a joint thing between the contractor, the engineers, and the owner in trying to see what was the best under the conditions, that the project became almost like a sculpture," said Williams. "You went in not knowing all the geological, rock foundation conditions, but as you went along you would find those out and then design it, very often in the field. It was like doing a work of sculpture on the site. After having seen the site, they'd come back and put their feet up and say, 'Well, how can we jointly do it?' The ultimate decisions would always be by Dr. Gaherty, head of Calgary Power, and in this case, Fred C. Mannix, because it was their money being risked."

"In those days, Dr. Gaherty was out here in Calgary frequently and always stayed at the Palliser Hotel," continued Williams. "He always had one of two or three suites there and he held long discussions into

Geoff Gaherty of Calgary Power Ltd. The shared vision of Gaherty and F.C. Mannix led to the electrification of southern Alberta through hydroelectric and coal-fired power generating facilities.

A western Canadian prairie coal mine after several years of operation and before reclamation.

1954 ▶

The first whooping crane nesting site in 30 years is discovered at Wood Buffalo National Park in northern Alberta. The bird, once thought extinct, begins a slow comeback.

1954 ▶

The Pembina gathering system includes the transmission line from Drayton Valley to Edmonton, Alberta, more than 840 miles (1,350 kilometres) of gathering system and 640 operating batteries.

wee hours of the night. Hours of the day meant nothing to him. Days of the week meant nothing; Saturdays and Sundays were just like any other day. As an individual, Dr. Gaherty was legend. He used to philosophize on anything. He was a genius in his own right. There used to be open discussions during the evening on many subjects. That was quite a tradition at that time, and much of our company's business was done in the Palliser Hotel. There was just a progression of the senior people from Calgary Power and people like Mr. Mannix from outside, or government people, and they'd discuss the issues of the day. They would come in and debate, discuss the pros and cons of where the province was going, what the issues were. The hotel room was a constant flow of paper and people, coming and going as the subjects would come up. With Mr. Mannix, much of the discussion would revolve around the issues in the province, the development of hydro projects and the involvement of the Mannix organization along with Calgary Power, getting what was the very optimum, the best development that you possibly could."

One prime topic of conversation in these Palliser sessions focused on how to meet Alberta's growing energy requirements and the likelihood that existing hydro-electric facilities could not meet the anticipated demand. "You had Leduc discovered in 1947 and the electrical loads just took off," Williams said. "Dr. Gaherty realized that even though they would like to stay with hydro, they were running out. And that it was not going to be long before all the good sites were going to go. By nature, in hydro, you develop the optimum sites first and

At Utility Mine, overburden has been removed by a dragline to expose the coal seam. A shovel now loads the coal into trucks for delivery to the tipple.

The buildings and tipple at the Wabamun Mine in 1953.

as you go on, the sites become more expensive, or they run out of them, because rivers in Alberta are not limitless in terms of hydro. So the realization was commencing in Dr. Gaherty's mind, back in the 1940s, that the day will come when hydro was going to run out and then what were we going to do? What were the alternatives?"

One alternative was coal. In the late 1940s, Mannix and Gaherty began discussions about developing coal-fired electric generating stations. These would be built close to large strip mines. Partly as a result of these conversations, Mannix purchased the Victory Mine at Lake Wabamun. This mine was located in the heart of the coal field west of Edmonton, Calgary Power's fastest growing load centre. Mannix also approached Gaherty with a study done in the 1920s concerning the use of the Pembina coal field as a possible source for a coal-fired power plant for the Edmonton area. This information came from Jack Sangwin and Bill Blackstock, two Mannix employees who were doing everything they could think of to salvage the Victory Mine, which was facing closure just two years after Mannix bought it. "Jack Sangwin had come up with a report made in about 1921 on the possibility of developing a large coal mine at Wabamun and building an on-site power plant there," said Blackstock. "We looked at it and said, 'Why don't we interest Calgary Power in this thing?'"

Gaherty and F.C. Mannix agreed to work together on the Wabamun project. The Mannix organization owned reserves in the area and could also provide the mining experience needed to operate the mine on contract.

1954 ▶

To operate the Pembina gathering system, Mannix Ltd. forms Pembina Pipe Line Ltd., a publicly traded corporation with a controlling block of shares owned by Mannix Ltd.

1954 ▶

An aerial view of the main pump station of the Pembina gathering system built by Mannix Ltd. and Sparling-Davis Company Ltd.

DETERMINED TO DO THINGS MECHANICALLY

"F.C. Mannix's interest was track, machinery on track, doing things with various machines," said Norris (Buck) Crump, president of the Canadian Pacific Railway from 1955 to 1962, and chairman and president until his retirement in 1972. "He reminded me very much of some of the railway conventions I attended in Chicago down through the years, where it was obvious that the Americans were determined to do things mechanically, regardless of what it cost. Mannix did a tremendous amount of development work on rail track maintenance. Tremendous."

In deciding to use a contract mining company, Calgary Power went against the conventional wisdom. Traditionally, the utility company both owned and operated the coal mine supplying a thermal generating station. "That was quite a normal pattern with utilities on the United States side," Williams said. "You just simply set up a mining division and go to work and mine it yourself. We would have been able to get the expertise, bring in the expertise for it, but typical of our basic philosophy, we said, 'No.' Our business was the production of electricity and the serving of customers with electric service, and the mining business is a totally different field. Why divert our attention away from our main business, when people like Mannix were experts already in this field? And, indeed, it might develop an industry or a company that could use its expertise internationally or outside. It was in Alberta's total interest to have Mannix develop, rather than have us develop."

Alberta was not the only province contemplating coal to produce electricity. Old-timers relate that Saskatchewan's premier, Tommy Douglas, asked F.C. Mannix to bid on the contract to operate Utility Mine, which would supply the new coal-fired Boundary Dam generating station near Estevan, Saskatchewan. This contract, which was the largest coal mining contract ever tendered in Canadian history, was awarded to Alberta Coal Company by Saskatchewan Power Corporation in 1956.

Meanwhile, F.C. Mannix, Si Fraser and Geoffrey Gaherty were negotiating the contract to develop and operate the coal mine that would fuel the Wabamun generating station in Alberta. Although this station would not begin burning coal until 1962, Calgary Power decided that thermal generating stations would be the future base of its systems.

"I think today the management of change is axiomatic," mused Marsh Williams. "The real successful ones should react to change ahead of time; be ahead, that's creative. Anyone can react after the fact and react on crisis, but it is he who can act ahead of time to avoid crisis that's the real creator. That's easily said, but it's hard to get done. Another thing is to have no fear to make decisions and move."

The Railroad Division and the Formation of Mannix International

While F.C. Mannix gambled that most of the future electrical use in Alberta and Saskatchewan would come from coal-fired generating stations, he also anticipated major changes in the railway industry. Lou Franco and F.C. Mannix worked closely in those first days of the Mannix Railroad Division. Since the market for new construction was limited, they decided to investigate track rehabilitation work. From Calgary, the two drove out to visit projects in progress in the surrounding area. For Franco, these visits were not a great deal of fun. "Every time we went by a railroad crew working, Fred would ask me, 'Is that one of our crews?'" Franco recalled. "I'd say, 'No.' And he'd say, 'Why isn't it?' And I'd say, 'That's the railroad's crew.' Fred would ask, 'Well, what are they doing there?' He used to just needle me with that until whenever I'd see a railroad crew coming, I'd want to hide."

1954 ▶

Hupp Ltd. builds the Progas Ltd. gas absorption plant at Big Valley, Alberta.

1954 ▶

Mannix Ltd. and C.L. (Dil) Robertson's dirt-moving outfit combine to form Mannix Robertson Ltd. Robertson, on left, is shown with Ray Decaire, day foreman.

"It Took Columbus Three Times!"

"In our early days, it was all very much trial and error," said Dick Peppin, who joined Mannix International in 1956. "We didn't have an engineering staff, so we did it out in the field. We weren't making very many points with the railroad officials at that time. But then the next morning, we'd try something different and get the equipment to work halfway. It was just a matter of improvising the first day. We would refer to it as, 'Tack it on the plow.' Try it out. If it doesn't work, take a hammer and knock it off and tack another piece on, until you find out just exactly what will work."

This trial-and-error method led to the creation of one of Mannix International's most oft-repeated slogans. "Lots of times, when we tried something, it would just irritate the railroad man in charge of the operation," said Peppin. "We'd have to pacify him by saying, 'Tomorrow is going to be a better day.' He would always give us another chance. The second time we broke down and tied up his railroad, he'd come back screaming and hollering, 'Get this thing off there!' We'd walk up to him and try to pacify him. We'd grab him by the arm and walk down the track to get away from the people. Then we'd tell him our famous saying: 'Remember one thing, Mr. So-and-So. It took Columbus three times!' Eventually, we'd get him to give us another chance."

The backup crew looking after tie renewals, tie plates and rail anchors on the Mannix International project for the Cotton Belt line near Athens, Texas.

As both Franco and Mannix knew, railways seldom used contract help for maintenance work. All railways had large maintenance of way departments, so only a limited need to hire contractors existed. Breaking into this market was a tough proposition, one made even tougher because the Mannix Railroad Division was brand-new and had absolutely no reputation in track rehabilitation work. F.C. Mannix understood all this perfectly well, of course. He realized that the new Railroad Division needed something to develop a competitive edge, an innovation that would enable it to gain a foothold in the track maintenance market. In conversation with Franco, Mannix suggested that perhaps the division could develop a machine to simplify one of the most tedious procedures in railway maintenance of way work — the process of reballasting sections of track. Both Mannix and Franco felt that the standard railway procedure for this task was hopelessly antiquated.

It seemed obvious to both F.C. Mannix and Lou Franco that the business of jacking up tiny sections of track and tamping the ballast was a basic problem that begged for a solution. Lou Franco believed that one way to get around this problem would be to develop a sled-like device that worked under the track. The track would be jacked up, and the sled inserted beneath it.

1954 ▶

Sparling Tank Ltd. builds a new conservation roof on an existing tank at the Shell Oil distribution plant near Toronto, Ontario.

1954 ▶

The Mannix-Raymond Concrete Christmas card sent from the Harmon Airfield construction project at Stephenville, Newfoundland.

MAY THE
Blessings of Christmas
REMAIN WITH YOU
THROUGH THE
New Year

The track would then be lowered onto the back of the sled. As the sled was pulled forward, it would raise the track out of its bed and grade the ballast that fell from the cribs. This machine would also be heavy enough to compact the ballast as it was pulled along. Fred Mannix thought this idea sounded promising. He told Franco to go ahead and try to develop such a sled.

The Mannix Sled, as this simple machine was eventually named, was not entirely Franco's idea. Like many basic inventions, the ballast sled was a design several people were working on simultaneously. Franco came across the concept in a railway magazine article about a Swedish track-raising machine that used the sled idea. Franco then learned that the Santa Fe Railroad was also working on a similar sort of device. This he found out from Rex Corley, a Mannix Railroad Division supervisor, then working out of Vancouver. Corley, who was originally from the American Southwest, was a friend of John Rushmer, the Santa Fe track engineer who developed that railroad's ballast sled prototype. After learning about this machine from Corley, Franco took a trip to the United States to see the Santa Fe sled at work. Franco was able to talk with Rushmer and returned to Canada with some drawings of the machine.

With the help of several Mannix engineers, Franco developed his own design and manufactured a rough prototype in one of the Mannix company's shops in Calgary. This first Mannix Sled was completed in 1952. The machine Franco developed was about 20 feet (six metres) long by 10 feet (three metres) wide and weighed about two tons (1.8 tonnes). It bore

The Mannix Ltd. Railroad Division Winnipeg office. Left to right, Jim Ainsworth, Muriel Combs, Ralph Lloyd, Lou Franco and Fred Heinzelman.

The 1954 rehabilitation of the Alaska Railroad finds the crews deep in the mountains of the Kenai Peninsula, south of Anchorage, Alaska.

little resemblance to the Swedish sled Franco had read about. It was also different in design from the Santa Fe sled. The great advantage of the Mannix Sled was that it eliminated the most tedious part of reballasting — the constant jacking up and tamping of small sections of track. The sled also greatly simplified tie replacement. As it was pulled along, the machine lifted the entire track structure up off the track bed, allowing ties marked for replacement to be knocked off and hauled out of the way as the track structure came off the back of the sled.

Despite early design problems, the success of the Mannix Sled enabled the Railroad Division to gain a foothold in the track maintenance business in Canada. "By the end of 1953, the Mannix company's Railroad Division had 10 projects in progress in Canada for the Canadian Pacific and the Canadian National," said Franco. The outlook for future business seemed so good that Franco decided to form a special Sled Rental Division within the Railroad Division. With the birth of the Mannix Sled and the formation of the Sled Rental Division, the Mannix company found itself in the track maintenance machinery business. They also found themselves with a patent dispute in Canada. "Patents were a very important factor," explained Bill Sharon. "We couldn't make our patents stick in Canada because the CNR refused to accept them as the sleds were developed by Mannix on ballast work for the CNR in southern Alberta. There was a fight going on, which we won in a sort of way, as it was a draw, I think. But our position in the States was protected."

1955 ▶

Mannix Gill Limited is named the prime contractor for the overall construction of the Battle River project located near the Vesta Mine. They build the coal-fired steam power plant.

1955 ▶

The Battle River work includes the construction of an earth and concrete dam to impound water for use in cooling the power plant.

Having formed the Sled Rental Division and established a reputation with the Canadian railways, Lou Franco felt that the next logical step was to penetrate the U.S. market. The question was how to establish a base of operations in the States. In 1954, a solution began to emerge. That year, the U.S. Department of Interior appropriated $4.6 million to rehabilitate the southern section of the Alaska Railroad. The Mannix company decided to bid on the 62-mile (100-kilometre) Seward to Portage job. Since Lou Franco had worked on the original Alaska Railroad rehabilitation work some years earlier, he was the ideal person to bid the job. He also had the Mannix Sled, which would greatly speed up the resurfacing work. Franco's experience and the new Mannix undertrack equipment gave the Railroad Division an edge over the competition. On May 11, 1954, the U.S. Department of Interior awarded the contract to the Mannix company.

J.W. (Jim) Christoff.

While assembling the construction crew for the work in Alaska, it occurred to Lou Franco and F.C. Mannix that it might be a good idea to set up an American subsidiary. This would simplify the accounting for the job as Mannix Ltd. would, of course, be paid in U.S. dollars. The subsidiary could also handle several upcoming Mannix Ltd. construction jobs in the United States. In short, an American subsidiary would not only mean they would be closer to their customers, it would also provide the company with patent protection. The name they chose for this American company was Mannix International. This Mannix subsidiary, the predecessor to Loram Maintenance of Way, Inc., was incorporated in Delaware in August 1954.

With the Alaska Railroad project successfully under way, Lou Franco needed another railroad engineer to bolster his team on the Railroad Division, which was still the real focus of operations. The man Franco selected was Jim Christoff, a bright, ambitious engineer who was then just 26 years old. Franco was a close friend of Christoff's father, Jim Christoff Sr. Lou Franco's father and Christoff Sr. both worked previously as section foremen for the Great Northern Railroad in Montana and were long-time friends. Franco often said that Christoff Sr. was the finest trackman he had ever known. It did not

"THERE IT IS! WE'LL MAKE IT!"

During Mannix International's early years, Jim Christoff was one of the primary sources of equipment modifications. "I remember occasions where I would be out on a job and would get an idea," he recalled. "It would probably be in a small town. I would go back to a motel, get some sandwiches, go in the room, lock the door, take the phone off the hook, and sit and sketch. The next morning we would go off and try some of those ideas. A lot happened that way."

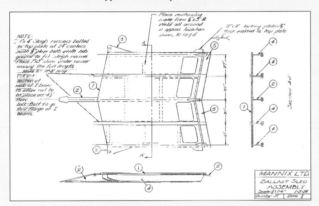

Christoff was also known for drawing out plans on whatever happened to be handy. "When you went out to dinner with Jim," recalled Earl Miller, "you'd sit there and have a couple of drinks, and then he'd get out his pen and make sketches on the tablecloth or napkin, trying to drum up ideas. But when it got right down to building something, he made a chalk drawing on the shop floor. He'd just make the sketch and say, 'There it is! We'll make it!'"

1955 ▶

Mannibec sponsors a joint venture with Miron Frères Ltée. to complete the Lachine Rapids and Dike section of the St. Lawrence Seaway. A deep water channel between the Caughnawaga Reserve and Lac Saint-Louis, Quebec, is constructed.

1955 ▶

The Pacific Great Eastern Railway Company has the outfit build new grade, line and switching-turnout facilities between Prince George and Dawson Creek, British Columbia.

take long for Franco to convince young Christoff to take the position. "Lou Franco had the capability of painting a beautiful picture on the side of anything," said Christoff. "Looking back on it, Lou Franco had something. If Lou Franco told you he could do something, you would believe it. Franco's effort as a promoter — and he was also a heck of a good railroad man — was what really got the Mannix Sled started as a device and eventually saved the railroad industry in North America and Australia hundreds of millions of dollars."

Late in 1954, Franco decided to make Minneapolis, Minnesota, his base of operations in the United States. He chose Minneapolis because it was close to Canada. It was also headquarters for several big U.S. railroads. In January 1955, Franco set up Mannix International's first official U.S. office at 360 Hoover Street in Minneapolis. These were just temporary quarters, however. In July of that same year, Franco moved the company's office to its first permanent home, 1154 Northwestern Bank Building, on Marquette Avenue, in the heart of downtown. This small office suite consisted of two small rooms with a couple of desks and telephones.

Meanwhile, Franco was coordinating activity on several other fronts. The most important of these was in the Calgary shops where Franco and his brother-in-law, Dick Stein, were developing a second piece of Mannix undertrack equipment. This was the Mannix Plow, a new

An early piece of Mannix undertrack equipment is about to be pushed under the section of CPR rail elevated by the two jacks. Once positioned under the rails, each side is attached to a winch cart by cables, then pulled along to clean ballast and the rail bed.

machine developed in 1954 and introduced early in 1955. As with the first jobs in Canada, the Mannix machines made it possible to resurface the track at the rate of one mile per day, triple the usual rate. It was not long before word about the Mannix undertrack machines began circulating through the industry. To resurface track and renew rails at a rate of more than one mile a day was such an astounding accomplishment that *Railway Age,* the leading industry journal in the United States, published a feature-length article with 15 photos, showing the Mannix Sled and Plow in action on the Northern Pacific lines.

While the sled and plow leasing operation in the United States was getting off to a successful start, Mannix International was undergoing major changes. Around the time that Mannix International set up its offices in downtown Minneapolis, Mannix management in Canada decided to move the Railroad Division headquarters from Winnipeg back to Calgary. In August 1955, shortly after this decision was made, Lou Franco resigned as vice president of the Mannix Railroad Division. This time, there would be no persuading him to return. Jim Christoff succeeded him.

While Lou Franco had a profound influence on the formation of Mannix International, he left the company when it was still in its infancy. On taking over Mannix International's sled rental operations, Jim Christoff faced tremendous challenges. The biggest of these was finding

1955 ▶

Weights are attached to a section of the Westcoast Transmission pipeline. Pipe is laid between Huntingdon and Kingsvale, British Columbia, and into the Vancouver area.

1955 ▶

In a joint venture with Dutton & Williams, Mannix engineers provide engineering and management services for the province-wide Alberta Gas Trunk Line. The provision of these services lasts until 1960.

new work. As head of Mannix International, Christoff spent most of his first few years travelling around the country. Since he was a railroad man, he always travelled by train and would go from city to city, carrying a few pieces of promotional literature in his suitcase. Eventually, he bought himself an 8-mm movie camera, shot film of the sled and plow in action, and used his homemade movies as a promotional tool. "Today, they call it marketing," Christoff laughed. "Back then, all I knew was we didn't have any work. I didn't really know how to go at the marketing. Nobody in Mannix really knew how, because most of Mannix's operations were in construction, where somebody advertises that they want something done, you go look at it and bid the work, and that's how you get the job. God, I would hate to look at those films now! They must have been horrible, but at the time they worked."

The films worked well enough that the fledgling operation outgrew its meagre facilities. The company's two-room office in the Northwestern Bank Building was barely enough for two people, and there were no facilities for equipment repair. This was a major problem because the sled and the plow were far from perfected, and it was too expensive to ship the big machines back to the Mannix shops in Calgary for modifications. "Suddenly we had work to do, and although one of these sleds or plows wasn't a delicate thing, it required a hell of a lot of maintenance during the course of a season," Jim Christoff said. "There wasn't any place to do that because all we had was an office in downtown Minneapolis."

In November 1956, Jim Christoff solved both problems of having too small an office and no shop. The corporate offices were moved to 4020 Minnetonka Boulevard in Golden Valley, a suburb west of downtown Minneapolis. Christoff's solution to the shop problem was to lease a small lot in New Brighton, a North Minneapolis suburb 15 minutes from the new office. The lot was next to a rail spur and came with a building — that is, a building of sorts. "There was a pole-type constructed building there, so I made a deal with the owner," Christoff explained. "I leased the ground, and we poured concrete to make a floor inside of the building, and that was what we used as a shop."

Without heat, insulation or plumbing, conditions in this first shop were primitive, to say the least. Much of the repair work was done in the slack winter months, and temperatures in Minneapolis in January and February often stay well below zero for weeks at a time. To go along with all its other charms, the shop was also close to the stockyards. This fact became all too obvious whenever the wind was from the north. Still, Mannix International was operating on a shoestring budget, and the lease on the property in New Brighton was cheap. Jim Christoff figured that somehow the company would manage.

Having found a shop and a new office, Christoff's most pressing problem was building up his staff. When he had taken over Mannix International in 1955, he had inherited just a couple of employees. His key man was his own father, Jim Christoff Sr.,

"THE COMPANY SURE LOOKED AFTER JIMMY"

When Jimmy Nairn retired in 1955, after 35 years with the company, he was not forgotten. Pansy Strange recalled her years with Mr. Nairn with great fondness. "The language he used!" laughed Strange. "We were on the third floor of the Credit Foncier Building, and we had complaints from the second floor about Jimmy's language. He wasn't quiet about it. I can remember when he used to get directives from these young fellows in the accounting department. He'd read these things and say, 'Those young so-and-sos! I was doing books before they were ever thought of.' And he would throw the paper down on the floor and jump up and down on it. Then after he had cooled down a little bit, he'd pick it up and read it again. He'd say, 'By God, they're right!'"

"The company sure looked after Jimmy when he was in the home," continued Strange. "They used to have those big Christmas parties in Calgary, and they'd ask me if I would bring Jimmy down. They would bring him to the airlines, I would look after him on the plane, and Fred Fenwick would meet him at the other end and take him home. Jimmy would just go to these parties and sit and stare. Everybody would come and talk to Jimmy; he loved it."

1955 ▶

Empire Development Company Limited is formed to operate an iron ore mine on Vancouver Island, British Columbia. Empire markets the ore to the Japanese steel industry.

1955 ▶

Further hydroelectric development sees Mannix crews employed on the Ghost River Dam project near the Canadian Rockies.

whom Lou Franco had hired shortly before he resigned from Mannix. One of the few seasonal workers was Neal Peppin, who ultimately turned out to be the source of another company father-son connection. Peppin's son, Dick, the future president of Loram Maintenance of Way, Inc., joined his father at Mannix International in 1956.

Dick Peppin was born in 1932 in Delano, Minnesota, a small farming town, but grew up in the Minneapolis area. In 1950, at age 17, Peppin joined the Marines and that fall was sent to fight in Korea. While there, he was twice wounded near the Choisin Reservoir. During his last two years of duty, he was assigned to the Marine Corps Color Guard for President Dwight Eisenhower in Washington, D.C. After his discharge from the service in 1954, Peppin returned to Minneapolis. Having been employed part-time by a building contractor in high school, he hoped to find work with a heavy construction company, but jobs were hard to come by. When his father told him there was an opening at Mannix International, Peppin decided it would be interesting to find out what railroad work was like. Peppin joined the company as a sled supervisor. Like all new hires, he was assigned to work with Jim Christoff Sr. for training.

It was Christoff Sr. who first spotted the talent that eventually led Peppin to the presidency of Loram Maintenance of Way. "My dad kept telling me about Dick Peppin," Jim Christoff recalled. "He would say, 'He don't know a damn thing about this railroad work, but that's the best man you've got.' And that's when Dick Peppin started getting more attention than some of the rest. He wasn't a guy who just worked from eight to five. He was very hard-working. Looking back on it now, I damn near put the guy in the hospital a number of times because I was so demanding of him."

Jim Christoff was also very demanding of himself. Besides making sales calls, he went out on every job to see first-hand what problems existed. "I would go out on every job because, in reality, the stuff we had, unless the conditions were just right, really wouldn't work that well," said Christoff. "That was what brought along the improvements to the sleds and plows."

Peppin agreed that these early years could be trying. "I think that most of our heartaches came in the early stages of the company," he said. "With the under-track equipment, everybody figured at first that you just jacked the track up, put the equipment underneath, set the track down, and then went about your business. We never thought that the equipment would operate differently in different soil conditions. On several of our jobs, on the first or second day, the equipment would either float higher on top of the ballast than we expected, or it would go down to China. If it went down to China, it was a disaster."

For a small operation like Mannix International, the trial-and-error method of correcting equipment problems in the field was a basic act of survival. "When I first started with the company, a $50,000 contract was just like manna from heaven," explained Peppin. "This was something that you'd marvel at. You'd say, 'Jeepers!

R.A. (Dick) Peppin, second from left, a member of the U.S. Marine Corps Color Guard for President Dwight D. Eisenhower.

1955 ▶

The Cheakamus Power project for B.C. Electric Co. Ltd., a joint venture with Stolte International Co., includes a 6.7-mile (10.75-kilometre) tunnel that connects with twin penstocks for the drop to the powerhouse.

1956 ▶

The Soviet army crushes the Hungarian revolt. Canada provides free transportation to Canada for Hungarian refugees.

We've got a contract. Now we've got to produce like we said we could!' And that would put the monkey on our back again. It was through good, hard work and people that put their heads together, that we kept our nose above water."

Impacting the Nation
"Work harder, do better, and not back away."

While Mannix Ltd. made remarkable strides during the early years of the Fifties, F.C. Mannix was the first to give credit to his people. "I don't look at companies as such," he once reflected, "as I don't think it takes companies to develop projects. It takes people within the companies to initiate and develop projects and to realize the opportunities available." To F.C. Mannix, "the important thing is to recruit and train new people to carry on projects at hand and to get on to new things."

This philosophy would attract an outstanding cadre of people. Mannix alumni include a remarkable group of people who became prominent Albertans including Chip Collins, Peter Lougheed, Harold Milavsky and David Wood.

After overseeing Mannix coal operations in the 1960s, Collins joined Premier Peter Lougheed's government as deputy treasurer. "Fred was a strong leader, a very forceful individual with a charisma that is very, very difficult to describe," Collins said. "It was a certain charisma that any leader of men has to have and Fred Mannix had it in spades. Every good leader I've worked for had the ability to inspire people and make them work harder and do better as a team than they were capable of doing individually. There's no doubt that Fred had that ability. In some way that I do not understand, he would inspire people to work harder, do better, and not back away."

Peter Lougheed worked for Mannix for five years, hiring on in 1956 as an assistant secretary and legal assistant to Everett Costello. "It was an invaluable experience," Lougheed said. Fred C. Mannix "wasn't afraid to take on large corporations, large organizations.... I saw him many times eyeball to eyeball against the big eastern corporations — and they blinked. If a man interested in politics said to himself, 'What would be a good thing for a future premier to do,' I'd have to say: lay the foundation by spending five years with Mannix.... Fred Mannix places a high value on personal initiative, and respects and encourages those who display that. He has a strong feeling that the most significant thing that can happen in this country is for the individual

An Immeasurable Loss

On Sunday, December 9, 1956, Trans-Canada Airlines Flight 810, heading east out of Vancouver, turned back in the vicinity of Hope, British Columbia, because of engine trouble. The last radio report was made to the Vancouver air control tower at 7:10 p.m. After that — silence. Sixty-two travellers were aboard, including Karl W. Collett, a director and executive vice president of Mannix Ltd. Extremely poor weather conditions hampered an immediate search. By January 1957, no trace of the plane had been found.

"We note and honour, as best we can, a man who has meant an immeasurable amount to the company, and to us as individuals," wrote F.C. Mannix in the January 1957 issue of *The Mannix Story*. "Karl Collett was a friend, a doer, a man of action, a builder in the very finest sense of the word. It is hard to realize that he is gone; that such a wonderful sincerity and tremendous vitality can be seen only in memory as it surely will all the balance of our lives.

"To a very great extent Karl was responsible for the introduction into this company of a larger, faster concept of dirt moving; his arrival marked the beginning of a post-war era of the biggest and most important projects we ever attempted. Also, to a very great extent, Karl was responsible for the training of some of our ablest superintendents, and for instilling into all corners of our organization the desire to get the job done, on time. I think I speak for all of us when I say it has been a great personal experience to have known Karl Collett. His loss has been greatest to his family and to those of us who knew him — but it has also been an immeasurable loss to the construction industry throughout North America. "

1956 ▶

The first section of pipe to be laid by Mannix crews is unloaded at Richardson Station, Saskatchewan, for the TransCanada pipeline.

1956 ▶

With construction costs approaching $1 million a mile, Trans-Canada Highway construction clears the summit of the Rockies through Banff and Yoho national parks.

to create and to control his own economic destiny. Literally hundreds of people, using the experience they gained working for him, have moved on to set up a whole range of independent companies. The alumni of the Mannix company are really something. He's created an impact on the whole nation."

After leaving Mannix in 1961, Lougheed practised law in Calgary while pursuing a political career. In 1971, a Lougheed-led Progressive Conservative party toppled the Alberta Social Credit party after 36 uninterrupted years of rule. One person who helped Lougheed trumpet his voice was David Wood, Mannix's public relations person for 13 years. After leaving Mannix, Wood served as a Lougheed public relations and television advisor.

Another of the major players in Alberta who was influenced by F.C. Mannix was Harold Milavsky. After leaving Mannix, Milavsky went on to head Trizec Corporation in 1976. Soon after taking over as president and chief executive officer, Milavsky turned the nearly bankrupt firm into one of the giants in the real estate field with a 1981 book value of $2.5 billion.

Milavsky joined Mannix in 1956. "At that time, I was working as an internal auditor for Mannix," he recalled. "I was about 26 years old. For a young fellow from Saskatchewan, it was very exciting to be involved in the building business, where you could see the coordination between people and the tangible results of your efforts. When the construction company bid on a major job, they were very well organized and all the disciplines were represented in the process. One time a bid meeting was taking place on a Saturday morning, and all these various people came together in the boardroom. For some reason, though, there weren't any financial people at that particular meeting. Fred Mannix said, 'Well, damn it, if you can't find a financial man, I'll find one for you.' He was gambling that I would be in my office on a Saturday. And, as usual, he was right. The phone rang and I heard Fred say, 'Harold, get over here. We've got a bid meeting going on and we need some financial help.'

A.F. (Chip) Collins.

E. Peter Lougheed.

H.P. (Harold) Milavsky.

"So I hurried over and did the work they wanted. Fred would remember those kinds of things; that's how he would judge your performance. So that was my next step within the organization. I became the treasurer and controller of the construction company. I had an inkling of what they were going to offer from the rumours that go around an organization. I had made up my mind that if this position were offered to me, I really wasn't ready for it. It was too big a jump for me, and so I would turn it down. But it wasn't presented as to whether I wanted the job or not. Fred just said, 'This is what we're going to do.' He had more confidence in me than I did. I worked every night for the next two years just to prove that he was right. When Fred recognized talent, he gave you the opportunity to express yourself. That's what he did with me. I owe a lot to him for having confidence in me. He had more confidence in me than I did, and he gave me the opportunities. When you're thrown those challenges, you say, 'Well, if he's put that kind of faith in me, I better prove he's right.'"

F.C. Mannix put not only his faith, but also capital, in his friends' private enterprises. "Back in the Fifties, Fred C. had a lot of friends who had gone into business for themselves as small contractors," said Gordon Coates, a quarter-century veteran of the construction company. "They weren't adequately financed; they couldn't get bonding assurances. Fred, through his loyalty and friendship, was quite prepared to assist them. You see, most of them had worked with him as operators or worked for him directly. He admired them and liked them, so when they got into the contracting business, they'd come to him for help. He'd help them indirectly by bidding the project they were pursuing in our name, and then subcontracting to these people. He had the ability to take those very capable people and meld them together and get them to work together, even though they didn't necessarily agree with each other. He sure as heck could get the best out of everybody."

1956 ▶

Elvis Presley makes his television debut at age 27.

1956 ▶

Egyptian President Gamal Abdel Nasser nationalizes the Suez Canal. Britain, France and Israel attack Egypt to retake the canal. Ships sunk during the battles block the canal for months.

While some moved on to set up independent companies, many more stayed on, choosing to make the Mannix outfit their life's work. "The greatest thing that happened to me was when I went to work for the Mannix company," said Dan (Frenchy) Hamilton, who joined the outfit at Sept-Îles. "That's all I've done in my life. I don't think a lot of people know how important the Mannix family is in Canada. F.C. Mannix was one of the greatest guys. He was a builder, a real builder. One thing I remember about F.C. was how he'd come on the job and how pleased he was just to see how I was doing. He'd say, 'Keep it going, Frenchy.' He gave you all the confidence and support in the world. How the hell could you back off? I mean you'd go harder if you could. He was that way with every man who worked for him, even the working guys. It may be a little embarrassing to say this, but everybody has heroes and F.C. Mannix was my hero. I sort of worshipped the guy because of who he was and his kindness to me. Even if you weren't the greatest success, if you'd done your best, you were great as far as Mr. Mannix was concerned. He always treated me great, like I was somebody. He always treated everyone like they were part of his family."

"One day, we were walking down the street," recalled Lou Franco, "and he just asked me to come home to dinner with him. I said, 'Oh, Fred, I don't know. Margie doesn't know I'm coming.' He said, 'Don't worry about Margie. It will be all right with her.' Then we met an old man in dirty overalls. Fred had known him since he was a kid, and he said, 'Hello, Jack, how are you?' and they shook hands. Then Fred said, 'Lou and I are going home for dinner. Come with us.' The fellow said, 'Oh, no, Mr. Mannix, look how I am.'

"'It makes no difference,' Fred said. 'Anything we've got in our house was made by guys like you, with clothes just like those you're wearing. You're welcome in our house.' So we went to his house and Margie couldn't have treated us nicer, especially him. She went out of her way to make him feel comfortable. We had a big steak dinner and a few drinks. That's the kind of fellow Fred was. He didn't forget the guy who was out there working, and he knew every one of those guys by their first names. He treated them like friends, not employees."

Having successfully brought full ownership of the outfit home to Canada, and having built some of the most historic projects ever let in Canada, it was time for F.C. Mannix to ready his "family of a company" to meet the challenges of the future.

"THIS FAMILY OF A CONSTRUCTION COMPANY"

"We married men who became company men. You were expected to cope, to be there with small children, to tend the fire," said Mary Fenwick. "Your concern was that your husband was happy, that he liked his job. But I know I had a little resentment that the company was so important in Fred's life. People say 'Divorce,' but I say, 'Divorce, no. Murder, yes.'

"I think from time to time most women whose husbands worked for Mannix have had that thought run through their minds. You'd get riled at times, but the people you met and the genuine relationships you built got us over our anger. I could go and tell Vi Wagar, 'To hell with the construction company,' and she knew I didn't mean it. But she'd listen to me, and then we'd celebrate being part of this family of a construction company.

"Something else was reassuring to wives, and it was almost an unsaid thing. If anything ever went wrong, you knew that somebody would step in and make sure things went well. Our son went into the hospital with polio when he was 15 months old. They said, 'We don't know whether you'll have a son for 24 hours.' Jimmy Nairn came over and said, 'Don't worry, Mary, no matter what you need, it will be there for you.' It was a very strengthening thing; it washed away all that resentment that someone was getting more of your husband's time than you were. In the crunch, you knew you could depend on either the people in the company or the company rallying around you. That goes today. I think if something terrible happened to Fred or myself, the company would say, 'What can we do to help, because you are part of our family.' That's a powerful feeling that's disseminated, and I felt it very early on in my life as a company wife."

1956 ▶

The Toronto Board of Education withdraws the book Little Black Sambo *from city schools because of racist content, an early acceptance of the individuality of people of colour.*

1956 ▶

Farley Mowat's Lost in the Barrens *wins the Governor General's Award for best juvenile novel.*

KEEPING THE FLAME ALIVE

1957– 1967

*I was at university when Dad got sick. But I was on the board of directors
at Loram and I saw all the internal debates and problems. It was just a miracle to have
Brock and Everett in the top slots. They were an ideal combination. They made the
transition from an owner concept to a professional management concept work.*

*Their mission was to hold the organization together. They did an unbelievable job
of carrying on business as usual and providing leadership during that period.
It was certainly a traumatic time for Everett and Brock and Dad,
but it didn't disturb the outfit. There was no great crisis.*

— Fred P. Mannix

*Left: Everett Costello (left) and
Brock Montgomery (right) at Shuswap
Lake, Sorrento, British Columbia.*

*Right: Sputnik I, the first man-made
Earth satellite, is launched by the Soviet
Union on October 4. It radios information
to Earth for 21 days.*

In 1957, the Soviet Union launched *Sputnik I,* the first artificial earth satellite. The Space Age had begun, but so had the age of the intercontinental ballistic missile. "Mankind, through the roaring thrust of a Russian rocket Friday, burst the bonds of gravity and stood on the black, cold threshold of space," commented a *Calgary Herald* editorial of October 8, 1957. "While the world rejoices at man's unlocking another secret of nature, the free world's jubilation is marred with foreboding and dread. Moscow to New York in sixteen minutes. That is the rate at which the Russian satellite is moving, and that is the length of time it would take a satellite carrying a nuclear-equipped weapon to travel that distance when — not if — it is possible so to equip and launch such a weapon. So it is that feeling in the western world about the Russian feat is tinged with fear; not the honest fear of men standing on the threshold of the unknown, but the sickly fear that this latest advancement of man will be turned upon him as yet another weapon."

"I Am Watching the Earth. The Visibility is Good."

In 1961, a young Russian astronaut orbited the world, radioing back re-assurances along the way. He landed safely after the first human conquest of space. It was one of history's greatest scientific accomplishments.

Nile River Delta from space.

Mankind's first space traveller, Major Yuri Gagarin, a 27-year-old father of two young children, was in orbit one hour and 29 minutes. He whistled around the globe at more than 17,000 miles (27,000 kilometres) an hour — six times faster than man ever travelled before — until reverse blasts permitted his five-ton spaceship to settle back to earth by parachute.

Moscow went wild with celebration at the news of Gagarin's successful return to earth. Loudspeakers blared out the announcement throughout the city, students cheered in Red Square and Radio Moscow broadcast special songs marking the flight.

It was in this shadow of a nuclear cloud that some of the sharpest skirmishes of the Cold War were fought. In the spring of 1961, when Cuba's Fidel Castro — briefly an American hero after he won power in Cuba — aligned himself with the Soviet Union, the United States invaded Cuba. This invasion by American-trained Cuban exiles, which was supposed to trigger a pro-American uprising in Cuba, was an ignominious failure.

In the summer of 1961, German Communists solved the problem of refugees who were defecting from East Berlin into the West zone — they simply built a wall. Thrown together almost overnight, the Berlin Wall served to further divide that divided city. Anyone who tried to leave the East zone without permission was shot.

But it was in the fall of 1962 that the world came closest to the Third World War. When American reconnaissance planes discovered that Soviet nuclear missiles were being installed in Cuba, President John F. Kennedy imposed a naval blockade. A confrontation between Soviet and American ships could have started a war, and for a tense week the armed forces and civil defence services on both sides stood on alert. Finally, Soviet Premier Nikita Khrushchev agreed to withdraw the missiles from Cuba.

There were other struggles and crises in the Sixties. The Vietnam War divided American society, which also saw the rise of the nonviolent campaign for black civil rights in the South. Civil wars were fought in Nigeria and the Congo. Rhodesia's white regime broke away from Great Britain rather than grant more power to the black majority and France gave up on a long, nasty struggle and granted Algeria its independence. Canadian troops were part of a UN force that did the sometimes dull, sometimes dangerous job of keeping the peace between Greek and Turkish factions on Cyprus. China was turned upside down by the Red Guards in Chairman Mao Tse-Tung's cultural revolution. Israel triumphed in the Six-Day War with Egypt and Syria in 1967. In Czechoslovakia, a new spirit of liberalism took root.

A generation of political leaders passed from the scene in Canada and Quebec became the focus of concern about the country's future. John Diefenbaker was still prime minister in the early Sixties, but his Conservative government was in trouble. The economy was faltering, and relations with the United States were testy. The election of 1962 destroyed Diefenbaker's majority. He carried on, but in 1963 his government was defeated in the Commons on the issue of providing American-controlled nuclear weapons for Canadian forces. Lester Pearson and his Liberals won the 1963 election. Four years later, Diefenbaker lost the Conservative party leadership to Robert Stanfield.

But like a gaily coloured balloon, rising above the political machinations of the world rose the euphoria that accompanied Canada's centennial celebration. Canada's birthday fair, Expo 67, attracted more than 315,000 people on its first day, almost three times the number expected. The success of Montreal's world's fair gave the nation a new sense of confidence.

1957 ▶

John Diefenbaker, Canada's first Conservative prime minister in 22 years, is elected.

1957 ▶

Prime Minister Diefenbaker appoints Canada's first woman Cabinet member, Ellen Fairclough of Hamilton, as secretary of state.

"The way to do things is to be ready. That was the start of Loram."

In 1957, Mannix Ltd. reorganized as the Loram Group, a corporate family of companies. The name Loram, which was coined by Everett Costello's secretary, Francis Boyd, was an acronym for **LO**ng **RA**nge **M**annix. The Loram Group's principal operating companies were the coal company, whose name changed from Alberta Coal Company Limited to Alberta Coal Ltd., Pembina Pipe Line Ltd., Mannix International Inc., and the construction company, which was renamed Mannix Co. Ltd.

The reorganization of 1957 was a vital step in the outfit's evolution, one which prepared the organization to meet future opportunities. "F.C. Mannix must be regarded as one of the most successful businessmen that we have seen in this country," commented R.J. Burns, then legal counsel with Macleod Dixon. "He took a medium-sized firm and made it a tremendous outfit. He activated an organization. He had a tremendous drive and he attracted people who were the same breed of people. He could transmit that attitude of 'Get the thing done and give it hell!' It doesn't matter if it is Saturday, Sunday or Christmas, the pipeline goes through!"

"I think Pembina made it apparent to F.C., if he hadn't thought of it before, that the way to do things is to be ready," continued Burns. "That spread to the coal company. For instance, when Calgary Power wanted to put a coal-powered power plant at Wabamun, guess who owns the coal rights? Mannix. That put him in the position to say to Calgary Power, 'We will build your power plant; we will operate the coal mine, which is literally under the power plant, and supply the plant with coal.' They did the same thing in Saskatchewan. To a large extent, the secret to Mannix's success has been just this sort of thing — to think five, ten years ahead and visualize what could happen and then position yourself to bring it about, or have a piece of the action when it comes about. The way to do things is to be ready. That was the start of Loram."

Overall management of all Loram subsidiaries was the province of Loram Ltd., over which F.C. Mannix presided as president. Jim Scott, who had headed the project group that developed the successful bid for Pembina Pipe Line, was the vice president of operations. Eric Connelly was vice president and treasurer. Everett Costello, F.C. Mannix's most trusted advisor, served as vice president and secretary.

E. Creswell J. (Cres) Oates, who joined Mannix Ltd. in 1954 as F.C. Mannix's personal assistant, was the main architect of the reorganization. "The policy of a corporate complex should always be to distribute your assets so they are not endangered by having all of them in one company," he explained. "This is true for any construction company. It's a very risky business. You can lose your shirt on these major contracts. If these operating companies were all subsidiaries of the construction company, you were going to put everything at risk, and that is just not a logical thing to do. Instead, you spin the subsidiaries out and each one stands on its own feet. If anything should happen, you're not going to have all your assets go down the drain."

"Cres Oates had some very, very smart ideas," admired Eric Connelly. "He was the man who dreamed up the idea of Loram, and in the process of that I came in to refine it a bit. I drew up the documents which set the company up. The thing was to divide things up, and to get more direct thinking into the operation of the coal business. The coal company was more or less an orphaned child. Si Fraser was president of Alberta Coal, but he was bright enough to know that his expertise was limited, so he hired Chuck Doerr to manage the operation, and Chuck was just outstanding. We were entering into the era of the huge draglines, and Chuck Doerr had this expertise. He knew the costs and so on, and none of the rest of us did. So that left Si Fraser to do the wheeling and dealing. The company was very fortunate to have him and his type of thinking at that time."

F.C. Mannix, standing, with W.F. (Bill) Sharon.

1957 ▶

The signing of the Treaty of Rome begins the European Common Market.

1957 ▶

On November 3, the Soviets launch Sputnik II with Laika, a dog, onboard. Laika is the first Earth life form to travel in space.

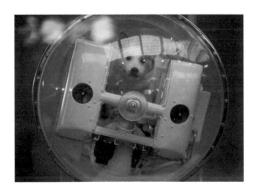

"WE OUTWORKED THEM ALL"

"One of the key reasons to the success in that period of time is that we outworked everybody, really," recalled Peter Lougheed. "We'd fly halfway across the world, we'd fly to New York, and we'd be up for a breakfast meeting. It was always a contest to see who could organize the earliest breakfast meeting. We were very determined people, and we worked damned hard. That was the nature of the success of the outfit. We all went to work on Saturday morning automatically. Saturday morning everybody just went to work. It wasn't a day off."

Left to right, Gordon Walker, Cal Baker, Ben Goodman, Tom Oxman, Peter Lougheed and Bill Sharon.

"The real secret, which is what Fred instilled in everybody, was hard work," continued Lougheed. "Maybe you didn't have quite as much financial strength as somebody else and maybe you didn't have some of the other assets or maybe you weren't as closely connected as some of the competitors. But we outworked them all. I've always attributed that to Fred's motivation to do just that. You can do a lot in this world by outworking people, and that was what he brought to it. We outworked everybody else. Steadily. And F.C. Mannix was the one who inspired that.

"This was a very unique organization. During the time I was involved with it, it was very much a dynamic period for the company. Not so much in profits or dollars earned, but in terms of activity and in terms of survival. We dealt with competitors all over the world. I would say today, without any equivocation, that perseverance being part of hard work, you persevered."

One of the primary reasons behind the formation of Loram was that the company was getting into activities far from the founding field of construction. The desire was to maintain the focus of each operating company. "Fred wanted to change it so that there was one control over the various companies," explained Brock Montgomery. "He also wanted to get the construction company back into construction and nothing but construction."

With the senior advisors of Mannix Ltd. now concentrating fully on the non-construction aspects of the operations, a vacancy developed for a senior officer who would devote his sole energies to the construction side of the business. W.F. (Bill) Sharon was appointed executive vice president of Mannix Co. Ltd. on April 6, 1957.

A hard-driving, chain-smoking engineer, who drank up to 20 nerve-jolting cups of coffee a day, Sharon brought a wide and varied background to the Mannix outfit. He began in the construction business as a labourer for the Conradi Construction Company in the 1930s. From there, he moved to the Sault Structural Steel Company where he served as a job superintendent and field erection engineer. He earned his B.Sc. in civil engineering from Queen's University in 1938. Between 1939 and 1945, Sharon served in the Canadian Army. He was promoted to major in 1944 and commanded the Ninth Field Squadron of the Fourth Canadian Armoured Division as it fought its way through northern France. For his actions in the fighting around the Brugge Canal in Belgium, he was awarded the Military Cross. Following the war, Sharon worked for Dominion-Bridge Iron Works of Calgary. In 1951, he joined Sparling-Davis Company Ltd., a manufacturer of petroleum storage tanks. He served as vice president and general manager until elevated to president after Mannix Ltd. acquired that organization.

Sharon explained the impact of the 1957 reorganization. "Mannix Ltd. had been purely a construction company, but it was carrying out coal work and it did the promotion for Pembina, all under Mannix Ltd.," he said. "Fred Mannix was a pretty astute businessman. He saw that the senior executives of Mannix Ltd. were spending a lot of time on deals that were outside the operational role of the construction company. The net result was that senior executives were not paying attention to the basic business and junior executives were not making decisions because they didn't have the authority. Now, that didn't mean that those secondary people didn't have the competence, but the structure was set. So the construction business was suffering.

1957 ▶

Empire Development Company Limited, formed in 1955, begins development of an iron ore mine on Vancouver Island, British Columbia, in 1956 to produce ore for the Japanese market.

1958 ▶

James Gladstone, a Blood band member of Cree and Scottish descent, is appointed to the Senate, a first for any band member.

"When I got there in 1957, the policy was that we couldn't take in any more work because our volumes were well beyond what the company was considered capable of doing. We had a hiatus of bidding for six months. There's no doubt about it, we were way over our capacity in 1957. The company's cash requirement was just at the limit, so it was a sound policy to put the cap on for that year. But people hadn't thought the thing through, about the changing nature of the company. I started analyzing this, and I realized that this volume that we had was not the volume that was going to be done in the current year, but it was going to be done in succeeding years."

"It was about that time that they were emerging into big jobs," continued Sharon. "Earlier, a contract would be started in the spring and finished in the fall, generally speaking. But they were getting more and more into these two- and three- and four-year jobs. So I was able to establish a policy where, when we took a job, we would project the progress of the work for each year the job was supposed to last. Then for any given year, we looked at the volume that would actually be done that year before we started putting a cap on our total capacity for that year. Until then, Loram wouldn't allow the construction company to bid, because we had more work than we could handle. In January of 1958, we suddenly found ourselves with around $350,000 worth of work, when we needed at least $15 million to keep alive. So '58 was a very lean year because we were desperate for work."

Not long after the reorganization, five-year plans became the name of the game. "The one-year budget was pretty fixed, and the five-year was your hopes and intentions — 50 per cent hope, and 50 per cent intention," explained Sharon. "You see, the thing with any construction company — I've always felt and I think Fred felt this way too — is that you should have a little bit more work in any given year than it could handle. That's the only way to expand and keep your people busy. Mind you, although there had been joint venture work earlier, we were getting more and more into joint ventures because the joint venture philosophy is you spread your risk. You take 10 per cent of a $100-million job, and that's only $10 million worth of volume spread over five years. That's $2 million a year, which means that you can go on another joint venture and another. That way, you can spread your risks substantially over 20 projects, whereas if you had a huge project all by yourself, that would put a cap on your ability to take on any more work."

"EVERYBODY WANTS EVERYTHING RIGHT NOW!"

"The way I felt about my position and everybody's approach to women when I was there was that they treated me like a person — not as a man or a woman but just a person," said Mary Sharon, who worked at Mannix Ltd. keeping the records for the field equipment from 1951 to 1959, until she married her husband, Bill Sharon.

"I never found when I was working there, at any time, that if I had something to say, it had less importance because it was said by a female," Mrs. Sharon recalled. "Now, I may have been naive at that time, but this was

Mary Sharon with Jack Bruce.

before people started thinking a great deal about women's place in the world and that sort of thing. After I left, I remember being at government meetings and different meetings. I was at human rights meetings at the university and I said, "I just don't believe that that's how it happened because I worked in a man's world for years and not once was I ever excluded because I was a woman. I doubt that any of the men ever thought about it."

What people thought about was completing the work. "When there was a bid going on, everyone was involved in the bid," said Sharon. "Everyone stayed there at night, sometimes until two in the morning. There was an excitement about it. They hired a fellow who had something to do with accounting. He had worked at Income Tax. I remember being there one night with him. He just about went out of his mind. He was so frantic at people walking by his desk so fast because everybody was. After a while he said, 'I just can't stand this job! Everybody wants everything right now!'"

1958 ►

U.S. President Eisenhower orders U.S. army troops to enforce the desegregation of Central High School in Little Rock, Arkansas. The forces protect the first African-American students to attend the previously all-white school.

1958 ►

Mannix-O'Sullivan Paving Company Limited is merged with O.K. Construction Ltd. The resulting company is called O.K. Construction Ltd.

"By implementing these policies, we really turned the company around," said Sharon. "We were right near rock bottom in the construction company in 1957. From the bottom line appearances, we were way down on our profits. We had no profits in 1958, and in 1959 and 1960, we actually showed a loss. We had a loss of $1,231,000 at April 30, 1959, and at April 30, 1960, our working capital was down to $137,000. But from there, we started showing profits and building the whole thing back up again."

As the group repositioned itself, it became clear that management by committee simply did not work. "When they first formed Loram it got run by a committee of Connelly, Costello and Scott," explained Montgomery. "They'd have a meeting and vote when something new would come up. But it didn't work. Fred realized it wasn't working so he brought in a fellow, Reginald H. Williams, and made him president in 1960. He lasted about a year. He was head of Canadian Westinghouse, Northern Electric Canada, the subsidiary of the American company. His idea of having a management meeting would be five or ten minutes."

"Williams was right in over his head," agreed Sharon. "He had grown up in a bureaucracy and he just couldn't understand it." Williams resigned after a year. On September 22, 1961, Everett Costello became president of Loram Ltd. and Brock Montgomery was named executive vice president. Little did they realize they were about to face one of the most traumatic times in the Mannix outfit's history.

"He just worked too damned hard."

F.C. Mannix dons a hardhat while viewing an atomic power station in England.

"In 1956, Mr. Mannix set up a separate office called Bowfort Services Ltd. to look after his personal investments," recalled David W. McClement. "He brought in Cres Oates to run it. This was when they were dividing the group up and separating out the construction company. I was hired as the chief bookkeeper. As soon as I started, we got organized on long-range planning to perpetuate the outfit. F.C. Mannix was in his early forties at that point, and it was unusual for a guy to do detailed long-range planning to perpetuate an outfit that early in his life. When Bowfort started up, the children were very young. However, that has always been a part of F.C.'s life. He does a lot of planning. That's probably the secret to his success."

Always working, F.C. Mannix travels with his portable desk, complete with stationery, pens and the well-used aspirin pack.

While F.C. Mannix made long-range planning an integral part of his life, he was not a man to include rest and relaxation in those plans; he quite simply lived to work. For F.C., the opportunity to accomplish something drove the work ethic. "The management techniques around here have all evolved through hard work," commented McClement. "In other words,

TRADE MISSION TO BRITAIN

"Two Calgary men will be included in the fifty-man sponsored trade mission to Britain. Among the industrialists and well-known businessmen chosen to make the month-long tour of Britain's industrial centres are: A.G. Bailey of Calgary, president of Bailey-Selburn Oil Co., and F.C. Mannix, president of Mannix Ltd.

"Creation of the mission was one of the steps agreed upon during the Anglo-Canadian ministerial talks in Ottawa early last month. It is the first step to be taken in the Federal Government's proposed trade switch. On the mission's shoulders will be the task of judging whether in fact Canada can make a big switch of imports from the United States to the United Kingdom." — CFCN Radio News Bureau, November 9, 1957.

1958 ▶

The Government of Canada expands the Namao Airdrome Runway with help from O.K. Construction. This $2.8-million project runs until 1960.

1958 ▶

Mungo Martin carves the world's tallest totem pole from a single log at Beacon Hill Park, Victoria, British Columbia. It stands 126 feet (38.28 metres) tall.

there is nothing magical about the techniques. They have all evolved through hard work and much sweat and tears. It was hard work and a dedication to accomplish something — a great desire to accomplish something.

"I don't know of anybody I've ever been associated with that worked harder than F.C. did during the time when he was going strong. I have never met any man in my life that worked anywhere near as hard as him. He was a fellow that worked 24 hours a day, seven days a week. Everything he did was related to the business. I feel that explains partly why he got sick. He just worked too damned hard and he never balanced it off to have a little relaxation. Even when he relaxed, he worked. I couldn't keep up with him. When he was relaxing, I wouldn't want to keep up with him for more than five minutes. Then, in 1962, in the fall of '62, he had a sickness, a blockage of a major blood vessel, so he had an operation to clear it out."

When F.C. Mannix was barely 50 years old, he was diagnosed with a potentially life-threatening blockage in his carotid artery. The operation he elected to have was very new and the odds of survival were slim. At that time, only eight similar operations had been performed. Seven patients had died; the one survivor was paralysed from the waist down. F.C. Mannix's operation was number nine. After weighing the risks, F.C. Mannix bet on beating the odds. After 14 hours on the operating table, and six weeks in intensive care, once again, he pulled up aces.

The Keepers of the Flame
"They ran a tight ship."

Although F.C. Mannix made a strong recovery from surgery, his doctors advised him to reduce his involvement in the day-to-day management of the Loram Group's operations, bluntly stating, "keep working and you'll be planted." Accordingly, F.C. Mannix began to devote more time to his family and long-range planning. Everett Costello and Brock Montgomery then shouldered the demands of the day-to-day business, playing key

Everett W. (Ev) Costello.

Brockwell L. (Brock) Montgomery.

roles in managing and refining the structure of the business during this difficult time. However, F.C. Mannix, as chairman of the board, continued to be responsible for all major decisions and for providing the overall direction for the Loram Group's activities. He also remained the source of inspiration that empowered the organization.

"When Fred Mannix got sick in 1962, it was a very, very difficult time," Everett Costello said. "Basically I set policy guidelines and Brock was responsible for operations. Together, our overall goal was to hold the outfit together and make sure we didn't lose the whole damn thing. Initially, we were just going to hold things in place until Fred came back full-time. But he never did. Eventually, the young fellows, Freddie and Ronnie, came along and gradually took over."

During this time of transition, the role of Loram caused some spirited debates. "There has always been a conflict in the outfit about the exact function of Loram," explained Costello. "That has gone on from the very beginning. Loram, in effect, owned things and was in position to run everything. Over the years, though, we laid down the policy that, while Loram would retain overall control, each subsidiary company would be fully integrated, fully operational, and look after its own affairs. So we didn't run the construction company, but we controlled it. The president of the construction company would review his policy manual every year and endeavour to make changes in it. We would then review and approve those changes. Every year, he would try to get more power. And, by and large, we gave it to him. Gradually, we loosened up from the strict attitude we had when we moved in."

One of the areas of conflict was that "the construction company wanted to get twice as big as it was," Costello said. "The coal company wanted to get ten times as big as it was. The pipeline company wanted to get ten times as big as it was. It was a very difficult thing to hold them all down. I sure as hell was not looking for that kind of rapid expansion. Fred Mannix was against it and I am a lot more conservative than he is. I wanted to take

1958 ▶

Selective breeding of Norman horses brought to Quebec in 1665 results in a unique breed of horse, the Canadian. The animals are hardy, gentle and intelligent.

1958 ▶

The National Research Council of Canada designs and employs one of the earliest cesium beam atomic clocks. It is accurate to a few millionths of a second per year.

THANKS FOR THE MEMORY

In the fall of 1957, Mannix Gill Limited rented an ALWAC III-E digital computer — with an amazing memory capacity of 8,192 words — from Alwac Corporation of Hayward, California. Mannix Gill then established a Computer Service Centre for this machine, which was thought especially suited for engineering problems because of its memory. A number of other companies, including Calgary Power, TransCanada PipeLines and Imperial Oil, expressed interest in sharing what is believed to the first computer in Calgary.

By August of 1958, however, Mannix Co. Ltd. concluded the lack of consulting work and failure in selling the services of the device doomed this experiment. Canadian Engineering Surveys then entered a joint venture with Mannix Gill and began using the computer in their consulting operations.

By late 1963, the Loram Group's statistics and records became so voluminous that new in-house equipment was installed to handle them — an IBM-407 accounting machine. In 1965, the company made another significant change, making use of an IBM-1401 computer at the IBM Data Centre in Calgary.

things slow and easy. We held the construction company down to a volume of $40 million a year. It was our policy and we held them to that for four or five years."

Brock Montgomery concurred, adding, "The policy at Loram at that time was that everything over so many dollars a contract had to be approved by us. Each company was responsible for its own financing. If they got in trouble, the only assets that they could give for borrowing money would be their own assets. One of our biggest policies was to limit the amount of money that any of our company presidents could commit to a given contract. In other words, they could break their own company, but they couldn't break Loram. However, whatever a given policy might say, we always made it a practice to finish the job. But the operating presidents always wanted bigger jobs. I don't think the presidents of our companies understood, or wanted to understand, that you couldn't be a big shot, and be a solid one, unless you had the wherewithal to look after some bad jobs. And those were our biggest problems."

"Now, Fred C. used to go and barge around all the companies," continued Montgomery. "He would go and pep talk them. He would always tell them to get more work. He was doing the right thing. He was pushing them. We were controlling them. They resented the control that we had. They said that if they were on their own, they could make better deals and decisions."

"We used to have some very interesting board meetings," recalled Bill Sharon. "Since we were an operating company, our interest was not the overall interest; our interest was the interest of the operating company. Loram was the overall interest, and sometimes the overall interest and the operating company's interests didn't exactly coincide. Under those circumstances, we had substantial battles.

"Fred was always ten miles ahead of Loram, and five miles ahead of me. He'd come in with some idea of his that I wouldn't agree with, and we would argue about it, and eventually he would say, 'God damn it, Bill, if you feel that strongly about it, then do it your way.' Then he'd give a grin and say, 'But, by God, it had better work!' And that was it. That was the end of it. And you made it work; you really broke your backside to make it work. He had the ability to back down and grin and give you the impression that, really, he hadn't been that serious about things in the first place."

"I remember one directors meeting when Reg Williams was with us," continued Sharon. "At that time, there were four directors plus Fred C. from Loram and then an equal number from the construction company. Fred was the chairman. Every monthly directors meeting, we brought a division manager in to question him on the affairs of his division, and sometimes Fred could be a miserable so-and-so. This time, Fred started heckling this division manager and nagging him to the point where the division manager was just getting more and more flustered. This was getting us nowhere, so I finally had to stop it. I hit the desk as hard as I could and said, 'God damn it, Fred, leave the man alone and let me run the meeting! Or if you want to come and sit here,

1959 ▶

Montreal Canadien Jacques Plante is the first professional hockey goalie to wear a protective mask during a game.

1959 ▶

Cuban revolutionaries, led by Fidel Castro, overthrow the Fulgencio Batista government. Castro visits Montreal in April.

you can run the meeting.' Fred looked at me and he grinned, and he stayed quiet from then on. But that night Reg Williams phoned me and he said, 'Bill, I'm sorry. I don't imagine you'll be lasting very long.' He just couldn't understand how Fred had the ability to take that sort of thing. But Fred knew he was wrong. Now, Everett could never take that sort of thing. No, he couldn't. Everett didn't have that ability to back down in a situation like that and make it appear that he wasn't backing down."

"I felt that Loram was increasingly interfering in things that were just not part of its brief, so I left Mannix Co. Ltd. in 1962," Sharon said. "We were having a directors meeting. Everett Costello said to me, 'I want to see you before the meeting.' He told me that I had to watch my expenditures and that my expenses were just too high. I told him that I didn't think that was the real issue at all. I said that I felt he was just upset with the way I was running things. I also said that I didn't think that there was really any room for me in the organization anymore. So I submitted my resignation right then. Costello said, 'You just can't leave your people up there in the air.' So I said, 'Okay, you're right,' and I went to Cal Baker, who was the general manager, and said, 'Cal, I want you to take over this meeting. I have just submitted my resignation.' So you can see that that particular day was very dramatic." Following Bill Sharon's resignation, C.P. (Cal) Baker was named executive vice president of Mannix Co. Ltd. in the spring of 1962. By year-end, Baker was elevated to president.

As keepers of the flame, Montgomery and Costello took their role very seriously, demanding a lot not only of themselves, but of others. "They ran a tight ship," said Paul Christensen, who joined the Mannix outfit as an accounting clerk in 1958 and became internal

auditor of Loram in 1962. "I would say, without being negative or derogatory at all, that Brock and Everett might have been very hard for people to get along with. They were tough on people. They wanted to know what was going on. They were hard-nosed guys. They were very cautious, careful in their approaches to things. I don't think either one of them were gamblers, in the sense that they would have ever done anything very foolish anyway, had there been no other restrictions. They were tough people and demanding. But they also put out a lot themselves, so they could be demanding."

Edna Hunt, who joined the company in 1967 as secretary to Ev Costello and Brock Montgomery agreed, adding, "I remember one day Mr. Montgomery called me in and said, 'Now, Edna, I just want to alert you that Mr. Costello is a man who can put you in your place with three or four words.' He said, 'I just don't want you to be hurt if it should happen to you.' Well, I heard Mr. Costello on the phone one day with AGT [Alberta Government Telephones]. He straightened that gentleman out with four words. I think that AGT knew exactly where they stood when he was through. I do believe it was a characteristic he was noted for. When Mr. Costello spoke, he meant business."

"I've seen days when Mr. F.C. Mannix would come into Mr. Costello's office, and the door would close," continued Mrs. Hunt. "They'd have their conversation, and voices might rise. Mr. Mannix would be on his way out and Mr. Costello would come to the door and say, 'Fred, you get back in here! I'm not through!' And Mr. Mannix would go back in. Then Mr. Mannix would walk out grinning at me. He'd say, 'Well, he's hard today,' and away he'd go."

Edna Hunt, secretary to
Ev Costello, Brock Montgomery
and F.P. Mannix.

1959 ▶

The crash position indicator, a system for locating downed aircraft, is developed by Harry Stevinson (right) and David Makow (left) of the National Research Council in Ottawa.

1959 ▶

Queen Elizabeth II and Dwight Eisenhower, president of the United States, officially open the St. Lawrence Seaway.

The Shuswap Conferences
"A very gentle, warm weekend"

While Ev Costello and Brock Montgomery may have been known as hard-nosed managers, they instituted a management retreat — the Shuswap Conferences, the forerunner of Loram's Presidents' Conferences — that, to this day, is remembered with genuine affection and warmth.

"I think the vision that Costello and Montgomery had, what they were trying to do with the conferences and how they went about it, was way ahead of their time," F.P. Mannix said. "Organizations are, after all, people. There are an infinite variety of ways of dealing with people, but they all stem from leadership. Montgomery and Costello were good leaders, especially Montgomery — he was a great leader. He understood those things. Men and management issues were all second nature to Brock. It was mostly his show. Dad had very little input as we were dealing with operational issues and Brock was the operational guy."

"The driving force was that it was tremendously difficult to get any company to deal with any other company; that was the last person they would deal with," David McClement said. "So a big factor in starting the conferences was to try and get them so they knew the person because we thought that when they knew each other, they would use each other. This was when the construction company was big and it was felt that it would be a great thing to be able to feed off it. It went back to the General Motors concept where they had all these divisions working off the other. This was a very mini thought of that, but the idea was the same. Also, I think they were trying to get them so they were sort of like a family, rather than a cold company."

The Shuswap Conferences were held at the Costellos' summer place on the shores of Shuswap Lake at

Top: Margie Mannix and Ev Costello take a morning stroll at Shuswap.

Above: Shuswap Lake recreation includes powerboating, fishing and rowing for relaxation.

Sorrento, British Columbia. At this comfortable, unpretentious home with lakes for swimming and boating, grounds for walking and decks for sharing an evening drink, the Shuswap Conferences not only provided top management a forum, they were the perfect setting for bringing the group closer together. "The social aspect of the conference wasn't the first emphasis, mind you," recalled Fred Fenwick, an early conference participant, "but it was important to build a community, a feeling of being together and being part of a family. The focus was the fellowship between the presidents, meeting as a group, so that the presidents could appreciate that they were members of a group and therefore could turn to the people in that group for advice or strength or solutions to their problems. Because with the diversity of the group, there was a great wide range of expertise. In addition, since half the time was recreation, you got to know these people along with their wives. Subsequently, you were able to meet the other presidents on a more personal basis because you had met with them and had fun with them."

"The conferences at Shuswap were absolutely wonderful," agreed Fred's wife, Mary Fenwick. "They weren't really like a conference, they were more like a family picnic. The whole ambiance was just getting together and relaxing and having a very pleasant time. The men were drawing together in their work area and the women were getting together in a very casual setting. It was a very gentle, warm weekend. It was a totally different experience. The men would come out after the meetings and Everett Costello would say, 'Okay, who wants to go around the lake?' There was none of, 'I can't go because I'm low on the totem pole.' It was, 'I'm here, so I can go.'"

"The personality of Florence Costello was a very strong influence, drawing people together," continued

1959 ▶

The Dalai Lama (in dark robe), the spiritual leader of Tibet's Buddhists, escapes to India following a failed uprising against the Chinese garrison at Lhasa.

1959 ▶

The Mannix-built, giant steel parabolic reflectors of this Distant Early Warning (DEW) Line station face the Soviet Union across the Arctic Ocean. The DEW Line stations are erected between 60 and 75 degrees north latitude and 65 and 140 degrees west longitude.

Mrs. Fenwick. "You were in awe and wonderment of her husband because he was a brilliant man, but Florence was just a very gracious lady. She was a very family-oriented woman and her children were very important to her and her friends were very important to her. Florence was one of my favourite people because she was so down-to-earth that you didn't feel that you were visiting someone you had to be very careful about being with. She had a warmth and gentleness about her that made you really feel that your presence was important, that when you went to the conference you brought yourself, which meant something. She made you feel welcome and very much a part of it. And not all of us can do that with people.

"There is a story a musician once told me. He said if you give a Stradivarius to someone who plays it badly with wrong tunes and discordant notes, the violin's wood absorbs that and you can never again play really good music on it. He said homes are like that, that if you go into a home where there is love and good feelings and people care about each other, that is woven into the fabric of the home and you walk into it and you are enveloped. Florence is the type of person who has that ambiance in her home."

Florence Costello recalls those early years at Shuswap with a great deal of humour and warmth. "The first year was rather funny," she said. "I had my table set with flowers and candles. But then Ev got a man who cooked for the construction camps. When he arrived, off went the flowers and candles and he put bottles of ketchup and Worcestershire sauce and mustard and toothpicks on the table, and spoons in a glass. I remember Katie Fraser and I being in the kitchen and watching this cook peel potatoes into a great big pail. The food he served was construction food, great big plates of potato salad and cabbage salad and cold cuts and nothing pretty.

Top: Brock Montgomery,
Margie Mannix, F.C. Mannix and
Buster Richardson on the Costello dock
at Shuswap Lake.

Above: Joyce McClement (left) and
Florence Costello swap tales.

"I was upset about this so I told Ev, 'I don't mind you having the meeting here, but this is my home and I don't want to be ashamed of how they're doing things.' I said, 'I can do a lot better than that.' So Ev said, 'Okay, you take over.' And I did and we got Mrs. Gates and her two helpers. They were with us every year from then on, and it was marvellous. I got my flowers, things were done nicely, and the food was good."

"The first year we hadn't added our extra bedrooms," continued Mrs. Costello. "We had a living room, kitchen and a dining room in one house, and then we bought the little house next door and it had two little bedrooms. We had one couple in each bedroom and a third couple on the pullout chesterfield in the living room. Ev and I slept on cots in the dinette area, and we had two couples sleeping down in the basement. We had a trailer across the road and we had two couples up there, and another two couples in a funny little cabin. Then Joyce and David McClement wouldn't ever move out of the little boat cottage because they loved it, so they always stayed there. And John Rockingham always stayed in one of the little cottages because everybody said he snored so loudly that he had to be by himself."

As Mrs. Costello explained, it was a very small, intimate gathering. "When you were in the company, the ultimate was to be invited to the meetings," Graham Pollock said. "Boy, that was really something. I can remember the first year that I went, I thought that was really tremendous. My eyes were as big as quarters with all the things that were going on. The conferences were deliberately kept small by the Mannix family. There were the wives, but attending the meetings there were never more than ten of us and quite often less than that. So it was high-level and it was a small group where everybody had lots of chances to say their piece and hear everybody out."

1959 ▶

A Mannix Co. Ltd. joint venture with Standard Gravel Ltd. begins construction of a new Calgary plant for Firestone Tire & Rubber Co. of Canada Ltd.

1959 ▶

Doctors Mary and Louis Leakey examine skull fragments and stone tools found in Tanganyika's Olduvai Gorge. The find suggests a man-ape lived at least 1.78 million years ago.

"I don't think it's possible to overestimate those early conferences," added F.P. Mannix. "There was a lot of status and prestige that went with them with the group of companies. There were only two occasions really — the Christmas party and the Presidents' Conferences — where the people got to bring their wives, so as a social event, it was a very relaxed atmosphere, but it was a very important occasion. It was also the only time that the women as individuals were visible. When they were at the Christmas parties, they were there in a supportive sort of role, whereas at the Presidents' Conferences, they had their own activities. So for the wives, the Presidents' Conferences were probably more important than we ever realized, in terms of getting their overall support for what was going on. And there was a sort of camaraderie that developed among those women in that regard. They had a sense that they weren't alone, that there were other gals who had the same issues and the same problems."

Mary Fenwick agreed wholeheartedly, adding how the conferences helped the wives put many things into perspective. "I think what the Mannix Group had from their men was something that a lot of people could never understand," she said. "We'd all complain and bitch about not seeing our husbands enough because, oh, my lord, they were never home. I used to kid Fred and say, 'You've been married to the company for longer than you've been married to me,' but it was true. What the conferences helped you to understand was why the work took so much of their time and why it was so important. And it wasn't a laid-on thing. It was a very family-oriented thing."

No story is perfect and memories can sometimes bathe the "good old days" in a golden light, but even with that understanding, the social aspect of the Shuswap Conferences was an important step in building the collegial atmosphere that was so important to the group's success. "There were a lot of problems in those early days, too," explained F.P. Mannix. "All sorts of different things happened, which aren't talked about too much, personal confrontations and that sort of thing. In those early days, there were lots of issues of precedents and prestige. There were turf wars that extended from the fights in the office to these functions, but as time went on and the outfit got more professional, those diminished. They were just part of getting over the hurdles and trying to do something in terms of building a collegial atmosphere."

One of the benefits of building such an atmosphere in the informal setting of a retreat, is that it can provide people with unexpected opportunities to work on developing a sense of cooperation and mutual trust — opportunities seldom presented in an office setting. Brock Montgomery recalls one rather humorous example of this principle in action. "I took General Rockingham home one night," he said. "We were both of us pretty tight. It was about 200 or 300 yards from Costello's place over to the cabins and we had to go around the lake because we didn't know where to turn off on the road up at the top. So I told him, 'You don't have to worry, all we have to do is keep our right foot in the water and we'll get there when we find it.'" But, just when you think that mutual trust and cooperation were indeed achieved, Montgomery added, "It was his right foot. My feet weren't in the water!"

From left, Donna Millican, Katie Fraser, Margie Mannix, Edith Baker, Barb Connelly, Florence Costello and Edith O'Keefe.

1959 ▶

Following the discovery of oil in Libya, Mannix crews unsuccessfully present proposals for pipeline development.

1959 ▶

The Glenbow Foundation excavates an ancient buffalo jump on the FM II Ranch, owned by F.C. Mannix and Rod McDaniel. The jump and Native camp are hundreds, if not thousands, of years old. The jump is one of only three known on the Bow River, and one of only 14 in all Western Canada.

Some Very Lean Years

When people recall the 1960s, they often remember a period of unbroken economic growth and prosperity. In reality, this period of relative affluence did not begin to take effect until 1963 and 1964. The decade began with Canada still in the grips of a marked depression. The average number of daily shares traded on the Toronto Stock Exchange fell from six million in 1956 to only two million in 1960. By 1961, 500,000 Canadians were out of work. This was the highest unemployment rate in Canada since the 1930s and the highest unemployment percentage of all industrialized western nations.

Unemployment was caused by the changing face of Canadian industry and a decrease in the nation's international trade. Postwar Germany and Japan were becoming formidable competitors in the world market and the United States, due to her own depressed economy, was buying fewer Canadian exports. As 60 per cent of Canadian exports went to the United States, this was a severe blow to Canada. Due to the sluggish economy, American investment in Canada also fell in the early 1960s. This, too, hurt the economy as almost three-quarters of the $20 billion annually invested in Canada came from the United States. Americans owned or controlled 39 per cent of Canadian manufacturing, 57 per cent of the Canadian petroleum and natural gas industry and 46 per cent of mining and smelting.

"I was the administrative assistant for all the construction divisions at that time," recalled Ben Kessler. "My job was to do the write-up on the documents and then assist in putting the bid together, so I was in a position to read most of the important documents circulating through the company. I can tell you that we had some very lean years in there in the 1962 to 1964 area. Things were particularly hard for the Railroad, Highway, and Pipeline divisions. The Railroad Division went at least two years and never had a job. In the Highway Division, they were wondering if they would ever get any more work. We once bid on 14 jobs in one week for the Department of Highways in Alberta. And we came out high bidder 14 straight times. We pumped those bids out like we were in a factory, and it was very, very disheartening to do that and not get any of them."

By 1963, the economy began to recover and more work became available. In 1965, the Canadian construction industry made up 20 per cent of Canada's gross national product and was Canada's largest employer. However, the construction industry was becoming increasingly subject

THE DEW LINE
"It was all outdoors, of course."

The Distant Early Warning (DEW) Line had its origins in the mutual defence agreement between Canada and the United States. Signed in 1958, the agreement established the North American Air Defence Command (NORAD) to protect North America from air or missile attack. As part of this agreement, Canada allowed the United States to build a line of radar warning stations from Alaska across the Canadian Arctic. Mannix Co. Ltd. won the contract for general building construction and for building the steel parabolic reflectors.

"The most difficult task we had was to construct the two microwave-type towers," said project manager Matt Roach. "They resembled movie screens in a drive-in theatre. They were about 80 feet (24 metres) high and 70 feet (21 metres) wide. Because they were microwave towers, every screw had to be insulated. We had specially designed tools for the task. They are common tools today, but in those days we had to make them. We had screwdriver guns with clips that the guys could put the screws in. Then they would just have to hold on to the gun. You couldn't really handle those small screws — not with the mittens and heavy clothing.

"We constructed those towers in January and February. There were days when we had weather of 60 below zero, and the wind would gust to 100 miles an hour. Sometimes you could only stay out and work for 10 minutes at a stretch. It was a very difficult task. It was all outdoors, of course. To get people from the campsite to the work site, we put up rope lines. If we had a whiteout, you had to follow them or you would stray out into the snow. Yes, it was difficult. But we had a deadline and we managed to get it all done."

1959 ▶

The Alberta Gas Trunk Line system is being laid to allow the collection of Alberta natural gas for export. Mannix crews' peak welding speed is 7,557 yards (6,919 metres) per day.

1959 ▶

A Mannix joint venture assists with the management and engineering for the gathering grid and main pipeline of Alberta Gas Trunk Line. Innovations include the bi-directional pipe carrier and the cost-saving use of Athey tracks from the 1930s to form another type of pipe carrier pulled by a Cat.

"One of Those Funny Things That Happen in Construction"

At Squaw Rapids, Mannix crews faced the challenge of closing off the Saskatchewan River. "The way you normally build an earth-filled dam is to build a cofferdam about halfway across the river,"

explained Newt Yeomans, who joined Mannix Co. Ltd. in 1960. "You then build the earth-filled dam inside that cofferdam. When you dam off the other half of the river, you put the water through the spillway which you have already built. But without any rock or anything like that to close the other part of the river, you have a very difficult problem. At Squaw Rapids, we only had this glacial till. It's the kind of material that will easily wash away in the river action.

"So we went down to Washington State University. We did a model study on how to close the river. After studying these results and findings, we came back to the dam site. At first, we just didn't know how we were going to build this thing. The principle we were working on was to put down 'fingers' to gradually close the river and dissipate its force. We hadn't quite solved our problem, but then we ran into one of those funny things that happen in construction.

"It was just about the time when pretzels were starting to be sold as snacks. A labour foreman suggested that instead of having the 'fingers' go straight, we should make the configuration like a pretzel upstream of the dam. Then all the deposition would take place there and we wouldn't have the problem. So that was exactly what we did. To my knowledge, it was the first time that system had been used in Western Canada. We also saved close to three-quarters of a million dollars over what we had allowed in the estimate."

to a continuing squeeze on profits caused, in part, by growing industry competition. In 1965, for example, the Canadian construction industry dollar volume set a record of approximately $9 billion, with a capacity for even greater volume. The year before, a slightly lower volume forced 148 construction firms out of business due to increased competition.

In 1965, after serving three years as president of Mannix Co. Ltd., Cal Baker left the outfit. He was succeeded by 37-year-old Graham Pollock, a 17-year veteran with the Mannix Group of Companies. "When I was made president of Mannix Co. Ltd., I tell you, I was the most surprised guy in North America," Pollock said. "It was a thrill but it was also a bit frightening for me. To this day, I'm not entirely sure why Fred C. Mannix picked me. I think he was beginning to realize that his sons would be coming into the company soon. Maybe he thought that he should start getting some younger guys in who would be mature, but not too old, by the time that Freddie and Ron were ready to come in. Anyway, I stayed on as president of Mannix Co. Ltd. for the next seven years."

Pollock's promotion reflected the enormous changes in the evolution of the construction business. Cal Baker was a product of the earlier rough-and-tumble era of construction. A master mechanic from Morrison-Knudsen, he learned his trade in the field. Pollock was known for his expertise in administration and finance. In his first year as president, he put a great deal of energy into ensuring that the company profited from its hydroelectric projects on the Columbia River. He also led the move into Alberta's rapidly expanding natural resources development industry.

Graham J. Pollock, president of Mannix Co. Ltd.

1959 ▶

Major-General Georges Vanier becomes the first francophone appointed Governor General.

1959 ▶

The new Ransomes & Rapier 1350-W dragline at the Whitewood Mine is assembled by a 45-member Mannix team in six months. When completed, it will be the largest dragline in Canada.

The Story Behind the Great Canadian Oil Sands Project
Frank O'Sullivan —
"the best salesman you ever did see"

In the mid-1960s, Mannix Co. Ltd. embarked upon a series of historic jobs that opened up the province's incredibly rich oil sands country. Begun in 1964, these projects included site clearing and grading work, constructing the Athabasca River Bridge and the tar sands access road, and laying the Great Canadian Oil Sands pipeline. In 1967, Mannix Co. Ltd. took on another major contract in the oil sands area, removing overburden.

Frank O'Sullivan.

Located along a stretch of the Athabasca River above Lake Athabasca, almost due north of the town of Fort McMurray, the oil sands are known as the world's richest sand pile — 250 billion barrels of oil are believed to lie in an area covering 30,000 square miles (77,700 square kilometres). Although most of this territory is covered by large quantities of overburden, muskeg and forest, the presence of oil along the banks of the Athabasca River has been well-known for two centuries. In 1788, Peter Pond noted in his exploration journals that the area contained notable deposits of "tar sands." In 1793, Alexander Mackenzie wrote about how the Indians used this "tar" to gum their canoes.

Site preparation and overburden removal near Fort McMurray, Alberta, for Great Canadian Oil Sands.

Over the centuries, this treasure remained largely unexploited. The challenges inherent in extracting oil from the sands, ridding the oil of impurities and getting the oil to market, defeated technology. Then, in 1950, the Alberta Research Council, the National Research Council and the Dominion Bureau of Mines commissioned the Blair Report. This report, which analyzed work done to date, concluded that economic exploitation of the area was now a feasible endeavour.

The Blair Report intensified interest in the region and, by 1952, several oil companies possessed permits covering about 50,000 acres (20,200 hectares) each. When Lease Number Four revealed the greatest concentration of oil deposits, the firm of Great Canadian Oil Sands Limited (GCOS) was formed to develop it. After 10 years of engineering studies, investigation and applications, Alberta granted GCOS the first permit allowing the commercial development of the oil sands area.

Frank O'Sullivan, a long-time associate of the Mannix organization and a partner in the Mannix-O'Sullivan paving firm, played a significant behind-the-scenes role in obtaining the GCOS permit. "O'Sullivan was a real negotiator and scrounger," recalled Eric Connelly. "He made friends all over the place, particularly with Mr. [E.C.] Manning. The highlight of his deal was that he discovered that the Province was trying to develop the tar sands. O'Sullivan was the man who sponsored this opportunity."

Bill Sharon agreed, adding, "O'Sullivan became sort of our representative at large. He is the best salesman you ever did see. I'm not exaggerating when I say he'd walk into the president of the United States' office if he had a deal, and he'd sell the deal to him." While it is not known whether O'Sullivan ever walked into the president of the United States' office, the story goes that he walked right into J. Howard Pew's office — the chairman of the board that controlled Sun Oil Company in Philadelphia — and boldly presented his case for the oil sands.

For Frank O'Sullivan, the oil sands had long been a source of fascination. "I first started thinking about the oil sands in 1949," he recalled. "I attended a symposium in Edmonton that included a trip up to Fort McMurray to see the area. We went on a barge on the Athabasca

1960 ▶

British engineer Sir Christopher S. Cockerell celebrates the successful crossing of the English Channel by his SRN-1 hovercraft.

1960 ▶

Canada's first ever Olympic skiing gold medal is won by Ottawa's Anne Heggtveit. She also wins the world slalom and alpine combined titles.

River and the oil sands were 200 feet high on either side. On a hot day, you could see the sticky oil running down to the river. My mouth watered thinking of the possibilities if it could ever be developed.

"A few years later, I had a meeting with Ben Goodman, who was vice president and chief engineer of the construction company at the time. Ben said, 'Frank, we'd like to have you work on this oil sands project because there could be some work in it for us.' So I went to see Tom Clarke, who was managing director of the outfit that became GCOS. He was running a project that was trying to get off the ground. A lot of money had been spent, but nothing really had been done. They were applying for a permit from the government to build a plant. If their operation became viable, then there would be a lot of work in it for Mannix."

"At that same time, Cities Service Athabasca, which is now known as Syncrude, was also applying for a permit," O'Sullivan continued. "That company was a consortium of Imperial Oil, Cities Service, Atlantic Richfield and Gulf, so they were well financed. In comparison, we were like little David. Everybody thought that Cities Service Athabasca would get the permit, but I had been talking to Premier Ernest Manning. Ernest told me, 'Frank, I like what you're doing. I like the people you're associated with. If you can hold on long enough, we're going to give you a permit.' Of course, I couldn't tell anybody about that conversation. At the time, it was strictly in confidence between Ernest and myself. But

Top: Giant LeTourneau L700 151D front-end loaders dump overburden into Wabco 150-ton trucks.

Above: One of 17 Mannix 657 Caterpillar scrapers chews through overburden to expose the riches of the oil sands.

I knew we were going to get the permit if we just stayed with it.

"So I went to a young lawyer we had in the office. I asked him to write a letter of intent for me. The letter stated that if and when the permit was granted to GCOS, then Mannix would build the road, the bridge, the pipeline and do the stripping — the whole bit, all the way down the line. The lawyer told me, 'If you get GCOS to sign this, and get a permit, then you've got us quite a job.' That young fellow was Peter Lougheed. He was just starting out at that time. With that letter, I took off for New York and got hold of Tom Clarke. Tom said, 'Look, Frank, we're broke. We've only got $50,000 left. There's no more coming in. I've got nine kids. I've got to quit.' So I said, 'Don't quit for a while, Tom. Let's see what we can do.' And I got him to sign the letter."

"Seventy-five per cent of the lease was owned by Sun Oil Company in Philadelphia, so I went down to Philadelphia," O'Sullivan said. "It will never happen again in a lifetime, but I got to see Mr. J. Howard Pew, who was the chairman of the board that controlled Sun Oil. He was about 80 years old at the time. I went up to see him at his office on the 19th floor. The elevator only went to the 18th floor. A guard took me the rest of the way. Very few outsiders got in to talk to Mr. Pew, but I spent five hours with him. I remember he had a secretary named Mrs. Baker. She was about 75 then. She had an old steam kettle and she brought us a cup of tea. Mr. Pew asked me every question he could think of. When I looked at him, it was as though he could look right

1960 ▶

Soviet Premier Khrushchev inspects debris from the American U-2 spy plane shot down while flying over Soviet territory. The flight increases Cold War tensions between the two countries.

1960 ▶

Saskatchewan Power Corporation and a Mannix Co. Ltd. sponsored joint venture begin development of the main stem of the Saskatchewan River. The Squaw Rapids Dam and part of the earthen dike system under construction is shown.

through me. He knew all the answers already, but he kept asking me questions.

"Finally, he said, 'Young man, down the road, these oil sands have got to be developed. They are bigger than all the other known deposits of oil in the free world put together. If we don't develop them, 20 years from now, the Arabs are going to have us over a barrel. Whatever they want to charge us for oil, we will have to pay. We will not be in a position to negotiate with them at all. Young man, you have got a challenge. We can put a plant in and make it successful. It'll take 10 years to do it. How much will it take to keep the parking meter ticking until we get a permit?' I said, 'Mr. Pew, it could cost $5 million.' He said, 'You have it. Young man, how much to build a plant once you have the permit?' I said, 'Mr. Pew, our estimate for 25,000 barrels a day is $125 million.' He said, 'Okay, we'll give you $67.5 million and we'll raise the rest by seeing to your financing.'"

Frank O'Sullivan's bold elevator ride to the top had paid off. "The Great Canadian Oil Sands project was sponsored by J. Howard Pew and the Sun Oil Company," Graham Pollock said. "Mr. Pew saw a great potential there and he was determined to see that the project got off the ground. Frank O'Sullivan got the letter of intent assuring that Mannix would do the bridge, the road, the stripping and the dikes. And Sun Oil kept their word to us throughout. We continued to work up there for many years, and they honoured their agreement, which was only a simple letter — we never had a formal contract. They were very honourable people and we tried our best to do a good job for them."

Part of Mannix Co. Ltd.'s contract with Great Canadian Oil Sands was to strip the overburden off the

To speed the GCOS work,
657 Cat scrapers are used in tandem
or pushed through heavy conditions
by Caterpillar dozers.

tar sands. "I was the project manager for that job," said Henning Jensen. "It was my first job with the Mannix Group. The worst problem up there was the cold winter weather. We had periods of 40 below. Sometimes, it got even colder and that could last for weeks. It was a challenge to men and equipment. You put on heavy winter clothes and you never shut the equipment down. In fact, you only shut something down to get it inside to service it. Other than that, everything was working 24 hours a day, seven days a week. It was a tough job, but it had its rewards. By the time we left Fort McMurray in 1974, the Mannix company had handled more cubic yards than had gone into all the hydroelectric projects in Alberta combined. If I remember right, with the overburden, the tar sands and the tailings, we handled over 100 million cubic yards."

"It was a large job in terms of quantity and quality of equipment, too," continued Jensen. "We had probably the biggest fleet of 657 Caterpillar motor scrapers put together at that time. We had 17 of them. It was also the first time that the Mannix or Loram companies got involved with large diesel electric mining trucks. We switched over to those in 1972. They were a step up from the 120-ton mining trucks. We loaded those trucks with 15-cubic-yard front-end loaders from LeTourneau. They had a diesel electric drive, which had never existed before in front-end loaders. We made 20 major improvements on the loaders alone, just local improvements. Most of those have now been adopted by the manufacturer."

"That job was another milestone in the Mannix development of using big equipment," agreed Graham Pollock. "We used bottom dump trailers up there. Our investment in equipment was many, many millions of

1960 ▶

Echo I, the world's first communications satellite, is shown atop its launch vehicle.

1960 ▶

Geraldyn (Jeffie) Cobb is the first woman to pass the U.S. astronaut tests and qualifies to become the first female astronaut. Under the NASA program, "Women in Space Soonest," she nearly becomes the first woman to voyage into space. The first female U.S. astronauts are not formally selected until 1978.

dollars. We also helped develop the equipment itself. For example, we helped develop tires that would handle the equipment. So Mannix was given credit by the equipment manufacturers for helping them develop machines to move such large volumes of earth."

"That was an exciting time," said Dick Hermann, who joined Mannix Co. Ltd. in 1964 as a project engineer. "I remember reading in school about the tar sands and visualizing in my mind pictures of the tar sands and of animals getting trapped in them. So I really found it quite exciting to be there and see it firsthand. This was literally the commencement of the exploitation of that area."

Pembina Pipe Line Goes Looking for New Business Ventures — "They didn't want to see anybody who wasn't a major oil company."

As construction on the Pembina field's infrastructure continued throughout the 1950s, Pembina Pipe Line Ltd. began to look past this great Alberta oil field toward other business opportunities. The company's first attempt at expansion was an idea for a gas liquids gathering system and pipeline. And here, once again, Pembina found itself bucking the major, established oil companies.

In the late 1950s, realizing that Alberta had an abundance of natural gas and more natural gas byproducts than the local markets could bear, Pembina commenced a study on how to use pipelines to move natural gas byproducts. Pembina's detailed, international market survey, which took Alberta's petrochemical and fuel requirements into account, showed that most

Some members of the Pembina Pipe Line Ltd. brain trust, from left, F.A. Madill, Harry Booth, James A. Scott, J.S. Slater and F.C. Mannix.

As the Pembina field expands, the number of oil well headers increases.

of the gas liquids and byproducts could best reach markets from a tidewater or Great Lakes terminal. Pembina then considered ways to economically transport gas to eastern Canadian and export markets. What they concluded was that pipeline transportation was both technically and economically sound.

Pembina then took their tentative plans on the road. "I got my first exposure to some heavy-duty negotiating when I accompanied the negotiating team down to Chicago to negotiate with Standard of Indiana on the joint venture arrangement to build the whole project," Bob Sanders recalled. "It was a fantastic experience for a young engineer. We negotiated a stack of documents six inches thick. But there was a lot of opposition to the idea because it really would have given Standard of Indiana a stranglehold on this source of supply for natural gas liquids in the Chicago area, and Standard of New Jersey and Gulf Oil Co. were not particularly pleased with that prospect. We had opposition from them and from Continental Oil Company as well. They just objected because they didn't want to see anybody who wasn't a major oil company doing anything in Canada."

During 1959, the company made the appropriate applications for starting the Foothills Product Pipe Line system. A new, wholly owned Pembina subsidiary, Westalta Products Pipe Line Ltd., applied for a permit from Alberta's Department of Mines and Minerals to construct the system. Hearings were conducted until 1961.

Meanwhile, the Pembina system continued to grow. In September 1959, the Alberta Oil and Gas

---

1960 ▶

Calgary Power Ltd. and Mannix Co. Ltd. begin the Brazeau hydro development in the Rocky Mountains southwest of Edmonton. When completed it will be Alberta's largest single hydroelectric and water control project.

1960 ▶

Dr. Theodor Maiman, the research physicist who perfects the laser, looks at the ruby used to create the first laser beam.

Conservation Board approved a plan for the field's producers to "unitize" a large portion of the field. Under unitization, producers agreed to consolidate many small batteries into fewer, larger batteries, to be run by a selected unit operator. The system also facilitated more efficient water flooding on petroleum reservoirs formerly tapped and managed independently by two or more producers. Fewer batteries meant lower costs. Moreover, the greater the production, the more oil travelled through the pipeline, generating more revenue. The results quickly began to appear. In 1960, Pembina had gross revenues of $5,974,000, a six per cent increase over the previous year. Throughputs also increased about seven per cent, to an average of 110,400 barrels per day.

Throughputs would increase even more thanks to the government's newly enacted National Oil Policy. In 1961, changes in Canada's National Oil Policy raised the Pembina field's production to 121,550 barrels per day. No sooner had the new oil policy gone into effect, however, than the government switched gears. In 1962, through an arcane system of provincial production regulations, the valves were tightened on Pembina's wells, cutting field output to an average of 113,580 barrels per day. Meanwhile, Pembina was undergoing its first major internal upheaval. In 1961, Pembina president, Jim Scott, left the company. He was replaced by Eric Connelly.

Under Connelly, the pace of automating field gauging accelerated. In the late 1950s and early 1960s, the company developed its Lease Automatic Custody Transfer, or LACT, system whereby oil in the batteries was measured on a meter. At the end of 1961, 60 per cent of the Pembina system was under automatic custody transfer, and the next year, 72 per cent. The company also installed equipment to control the main pump station remotely from facilities in Edmonton. To the men in the field, automation made a major difference in how they worked. But for the company, even greater change appeared on the horizon.

Pembina's efforts to grow by establishing a gas liquids gathering system and pipeline were stymied. While the Mannix organization had convinced government that it could build and operate the Pembina system, it could not sway the bureaucrats and officials on the natural gas products pipeline. The permits were denied in 1961. Several other proposed projects also met with government resistance.

PEMBINA CRUDE

"I think Pembina is probably still one of the largest oil gathering systems in the world in terms of aerial extent, and certainly one of the most complicated in terms of the number of delivery points," explained civil engineer Gordon Brown. During the late Sixties, Brown was a member of the Mannix group requested to produce a proposal for the development of a new oil field in southern Siberia, a place called Pravdinskoye. This proposal, which was ultimately unproductive, was sponsored by the Soviet Union Oil Ministry.

"One of the things about the Pembina system is that a lot of the crude oil they had initially gathered was what they technically call a non-Newtonian fluid — it's a fluid that doesn't behave as a fluid," Brown said. "There was no body of scientific knowledge on how to handle this fluid called thicksotropic fluid.

"If you have ever tried to stir a can of latex paint, you'll know that when you begin, the paint is so solid you can stand the stirring stick up in it, and after a certain amount of violent agitation it becomes quite liquid. That's what this Pembina crude is like — it takes a tremendous amount of power to overcome that initial resistance to flow, but once that happens the flow occurs relatively easily. Getting this stuff to flow was done by brute force, but through examination and looking at all these empirical relations, a theory was developed over a period of time. Pembina pioneered that in Canada, certainly."

1960 ▶

The Calgary Firestone plant is completed in October.

1961 ▶

An earthquake near Concepción, Chile, creates tsunamis (tidal waves) that race across the Pacific Ocean. Shown is damage at Hilo, Hawaii.

The Move into Oil and Gas Production
Eric Connelly Goes to Work

Without other opportunities to expand the pipelining business, Pembina could not grow. Realizing that Pembina could not stake the organization's future on pipelines, Pembina management decided to move into oil and gas production. "As the Pembina field was more fully developed, and the opportunity for the expansion of the pipeline system decreased, we looked for additional pipeline opportunities," explained Harry Booth, who was then general manager and controller. "But they just weren't available. We weren't successful in that area. The Westalta-Foothills deal, of course, was a major example of that. Getting into the oil and gas producing side of the business, then, really followed from our inability to be able to expand the pipeline side of the business. So a deliberate decision was taken to establish ourselves as a company on the same competitive basis as producing oil companies."

Here, Pembina faced an enormous obstacle. At that time, a pipeline company had a great disadvantage compared with oil and gas enterprises. "There was absolutely no use of our trying to get into the oil business in Alberta, because the other companies could offset the costs of all their development and drilling against their revenue," explained Eric Connelly. "We couldn't do it." So Connelly went to work, trying to organize support in government that would enable Pembina to move into the oil and gas exploration and production business. Next to the formation of the company, the changes he helped persuade government to make were perhaps the most important development in the history of Pembina Pipe Line Ltd.

Canada's Income Tax Act required modification if Pembina was to grow in the oil and gas producing business. "I threw up an awful lot of smokescreens, but I couldn't get far in generating help or support from Canada's oil companies," Connelly said. When Connelly approached Imperial Oil and tried to buy their oil in the Pembina field, Imperial told him that they already had enough competitors in the business. Yet these same Imperial officials were frequent complainers to Premier Manning that Pembina be denied additional pipeline contracts unless Pembina took more risks and entered the exploration business. In other words, since major oil companies made up the Canadian Petroleum Association, it would not support Pembina. And even though Connelly sat on the board of directors of an organization of independent oil companies, he could not count on their help either, as the independents depended on the majors for farm outs.

An early Pembina pump station control room.

Still, Connelly persisted. He enlisted the help of Gordon Brown, a young Alberta civil engineer who had worked for Sparling-Davis, spent some time with a major oil company in Eastern Canada, and returned to the Mannix Group in 1960. Connelly and Brown wanted to change the income tax law to allow a pipeline company to charge exploration and production expenditures against its pipeline earnings. The Pembina team found a precedent to help make its case. "Steel companies were allowed to spend money on prospecting for new iron ore bodies before their income was taxed," explained Brown. "The rationale was that if we didn't continue to find new iron ore bodies, our steel manufacturing would eventually die. We were able to make the same argument for pipeline companies."

A change in government temporarily delayed a decision on the matter. Then, although the Tax Department acknowledged the wisdom of the position, opposition developed. Connelly promptly enlisted the support of five other

1961 ▶

A Mannix Co. Ltd. sponsored joint venture begins the $10.7-million, two-year Grand Rapids grouting project to prepare a dam foundation for Manitoba Hydro.

1961 ▶

East Germany erects the Berlin Wall.

companies, all of whom owned pipelines and endured business conditions similar to Pembina's. With the help of Mannix's Ottawa attorney, Ross Tolmie, Connelly brought his ad hoc group of petitioners to Walter Gordon, the minister of finance who was responsible for changes to the Income Tax Act. The amendment passed. Said Connelly, "At no time did I ever go in and ask for something for ourselves that wouldn't benefit the country generally. I'd been taught that. It wasn't any brains on my part; I just went in there and handled it that way."

Thus able to write off exploration and production expenses against its growing earnings, Pembina began purchasing oil and gas properties. Pembina's first major acquisition came in 1963 when it bought Asamera Oil Corporation's interests in the Etzikom gas field and South Alberta Pipe Lines Ltd., which it split 50-50 with Midcon Oil and Gas. The acquisition of the 50 per cent interest in South Alberta Pipe Lines was a major turning point. "That was really the beginning of Pembina's entry into the oil and gas side of the business," said Booth. Soon after the South Alberta Pipe Lines acquisition, Pembina management began hiring staff who were well versed in the oil and gas exploration business and knew how to assess properties. "About that time I hired Dr. Tom Parks, who had been the head of Sohio's exploration operation here in Calgary," said Booth. "Henry Acteson, who is a very good petroleum engineer, also joined the department. So we put a small group together to start up an oil and gas operation. From that time on, we really started in a more orderly way to acquire oil and gas interests."

The Search for Land

In 1964, to meet higher demand from the city of Medicine Hat, and to help supply an expanded Northwest-Nitro Chemicals plant, Pembina purchased additional gas reserves in the Medicine Hat field, which straddled the South Alberta pipeline route, and in the Dunmore field, about 12 miles (19 kilometres) southeast of Medicine Hat. The company also purchased the oil and gas interest of Zenmac Metal Mine Ltd. in Alberta, and participation in the Mitsue oil field of northeastern Alberta.

Only a healthy company could make such purchases, and Pembina grew stronger and healthier with each passing year. It had gross revenues of more than $7 million in 1964, and net earnings of more than $1.5 million. It tied in two additional fields in the Pembina system, and breathed a sigh of relief when a new Alberta Oil and Gas Conservation Board study promised to at least maintain the same volume of production allowed from Pembina wells in 1965 as 1964. Thus, by the mid-1960s, thanks in large measure to Eric Connelly's efforts, Pembina began to emerge as a power in oil and gas production as well as pipelining. However, its new role, as Pembina soon discovered, brought it squarely into another oil and gas thicket — the acquisition of property.

Feudal barons and British royalty of centuries past knew from where one drew wealth. Military and civil power may have enforced the collection of wealth, but riches

NO FUEL LIKE AN OLD FUEL

In the pioneering days of Pembina, "your responsibilities were such that today you would have some fancy title," said P.G. Clarke. "Titles are great if you are able to do the work, but if you're not able to do the work, a title isn't going to help any." Brock Montgomery concurred wholeheartedly with this sentiment, adding, "I went around for two months down in the southern United States and Chicago trying to sell this pipeline to prospective purchasers without any title. I didn't have or need a title to talk. I didn't know what the hell I was talking about."

B.L. Montgomery.

"One of the funniest stories I think I've ever heard," said Clarke, "was with Pembina at the start of the Westalta project. It was at a meeting with the brass, with the senior pipeline officials for a group that took in a lot of the major oil companies. Brock was chairing the meeting and started talking about carbohydrates, meaning hydrocarbons. Well, at coffee break, somebody said to Brock, 'It's not carbohydrates. It's hydrocarbons.' Brock said, 'Well, I'm sure glad you corrected me.' He got back in, and he reopened the meeting by saying that he apologized for saying carbohydrates when he really meant hydrogen carbides!"

1961 ▶

The S.S. France is launched. Shown at New York, she is the longest, and last, of the great transatlantic passenger liners.

1961 ▶

After lifting the rails and ties, a Mannix International Autotrack positions undertrack equipment in the state of Texas, one of the 28 U.S. states in which Mannix International equipment has worked.

flowed primarily from land. Ranchers and railroad men knew the value of real estate. So too did oil men. When Pembina purchased many properties that were already producing oil and gas, it also sought to lock up exploration and production rights on as much land as possible. For the company, the 1960s were notable for what one might call its "territorial expansion."

In 1965, Harry Booth took over as Pembina's president, while Eric Connelly stepped up to become chairman of the board. Booth continued the company's acquisition of crude oil and natural gas producing properties. Pembina's production in 1965, after deducting for royalties, amounted to 122,100 barrels, compared with 14,000 barrels in 1964. This came from 17 net oil wells — the company, of course, owned multiple smaller interests in many wells; the net figure is the sum of the percentages owned — that produced an average of 449 barrels of oil per day. Pembina also held ownership in 38.8 net natural gas wells, all in the Medicine Hat area. Together, these properties produced a daily average of 10 million cubic feet of gas (283,218 cubic metres) per day, up from 4.1 million cubic feet (106,105 cubic metres) daily in 1964. However, throughputs from the Pembina field dropped more than 2,500 barrels per day, due mainly to government regulations. Oil and gas production helped the company increase its overall revenues by nearly $400,000 over the previous year, to nearly $7.5 million in 1964.

With demand for Alberta crude in a temporary decline and the Alberta Oil and Gas Conservation Board still tinkering with Pembina field production allowances, Pembina redoubled its efforts to expand. It acquired crude oil reserves in the Swan Hills field by purchasing an interest in the Deer Mountain Unit. It acquired the natural gas leases on 106,983 acres (43,296 hectares) around Medicine Hat, on which 31 net natural gas wells were either completed and producing, or were capable of producing. Pembina also acquired, in permits or leases, other or additional interests in British Columbia, Alberta and the Northwest Territories, which together totalled nearly 290,000 net acres (117,000 hectares).

Erven Rendflesh thiefing the tank looking for water, hydrometer density and oil temperature.

The next year produced similar additions as Pembina's land and property-buying fever continued. Names like Boundary Lake, a gas field in British Columbia, and Provost and Cessford in southern Alberta, were added to the company's roster. Possible oil-bearing acreage was obtained in the Rainbow Lake, North Zama, Hay Lake, Bistcho and Mitsue areas of Alberta, in the West Peejay and Beaverskin areas of British Columbia, and in the "Winnipegosis reef trend" in Saskatchewan.

Pembina participated in the drilling of 15 wells in 1966, six of which were completed as oil wells and four as gas producers. At the end of the year, one well was considered suspended, another under test and three were dry holes. All in all, when the petroleum industry average was only one successful well for seven drilled, the results for 1966 were heartening.

The next year seemed as if it might be even better for Canadian oil men, but not so promising for world peace. The world's oil supply appeared once again headed for disruption. In six days of skillful and daring fighting, Israel, under pressure from its avowed Middle East enemies, made large territorial gains in the Gaza Strip, the Sinai Peninsula, Old Jerusalem, the Golan Heights and Jordan's West Bank. Halfway around the world, political instability created a strengthening demand for western Canadian crude.

1961 ▶

New York Yankee Roger Maris, standing next to Babe Ruth's plaque in Yankee Stadium, breaks Babe Ruth's single season home run record. Maris hits 61 dingers, one more than Ruth.

1961 ▶

Continuing to help lay the Alberta Gas Trunk Line system, Mannix crews work from Priddis to Rocky Mountain House and from the Crowsnest Pass to Carway on the U.S. border.

Drayton Valley Becomes a Home
"The spirit of the community is exceptionally high."

While the corporate Pembina Pipe Line expanded, its people in Drayton Valley, where the company truly began, settled in. Skid shacks were replaced by three-bedroom homes and scattered trailer parks gave way to well-tended residential areas. The pleasant change occurred relatively quickly. But for a brief period, the discovery of the Pembina field spawned a rush of humanity that threatened to turn Drayton Valley into an archetypical boomtown — seedy, rough and as the crusty old maxim went, no place for a lady.

The original residents of the area had mixed feelings about all this. The oil business provided jobs, money and services. But some of the services, such as those proffered at the Wildcat Cafe, were of the type family folk could do without. The town clearly had a raw appeal for the young and footloose. And yet, as early as 1955, men had begun bringing wives and children to town, while single men were finding brides. It was time for Drayton Valley to come into its own.

By 1956, the Alberta government gave Drayton Valley "new town" status, with the passage of the Drayton Valley Townsite Act, a measure made retroactive to March 1, 1954. This set forth the legal forces and conditions for careful subdivision, which in turn set the foundations for solid city planning. Incorporated as a village in February 1956, the hamlet was initially administered by a board composed of residents. Four months later, it became an official town, with council and mayoral elections held in March of 1957.

Most planning functions were overseen by the Edmonton Regional Planning Commission, while the town established a Municipal Planning Commission and Development Appeal Board. Thanks to planning, nearly every street in Drayton Valley was paved. A large, modern sewage treatment plant, a fine hospital and five schools serving nearly 2,000 students were established. That the town reached this maturity in such a brief span of time is remarkable. Noted the town's general plan of 1967, "The spirit of the community is exceptionally high, the participation in the affairs of the community on the part of citizens, as well as clubs and other organized groups, is equal to, if not higher than in other older centres." How this came about, suggested the report, was partly attributable to "some outstanding citizens, both inside and outside the administration who provided the community with leadership." A significant portion of those "outstanding citizens," to be sure, came from Pembina Pipe Line.

Johnny Carroll, who joined Pembina in November 1954 as station chief at the main pump station at Buck Creek, relates a story that exemplifies Pembina's community spirit of taking care of not only each other, but also other members of the community. "One night in late autumn, on the way in from Drayton Valley, my wife and I came across an ambulance stalled in the road," he recalled, "so I hooked onto it with our car and towed it

Top: Employee houses on 49th Avenue, Drayton Valley.

Above: The Drayton Valley Hospital decorated for Christmas, 1959.

1962 ►

The Soviet missile buildup in Cuba causes a crisis that moves the world to the brink of nuclear war. Canada prohibits Soviet planes from refuelling at Canadian facilities and supports the United States.

1962 ►

In response to increased Cold War tensions, some students are taught to "duck and cover" to survive a nuclear explosion.

THE PEMBINA ANNUAL GOLF TOURNAMENT

In the late spring of 1962, Eric Connelly, president of Pembina, suggested that Pembina's Drayton Valley employees go to Jasper for a weekend golf tournament. Earlier, Pembina groups played golf in Red Deer, Lacombe, Mulhurst and Edmonton, but by formalizing the annual event and moving it to the world-famous Jasper Park Lodge, the chance to hit a ball around a golf course with friends from work was elevated to a memorable occasion.

Although the focal point of these weekends was golf, they were really a social event. In those early days, many employees never played golf. In true Pembina spirit, they learned to golf right during the tournament. When the tournament first went to Jasper, the field men all bunked in one cabin just north of the clubhouse. The highlights of those years included poker games and singing well into the wee hours of the morning. The later they sang, the better they sounded, or so they claimed.

"The tournament established a relationship where the people see that the company just doesn't look upon you as somebody that comes to work at eight o'clock in the morning and goes home at four o'clock," said John Poloway. "I think it indicates that the company has an interest in that individual. They try to have this relationship with their employees and I think we certainly have it within the company. We work more as a family unit than as an employer-employee relationship. It's a relationship that's hard to describe, but it's there. You feel like you're part of the company, not just something within the company. You're part of the whole thing that moves, that makes the company go round."

into town. Dan Greger, who had been on the road with us, stayed behind me just in case something went wrong. We took that ambulance right into General Hospital."

"I found out later that the ambulance was going to charge the lady," Carroll said. "I told them if they did that, then I'd charge the ambulance for towing them. She must have froze to death in that ambulance — there was no heat, because the motor wasn't running. I must have towed them about 40 miles, so I thought they had an awful nerve trying to charge her. Eventually, they didn't. She was on relief or something like that. She was in no position to pay for an ambulance, anyway. But I always thanked Greger for staying behind me because you never know when something else could go wrong."

Despite such valiant rescues, most of the early Drayton Valley social activities, as one might expect, revolved around company functions. In July of 1955, the company held its first picnic, a corn roast at Violet Grove. Because their families were still living in Edmonton or other locations far from Drayton Valley, quite a number of employees didn't have the wherewithal to attend. Jim Scott, Pembina's first president, came to the corn roast, looked around at the children and wives who were there, and decided to organize the next one better, to ensure that every employee could make it.

"He said we were going to have a barbecue next time, and he set it up for Isle Lake," recalled John Poloway, who joined Pembina in 1954 as a pump mechanic. "The company bought steaks, provided buses for anybody who needed transportation and anybody who wasn't working was expected to go. They got Shetland ponies for the kids to ride, and this whole event was dedicated to the employees and their families, to recognize the year's achievements. That's how the company barbecue tradition got started."

For the men in the field, the year's achievements were marked day by day. "When we initially started," explained Poloway, "there was no such thing as looking at the clock. If you went to work at eight in the morning, and you had a problem, you didn't come home until the problem was solved." When Poloway first came to Drayton Valley and got a taste of the working conditions, he questioned his wisdom, saying to himself, "What an idiot. I left a good job at Texaco to come here to what?" But soon he came to appreciate his fellow Pembina workers. "I had an opportunity to meet really beautiful people to work with and establish lifelong friendships," he said. "Because we were all part of

---

1962 ▶

This Calgary Power Ltd. sign tells the story of the Brazeau Dam.

1962 ▶

The Portage Mountain Diversion Tunnels are built for B.C. Hydro & Power Authority some 500 miles (800 kilometres) north of Vancouver, British Columbia. The Drake, Mannix, Kaiser and Gilpin joint venture builds the massive tunnels in only nine months.

something, we grew together. You can get into a big company in Edmonton, or wherever, an organization that has 3,000 or 4,000 people, and you never know that many of them."

One of the ways people got to know each other better, was on the golf course. By 1962, the company had established its annual golf tournament at Jasper Park Lodge. "They always seemed to treat the personnel as people, not just numbers," said Carroll. "They always had what they called a steak barbecue in the summer for the whole family, and put on a Christmas party for the kiddies. They had the golf tournament at Jasper every year. I think the morale of the personnel was always fairly high. You have your highs and lows in any company, but here it was mainly on the high side."

The longevity of service by employees in the Drayton Valley pipeline operation is clear evidence of this bond between Pembina and its people. "There are a lot of younger people who have grown up here," explained Reg Samis, who joined Pembina in 1955 as a gauger, "and after seeing Pembina in the community, would like to work for us. They apply for jobs, and real good people, too. But we just don't turn over that many people, so it's hard to hire many new ones."

"One other thing that went over good with Pembina was, rather than being unionized, they had an Industrial Council," explained Carroll, "where the men elected delegates and the company appointed delegates. We had meetings once a month to iron out any difficulties or things that the men thought should be brought to the attention of management. Wages were discussed, but always on a friendly basis. There were times when management didn't go along with what the men suggested, but mainly the thing went along smoothly."

Rarely in its history has Pembina been forced to let many of its people go. The downturn in oil demand in 1957 led to one of the few significant work force reductions, roughly 30 in Drayton Valley. And automation of gauging facilities, started the next year, kept the staffing lean. Those who did leave the company were often not replaced. "If you look at the seniority list," said Samis, "there's hardly anyone who was hired between 1958 and 1968."

However, not every Pembina employee was thrilled by Drayton Valley. "I know an awful lot of people who came out here and this was the last place in the world they wanted to go," said Poloway. "Office people and the like don't get to see that much; and, of course, in Edmonton or Calgary you have a lot of social life, and you can go see professional hockey and football."

The Mannix Co. Ltd. float in the annual Drayton Valley parade.

On the other hand, many were content with the slower pace in Drayton Valley. "You could bring up your family in a relatively good environment," said Poloway, "and the children weren't exposed to a lot of things that kids get exposed to in Edmonton. And the education system here is good. You knew your teachers and you socialized together, which was good."

Pembina's people pitched in to the community. Many of them joined the volunteer fire department, and some worked as auxiliary members of the Royal Canadian Mounted Police. For a time, Pembina had its own adult hockey team that played in a commercial league, two or three times a week. However, it became highly competitive, with teams like Edmonton's Oil Kings, laced with men who were real hockey players disguised as engineers.

1962 ▶

Canada's Alouette 1 is the first satellite developed by a country other than the United States or the Soviet Union.

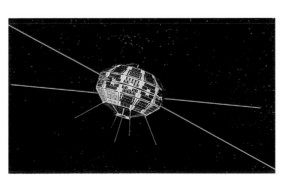

1962 ▶

Canadian communications theorist Marshall McLuhan coins the term "global village" when describing the world's electronic interdependence.

Pembina then sponsored a juvenile hockey team, with a focus on youth. "The company was very supportive of sports for children, as well as personnel," said Carroll. "Like with hockey, they'd drive them or supply transportation." Pembina provided uniforms and company volunteers constantly refereed games in Drayton Valley. The company also became involved in Little Canadian Football, for boys ages 6 to 14. Along with hockey and football, Pembina's people also were an important part of Drayton Valley's Neptune Club. The town got a swimming pool in 1963, and the local swim club performed well in races throughout the province.

The company's Len Charbonneau, along with Buck McDonald, Slim White and others, started Drayton Valley's golf course, raking rocks, cutting roots and clearing enough room for only two or three holes at first. Company trucks were used to help the night and weekend efforts that led to the Pembina Golf Club. Pembina and its employees also "built a curling rink at Buck Creek," Carroll said. "The company donated I think it was $500, and the rest we raised by selling shares. Everybody put in $50 and then we did all the work. We built it right from the ground up. It was a good thing for winter entertainment."

There were silly moments, too. The Oil Wives Club of Drayton Valley — to belong, a woman's husband had to derive 75 per cent of his income from the oil business — put on monthly skits and dances. Hawaiian Night, with everyone dressing up in Hawaiian clothing in the dead of winter, had that certain touch of levity that made times lighter. "We'd go down for a dinner and dance and a half-hour show and they were really good," recalled Poloway. "It seems we used to go out every Friday night. If it wasn't the Oil Wives, the ski club or the hockey team would have something."

"It seems like Pembina was important in all of the community projects; whether it was sports, or anything, Pembina and its people did more than their share," said Samis. While Pembina's people were quite visible in activities that supported their community, they also quietly, and anonymously, contributed in other ways. "Even some of our employees didn't know about certain contributions within the community," said Poloway.

"Slim White, for example, was one who did many things behind the scenes," Poloway said. "One day he and a man named Syd Mitchell heard of a family that didn't have anything whatsoever for Christmas. Well, they just looked at each other, and without saying a word, headed out. I learned later that those two took it upon themselves to see that the family enjoyed a proper Christmas. This is the type of thing that is part of the company. We don't print it in the paper or make announcements, but it's part of being in the community."

The Tale of Empire Development

By all accounts, Pembina was a phenomenal success. Between 1954, when the project began, and 1955, Pembina's stock shot up in value from $4 a share to a whopping $67 a share. For the people at Loram, these were heady days. "We were living in a different era then," recalled J.D. (Don) Mawhinney, who would become legal counsel to Empire Development Company, Loram's iron ore mining company in British Columbia. "Things were very, very prosperous. Everybody was very bullish. People were a little more reckless. It was difficult for people not to make money."

Fuelled by the optimism of the times, which seemed to offer unlimited possibilities for growth, and buoyed by their success with Pembina, in 1955 Loram jumped headlong into the risky world of international metals mining. Mining lore is full of stories about fortunes made overnight — bonanza discoveries that turned poor prospectors into millionaires and small mining companies into giant corporations. But for every story about fortunes made in this fabulous industry, there are thousands of tales about fortunes lost. The history of Empire Development Company Limited is one such tale.

In the early 1950s, Fred C. Mannix made a trip to Japan to investigate business opportunities there. While Mannix was mainly interested in finding new markets for his construction company and its coal mining subsidiary, he discovered that one of the highest priority items for the Japanese was iron ore. Japan had recently begun importing small quantities of iron ore from two mines on the British Columbia coast. The Japanese steelmakers Mannix met told him that they were quite interested in finding additional sources of iron ore in Western Canada.

"The Japanese were insistent that we go over there to Tokyo, and we did," F.C. Mannix explained. "The people we were dealing with were very big and had lots of opportunities there. They wanted to import iron ore, so we went over to see them, to see what they had and what they could take. Then we came back to look around and see if there was any iron ore, and we bought the Empire Development property. We bought it from some outfit on the coast, a man by the first name of Cowan."

1962 ▶

The Orient Express runs its last trip after 79 years of service.

1962 ▶

Vinnell, Mannix and McNamara begin the Lower Monumental Lock and Dam on the Snake River in Washington state. Once concrete work is mostly completed in this small peninsula, tubular steel sheet pilings will divert the river flow to allow construction across the remainder of the river to begin.

J. Cowan Adam was the president of Quatsino Copper-Gold Mines Ltd., a B.C. mining company that had been mining copper on Vancouver Island since the 1930s. British Columbia did not produce any iron ore to speak of until the mid-1950s, as local developers largely ignored the iron ore in order to concentrate on the rich deposits of copper also found in the area. However, in 1932, in the course of exploring for more copper, Quatsino crews made another magnetite discovery. While working on the side of Merry Widow mountain, they sank a 1,000-foot (305-metre) drill hole through 45 feet (14 metres) of magnetite ore, some 750 feet (230 metres) below a series of magnetite outcrops. The deposit remained untouched for the next two decades for several reasons, however. With the onset of the Depression, Quatsino lacked the resources to exploit this discovery, and the inaccessibility of the deposits seemed an insoluble problem for the technology of the day. In addition, the abundance of cheap iron ore on the world market in the 1930s and 1940s prohibited additional work by the Quatsino crews.

In the 1950s, efforts to exploit the economic potential of these deposits were renewed. Quatsino acquired holdings of some 63 claims in the area, including options on the Merry Widow and adjacent Kingfisher claims, properties that were to form the heart of the Empire Development project. In 1950, Quatsino hired consulting mining engineer Henry L. Hill to diamond drill two main claims: Merry Widow No. 5 and the Kingfisher fraction. The results were encouraging enough to prompt more drilling in 1951. In that year,

An aerial view of the Empire Mine locale.

4,422 feet (1,348 metres) of closely spaced vertical holes proved the existence of up to 500,000 tons (454,000 tonnes) of ore. In 1952, Quatsino undertook an additional exploration program, drilling another 4,471 feet (1,363 metres) of vertical holes, which proved an additional 500,000 tons (454,000 tonnes) of ore. The company also undertook a magnetometer survey, which indicated that the ore body might contain another 1.5 million tons (1.36 million tonnes). Preliminary assays showed that the ore was a rich 58 per cent iron and contained very little silica and other impurities.

In 1955, Mannix Ltd. learned about Quatsino's iron ore property. After examining geological and preliminary engineering reports prepared by various consulting firms, Mannix sent a team of engineers to examine the potential mine site. They returned with a report that was glowingly optimistic. Early in 1956, Mannix and Quatsino agreed to form Empire Development Company Limited to mine the property. To secure contracts with Japanese steel companies, Mannix and Quatsino signed an agreement with C.T. Takahashi, a Japanese trading agent. By that spring, negotiations with the six largest steel companies in Japan — Yawata, Kawasaki, Sumitomo, Nakayama, Amagaski and Nippon Kokan — were under way. On May 11, 1956, Mannix and Quatsino signed an agreement which stated that Quatsino would lease the property to Empire in return for a 40 per cent interest in the proceeds. Mannix, through the wholly owned subsidiary, Empire, would be responsible for construction of all the mine facilities and infrastructure, and would operate the mine.

1962 ▶

Mannix pipeliners help construct the Imperial Oil Swan Hills gathering system. The crews lay the system in the dead of winter during one of the longest, below-zero cold spells in 50 years.

1962 ▶

Mon-Max Services Ltd. is formed. This 50-50 partnership with Montreal Engineering designs and builds gas and sulphur processing plants, gas compressor installations and LPG storage facilities. Shown, from left to right, are Dave Hoeppner, Ted Starr and Bob Barratt.

After the signing of this agreement, Brigadier-General Alan B. Connelly, who would become Empire's president, went to Japan with one of Quatsino's vice presidents to complete negotiations with the Japanese buyers. Meanwhile, Connelly's brother Eric was developing an inspired scheme for financing the project. All capital costs for starting up the mine would be put up by a consortium consisting of the Industrial Development Bank and a large group of private investors. Mannix Ltd. would not have to contribute a cent to Empire but would effectively control the entire operation.

By June 1956, Alan Connelly returned from Japan with a three-year contract. The Japanese steel companies would pay nearly $12 million for about 1.4 million tons (1.27 million tonnes) of iron ore to be delivered to the dock at Port McNeill over the next three years. Mannix engineers figured that capital costs to start up the mine would be $3 million, and operating costs would be around $4.30 per ton of ore. This meant that Empire could expect to pay off all its creditors in the first year of operation, and generate about $3 million in profits in its first three years of operation. While this was hardly big money, it was not too bad a return on an investment of zero dollars. Since the geological studies showed possible additional ore reserves of another million tons (900,000

Drilling into rock to set CIL Hydromex explosives to blast material over the iron ore deposit.

tonnes), it was projected that the mine would generate at least another $4 million in profits before it was shut down.

If this arrangement sounds too good to be true, it most definitely was. The Empire project came with two very big ifs. The first one had to do with the geology of the deposit. The entire project was based on the assumption that the original exploration work and the Mannix feasibility study had proved that the ore deposit could be profitably mined. Unfortunately, this assumption would quickly prove wrong.

The second big if had to do with the Mannix company's capital cost estimate for starting up the mine. If these costs had been correctly estimated, Empire Mine could be expected to be a nice source of revenue for the next few years. If, on the other hand, the estimate was to prove too low, someone was going to have to make up the difference. Since all the capital for mine start-up was being provided by outside investors and a bank, Loram Ltd. had been required to guarantee that its estimate for the construction of the mine and associated infrastructure was indeed correct. Even though Mannix Co. Ltd. would not contribute any of the original capital costs, its parent company, Loram Ltd., would have to pay any cost overruns incurred in starting up the mine — a condition which would soon prove very, very costly.

1963 ▶

Mannix Construction Inc. joins joint venture partners Vinnell, McNamara and George A. Fuller Company to build the John Day hydro project spanning the broad Columbia River between Oregon and Washington. The construction will run until 1968.

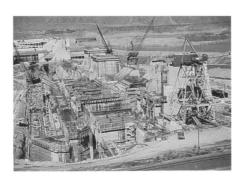

1963 ▶

When completed, the $70.5-million John Day project includes a hydroelectric dam, lock, fishladder, access road and rail spur. A tug pushing four barges powers out of the giant lock.

What Seemed Like a Good Idea at the Time

Fred C. Mannix's belief that Japan could be a rich market for Canadian natural resources was extremely perceptive. Like several of the concepts behind the Mannix operations in the 1950s, this idea is now seen to be way ahead of its time. Japan was rapidly turning into one of the world's industrial giants. Lacking natural resources within its own borders, Japan needed resource-rich trading partners to fuel its tremendous economic growth.

Of all the stories of postwar Japanese growth, few are as inspiring as the saga of the Japanese steel industry. As World War II drew to a close, only three of Japan's 35 blast furnaces were still in operation. This did not last for long though. With an infusion of capital from the major Japanese banks and the dedication of the country's foremost engineering and managerial talents, the native steel industry soon began to recover. By 1949, this once devastated industry had equalled its prewar production figures. By 1954, that figure doubled. In 1956, Japan surpassed Great Britain as the world's largest shipbuilder. By 1957, Japan was widely recognized as the world's foremost steel producer, both in terms of quality and quantity of product. At the time the Empire project was getting under way, it was estimated that Japan would require around 15 million tons (14 million tonnes) yearly of imported iron ore to keep its plants operating.

F.C. Mannix was also aware that the Canadian mining industry was growing at an extraordinary rate during this period. Between 1950 and 1955, the metallics sector of this industry increased its value of output from $617 million to $1 billion, a jump in productivity of over 60 per cent. During this time, iron ore went from being an insignificant part of Canada's mineral production to one of its leaders, approaching the value of zinc and far surpassing lead, the two leading metals of the previous decades. Between 1950 and 1955, Canadian iron ore exports increased from two million to 13 million tons.

A Risky Business

The process of putting a new mine into production is a lengthy and complicated one, requiring a complex combination of scientific knowledge, engineering and construction expertise and good financial planning. The first step in the mine development process is exploration, which is one of the most risky businesses in the world. Statistics show that exploration work yields few mineral discoveries, and only a few of these discoveries actually become working mines.

Exactly how difficult and risky it is to develop a metals mine was discovered by Mannix Co. Ltd. in 1956. The Empire project was located in the north-central section of Vancouver Island, British Columbia, midway between Quatsino Sound on the west coast of the island and Port McNeill on the east coast, about 243 miles (391 kilometres) northwest of Victoria. The Empire property lay on the eastern flank of the Merry Widow mountain at an elevation of 2,700 feet (940 metres) in a region dependent upon forest products for its economy — the area surrounding the Empire claims was owned by MacMillan Bloedel, the largest lumber company in Canada. The Empire Mine lay in rolling and heavily wooded country with pockets of dense underbrush in an area without paved roads or easy access. To reach the work site, miners and engineers had to take a float plane to Benson Lake, two miles (three kilometres) south of the property, and then hike along a four-mile (six-kilometre) trail through heavy undergrowth.

To further complicate matters, the Empire property lay in an area with an inhospitable climate. Annual rainfall was in the vicinity of 100 inches (250 centimetres) and snow could be expected as late as May. The dry season only lasted from May to September. But even during that period, rainfall in the neighbourhood of 10 inches (25 centimetres) or more was considered commonplace.

Perhaps because of the inhospitality of the site, the Empire deposits remained untouched until Mannix Ltd. prepared its report on the possible ore reserves at the Merry Widow and Kingfisher claims and the economic feasibility of surface mining operations. "Late in 1955, your directors entered into negotiations with Mannix Ltd., one of Canada's leading contractors, who have extensive experience in strip mining operations, as to the possibility of bringing your iron ore properties into operation," wrote J. Cowan Adam in a letter to Quatsino's shareholders dated August 1, 1956. "Following extensive investigations by Mannix engineers and their consultants, a contract was entered into by your company and Mannix Ltd. for the formation of a company by the name of Empire Development Company Limited for the purpose of bringing your properties into production."

People who are involved in the development of resources are generally optimistic and positive people, sometimes it is hard for them to imagine just how bad things can get. Unfortunately, Empire was about to prove exactly how bad things could get. Almost from day one, everything that could go wrong, did.

1963 ▶

Branding time at the Diamond 7 Ranch near Empress, Alberta, is also a time of great food. Here the kitchen staff and children take time to pose for a group shot.

1963 ▶

Hockey great Gordie Howe, number 9, scores his 545th goal to pass Montreal Canadien star, Maurice (Rocket) Richard, as the NHL's leading scorer.

To begin with, the report based on what Adam terms "extensive investigations" was highly optimistic. Since 1932, Quatsino had only spent about $200,000 on the exploration work and completed less than 10,000 feet (3,048 metres) of drilling. This represents an exploration effort that would ordinarily be considered adequate for nothing more than an initial investigation of the property. Normally, an experienced exploration company would then proceed to a more detailed study of the ore deposit, involving a considerably greater amount of drilling. If results from this more intensive drilling program were promising, the next step would be trenching and excavation to get a clearer idea of the extent of the ore body and its minability.

The optimism of this report also showed a lack of understanding of the economics of the iron ore mining industry. Iron is the most suitable metal for construction and manufacturing because of its strength and ready availability. It is the fourth most abundant element in the earth's crust. While iron ore deposits seldom appear in concentrations that are minable, they are common enough to make iron very inexpensive in comparison to other metals such as copper. Iron ore is a bulk product of relatively low value in comparison to other metals, and transportation and processing account for a good portion of its final selling price. Since iron ore mining is a very low-profit operation and the competition is tough, an iron mine has to have low operating costs just to have a shot at making a profit. Furthermore, to generate revenues of any significance, the mine needs to handle large tonnage.

The iron ore in Eastern Canada is found in huge deposits. In 1955, the Iron Ore Company of Canada, for instance, owned 45 iron properties near Schefferville on the Quebec and Labrador border, with some of these properties containing as much as 50 million tons (45 million tonnes) of ore each. In open-pit mining operations of this size, with reserves in the one-billion-ton (900-million-tonne) range, significant economies of scale come into play. The greater the tonnage handled per day, the lower the fixed operating costs per ton of ore.

The Empire property, with a mere two million tons of possible reserves, was an extremely small iron ore mine. Fixed costs could be expected to be higher just because of the size of the operation. Since the geology of the ore body was one of the most complex of any commonly associated with iron ore, the cost of operating the mine could be expected to be even higher still. When the rugged terrain of the mine site is also factored into the equation, it can be seen that the potential for any sort of profit margin was optimistic, at best.

To make matters worse, by the time the decision to start up Empire was made, although only a relatively short time had passed, the market had shifted. By the mid-1950s, it was apparent that the iron ore mining industry, which was already heavily competitive, was going to become more so. At the start of the decade, it had appeared that world output was not going to be able to keep up with demand, as the world economy recovered from the war years and industrial growth started to boom. But by 1956, huge discoveries of iron ore had been made in Africa, Brazil, Australia and the west coast of South America. As these new mines began to come into production, worldwide supply began to exceed demand.

Empire Mine railcars about to enter the underground shaft, just around the corner.

1963 ▶

Lester B. Pearson is elected prime minister of Canada.

1963 ▶

Mannix crews work on the Lakehead pipeline in Minnesota.

As a result, the Japanese steelmakers were in the process of diversifying their sources of supply. Japan no longer desperately needed B.C. iron ore. By 1956, British Columbia represented a small, alternate source of supply, which could be played off against other sources in an effort to keep prices down. Thus, Empire was started up at a time when an already tough business was becoming even tougher. The Japanese market was becoming increasingly competitive. The margin for profit was lower than ever, while the margin for error was greater than ever.

A Desperate Deadline
"Seventy-five feet of road slipped into the lake."

According to the terms of the contract between Empire Development and the Japanese steel mills, the first iron ore shipment was to be ready at Port McNeill in March 1957. In order to meet this deadline, and to avoid heavy penalties for any shipping delays, the mine had to be producing no later than February 1, 1957. However, the construction effort was soon bogged down and running substantially over budget. "We got into a real mess on that one," remembered Eric Connelly. "We started losing money right from the very first day." A combination of reasons caused this loss. The original estimates were far too low, the weather was horrendous and, because of the tight deadlines, work was pushed forward with undue haste and wastage.

One of the biggest problems with Empire began with the original estimates. "The Mannix people sent one of their junior engineers up to British Columbia to look over the conditions and prepare an estimate on the construction job," said Eric Connelly. "Well, that turned out to be a key mistake. They should have sent someone more senior. This engineer found another mine that had been operating in the area. He found out what their costs were for machinery use, for bulldozers and so on, and he used that figure. But he didn't dig into it. He didn't realize it was just their operating costs that they had used. There was nothing there for major overhaul, nothing for depreciation, nothing for camp costs. All of that had been absorbed in the overall mine operation."

"As a result," Connelly continued, "this guy came up with an estimate which was about 50 per cent of what it should have been. There was another junior engineer who was working in our office in Vancouver. He brought these problems to our attention, but nobody would listen to him. They were just too anxious to get this job going."

Another serious difficulty involved a tremendous cost overrun in constructing the road leading from Port McNeill to the mine. "The gentleman who was designated by Fred C. Mannix to head up the Empire Development operation was a chap by the name of Jim Scott," explained Don Mawhinney. "He was, as I understand it, the one responsible for the development of the Pembina operation, which proved to be extremely profitable and provided a great part of the development of the Mannix companies. Having been successful in that, he was designated to run the Empire Mine venture.

"I was told that in order to determine the cost of constructing the road, Scott went to the major lumber companies in British Columbia and asked them what their experience had been with constructing roads for logging and lumbering in similar areas. Well, one of the things about lumber companies is that they don't always exactly know what their road costs are, because a lot of their costs are really buried in logging operation costs. So the true cost of constructing a road may be much more than what is apparent in their figures for that type of construction."

On the basis of that information, Scott concluded that, rather than entering into a fixed-price contract for the construction of the road, he would enter into a cost-plus contract with a relatively small firm. It ended up that the road cost $2 million rather than $1 million. Of course, that extra $1 million had to be put up by Loram.

Once actual construction began, the crews faced inclement conditions from the first day to the last. The road crews expected the normal difficulties of hacking a pathway through 10 miles (16 kilometres) of dense virgin forest. They did not expect, however, that constant rain would turn that forest into an almost impassable swamp. To solve that problem, they decided to create a supporting tote road for equipment and supplies. Soon, even this rudimentary task bogged down in the onslaught of continual rain and flash floods. As the soil became saturated, even dozer tractors found it extremely difficult to blaze a trail behind the clearing crews.

In such conditions, equipment could not be hauled on a typical tote road. Instead, the crews had to build a fully stabilized haul road as they went along. To facilitate this task, they used quarried rock as base material to depths of up to six feet (two metres) and put giant cedar trees on top to make a corduroy road. Not surprisingly, the work slowed down to a crawl. In fact, the lead tractor for the road crews did not even

1963 ▶

Canadian golfer Marlene Stewart Streit wins the Australian Open to become the only woman to win the Australian, British, Canadian and U.S. opens.

1963 ▶

Mannix Construction Inc. sponsors a joint venture with Standard Gravel and Surfacing Contractors Inc. to build the underground powerhouse at Boundary Dam in northeastern Washington.

THE MOLE AWARD

"Mannix Company Ltd., one of Canada's largest heavy construction firms, is the first company outside of the United States to be admitted to the Hall of America's Builders.

"The citation was made at the ninth annual America's Builder Recognition Night at Los Angeles recently, and recognized the Canadian organization's 'significant contributions to the building of our World of Today throughout heavy engineering and construction, not only in the United States but at numerous places and on numerous projects throughout the Earth.'" — *Oilweek*, July 17, 1961.

reach the base of Merry Widow mountain until November 15. Because of these delays, Empire officials flew to Japan to try to negotiate a delay of the original shipping schedules. Reluctantly, the Japanese agreed to slip the original February 1 operating date to the middle of March 1957. The first shipment was also delayed until early April of that year.

Back in British Columbia, however, the rain and snow continued to fall. From September 1956 until May 1957, unusually severe weather conditions impeded the progress of construction. The project's weekly progress reports give some indication of the conditions being faced. The October 23rd entry reads: "Rains of unprecedented severity. The Raging River also rose and removed the bridge just north of Iron Lake, cutting communications with the head-end for a day." The November 12th report states: "Rain all week. Maynard Lake rose six feet in 12 hours and Raging River eight feet in 12 hours. The river held its flood crest for almost five hours." On December 15, the report recorded: "Heavy rains for the past week — slides on all roads including Alaska Pine's."

For the month of January, the reports state that rough weather prevented work on the wharf and that the combination of heavy snow and rain curtailed further operations inland. The report of February 25, 1957, mentions that "75 feet of road slipped into the lake and several other sections are threatened. It was required to relocate some 500 feet into solid rock bluff." For March 16, the report states: "Gales at wharf for two weeks prevented pile driving."

But the Empire team was determined to keep going forward at all costs to avoid the severe penalties called for in the contract if the schedule was not met. There are stories, for example, about people building roads through muskeg areas. They were actually burying equipment as part of the roadbed to keep on moving the road closer to the mine site.

Despite efforts to speed up work on the road, progress bogged down and the target date for the first shipment became increasingly unlikely. So further negotiations took place with the Japanese in January 1957, at which time, the target date was rolled back to the fall of that year. This revised schedule called for the mine to be in operation by late August. It also called for the first Japanese ship to come into Port McNeill for loading on September 25. Although a clause in the sales contract said that the Japanese could claim damages for nonfulfillment, the Japanese decided to take no such action as long as, in the words of one memo from 1957, "Empire worked steadily toward completion of its tasks."

In the first few months of 1957, the construction continued to move forward, still hampered by the combination of bad weather and rough terrain. As the work crews clawed their way forward, costs began to soar. With the price of equipment, labour and supplies all running well above the original estimates, the initial $3-million financing began to run out. That spring, it became time for the Mannix outfit to honour its pledge to cover any cost overruns. On April 24, 1957, Loram Ltd. made the first such cash advance to Empire in an attempt to keep the new company in business. "With the cost of the road running at least $1 million higher than the original estimate, Loram had to put up the extra money," said Mawhinney.

1963 ▶

Mannix Highway Division crews grade right-of-way on the original Great Slave Lake Railway line for the Canadian National Railways. The work is called the Pine Point Grading.

1963 ▶

The Pine Point Grading project approaches 61 degrees north latitude in the Northwest Territories.

By the time construction was completed, the total bill was enormous. The road and tramway cost $1,892,000, while the wharf and loading facilities cost $480,000. The construction of buildings and ancillary structures consumed another $827,000. The cost for installed machinery and equipment was $1,316,000. The purchase of mobile equipment required another $455,000. Pre-production expenses had taken up $625,000. Empire also spent $57,000 on the still uncompleted tote road up the side of Merry Widow mountain. There was also $88,000 in miscellaneous expenses and $309,000 for working capital. The bill came to $6 million, double the amount projected in the feasibility study.

Finally, construction was completed on September 13, 1957, and ore was treated at the mill and shipped to Port McNeill. On September 25, the first Japanese freighter arrived and was loaded with iron ore. While one would hope that this first shipment of iron ore marked the end of Empire's troubles, in actual fact, it simply marked the beginning.

"In the free enterprise system, you have the opportunity to make money and an equal opportunity to go broke."

If the plans for Empire had gone as originally forecasted, September 25 would have signalled the turning point in the fortunes of the mine. On that date, Empire would begin extracting iron ore at a cost of a little over $4 a ton and selling it for over $8 a ton, quickly reaching the break-even figure of 700,000 tons (635,000 tonnes) of concentrate. At that magic point, the company would liquidate its debts and start to roll up some impressive profits. The bankers would be repaid their loans, and the shareholders would start collecting their dividends. But nothing even remotely resembling that rosy scenario was about to happen.

For the next four months, the workers at the Merry Widow Mine tried to make the early optimistic estimates of the mine's profitability come true. Between that first shipment on September 25, 1957, and the last shipment in early January 1958, 110,385 tons (100,139 tonnes) of ore were milled. From this total, 74,259 tons (67,366 tonnes) of concentrate were produced.

Despite the best efforts of the mine and mill crews, though, these shipments did nothing to alleviate Empire's crushing burden of debt. In fact, a shocking reality began to sink in for the people of Empire. Instead of making money on each ton of ore shipped, they were progressively falling even further into the red. It soon became apparent that the original cost estimates for mining and milling the ore were incorrect. In 1956, the cost estimates indicated that it would take something like $4.30 a ton to mine and mill the ore. As the mine struggled to get under way and the work crews laboured to keep the equipment operating in the rain and the slush, actual costs were soon running closer to a catastrophic $13 a ton.

Empire Mine was also beginning to provide some basic instruction in the geology of iron ore deposits. As a result of the complex nature of the main ore body, the mining crews soon realized that it

A P&H shovel and dump truck prepare to remove additional overburden as the underground iron ore mine is converted to a strip mine.

1963 ▶

U.S. President John F. Kennedy is assassinated.

1963 ▶

The California State Division of Highways hires the McNamara and Mannix Co. Ltd. joint venture to relocate the four-lane San Luis Highway, U.S. 101, southeast of San Francisco. The project runs until early 1965.

New highway

Existing highway

was extremely difficult to get the ore out of the mountain cheaply. Since the main iron ore deposits did not lie horizontal to the ground, unexpected quantities of dirt had to be removed. Furthermore, it was discovered that the ore lay in pods. "A great deal of the hopes for Empire's prosperity lay in the belief that the mining consultants whom Mannix had originally retained to give an opinion on the ore content of the property had more or less accurately assessed the content of the property," said Mawhinney. "Unfortunately, it turned out that they had not taken into account the placement of the ore in the property. If an ore body lies horizontal to the surface of the piece of property, say three feet down, you only have a very small amount of waste to remove before you start mining the iron ore. Whereas, if that same ore body were standing perpendicular in the ground, you'd have a tremendous amount of waste to remove to get the ore out of the ground. So the placement of the ore had a profound effect on the economics of the mine."

The Industrial Development Bank (IDB) was rapidly coming to the conclusion that Empire was essentially bankrupt. On June 2, 1958, the IDB sent a letter to Jim Scott informing him that a loan of $2.2 million extended to Empire in 1957 had been cancelled. Furthermore, since Empire had been unable to meet its payments

The excessive overburden is stripped, stockpiled, then loaded off this cable and log platform into large haulers for off-site disposal.

on the original credit of $1.6 million advanced to it by the IDB, that entire loan was declared in default. The IDB agreed, however, to loan an additional $200,000 to Empire to help it meet its operating costs under the new mining contract for 1958-1959. The terms of this loan were severe. Among other things, Loram was required to put up a debenture that encumbered all of Empire's fixed assets. Loram was also told to assign to the IDB all proceeds from ore shipments to Japan before any of these proceeds were assigned to Mannix Co. Ltd. The IDB further instructed Scott to begin submitting monthly balance sheets and statements of profit and loss.

Meanwhile, Empire's debts to its trade creditors were skyrocketing. By the first of the year, Empire owed roughly $650,000 to more than 126 creditors. And these people were not stock investors. Instead, these trade creditors included a number of small to mid-sized Canadian businesses depending on their work with Empire to meet their payrolls. Their plight was a profound source of concern for Fred C. Mannix.

"Presumably, the big investors could write off any of their losses on Empire against other gains," said Mawhinney. "However, Fred C. Mannix was always concerned about the trade creditors. I think it always bothered him that these creditors were out of money because of an endeavour by one of his companies. This

1964 ▶

Increasing its individual identity among all nations, Canada struggles to create its own, unique flag to replace the Red Ensign. F.C. Mannix personally finances this unsuccessful effort of John Kingsmill.

1964 ▶

Great Canadian Oil Sands begins the development of the Athabasca oil sands. An early Mannix project is the head shaft, dug by hand to determine the depth of the oil sands.

particularly applied to those smaller creditors who were really hurt by Empire's insolvency. These were the people who had rented their trucks or done contract Caterpillar work or supplied goods to the mine, the smaller businessmen who had become involved in the project. They were the people who would be genuinely hurt by the operation. And Fred was determined that they should be paid back."

On January 14, 1958, the Empire Mine shut down its operations. It was estimated that the yearly cost just to maintain it in an inoperative state would be close to $100,000. It was now no longer a question of how big a profit the enterprise would turn. Rather, it was a matter of whether Empire Development should continue to operate at all or be shut down permanently. As far as several people in Mannix management were concerned, it seemed a good time to cut one's losses in Empire and get out of mining operations in British Columbia in the most expeditious manner possible. "At that time," recalled Eric Connelly, "I told Fred Mannix, 'Let's withdraw and forget about this thing. Let's take our loss and walk away.' Having to persevere with the Empire thing certainly cost us a lot of money. It also forced us to change our pattern in other ways. Up until that time, we had been riding fairly high with the Pembina deal. Now we had to carry on as best we could. For a long time, then, we didn't have any money to get into other ventures. We just really couldn't look at anything new.

"But again, the old teaching of his father came into play. It was that idea that we finish a job if we only come off with our knapsack. So Fred went in there and said, 'No, no, we'll take over responsibility of this job and also the ownership and so forth.' That's the kind of thing that I admired him for, but it was a tough time."

"The question was, how were we going to deal with these debts?" continued Connelly. "We decided that we would try going to the government for help. We went to see W.A.C. Bennett, the premier of the province of British Columbia, about our problem. They called him Wacky Bennett. He was very much identified with the social credit movement and all of that. So we sat there and told Mr. Bennett that we wanted to be relieved of the heavy royalties that the Province wanted to assess against Empire ore. We asked to be so relieved until we had met our other obligations and paid off our debts. Bennett told us that he wasn't going to relieve us of any of it. He said, 'In the free enterprise system, you have the opportunity to make money and an equal opportunity to go broke.' And that was his answer to that."

"And they were all paid 100 cents on the dollar."

The decision was made to continue the Empire operation and attempt to get the mine back up and running. First, Loram had to convince the operation's creditors that the mine was still potentially solvent. This meant trying to get some kind of temporary relief from the immediate burden of principal and interest payments to the Industrial Development Bank. Next, they would have to significantly reduce costs and increase the mine's overall efficiency. Finally, they would have to renegotiate the base contract with the Japanese steel mills. This last step was particularly crucial. Without a substantial increase in the price of Empire ore, there was no prayer of recovery for the tottering operation.

To put the pieces of Empire Development back together again, Fred Mannix called on Cres Oates. "In early 1958, Fred Mannix sent Cres Oates out to Vancouver to assess the situation," Mawhinney said. "Cres was a very fascinating man. He was a teacher by profession. He went to the University of British Columbia, where he got a master's degree in history. Then, he taught in the British Columbia high schools. From childhood right through his teaching days, Cres was always wheeling and dealing in something. He started off by selling canaries at the Pacific National Exhibition. He wheeled and dealt in property. He bought and refurbished cars and resold them to teachers. Then he got into the business of financing the purchase of cars for his fellow teachers. Ultimately, he got into the stock market."

In addition to his role as Fred C. Mannix's personal advisor, Cres Oates served in a number of capacities for the Mannix Group of Companies. Joining the outfit in 1954, he had gone on to become a director of Loram Ltd. and a director of Pembina Pipe Line Ltd., as well as serving as a director and chairman of the board for Empire Development. Oates also took on the responsibility of serving as a director and treasurer for a number of personal companies associated with the affairs of Fred C. Mannix.

Cres Oates turned out to be the perfect person to try to salvage Empire. After putting an arrangement with Empire's creditors in place, he set about improving the mine's efficiency and lowering its costs. First the mining facilities and equipment were rehabilitated. Next, Oates managed to induce the Japanese to agree to a new contract calling for $9.70 per ton of concentrate, a price increase of about 85 cents per ton over the old contract. With this new contract in hand, Empire could

1964 ▶

To reach the oil sands deposits, Mannix crews build a road from Fort McMurray, including a bridge across the Athabasca River, using many reinforced concrete supports.

1964 ▶

Northern Dancer is the first Canadian-born horse to win the Kentucky Derby.

turn its full attention to stabilizing Empire's position with its most significant creditors. In the course of these negotiations, the Industrial Development Bank announced that it no longer wished to retain its position as the senior creditor over the 10-year period of the Creditors' Compromise Arrangement. Representatives of the bank invited Loram Ltd. to come up with a strategy to purchase their interest in the Empire deal on some type of discounted basis.

On May 12, 1959, Fred C. Mannix, Eric Connelly, Cres Oates, Everett Costello, Peter Lougheed, Cal Baker and J.M. Ferguson met and decided to make the following proposal to the IDB. In exchange for its position as the senior creditor, the IDB would receive $850,000. Payments, which were to be made in three installments, were scheduled for 1959, 1960 and 1962. In order to share the burden somewhat, Loram turned to its Japanese trading partner, the firm of C.T. Takahashi & Co. Inc. Together, these two companies made their offer to the IDB in the spring of 1959. Loram and Takahashi offered, in effect, a deal of 50 cents on the dollar for the IDB's first mortgage bond and the IDB accepted the deal.

With the IDB out of the picture, and the relationship with its other creditors stabilized, Empire could now negotiate a long-term arrangement with Mannix Co. Ltd. to operate the mine, mill and loading facilities.

When completed in 1967, the spectacular, curved-face, thin-arched Boundary Dam stands as a testament to those who built it.

But it seemed for every step forward, Empire took two steps back. First, it became apparent that the iron ore at Merry Widow contained excessive amounts of sulphur. As do all contracts for iron ore, Empire's contract contained strict specifications for the quality of the ore. Each shipment was to contain a minimum of 56 per cent iron per ton. In addition, no shipment could contain more than the specified percentages of certain impurities. For example, any shipment containing more than 0.20 per cent sulphur would be subject to penalties. A shipment containing more than 0.35 per cent sulphur or 0.05 per cent copper would be rejected outright and Empire would have to pay the shipping charges. Shipments from Merry Widow began to approach, then exceed, the 0.20 per cent penalty point.

If the excess sulphur wasn't a bad enough headache, the miners at Merry Widow soon found another problem. Beginning in early 1961, assays of the ore milled began to show unusually high levels of copper. As specified by the contract with the Japanese, excessive copper also carried a payment penalty. The rejection point here was 0.05 per cent. In the spring and early summer of 1961, the assays of Empire ore showed copper levels as high as 0.08 per cent.

Whether the copper, in fact, posed a major problem was questioned by a number of Loram personnel. They felt that the copper was not a contaminant in the

1964 ▶

Canadians share peacekeeping duties on Cyprus with Sweden, Ireland and Britain. A British soldier watches a burning building.

1964 ▶

Mannix Co. Ltd. pipeliners tackle the Hussar to Carstairs pipeline loop in central Alberta.

same sense as sulphur since copper is valuable in its own right. It was argued that the Japanese were in an ideal situation: they could charge Empire for copper penalties while separating the copper in Japan and using it themselves. It was felt by many that where they were receiving a penalty, in fact, they should have been getting a bonus.

Throughout this time, efforts were under way to ensure a continued future for Empire Development. A series of exploratory efforts were carried out in a desperate attempt to find a major discovery, the kind of big strike that would bring in profits for years to come. Empire was confronted with debts of approximately $4.25 million in principal and $460,000 in interest for a total just short of $5 million. Considering that debt, Empire required deposits that could be measured in the millions of tons.

But those deposits, if there were any, remained hidden deep within the earth's crust. "Possibilities of finding ore suitable to open-pit mining have virtually been exhausted," wrote John C. Lund, head geologist. "The writer concludes that if any sizeable mineralized body exists, it would probably occur at considerable depth. The economics involved in finding and exploiting such a body are prohibitive, and the writer feels that no further exploration is warranted." In a sense, the admission that there were no major discoveries in the future signalled the end of the Empire Development project. With no additional discoveries in sight, and no reason to anticipate any improvement in the costs of mining and milling the contaminated ore, the directors of Empire Development made the decision to shut down the mine in August 1967.

By most accounts, Empire had been a financial disaster. "They told us we could get one and a half million to two million tons of ore, so we went in and had a hell of a time getting out a million tons. And we lost almost four or five million dollars getting out that million tons," F.C. Mannix said. Yet while Mannix lost a small fortune, some of which was recouped through tax manoeuvres, F.C. Mannix was insistent that the small creditors in Empire lose not a dime.

BRINGING RANSOMES & RAPIER LTD. TO NORTH AMERICA

The negotiations between Calgary Power and Alberta Coal on the contract to operate the Whitewood Mine were completed and the contract signed early in 1959. Under the terms of this contract, Calgary Power was to purchase and own all the major mine equipment. Chuck Doerr and Gerry Gerow were the principal consultants for the mine's design and equipment selection. A major decision was the type of dragline to purchase. In the late 1950s, there were only four companies in the world making large draglines. The three largest of these firms, all in the United States, were Bucyrus-Erie, Marion Power Shovel, and Page Engineering. The fourth was a British firm, Ransomes & Rapier Ltd. As is still true today, Bucyrus-Erie and Marion were the leading manufacturers of big electric shovels and draglines. But in 1959, a used

Ransomes & Rapier walking dragline became available in England. This was a 1350-W, a machine having a 33-yard (25-cubic-metre) bucket and a 233-foot (71-metre) boom.

"That was going to be the first Ransomes & Rapier machine to be used in North America," Marsh Williams recalled. "So it was looked on as quite a brave step to take at that time. Theron Gerow, who was our consultant from Minneapolis, was an elderly man, in his seventies, and to get him to accept Ransomes & Rapier was very major because his whole history was Marion and Bucyrus-Erie. He was a very salty old man, and you certainly knew where he stood at all times. Eventually we sent him over to England to see the Ransomes & Rapier work. He came back quite excited because where the American machine only had one motor on a particular piece, they had two. Ultimately, we chose to go with Ransomes & Rapier on price, but we satisfied ourselves that technically it was a very sound machine. The second one ever brought to North America went to Minto, New Brunswick, so there were only two that ever came over here."

1964 ▶

Mannix pipeliners build a portion of the Dresden to London, Ontario loop for Ontario Natural Gas Storage and Pipelines Ltd.

1964 ▶

Mannix Co. Ltd. sponsors a joint venture for B.C. Hydro & Power Authority to build the Duncan Dam, the first hydro development of the Columbia River in Canada. This $16-million project runs to 1967.

Red Flannel in August

"We brought our first Komatsu to Canada in 1964 at Taber," F.P. Mannix recalled. "When they brought that first tractor over, we couldn't run it for more than one half-hour because they had set it up for the Arctic.

"The Japanese knew so little about Canada, that they didn't understand that during the summer in Taber, the temperature is over 90 degrees above. They had no concept of that. The mechanical engineer they sent over came in red flannel underwear. He was ready for the worst. He had a parka and red flannel underwear for August in Taber."

"After Empire shut down, Fred Mannix had Cres Oates identify creditors who were really hurt by Empire's insolvency," explained Mawhinney. "Many years later, after these people never expected that they would receive any money, lo and behold, Cres Oates came along to them and said that they were going to be paid out in full. If my recollection serves me correctly, I think that something like $700,000 was paid to these various smaller creditors who were genuinely hurt by the operation.

"There was some trouble in finding them all. But Cres, who was then on a sort of consultancy retainer from Fred Mannix, had plenty of free time on his hands. He tracked them down through various sources, talking to one and then another. And they were all paid 100 cents on the dollar. To me, it was a very magnanimous gesture. There was no need to do it whatsoever. By that time, it was all past history. I think Fred did it as a gesture out of his own heart because he wanted to see these people made whole."

While the Empire affair was put to bed in the Sixties, the lessons learned from the experience would continue to echo throughout the Loram Group of Companies for many years to come. And, as painful and costly as the experience was, Empire paved the way for Gregg River, the group's metallurgical coal mine.

The First Attempt to Market Gregg River Coal to Japan

In the mid-1950s, Bill Blackstock did a small amount of exploration on a property that would eventually have great significance for future developments at Alberta Coal. This work was done in the Coal Branch at the old Gregg River Collieries mine, then owned by the Cadomin Coal Company Ltd. Phil Shirley, who started out working on drilling rigs in the Crowsnest Pass for Mannix back in the 1940s, went along on several of Blackstock's initial exploration expeditions to Gregg River. "Cadomin Coal originally owned that, and each summer they'd do a little work on it," Shirley recalled. "Because the mine was short of engineering personnel, they asked Mannix if they could send somebody up to survey all these pits and openings to put on their maps. That's what I did for them when I went up there the first time. We were up there for about two weeks at that time."

This first trip turned into a series of visits to Cadomin. "Bill Blackstock always left Calgary at night," Shirley recalled. "You had a two-lane highway to Edmonton, narrow and winding, and 40 miles out of Edmonton, you had a gravel road right into Cadomin. We got in about six o'clock in the morning, went to work, and left the same day. Hours didn't seem to mean too much to us."

The market that F.C. Mannix and Si Fraser envisioned for the Gregg River property was the metallurgical coal market in Japan. This idea developed out of two circumstances. The first was the transportation costs for coal. In Eastern Canada, there already existed a large market for coking coal, but Canadian steel makers imported most of this coal from the United States. The primary reason for this was that rail freight charges made western Canadian metallurgical coal too expensive to compete with mines in the eastern United States, which were much closer to Ontario. The freight charge per ton of coal to Eastern Canada was actually much more than the cost to Japan, which involved a

1964 ▶

Joint venture partners Henry J. Kaiser Co. (Canada) and Mannix Co. Ltd. construct the Montreal Subway. This $4.7-million project runs from August 1964, to January 1966 and is operational for Expo 67.

1964 ▶

Manitoba Hydro hires the outfit to perform investigative drilling along the Churchill and Nelson rivers for future, potential hydro projects. The remote location is reached by boat or float plane.

700-mile (1,126-kilometre) trip by rail to Vancouver and then a 4,300-mile (6,920-kilometre) ship voyage to Yokohama.

F.C. Mannix was also interested in Japan because of the Empire Mine. Although the Empire Mine experience turned out to be a financial disaster from the beginning, F.C. Mannix continued to believe that, with a better managed project, the Japanese market for either iron ore or coking coal was worth more investigation. Nothing came of the early exploration work at Gregg River, however, although a test sample of coal from the property was sent to steel companies in Japan in 1956. Meanwhile, several other western Canadian coal mining companies were beginning to explore the Japanese market. In 1957, a delegation led by Mr. Kawada, president of Nippon Kokan Kabushiki Kaisha (NKK), came to Canada to visit metallurgical coal producers. Later that year, Canmore Mines Limited was awarded the first small contract for Canadian coal to be delivered to Japan, a shipment of 4,000 tons (3,629 tonnes) of semi-anthracite.

In 1958, Alberta Coal acquired the option to buy the Gregg River property from Cadomin Coal Company. The year also saw numerous developments in the Canadian-Japanese coal trade. Representatives from several western Canadian coal mining companies made a government-sponsored trip to Japan to discuss the market for metallurgical coal with Japanese steel producers.

Mannix representatives visit the NKK steelworks in Japan, 1961. Bottom row from left, Cal Baker, F.P. Mannix, F.C. Mannix, Si Fraser, Bill Bandeen, Charles Crawford and Rinjiro Kaku of NKK. Hisao Makita is fourth from right in top row.

From the standpoint of western Canadian metallurgical coal producers, however, the single most important event in 1958 took place in Australia. That year, the Japanese steel companies signed the first large contracts for coking coal from Australia. These contracts brought Alberta Coal's plans for developing the Gregg River property to a complete halt. "When the Australians started to ship coal to Japan, they killed us," Bill Blackstock explained. "The Australian coal was a better coking coal, and they were selling it a lot cheaper. So we weren't able to make a deal with the Japanese at that time. We spent quite a bit of time and effort trying to get that mine into production, but once they turned us down, we were out."

In 1959, to help make western Canadian metallurgical coal more competitive in the world market, the Dominion government introduced a railroad freight subvention, which paid $4.50 per ton of the railway charge to move coal to the coast. Because of these developments, F.C. Mannix decided to visit Japan in 1961 to investigate markets for metallurgical coal and iron ore. "I stopped off in Hawaii on the way, and I got my ankles sunburned and I couldn't walk when I was going to Japan," he recalled. "We never negotiated anything. It was just discussions and social meetings, but I had to use my slippers instead of my shoes." For more formal occasions, such as a visit to the NKK steelworks, Mannix wore a pair of tennis shoes.

1964 ▶

Mannix Construction Inc. sponsors the $28.5-million joint venture to build the Boundary Dam and underground powerhouse in this narrow gorge on the Pend Oreille River in northeastern Washington.

1965 ▶

The U.S. Army Corps of Engineers contracts for the construction of Little Goose Lock and Dam. The $72-million project will be completed in 1970.

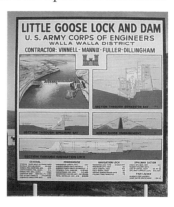

MISSED OPPORTUNITIES

Not long after F.C. Mannix's trip to Japan in the early 1960s, the Japanese steel companies decided to send a delegation of their own to meet with Mannix personnel in Vancouver. "The Japanese sent over their group, we sent our group, and they met on neutral ground in Vancouver to assess where we dovetailed," Charlie Crawford explained. "What the Japanese were looking for, basically, was iron ore and coal. Nobody except Fred was really for this deal. Eventually, the Japanese sent a delegation over to tour the oil fields and coal mines and I was delegated to take them around."

While this exchange of visits did not lead to anything concrete in the way of deals to develop iron ore or coal mining properties, the Mannix organization did get offers to handle Canadian business development for two relatively small companies. In retrospect, these offers might have been interesting if Mannix management had decided to pursue them. One was with a small automobile manufacturing company, the other with a manufacturer of heavy construction equipment.

"We could have had, probably, the North American agency for Toyota cars," Charlie Crawford said. "But all of us said, 'Who the hell would buy these puddle-jumpers?' Another one that we could have had was Komatsu, but we thought, 'Who would use one of those when they can get a Caterpillar?' Those were some of the less wise business decisions, which were, out of hand, not even considered."

The coordinator for this trip to Japan was Charlie Crawford, F.C. Mannix's executive assistant. "We were just looking for business opportunities on the Pacific Rim, although nobody used that term in those days," he recalled. "This was Fred's foresightedness. It was obvious to him that Japan was our natural trading partner. When we went over there, we were the first private individuals ever to go there from Canada. We were not government-sponsored. Young Freddie went, too. I suspect that Freddie really got broken in on that deal."

Although these talks did not lead to any contracts, they did produce one extremely important result. They established an absolutely crucial relationship with a man who in just two decades would turn out to be one of the most powerful executives in the Japanese steel industry. This was a relationship founded on trust and mutual respect, and the importance of this connection confirms the farsightedness of Fred C. Mannix's original idea of seeking business opportunities in Japan.

"Gregg River really goes back to the time when my father first started going over to Japan in the 1950s," Ron Mannix explained. "On one of his trips, he visited the Kawasaki steelworks, which were an old set of works belonging to NKK. The manager at Kawasaki at that time was a man named Mr. Hisao Makita. There was also a samurai named Kin Kishimoto, whose trading company would be bought by the Okura Trading Company. Kin was a promoter and a wheeler-dealer, and I think he had a very good sense of who the rising stars in the NKK organization were. Consequently, he suggested that we get to know this Makita."

"My father and Makita ended up having some good times together and became friends," Ron Mannix continued. "Ultimately, Mr. Makita became chairman of the board of NKK. He was a very astute and long-term thinker in terms of strategy and organization, and he led the NKK outfit to be the second-biggest steel producer in Japan. So going back historically, there was a relationship between NKK and our company that was created many, many years ago. Hisao Makita would be a key figure in the future of the Gregg River property and the whole development of Canada/Japan relations."

1965 ▶

The Vinnell-Mannix-Fuller-Dillingham joint venture begins spillway construction on the Little Goose Lock and Dam.

1965 ▶

Britain's Mary Quant invents the miniskirt. Here, two women stare at the creation.

Alberta Coal Ltd.
Becoming Canada's #1 Coal Producer

The year 1957 inaugurated a new era for the western Canadian coal mining industry. In 1957, Alberta Coal personnel began developing the Utility Mine, located near Estevan, Saskatchewan. At the same time, Alberta Coal was working with Calgary Power on the plan for the Whitewood Mine, near Wabamun, Alberta. These two mines were soon to become the largest surface coal mines ever put into production in Canada up to that time.

The start-up of the Utility and Whitewood mines came at a time when the coal mining industry in Canada appeared to have faded away. After the brief postwar boom when national output rose to an all-time high of 19.1 million tons (17.3 million tonnes) in 1950, production steadily declined as mine after mine closed, as the railroads switched to diesel fuel and industry converted to electricity and gas. In 1962, Canadian coal production dropped to a mere 10.2 million tons (9.25 million tonnes), the lowest production since 1906. This figure would be the bottom of the trough, however. The development of Utility and Whitewood marked the beginning of a new era. Alberta Coal's role in the development of the market for thermal coal for electric generating stations in Western Canada was a key factor in the revitalization of the western Canadian coal mining industry. By 1963, the four mines operated by Alberta Coal produced close to 20 per cent of all the coal produced in Canada.

Top: A meeting of Alberta Coal staff in 1967 includes from left, Ed Panchysyn, Woody Wood, Mac Summersgill, Sherman Lang, Gerald Thompson and Chip Collins.

Above: Alberta Coal Ltd. forms Utility Coals Ltd. to operate Saskatchewan coal properties.

With the opening of the Utility and Whitewood mines, Alberta Coal emerged, seemingly from nowhere, as one of Canada's largest coal mining companies. While the development of Utility and Whitewood was a group effort, Chuck Doerr, Alberta Coal's general manager, was the catalyst that took both these major deals from the realm of possibility into actuality. Doerr's knowledge of large-scale surface coal mining and its operating costs gave Alberta Coal the competitive edge it needed to move into a much larger scale of mining operation. Having played a key role in the start-up of the two largest surface coal mines in Canadian history, Doerr was not content to rest on his laurels. Shortly after production at Whitewood approached one million tons (900,000 tonnes) per year, Doerr alerted Loram management to a possible acquisition of two new coal mining properties. The company Doerr targeted was his former employer, Great West Coal.

The negotiations with the owners of Great West Coal, the Paterson family out of Winnipeg, remained a tightly kept secret until August 6, 1964. Then, Alberta Coal, through a specially created subsidiary called Loram Coal Ltd., made a tender offer to purchase all outstanding Class B shares of Great West stock for $5.85 a share. This offer brought in all but about 6,000 shares, giving Alberta Coal a controlling interest in Great West. On September 1, 1964, Alberta Coal officially assumed control of the company and the Klimax and Roselyn

1965 ▶

Hamersley Iron Pty. Ltd., Australia, requires a railway to open their iron ore mine in extreme northwestern Australia. A Morrison-Knudsen sponsored joint venture with Mannix Contractors Pty. Ltd., one of several participants, builds 180 miles (290 kilometres) of new railway grade, 193 miles (310 kilometres) of track and associated bridges, yards and appurtenances. This $17-million project runs until July 1966.

mines came under the Loram umbrella. In 1965 and 1966, Loram Coal Ltd. purchased all the remaining Class B shares not acquired in 1964 and all outstanding Class A shares. This enabled Alberta Coal to privatize Great West. Great West's sales organization was reorganized as an Alberta Coal subsidiary named Great West Coal Sales Ltd. The Klimax Mine in Saskatchewan and the Roselyn Mine in Alberta became part of the Alberta Coal subsidiary, Battle River Coal Company Limited.

For Alberta Coal, the acquisition of Great West was a bold move, one involving a fair amount of risk. For the short term, the deal did not look particularly promising. On the positive side, the purchase price of Great West shares was low and most of the financing for the deal came from a loan from the Dominion Coal Board, which was working desperately to salvage the nation's coal mining industry. On the negative side, the Klimax and Roselyn mines were obviously not selling enough coal to repay the acquisition costs, and future prospects for these two mines were questionable. But, as with previous property acquisitions, senior management of Loram and Alberta Coal were taking the long-range view.

Reserves were the key to the Great West deal. The Klimax Mine property covered most of the north-central portion of the Estevan coal field between Estevan and Bienfait, Saskatchewan. These reserves were both north and south of the CPR and CNR lines. Great West's holdings also swept southeast through the old Western Dominion mine properties. These lay to the west of the railway spur south of

Top: An early coal hauler at the time Alberta Coal wins the contract to supply the new Wabamun generating station from the Whitewood Mine.

Above: F.C. Mannix is dwarfed by one of the prairie mine shovels.

Bienfait. Near Roche Percee, Great West's property connected with a large block of reserves that extended from around the Old Mac Mine all the way to the southeastern corner of the coal field. In Alberta, at the Roselyn Mine, Alberta Coal acquired some of the highest-quality reserves in the Sheerness coal field. These reserves were more than adequate to support a large coal-fired electric generating station.

The acquisition of Great West Coal united many people into one staff with decades of connections in the coal mining business. The takeover of operations at Klimax and Roselyn produced few discontinuities. In some respects, however, there was a tremendous change with the new ownership. For new Alberta Coal employees like Cap Jenish, with no previous association with the Mannix organization, the takeover brought some interesting perspectives on a different corporate philosophy. When Jenish first learned about the sale of Great West, he asked Woody Wood what to expect. "Woody said, 'I'll tell you one thing you can expect,'" Jenish recalled. "'F.C. Mannix has never made a bad move in his life, and I don't think you're going to have anything but good things to look forward to.' I found that they were aggressive, a company that liked to have challenges, so I did see considerable change, particularly compared with the Patersons. All of a sudden, things turned around and started to go. So it was certainly different from working for the Patersons.

"But the biggest difference for me was the difference between Sinclair Coal and the Mannixes. Sinclair was the type of

1965 ▶

Concrete and asphalt giants working in tandem, O.K. Construction and Crown Paving are joined into one operation named Alberta Concrete Products Co. Ltd.

1965 ▶

Joint venture partners Perini Pacific Limited, Northern Construction, J.W. Stewart Ltd., Mannix Co. Ltd. and Morrison-Knudsen begin construction of the 45-foot-high (13.7-metre) Mica Creek diversion tunnels for B.C. Hydro.

BURN-A-BAGS

With the disappearance of the domestic market for coal, it was evident that Mannix's Majestic Mine was just about finished. There was, however, one last desperate attempt to develop a market for the mine — Burn-a-Bags.

"Someone had the brilliant idea that we might go into the small retail market for fireplaces and also for barbecues, which were just coming into popularity," explained Dick Wilsey, who joined Alberta Coal in 1958 as master mechanic. "I think this was probably our sales organization. They conceived the idea of packing this coal in paper bags and then selling the

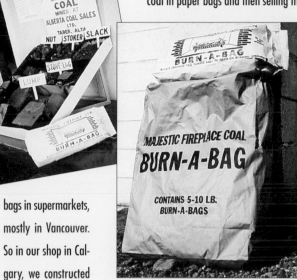

bags in supermarkets, mostly in Vancouver. So in our shop in Calgary, we constructed a machine to weigh out and load this coal into paper bags. Then the bags were loaded into a boxcar and shipped to our storehouse in Vancouver. I think they sold in the stores there for 35 cents. They probably contained three or four cents worth of coal. Since the paper bag was probably a nickel and shipping something like 15 to 20 cents, the coal was the least part of the cost of material we were selling that way."

company where they taught you things, but there was no personal touch. When Merl Kelce came down, he didn't know who I was. I was just an employee. When the Mannixes took over, they made an effort to get to know everybody on a personal basis. When they came around, they knew your name and they would talk to you.

Left: Chuck Doerr built and operates this working model of a Bucyrus-Erie dragline at the Calgary Power Ltd. display at the Calgary Exhibition and Stampede.

Below: Mr. Klimax, the Marion dragline, strips overburden near the tipple of the newly acquired Klimax Mine between Estevan and Bienfait, Saskatchewan.

1965 ▶

Sir Winston Churchill dies.

1966 ▶

In 1966, Alberta Coal Ltd. becomes Canada's number one coal producer. During the previous decade, the Mannix coal miners produce 17,274,714 short tons (15,671,275 tonnes) of coal.

Ed Panchysyn's Hat Dance

On June 16, 1959, Alberta Coal Ltd. bought out West Canadian's interest in Battle River Coal and acquired all outstanding shares held by the other 15 minority shareholders. Although this ended the Mannix-West Canadian partnership, one extremely important West Canadian manager stayed on with Alberta Coal. This was Ed Panchysyn. Panchysyn was sent over from West Canadian to manage Vesta Mine in 1953. There he oversaw the renovation of the mine's tipple and supervised the erection of a Bucyrus-Erie Walking Monighan 560 dragline. He remained at Vesta until 1961. He then transferred to Calgary as assistant manager of Alberta Coal. Panchysyn quickly moved up through the ranks, eventually becoming vice president in charge of exploration. Before his untimely death in 1978 while touring coal mines in Germany, Panchysyn was responsible for acquiring most of the major coal reserves Manalta now controls.

Although Panchysyn was known as an extremely fair person and an excellent manager, he was also known to have a temper. One of the things he quickly became famous for was his rather unusual behaviour when he was angry. "If Ed lost his temper, he would throw his hat down and jump on it," Roy McBride recalled. "After he'd jumped on it, he'd put his hat back on, and then he was in complete control again." According to McBride, Panchysyn usually had pretty good reason to be upset when he did lose his temper. There was the time, for example, when a Cat operator was busy piling up a large quantity of coal that was to be later crushed to a smaller size. The problem was that someone had inadvertently left the chute to the crusher open, so the coal was dropping down onto the crusher belt below. The Cat operator apparently never noticed that no matter how much coal he pushed into the room, the pile never grew larger.

I've noticed that with the Mannixes it's the personal touch that makes the difference, knowing you personally. So there was a big difference, a big change."

Following the acquisition of Great West, there were some important changes in Alberta Coal's senior management. On July 2, 1965, Chuck Doerr was promoted to president. Si Fraser became chairman of the board, replacing Everett Costello, chairman since 1961.

From the moment Chuck Doerr joined Alberta Coal in 1955, the company's central focus was to develop new mines and improve existing mining operations. In the mid-1960s, there was another major effort under way, one that was much less visible than the ongoing mining operations. This new focus was exploration for new coal properties, directed by Ed Panchysyn. Before Panchysyn's arrival in head office, exploration was a relatively minor aspect of Alberta Coal's operations. In the 1950s, most of the exploration work that Bill Blackstock did was on properties already owned or mined by Alberta Coal. Very little work done by Blackstock was aimed at identifying new properties for possible acquisition and business development. After Panchysyn became chief engineer in 1962, he started an aggressive program of exploration. He also began to acquire leases. Despite his lack of formal training in geology, Panchysyn possessed an almost uncanny ability to predict precisely the location of large coal seams in specific geological structures.

The reserves that Alberta Coal acquired in Alberta, Saskatchewan, Ontario and British Columbia were huge. Panchysyn's approach to exploration was like big-game trophy hunting. He was interested in only the most massive targets. The importance of Panchysyn's efforts was immediately recognized by Chip Collins

1966 ▶

Canadair begins production of the CL-215 water bomber, a plane capable of scooping up water while in flight, then dumping it on a fire.

1966 ▶

Mannix Co. Ltd. continues mine stripping operations. One contract for Texas Gulf Sulphur in Ontario finds D-8 and D-9 Cats pushing a Euclid TS-24 scraper.

when he joined Alberta Coal as general manager in 1965. "Ed was the professional coal locator and engineer, and a good one," Collins said. "One of the things that he and I decided was that the coal company's future depended on coal reserves. We were going to take every dollar that we could squeeze out of Fred C. Mannix to buy reserves. Nobody, I think, ever knew quite how many millions of tons of coal reserves Panchysyn and Collins purchased and squirrelled away in the archives. Those were all obtained with a very long view. Those reserves weren't marketable then, but we knew that someday they would be."

F.C. Mannix, who started buying coal properties in 1946, did not need to be convinced of the importance of Panchysyn's exploration efforts. He was clearly aware that reserves were the future of the company. "Ideas are one thing, but you have to have somebody who will back them," Phil Shirley commented. "That happens in a private organization where you have somebody who will take a gamble. I think Fred Mannix was a gambler. I also think he was very fortunate to have some very good people working for him. It was quite an undertaking for Alberta Coal to get a jump on the other companies. In the 1960s, there were very few people looking for coal. For results from anything you do today in exploration, you're looking 20 years down the road. Ed Panchysyn could look into the future. In the coal business it takes people like Chuck Doerr and Ed Panchysyn. You just have to look into the future and have faith, because there's no quick return to it. Ed believed in coal. That was his life."

When Alberta Coal Ltd. was formed in 1957, the company's mines produced 414,433 short tons (375,965 tonnes). Within a decade, the company increased production more than 800 per cent to become Canada's leading coal producer. In 1967, Chuck Doerr, the man who played such a pivotal role in this rapid growth, left Alberta Coal. It is impossible to exaggerate the importance of the contribution Doerr made to the development of the company. Before his hiring in 1955, there was essentially no Mannix coal mining company. Within a few years of becoming general manager of Alberta Coal, Doerr helped lay the foundation for the organization that would become Canada's leading coal mining company.

After Doerr left, Loram senior management had difficulty finding an executive with coal mining experience to replace Doerr as president.

WHOA, NELLY

During the late 1950s, Bill Blackstock directed Alberta Coal's exploration activities. Blackstock's drilling crews used four-and-a-quarter-inch (11-centimetre) seismic drills to locate the coal. But the real mainstay of their equipment was the horse auger. "The horse auger would drill about a two-and-a-half-foot hole," Blackstock explained. "You'd drill right through the coal and then you'd go down into the hole yourself and cut the sample off the side of the hole. Yes, right down in it, because it was two and a half feet in diameter. You could bring out a bucket of this material and

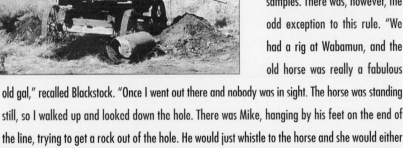

keep doing it until you drilled through the coal."

The horse auger required a two-man crew, with one person remaining on top to direct the horse while the other person was lowered into the hole to take the samples. There was, however, the odd exception to this rule. "We had a rig at Wabamun, and the old horse was really a fabulous old gal," recalled Blackstock. "Once I went out there and nobody was in sight. The horse was standing still, so I walked up and looked down the hole. There was Mike, hanging by his feet on the end of the line, trying to get a rock out of the hole. He would just whistle to the horse and she would either back off and let him down the hole or hoist him up out of the hole. That was how he was operating because that particular day his partner hadn't come.

"I said, 'No more of that.' The one thing you've got to watch is when the barometer is falling because when the atmospheric pressure is coming off, the methane gas will come out of the coal. If that had happened to Mike, he wouldn't have been able to call to the horse to get him out of the hole."

1966 ▶

Canadian centennial celebrations start at midnight on December 31, when the Centennial Flame is lit in Ottawa, Ontario. The gas torch, once lit, is intended never to be extinguished.

THE ORIGINS OF RECLAMATION

Alberta Coal was one of the first coal mining companies in Western Canada to develop reclamation programs. Reclamation at Alberta mines got started at Vesta when Roy McBride, then the electrical foreman, started experimenting with reseeding spoil piles. "I was the first one around there with a farm background, and I did quite a little experimental planting, every kind of grass that you could think of, trees, and various other plants," McBride explained. "I became convinced that we could get growth on the spoil piles if they handled it right. One of the essentials, though, was to save what topsoil there was, as far as possible. Of course, back then, the company was operating on a very close margin. There wasn't room for financing much reclamation. But after I became manager in 1964, I made trips to the States and became convinced that the handwriting was on the wall. If mining was going to continue as an industry, we would have to develop some reclamation policies.

Roy McBride at Vesta Mine, Halkirk, Alberta.

"From then on, there was more consideration of reclamation. The company started to allow for it in the budget. I'm still quite proud of those first trees we planted there along the main highway to the north. A lot of things we tried didn't work, but I think we laid the foundation. I take some pride in that."

Reclamation programs began at Whitewood in 1963 and at Utility in 1966. A good example of these early reclamation efforts is Manalta's work at the Majestic Mine at Taber. After the mine was closed in 1966, the company filled the pit and levelled spoil piles to restore the landscape to its previous condition. At the request of the Taber Fish and Game Association, one portion of the pit was only partially filled in, then flooded to create a small lake. The lake was then used as a hatchery by the Fish and Game Association.

Si Fraser, the chairman of the board, was named president in 1967. His two-year tenure would be tragically short, however. He died within three short months of being diagnosed with lung cancer, running the company from his bed until his final days.

Mannix International
"We're going to make some history today!"

While Mannix Co. Ltd. was working on historic projects such as the oil sands, Pembina was dramatically changing the oil and gas industry and Alberta Coal was growing into Canada's largest coal producer, Mannix International's most pressing problem was finding a proper truck at a good price.

Despite the major growth of her sister companies, having little budget and no real engineering staff continued to be a fact of life back at Mannix International's shop in New Brighton, Minnesota. One of the first problems that Jim Christoff had to solve was how to get the heavy undertrack machines loaded and unloaded from the flatcars on which they were shipped back to Minneapolis for maintenance. Christoff figured

Mannix International's new Minnesota facilities are visited by, from left, Fred P. Mannix, Graham Pollock, George Ballinger, Maureen Mannix, Ron Mannix, Earl Miller and Dick Peppin.

1966 ▶

Great West Coal Company Limited, one of Alberta Coal's coal-producing companies since 1964, is amalgamated into Battle River Coal Company Limited.

1966 ▶

J.L.E. Price builds the Australian (shown) and Kodak pavilions for Montreal's Expo 67.

that a truck with a winch and cable, like those on a gas station tow truck, would be just the thing for handling the sleds and plows. Since the company did not have the funds to buy a real tow truck, Christoff sent Dick Peppin out to find a used truck they could juryrig.

Peppin got an excellent deal on an old Pepsi-Cola delivery truck. With its Pepsi-Cola logo emblazoned across its sides in red, white and blue, the truck was a little gaudy, but the engine was in good condition. Christoff then directed Peppin to "get some steel and build an A-frame on the back of the thing so we could put on a winch to run cable from," said Christoff. "I'll never forget, Peppin came back out with a huge hunk of pipe in his hand. I said, 'Jesus Christ, we're not going to pick up the Queen Mary.'" But the winch would have to pick up pieces of equipment weighing over two tons (1.8 tonnes). As it turned out, Peppin's extra-heavy-duty boom-and-winch arrangement on the rear of the truck worked out perfectly.

The Pepsi-Cola truck proved to be a great investment, although it did manage to produce the occasional odd adventure. It was difficult to start in cold weather. Sometimes it had to be towed to get the motor running. Once, when the truck was being pulled, the fully extended boom at the rear took out all the telephone and electrical lines running into the shop. The truck caused more excitement when Mannix International received its first double-track plow.

The standard Mannix Plow would not work on double tracks since it pushed fouled ballast off to both shoulders of the track. On double tracks, any ballast

GANDY DANCERS

Around the turn of the century, the leading manufacturer of hand tools for track work was the Gandy Manufacturing Company in Chicago. It is probably from this company's name that the term "gandy dancers" came to be used for railroad section gangs. Through much of the first half of the twentieth century, maintenance of way practice was still heavily dependent on large crews of gandy dancers. Crews of 100 to 150 men were not uncommon on big out-of-face resurfacing jobs. Even with all these men, the work progressed at a snail's pace. To be able to resurface one-third mile (one-half kilometre) of track in a day was considered exceptionally good.

There were about 214,000 miles (344,000 kilometres) of main line track in the United States in 1950. Including branch lines, turnouts, sidings and yard tracks, the total amount of railway line in the United States came to about 355,000 miles (571,000 kilometres). If all this track was laid out in one continuous line, it would form a railway long enough to circle the earth at the equator more than 14 times. Imagine 100-man crews resurfacing this enormous expanse of track using hand-operated track jacks, shovels, picks and lining bars, moving along at the rate of less than a third of a mile (one-half a kilometre) per day, per crew.

removed from the tie bed had to be pushed to the outside shoulders of the two tracks, since earthmoving equipment could not operate between the two sets of tracks to remove the fouled material. To remedy this problem, the plow was modified with different grader blades. These could be adjusted to push all the ballast off to either side of the track. The Calgary shops developed the machine and put it in service across Canada in 1956.

In 1957, the first double-track plow was shipped to Minneapolis. When the Mannix crew tried to move the machine with the winch on their Pepsi-Cola truck, they immediately made a horrifying discovery. "The double-track plow weighed about twice as much as the others," Christoff said. "When we went to load it on the flatcar with the winch on our truck, the whole front of the truck went up in the air. Everyone working at the shop had to get on the

1966 ▶

The National Research Council of Canada develops a bomb sniffer small enough for practical use. It will fit in an attaché case and detect explosives in parts per trillion.

1966 ▶

Manalta Holdings Ltd. is formed to consolidate management and services for various properties, office buildings, ranches and investments. It operates a cross-breeding program of registered purebred Hereford and Angus cattle.

front bumper to keep the truck down so we could jockey the plow over to the flatcar to load it."

The double-track plow's notoriety was not limited to the new ritual for loading and unloading, however. Out in the field, it proved to be even more difficult. "When we got it out on the job, the first thing that happened was that the plow dove down in the ground and almost turned over," Christoff recalled. "So then we spent hours and hours making field changes. We would work 20 hours a day for six, eight, 10 days in a row to try to satisfy the railroad so they would keep using this piece of equipment."

Although the double-track plow turned out to be one of the least successful Mannix undertrack machines, Mannix International was already starting to develop a totally new product that represented a considerable advance over the basic sled and plow concept. While the sled and plow were slowly being perfected, the company's improvisatory approach ultimately led to the creation of their second generation of undertrack equipment — the Mannix Autotrack. The basic idea was to create a machine that would ride on top of the rails while guiding either a sled or plow, which would be moving below the track. The autotrack would automatically align the track and also eject failed ties out to the side of the roadbed.

The first prototype of the autotrack was developed during 1958 and 1959. The first contract for the machine came in 1959. While the basic notion was sound, there were still a few problems to work out.

Left: The Mannix Autotrack. After the track is raised, hydraulic arms swing a sled beneath the rails and ties to work on the roadbed.

Right: The Mannix Autotrack is about to begin undertrack repairs. On both sides of the track, cables run forward to a winch cart. The winch cart provides the propulsion for the autotrack.

Left: Looking from the winch cart back to the autotrack. The winch cart is embedded in the track structure so it can pull the autotrack and undertrack equipment up the track. Simple, but revolutionary in its time.

"Our very first autotrack job was in Normandy, Texas," Peppin recalled. "We were so proud of it when we shipped it from Minneapolis. When we got to Texas, we unloaded it and put it on the siding. The next morning, we were supposed to go to work and be the first machine out. Everybody was very proud. Jim Christoff's famous saying was, 'We're going to make some history today!'" As it turned out, the Mannix crew would have to wait for another day to make history. "We couldn't even get it out of the siding," Peppin said, "and about 60 or 70 men were waiting for us to go to work so that they could get their equipment out. We finally had to push it out by hand, let the other equipment out, and then push it back into the siding and go to work on it."

"That's it! That's it! We're going to celebrate!"

Despite this inauspicious beginning, the Mannix team got the autotrack working and completed this first job successfully. The process of working out the flaws in the design continued through 1959. Throughout this learning period, the Mannix autotrack crew worked a brutal schedule to allow time to make adjustments to the machines. "We generally started very early in the morning to run this equipment," said Christoff. "I'm talking about starting at 3:30 or 4:00 in the morning. That way, we could get so far ahead that we had to stop for the day to let the railroad crews catch up with the back work so the trains could go over the finished track.

1966 ▶

Mannix pipeliners build a 265-mile (426-kilometre) pipeline from Fort McMurray to Edmonton on the GCOS project. Later this year they connect the GCOS facility and Fort McMurray with a pipeline extension.

1966 ▶

The Alberta Resources Railway Corporation hires Mannix Co. Ltd. to start clearing, grading, laying culverts and building bridges for a rail line to be built west of Hinton, Alberta.

Then we would work all afternoon or at night, either making changes to the autotrack or repairing it so that it would be ready to go the next day."

Upon successful completion of the autotrack prototype, Christoff submitted a proposal to head office in Calgary, asking for funding to begin manufacturing the machine. The basic policy of Mannix management in Calgary was that Mannix International had to stand on its own. Calgary was extremely reluctant to put any outside dollars into the operation. "By God, we did a hell of a job with little or nothing in those days," Christoff recalled. "It was a case where you battled the people in Calgary to get the money to build some stuff so you could go out and take in more money from the customer. That was the kind of circle it went in. We ended up spending about $50,000 for all four of those machines. So then we were in the manufacturing business in this old pole building with the concrete floor in New Brighton."

The decision to begin manufacturing the autotracks marked a major turning point for Mannix International. Christoff set up a tight production schedule to meet his commitment to the railroads for the new autotracks, at one point operating triple shifts, seven days a week. Because the office and the shop were in different locations, Christoff and Peppin took turns supervising the shop team, which included Boyd Croonenberghs, Kenny Lowell, Dick Ingram, Steve Andrews and Lloyd Hamilton. They comprised the nucleus of personnel to manufacture the equipment and operate it in the field. By then, Christoff had hired several mechanics and welders to round out the engineering team. Two key new people brought into the organization in 1959 were Earl Miller and Leonard Lawrence.

With the development of the autotrack, Mannix International evolved into a much different kind of company. Starting out as a small division of a heavy construction company, leasing two fairly simple undertrack machines to railroads, it slowly evolved to establish its

SELLING MAINTENANCE OF WAY
"'It's not possible,' they'd say."

Although the equipment developed by Mannix International revolutionized railroad maintenance of way, selling the equipment was not an easy matter. "I went to Omaha to see John Bunjer, the chief engineer of Union Pacific," Jim Christoff recalled. "I had been there maybe half a dozen times, and even though I would call ahead for an appointment, he would never be there."

This time, Christoff arrived at eight in the morning, absolutely determined that he was going to see Bunjer. "Bunjer's man out in front was a fellow by the name of Bates, and once again, Bates gave me the big runaround," said

Jim Christoff, fourth from right.

Christoff. "So I told Bates, 'There is a sporting goods store near here, and I am going to go down to that sporting goods store and I am going to buy a tent and I am going to pitch the God damned tent in the lobby and I am going to stay here until I see him!' John Bunjer heard me talking and came out of his office and said, 'Well, come on in here.'" In 1959, Mannix International got its first contract from Union Pacific.

"It was a terrific challenge because it was something new," Dick Peppin said. "Nobody had any idea of what we were doing. We'd tell them that we could plow a mile of track, put in 500 or 700 ties, and put that track back with the sled in a day's time. That was unheard of at that time, and nobody would believe you. 'It's not possible,' they'd say. Many of the railroad personnel were the old-timers. All they knew was the pick and shovel. They were afraid of any piece of mechanized equipment. When they retired, a new door was open for us. It was just a matter of being persistent. But they were tough days."

1966 ▶

In its fifth year of success, Mon-Max completes two sulphur recovery units, including the largest single-train unit in the world at Whitecourt, Alberta.

1966 ▶

The scale of the Whitecourt plant is illustrated by this immense engine delivered to the site by rail flatcar.

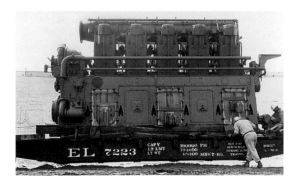

name as a developer of innovative maintenance of way machinery. By 1960, 25 railroads in the United States had used Mannix undertrack machines. Fourteen auto-tracks were manufactured and in use on jobs throughout the country.

Mannix International found itself with the makings of a good product line but with no real place to manufacture its machinery. So Jim Christoff headed up to Calgary to do battle for funds to set up an adequate plant. Christoff returned with a modest budget of $80,000 and set about finding a site for the new facility. The location he finally settled on was a five-acre (two-hectare) plot of land at 2500 Nathan Lane North, in Plymouth, a northern suburb of Minneapolis, not far from New Brighton. This was to be quite a bit bigger than the old shop but still a fairly small structure.

Christoff continued to run a frugal operation as Mannix International moved into the manufacturing business. The power trains for the first autotracks used old Ford and Chevrolet transmissions scrounged from the dump or bought secondhand. Since the shop had no saws or flame-cutters, all metal had to be hand-torched. Angle

J.W. (Jim) Christoff, wearing glasses, helps with on-the-job adjustments to a Mannix Autotrack.

iron was initially used to construct the frames for the autotracks because it was cheap. All these economy measures resulted in a 12-ton (10.9-tonne) machine that was put together at a cost of only $17,000.

"During that time, everyone would incorporate ideas into these machines. So a lot of people had their fingers in what the machine actually came out to be," recalled Glenn Shannon, who was hired to work in the engineering department in 1960 and eventually became the company's production manager. Meanwhile, Christoff continued to rely on his tried-and-true method of drawing out plans on whatever happened to be handy.

One example of this unique research and development process was the Mannix Undercutter Cleaner, a specialized machine developed in 1960. The undercutter was a spin-off of the basic autotrack and sled design, meant for jobs where the railroad wanted to lower the track height. The idea was to follow a sled with a cutting device. The cutter would break up the ballast under the ties, undercut it, and throw the undercut ballast to the track shoulders. "The first undercutter was a big tube with a bunch of

1967 ▶

One hundred years of Confederation are celebrated throughout the land, including the cutting of a huge birthday cake by Queen Elizabeth II.

1967 ▶

Taking a break during the Diamond 7 Ranch branding are, from left, Bill Kabeary; Alec Gillespie, general manager; Dooley Allen, foreman; and Jim Ball.

cutters on it," said Shannon. "We worked for weeks on that thing. I came in one Saturday and made the teeth for it. I said to Jim, 'I don't think this is going to do it.' We pulled this undercutter behind a truck to test it, and stuff was just flying all over. Jim was yelling, 'That's it! That's it! We're going to celebrate!' Somebody went out to get us beer. I told Jim that it wasn't going to work. That was the wrong thing to say to Jim. He got madder than heck. When they came back with the beer, he gave everybody in the shop one, except me." Shannon turned out to be right, however.

While Mannix management in Calgary debated whether to continue funding the undercutter cleaner, Jim Christoff was deciding to resign from Mannix International. He left in late 1964. During the period that Christoff ran Mannix International, mechanization completely transformed the maintenance of way business. In the late 1940s, U.S. Class I railroads annually charged more than 600 million man-hours to maintenance of way work. By 1964, that figure was reduced to 200 million man-hours, with savings to the railroads of hundreds of millions of dollars.

R.A. (Dick) Peppin, second from left, the new executive vice president of Mannix International.

In 1981, Jim Christoff was named the National Railroad Contractors and Maintenance Association's Man of the Year. He attributes much of his success in later life to the experience he gained working at Mannix International. "Of all the people who influenced me, I remember first of all Lou Franco and secondly, and maybe more importantly, Fred Mannix because of the way he had of handling me," Christoff said. "Fred made me want to do the best that I could do. I think that is the reason Fred was so successful. Fred kept surrounding himself with the kind of people who might not necessarily have thought the way he did, but who had some get-up-and-go and wanted to live and work and do things, accomplish things."

To replace Jim Christoff, Loram management in Calgary wanted someone with the same type of energy and desire to accomplish things. Early in 1965, Brock Montgomery flew down to Minneapolis to offer Peppin the job of executive vice president, Mannix International's top job. Much to Montgomery's surprise, Peppin said he did not want the position. Peppin, with no post-high school education, felt he did not have the background in either finance or

1967 ▶

Christiaan Barnard performs the world's first heart transplant at Groote Schuur Hospital, Cape Town, South Africa.

1967 ▶

The Order of Canada, recognizing exemplary achievement in major fields of endeavour, is instituted by the federal government on the centenary of Confederation.

"What Can You Do to Solve This Problem?"

"When I first started going to the Shuswap Conferences, I was a little bit gun-shy because the older people were there and they had things to talk about and I didn't have anything to talk about at that time," recalled the head of Mannix International, Dick Peppin. "I more or less sat back and was a little mouse in the corner, come my turn to talk. But the coal company would always say they mined so many tons of coal and the oil and gas company would say they'd pumped so many cubic feet of gas and so many barrels of oil, so I would tell them, 'Well, I didn't do either of those

Mary Peppin, Brock Montgomery and Dick Peppin at Shuswap.

things, but I put in 20 million ties this year,' so there would always be some little dig. At that time, I was the only one with a small company, you see, and of course, everyone wanted to know how we were doing.

"It was quite an experience, especially when Mr. F.C. Mannix would say, 'Come with me, Peppin, we're going to go out and take a little ride.' I'd think, 'Well, what are we going to do? Drive off the end of a mountain or something?' But we'd go out and take a look at some railroad track right close by and he'd say, 'What can you do to solve this problem? Why don't you get on the ball and get that taken care of?' He was real good that way, he always used to have a little something to say about the business you were in and how you were going to solve the problems and so forth."

engineering to run the company. "Brock kept saying he thought Richard could handle it just fine," recalled Dick's wife, Mary Peppin. Montgomery refused to take no for an answer, and finally Peppin said he would give it a try.

Although Peppin lacked formal business training, he possessed a natural flair for handling finances. His first budgets, however, were so peculiar that they are now corporate legend. Brock Montgomery recalls that Peppin came in those first years with forecasts for annual revenue of around $3 million. This raised eyebrows in the boardroom because Mannix International was still a very small company. While the Mannix Sled, Plow, and Autotrack were revolutionary machines, revenue throughout the Christoff era grew slowly. By 1964, it only reached the neighbourhood of $300,000.

While Peppin's forecasts for millions in revenue those first years were totally fantastic, somehow his forecasts for profit always turned out right on the mark. Finally, Calgary realized Peppin had another set of numbers to actually run the business. "I think it took us two years to figure that out," Montgomery said. "One day I said, 'Dick, what the hell do you mean by your budget?' 'Well,' Dick said, 'the budget is what we've got to do.' You see, Fred Mannix used to get at Dick and say, 'Dick, you should have $3 million of business down there. No reason why you can't.'"

"I asked Dick how he could come up with all these forecasts that said he was going to make money, and somehow he still did," Montgomery said. "'Oh,' Dick says, and he reaches down in his bag and pulls out a real detailed budget of what he knew he was going to do, what he could actually do! As far as I was concerned, that was the first time Dick knew what we meant by budget. He had thought budget meant what he was supposed to do — not what he figured he actually could do!"

Passing the Torch

When F.C. Mannix's health in the Sixties forced him to take a less active role, the outfit survived with no great crisis. "Brock and Everett did an unbelievable job of carrying on business as usual and providing leadership during that period of time," said F.P. Mannix. "I just don't know of any other team that has accomplished what Brock and Everett have, and I've seen other outfits through Canada, some in the States, and even some in Europe.

"Their mission was to hold the organization together, but I think major progress was made during Brock's and Everett's tenure.

1967 ▶

Montreal hosts Expo 67, the world's fair, and some 50 million visitors during the year.

1967 ▶

The Quebec separatist issue, smouldering for decades, bursts into heated controversy when French President Charles de Gaulle shouts to a frenzied crowd in Montreal, "Vive le Québec! Vive le Québec libre! Vive le Canada français! Vive la France."

They got the Income Tax Act changed, and we started spending money in oil and gas on an oil and gas banking basis. They got the relationship with Home Oil and Dome to start the exploration, and they brought in Tom Parks, who was our first geologist, to get us in a land play. They constantly worked at trying to improve business and get the maintenance of way company and the coal company going. They were certainly great supporters of trying to do more exploration. In fact, the majority of our coal was picked up during their tenure. They were aggressive in keeping the construction company competitive."

"That isn't just holding ground," continued F.P. Mannix. "If that's holding ground, you'd sure hate to be in an advance mode, because you'd really be busy. Sure, we had all sorts of turmoil and problems, but they held things together during that period. Brock and Everett were on trial 24 hours a day, seven days a week, and that's a tough position, no question about it. Their philosophy was to try and hold the thing together until Ronnie and I could get there, and, of course, that's one of the reasons they pushed me as hard as they did."

Not only did the outfit survive, but its future leaders learned an invaluable lesson from the experience. "If there's a lesson to be learned from that, it is this — notwithstanding the bumps here or there and everywhere — if you have a system that's working, then business will just carry on, even when things could have been traumatic," said F.P. Mannix.

While Everett Costello and Brock Montgomery were carrying the torch, David McClement was working on the succession structure. "F.C. Mannix's great hope was that his sons would carry on," said R.J. Burns. "I think he had developed a sense of dynasty that he carried on from his father and he hoped that Freddie and Ronnie would carry on from him. It is a tremendous sense of 'the outfit,' as they call it over there, that it has got to continue and be kept within the family, if at all possible." F.C. Mannix's dream was not only possible, it was about to become reality.

THE LOCKHEED LODESTAR RETIRES

Mannix Co. Ltd.'s Lockheed Lodestar was destined to become as much a part of the company's history as any piece of machinery ever could. Purchased in 1948, it was retired from the Mannix fleet in 1963.

CF-TDI completed two million miles in Mannix service, all in North America. It travelled from the northern tip of Ellesmere Island in the Canadian Arctic to Mexico City, and from St. John's, Newfoundland, on the continent's easternmost tip, to Anchorage, Alaska, almost as far west as Hawaii. It flew nearly every veteran Mannix employee, leading businessmen from all parts of the world, dignitaries, rulers of state, welders from Oklahoma, Grey Cup guests — even Minto, the grizzly bear.

Hal O'Keefe standing in front of TDI.

Shortly after acquiring TDI, maintenance engineer Rudy Strick joined the Aviation Department. He became responsible for the entire maintenance program on all aviation equipment — a program that contributed to a remarkable safety record of 15 completely accident-free years.

Hal O'Keefe was the captain of the TDI from the beginning. Since this represents a continuous service of 15 years as captain on the same plane, the Lockheed company feels a record may have been established. Whether he established a record or not is in some way immaterial, as this tall, gentle man had a way not only with airplanes, men and bears, but with small children as well.

"The first time I ever remember flying, I was maybe five," said F.P. Mannix. "Hal came back and gave me a blanket. He said that there were about four things you could do on an airplane, but one of them was sleep, and I was going to sleep. So he put the oxygen mask on me, blanketed me down and said, 'Sleep.'"

1967 ▶

Continuing railway construction in Australia, Mannix crews help build the Mt. Newman Railroad.

1967 ▶

Israeli soldiers look west across the Suez Canal following their sweep across the Sinai into Egypt during the Six-Day War.

THE DAWN OF A NEW AGE

1968 – 1977

*I used to take Maureen and Freddie and Ronnie and get in an airplane
and visit all the jobs with them. It was very interesting for the people on the jobs
to see the kids — well, they were young adults by then — and to see how they had developed
and to know that they would soon be running the Mannix empire.*

*The three of them enjoyed it, and the people on the jobs enjoyed meeting them.
Then, not long after that, they started getting involved directly in doing work on the jobs.
So their whole life was part of the company and being on the jobs.*

— Graham Pollock, president of Mannix Co. Ltd.

Left: The 600 people attending the 1966 Mannix Calgary Christmas party share a laugh after Ron Mannix makes his entrance on a diminutive tractor. Maureen and F.P. Mannix, foreground centre and right, extend their congratulations.

Right: Apollo 11, with U.S. astronauts Neil Armstrong, Edwin Aldrin and Michael Collins, voyages successfully to the lunar surface and back.

L ike most decades, the Sixties left a lot of unfinished business. But there is one achievement of the Sixties that seems most likely to be remembered a few centuries from now, if anything is remembered — at 7:58 p.m. MST on Sunday, July 20, 1969, Neil Armstrong left his footprints in the lunar dust and the history of mankind. The first explorers to land on the moon completed the grandest adventure since the discovery of the New World. Armstrong and his fellow astronaut, Edwin Aldrin, unveiled a stainless steel plaque bearing these words: "Here men from planet Earth first set foot upon the moon, July 1969, A.D. We came in peace for all mankind."

The *Calgary Herald* editorial on the moon landing opened with the words of a Canadian pilot, John Gillespie Magee Jr.:

*I've tapped the windswept heights with easy grace,
Where never lark, or even eagle flew;
And, while with silent, lifting mind I've trod
The high untrespassed sanctity of space,
Put out my hand and touched the face of God.*

"THE EAGLE HAS LANDED"

On a summer day in 1969, while Apollo 11 circled 69 miles (111 kilometres) above the surface of the moon in lunar orbit, the Eagle separated from the command ship to start the dangerous descent to the moon. The two astronauts, commander Neil Armstrong and pilot Edwin Aldrin, stood upright in the tiny moon bug as they flew down to the lunar surface. They controlled the Eagle manually, having disengaged from computer control when it appeared they would touch down on a boulder-strewn area. They landed on a smoother area some ways from the site originally selected. Neil Armstrong's words crackled back a quarter million miles through the depths of space. "Houston... Tranquillity Base here. The Eagle has landed."

It took 10 minutes for Armstrong to get through the hatch and work his way to the alien, eerie surface of the moon. Through the magic of television, an estimated 500 million people around the world watched man's greatest adventure. A ghostly figure, his movements like a movie in slow motion, moving cautiously in his bulky suit,

Armstrong announced, "I'm going to step off the LM now...." One could almost feel people around the globe hold their breath. Still holding the ladder with his right hand, Armstrong achieved immortality when he gingerly touched the moon with his foot, proclaiming, "That's one small step for man, one giant leap for mankind." Their hearts filled with awe and wonder, people everywhere breathed a sigh of relief.

Twenty minutes later, Aldrin became the second earthling to plant his footprints on the moon. Carrying a portable television camera, the astronauts beamed back pictures of uncanny clarity. Armstrong, the 38-year-old mission commander, gazed around at the stunning lunar landscape, and radioed back to Earth, "It has a beauty of its own. It's very pretty up here."

"There's a new meaning today to those soaring words written by a young Canadian air force pilot before he was killed in 1942," commented the editorial. "Little did he know that the words he wrote describing his own experience were almost prophetic even to the use of the word 'eagle.'...Here is man, with this incredible intellectual ability, surpassing technological skill and vast material resources, able to burst the bounds of earth and set foot on a distant planet, and with all this he is not capable of living in peace with himself.

"From the moon's surface, he could look back at his earthly home and know that several wars were raging there, that one of them had been triggered by a silly soccer game. Truly, God must be shaking his head.... Today, then, at the dawn of a new age, let us all pray that the intelligence which took man to another planet can be used — somehow — to make a better one of his own."

The Tenor of the Times

While the Eagle's lunar landing signalled a new era in the Space Age, in Alberta the end of the Sixties ushered in a new era in politics. After 25 years in power, Premier Ernest C. Manning resigned in 1968 and was succeeded by Harry Strom. In 1971, Peter Lougheed, leader of the Alberta Progressive Conservative party, swept into office.

Meanwhile in 1968, after contesting the Liberal leadership, Pierre Elliott Trudeau, politician, writer and constitutional lawyer, was elected as Canada's 15th prime minister. In the ensuing general election — which was dominated by "Trudeaumania" — his government won a majority. "It seemed to me, reading the press in the early stages a couple of months ago," commented Trudeau, "as though you guys were saying, 'We dare the Liberal party to choose this guy Trudeau. Of course, we know they never will, but we'll just dare them to do it....' And what happened, I think, is that the joke blew up in your face and in mine. People took it seriously." Thus he began a period in office which was to last longer than any other prime minister's save Mackenzie King and Sir John A.

1968 ▶

During the winter, pipeline crews build the section of the Peace River pipeline between Valleyview and Zama Lake in northwestern Alberta. Work continues with temperatures as low as -51°F (-46°C).

1968 ▶

The "Prague Spring" of 1968, a loosening of Communist controls in Czechoslovakia, is shattered when Soviet tanks and Eastern Bloc forces occupy Prague and overthrow the government.

Macdonald. Many thought Trudeau was the man for the times. Here was a Quebecker willing to face down the Quebec separatists. Even so, he and western Canadians did not get along. In the Seventies, this mutual lack of understanding would become a serious problem.

Shortly after assuming power, the Trudeau government launched its first attempt to combat the ravaging effects of inflation by creating the Prices and Incomes Commission under the direction of Dr. John Young. Although possessing no direct power, this advisory group asked both business and labour leaders to institute a policy of mutual restraint regarding wages and prices. When this program appeared to be failing, Dr. Young sponsored a national rally of more than 250 business leaders to support the voluntary effort of holding down prices. It generated a great deal of rhetoric and perhaps little else. F.C. Mannix spoke for many private entrepreneurs when he said, "The most difficult obstacles are to cope with government interference and management."

Government intervention in the private sector became an issue of the times. It spawned bitter controversies including government control of foreign investment in Canada. For members of the government, these controls were prompted by the desire to ensure Canadian economic independence. Many individuals in the private sector, however, interpreted the situation in an entirely different manner. One frequently heard complaint was that Trudeau's ministers were not displaying a true sensitivity toward the delicate relationship between Canadian firms and outside investors. Other business leaders raised a considerably more serious accusation — they claimed the government was using the issue of foreign investment as a smoke screen to hide its true intent, the nationalization of Canadian industry.

The running skirmish between the federal government and Canadian business began in earnest in 1968. That year the government issued the Watkins Report, which called for more business competition in general, coupled with higher tax rates and more stringent regulatory

A STRONG WESTERN VOICE

"One Prairie Province," a three-day conference, was sponsored by the University of Lethbridge and the *Lethbridge Herald* in May 1970. The keynote speaker, James A. Richardson of Winnipeg, expressed the view that the study and research that had gone into the preparation of the many papers and speeches should be continued and expanded by a new organization. As a result, a number of concerned western Canadians, drawn together by Richardson, Fred C. Mannix and Max Bell, a Calgary publisher and industrialist, established the nonprofit Canada West Foundation.

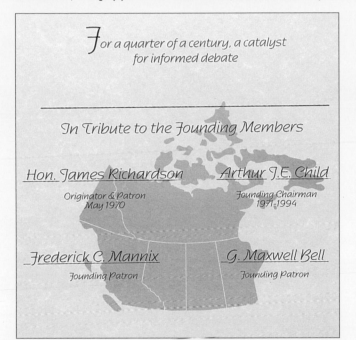

For a quarter of a century, a catalyst for informed debate

In Tribute to the Founding Members

Hon. James Richardson
Originator & Patron
May 1970

Arthur J.E. Child
Founding Chairman
1971-1994

Frederick C. Mannix
Founding Patron

G. Maxwell Bell
Founding Patron

"F.C. Mannix was one of the primary founders of the Canada West Foundation," explained Chick Thorssen, executive director of the Canada West Foundation from 1972 to 1974. "He put up the bulk of the initial money to get it off the ground."

"I believe we have as much integrity in Alberta as anyone in Ottawa," F.C. Mannix commented. "We can find people who will be dedicated and as industrious as easterners. Everyone seems to think by having centralized and remote control that this solves problems. I disagree. Self-discipline is the only salvation for operation of any business or arm of government and we should have it."

"He was a dedicated westerner," admired Doug Gardiner, director and vice chairman of the Royal Bank of Canada. "He has done so much in a quiet background, not front and centre, because that's not his makeup. But he has done more to make sure the West was well represented and well looked after, fighting the battles with the easterners. You would just bring the subject up, and away he would go talking about the 'wicked East.'"

1968 ▶

On April 1, Mannix International Inc. completes construction of its first shoulder ballast cleaner. By the next year this new machine creates $122,000 in revenue for this subsidiary.

1968 ▶

In May, riots plague much of Paris. Universities are closed, streets are barricaded and fires burn through the night. In June, Gaullists win a clear majority in elections while radicals lose seats.

controls for foreign-owned firms. Four years later, the government published the Gray Report. This report presented an even more critical assessment of foreign control of Canadian business affairs, calling for a national tribunal that would review and regulate takeovers, licensing, franchising and investments in Canada by existing foreign-owned firms, as well as foreign investments made by Canadian-owned multinationals.

In 1973, two major events fuelled the private sector's fears that Ottawa was pursuing a policy of nationalization of business. That year, the government purchased de Havilland Aircraft of Toronto from Hawker Siddeley, a British firm, and acquired Canadair from General Dynamics of the United States. With these two transactions, the government effectively nationalized the Canadian aerospace industry. Then, in December 1973, the government set up Petro-Canada, a national petroleum company whose purpose was to arrange for oil imports and to develop Canada's internal oil reserves. While Petro-Canada's stated mission was to make Canada energy self-sufficient, some in the private sector believed the creation of Petro-Canada was a government attempt to enter the oil business in direct competition with private firms.

Events in the Middle East in the fall of 1973 temporarily interrupted the dispute between the private sector and government and had a dramatic impact on Canada's economy. Following the outbreak of the Yom Kippur War, the Organization of Petroleum Exporting Countries (OPEC) announced an embargo on oil shipments to the United States and other Israeli allies. At the beginning of the decade, Iranian oil unloaded in Montreal sold for $2.50 a barrel. By November 1973, the price of imported crude oil in Canada soared to $7.50 a barrel. By the end of 1974, crude cost $10 a barrel.

The ensuing energy crisis sent Canada into a sharp recession marked by record high inflation and unemployment, double-digit interest rates and sluggish economic growth. As jobs became scarce, a spirit of militancy took hold among Canadian unions, particularly in the two traditional strongholds of the Canadian union movement, Quebec and British Columbia. When demands for 20 to 80 per cent wage increases were not met, strikes and lockouts broke out across Canada. Lost man-days were four times higher than the early 1960s.

In the fall of 1974, the struggle between government and private industry resumed with the creation of the Foreign Investment Review Agency (FIRA). This agency was given the power to screen and approve any new activities by foreign-owned firms that could affect internal Canadian economic affairs. FIRA would monitor all takeovers and transfers of ownership of Canadian firms involving outside interest. It would also review direct foreign investment in new businesses and foreign expansion into new markets. FIRA would transmit its findings and recommendations to the federal cabinet in Ottawa.

Although intended to monitor foreign investments for the benefit of Canadian firms, this measure set off a fresh wave of controversy regarding the government's attitude toward the private sector. Many business people felt the procedures were more arbitrary and rigid than in any other industrialized nation. They argued that FIRA would only serve to cripple Canadian business by cutting it off entirely from foreign capital. In response, supporters of the measure pointed out that FIRA was approving more than two-thirds of the cases it reviewed. Whatever the facts of the matter, this controversy eloquently illustrates the lack of communication between private enterprise and the federal government.

This, then, was the tenor of the times. It was a time when leaders of a new generation came face to face with the hard, complex realities of political separatism and economic upheaval. For the third generation of the Mannix family in business, in many ways, it would be a trial by fire.

The Decision to Perpetuate the Outfit

History has an odd way of echoing through time; the past and future can sometimes be heard in the present. For the Mannixes, this was particularly true in the case of succession planning. For instance, like his father before him, F.C. Mannix was once presented the opportunity to sell the family business at a time when his children were too young and inexperienced to take over the outfit.

Back in the late Fifties, the Mudd family, of Harvey Mudd College and Claremont College, expressed an interest in buying the company. "The Mudds owned a big mine in Cypress," explained David McClement. "They were looking for diversification at that time. They had quite a long discussion on that deal for five or six months. It was felt that maybe they would do the same kind of thing that had been done by F.C.'s father earlier, when F.S. had sold the controlling interest of the company to Morrison-Knudsen so Fred C. would be able to continue to work in it. The Cypress people looked at the construction company but finally they just didn't think that the margins were great

1968 ▶

Mexico City police escort an arrested student demonstrator during riots in the city. Police fire into the crowd at Tlatelolco Square. Police report 40 killed; others claim up to 700 killed.

1968 ▶

The Newfoundland joint venture with Curran & Briggs builds the Whitebear Diversion and Victoria Canal southwest of Grand Falls-Windsor for the Bay d'Espoir hydro project.

enough for them. They turned it down in '58 or '59. The Mudds actually passed up a great bargain. That was one of their mistakes in their career."

"So there was one position that maybe the best way to perpetuate the outfit was to sell it to an outsider and let the family catch their own rabbits, however they came into the picture," McClement said. "The question would have been how the younger generation would go about moving back in later to regain control. In other words, it would have been up to them to come back and take it over, like F.C. regained company control from Morrison-Knudsen. Certainly, that was not my view. I was a major proponent of trying to get the estate planned. I didn't see why we couldn't make the estate self-perpetuating, to do it from the inside. I felt very strongly that the outfit should be perpetuated. I was of the view that the children should be given the chance to keep the outfit going."

McClement was then charged with coming up with some long-range planning to perpetuate the outfit. "At that point, we had estate taxes to worry about, which were very onerous," he said. "The taxes could wipe out quite a bit of the estate. That was also a concern because of F.C. Mannix's health at that point. So we sort of had a double whammy to think about." As the payment of the estate tax could cripple the entire organization, McClement recommended that the Loram Group adopt a common recapitalization procedure known as an estate freeze. This plan both effectively eliminated the disastrous estate tax exposure and provided a mechanism for transfer of Loram organization control to the next Mannix generation.

While an estate freeze may have been a common recapitalization procedure, the actual succession planning itself was not — the lack of succession planning is one reason why 70 per cent of all family firms do not continue as family firms beyond the tenure of their founders. But even with proper succession planning, the odds were stacked against the Mannix family surviving

Above: F.P. (Fred) Mannix.
Below: Maureen G. Mannix.
Bottom: R.N. (Ron) Mannix.

the transfer of the business to the third generation. The odds of F.C. Mannix carrying on the business his father had founded were three in ten — seven out of ten family businesses crash shortly after takeoff and do not survive transfer to the second generation. By the time of the transfer to the third generation, these odds plummet to a rather daunting one in ten. However, as time has shown, the Mannix family is no stranger to beating the odds.

"Those three kids were as different as day and dark."
Frederick Philip Mannix, the eldest son by six years, Maureen Gail Mannix and Ronald Neil Mannix grew up surrounded by the reality of a family business. For them, the employees of the Loram Group were an extended family. At the same time, Margie and Fred C. Mannix took pains to give them as normal a childhood as possible, allowing them to develop as individuals. "Those three kids were as different as day and dark," recalled Evelyn (Nursie) Hayward, who helped Margie Mannix look after the children. "Freddie was a very obedient, very nice child to handle. He had one or two faults, but not many. Maureen was a little spitfire and yack, yack, yack with that red hair. But she was very honest and very fair. And then we had Ronnie. He jumped around a little bit more. He was a real doer, that kid. There were things about them that you would know that they were family, but you could never say they were three peas in a pod. No way."

A large part of the children's upbringing was rooted in the land. "The Mannix family had deliberately stayed out of real estate, largely because of Everett Costello's antipathy toward such investments," explained Stan Waters, who joined the outfit in 1975. "Costello's father had been active in real estate in Calgary during the previous booms and had lost heavily. This had so coloured young Everett that he had convinced the Mannix family that the last thing they ever wanted to get into was real estate. I think that, to some extent, also coloured the views of the Mannix family when they ignored great opportunities for acquiring real estate in the '50s and '60s

1968 ▶

The electrical generating capacity of Calgary Power Ltd.'s 13 dams and plants reaches 1.7 million horsepower or 13 million kilowatts. Of the 11 structures shown, Mannix crews helped construct eight. Total Mannix-built capacity is 1.5 million horsepower or 12 million kilowatts.

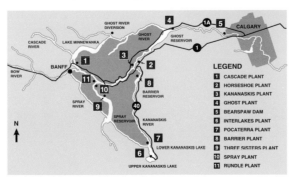

1968 ▶

Mon-Max Services Ltd. constructs an addition to the Jumping Pound, Alberta, gas plant for Shell. The facility includes a refrigerated lean-oil absorption LPG recovery plant.

and did not become major landowners, landholders and developers."

While F.C. Mannix decided not to pursue landholdings in a major way, finding property for a home for his family was a major priority. "He found the property at Fish Creek," explained Waters. "The 1,200 acres along Fish Creek became the centre of his home site where he lived happily for many years."

"The cattle operation as I knew it at the time, was started at the FM #1 property, or Fish Creek, the home ranch with F.C.," added Fred Fenwick who managed Manalta Holdings, the Mannix ranching and real estate subsidiary, during the '70s. "That would date back into the '50s when there was maintained a purebred Hereford herd. We were breeding, raising and showing cattle. We showed cattle in the Calgary Stampede and other areas off the FM #1 property."

"It goes back to the grandfather, of course," said Fenwick. "He had a farm at Rockyford, Alberta. The genesis of the original western Canadian contractor was a farmer. He farmed in the early spring and then took his horses and his wagons and did contracting. He returned to the farm in the fall to harvest, put up his wagons, put his horses away, feed them and wait till the next spring. Then he'd do his planting and then go back out contracting. So there was always a strong family tie to agricultural property and the idea of raising agricultural crops, be they cereal grains or cattle or anything. The two boys were raised on the FM property in an agricultural setting with horses and cows. They had something of everything there. Freddie and Maureen were in 4-H; they raised their calves and showed them. So there's always been that basic interest that there would be a home and the farm where at some point if necessary one could go back to live."

While the children were raised in an agricultural setting, like their father and grandfather before them, they were exposed very early on to the ways of business. "They learned the business from the bottom up, and they were very proud of it," recalled Hanna Hunter, a Mannix family helper. "When he was 12 years old, Freddie started going to work on his holiday. He shovelled coal at 15. Ronnie worked 16 hours a day driving a scraper. Maureen didn't go out on a job site, but she worked in the office. She knew a lot about it, but not the physical. I don't think any of the guys who were shovelling cement would have liked a woman there. It wasn't the time for it."

"It was always the plan that Freddie and Ronnie were going to run this outfit as soon as they got into shape to do it," explained Brock Montgomery. "They were going to take over. Now, how they were going to take over, we didn't know. Fred C. decided, and we agreed, that Freddie would go in and run the outfit for a period of ten years, and not much longer, as president of Loram; directly running it. Then Ronnie would come in, if and when Ronnie was ready at that time, and he would take over and run it as president."

"F.C. made the program, and we, Everett and I, developed the steps," said Montgomery. "F.C. had young Freddie and Ron out in the field learning how the work was done. They were out each summer. Each summer

Top: The Mannix family at Camelback Inn, Arizona, in 1957. From left to right, F.P., Margie, F.C., Maureen and Ron Mannix.

Above: The FM Ranch at Fish Creek, Calgary, Alberta.

1968 ▶

Ernest Manning retires as premier of Alberta after 25 years. His pragmatic stewardship brings Alberta into the modern era.

1968 ▶

United States troop strength in Vietnam reaches 500,000, the maximum number deployed in the conflict. The death toll reaches 30,000.

they were, at Ev's suggestion and mine, stepped up to a little more demanding job, to the point where they were made foreman or were directing certain parts of the job. They were forced into it — to learn something about it. They had to learn a lot of things in a short time. Actually, they both did very well at it, but they progressed from a Cat operator to a foreman much faster than anyone else would have done because it was pushed that way. So they got a pretty thorough grounding in the actual way work was carried out in the field."

"Both Fred and Ronnie also got an awful lot from F.C., personally," continued Montgomery. "Unconsciously they knew more about the operations and operating companies. Fred used to take young Freddie with him. Even when he was going to high school, he would take him to New York and take him along with him when he was doing a joint venture deal. Freddie would be tagging along, somewhere. It wasn't just Freddie, it was both of them. Ronnie got the same deal. That gave them a lot of exposure."

The First-Born's Apprenticeship

Frederick Philip Mannix was born February 24, 1942, in Calgary. "When I saw F.P. in the bassinet, he looked just like Grandpa to me," recalled Bob and Alice (Mannix) Kramer's daughter, Marilyn Kramer Acteson. "Grandpa was so thrilled with F.P. being the first-born son and having the Mannix name."

When F.P. was five years old, his father and grandfather took him out to visit the job at Spray Lakes. In typical Mannix style, visiting a job site involved an adventure with a car. "I went up with my grandfather, my dad, Karl Collett and Si Fraser," Fred P. Mannix recalled. "My dad had a brand-new, red-maroon Chrysler. It was the first time it was driven. We drove up the Banff Highway and looked at the job. We spent most

Fred C., Fred P., Maureen and Ron Mannix enjoy an equestrian outing at Fish Creek.

F.S. Mannix with his first grandson, F.P. Mannix.

of the day there. Then we drove back down. We left the old highway at Morley Flats and drove up toward where the present highway is. We went and looked at the gravel pit we had in there. We were supposed to be back in town for dinner, but by the time we looked at those two jobs, we were late. They got talking about the car — the car went to 120 on the speedometer — and my grandfather said to my dad, 'Ah, there's no way this car will do that.' And Dad said, 'You want to bet?' So he floored the car and we came in at about 120 miles an hour. When we got into town, the engine was cooked. We got home, but that was the last the car moved. They had to come and tow it away the next day."

The next job the young Fred P. remembers visiting was Kenney Dam in British Columbia. "When I was about ten years old, I flew up with Dad on one of the Lodestars we had and we looked around the job," he said. "We met Karl Collett on the job site and then we flew down to Kamloops. We stopped in Kamloops because we were building part of the Trans Mountain pipeline. That was the first time I had been in Kamloops. The office was right across from a beer parlour. It was so hot that I went outside to sit in the shade. All of a sudden, there was a great big bang, and a bunch of people came roaring out of the bar across the way. One guy went into the little store a couple doors down the way and came back with a dozen eggs. He cracked an egg and fried it on the sidewalk. That's what the argument over in the bar was all about. It was so hot, you could actually fry an egg on the sidewalk. My friends wouldn't believe me when I got back to school."

One of young Fred P.'s friends who listened to the stories he brought back from his early "business" trips was John Jennings, whose father introduced the Mannixes to the Fish Creek property. "I grew up across

1968 ▶

After winning the Indiana, Nebraska and California primaries in his quest for the U.S. presidency, Robert F. Kennedy is assassinated.

1968 ▶

Western Auto-Par Distributors Ltd. changes its name to Check Products Ltd. This company, formed in 1967, developed and markets a line of Teflon-based additives for aircraft and automobile engines. In 1971, it will join the Mannix family of companies.

the street on Talon Avenue," recalled Jennings. "One of my earliest memories was sneaking cigarettes with Fred and smoking them under our porch. I went to school with Fred all the way to Grade 13 — Strathcona [School for Boys] and Ridley College. Fred and I grew up in a very parallel way and I saw a lot of him — school, riding, summer camp. I grew up acutely aware that there were way more pressures on Fred right from the very early times when he was 8, 10, 12; that he was the heir apparent. He would be going off to these, to me, mysterious meetings with 'these men.' Ron was involved with that to some degree, but with a difference. Fred was under the pressure. This was something that, whether he liked it or not, he was going to do."

"What amazes me is how I grew up across the street from one of the country's great economic success stories as it emerged in the 1950s and I was almost completely oblivious to it all," Jennings continued. "Perhaps not so strange when I was a child, but I didn't really know until recently the extent of what was created from rather humble beginnings after the Second World War. But what hits me now with great force is the lack of pretension and pomposity involved in the creation and forging of one of Canada's great economic empires. And what needs stressing perhaps above all, is that this empire was built without losing humanity. I wonder if this could be said as forcefully of any other Canadian corporation."

The Mannix family lack of pretension can clearly be seen in young Fred P.'s on-the-job training program. At the tender age of 12, Fred P. was put to work at the main camp at Sept-Îles. There he hauled garbage, dumped waste steel, helped the cook, filled the potholes in the airstrips and served as water boy on the steel gang. During the evenings, he wrote letters to his folks back

Top: Maureen Mannix is protected from the wild things of suburban Calgary by John Jennings (centre) and F.P. Mannix.

Above: A pastoral interlude.
Young F.P. Mannix and his horse.

home, telling them about the events at camp. These letters, and his tenure at Sept-Îles, came to an abrupt end when young Fred P. wrote home about how one of the men had a new "wife" arrive every week from Montreal.

"When my mother heard about this, she went to my dad and said, 'You send that airplane down and you get my son out of the bush,'" recalled F.P. Mannix. "So one day I looked up and there was Hal O'Keefe, our chief pilot. He said, 'Hi, Fred. How are you doing?' I said, 'Oh, fine, what are you doing here?' He said, 'I've come to get you.' I said, 'Summer isn't over yet. School doesn't start for another three weeks.' And he said, 'Your mother says you are to come home.' So home I went."

"The day before I left, Buzz Pickard, Jim's brother, took me fishing for salmon," F.P. Mannix said. "The first fish I hooked pulled me off the rock and into the river and I went down through the rapids. I wasn't going to let go of the rod because I knew it was Jim Pickard's best rod. Buzz Pickard was running down the side of the river yelling, 'Let go of the rod, you dumb kid!' because he thought I was going to drown. He thought he was going to drown the boss' son, and that would be the end of him. I went underwater and I finally had to let go of the rod. We carried on fishing with the other rod we had. Buzz Pickard held me from behind and we caught a fish bigger than I was, probably a 45- or 50-pound fish. I wanted to take this fish home to Mother, seeing how I was going home the next day with Hal O'Keefe. So we left Seven Islands with this fish onboard in the hold of the aircraft.

"We just about got to Quebec City when the right-hand engine caught on fire. Hal O'Keefe, being an old bomber pilot, sideslipped the airplane to keep the flames away from the inboard fuel tank. We had

1968 ▶

Walter Carr, Alberta Coal Ltd., with Mr. Klimax, the 1,700-ton (1,500-tonne), 10-storey Marion dragline, during their eight-mile (13-kilometre) walk from the Klimax Mine to the Boundary Dam power station to assist in overburden stripping. En route they cross three rail lines, two rivers, two major highways, several power lines and numerous smaller roads.

1968 ▶

Liberal Pierre Trudeau is elected prime minister of Canada. His government is the first majority government since 1958. He is shown with Andrea Spindel Wilkinson.

Lou Franco onboard who was the manager of the Railroad Division, and he really was petrified of airplanes. This, of course, just wasn't his cup of tea at all. In the middle of this sideslip, where you're on about a 45-degree angle and coming down out of the sky at a hell of a rate, I turned to Lou Franco and said, 'Lou, at this rate I'll never get my fish home to Ma.' He grabbed me — to this day, I still have the fingerprints in my arm — and said, 'Fred, forget the damned fish! I want to get me home to Ma!'"

"We made an emergency landing in Quebec City and Hal O'Keefe was out of his seat and had the door open and us out of that airplane just like peas out of a peashooter," said F.P. Mannix. "The engine was burned up and some of the bags were burned, and I lost my fish." The next two summers, Fred P. was kept close to home, working as a farm labourer.

In 1957, at age 15, Fred P. asked to be assigned to a coal mine as a labourer because he was interested in that side of the Loram Group's business. "I had a crew that summer that included Freddie Mannix," recalled Dick Wilsey, a master mechanic and electrician who hired on at Taber in 1958 after two decades' experience in coal mining. "And he was put to work. His job was cleaning up the machinery, and I have seen him up to his elbows in grease on this old machinery. On weekends I was driving back and forth, and I would frequently pick up Freddie and bring him home here and then pick him up again early Monday morning, or maybe it was Sunday night; it didn't make much difference. I'd pick him up and take him back again — that way both of us got back to Calgary for the weekend.

"He was very conscientious. He would do any kind of work that I asked him to do. He didn't care about how dirty it was or how hard it was. He wanted to learn all about coal mining, and believe me, he was learning it the hard way. I remember one Saturday — we were

Top: Fred P. Mannix with his fish caught near Sept-Îles, Quebec.

Above: A 10-year-old F.P. Mannix tells his mom a fish story.

working Saturdays in those days — I suggested to him, 'Let's quit an hour or so early to be able to get back home at a decent time for a change.' No, Freddie didn't want to do that. It was a little bit before quitting time and he wanted to be sure he got his full hours in."

Fred P. recalled that the worst part of the job that summer was working in the tipple. "I was shovelling bug dust [finely crushed coal] underneath the screens and picking bone [rock] off the belts," he said. "Of course, shovelling bug dust is pretty tough when it's 90 degrees and you're in a tin shack. That bug dust is just like flour." For young Fred P., the fun part was learning how to blast. "When we were in the pit, we had a tractor with a drill, and I was putting the drill holes in the cap rock," he said. "We had a guy with a blasting ticket, so I was apprenticed to him to learn how to blast and I set all the dynamite under his supervision. We drilled all the holes, loaded them and shot all the cap rock ahead of the stripping. I wrote the exams there at the end of August and had the first level of blasting, so then I was a 'powder monkey.'"

The next year, at the age of 16, F.P. Mannix spent his summer working as a dozer operator at Brazeau Dam. The following year, he summered at Albert Canyon, skinning a D-4. "We were up to Albert Canyon and Freddie — Fred C. Mannix — come up there," recalled Hans Olesen. "I was the foreman there, and he and Gordon Coates come up this day looking the job over. All the foremen were in the foremen shack, in the office there, and he said, 'I'm sending Freddie — that's young Freddie P. — out to work up here this summer, and I want Hans to be his foreman.' One foreman said, 'Who the hell is Hans Olesen?' And he said, 'Well, I know Hans from way back. I used to run a Cat with Hans and we worked together for a long time. I want him to be Freddie's foreman.'

"So Freddie P. came out and they wanted him to sit at the same table we were sitting at, the foremen. Freddie said, 'No.' He said, 'I'll sit anyplace.' He wouldn't

1968 ▶

The television program "60 Minutes" debuts. Here Mike Wallace is shown interviewing the family of slain civil rights activist, Dr. Martin Luther King Jr.

1968 ▶

The magic and anticipation of the season is reflected in the faces of these children at the annual Calgary employees' Christmas party for children.

have anything to do with that. He was a good kid. On a Sunday, we would take the jeep and drive out in the mountains. Then we'd get to some old mines. Freddie would be looking around these old mines and he would find different things up there. He would be really interested in things like that. Every weekend we would wash our clothes together."

Young Fred P. spent subsequent summer vacations labouring as a pipeliner in the Drayton Valley oil field and working in the engineering department of the construction company. In 1962, he travelled to Japan and Australia with his father on business trips. In 1963, he served as assistant to the general manager of Manalta Coal. The subsequent two summers, young Fred P. worked as a pipeline labourer and line-up crew member on the Alberta Gas Trunk Line pipeline in Cochrane and as foreman of the south preparations crew for Alberta Concrete Products in Edmonton and Leduc.

After graduating from the University of Alberta in 1966 with a degree in commerce, Fred P. Mannix spent 1967 working full-time as project manager on the Alberta Resources Railway Section Seven, which included 35 miles (56 kilometres) of new construction. It was at this job that the sequel to a legendary story occurred. Years earlier, at Lake Minnewanka Dam, the cook had been fired before a replacement was secured. The result was that Margie Mannix cooked for about one day before the crew rebelled, fleeing to the nearby Chinese restaurant. F.P. Mannix would have a similar experience at Section Seven.

The story goes that the cook, whose name was Leon, was a very good cook. But the catering company fired him. The next day, F.P. Mannix was walking down the road when he saw Leon sitting on the tow bar of a trailer. When F.P. asked him what was the matter, Leon replied, "They fired me, but I don't have the money to move the trailer out of here." F.P. said, "Grease is grease," so he put Leon on the service crew. A week later, F.P. fired the catering company that had replaced Leon. He then got on the radio and said, "Grease is grease. Get that damn cook to stop filling the engines and feed the men in one hour!" His comments, which went out over the open airways, entered into the realm of legend.

Left: September 1964. Fred P. Mannix practising for the bull riding competition at the University of Alberta rodeo.

Below: Catskinner F.P. Mannix at the Albert Canyon, Alberta, project.

1969 ▶

The RCMP stops sled dog patrols. The dogs were mostly descendants of Siberian huskies donated by Walt Disney after filming *Nikki: Wild Dog of the North*.

One Of The R.N.W.M.P. Dog Teams
#2 Arctic Patrol.

1969 ▶

The North Sea oil field is discovered. It is the largest pool of oil outside the Middle East and lies 60 per cent in British territory and 40 per cent in Norwegian territory.

The First Step in the Transition to the Third Generation
"He was a very, very young man."

In 1968, Fred P. Mannix came in from the field. "I came in first as vice president of operations," he recalled. "I took Rocky's [John Rockingham's] place. Rocky went to Edmonton to run Alberta Concrete Products. Brock Montgomery had been general manager in Loram and within two months after I'd gotten married and returned from my honeymoon, Brock and I just switched. Brock went to vice president of operations and I was general manager. The idea was that Brock would backstop me and by putting me in as general manager, that was the best thing that could be done. It was a way of trying to accelerate my whole program. When Brock got sick — about the end of June, Brock had a heart attack — what it meant, and it sort of threw me, was that I was an operator right off the pump handle. I was doing what Brock was doing plus what I'd been doing. So I had the whole thing and I was working from seven in the morning until seven at night."

Edna Hunt, secretary to both Costello and Montgomery, vividly recalls the day the 26-year-old F.P. Mannix

Fred P. Mannix begins to take command of the outfit.

assumed the burden of his new responsibilities. "I walked into the office and Brock Montgomery's desk was cleared off," she said. "I thought, 'Oh, my goodness. What is going on?' I went in to see Mr. Costello and he announced that Fred P. Mannix was taking over Mr. Montgomery's workload, that F.P. would be the new vice president and general manager of Loram. Then Fred P. Mannix walked in. All of a sudden, I realized that he was going to be my boss. I was quite floored because he was a very, very young man. He could have been my son."

F.P. Mannix credits Brock Montgomery and Everett Costello for giving him the support needed to rise to the challenge. "Being a general manager at that age, I had lots of problems trying to deal with people much older than me who thought I didn't know anything and they knew it all," he said. "If I hadn't had the kind of support that Brock and Everett gave me, I would never have survived in that slot. But they knew all the wrinkles and they knew how to handle the various people. If someone was giving me a bad time, I'd say, 'Look, Brock, what do I do now?' And he'd say, 'Well, here's what I'd do.' There was always one thing that we were united behind. There were no cracks in the wall as far as trying to present an image to either the

outsiders or our own people. Even when I was wrong, they always supported me. Then, they would tell me privately, 'Now, you dumb bastard, go fix it.' That kind of public support was important to me."

In 1969, the first major step in the transition to the third generation of Mannix family management began when Fred P. Mannix became president of Loram Ltd. He was 27 years old. As every first-born will tell you, being the eldest, and therefore going first, is not easy; in many ways, you are the trailblazer for those who follow. You bear the heavy burden of responsibility and the trail is often strewn with hazards. For young Fred P. Mannix, the lack of a

1969 ▶

La Cie Mannix (Québec) Ltée., the Mannix Quebec subsidiary, completes the Alberta Resources Railway from near Jasper National Park to Grande Prairie, Alberta.

1969 ▶

The White Pass Railway, originally built in 1898, is a narrow-gauge railway between Whitehorse, Yukon, and Skagway, Alaska. Mannix Autotrack, winch cart and ballast tamper are modified to perform the track work.

"THE WHOLE THING WAS SO NEW"

In August 1968, a Honeywell-120 was brought in to handle the increasing data processing load for the Loram Group of Companies. By 1976, after 19 upgrades, a new Honeywell H66/10, with a front-end communications processor, was installed. "There was no textbook in this business," recalled Ed Bryant, who directed the Data Processing Centre in the Sixties. "The whole thing was so new there was no precedent or pattern to follow. Every application was a new subject and we had to experiment and feel our way into this thing."

"Mannix was one of the leaders in Canada, especially in adapting the computer to pipeline estimating," added Bob Marriott, a civil engineer and analyst programmer who joined Mannix in 1964, specializing in engineering applications. "The machines then were not what they are today, and it was costly. We rented our Honeywell for about $10,000 a month. Today, you could buy the equipment for a few thousand dollars.

"We went through our growing pains. Computers were being used in construction in the States, mostly for accounting functions, so we had to adapt them to pipeline estimating, and later on, to civil construction. The first time we used a computer for a bid was in spring 1965, on the Northern Natural job in the States. We ran a combination of 27 different estimates. Since that time, the Pipeline Division used a computer for all their estimates. It was about two years later that the other divisions adapted computers to their operations."

systematic, organized system with which to keep track of the family business was the first obstacle to overcome.

While Montgomery and Costello were united in their support of young Fred P., there was one area where no amount of support could help him — the sheer volume of paperwork. The challenge of jumping straight from the field into trying to grasp the intricate, myriad details of a multimillion-dollar business with literally dozens of subsidiaries was a physically exhausting one. "When I came in as general manager, I came in from the field," explained Fred P. Mannix. "I'd run the project at Section Seven, so I was well aware of the field things. But I, physically, couldn't read what Brock read in a day, but Brock didn't need to read it. He was so familiar with it that he knew where to go to look for what he wanted to see."

"We had no systems, as systems," he said. "I say that, but I'm not being disparaging. There were systems, but they weren't institutionalized. They weren't completely thought through. We had policy manuals, but they weren't complete. There was no overall policy. What happened during the Sixties, I call the institutionalization phase. The application of the computer during the Sixties was part of the institutionalization of the cost reporting and the estimating in the construction company. It happened as much in the construction company as it happened upstairs, but it was really dramatic at the top levels. For the first time we had an overall picture of the whole group of companies and there were some really dramatic things. It was obvious what you could do to reorganize things. Nobody really understood what we had because it had never been pulled together. Not that there was bad management or anything else, but you had to have an institutionalized approach to what was happening.

"We built an institution out of something that had been a group of individuals. If one guy got hit with a bus, the institution carried on. What you had was a transition from an individual operation. People are still important and you can't replace them, but when you institutionalize a lot of the information, it means that we aren't as vulnerable to the problems."

1969 ▶

The Concorde makes its first flight March 2 and its first supersonic flight October 1.

1969 ▶

J.M. (John) Rockingham is named president of Alberta Coal.

1969 ▶

Ho Chi Minh, leader of North Vietnam and lifelong Vietnamese independence advocate, dies at age 79.

Churchill Falls
The Largest Single-Site Power Producer in the World

Immediately after coming in from the field and taking over the reins of Loram, F.P. Mannix became responsible for Mannix Co. Ltd.'s involvement in what surely must be, to this day, one of the most ambitious construction projects ever attempted by humans. Designed to harness the massive hydroelectric power of the Labrador plateau, the Churchill Falls development project was projected to generate a staggering seven million horsepower.

Soaring some 1,500 feet (450 metres) above sea level, the Labrador plateau was shaped like a shallow saucer. Because of a few "dents" in this saucer, some water drained to other rivers, but mostly the drainage flowed through the Churchill River. The most majestic aspect of the waterway was the 245-foot (75-metre) Churchill Falls. With long stretches of rapids preceding and following the falls, the Churchill River dropped more than 1,000 feet (300 metres) over a course of 20 miles (32 kilometres) as it cut through the Labrador plateau.

A portion of one of the 21 dikes built at Orma and Sail lakes, Newfoundland, for the Churchill Falls hydroelectric project.

To harness this power, a channel system was built to augment, enclose and direct the flow of water into the upper Churchill River basin. Once enclosed within the Smallwood Reservoir, the water was directed into a fore-bay channel to flow into the power plant intakes of the newly created Churchill Falls power plant. To direct the river flow, diversion dams were built along the course of the Churchill River to retain the water on the plateau, preventing it from cascading over the rapids and down the falls. To hold the river flow upstream, more than 40 miles (64 kilometres) of low dikes plugged the dents in the saucer. Thus contained, the water filled the Smallwood Reservoir, covering an area greater than one-third the size of Lake Ontario.

The controlled flow of water was then directed from the reservoir through a new channel on the plateau to a forebay intake some 16 miles (26 kilometres) east of the falls. At that point, a flow of 49,000 cubic feet (1,387 cubic metres) per second, with a net head of 1,025 feet (312 metres), was obtainable above the underground power plant. The plant itself would be located one mile (1.6 kilometres) north of the lower Churchill River. At that location, the water would be funnelled to the plant down 11 penstocks, spinning the 11 turbines which would drive the 11 electric generators. From there, the water would go through a surge chamber and proceed along two tailrace tunnels before exiting into the lower Churchill River. All in all, Churchill Falls was a job of massive proportions.

As with any scheme of such scope and ambition, the Churchill Falls project required years of study, research and development before it reached the stage of actual construction. The first exploration of the Churchill River

1969 ▶

Mannix Construction Inc. builds the Wahluke Slope Railroad between Mesa and Mattawa, Washington, for the Northern Pacific.

1969 ▶

Harry Booth, left, resigns as president of Pembina Pipe Line. J.A. (Buck) McDonald, right, is appointed president.

"TO DO SOMETHING FOR CANADIAN ATHLETICS"

"My connection to F.C. Mannix was mostly through horses and horse shows," explained John Jennings. "The Mannixes were very much into the horse show business as my father was, and we always had seats together every year at the big Calgary horse show. Freddie, F.P. Mannix, and I used to work with a mad cavalry officer, Colonel Michael Gutowski, who at one point was the trainer of the Canadian Olympic team. Freddie and I both worked with him, then I went on into training for the three-day Olympic event.

"The reason I was able to make it onto the team was that F.C. Mannix brought over this really wonderful horse, Brygadier, from Poland. I needed two horses and I only had one, which had been donated to the Canadian team from some people in Boston, with the stipulation that I ride it. Then F.C. Mannix, out of the blue, bought this really terrific Polish horse and donated it to the team, again with the stipulation that I ride it. So that got me to the Pan-American Games."

"The horse was pronounced unfit by the team veterinarian and it was pulled just before the Pan-American Games in Winnipeg in 1967," Jennings said. "I was hoping to go to the Mexico Olympics in 1968 and that's when the horse was deemed lame. I took that supposedly lame horse down to the American Championships at Pebble Beach, California, and won. I went back the next year and won again on the same horse.

"So it was sad. It was sad for the Mannixes, too, because it didn't end as it should have, but still it was a really wonderful gesture. Fred C. Mannix did not want anyone to know that he had done anything. It was just one of those wonderful quiet gestures behind the scenes, partly that he knew me but partly that he just wanted to do something for Canadian athletics."

occurred in 1839. Although an 1863 geological survey revealed large deposits of iron ore, the area lay largely untouched until the 1950s. It was not until the completion of the Mannix-sponsored Quebec North Shore and Labrador Railway that extensive mining began in the area. In 1953, the British Newfoundland Corporation Limited (Brinco) was formed to help develop hydro-electric capabilities to support these mining operations. Soon, the channel concept was worked out on paper.

Mannix Co. Ltd. participated in many of the preliminary support tasks necessary for the proposed channel system to become a reality. In 1957, Mannix crews helped build a 105-mile (170-kilometre) road from the QNS&L Railway to the Churchill River just below the falls. In 1962, power from the Twin Falls development began to feed the Labrador mining operations. This was only a stopgap measure, however, as it was evident that as mining expanded, more power would be required.

In 1963, final studies for the Churchill Falls development began. The following year, H.G. Acres & Company Limited and Canadian Bechtel Limited formed a joint venture called Acres Canadian Bechtel of Churchill Falls (ACB). This venture provided engineering and construction management services for the Churchill Falls (Labrador) Corporation Limited (CFLCo.), a subsidiary of Brinco. In 1966, a letter of intent was signed between CFLCo. and Hydro-Québec, whereby Hydro-Québec promised to purchase most of the energy from the site. With a guaranteed market for its electricity, CFLCo. then permitted the actual start of construction.

Subsequent to this accord, Mannix Co. Ltd. became involved in two joint venture projects. As part of a joint venture sponsored by Dufresne Engineering Company, Mannix Co. Ltd. won Contract No. 12001. Begun in November 1966 and completed in the spring of 1967, this work included the completion of 16 miles (25 kilometres) of access road from Esker to Churchill Falls and construction of the first camp buildings for the arriving army of almost 5,000 labourers. In 1968, Mannix Co. Ltd. took on its

1969 ▶

The Montreal Expos are the first non-U.S. team to play Major League Baseball.

1969 ▶

Alberta Gas Trunk Line contracts with Mon-Max for the engineering design of 13 compressors with 49,900 total combined horsepower at four different stations. Compressor engines are delivered by rail.

1969 ▶

U.S. astronaut Neil A. Armstrong takes man's first small step on the surface of the moon.

second joint venture when Mannix-O'Connell built 63 miles (101 kilometres) of the Trans-Labrador Highway, stretching from Churchill Falls east toward Goose Bay.

In 1969, the pace of work at Churchill Falls quickened when Hydro-Québec agreed to purchase $5 billion worth of Churchill Falls electricity. This arrangement made Churchill Falls the largest single-site power producer in the western world. By the time of this agreement, more than five million tons (4.5 million tonnes) of rock had been excavated to form the underground powerhouse. The main focus then shifted to the creation of the dike system. In a joint venture with Brown & Root of Edmonton, and N.S. Curran & Briggs Limited of Ontario, Mannix Co. Ltd. won a $28-million contract for the construction of 40 miles (64 kilometres) of dikes.

For their portion of the joint venture, Mannix Co. Ltd. created 21 earth-filled dikes with a total length of more than 10 miles (16 kilometres). To complete the 21 dikes, the Mannix team would have to place more than 6.6 million cubic yards (five million cubic metres) of fill. Sixteen dikes were to be built in the Orma Lake area and five in the vicinity of Sail Lake — the most remote section of the entire development, more than 100 miles (160 kilometres) from the main power plant.

"The only really difficult thing about the job was the isolation," said project manager Joe Tonelli, who joined Mannix Co. Ltd. at Boundary Dam in 1964. "In one or two cases, guys just couldn't stand it. For the first six months, I couldn't stand it myself, I felt so enclosed. But I got used to it and stayed there for the whole three years. All in all, I think that when we left there, there was a closer feeling between all of us than there was in the beginning. In fact, I kind of wished we could have stayed for another year or two."

In the spring of 1969, more than 500 Mannix employees moved to the area, 340 of them reporting to the Orma Lake camp and the rest to Sail Lake. Under the direction of Tonelli, the Mannix team consisted of a number of Mannix veterans and one young member of the Mannix family. "I would say the outstanding people were Bev Ostermann, the project engineer; Mike McCarthy in administration and labour relations; Bud Burke and Gordon Geddes, master mechanics; Tony Archibald, general superintendent; Bill Wallace, the other general superintendent at Sail; Si Piedmont, who we brought in to assist these general superintendents; and Ron Mannix, foreman," said Tonelli.

"Ronnie Mannix would be out there first thing in the morning, and he'd be out there in the evening checking the second shift, because it ran in two shifts," Tonelli said. "We were working two 10-hour shifts, six days a week, through the whole project. Ronnie built a dike there, I forget which one now, but he took it on and just called for the equipment when he needed it. Rick Seemel of Bechtel was very pleased with his efforts. Ronnie built it from the bottom up to completion, without any repercussions or any additions or any remedial action. I was quite pleased when Rick Seemel came and informed me of this.

"Ronnie had a remarkable memory for names and he would mix with the men. He stayed in the bunkhouse when he could have stayed with me in my trailer, but he

BUILDING A DREAM

Back in 1948, a man by the name of S.D. Southern was earning the princely sum of $218 a month. While this was enough to support his family, it was not enough to realize his dream of sending his only child to university. But as necessity is the mother of invention, thus began a business. Started on a bankroll of $4,000 — $2,000 from S.D. Southern's mustering-out pay from the Royal Canadian Air Force and $2,000 from his son, Ron, who contributed money earned from summer jobs — the business was a small family venture. However, in classic entrepreneurial style, what the Southerns began by renting little yellow utility trailers

Maureen Mannix presenting a trophy at Spruce Meadows.

from their backyard, matured into one of Canada's premier corporations, ATCO Ltd. (Alberta Trailer Company), a multibillion-dollar company employing thousands of people worldwide.

Ron Southern and his wife, Marg, were architects of the vision that would become the equestrian centre, Spruce Meadows. At the first tournament in 1976, few realized that Spruce Meadows would change the face of show jumping in Canada, in North America and around the world. The Mannix family, long supporters of ATCO through leasing their equipment, were also original supporters of Spruce Meadows. Through their contributions, and those of many others, Spruce Meadows has grown to become the most popular show jumping venue in the world.

1969 ▶

Russian-born, U.S.-raised Palestine pioneer Golda Meir becomes prime minister of Israel. She will serve five years.

1969 ▶

On August 2, the F.M.R. (Fred and Margie Racing) Stable three-year-old, Wyn D'Amour, wins the Canada Derby in record time. He is the first horse raced out of the Mannix stables.

wanted to be with the men in the bunkhouse. He liked the odd poker game, too."

Mannix crews worked two 10-hour shifts six days a week, operating more than 275 pieces of equipment. In addition to dozers, tractors and graders, this fleet included 58 highway-type vehicles and major earth-moving equipment such as shovel-type excavators, 992 and 988 front-end loaders and 60-ton and 35-ton belly dumps. "We took the first really big loaders into that part of the country," said Bev Ostermann, who joined the company in 1961. "We had the 10-cubic-yard 992 Caterpillar loader. That was the biggest production loader commonly used in the industry, and we took the first of those machines in Canada into that job."

However, just as full-scale work began in 1969, a three-month QNS&L Railway strike delayed the arrival of most of this huge equipment fleet. "That first year was a bad one for us," said Tonelli, who had served as a rear gunner with the Bomber Command of the Royal Canadian Air Force during the Second World War. "It was like being on the front lines again in the war. We had no road to start with, so we had to rebuild the road. The equipment was taken across on skid pads. We flew the fuel in. Conditions were bad with no access, so we used helicopters, too. Food supplies also became a problem.

"Then we had the rail strike, which prevented our main fleet of equipment from coming in. After the strike was over, we started work on the set of dikes at Orma and a set of dikes at Sail. When we opened up the Sail area, we were worried about being flooded in the spring when the frost melted. To prevent frost penetration of the dikes, we used about five feet of gravel cover over the dikes. That resulted in an early start the following year." Despite starting several months late because of the strike, "We just kept building on that and ended up finishing the whole job four months ahead of schedule," said Tonelli. "The Mannix men took pride in their work."

A Quebec-based extremist group kidnaps British Trade Commissioner James Cross, top, and Quebec Labour Minister Pierre Laporte, bottom. Laporte is killed seven days later.

"The one very successful job we had at that time was Churchill Falls," added Mannix Co. Ltd. president Graham Pollock. "It started out as a $30-million fixed unit-price contract. At the time of the bid, it looked like a good job for us. But then we had the railroad strike which delayed the project. Well, we renegotiated with the Churchill Falls project people. We were able to convert it from fixed unit-price to cost-plus, with some bonus incentives. After the railroad strike, the project went very well and we made a lot of money. So it was one of the good jobs that balanced out some of the bad ones we had."

The Saga of Mount Wright — "I will now tell you a secret that you must not repeat."

As any construction veteran can tell you, the construction business is by no means a stable, predictable business. "In the construction industry, if you have four jobs, and two of them are running good, you can be sure that the other two have problems," aptly remarked Gordon Walker, who joined Mannix in 1954 as an engineer estimator.

Herb Donaldson, manager of special projects and development for Mannix Co. Ltd., mirrored this sentiment when he said, "You figure jobs and think you put in the right price and you're going to do well on them. But you can't seem to avoid the losers. There are always bad times or bad deals or unforeseen problems. So you can't have a 100 per cent success record in construction contracting. Construction is a very violent business; it has always been subject to violent economic swings."

During the 1970s, the unforeseen problems loomed larger, and more violent — not just in terms of economic swings, but actual physical violence — than anyone could have anticipated. With the Mount Wright project in Quebec, it can be argued that not since the Hart Highway job in the 1940s, would the Mannix philosophy of "finish the job, no matter what" be tested so severely.

The underlying political turmoil of Mount Wright can be traced to French President Charles de Gaulle's

1969 ▶

Mannix Engineering Ltd. is formed and soon renames itself Techman Ltd. The business is to develop improved engineering services for the operating companies and for independent companies.

1969 ▶

Expanding their successful central Alberta concrete operations, Lethbridge Concrete Products Co. Ltd. is incorporated to supply southern Alberta with ready-mix concrete and concrete blocks.

1967 visit to Canada. On the balcony of the Hôtel de Ville in Montreal, before a crowd of 500,000 people, the French leader made an address that provided separatists the best publicity in the world. It also shook English Canadians out of their Expo 67-induced complacency. Stretching his arms as though to embrace all French Canada, General de Gaulle proclaimed: "A great emotion fills my heart in seeing before me the French city of Montreal. In the name of the old country, in the name of France, I salute you with all my heart. I will now tell you a secret that you must not repeat. Tonight, here, and along my route, I have discovered an atmosphere of the same type as during the Liberation. Vive Montréal!" The cheers of the crowd prompted him to add, "Vive le Québec" — and then, after a pause, the four words that would send shock waves throughout Canada, "Vive le Québec...libre!"

Laporte's murder, which intensifies the October Crisis, is the federal government's justification for imposing the War Measures Act. Federal troops are sent to Quebec.

The reaction from English-speaking Canada was immediate. Prime Minister Lester Pearson denounced the French leader and accused him of an intolerable intrusion into Canada's domestic affairs. "The people of Canada are free," declared an angry Pearson. "Every province in Canada is free. Canadians do not need to be liberated."

As de Gaulle's visit made clear, the political situation in Quebec was approaching the boiling point. In 1968, René Lévesque formed the Parti Québécois, a political movement dedicated to securing some form of independence for the province. That same year, the legislature in Quebec changed its name to the National Assembly, an act that augured poorly for future relations between the province and the rest of Canada. In the autumn of 1969, there were riots in the Montreal suburb of Saint-Léonard. Touched off by a dispute over educational facilities in the area, these disturbances also revealed the depth and bitterness of the emotions involved.

With the beginning of the new decade, the people of Quebec went to the polls to express their vision of the future. On April 29, 1970, they voted in the Liberal government of Robert Bourassa. As Bourassa was thought to support some kind of continued relationship with Ottawa, his victory was largely interpreted as victory for the advocates of moderation.

It was not long, however, before the debate over Quebec's status moved out of the polling booth and into the streets. On October 5, 1970, the Front de libération du Québec (FLQ) kidnapped James Cross, a British trade commissioner in Montreal. In return for his release, the representatives of the FLQ demanded $500,000 in gold, the release of a number of alleged political prisoners, safe passage from the country for the kidnappers, and the reading of various FLQ manifestoes over the government-controlled radio and television. In response, the provincial government, adopting a policy of concession and compromise, agreed to negotiate with the kidnappers and held out the possibility of parole for some of the prisoners on the FLQ list.

1969 ▶

Mannix International Inc. becomes Mannix Construction Inc., Maintenance of Way Division. The company develops its first rail grinder, a 16-stone machine.

1969 ▶

Quarterback Russ Jackson leads the Ottawa Rough Riders to their third Grey Cup in the decade. Jackson is voted the most valuable player for the game and wins the Lou Marsh Award as Canada's outstanding athlete of the year.

While the Quebec government was still considering how to respond to the FLQ's demands, events quickly grew more complicated and desperate. On October 10, Pierre Laporte, Quebec's minister of labour, was kidnapped by a group which called itself the Chenier Financial Cell and was believed to be part of the FLQ organization. While the abduction of Cross was seen as an act of terrorism whose motive could be traced to anti-English feelings in the province, this second kidnapping was an entirely different story. Laporte was a Québécois, the second minister of the Quebec government and a very strong candidate for eventual Liberal party leadership. Thus, his kidnapping seemed a blow aimed at the provincial government itself.

At first, it appeared that the terrorists were going to succeed in their attempt to manipulate the government. A number of ministers flew their families out of the province. On October 14, a petition signed by 16 of the most prominent political, business and labour figures in Quebec urged the government to negotiate the exchange of political prisoners for the two hostages. On October 15, a boycott began at the Université de Montréal in support of the FLQ. That evening, in a rally at the Paul Sauvé Arena, a large gathering of supporters shouted, "FLQ, FLQ, FLQ, FLQ!" in support of the extremists.

By that point, the Bourassa government appeared about to collapse. Speaking before the National Assembly, Bourassa asked, "What do you want me to do?" A member of the Parti Québécois promptly answered, "You must immediately form a coalition government. That coalition government will negotiate with the FLQ. We haven't a minute to lose. It's your last chance."

Fearing that Quebec was on the verge of anarchy, the Trudeau government invoked the War Measures Act on October 16, declaring that a state of "apprehended insurrection" existed in Quebec. Under the emergency regulations, the FLQ was banned, normal liberties were suspended, and arrests and detentions were authorized without charge. This was a shocking event as it meant that people could be taken from their homes and put in jail with no specific charge.

Canadian Army units took up positions in Montreal, Quebec City and Ottawa. The next morning, a combined force of the Quebec police and the army began a systematic roundup that produced 436 people suspected of terrorist activities. In addition, the Trudeau government made it clear that there would be no bargaining with the FLQ or any other terrorist group. "Should governments give in to this crude blackmail, we would be facing the breakdown of the legal system and its replacement by the law of the jungle," Trudeau announced. "This government is acting to make clear to kidnappers and revolutionaries and assassins that in this country laws are made and changed by the elected representatives of all Canadians — not by a handful of self-selected dictators."

On October 17, Pierre Laporte was killed by his captors, his body left in the trunk of a car. Cross was held captive until early December and then released. Of the 436 people detained by Canadian authorities, 62 were brought to trial and 20 were convicted. Eventually, the men who kidnapped Cross and those responsible for the murder of Laporte were brought to trial and convicted.

The prompt use of military force crushed any possibility of an FLQ-inspired uprising in Quebec. But while stability was restored, the political future of the province still remained greatly uncertain. All observers appeared to agree that the Bourassa government had been severely compromised by its vacillation and weakness, but no one dared to predict what would happen next. It was in this climate of uncertainty and fear following the October Crisis, that Mannix Co. Ltd. undertook the mammoth Mount Wright development project in 1971.

"Mount Wright was supposed to be a great job."

The history of Mount Wright can be traced back to the mid-1500s, when French settlers in the eastern part of the province first discovered iron deposits along a number of riverbanks. By 1737, their descendants had begun to smelt bog iron in the St-Maurice district. Consisting of relatively small-scale operations, this activity extended into the last quarter of the 19th century. Large-scale development of the area did not get under way until the coming of World War II, when the demand for a native source of iron ore for the Canadian shipping and armament industries grew dramatically. After the war, this demand intensified, leading to the first major efforts to develop the Sept-Îles area of eastern Quebec in the late 1940s.

With the development of the Sept-Îles area well under way, mining firms began to explore the more remote reaches of eastern Quebec. In 1958, Quebec Cartier Mining began its development of the Mount Reed-Mount Wright area by awarding a contract to Mannix Co. Ltd. to build a 193-mile (310-kilometre) railway from Port Cartier to the new mining community of Gagnon. At the same time, Quebec

1969 ▶

Mannix pipeliners prepare to weld a loop section of big-inch pipeline on the Interprovincial pipeline near Regina, Saskatchewan.

1969 ▶

Further along the Interprovincial pipeline, a road-boring machine is about to begin a cut under a rural road.

1969 ▶

Production of coal at the Whitewood Mine exceeds two million short tons (1.8 million tonnes) for the first time.

Cartier started work on an immense concentrator plant in the Gagnon-Lac Jeannine area. Completed in 1961, this plant began to process some eight million tons (seven million tonnes) of ore annually.

As a result of these developments, iron ore production in Canada almost doubled between 1955 and 1965. By 1964, the resource value of Canadian iron ore was exceeded only by that of nickel and petroleum. With the advent of the 1970s, Quebec Cartier decided to further expand its mining and processing capabilities in eastern Quebec. On September 4, 1970, a joint announcement was made by Quebec Cartier Mining and Quebec Premier Robert Bourassa that Quebec Cartier would operate a new major iron ore mine near Mount Wright.

Located near the eastern border of Quebec, 80 miles (129 kilometres) from Gagnon, Quebec, and 26 miles (42 kilometres) from the towns of Wabush and Labrador City, Newfoundland, the Mount Wright mine site contained reserves to last an estimated 75 to 90 years. In order to exploit this rich potential, Quebec Cartier decided to build a large concentrator plant near the mine, along with a new housing complex and town site to accommodate the plant's workers and staff. The concentrator facilities would be able to produce 16 million tons (14.5 million tonnes) of high-grade concentrate each year. Once processed, the ore would be transported via the Quebec Cartier Railway for shipment to international markets. The mine was designed by a

In Quebec, the Mount Wright iron ore project crusher building is excavated from solid rock. The crushed ore conveyer tunnel exits from the bottom of the excavation.

Partial completion of the Mount Wright crusher building.

subsidiary of U.S. Steel, U.S.S. Consultants of Canada Ltd. (now Met-Chem Canada, Inc.).

In the spring of 1971, Quebec Cartier selected Mannix Co. Ltd. to head up the effort to construct the new processing plant. The scope of the work called for la Cie Mannix (Québec) Ltée. & Associates, a subsidiary of Mannix Co. Ltd., to provide site preparation and concrete foundations for the concentrator plant and associated facilities. The job also included such general contracting services as building roads, laying sewers and service piping, driving steel sheet pilings and caissons and performing miscellaneous electrical work. In total, the scope of the work called for the placement of some 120,000 cubic yards (92,000 cubic metres) of concrete, the handling of approximately three million cubic yards (two million cubic metres) of common and rock excavation, embankment and backfill, and about five miles (eight kilometres) of underground sewers, drains and service piping.

In April 1971, the Mannix team, led by Gerry Scraba, project manager; Vic Lemecha, project engineer; Vic Rhyorski, structural superintendent; and Bill Wallace, general superintendent, went to work. Vic Lemecha recalled how he came to be project engineer. "Gerry Scraba came to me and said that he was looking for somebody to go to Quebec with him to run this project. I said, 'God, Gerry, I don't even know where that part of the country is. I'm afraid to look it up on a map because I know it's somewhere in the boondocks.' But Gerry said, 'Oh, it's just a short jaunt,

1970 ▶

Alberta Coal Ltd. begins mining at the Highvale Mine near Wabamun, Alberta. Specially designed coal haulers help the mine become Canada's largest coal-producing mine.

1970 ▶

A.F. (Chip) Collins becomes president of Alberta Coal.

Vic, only 24 months. It's going to be an interesting job and it will pay you a whole bunch of money. You'll be project engineer and have six or seven engineers working for you.' Well, that got my attention.

"So eventually I decided to go. I arrived at the site on June 7, 1971. I had never been east of Winnipeg in my life, so when I flew to Montreal and stayed at the Hilton Airport Hotel there, boy, I thought I was king. I had a suit and a tie and was really dressed to kill. The next morning I flew up to a place called Wabush, Labrador. The first thing I noticed was that there weren't too many people there dressed in suits and ties — just work boots and work clothes and hardhats. They put me on a float plane to fly me over to the site. They threw me into the plane along with a bunch of toolboxes, carpenters and mechanics."

"So there I was, still in my suit and tie, with all these guys," said Lemecha. "Of course, they were all speaking in French and I didn't speak any French. We get to the work site and I got off the plane and everybody there was speaking French, too. Well, at that point, I was wondering what the hell was going on. I hadn't seen one friendly face so far. But we jumped in this truck and away we went. It's June so the mud was three feet deep and the truck got stuck in the mud. Naturally, everybody had to get off and push. So there I was in my oxfords and my suit trying to get this truck out of the mud. Finally, we got to the camp. I checked in and got my blankets and my keys. And that's where I saw my first Mannix people. I was so happy that they were from Calgary and spoke English."

"So there we were, out in the bush, working on the project," Lemecha said. "Mount Wright was supposed to be a great job, 24 months and $25 million. Everything was supposed to roll perfectly right to the end. No one could have known that we would become involved in all the problems in Quebec, particularly the tremendous battle that was coming up with the unions. No one could have known that we would be there until 1975 and that the job would end up running to about $75 million."

The wood and rebar formwork for the Mount Wright load-out silo. The walls of the foundation are below ground and the concrete footing rests on bedrock.

"It was more like fighting a war than constructing a project."

Mannix Co. Ltd. found itself in the middle of a political and cultural maelstrom at Mount Wright. And this, perhaps, constitutes the most tragic irony of this troubled project. For the forces of private industry and for the Liberal government in Quebec City, the Mount Wright project was meant to exemplify an enlightened spirit of cooperation between industry and government. It was also intended to symbolize the rich possibilities of a mutually beneficial alliance between French- and English-speaking Canadians.

But Mount Wright turned out to have practically nothing in common with either of these lofty ideals. On the contrary, the project was marred by the same spirit of discord and conflict that accompanied such events as de Gaulle's visit to Quebec in 1967 and the October Crisis of 1970. As the people of Quebec wrestled with such questions as possible sovereignty, the place of French culture within the larger Canadian scheme, and the role of English-speaking individuals and companies within the province, age-old feelings of bitterness, betrayal and anger reached the boiling point. At Mount Wright, these feelings

1970 ▶

Earth Day, April 21, is celebrated with public participation in cleanup programs and commitments to better the quality of life on Earth.

1970 ▶

Mannix Construction Inc. joins the Vinnell-sponsored joint venture to construct the third powerhouse at Grand Coulee Dam on the Columbia River in Washington. This $112-million project lasts until 1974.

found expression in an ongoing and often violent series of confrontations between the English-speaking owners and managers of the project and the predominantly French-speaking forces of organized labour.

Lemecha described how pressures and tensions began to mount. "In the first place, people working in the bush can only take so much of that kind of life to begin with," he said. "So we had a real problem with turnover. A crew would come in and spend six or seven months there and then they would go, and then we would have to bring in a completely new crew. We would turn over a new crew every six months. That was one of the main reasons why the project took twice as long to complete as it was supposed to. We would train a group of people and they would go through the learning curve. Then something would happen and they would all leave, and we would have to start over again."

"At the same time, we were continuously fighting with the unions," said Lemecha. "It was just constant, and if you've got that kind of situation, nothing gets done. That's not all. There were three different unions who were supplying men to construction projects in Quebec, and they all wanted to control the construction labour in the province. So the three of them were also fighting among themselves, besides fighting with us. To give you an example of how bad it was, there was a permanent town site being built for the concentrator plant operators about 10 miles down the road from the main site. The construction work on the town was staffed by a different union than the one staffing the plant site. One day, the plant site people decided that they were going to clean out the town site people. So, in the middle of the day, all work stopped and they commandeered all the company buses. About 300 people then motored down the road to the town site with baseball bats and pick handles and God knows what else. They just went down and ran those people right off the project."

"So you can see, it was more like fighting a war than constructing a project because you were continuously

THE BIGHORN DAM

While some of Mannix Co. Ltd.'s crews were busy constructing the third powerhouse at Grand Coulee Dam, others were building the Bighorn Dam for Calgary Power Ltd. Located across a natural gorge in the North Saskatchewan River Valley, 73 miles (117 kilometres) west of Rocky Mountain House, Bighorn Dam added an additional 150,000 horsepower of electricity, bringing Calgary Power's total installed hydro capacity up to 788,000 kilowatts. Bighorn Dam also created the largest man-made lake in the province. Known as Abraham Lake, in honour of Chief Silas Abraham of the Stoney Indian Nation, it stretches upstream for some 20 miles (32 kilometres).

"In the spring of 1970, I went up to Bighorn as project manager," recalled Alex Cummings. "Those were among the two greatest years of my life. It was a very successful job. It was also extremely interesting. It was a 300-foot-high earth-filled dam stretching across a canyon. It had all the aspects of some of the most massive dams built in the world, and we faced some challenges for getting the material up to the dam. It was also an interesting challenge as far as handling the water was concerned. Because it's a mountain-fed river, the North Saskatchewan has a lot of highs and lows. With all the pressures that went with facing the spring runoffs, the first years there were really exciting. We had some very interesting times with water lapping a couple feet below the crest of the cofferdam."

To celebrate the successful completion of the dam in 1972, the people at Bighorn threw a party. "That was really quite a party," Pansy Strange recalled. "It started at ten o'clock on a Saturday morning and ended about two o'clock on Sunday afternoon."

1970 ▶

The Maintenance of Way Division delivers a multipurpose machine and winch cart to the Government Railways of South Australia.

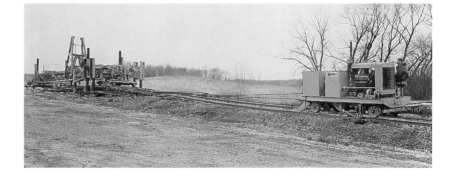

fighting with the unions," Lemecha said. "We had numerous supervisors who were threatened by anonymous phone calls, particularly the ones who had wives living in Wabush. Those women would get calls that somebody was going to pick up their kids on their way home from school and they would never see their kids again. You don't have to tell a lady that twice before she'd pack up her bags and her kids and her husband and was gone. So we lost a lot of supervisors.

"At first, we staffed the job with English-speaking people. We quickly learned we couldn't operate that way, so we brought in a lot of bilingual supervisors, mostly people who were from Quebec. But that didn't seem to make much difference to the unions, and soon these new supervisors were also being threatened. They were being threatened because they were seen to be a part of management, doing things like trying to get the job done, improve productivity and just supervise the work. After enough threats, they would just leave. A supervisor wouldn't show up for work one day. Somebody would go to look for him and find that he had cleaned out his trailer, gotten on the plane and gotten out of there."

A crane removes the inside slipform ring from the top of two storage silos at Mount Wright.

Then there was the incident when one of the Mannix supervisors was physically assaulted. "On that day, the work force all stopped working at the same time," explained Lemecha. "Then, a squad of people came up to the site led by a bunch of shop stewards and union leaders. They came into our project office, picked up our general superintendent, carried him to the gate, and threw him out on the other side and told him never to return. The work force got to be totally out of control. We had probably 1,000 men under our direct supervision, 1,000 people who were being paid to work for us, but the work that was actually getting done could probably have been done by about 100 men. We just could not control those guys. We had no security to speak of. It was supposed to be provided by the owner, but there was no effective internal police force. The closest law enforcement people were the Quebec Provincial Police, who were two or three hours away at Sept-Îles, and never showed too much interest in making the trip out to the site. So things began to get more and more out of hand. It began to look like we would never get the project completed."

There were many among the Mannix personnel who shared Lemecha's frustration. "I started setting up radio communications for the Mannix outfit in 1952," related Robert McNeill. "So I worked on a lot of projects for them over the years. I guess my least favourite job for Mannix was Mount Wright. That was some kind of place. Mostly it was about labour problems. Labour in Quebec was at a real bad point in those days. The workers were very unrestful at that time. They had guys packing guns and all kinds of stuff. The shop stewards didn't do any work. They did nothing but run around all blessed day raising hell. And they sure knew how to do it. It was a very bad place to work. I wasn't allowed to do anything down there with the communications system because the union people told me not to touch anything. I was warned about that. They told me that if I wanted anything done, even just to pick something up, I had to get somebody to do it for me."

"I remember one night we had one of three pumps freeze up and quit," McNeill said. "The management sent out one of those Herman Nelson heaters, a gasoline-driven heater, to warm up this pump so they could get it started. Well, they didn't send a pipefitter with the pump. Now why they had to have a pipefitter, I don't know. But they did send out three guys, which was more than enough to do the job. Well, the pipefitter came out with an axe and just

1970 ▶

Civil war erupts in Jordan as the Palestine Liberation Organization (PLO) attempts to take control of the country. PLO guerrillas are shown reading Mao's "little red book." King Hussein's Bedouin troops eject the PLO, who move to Lebanon.

1970 ▶

Also in the Middle East, Palestinian militants highjack and blow up BOAC, Swissair and TWA planes. They hold the passengers hostage for several weeks until Leila Khaled, a captured highjacker, and other Palestinian prisoners throughout Europe are released.

promptly destroyed the heater. He just chopped it all up and broke it to bits. Oh, they didn't fool around there. They were ugly."

"On the Quebec Cartier mining project, they were just one of many contractors that were there and it was just a disaster from the standpoint of labour problems and equipment problems," recalled Harry Duckett, a long-term provider of insurance for the Mannix outfit. "The people who were administering the project told me that they had a regular routine that they followed every Monday morning. When they came to work, they drained the crankcase and the transmission of all the machines and checked all the belts and the gasoline tanks. That was because they knew there was going to be sand in the transmissions and sugar in the gas tanks. There was constant vandalism by the people working there.

"The labour situation in Quebec was unbelievable. I remember they fired one fellow for a just cause. Unfortunately, the security people didn't know that he had been fired. They knew him and figured he was still working there. So, anyway, he goes in at 12 o'clock and walks up to the operator of a big crane. This guy says to the operator, 'I'm taking over for lunch hour.' The operator went to lunch and this guy took the crane and rolled it. Well, it was about a $250,000 crane and he just deliberately rolled it. Naturally enough, that is the kind of thing an insurance company doesn't want to pay for." Ben Kessler, who administered the company's insurance, recalls that at one time during the project there were outstanding insurance damage claims in excess of $800,000.

Paul Christensen also had vivid memories of Mount Wright. "I was the controller of the construction company at the time we were building the new concentrator for Quebec Cartier," he said. "That was during the most militant days of the Quebec labour unions. There were all kinds of violence going on up there. They beat up the foremen and superintendents and they sabotaged the equipment. Instead of working, people would just hide behind stacks of material. I used to visit the project

THE EIGHTH WONDER OF THE WORLD

Celebrated as the "Eighth Wonder of the World," Grand Coulee Dam is located in north-central Washington state. Although work on the initial structure was begun in 1933, the first water did not pour over the spillway until 1941. Upon completion, the dam formed the Franklin Delano Roosevelt Lake which extended 151 miles (243 kilometres) upstream to the Canadian border. In all, 100 million man-hours went into its construction. According to the initial design, there were to be two main power plants, each containing nine, 108-megawatt generators. In 1951, the last of these generators went on-line, giving the dam a total installed capacity of nearly two million kilowatts.

With the advent of the 1960s, however, and the signing of the Columbia River Treaty, engineers began to dream of creating a third powerhouse at Grand Coulee. Following the completion of the three Canadian Columbia River storage dams, this plan became economically feasible. The third powerhouse, which would be as long as three football fields and as high as a 20-storey building, would ultimately house a dozen 600-megawatt generators, the largest hydroelectric generators in the world.

On February 26, 1970, Walter Hickel, the U.S. secretary of the interior, signed a contract with Vinnell-Mannix that was worth well over $100 million, the largest amount ever awarded in the history of the Bureau of Reclamation. For this work, Vinnell-Mannix, with Vinnell as sponsor, took on two additional partners — Dravo Corporation of Pittsburgh, Pennsylvania, and Lockheed Shipbuilding & Construction Company of Seattle, Washington.

1970 ▶

The joint venture of M-K, Mannix and Oman extends the Hamersley Iron Railway 74 miles (119 kilometres). The project, called the Paraburdoo Railroad, includes grading, bridge structures, culverts, rail welding, ballast production and track laying. Shown are the first rails being laid.

1970 ▶

Another joint venture of M-K, Mannix and Oman in Western Australia is for Cliffs Western Australian Mining Co. Pty. Ltd. Known as the Robe River Iron Ore Project Railway, the two-year, $36-million project uses vast stockpiles of welded rail for the 130-mile (209-kilometre) job.

maybe twice a year. You had to go through a checkpoint to get on the site, but there was just a small company security force. They weren't very effective. They had certain rabble-rousers there who seemed to delight in causing trouble, and there was no real effort made to keep them off the work site. With those kinds of conditions, it was very hard on the morale of the people to work at a place like that. Gerry Scraba was the first project manager up there. There were others over the years — Joe Tonelli, Herb Donaldson and Vic Lemecha. Mount Wright is certainly one of the more memorable jobs in the company's history."

Mount Wright is not only memorable, it is legendary in its list of sabotage, heartbreak and tragedy. In November 1972, as a result of an accident at Silo No. 3, seven people were killed and a number of people were badly injured. In the spring of 1973, disaster struck the project a second time when the camp caught fire. "The fire pretty well destroyed the whole camp, so then we had to evacuate the work force," Lemecha said. "There was no place to live and no place to eat. Afterwards, there was considerable speculation that it was a case of arson. So then we had to build a whole new camp."

THE LOSS OF AN INDUSTRY GIANT

Many people in the Mannix outfit marked the passing of H.W. Morrison on July 19, 1971, with great sorrow. Those who knew him remembered him as a pioneer of strength, vision and substance in the construction industry. He extended courtesy, respect and attention to all men. "Mr. Morrison was just as courteous to the bull cook — the guy in the camps who got the food out and washed the dishes — as he was to the president of the United States, and he knew them both," recalled Eric Connelly. "Those early people in the construction business were just that way. They knew that their prosperity and everything else depended on their people."

From the age of 14, as a water boy with a Chicago construction firm, H.W. Morrison was destined to become one of the world's great builders. Hallmarks of his construction progress exist on every continent. In 1912, he founded Morrison-Knudsen in partnership with M.H. Knudsen, who passed away in 1943. Mr. Morrison, with his wife Ann always at his side, became president and general manager in 1939, and chairman of the board in 1960. He retired in 1968, assuming the honorary title of founder-chairman after 55 continuous years with the company.

The life of Harry Morrison and the history of M-K are as one, for each grew with the other. In the process, H.W. Morrison built not only great and enduring structures but enduring friendships. No man can build better.

"It was just like an evacuation in a war."
Joe Tonelli, who had replaced Gerry Scraba as project manager at the end of 1972, tried to put a stop to the atmosphere of anarchy surrounding the project. First he went to the unions. "They told us the problem was not with the contractor," he recalled, "that their problem was with the representative of the owners over such issues as wages."

Next, Tonelli went to the representative of the owner to ask if they wouldn't fence off the project and have clearance cards for the personnel. His request was turned down. "They wouldn't go for that," Tonelli said. "They said they didn't want to turn the project into a concentration camp, so we asked them to at least check out the personnel because we thought that quite a few of them had police records. The provincial police did come in and start interviewing certain ones. We lost quite a few workers who just disappeared because they did in fact have criminal records. That seemed to settle the job down somewhat, but not enough to get the production we were looking for. After I had been on the job for about six months, the company decided to move Herb Donaldson in to take over the project in the spring of 1973."

1970 ▶

A third Western Australia rail project is the Mt. Newman Railroad. Australian summer temperatures climb over 120°F (48°C) while crews simultaneously lay two 1,440-foot (439-metre) welded rails with the help of a Petitbone Speed Swing.

1970 ▶

The immensity of the Australian iron ore trains is shown. Three engines pull 170 ore cars followed by two additional slave engines pulling 60 more cars with a total weight of 30,865 tons (28,000 tonnes).

Herb Donaldson, a project manager who had been promoted to manager of business development for Mannix Co. Ltd., was not exactly thrilled with the prospect of being sent to Mount Wright. "At that time, the top people at Mannix decided that it would be a great idea if I went down there and actually managed the job," he recalled. "I didn't particularly want to do that because I reckoned that I had put in my time running projects as a project manager. As I didn't want the job, I became the area manager instead. But, in effect, I was the project manager."

Donaldson agreed to go to Mount Wright for a period of four months. After assessing the situation, one of his first recommendations was "that we shut the job down and start over again," he said. "The owner didn't want to do that, though. They said, 'No way.' So instead, we got organized and increased the number of bilingual foremen and reduced the size of crews they had to supervise. We ended up getting about one foreman for every four or five workers. I also had lots of talks with the owners in Montreal about all of our problems. While I was up there, I got the word that the unions were going to try and take over the job. We talked to the owners and said, 'We're not going to permit that.' So we moved out the whole crew and shut everything down. That meant we bailed out about 4,000 people. But it also meant that we could do what I wanted to do in the first place, which was to start all over again."

"When we shut down the project, we put all the people on buses and sent them to the airport in Wabush where they could get on a plane," Lemecha said. "It was just like an evacuation in a war. We had all these people in the airport and they were all trying to get out of there. Eventually, the owner came to us and said, 'What are you fellows going to do? Are you going to get this job done?'

Mount Wright supervisory personnel include, from left to right, V.J. (Vic) Lemecha, assistant project manager planning; H.L. (Herb) Donaldson, area manager; and W. (Bill) Julien, assistant project manager construction.

You've got nobody on site.' So we sat down with the owner and said, 'Look, here's what has got to happen. We have to get better security. We have to have better control of the work force. We have to have police on site so that we can enforce some of the rules and laws.' And, eventually, we were able to convince the owners that we were right and that these things had to be done. The owner then went to the Quebec government and said, 'Look. This is a big project. It's employing a lot of people. It we don't get it built, if we shut it down, you're going to lose a lot of jobs in this province.' Finally, we managed to talk both the owner and the government into working with us for a change. We restarted the project and brought in new people. Then things got going again."

Just as it seemed Mount Wright was finally under control, in December 1973, disaster struck once again. "I was in Montreal, about to go home," said Donaldson, "when I was told that someone had set fire to the camp for a second time. But, at least this time, it was an accident. Someone was smoking in bed. Unlike the first fire, this was not a designed catastrophe. Still, we were pretty well wiped out."

"At the end of 1973, Herb Donaldson was going to leave the job and they were going to appoint me to be his successor. Of course, they had also considered moving me from the site altogether," said Lemecha. "Some people figured I had probably had enough and was getting a little shell-shocked with all of this. But I certainly didn't want to leave the project. I wanted to complete the job. I had started it. I was there right from the beginning and saw it when it was just three feet of mud to where we had it under control and it was operating very, very well. So I wanted to see the thing through. At that point, I really thought that it was all going to be downhill all the way.

1970 ▶

Mannix Construction Inc., Maintenance of Way Division introduces its first tie inserter. This machine hydraulically inserts a rail tie in only 12 seconds and can travel up to 20 miles (33 kilometres) per hour.

A BANKER WITH A LION'S HEART

In March 1969, Arthur F. Mayne became Loram's first out-side director. A small-town Ontario boy who joined the Royal Bank of Canada in 1925, Mayne quickly became known for his brilliant facility for international banking. Appointed associate general manager (non-domestic) in 1955, by 1960, he was a director of the bank and headed the bank's international operations. In this capacity, Mayne was, in large part, responsible for the bank's successful exit from Cuba.

Following Castro's entry into Havana early in 1959, an anti-American backlash set in. In October 1960, all American banks in Cuba were expropriated. Despite the exemption of Canada's two banks from this order, Mayne reported that profitable operations in Cuba seemed unlikely, as Banco Nacional de Cuba began to assert a monopoly over all banking on the island. By December 1960, the Royal Bank negotiated an exit from Cuban retail banking. Unlike its American counterparts, the bank managed to repatriate its Cuban investment — about $8.8 million US.

In 1964, Mayne, then executive vice president, helped revamp the bank's corporate image. As a first step, the bank's venerable rampant-lions logo was replaced by a lion-and-globe motif, the now-famous "Leo." Working with bank president, W. Earle McLaughlin, and chief general manager, John Coleman, Mayne ushered in the age of modern management at the Royal Bank.

Mayne's financial advice, provided from his lifelong business experience — he was F.S. Mannix's banker during the end of the elder Mr. Mannix's career — contributed invaluably to the Loram board of directors. When Art Mayne passed away in Montreal on September 17, 1972, his loss was felt keenly by all those who knew him in his long association with three generations of the Mannix family.

That was after the first fire. I said 'Hell, there's nothing to this project. It's over, productivity is going great, and everything is going well.' When the place burned down the second time, I said to myself, 'My God, is this thing ever going to finish?' Some people just quit and said that they couldn't handle staying there anymore."

After the second major fire, Mannix mounted yet another airlift of crew off the project and built yet another camp. Despite all obstacles, Mount Wright was finally completed in the early part of 1975. And while the story of Mount Wright was painful from day one, ultimately, the project had a happy ending. "We eventually negotiated a revised contract with the owner, so Mount Wright turned out to be a very successful project for us financially," said Lemecha. "We left there with a very good relationship with the owner, Quebec Cartier Mining. As a matter of fact, a number of years later, we went back to that site and did more work for them."

Not only did Mount Wright turn out to be a success financially, it would serve as an invaluable lesson for future projects. "I would attribute our success at places like James Bay and Gregg River to what happened to us at Mount Wright," Lemecha said. "At that time, we

An aerial view of the almost completed Mount Wright iron ore facility.

1970 ▶

Mannix Co. Ltd. will construct the Bighorn Dam for Calgary Power Ltd. across this gorge on the North Saskatchewan River.

1970 ▶

The Bighorn Dam project uses Mannix-developed equipment innovations such as this push/pull on the front of a Cat 657 scraper. It allows the scraper to be combined with other scrapers for greater production.

were kind of a new generation coming into project management. We were relatively inexperienced at that kind of task. We really hadn't done it before. I was 30 years old at the time that I became involved, and I think that Gerry Scraba was about the same age. Most of our engineers were in their late 20s to early 30s, too. So we really went through the learning curve on that one. You might say that we had the misfortune of picking one of the worst jobs and worst times to go through that learning curve, but we sure learned a lot. So when we came to big projects like James Bay and Gregg River, we knew that we could use our experience from Mount Wright to make sure that those jobs would be successful." And that may well be the greatest triumph to come out of Mount Wright.

The Story of Mica Creek
"Against all odds, we did make it."

In 1973, C.L. (Dil) Robertson replaced Graham Pollock as president of Mannix Co. Ltd. Born in Calgary on November 26, 1926, Robertson attended high school there. At 19, he entered the world of construction. His first exposure to the Mannix outfit was as a member of the labour gang on the Barrier Dam project in the mid-1940s. After working for several other construction outfits, Robertson cofounded a firm that specialized in subcontracting highway construction projects. By 1952, Robertson took over sole ownership of this enterprise, which he named C.L. Robertson Ltd. For the most part, this company performed highway work as a subcontractor to Mannix Ltd.

C.L. (Dil) Robertson becomes president of Mannix Co. Ltd. in 1973.

Mannix Robertson Ltd., a Mannix subsidiary, was formed in 1954. Due to the increased highway competition, the firm was dissolved in 1958. Robertson then worked for several other construction companies before returning to Mannix in the Sixties, becoming construction manager in 1966. "That meant that I had the responsibility of working with the Highway Division, the Heavy Construction Division, the Pipeline Division, the Railroad Division and the Mining Division," Robertson recalled. "Shortly after I got that position, we were involved in a real bad project at Metaline Falls called Boundary Dam. It was an underground powerhouse and a thin-arched concrete dam. I've always said it was the first underground powerhouse built in the States, but it might have been the second. Anyway, we were in bad trouble on it. We were behind schedule and we were pretty heavily overrunning in costs. And one of the dictates I was given as construction manager was to go down and see what I could do to straighten Boundary out. Well, that was pretty tough for me because I had never been on a big concrete project

before, but I went down. I made two trips down and was impressed that there was a lot wrong with the job. Graham Pollock was the president of the construction company in those days and Graham said, 'Well, what are you going to do?' I said, 'We have to pull the project manager out of there.' He said, 'Well, that's fine, but who are you going to put in?' So I said that I was going to run it."

After taking the most unusual step of personally taking charge of the project, Robertson moved onsite. "I ran the job for six to eight months and there were two major problems," he said. "The job was behind schedule, it was overrunning, but we also had an intolerable situation with the owner, Seattle City Light. Our company had a great dislike for the owner's project manager, Robert Brown, and he didn't think any more of us. So I hit the job knowing that the crew was demoralized because they were being inspected so critically; anything they did, the owner was able to

1971 ▶

Bangladesh announces its independence from Pakistan. Sheik Mujib, pointing, leads the new country.

1971 ▶

The term "Silicon Valley" is coined and Intel Corporation of Santa Clara, California, introduces its first microprocessor chip, the 4004. The chip is shown both in a magnified image and its actual size.

Actual size.

find a problem with it. But I made a real point of getting to know Brown and making him feel that I liked him and making him feel that he was part of our problem — he had to help us get out of it. There was one other real important thing. My wife got to know Catherine Brown very well. They became friendly and did a lot of things together and I think that helped my association with Brown and helped the project. The long and short of it was that we were down about $6 million bucks and this was only a $28-million job; in today's money, it would be a $100-million job. It was a big job, it was a critical job, and we were able to finish just about on time. The owner was happy with us and we were able to get a claim settled. We still lost something like a couple of million bucks, but it wasn't as much blood as it had been before."

After his success at Boundary, Robertson was named vice president and general manager of Mannix Co. Ltd. in 1970. Two years later, he moved up to executive vice president and, in 1973, he became president. "Boundary was an important job in my career and it was an important job in the company's career," he said. "The reason it was important was that following right on the heels of that job, there was a big underground powerhouse going to be built at Revelstoke. So we were able to take all of the experience that we accumulated from running Boundary, and we had a crew that could go right into Mica Creek at Revelstoke. So we bid Mica."

Located near the confluence of the Columbia, Canoe and Wood rivers, 85 miles (137 kilometres) north of the town of Revelstoke, British Columbia, the Mica

The Mica Dam underground powerhouse excavation includes the construction of two manifold tunnels (one is shown), to direct the Columbia River flow from the powerhouse generators to the tailrace tunnels and finally back to the river channel. The varying contour of the manifold directs water flow.

Creek work site was a familiar place for Mannix crews. Between 1965 and 1967, they had helped drive two diversion tunnels to channel the flow of the Columbia River, the first step in the construction of the 800-foot-high (245-metre) Mica Creek Dam. On March 29, 1973, with the lowering of the outlet work gates, the dam became officially operational. In April 1973, as excavation of the powerhouse access and tailrace tunnels got under way, Mannix Co. Ltd. was awarded a five-year contract by B.C. Hydro & Power Authority to construct the Mica Creek underground powerhouse.

"Mica Creek was a challenge," said Dale Anderson, who left Peter Kiewit Sons' Company to join Mannix Co. Ltd. as project manager at Mica. "It was such a tremendous job. The Kiewit company had also bid the job but they were considerably higher than the Mannix company. Everyone was afraid of the tight schedule. When I accepted the job, everyone with Kiewit told me that I would never make the schedule. It was a very complex underground project. The logistics were also terrible. Most of the contractors who had bid the work felt it couldn't be completed in the time frame. To me, it was a real challenge."

Like the Mount Wright project, Mica Creek encountered labour disruptions. "We ran into some problems on the job," Anderson said. "There was an NDP government in power. They're labour supported, and the labour unions felt they had the upper hand in the province, so they decided to wage some jurisdictional wars. None of the employees were ours. They were supplied to us by Columbia Hydro Constructors, which was

1971 ▶

J.H. (Harry) Irving is named president of Alberta Coal.

1971 ▶

Ferguson Jenkins, the Chatham, Ontario, right-handed pitcher, wins the National League's Cy Young Award as the best pitcher in the league. In his 19-year Major League Baseball career, he is the only pitcher to have more than 3,000 strikeouts with fewer than 1,000 walks.

1971 ▶

Individuals who fish commercially continue to be an important part of Atlantic Canada's economy.

an employment agency that was set up by B.C. Hydro. In one year, we had 44 illegal work stoppages. We lost something in the neighbourhood of 275,000 man-hours. It was a tight schedule to start with, and when we met this sort of disruption, our schedule kept moving back. I think it was pride in the organization and pride in ourselves that prompted us to keep at it. We wanted to show the construction world that we were one outfit that could make an almost impossible completion date. And we made it. Against all odds, we did make it."

"I used to lose a lot of sleep over it but everybody on the team devoted a lot of effort," continued Anderson. "It was a very tight-knit community at Mica Creek. We were working around the clock. We had three shifts going for 24 hours a day. We worked 12 days on and two days off. So to let off a little steam, we would throw parties. On a quarterly basis, we'd have a rip-roaring party and everybody would just let their hair down and relax and get rejuvenated for another three months of hard work. That job brought together a lot of good young people. We brought other young engineers and supervisors, virtually from all across Canada. And they matured on the job because they were given responsibility. And they took on that responsibility and developed and matured as construction men. They got good training and developed a sense of camaraderie and a high regard for the Mannix organization itself."

"In 1975, I was given the job of manager of Heavy Construction Division, so I left Mica Creek," Anderson said. "But I want to say that I couldn't have done anything without the full support of the Mannix organization. They were proud contractors — particularly old F.C. Mannix. He was an entrepreneur and a hard-nosed old contractor that knew the business. He indicated to us on more than one occasion that he was very proud of the way we conducted ourselves and the way we performed on one of the major underground powerhouses in the world. It was one of the toughest."

Following Anderson's promotion, Mo Korol was named Mica Creek project manager in 1975. Under Korol's guidance, work progressed rapidly. After almost five years, stretching from April 5, 1973, to nearly the last day of 1977, Mannix crews excavated one million cubic yards (765,000 cubic metres) of rock, placed 250,000 cubic yards (191,000 cubic metres) of concrete, and installed almost 10 miles (16 kilometres) of piping and 11 miles (17 kilometres) of conduit and cable. They also transported 22,000 tons (20,000 tonnes) of machinery and equipment to the powerhouse for installation. During the five years, the work force averaged more than 700 people. It peaked at 1,600 in the summer and fall of 1974.

"It had a big impact on the group of companies."

While Mica was an extremely successful job for Mannix Co. Ltd., it also had a long-term negative impact on the construction company's future. "The Mica Dam project really affected the history of future events in Mannix Co. Ltd.," explained Alex Cummings, whom F.P. Mannix had brought in from the field to serve as Loram's vice president and general manager. In so doing, young F.P. Mannix continued a Mannix family management tradition — recruit good people and train them for the task at hand.

Born in Winnipeg in 1928, Cummings graduated from high school at Hamiota, Manitoba. He then went to work for Imperial Oil. In his six-year

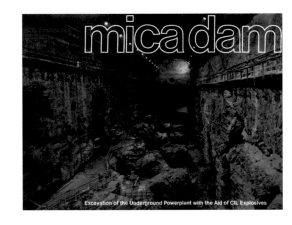

mica dam

Excavation of the Underground Powerplant with the Aid of CIL Explosives

Above: The interior of the Mica Dam underground powerhouse. Blasted out of solid rock, the powerhouse is shown after major benching is completed. Circuit breaker chamber openings are shown on the left with outlet tunnels to the lower penstocks on the right.

Below: The partially completed Mica Dam powerhouse.

1971 ▶

Alberta Coal Ltd. forms Gregg River Resources Ltd. to operate the proposed metallurgical mine at Gregg River, near Hinton, Alberta.

Gregg River Resources Ltd.

FIRST IMPRESSIONS

When F.P. Mannix was named president of Loram in 1969, one of his first acts was to recruit Alex Cummings as his vice president and general manager. After Cummings had wound up his affairs at Bighorn Dam, F.P. Mannix sent an airplane to take him back to Calgary. "I didn't even have a suit with me," recalled Cummings. "At a project site there is no need for that kind of thing, so the best I could muster up was a pair of cowboy boots, some western slacks and a western shirt." This rather relaxed form of corporate attire caused quite a first impression. Cummings, who stands well over six feet tall without his cowboy boots on, would be a hard man not to notice, even if he was not your new boss.

"I got to Calgary in the middle of the afternoon," Cummings said. "Freddie's first comment was, 'Haven't you got anything better to wear than that?' But, despite my appearance, he decided to introduce me to all the presidents. Back in those days, Loram had about nine companies; that meant nine presidents. So here I am in my cowboy boots and away we went. There was a very interesting reaction from most folks including Graham Pollock, who was president of the construction company. He was the chap I had been reporting to as project manager at Bighorn. Needless to say, he was quite shocked that he would now be reporting to me.

"Somehow, I got through that day. I do remember one amusing comment, however. Wally Gray, who was a very straight-forward fellow, was the controller of Loram. After my interview with Wally, he said to Freddie, 'Now I'm working for a cowboy!'"

tenure there he progressed from road man to chief surveyor. Recruited by Seismic Ventures, Cummings spent the subsequent four years managing seismic crews throughout Alberta. In 1955, he went to work for Burns & Dutton, where he gained experience as project manager in the heavy construction aspects of their business. In 1962, he joined Standard Gravel as senior estimator. In this capacity, he worked with Mannix on many large joint ventures. In 1969, Cummings accepted an offer to join Mannix as a senior estimator in its engineering department and in 1970, he was named project manager for Bighorn Dam.

"By the time 1972 had come along, we'd operated the project at less overall cost to the owner than we had anticipated doing," said Cummings. "We'd certainly operated it to the point where we knew we had made a good contribution to our shareholders' pocketbooks by virtue of the other things we did on the project to save money. I guess that, perhaps, found itself noticed around the outfit and that led to a communication that young Freddie Mannix sent me in July of 1972. That's when he suggested I come up as vice president and general manager of Loram. That announcement was a fairly great shock as far as I was concerned because it meant a little end-run on quite a few people. I realized the political implications of the promotion, but I had no idea of what the impact would be at the time.

"Freddie sent an airplane to pick me up at Bighorn. There was an airstrip there that could handle one of our aircraft, so I came to Calgary. That's how I started. Freddie led me into the general manager's office and sat me down at the desk and said, 'Here's your office and here are a few problems. Go to it.' Well, back in those days, Loram had nine company presidents reporting to me, one of which was my former boss. Then there was the staff of Loram, which would probably be at least six or seven people. So all of a sudden, I had 15 people reporting to me, few of whom I knew. As Freddie had told me earlier, the philosophy behind my promotion was that 'You can't train a person to handle people, but you can train a person to handle corporate affairs.' That was the philosophy they were using right off the bat. You kind of learn by doing. So, immediately, that's what I had to start doing."

"Mica Dam was bid right about the time I arrived in Loram," continued Cummings. "Graham Pollock was involved a lot in that project, in putting it together. We had formed a joint venture to bid that project which involved Kiewit, Zachry and several other major firms in the United States. The project was bid competitively on a firm-price or

1971 ▶

R.J. (Ron) White replaces Buck McDonald as president of Pembina Pipe Line. McDonald joins the Pembina board of directors.

1971 ▶

Ugandan President Obote is ousted by a military coup. Major-General Idi Amin, shown taking the oath of office, seizes power and begins to liquidate his opponents.

1971 ▶

Techman Ltd. provides studies for a pipeline from Prudhoe Bay, Alaska, to Edmonton, Alberta.

unit-price basis to start with. Having received the bids, the owner either decided that they were too high or else wanted to allow the bidders an opportunity to come back and take a second go at reducing the price of the project. I suspect it was strictly because the price was too high. At any rate, they requested proposals that would involve target-type submissions.

"In the process of developing a new bid, we decided to move our partners out of the picture. We thought the fee that would come to us as the sponsor would not be substantial enough if we had to share it with all the various partners — at least that's what we perceived at the time. So Kiewit, Zachry and the other partners were, one at a time, all generally crowded out of the joint venture. Since the project had changed from a highly risky job to a non-risk one, the decision seemed to have a reasonable logic at the time, so I supported the idea. Ultimately, we turned in a proposal that Mannix do the job on its own, and the project turned out to be quite successful on that basis. I guess with a few more years of experience in my new job, I would have realized the implications of what was going to happen in the future, but I didn't at the time. What did happen was that our relationship with the other major partners in the community was very severely and adversely affected for years to come. That decision, in fact, probably denied us the opportunity of joint venturing with those companies in other projects for at least the next three, four or five years. There are still some hurts around, as far as I understand. Business has long memories."

F.P. Mannix concurred, adding, "What happened was we put a joint venture together. Mica was called a fixed-price job. Then it was recalled and it was called a cost-plus-target job. And it became apparent that we made a basic error in judgment because we should have carried the exact same partners and the same relationship through to the other but we tried to cut them out of it. The result of that was a lot of bad will with the partners. Yes, we got the job and we made a bit of money, but it cost us more in terms of the relationship with partners."

"It had a big impact on the group of companies," F.P. Mannix said. "It was a hidden impact because it was at the top level. We got very defensive and very tough on approvals and making these guys tell us what they were going to do before they'd do it. We overreacted to that, frankly, but understandably, because here was a guy who had been trusted and he went off on his own — Graham Pollock went off and committed to things before he had approval from upstairs. In fact, it took three weeks until Loram heard about it. We just clamped down on the whole

outfit as a result of that experience. In some areas it was the right thing to do and in some it wasn't. We got very tough on controls, as a result of that experience, which was bad for the outfit in general terms. It was something that Ronnie had to correct when he came in, but it was directly related to that Mica experience."

Recruiting a Silver Star to the Outfit

In 1975, Brock Montgomery and Everett Costello began their retirements. At this time, F.P. Mannix temporarily activated a Loram Co. Ltd. subsidiary called Lorinco. In his capacity as president of Lorinco, Fred P. Mannix recruited David McClement and P.G. Clarke to be his two top advisors. "One day F.P. came to me and said, 'We'd like to have you come in with David McClement and myself,'" explained P.G. Clarke. "The name was given at that time as Lorinco. Now Lorinco was an offshoot of Bowfort/Loram, but it had never been active. I believe Lorinco stood for Loram Investment Company. In any event, Fred P. explained that the reason this was being set up was that F.C. wanted to become less and less active. Brock and Everett, who had been with F.C. throughout those years prior to Lorinco, were also in the stage of retiring. So rather than move into Bowfort and disrupt that as an entity, we set up in a new company that was independent of Bowfort, but was really performing the functions that Bowfort had handled before. We were the buffer now between Bowfort, who were three people who felt they wanted to retire and become less and less active, and the operating companies."

"This was the big thing, that Everett and Brock were getting out," continued Clarke. "We were replacing F.C., Brock and Everett, in the sense that they were still there, but they were very inactive in the day-to-day things. We took over what their functions had been. I acted as construction advisor to the president, who was Fred P., and David was the financial man. Fred P., Dave McClement and I were the three closest to what was going on at the time. We had to be fully knowledgeable about what was going on in the companies. All bids that went in by the coal company, on properties or whatever, by the construction company on construction projects, by Pembina on land purchases or development expenditures, the three of us sat down and discussed them. So underneath Freddie, the Lorinco group was reported to by all the active companies."

"David McClement, P.G. Clarke and I took over the role that Dad, Brock, Everett and David had done; David being consistent because he came with me," explained F.P. Mannix. "That meant we had to replace

1971 ▶

Dr. Gerhard Herzberg of Canada's National Research Council wins the Nobel Prize in chemistry for his work identifying molecules in space.

THE KEEPERS OF THE FLAME RETIRE

In 1975, Everett Costello and Brock Montgomery retired from active management. Their combined service with the Loram Group exceeded 60 years.

When Everett Costello joined Fred Mannix & Company, Ltd. as assistant secretary and general counsel in 1946, the company's head office was located on Seventh Avenue West "over the cafe," and numbered eight people. A lifelong friend of F.C. Mannix, Costello dedicated his working life to the development and preservation of the Mannix family business. Serving as a director, counsellor, chairman and confidant, Costello remained in the saddle until the third generation held the reins firmly in hand.

Brock Montgomery's association with the Loram Group began in 1948. In 1950, when the group entered big-inch pipelining, Montgomery was appointed field engineer on the Mannix section of the Trans Mountain line from Edmonton to Vancouver. He then worked on most of the subsequent lines built by the company. After a three-year stint with Bechtel Corporation of San Francisco as project manager on Canadian pipelines, Montgomery returned to the Loram Group to research and design pipeline gathering and transmission systems. In 1961, Everett Costello appointed him vice president and general manager of Loram. After 1968, when his health dictated a slowing of pace, Montgomery helped hold the outfit on track by serving as vice president and director of Loram and other companies in the group for many years.

me as president of Loram. I had two candidates in mind. The first was Wally Gray [assistant general manager of Loram], who died suddenly of lung cancer. The second was Graham Pollock. Graham had screwed up on Mica. Instead of firing him, we tried to salvage him, moving him up to Loram to become president. But then Graham quit before he could become president. What happened was that every week I consulted with the older generation. Usually on Thursday at 10 a.m., I took Graham with me to Bowfort's office. I remember I had 73 items on my weekly list to go over with McClement, Costello and Montgomery and Dad for advice. There were magnificent problems. Everywhere you looked there were alligators and snakes. We met until 6:00 p.m., but I was elated because we got all 73 items on my list covered.

"When Graham and I got in the elevator, Graham turned to me and said, 'Christ, Fred, those guys tore you to pieces! They called you a dumb so-and-so. They called you every name in the book!' I said, 'That's just the older generation's construction talk, it's not personal. It wasn't an attack of me." But Graham said he could not work that way. He quit on Monday. So I went from two candidates to zero." F.P. Mannix then went searching outside the organization. He found someone with 35 years' experience as a leader of men — retired Lieutenant-General S.C. (Stan) Waters.

Stan Waters was born on June 14, 1920, in Winnipeg. In 1941, while attending the University of Alberta, he enlisted in the ranks of the Canadian Armed Forces. For the next 35 years, he would hold every commissioned rank from second lieutenant to lieutenant-general. Waters served with the First Canadian/U.S. Special Service Force and the First Canadian Parachute Battalion in operations in the Aleutians, North Africa, Italy, southern France and Germany. For gallantry in action at Anzio, Italy, he was awarded the United States' Silver Star. Waters, who earned the nickname "Muddy" while in the army, spent his postwar service in command and staff appointments in Canada, Germany, India, Pakistan, Belgium and the United States.

Stan Waters, shown in 1957 as a Lieutenant-Colonel of the Canadian Army. He becomes president of Loram Co. Ltd. in 1976.

1971 ▶

Papa Doc Duvalier, Haiti's president, dies after 13 years of dictatorial rule. His son, Jean-Claude (Baby Doc), becomes "president for life" and continues the repression.

1971 ▶

Canada, through an act of Parliament, begins her long, and sometimes torturous, conversion to the metric system.

In 1972, Waters was promoted to the rank of lieutenant-general and assigned to National Defence Headquarters as deputy chief, defence staff. He was appointed commander, mobile command in 1973, where he served until July 4, 1975. Soon after retiring from the army, he joined Loram. "I had been in discussion with Freddie [F.P.] Mannix for several months about possible employment in the Loram Group of Companies," Waters said. "I was looking at several job opportunities, but I'm from the West — I'm an Alberta boy, and I was trying to get back to Alberta. This was the most attractive opportunity I had, although I was seriously considered for ombudsman in this province, which I think would have been a very unfortunate choice because I tend to be hard-nosed and inflexible." Not long after joining Loram, "much to my surprise, I was made president of the Loram Group."

F.P. Mannix explains how the decision was made to make Waters president. "I hired Stan Waters for two reasons," he said. "First, it was two years before Ronnie would be ready to come in and, as a military man, Waters was used to two-year commands. Secondly, I hired him because we needed a disciplinarian who would take over from me and help with the succession plan for Ronnie. Waters didn't even know what he was coming for. I had him do a three-month complete operational audit which consisted of two internal audits, engineering and operations, and he spent five weeks auditing the offices. At the end of his two-day report to me, when he told me all the things he thought were wrong, I said, 'Fine. Now you go fix it. You're president.'"

January 1, 1975, the Mannix construction company, Mannix Co. Ltd., changes its name to Loram International Ltd.

Loram International Ltd. Tackles "the Project of the Century"

On January 1, 1975, Mannix Co. Ltd.'s name was changed to Loram International Ltd. Although the company operations would remain the same, the announcement was a sad day for many old-timers. For the first time since F.S. Mannix's horses proudly bore the Mannix "M" on their backs, the letter "M" would no longer grace the construction company's name.

Not long after the name change, bids were called for the construction of a huge underground powerhouse in Eastern Canada. The experience of Boundary and Mica gave the group the confidence to bid. "On April 1, 1976, we were awarded the LG-2 project in northern Quebec for the James Bay Energy Corporation," said Gary Donnelly, who left Peter Kiewit & Sons' Company in 1973 to join Mannix as Mica Creek general superintendent. "I was assigned as project manager. It was part of the James Bay megaproject. In Canada, we called it the project of the century."

The goal of this megaproject was to develop the extensive hydroelectric capabilities of the La Grande Rivière as it ran through the heart of the 400,000-square-mile (1,036,000-square-kilometre) James Bay region. From the town of Fort George, the La Grande flowed eastward more than 535 miles (861 kilometres). The drainage basin of some 916,000 square miles (2,372,440 square kilometres) covered almost one-tenth of the province. The driving force behind this endeavour was the James Bay Energy Corporation (Société d'énergie de la Baie James), a subsidiary of Hydro-Québec and the James Bay Development Corporation. Their plans called for the construction of four powerhouses and two major diversions along a 288-mile (463-kilometre) stretch of the La Grande. Once in place, the four powerhouses would total an installed capacity of 10,000 megawatts.

Budgeted at $14 billion over 14 years, the work involved 50 million cubic yards (38 million cubic metres) of excavation and 190 million cubic yards (145 million cubic metres) of fill. The job required the construction of more than 1,000 miles (1,600 kilometres) of new roads through the wilderness of northwestern Quebec. It employed

1972 ▶

Team Canada narrowly wins the first Canada-Soviet hockey series.

1972 ▶

Sectarian violence flares in Northern Ireland. Protesters and police are shown a week after Bloody Sunday, the day when British troops killed 13 Roman Catholic demonstrators in Londonderry.

approximately 16,000 workers and required more than $500 million worth of construction equipment. For ease of identification, each of the four powerhouses was given its own designation number. "On the La Grande, there were to be four main sites," explained Dale Anderson, who was intimately involved in the bidding process. "Instead of saying La Grande Site Number One, and La Grande Site Number Two, it was easier to use abbreviations. So they used LG-1, LG-2, and so on."

For Loram International Ltd., the initial bidding effort for James Bay focused on winning the contract for the LG-2 powerhouse. Situated 720 air miles (1,160 air kilometres) northwest of Montreal, on the south bank of the La Grande Rivière, LG-2 had a designed capacity of 5,328 megawatts. Located 450 feet (137 metres) underground, the power-house was divided into east and west sections. Each section contained eight generating units. Main access to the powerhouse would be provided by a tunnel 38 feet (11.5 metres) wide, 30 feet (nine metres) high, and 3,270 feet (997 metres) long. Four 3,800-foot (1,158-metre) tailrace tunnels would carry the water back to the La Grande Rivière. LG-2 would be the largest underground powerhouse in Canada and the fifth largest anywhere in the world. Its 16 turbogenerators would produce 35 billion kilowatt-hours per year — enough electricity to serve a city of four million people.

"The major one was LG-2," said Anderson. "It was the control structure for the whole job. At that time, we were the only contractors in Canada with recent experience in underground powerhouses so we joint ventured with Morrison-Knudsen. On the first job, LG-2 East, we could

An overall map of the James Bay hydroelectric power project. The powerhouses are shown as LG-1 through LG-4.

not come to a consensus of agreement on what the price should be. We capitulated to M-K and we were pretty high on the job. When it came time to bid the second LG-2 underground powerhouse, LG-2 West, again, we couldn't agree on what the price should be. We offered M-K the opportunity to accept our price and stay in the joint venture with us, because we did not want to add the additional money that they wanted. They declined, so they left the joint venture. We were virtually left to do the job on our own and we left with very little money on the table. We were just marginally below the next bidder."

Shortly after winning the bid, the joint venture team of la Compagnie Loram (Québec) Ltée. and Komo Construction Inc., commonly called Loram-Komo, began work on the west powerhouse at LG-2. La Compagnie Loram, a wholly owned subsidiary of Loram International Ltd., was the sponsor.

James Bay proved to be a highly successful job, in part because of the group's recent experience at Mount Wright and Mica. With the memory of those experiences still fresh, Mannix staff watched the political developments in Quebec apprehensively. In the fall of 1976, René Lévesque and his Parti Québécois swept to their first electoral victory. Given the separatist tendencies of this party, many observers in Quebec wondered if Lévesque's election might trigger another period of instability. There was real concern that the province would plunge into a period reminiscent of the dark days of the October Crisis of 1970.

For a while, it seemed the James Bay project might fall victim to the confrontation and violence that had plagued the Mount Wright project. Before the 1976

1972 ▶

Alberta Coal Ltd. is reorganized and renamed Manalta Coal Ltd. to reflect its broader market.

1972 ▶

The compact disc is invented by RCA.

arrival of the Loram crews, there was a series of disturbing incidents near the LG-2 work site.

"In the early to middle 1970s, there was a lot of labour trouble in Quebec," Gary Donnelly explained. "In fact, the year before we came in, they had burned down the camp at LG-2. They had a camp for roughly 2,000 men with a big kitchen, and a bunch of hooligans burned down the whole bloody thing. Fortunately, there was a judicial inquiry into the crime shortly after that. As a result, the unions had cleaned up their act quite a bit by the time we got there. We still had one strike in the first few months we were on the job. When that happened, we were concerned that things might get violent. We decided that it was impossible to continue work, so we shipped everybody out. If we had kept working, things might have gotten rough. We had a pretty interesting time there for a while. But things soon changed, and it became a good climate to work in. The government came up with a law or two to keep things under control, and we knew how to handle the situation because of our experiences at Mount Wright."

"There was a real strong nationalistic feeling in Quebec at that time," Donnelly said. "There was a widespread feeling that Quebec should be in charge of its own destiny and that it didn't need any foreigners from the rest of Canada coming in to help. Despite this feeling, though, they didn't really have the experience to build something like LG-2 entirely with French people. I think that a lot of the top brass in Quebec knew that, even if it wasn't common knowledge with the unions. The unions tended to take the opposite view. They put a lot of propaganda in the newspapers, things like, 'We don't need people named Donnelly building this project.'"

"But we never faced anything like what happened at Mount Wright," Donnelly said. "We took a number of steps to prevent that kind of thing. To overcome some of that nationalistic feeling, we got a joint venture partner that was French. The authorities wanted

THE BIRTH OF THE PERSONAL COMPUTER INDUSTRY

In 1975, a small Albuquerque firm named Micro Instrumentation and Telemetry Systems (MITS) started a revolution in the computer field with its introduction of the Altair computer. Named after a Star Trek episode entitled "A Voyage to Altair," this first computer used Intel's eight-bit microprocessor and was sold primarily as a kit to be assembled by the user. While futuristic in concept, the Altair was not so futuristic in other respects such as its input/output system, which consisted of switches and lights. Having no video display or keyboard, the Altair definitely belonged to an era in which the term "user-friendly" had yet to be invented.

While the Altair computer's technology was fairly primitive, this new product marked a major turning point in the history of computing. The Altair's primary claim to fame now is that it led directly to the formation of two companies whose names would become synonymous with the term personal computer. In 1975, the Homebrew Computer Club, the first personal computer users group, was formed and began meeting once a month at the Stanford Linear Accelerator to discuss ways of using and improving the Altair. Among the founding members of this group were Stephen Wozniak, Steven Jobs and Bill Gates.

That same year, Gates and another member of the club, Paul Allen, adapted BASIC for the Altair and sold it to MITS. Later in 1975, Gates founded Microsoft, which was destined to become the largest software company in the world. Meanwhile, Wozniak and Jobs, who felt Altair needed considerable improvement, were designing their own personal computer, the Apple I, which they introduced in 1976. In 1977, Apple Computer was formed in Cupertino, California, and the company introduced its now famous logo and Apple II, the first true personal computer and the product that launched the entire personal computer industry. At the end of 1977, the company's first year of business, sales of the Apple II had reached $2.5 million. Just two years later, Apple's sales surpassed the $70-million mark.

1972 ▶

In British Columbia's Fraser River Canyon, the CNR suffers from rock falling from cliffs above the tracks. Mannix Co. Ltd. provides rock bolts, hydraulic scaling and sprayed concrete (shotcrete), to solve the problem.

1972 ▶

Canada's Anik-A1 is the world's first geostationary domestic communications satellite.

Quebec involvement in Quebec work. They didn't particularly care for a company coming out of Calgary and having 100 per cent of the work with all the profits going back to Alberta. To avoid those kinds of feelings, we got into a joint venture with the Komo company, out of Quebec City. We still had financial control, since we held about 75 per cent of the project. So that gave us control as far as decision making was concerned. We were the sponsor and they were mostly a financial partner. They did, however, give us two engineers who spoke French, which helped us a great deal."

"Of course, the language problem was always a potential sore point," Donnelly said. "One of the most difficult things about the job was that you had to speak French. Most of us weren't conversant in the language at the time we were awarded the contract, so we hustled just about all of the anglophones off to French school for a three-week crash course. In retrospect, those courses were a key to our being able to function on the job. We also took steps to keep troublemakers away from the work site. We didn't want any thugs around, so we restricted access to the job. There was a list of people who weren't to be hired based on past experience. When we were at Mount Wright, we had developed a pretty reliable work force. We had a list of 600 or 700 employees that we used. We knew they were good people and that we would have no problem with them."

In addition to the precautions taken by the Loram people at the job site, the Quebec government

An interior view of the partially completed LG-2 underground powerhouse.

also took measures to ensure that work proceeded smoothly. With unemployment levels rising through the province, it was apparent to everyone concerned that the continuation of the James Bay job was vital for the provincial economy. As a spokesman for the Construction Association of Montreal said during the course of work, "Without James Bay, Quebec's economy would probably go down the drain. One of the only places people are working is James Bay."

The government may also have hoped to use the time-honoured art of political patronage at James Bay to ensure its continued electoral success. That may be one reason why the government awarded the project's 14,000 workers a significant pay boost in 1980. The result of this pay raise was that the James Bay workers made five per cent more than other construction workers in the province. At the time, many people argued that this extra pay for "remote project" work was an attempt to influence the upcoming referendum on Quebec's separatist status. Whatever its purpose, the pay hike made James Bay an even more attractive place to work for the construction workers of Quebec.

With labour peace assured at James Bay, the Loram team could safely direct the project toward its scheduled completion date. By the end of 1977, the project was 35 per cent complete. In July 1977, the Loram-Komo team won an additional contract at James Bay to do work on the Eastmain-Opinaca-La Grande (EOL) diversion scheme.

1972 ▶

Terrorists attack the Israeli Olympic team in Munich.

1972 ▶

The women who help make the Maintenance of Way Division successful attend the annual Christmas party in Minnesota.

"The project turned out to be a real winner," said Anderson. "We were able to take our people from Mica and put them right on that job, and they just did a helluva job. It was a target job and we finished below budget and ahead of schedule. The owner was very pleased with the way Loram International performed."

By the late 1970s, Loram had developed an incredible large-project experience. At the time of completion of the LG-2 project, only 12 underground powerhouses of any magnitude had been built in the world. Loram crews had built three of them — Boundary Dam in Washington, Mica Creek in British Columbia and LG-2 in northern Quebec. However, by the mid-1980s, this experience would no longer be required in a radically changed construction business.

Pembina Capitalizes on the Learning Curve
The First Attempt to Take Pembina Private

If only a single trait could be used to characterize Pembina Pipe Line's employees and management, one ability — a company theme perhaps — was Pembina's skill in learning from mistakes. Throughout its history, the company and its people made errors, quite a normal behaviour in both business and life. However, the same mistakes were seldom made twice. In fact, Pembina consistently profited from its mistakes, capitalizing on knowledge gained to reach successes it might not otherwise reach. The history of Pembina Pipe Line is replete with examples of men flying by the seat of their pants, getting into trouble, learning their way out and evolving into masters of that particular art or discipline.

During the late Sixties and on into the Seventies, Pembina also demonstrated one of the other great strengths of the company — that while people were integral to the operations, no one person was irreplaceable; the organization could operate despite changes in top management. This quality can clearly be seen in the fact that even though Pembina was led by several different presidents between 1968 and 1977, the company continued to run smoothly.

In 1969, Pembina president Harry Booth left Pembina and was succeeded by J.A. (Buck) McDonald. A Mannix pipeline veteran with 15 years' experience in the field and mud around Drayton Valley, McDonald had risen through the ranks to become general manager under Booth. A tremendous field manager, whose interest in people established a great esprit de corps among Drayton Valley employees, McDonald had been trained as an engineer. He played a key role in Pembina's switch to automatic gauging.

In 1971, when McDonald moved up to Pembina's board of directors, he was replaced by R.J. (Ron) White, a 20-year veteran of the oil industry. White ran the company for two years, overseeing the amalgamation of Pembina and its wholly owned subsidiary, Pembina Products Pipe Line Ltd. He also guided the company exploration activities in the Western Canada Sedimentary Basin, Northwest Territories and Arctic islands, along with a couple of new areas — the offshore Atlantic and St. Lawrence

"I WANT A GREYBEARD AROUND TO HELP THE BOYS"

In 1976, W.D.H. Gardiner, deputy chairman and executive vice president of the Royal Bank of Canada, joined the board of directors of Loram Co. Ltd. Gardiner's 40-year career with the Royal Bank began in Walkerville, Ontario, in 1935. He became director of the bank and was appointed vice chairman in 1973.

"I met Fred C. Mannix through Art Mayne," Gardiner explained. "At that time, Fred C. Mannix had asked Arthur Mayne to be the outside director to help him bring the boys along. Then Art Mayne died very early in the game with cancer. About a year after his death, Fred said, 'Doug, if you don't mind, you better come along and take Art's place here because we would like to talk to you. If anything happened to me, I want a greybeard around to help the boys.'"

"The first really serious thing I got involved with was when Fred C. decided that he would buy out Hudson Bay Mining's interest in Western Decalta," recalled Gardiner. "We put that together, encouraged by both the boys, I must say. We had David McClement do a lot of homework on it, and everything he turned up verified our reasoning. It was typical of Fred C. that he saw this opportunity. At that stage of the game, things weren't that cheery looking.

"Anyway, Fred C. had the courage to do it and it translated itself into an extremely good investment. Fred C. talked our president, John Coleman, who was a very imaginative fellow, into giving him all this money. He gave it to him, and away he went. Fred C. didn't have much to offer him really, other than what he was buying. Just amazing."

1972 ▶

Maintenance of Way crews rehabilitate part of the B.C. Railway with the new tie inserter and an autosled. Two operators of the autosled can sled the track bed, eject failed ties and align the rails.

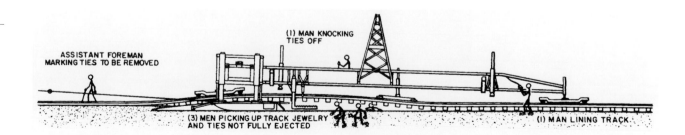

lowlands. White left in early 1973. In October 1973, T.H. (Tom) France was named president.

Two years later, in 1975, Loram Co. Ltd. management initiated a deal which would have had a tremendous impact on Pembina — the bid to buy the 47 per cent of Pembina stock not held by the Loram Group. This move to take Pembina private, which clearly was desirable as there never was an intent to have a public company, failed. Asked about the deal, Lorne Gordon, then a vice president of Loram Co. Ltd. and a director of Pembina Pipe Line, shook his head and said, "I'd like to tell you about it but you wouldn't want to see me cry." Although painful even in retrospect, the attempt to take Pembina private was highly instructional.

The decision to make the bid came about because, for one thing, 1975 seemed an especially opportune time to buy up the Pembina stock, for oil stocks were seriously depressed. Why oil stocks dropped in Canada, when petroleum companies in other parts of the world began to thrive, can be traced directly to the responses of the federal and provincial governments to global events.

In 1973, still another Arab-Israeli war had broken out. This time, on October 6, the day of Yom Kippur, the most solemn day on the Jewish calendar, Egypt and Syria attacked Israel. The active phase of the war ended in 18 days, but not before Israel counterattacked, drove back the Syrians and pushed Egyptian forces across the Suez Canal. Although such conflicts had become almost routine, this one had an enormous economic impact that sent shock waves far outside the region. On October 19, Arab oil-producing nations decided to "punish" the United States for its military and political support of Israel, and placed an embargo on oil exports to America. The ban lasted until March of 1974, long enough to depress petroleum supplies in the United States and create more than a bit of panic. Motorists lined up at service stations to guarantee that their

L.B. (Lorne) Gordon,
vice president, Loram Co. Ltd.

automobile tanks were full. Moreover, the embargo occurred at a time when worldwide demand for energy had increased beyond the ability of petroleum producers to meet it.

Since the end of World War II, oil producers had remarkably stayed a step ahead of demand, which kept prices stable. Now, major oil producers had some leverage in the marketplace, and the Organization of Petroleum Exporting Countries, or OPEC, began to take advantage of the disparity between supply and demand. Oil that was selling for less than $2 a barrel for a couple of decades hit the $5 and $6 level, a 150 per cent increase, which then seemed incredibly disastrous for consumers and industry. In the United States, oil companies began to reap much higher earnings. But in Canada, Ottawa and Alberta commenced to war over sharing the increasingly rich petroleum pie, with little mind for the health and rewards due the companies performing the real work of bringing energy from the ground. As a result of the government skirmishes, royalties were disallowed as an expense in calculating taxable income. This seriously affected the industry and, by 1975, stocks in Canadian oils plunged. It was a good, and cheap, time to take a company private.

In this climate, Loram Co. Ltd. went to work figuring an appropriate bid for Pembina Pipe Line. Researching every takeover from the previous 20 years, Lorne Gordon and his advisors reached a figure of $3.75 per share, a premium of 63 per cent over the company's trading value at that time. "It was the highest premium ever offered in a takeover bid," said Gordon, "and we hung our hat entirely on that fact." What Gordon and Loram management had not considered was that the stock might really be worth much more than its market value. Sophisticated investors, including the 16 pension fund or insurance companies which held 25 per cent of Pembina's stock, were not pressed for money, knew oil stocks would continue to pay dividends, and

1973 ▶

A Mannix-sponsored joint venture builds a massive canal system to divert Churchill River water to the Nelson River for Manitoba Hydro. The $28-million South Bay Channel Diversion project runs until 1976.

1973 ▶

The Long Spruce generating station — a dam, spillway and powerhouse — is built on the Nelson River to help meet the increasing demand for electricity. Mannix Co. Ltd. helps construct this $102-million facility.

knew that the government's policies were only temporarily depressing oil stocks. Aware of Pembina's long-term value, they were not impressed by the premium. Consequently, the bid went bad.

"It was an incredibly terrible experience in every way," said Gordon. "Whenever I reflect back on it, I just have to shake my head. I was the project manager, and there's no question I carried into that project a very high level of ignorance. I can remember being in one of the critical board meetings in 1975, during the bid. The total exposure for us, the total size of the transaction, was about $16.5 million dollars. I had it explained to me many times by Mr. Mannix Sr., as well as by Brock Montgomery and Everett Costello, that this was the biggest transaction that the Mannix Group had ever undertaken. I mention that only to point out the difference in the size and the complexity and the magnitude of the Loram Group. In 1975, $16 million was far and away the biggest transaction that had ever been done, and I think it virtually scared everyone. It certainly scared me."

"Anyway, the bid went badly," said Gordon. "We did absolutely everything wrong. Somebody standing on the side watching the transaction would have been overwhelmed by our stubbornness. It's my opinion that we could have done the transaction for $4.50 a share. I can tell you that this view is not shared by others. Our bid price was $3.75 a share, but I'm absolutely convinced we could have done it for $4.50. We had a main opponent during the bid, named Bill Riedle, who was representing all of the institutions who were opposing our bid. In the last board meeting we had during the bid, we got a call. I went to the telephone, and it was Bill Riedle. He told me he would deliver the stock for $4.50."

THE SLIM WHITE MEMORIAL SCHOLARSHIP

Slim and Dale White.

If Pembina's W.F. (Slim) White had any character flaw, it might be pride, although it is questionable whether doing what one claims one can do is a flaw. For example, while sitting in a bar one day after work, White listened while other men bragged about athletic prowess, in particular, basketball.

"Slim was about 6'1", wasn't heavy, and kept in pretty good shape," recalled John Poloway. "He hadn't played basketball in years, but he proceeds to tell these guys that he could go right out to the high school gym, without any practice, and stand at centre court and make 15 out of 20 baskets." The men at the bar laughed at White. But such a true and wondrous sporting proposition could not help but stimulate the wagering instincts in the crowd. They bet White a case of beer that

he couldn't do it. Since the high school principal happened to be sitting in the bar, the keys to the arena were immediately at hand.

White, the principal and the doubters headed for the school. Parking himself at centre court, Slim heaved a shot. Good. He heaved another. Good. Again and again he shot, until he made 18 out of 20. Good enough, by far, to win the case of brew.

White was eventually promoted to Pembina's pipeline superintendent. When he died in 1974, the loss cut deep. "I considered him to be one of the best people that I have ever met," said Poloway. Shortly after Slim White died, Pembina Pipe Line established a memorial scholarship in his name at Drayton Valley's high school.

"I went into the board meeting, put that offer on the table, and it was turned down for all kinds of reasons — not because the $4.50 price was too high, but because of all kinds of emotional reasons," Gordon said. "We weren't going to change our price, the price was right, the premium over market was right, and so on. So, as a result, we did not buy the Pembina stock for $4.50. I think that that decision cost a lot. It was a $50-million error as a minimum, but perhaps even larger than that. It's just hard to imagine. There is no question in my mind that had all of the people worked together to try to reach an objective, we could have very easily succeeded at that bid, despite our errors.

1973 ▶

R.C. (Dick) Hermann becomes president of Manalta Coal.

1973 ▶

The Jenpeg Power Facilities project on the west channel of the Nelson River is built for Manitoba Hydro. It will help control Lake Winnipeg discharge and produce electricity through horizontal bulb-type turbines, the first installed in North America.

ADVENTURES IN THE DEEP

While the early years of Pembina were marked by struggles in muddy terrain, those toiling for certain subsidiaries of Western Decalta had it no easier, struggling in the cold, murky waters of Lake Erie. Consider one Michael Schoger, who, in 1958, joined Consolidated West Petroleum as an underwater diver.

"When I started," Schoger said, "the company was at its peak. Their subsidiary, Underwater Gas Developers, had 12 drilling towers and barges with 100-ton cranes aboard. I worked long and very treacherous jobs. We had sunken boats, we had people drown, people hurt. The conditions were primitive. We worked from seven in the morning till midnight. Once, at three in the morning, I went down to recover a drilling bit. They had no other drilling bit, so I had to go and get it. I got $25 a diving day, plus a small salary. But I couldn't wait to get into the helmet, even for nothing. Money doesn't mean anything when you love your job."

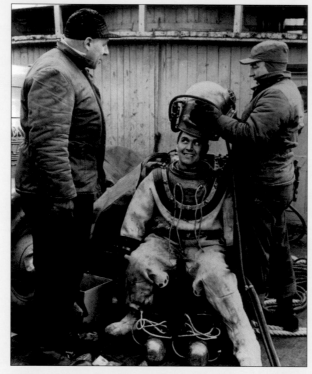

Schoger came to the Loram Group in 1976, when Loram Co. Ltd. purchased Western Decalta. One day, "my boss Bill Barnett, who was manager of production, called from Calgary to tell me to plug some eight wells," Schoger said. The cement unit, pumps and other equipment were estimated to cost thousands of dollars. "Then here comes Crawford from Calgary," said Schoger. "Del Crawford was a young engineer from Calgary who worked for Western Decalta in 1971. He said, 'Mike, we'll get a plastic hose and put a chunk of pipe on the hose, and we'll put in the cement that way.' Now, you should see the beautiful work we did. We plugged the well with cement for a heck of a lot less money. When government people noticed our work, the inspector said, 'God, Mike, I've never seen that before. Your idea?' I said, 'Heck, no. Those cowboys from Calgary, when they work up in the bush, they have to know how to help themselves, and I learned it from them.'"

The timing of the bid was right; it was exactly the right time to have made an attempt to do what we were trying to do. But we were so busy fighting amongst ourselves that we didn't do it."

Despite mounting resistance on the street, and plenty of heated internal debate at Loram Co. Ltd. board meetings, the company pushed on toward making its offer. Loram's board tried to convince the institutions that they could take the money and invest in other oil stocks. But the arguments were academic; the institutions would not budge. Not even Loram's own banker. "They would be banking the transaction, and had every reason to want to support us," explained Gordon, "but they also were a major Pembina shareholder, holding it in the bank's pension fund. The opinion within the bank was that they could not tender their stock to our offer because the price was so unreasonable and they would be perceived as doing something they shouldn't be doing."

One indication that the street's resistance to the bid would be firm and resolute was that Loram Co. Ltd. had difficulty acquiring a dealer/manager for the effort. Early on, the company's request for a dealer/manager was rejected by Wood Gundy, a noted investment banking firm. Loram then turned to Dominion Securities, which also expressed reservations. Only after much cajoling by Gordon, did Dominion's chairman of the board Frank Logan agree to handle it. For a week or so, Dominion staff people did their own evaluations of the bid and tested the water by feeling out the institutions. And yet, just as Loram and Dominion decided to go ahead with the offer, still more opposition developed.

Bill Riedle of Alfred Bunting & Company, a small brokerage firm in Toronto, had followed Pembina's stock for years. His firm specialized in dealing with institutional investors, and had a track record of defeating unreasonable takeover offers. Riedle and Bunting immediately took a high and public profile in the media against the bid. On a Friday, Logan had supposedly agreed conclusively that

1973 ▶

Sandy Hawley of Oshawa, Ontario, shown in a later photo, becomes the first jockey to win 500 races in a season.

1973 ▶

OPEC embargoes oil to most of the Western World and raises the price of crude oil 300 per cent, leading to a major energy crisis.

Dominion would handle the deal. But the following Monday morning, Gordon received a call from a Dominion senior vice president, saying that Dominion had second thoughts and was backing out. Insiders suspect that Riedle had lined up the institutional investors against the offer, thus scaring Dominion away from the deal.

Loram then turned to Brawley Cathers, a virtually unknown firm. This company did, however, employ a man named Doug Armour, a hard worker with much enthusiasm, who made up for Brawley Cathers' lack of muscle. Still, Loram had made its $3.75 bid and it was too late to change it, at least in the minds of Loram board members, who philosophically locked onto the idea that their price was right. "We were right, all right," said Gordon. "The problem was that none of our shareholders thought we were right." During the 35-day acceptance period following the offer, Loram management counted the incoming tenders. The chore was easy — very few arrived. Less than half the shares needed to complete the takeover were tendered for the $3.75 bid. As a result, Loram did not buy any of them.

According to F.P. Mannix, there were underlying reasons for the adamancy of the Loram board in sticking to their original price. "The biggest shareholders were institutional holders of Pembina stock," he explained. "The stock market went all to hell in a handbasket in October the year before we made the offer and Pembina's stock was down. Under the pension fund rules, when the stock goes under a dollar, the guys have to write it off to nothing and they have to take their losses right away. There were five of the pension funds that called me up and said, 'You can't let this stock go below a dollar.' I was president of the holding company and I said, 'We've never interfered in the market before, and we're not going to now. Besides, the market out there sets the price, not me.' They were all upset about this and were saying you've got to buy us out, you've got to do this and so on. They all wanted a special deal. They were just adamant that we had to do something. It was the closest thing to blackmail you could find without being able to throw them in jail."

"We said we can't do something with you without dealing with the whole public," continued F.P. Mannix. "We put together an offer and we had the offer ready to go just before Christmas. Then we discovered, because the stock was listed on the Montreal Stock Exchange and the new legislation had come in in Quebec, that we had two problems. The first was we didn't have current engineering reports on the reserves and the second was we had to translate all this into French. The offer which we had been planning to come out with on the first week in January, we had to put off while we got these two issues solved. It took months just to get everything translated into French alone. Then we went to the street with the second highest premium ever recorded on the TSE.

"Of course, by then, the market had turned around, the stock had improved a bit, and all these five guys turned us down. They would not tender their shares. They were playing a game. They wanted to see how much more they could squeeze out of us. Lorne rightly made the point that even if we had paid 75 cents, in the long term we would have made more money because of the fact that we later paid much more for the company. But it became a

"THEN I WENT DOWN WITH THIS PAIL ON MY HEAD"

"When I first came to Port Alma, I loved to sit with those old-timers," recalled Mike Schoger. "You would not believe how these guys were diving way back at the very beginning.

"Merv Presley was a man in his eighties. Old Merv worked for Union Gas all his life. He told me, 'Oh, God, Mike, I used to dive on the first wells with a pail over my head. We couldn't get a diver so we rigged up a pail and put a nipple on it and ran an air hose to the top. I had to go on my knees, because if I went head down, I'd drown. At first, I started to rise to the surface, so I put some weight around my waist. Then I went down with this pail on my head, and they pumped the air down to me.'"

1973 ▶

T.H. (Tom) France is named president of Pembina Pipe Line.

1973 ▶

Chilean President Salvador Allende, the first freely elected Marxist in the Western Hemisphere, is killed in a military coup after three years in office.

matter of principle with me and Dad. I guess I was the most pissed off because I had done all the work to get ready and then to have these guys, who originally wanted special treatment, turn it all down when they'd been so adamant that we had to do something really made me mad. Dad just said, 'Forget it. Carry on and do what you're doing.' So we withdrew the offer."

The Acquisition of Western Decalta
"It would be fair to say that Mr. McClement was there first."

Loram recovered quickly. About the time Pembina began investigating new ways to expand its exploration activities, Western Decalta Petroleum Co. Ltd., an oil and gas exploration company, launched a search for a new shareholder to replace Hudson Bay Mining and Smelting, which owned 43 per cent of the company in convertible debentures and common stock. In an attempt to rid themselves of what they felt to be stifling controls, Western Decalta managers Charles Lee and Al Ross went looking for a "white knight," seeking a company more compatible with Western Decalta's goals and people, to buy out Hudson Bay's interest. For a brief time, it appeared as if Brascan would be that knight, but at the last moment, Brascan called off the deal.

When the Western Decalta and Brascan deal fell apart, Decalta's Al Ross, who once worked for the Mannix organization, contacted Fred C. Mannix. Ross, who knew that Loram was looking to increase Pembina's oil and gas exploration and production activities, thought the company might be interested in Western Decalta. They were. Not long after Ross' meeting with Fred C. Mannix, Fred P. Mannix placed David McClement in charge of the transaction.

Ronnie Fraser, Hudson Bay's chairman, was amenable to a Loram takeover. However, the deal was fraught with legal and technical difficulties because Western Decalta was listed on both the Canadian and American stock exchanges. The Mannix Group wanted to structure their offer so as to force unwilling shareholders to yield. "Under Canadian law, if you proceed in a proper manner and are successful in buying 90 per cent of the shares of a target company within four months of your bid, then you have the legal right to buy the balance of the stock at the same price," Lorne Gordon explained.

Aside from its dual listing on the Canadian and American stock exchanges, Western Decalta presented the Mannix Group with other difficulties, for it controlled a number of other public subsidiaries. These included Petrol Oil & Gas Company Ltd., Consolidated West Petroleum Ltd., Western & Texas Oil Co. Ltd. and South Brazeau Petroleum Ltd. All public companies, each of them had cash accumulations. It was essential to gain 100 per cent control of this cash and subsequent cash flow in order to service the debt involved. However, the deal hit a snag when one of Western Decalta's directors, a Hudson Bay nominee named Ralph Henson, a Toronto broker, claimed a commission on the transaction, because he had spoken with Gerry Thompson, then the general manager of Pembina Pipe Line. Henson insisted that it was he who had first made Pembina and Loram aware of Decalta's availability.

In drawing up an option agreement to buy Hudson Bay's interests in Western Decalta, Gordon, McClement and Buz Fenerty, Loram's attorney, included a condition that Loram would not have to pay any commissions arising out of the transaction. An amended option agreement required Loram to make a substantial starting payment, around $2.1 million, and the group wanted to avoid any additional costs. "We became concerned that with so many brokers and people involved in this whole deal, we might face a tremendous

Pembina Pipe Line purchases controlling interest in Western Decalta Petroleum Limited in 1976.

◄1973

The General Contracts Division and Railroad Division join together to design and build the Aquitaine Ram River Railway to transport sulphur from Aquitaine's Ram River gas plant. The construction includes two major river crossings. It is completed in 1975.

liability for commissions," said Gordon. This is a fairly common form of protection that takeover companies often insist upon. And the Loram Group made its point without even being sure whether anyone would actually request a commission, for Henson's claim was not yet formal. But Henson finally did make it official, asking for $50,000. Although this was a relatively small amount, considering the overall size of the transaction, it turned into a major stumbling block.

After days of sitting in Hudson Bay's boardroom negotiating with Ronnie Fraser on commissions and other details, Fraser finally said that his company could not indemnify WesDec Petroleum Ltd., the company formed by Loram specifically to acquire Western Decalta, against commission claims. Gordon and Fenerty, with patience bankrupt, packed up their briefcases and started to walk out. Before they even got to the door, Fraser called them back. After going eyeball to eyeball, Hudson Bay blinked. It would pay any commission claims.

Loram had secured Wood Gundy as the lead dealer/manager, despite the bad blood developed the previous year over the attempt to take Pembina private. Negotiations went around the clock, between all the various parties, for nearly 60 days. The sticking point was the price Loram would pay for the Decalta stock. There was a concern that all shareholders would not receive an equal share price because of the $2.1-million payment to Hudson Bay. Once this matter was settled, the deal moved forward without a hitch, and the 90 per cent figure was easily reached.

"We borrowed $76,675,000 and Loram put up $10 million cash and a $20-million guarantee," explained Gordon. "Certainly, in Loram Group history we had never done a transaction of this size. In fact, in Canada this ranked as one of the largest takeover bids of its time. At the time it was done, there were maybe three in all of Canadian history before 1976 that exceeded the total value of this, because to that $76 million you had to add the debt that the company had, and that brought it close to $100 million.

"Interestingly enough, we closed our bid on a Friday. The following Friday, Ocelot bid for Alberta Eastern, and that transaction was a $115-million transaction. In the two or three years that followed, there was a virtual avalanche of takeover bids that ended up dwarfing the WesDec bid, but I think it would be fair to say that Mr. McClement was there first."

The Odd Couple
Merging Pembina and Western Decalta

Although the acquisition went off without a hitch, mergers and acquisitions are risky business; research indicates that between 65 and 85 per cent of these deals fail to achieve their value. The immediate task facing Loram was to put Western Decalta to work to service the debt incurred in the takeover. "In Canadian terms, I think we invented the highly leveraged takeover," Lorne Gordon said. "The transaction had a total value of about $85 million, of which $10 million was equity and the balance was debt. So there were very important implications to Western Decalta. When you take a company and suddenly thrust upon it $72 million worth of new debt, that company has to service that debt."

Western Decalta had grown on the philosophy of acquiring oil and gas reserves at the lowest possible cost, seeking out undervalued companies and buying stock. "They didn't mind putting part of their cash flow into acquiring stock of public companies, even if they didn't get controlling interest," Gordon explained. "They would usually continue to buy until they had a control position, and then just stay there. They didn't have the kind of motives that we did, trying to sweep out the rest of the shareholders."

Western Decalta was merged with WesDec Petroleum Ltd. and its name was changed to Western Decalta Petroleum (1977) Ltd. Loram then went after Decalta's public company subsidiaries — all oil and gas companies — using a variety of financial techniques to buy up the stock in each and take them private, all but Petrol Oil & Gas Company, which would be sold in 1982 to Universal Exploration Ltd.

Next, the Mannix organization had to somehow integrate this new company with its existing operations. The Loram oil and gas interests effectively owned 53 per cent of Pembina. They also owned 100 per cent of Western Decalta. The two companies were totally separate legal entities but somehow, the staffs of the pair had to be combined. The task of managing both organizations fell to Al Ross, president of Western Decalta, who was also named president of Pembina Pipe Line, replacing Tom France. The decision was then made to run Decalta out of Pembina, rather than the other way around. "Since Decalta was 100 per cent owned, it had no outside shareholders," Ross explained. "If we had done it the other way, how would you explain to shareholders that they no longer had any management, that their company was being run by a private group? It just didn't make sense to do it any other way than manage Decalta out of Pembina."

1973 ▶

This is only one of six hydroelectric generating units in the Mica Dam powerhouse that Mannix crews dig and blast out of solid rock.

1973 ▶

The construction of the Mica Dam underground powerhouse for B.C. Hydro & Power Authority occurs north of Revelstoke in an area rich in wildlife.

The job in combining the two companies was eased by the fact that there were not many overlaps. Although Pembina owned numerous oil and gas properties, it operated only a few gas operations in the Medicine Hat region. The company had only two geologists on its staff. Decalta had a large field staff and accounting group, as it managed nearly 800 wells. Pembina still derived most of its income from pipelining, while Decalta was mainly involved in oil production, with commensurate staffing for each activity. So, "it wasn't as though you had two completely filled up staffs of two companies," said Ross.

There were, of course, some disparities. Initially, Western Decalta managers seemed to be the survivors, while Pembina people were shuffled to lesser positions. However, on the whole, the merger went rather smoothly, and within a year, many Decalta people reached retirement age and left, opening spots for Pembina employees. In fact, although some people quit, it usually wasn't for lack of a job. "That was one of the good parts about the whole situation," said Ross.

One of the bad parts was that Western Decalta had to service the debt incurred to acquire it. "The exploratory effort that Decalta used to have shifted over into Pembina," explained Ross. "And Pembina's main thrust was developing more oil and gas properties, because you couldn't find more pipelines. You ran the pipeline as effectively as you could and made as much money out of it as you could, but that money would then go into exploration and development."

"After about two years we started to lose quite a number of our old employees," explained Western Decalta's Les Elhatton. "They went to companies that had stock options or something equivalent. And that was really the main reason, because the Mannixes are great, great people to work for and be around, except that the group in Western Decalta were not used to their type of operation. They were not used to having to report to somebody who owned all the money.

The new corporate logo for Western Decalta Petroleum (1977) Ltd.

A.H. (Al) Ross, president of Western Decalta, is named president of Pembina Pipe Line in 1977.

"Let me tell you, if I owned all the money, they would report to me, too, and I'd be very slow, so this is easy to understand. The thing is, these guys weren't used to that. But, of course, when you were working for the Mannixes, they wanted to look at every major expenditure of $250,000 or over, and you had to get their approval. That slows things down and in this business, you can't afford to be slowed down because it's too competitive. Somebody else will have nipped in there and got it, and when that happens, it's very discouraging to the people who have done all the work, because they really haven't had a shot at it."

After two and half years, Al Ross decided to go elsewhere. During his time with the Loram Group, he helped join Pembina Pipe Line and Western Decalta. In a sense a classic odd couple, one a public company, one private, they somehow worked well together. One might even argue that the purchase of Decalta by the Mannix organization was something of a gift to Pembina's other shareholders. The marriage of the two clearly helped Pembina Pipe Line continue to grow.

Frustration Follows Victory at Gregg River
"We want to start talking about selling some coal."

While Pembina was growing through the acquisition of Western Decalta Petroleum, Manalta Coal searched for opportunities to export coal. Primarily a domestic coal producer for power plant development, the company continued its pursuit of the export coal market as it began to open up in the late 1960s and early 1970s.

However, through the 1960s, Manalta Coal's attempts to market its Gregg River metallurgical coal property, the Gregg River Mine, remained on hold. Manalta was not alone in its stymied efforts, however, as all western Canadian coal producers were meeting with minimal success in negotiations with the primary buyers in the Japanese steel mills. Then, in 1967, Coleman Collieries succeeded in gaining the first long-term contract to export western Canadian coking coal to Japan.

1973 ▶

Westcoast Transmission Co. Ltd. contracts with Mannix crews to lay pipe from Chilliwack to Fort Nelson, British Columbia. This $15-million project is completed by year-end.

1973 ▶

The fourth Arab-Israeli war erupts on the Jewish Holy Day of Atonement. The Yom Kippur War will last 18 days and claim more than 18,000 lives.

The next companies to negotiate long-term contracts were Kaiser Resources (later named Westar Ltd. and now Elkford Coal), Luscar-owned Cardinal River Coals, McIntyre Porcupine Mines (owned by the Keck family of Texas through Superior Oil) and Canadian Pacific's Fording Coal.

In 1968, Ben Goodman, former Mannix Co. Ltd. and then Loram executive, was named to head the development of the Gregg River project. Goodman transferred from Loram into Alberta Coal as vice president of development. Nothing much at all happened with the project until 1970 when F.C. Mannix and Ron Mannix, then in his senior year at the University of Alberta, flew to the world's fair in Osaka, Japan. While in Japan, F.C. Mannix stopped by NKK to see an old friend, Hisao Makita, now chairman of the board. "That goes back to the time that Father and Freddie went over to Japan in 1961," Ron Mannix explained. "They went to visit the Kawasaki steelworks, and the manager

Si Fraser, left, with F.P. Mannix, right, at the NKK steelworks in Japan in 1961.

there at that time was Mr. Makita. Father and Makita ended up having some good times together and became friends. So there was a relationship created many, many years ago. Because of my father seeing Makita again, our interest was piqued very significantly in terms of pursuing this again. I remember Father phoning up and having Ben Goodman come over to Japan. He said, 'Send some people over here. We want to start talking about selling some coal.'"

Shortly after this call, Goodman was on a plane to Tokyo. "I arrived in Japan and went to the Imperial Hotel, where Fred and Ronnie had their suite," Goodman recalled. "Fred had arranged meetings with the Mitsui people to sound out the possibility of opening up a mine for coal." Goodman, who was quite familiar with F.C. Mannix's negotiating style, became the person selected to handle the talks with the Japanese steel companies. "Fred insisted that I be the man to head up the negotiations," Goodman said. "So I spent the next four years commuting to Tokyo and back. I was in Tokyo 17 times." Because of the financially disastrous experience with the Empire Mine, Loram senior management was not about to rush ahead with marketing the Gregg River project until all the technical details had been carefully examined.

Loram senior management also did not want any start-up problems similar to what other western Canadian metallurgical coal companies holding big contracts with the Japanese were experiencing. Nearly all the mines had immediately run into serious difficulties, primarily due to insufficiently detailed exploration activities. In addition, the wash plants which handled the western Canadian metallurgical coal were poorly designed, a fact which resulted in penalties on price. The major problem was that the raw coal delivered to the preparation plants was neither chemically nor physically as had been anticipated.

1974 ▶

Coleman Collieries Ltd. hires Grande Resources Management to develop and mine the Tent Mountain No. 4 pit. Approximately 875,000 short tons (794,000 tonnes) of metallurgical coal are mined annually at the site.

1974 ▶

Argentine dictator Juan Perón dies. His vice president and third wife, Maria Estela (Isabel) Martínez de Perón, becomes the first female chief of state in the Western Hemisphere.

Fortunately, Alberta Coal had Ed Panchysyn. Panchysyn had considerable experience with metallurgical coal mining from his years with West Canadian, a pioneer in coal-washing technology since the days when Gus Vissac was the company's chief engineer. Because of this experience, Panchysyn insisted on an extremely thorough exploration program at Gregg River. "In terms of the philosophy and doing the exploration, Ed Panchysyn was the key guy at Gregg River in the early days," F.P. Mannix said. "Ed had worked with companies that had washed coal, and he knew what the problems were. So the theory was that we were going to be so well prepared, so organized, and so knowledgeable that we would eliminate most of the risks. We were more cautious than other people, but I think that was because we had already dealt with the Japanese at Empire and we understood the credibility risks and how they thought. We were also mining more coal than other people. We had mined at Gregg River in the '40s, and we knew what the problems were."

On December 17, 1971, the Gregg River project was reorganized through the creation of an Alberta Coal subsidiary, Gregg River Resources Ltd. A key addition to the Gregg River team was Bob Sanders. Sanders, who joined Mannix Ltd. in 1956, was previously a senior manager for Pembina. He then worked in Loram on natural resource development. Sanders immediately began working on Gregg River Resources' technical presentations. "We made our first trip over to Japan in August 1971, to introduce the Gregg River project to the Japanese steel mills," Sanders recalled. "There had been a couple of previous visits by coal company people,

Congratulations following the 1974 basic agreement to market Gregg River coal to Japan. Japanese delegates watch with approval as S. Kametaka, Kobe Steel, standing left, and T. Nemoto shake hands with J.T. (Jack) Wood, Gregg River treasurer, left, and Gregg River president R. (Ben) Goodman. Standing right are E. Mekata and T. Kinoshita, Mitsui & Co. Ltd.

but it was not until 1971 that we really became serious about putting a deal together." Despite the quality of the technical presentation, the initial talks did not produce much. The main stumbling blocks were financing arrangements and the Japanese companies' request for equity in the project.

In 1973, the Japanese market for coking coal climbed to nearly 11 million tons (10 million tonnes), about half Canada's total yearly coal production. With many metallurgical coal projects in the exploration or development stage, the Gregg River project was certain to face heavy competition in the coming years. By 1974, Ben Goodman, who had travelled between Canada and Japan constantly since 1971, was worn out. In the summer of 1974, Goodman gave up. "I was there three weeks," he recalled, "and finally I said, 'I've had enough of this. It's going to wear me out. I'm going back, contract or no contract, and if that means I've got to quit Mannix, I'm going to do that, because I can't stand this anymore.' So I called Calgary and told them I was coming home. That evening, the Mitsui representative came to my hotel room and said, 'I hear you're going back tomorrow.' I said, 'Don't feel too badly about it. We've all done our best, but we apparently can't get to first base with the steel companies. But my plane reservation's been cancelled. You get someone to fix that.' So he got that fixed up and came back, and then his face burst into a smile. He said, 'I've also come to tell you that the steel mills have agreed to all of your requests.' I said, 'Are you joking? I'm leaving tomorrow.' He said, 'I know. The signing ceremony is going to be tomorrow morning.'"

1974 ▶

Mannix Co. Ltd. returns to the Athabasca River near Fort McMurray, Alberta, to build a second bridge across the river. Syncrude Canada Ltd. contracts for the $8-million, two-year project.

1974 ▶

Hammering Hank Aaron of the Atlanta Braves baseball club hits his 715th career home run, breaking Babe Ruth's lifetime record. Many thought Ruth's record would never be eclipsed.

Goodman immediately called Calgary with the good news. The Japanese had agreed to sign a letter of intent, outlining the terms for a 15-year contract for 21 million tons (19 million tonnes) of metallurgical coal. Deliveries were to start in 1976 with an initial price of $32.24 per ton. The Japanese also agreed to supply a $20-million loan for the mine's capital costs, then estimated at $60 million. "This was about a $700-million contract, which is something you don't sneeze at," commented Goodman.

The euphoria over the signing of the 1974 letter of intent for Gregg River proved short-lived, however. Soon after Goodman's return to Calgary, the company applied for a mining permit with the provincial government. In September 1974, Manalta received word that the decision on the application was deferred indefinitely. The province had decided to reassess its policies on land use and resource development on the eastern slopes of the Rockies. According to F.P. Mannix, "This was Peter Lougheed's way of not being seen as favouring his former employer." Whatever Lougheed's motivations, one thing remained clear. Until a new policy was formulated, a moratorium on all new mining projects in the mountains was instituted. Because of the complexity of the environmental studies needed for developing the new provincial coal policy, the moratorium was projected to last for at least two years.

The eastern slopes moratorium was a tremendous disappointment. It also created a serious problem for Manalta. Since the letter of intent called for coal deliveries to start in two years, purchase orders for about $50 million worth of new mining equipment had been immediately signed and a used preparation plant had been purchased in the United States. All these contracts required cancellation. This was a bit tricky since the contracts for large equipment contained provisions invoking stiff financial penalties for cancellation. The task of getting out of these commitments fell to Mike Mears. Mears, who previously was executive assistant to Fred P. Mannix in Loram, joined the Gregg River project team in 1973 as purchasing coordinator. "It was then my job to sell all this equipment," Mears said. "I think out of those millions of dollars of equipment, we only lost about $50,000 in foreign exchange. But it took about a year to clean that up."

By 1976, the Alberta government under Lougheed finally released its policy statements on coal mining in the province. The policy prohibited mining in certain areas and allowed only underground mines in other areas. Although plans for the Gregg River Mine were not affected

by the new policy — it was mining in an old mining area of the province for which the government had issued a mining permit — the project once again went into limbo. By this time, the effects of the 1973-1974 energy crisis had spread around the world. The Japanese steel industry was mired in a major recession. Across the globe, steel production was down. World coking coal supplies climbed, forcing coal prices down. In 1977, Manalta representatives resumed negotiations with the Japanese, but the talks were not encouraging. Given the depressed market conditions, the Gregg River project ceased to be economically viable. Japanese steel makers advised Manalta and other Canadian coal producers that they did not anticipate the steel industry would recover until the 1980s.

Alberta Coal Becomes Manalta Coal

In 1969, John M. Rockingham was named president of Alberta Coal. Like Stan Waters, Rockingham had a truly impressive military record. Born in Sydney, Australia, in 1911, Rockingham was educated in Australia, Nova Scotia and Barbados. During his twenties, Rockingham served with the Canadian Scottish Regiment.

When the Second World War broke out in 1939, Rockingham was a lieutenant with the First Canadian Scottish Regiment. He rose through the ranks to lieutenant-colonel with the Royal Hamilton Light Infantry, serving in the United Kingdom and Europe. During the war he was awarded a C.B.E., D.S.O. and Bar. He was made an officer of the Leopold I with Palme (Belgium) and also awarded the Croix de Guerre with Palme (Belgium). Between World War II and the Korean conflict, Rockingham served in supervisory capacities for three transportation companies in British Columbia. In 1950, he was named commander of the United Nations Twenty-Fifth Brigade (Canada). He was made commander of Canadian troops in Korea in 1951. He was awarded the U.S. Legion of Merit and C.D. (Military Division). In 1952, he attended the Imperial Defence College in England and was appointed commander of the Third Canadian Infantry Brigade in 1953. He then served with the First Canadian Infantry Division and was appointed G.O.C., Quebec Command, in 1957.

In 1966, Rockingham came on board as vice president and operations manager of Loram. He recalled how the switch from military to civilian life came about. "I was in the army and I got into a slight argument with the minister of defence, who was then Paul Hellyer,"

1974 ▶

Shell Canada relies on Mannix skill with draglines and hires them to construct a walking dragline for Shell's tar sands operations.

1974 ▶

U.S. President Richard Nixon resigns in disgrace to avoid impeachment over the Watergate break-in and cover-up.

he said. "So I called 'old' Fred, F.C., who was then running the outfit; young Freddie and Ronnie were at university. I had known F.C. before I left the army because I used to ski with him, and we were quite good personal friends. So when I got into this fight with Mr. Hellyer and left the army, F.C. said, 'Come work for me.' I don't think he had the faintest idea of what I was going to do, but I came anyway and I became vice president and operations manager. In those days, there was the president of the company, the general manager, vice president of operations, and vice president of administration. So that was all of four people. I think the hiring of me was strictly an experiment to see if a senior serving officer would make it and could man an industry, and after me there were several — Bob Jones, Stan Waters and Geoff Corry. Geoff Corry was my ADC in Korea."

Before moving into Alberta Coal, Rockingham shut down Empire Mine, the Loram Group's hugely unsuccessful iron ore mine on Vancouver Island. He also briefly headed Alberta Concrete Products, the group's concrete company. Loram senior management regarded Rockingham as something of a trouble-shooter. "We were having trouble and looking for some-body to run the coal company, so we brought him down from Edmonton and he ran Manalta Coal for about a year," Brock Montgomery explained. "Rockingham was always good at running something for a year or a year and a half and straightening those things out. He was a good military man."

While the decision to bring Rockingham in as president of Alberta Coal seemed logical to Loram, it mystified just about everyone in Alberta Coal.

In 1970, John Rockingham, Chuck Doerr and Mac Summersgill, left to right, visit the Whitewood Mine at Wabamun, Alberta.

"Rockingham then came in from left field for a short period," Chip Collins recalled. "To be perfectly blunt, I've never been quite sure why that occurred." Titus Oates held a similar opinion. Oates, who helped Rockingham shut down Empire, joined Alberta Coal in 1968 as an assistant to Ben Goodman, who was vice president, business develop-ment. "Rockingham was a good friend of mine, but the reason for his elevation just escapes me," Oates said. "He had no experience, period, except as a general in the army. He was a front man. He was the most highly decorated Canadian in the Korean War, and he was decorated in the Second World War. He was a very good military man, but I don't know what his qualifications were otherwise."

During his tenure, Rockingham conducted crucial negotiations for the coal company with Calgary Power Ltd. on the new Highvale Mine which supplied coal to the Sundance power plant. "When I first joined the coal company," he said, "there was only one mine at Wabamun Lake. It was on the north side. Calgary Power built a powerhouse, called Sundance, up on the south side of the lake, and we were supposed to supply them with coal. That new mine was the Highvale Mine, and it was located at Seba Beach. The general man-ager had been negotiating for months with Montreal Engineering which had always done a lot of work for Calgary Power.

"The chairman of Calgary Power then was Harry Thompson, and he was a great friend of the Mannix family. I became very friendly with him, and one day he called me up and said, 'For goodness sake, can you come up and see me for a minute?' I did, and he said, 'Let's get rid of this contract.' It was very complicated. We were

1974 ▶

Bill Fofonoff, left, and Bill Couch, right, are honoured for 25 years' service.

1974 ▶

From left to right, Mary Fenwick, Jimmy Nairn, Pansy Strange, Everett Costello and Vic Fabri at the Christmas party.

going to charge the coal company for operating the dragline, which belonged to us, and there were all kinds of complications. We talked for about a half an hour, and by the end of that half-hour, we got the contract settled. I guess the general manager wasn't very happy about that, because he'd spent six months on it and had gotten nowhere."

While Rockingham's tenure at Manalta Coal lasted but a year, he quite enjoyed the experience. "When we started up the Highvale Mine, everybody outside of the company said, 'You'll never get the crews to work there,'" Rockingham said. "But, of course, we did, and we had lots to spare — trained dragline operators and truck drivers and shovel operators. The reason why Mannix had such great ease in getting skilled workers for this job was simply F.C.'s reputation. He had been mining coal for a long time and he was very keen on it. I think he thought it would be steady, unlike the construction company, which made for them millions of dollars one year and then nothing the next year. I think they just sort of said, 'That old coal company goes on and on forever.' They finally got this Highvale Mine operating and, at the same time, as I was negotiating this deal, all of the rest of the coal operation was working on the other side of the lake at Whitewood. So then Whitewood was operating and we had mines working all over the place."

When, in 1970, Rockingham was moved back into Loram, Chip Collins became president of Alberta Coal. In 1971, Collins resigned to take the position of assistant treasurer for the Province of Alberta. This appointment came from former Mannix employee Peter Lougheed, the new Alberta premier, who wanted a top administrator to help him control the finances of the new Conservative government. Collins was succeeded by J.H. (Harry) Irving, previously executive vice president of Alberta Concrete Products and vice president, operations, of Loram. Like both Rockingham and Collins before him, Irving had no experience in the coal mining industry.

In 1972, the company was renamed Manalta Coal Ltd. The following year, Manalta's president, Harry Irving, switched places with Dick Hermann, president of Alberta Concrete Products, the company Irving left in 1971. Hermann viewed his transfer into Manalta Coal as a tremendous opportunity. "I was personally rather interested in the coal industry," he said. "Harry and I had some conversations, and then there was some conversation with others, and we ended up making the switch. During my activity in Loram previously, the coal company was one of the groups that we were involved with. The reason I found it interesting was not the mining so much, although that in itself is interesting to somebody with my background, but the international aspects of the coal trade and the possibilities for expansion. I really saw the job as a good opportunity to become involved in the coal business. I perceived the industry as something that would be growing, with lots of scope."

"THEY SHOULD HAVE SENT SOMEBODY WHO HAD NEVER BEEN IN THE BATTLE"

Brigadier John Rockingham, on left.

While recruiting seasoned military men to the outfit no doubt brought a lot of experience to the table, it also brought its humorous moments. General John M. Rockingham, highly decorated in battle, joined Manalta Coal not long after his retirement from service. He recalls one of those moments.

"Whitewood was operating and we had mines working all over the place," he said. "We had about a half a million tons of coal to spare at that point and we were trying to get rid of it. Somebody said, 'Maybe you could sell to the Germans,' who were running out of high-class coal. So I went over to Germany.

"I got off the airplane in Hanover where the agent who was selling was, and I'll be damned if he didn't call me by name immediately. I looked at him, and he said, 'I was the chief of staff here when you accepted the surrender from Admiral Von Blessing. I was his interpreter. You were the formation commander.' I thought he was talking about Emden. I said, 'Oh, you've made a mistake. I was there, but I wasn't the formation commander.'

"'Well,' he said, 'I can remember,' and he described the exact clothes I had on and everything I said that day. So naturally I didn't sell him any coal and decided I'd better get out of there. They should have sent somebody who had never been in the battle."

1974 ▶

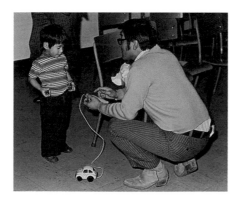

J. Fujino from Techman, and his son, at the Calgary employees' Christmas party for children.

1975 ▶

The Mannix name and shield are retired after 77 years.

The Second Son's Apprenticeship

While Fred P. Mannix's training program had been accelerated, so too had his younger brother's. Born February 25, 1948, Ronald Neil Mannix literally grew up with the outfit. Although the days when his grandfather's business depended upon horses had long faded into history, young Ron learned early on the way of horses. "Toby was Ronnie's horse," recalled George Reid, F.S. Mannix's attendant and driver who, following the death of the elder Mr. Mannix, worked at Fish Creek as ranch manager for F.C. Mannix. "Toby used to lead the Stampede Parade. He was a beautiful horse, he was. But, he was a great big horse. Ronnie was about three when Ed Fraser, Si Fraser's brother, taught him to ride. No saddle, and his feet would stick straight out on either side of this big horse. Ronnie would be kicking and jumping, but the horse would go right along with him. The horse just knew that he had a little one on his back."

"I never will forget the time they moved out to the farm and Ed Fraser was teaching the kids to ride," said Evelyn (Nursie) Hayward, who helped Margie Mannix with the three children. "I could have choked him. He let Ronnie get up on that big horse, Toby. Maureen was on Hotfoot, Freddie was on Featherfoot and they left the farm and went up to the airport. They came back at 9:00 at night. And here is poor little Ronnie, four years old, sitting up on old Toby with his little legs stuck straight out on either side of this big, fat back on this horse. Poor Ronnie was exhausted. That was too far to take a little kid. He didn't have stirrups or anything. He was riding bareback on that horse for 20 miles. I don't know why Ed ever did that. I told him, 'That's no way to treat that little boy.' He said, 'Well, he's a boy and he's going to grow up. He may as well learn now.' I was so furious with him!"

A young Ronnie Mannix.

Maureen and Ronnie Mannix on Hotfoot, Maureen's first horse.

During their childhood at Fish Creek, Fred P., Maureen and Ron joined the Pony Club. "Because of the Pony Club, we started building all the jumps," recalled Maureen Mannix Eberts, who became quite an accomplished competitive equestrienne. "The more jumps we built and the further we went in the Pony Club the more difficult the jumps became. Then we started having competitions on our property. We had a Fall Hunt. The Pony Club taught us how to hunt as the real system goes. We didn't have hounds and we didn't have foxes, still we had to know what all the different positions were. It worked out really well in that Ronnie would be the fox. He would leave a half-hour before everybody else. He would take whatever course he wanted to and he would lay a paper chase. Every now and then, he would drop a handful of paper. That was the scent. Then there would be three or four kids who were assigned to be the hounds. They had to find the paper so that we knew where the route went. The third person would be the Master of the Hounds. He had to keep these hounds close to the trail which was supposedly preset, although foxy Ronnie might go a little wrong."

"The Fish Creek Branch became a very successful branch of the Pony Club here in Calgary," recalled Marg Ellard, who, along with her husband Ray, leased a cottage from the Mannixes at Fish Creek. Mrs. Ellard, a former Stampede Princess and great friend of Margie Mannix, set up the Fish Creek stable, looked after the Mannix horses, and helped establish the Mannix annual Fall Hunt. "Mrs. Mannix and I would go out and build the jumps. We would always have a little assistance from Ronnie, who would run through the bush with a machete. He was forever trying to build jumps.

"There's another little incident about Ronnie. He got a beebee gun for his birthday one year. One day we

1975 ▶

The CN Tower in Toronto is the world's tallest freestanding structure.

1975 ▶

For the first time, the maintenance of way operations are set up as an independent operating company, no longer part of the U.S. construction affiliate. The company is named Loram Maintenance of Way, Inc.

were just leaving the house with Don and Luella Wilson, Mr. Mannix's sister. I was leaning over the hood of the car and we were just talking. All of a sudden, kerpow, and I thought my leg was broken off. And here was this charming little redheaded, round face from behind the tree with a beebee gun. He had shot me in the bum with it!"

From jumps, young Ron tackled a much more ambitious project — a secret fort. In this, his efforts quite resembled some of the earthen-mound fortifications built by his Norman conqueror ancestor, John de Courcy. "When he was quite young, Ronnie built an incredible hut," recalled the Ellards' son, Norman. "It was built into the bank of the hill which was exactly opposite the Mannix house. He had dug this thing about four feet into the ground, built branches, and then packed it with mud. For numerous years, some of us didn't even know it was there. Ronnie's youthful creation was really quite incredible. It was right on the side of a cliff. He called it his fort."

Along with his fort, young Ronnie enjoyed a swimming hole. "We dug a hole in the creek so the kids could swim," recalled Mannix construction veteran Hans Olesen, who started with the company back in 1935. "Ronnie used to come out there. He was only about nine years old. He would bring his lunch kit out there and he would stand behind the dragline and watch. He said, 'Don't you get tired of this, Hans? Don't you get tired of working all the time?' I said, 'I have to — I get paid for it. If I get paid, I got to work, you know.' Anyhow, he was always around there asking questions. He said to me this day, 'Will you work for me when I get to be boss? I'll give you $20,000 a year.' Oh, he was a nice kid."

"He was just one of the boys," said Mannix family friend Vera Holdsworth. "With a lot of boys of successful fathers, you'd hear about it. Ronnie was never

Top: Margie Mannix
with her young son, Ron.

Above: Ron Mannix during an
equestrian competition at Fish Creek,
riding his favourite horse, Brownie.

like that. He was so down-to-earth. He never mentioned anything about it. He was just a real good all-around boy." While Ron may have been a good all-around boy, he was also a Mannix. "In 1929, I went to St. Hilda's Girls School where I met Luella Mannix." Mrs. Holdsworth said. "We became very good friends. I would go to their home on Talon Avenue. That's where I met Fred C. Mannix. I recall that John MacKenzie went to St. Mary's Boys School with Fred. Many times the principal, Father Cameron, would tell John to go down to Rosie Herlmer's Pool Hall and bring Fred Mannix back to school. That happened on many occasions.

"In 1959, 30 years later, my son Ronnie and Ronnie Mannix became great friends. They went to Strathcona and Ridley College and to St. Mary's School together. They had lots of fun times. One time, too much fun. It was a school night. Ronnie took his mother's car out and picked up my son and Dr. McManus' son, Doug. Two hours later, I got a call from Margie Mannix saying, 'Did you get a call from the police? They've just phoned and said they've got your Ronnie and my Ronnie and Doug McManus in jail.' The boys had taken a case of beer, went down a lane and were having a drink. A police car went down the lane and saw the big car those boys were in and they took them off to jail. They thought they had stolen the car. Between Margie crying and me crying, she told me, 'Fred is in the East. Shall I get the lawyer now?' And I said, 'Wait. I will phone Dr. McManus and ask him what he is going to do about Doug. I phoned him up and he said, 'We're going to leave them there. I'll phone Margie Mannix right now.' And then I got a call from Margie and she said, 'We can't leave them there all night.' I said, 'Oh, Margie, I think we had better listen to Dr. McManus.' The three of them were all out by eleven

1975 ▶

After decades of fighting French and American forces, the Communist-backed North Vietnamese and Vietcong forces defeat the South Vietnamese army and unify the country.

1975 ▶

The Minnesota shop for Loram Maintenance of Way includes a four-torch gas-cutting machine set up by Glenn Shannon.

in the morning. So we had wonderful boys and nothing happened after that."

While most boys his age spent their summer vacations hiking, swimming or golfing, Ron Mannix spent his summers working in the field. Beginning his career as a farm hand at the FM Ranch, he progressed to mechanic's helper at the Ogden Shop. He spent successive summers working on heavy construction, pipeline and railway projects. It was when he worked as a labourer at Duncan Dam that his life almost came to a premature end. "Duncan Dam was the one that Ron was sent down to," recalled Christine Vennard. "Ray supervised it. I remember Ron went through a conveyer belt and nearly slid into one of the belly dump trucks. Well, he came out of there safe and sound and we thought, 'Wasn't that awful!' Margie came down with Fred and everybody said, 'Thank God that he survived that one.'" After surviving Duncan Dam, young Ron served as an equipment operator at Fort McMurray and as a cleanup foreman on the Interprovincial pipeline. Subsequent summers were spent as assistant superintendent for the B.C. Railway project at Hixon and as foreman on the Churchill Falls project.

Like his brother, Ron Mannix understood why this field experience was so important. "Because of the people and the principle of understanding the operations, it is necessary to go out and work in the companies," he said. "You cannot talk too little about, or value highly enough, the necessity of what's happening in the operations, because no matter how you look at it, that's ultimately what makes the money. It's off the end of the shovel teeth, as Freddie would say, or the pipeline welding, or the drilling of the oil. If those operations are screwed up, everything else goes down the drain. People are the single

F.P. Mannix (second from left), R.N. Mannix and George Ballinger (right), discuss a maintenance of way problem with an autotrack operator.

most important asset in the whole outfit. We have to have all the things that sound so trite — the honesty, the loyalty, the integrity — and it requires an understanding of how to deal with people. That is one thing that to a great degree Father tried to instill in Freddie and me and ensure that we have a sensitivity toward."

On graduation with a bachelor of commerce degree from the University of Alberta, Ron Mannix undertook a year's management training with Loram Co. Ltd. and travelled extensively. In 1973 he was appointed manager of Manalta Coal's Klimax Mine at Estevan, Saskatchewan. "Ronnie Mannix was just graduating out of university at the time," said Loram executive Alex Cummings. "One of the things I was charged with was coming up with a program to start getting him business exposure. We thought about the rather simple way that Freddie had come through the construction company. Even though his period there was very brief, there was nothing wrong with that method. But we wondered why would we want to bring the second member of the family through the same route. I suspect it was more Brock and I who finally decided that we should do something different and bring Ronnie through the coal company. The only way we could do that was get Ronnie out running a mine. So the Klimax Mine in southern Saskatchewan was selected."

One person who got a firsthand look at Ron Mannix's entry into the coal business was George Chapel, one of the top engineers in Mannix Co. Ltd., who moved into Manalta as chief engineer in 1973. Chapel, who would be a key figure in future development at Manalta, joined Mannix Co. Ltd. in 1962 as student engineer in the work-study program started by the company in the 1940s.

1975 ▶

Spanish dictator Generalissimo Francisco Franco dies after 36 years in power.

1975 ▶

The crib skeletonizer is developed. This machine clears fouled ballast between the rails to the shoulders where it is picked up by the shoulder ballast cleaner, cleaned and redeposited amongst the ties, improving drainage and adding years of life to the rail bed.

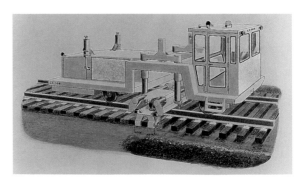

After receiving his engineering degree from the University of Manitoba in 1964, he worked as an engineer on several Mannix Co. Ltd. jobs, including the site preparation work for the Kidd Creek Mine at Timmins, Ontario, the Alberta Resources Railway and the Mt. Newman Railroad in Australia. He then moved into head office.

Chapel vividly remembers the meeting where Ron Mannix presented his first budget for the Klimax Mine. "Ronnie came in and he had done a lot of work on it," Chapel recalled. "He may not have been perfect, but that was his first crack at it. He worked hard. Christ, he was there almost seven days a week. He had just been married, and he was always spending time in the office."

In 1974, after completing his year of training in mine management at Klimax, Ron Mannix moved back to Calgary, where he was named manager of the thermal coal division in the head office. The focus in head office in Calgary was on renegotiating existing contracts and potential new contracts for the near term, so responding to the explosion of thermal coal marketing opportunities in the wake of the energy crisis became Ron Mannix's responsibility.

One of Ron Mannix's principal concerns on arriving in the head office was that Vesta, Sheerness and Klimax lacked the capability of taking on new contracts with existing equipment and Utility needed additional capacity. All four mines struggled along with the same antique machines they had back in the 1950s, plus equally antique hand-me-downs from the larger mines and the construction company. At Vesta, the only major attempt to upgrade equipment had been the acquisition of the Bucyrus-Erie 15-W, a machine which was about 20 years old when it arrived in 1962. At Klimax, the course of history actually seemed to be going backwards. After the Marion 7800 was moved to Utility, the Bucyrus-Erie 500-W, which Chuck Doerr purchased back in 1950, was taken out of the bone yard and put back in operation.

A successful morning on a day off at the Churchill Falls project.

Wayne Kelly, who transferred from Mannix Co. Ltd. in 1970 to become the first mine engineer at Klimax, was stunned when he first arrived at the mine. "I thought I was stepping back into the Dark Ages," Kelly said. "Before, I was on construction in Newfoundland and British Columbia where all the equipment was brand-new when they moved it in. When I came into Estevan, all the dozers still had cable blades on them, and I kind of wondered, 'How long is this going to last? Surely they can't operate on this for very long.'"

According to F.P. Mannix this was a deliberate policy. "It was a capital versus operating cost tradeoff," he explained, "and one of the key elements to developing the coal company. The new equipment was first used on high-production construction jobs, then on low-production construction jobs, then on important mines, then passed down to the coal company. Contract mines where high performance was required got new machines, while the other mines got several old machines. With their great shops and mechanics, they used the several old machines to keep one running."

Ron Mannix was about to blow that capital versus operating tradeoff right out of the water, however. One of his first acts as division manager in 1974 was to visit Bucyrus-Erie's headquarters in Milwaukee, Wisconsin. Accompanying him was Mac Summersgill, manager of operations, with overall responsibility for day-to-day supervision of the company's mines. After Bucyrus-Erie explained that demand for draglines was starting to shoot up, Mac Summersgill and Ron Mannix made commitments for three machines. On May 4, 1974, they signed purchase orders for a 90-yard 2570-W for Klimax, a 60-yard 1570-W for Vesta, and a 30-yard 1300-W for Roselyn. The total cost of these three machines was approximately $55 million.

Ron Mannix's decision to go ahead and sign these purchase orders would probably have seemed reasonable

1975 ▶

U.S. Apollo and Soviet Soyuz spacecrafts rendezvous 140 miles (225 kilometres) above Earth. Left to right, Thomas Stafford, Aleksei Leonov and Donald Slayton share a visit.

1975 ▶

Heritage Park Society in Calgary hires Loram International Ltd., the recently renamed Mannix construction company, to build a nostalgic electric streetcar line to transport park visitors in a restored electric trolley.

to Loram management, except for two minor details. Manalta at that point had no assurances of any sort for contracts at any of the three mines, and the younger Mannix had not checked with anyone in Loram before he signed on the dotted line. These two details did not go unnoticed.

"I remember Dick Hermann giving me a call one day and saying, 'Ronnie's committed us to the three draglines down there,'" Alex Cummings recalled. "Before that, we didn't really have a coal contract to pay for any of the draglines, but we had positions in the production lineups, as did everybody else. We were all fighting to hold our capability of being able to react to new opportunities to mine coal. Harry Irving had originally recommended this, as a matter of fact, and then it progressed along to the point where we had to make commitments to Bucyrus-Erie.

But Ronnie didn't have Loram director approval, he didn't have anything, and he had gone down to Bucyrus-Erie and committed us to what then was a big bunch of money. It was going to break the coal company if we weren't careful. Dick came up sort of laughing about it, but of course, I was the guy who had to break the news to the fathers of confederation here, and wow, there were big problems then. Big, big problems."

Although Cummings' announcement immediately produced some fairly exciting moments in the boardroom of Loram, Ron Mannix's decision to order $55 million of equipment with no coal contracts in place was not as crazy as it first appeared. Under normal circumstances, it takes several years to manufacture a big dragline, which contains as much iron as a good-sized steel-frame building. The circumstances in 1974, however, were anything but normal. In the late 1960s, total worldwide sales of big draglines were less than 20 machines a year. In the early 1970s, however, sales began to climb, with 18 units sold in 1971, 26 in 1972, and 43 in 1973. Following the OPEC embargo in 1973, the market for draglines literally exploded. In 1974, Bucyrus-Erie, Marion and Page collectively received an astounding 106 orders for draglines, with 95 of these placed by North American mining companies.

Now, if the world's three dragline manufacturers' combined production capacity equals 20 units a year, the coal mining company with purchase order number 106 would probably not see its new machine for quite a while. This, of course, would be a serious problem if that same company had just signed a large new contract calling for coal deliveries to begin in a couple of years. On the other hand, a company counting on winning a new coal supply contract to finance its new $20-million machine would not be in such a wonderful spot either if that new contract failed to materialize. Ron Mannix's position was that the first of these two worst-case scenarios was by far the most undesirable. The problem then became winning the contracts that would pay for the three draglines. That problem was soon to fall squarely in Ron Mannix's lap.

R.N. Mannix working as cleanup foreman on the Interprovincial pipeline project from Moose Jaw to Kerrobert.

1975 ▶

William H. Gates III, 19, shown, and Paul G. Allen, 22, found Microsoft. Gates will be a billionaire before age 30 and the richest person in the world by the late 1990s.

1975 ▶

Disco, a style of popular music and dance, sweeps over much of the world. Sister Sledge, one of many disco groups, is shown.

In November, after less than a year as president, Dick Hermann announced that he would be leaving Manalta Coal. With Hermann's resignation, Loram senior management made a bold decision. They decided to immediately move Ron Mannix into the presidency of the largest coal producer in Canada, further accelerating his already accelerated management training program. On November 20, 1974, Ron Mannix became president of Manalta Coal. He was 26 years old.

R.N. Mannix becomes president of Manalta Coal Ltd. in 1974.

"So we ended up with new mine managers everywhere and were off on a whole new adventure."

Ron Mannix's first act as president was to select Bob Sanders as general manager to replace Gordon Coates, who returned to a management position in Loram International. Another new addition to Manalta's management team was Paul Christensen, the vice president, finance, who previously was controller of Mannix Co. Ltd. Ed Panchysyn continued as vice president, exploration, and president of Master Explorations Ltd., an exploration subsidiary set up in 1969. Mac Summersgill, the operations manager since 1973, and George Chapel, the chief engineer since 1973, remained in their positions.

The purchase of the three draglines made obtaining new contracts for Klimax, Vesta, and Roselyn the top priority in Manalta's marketing efforts. Of these three mines, Klimax came first. In 1975, Ontario Hydro called for coal supply bids for the two new 150-MW lignite-fired units to be added to the Thunder Bay generating station. The contract was to run for 15 years, with annual production around 1.5 million tons (1.4 million tonnes). Although Manalta lost to Luscar, the company decided that Klimax would still get a new dragline. Manalta did, however, go to Bucyrus-Erie to renegotiate for a smaller machine and switch production decisions to delay delivery of the smaller machine. Bucyrus-Erie obligingly found a customer willing to swap its position for a 60-yard 1570-W for Manalta's position for the 90-yard 2570-W.

Later in 1975, Manalta received more bad news. The first unwelcome development affected plans for the Mercoal and McLeod River properties. Manalta was attempting to market this coal to Ontario Hydro's thermal generating stations on Lake Erie. Ontario Hydro again awarded Luscar the 15-year contract. About this time, Alberta Power and Calgary Power shelved plans for the Sheerness generating station until later in the 1980s. This decision effectively killed the new dragline for Roselyn. With the short-term contract for the Queen Elizabeth generating station to run for only a few more years, there was no need for any more stripping equipment at Roselyn. The task of getting rid of the 1300-W fell to Mike Mears, who was becoming quite good at selling mining equipment. "I travelled all over the U.S. and even up into Alaska," Mears said. "Finally we sold that 1300 to a family-owned coal mining company about 80 miles from Fairbanks."

With the sale of the 1300-W, just one dragline needed taking care of, the 1570-W for Vesta. The financing of this purchase was entirely dependent on negotiating a new contract for coal supply to the Battle River generating station. This was a critical issue because by 1976 it had become obvious that the existing contract with Alberta Power was a disaster. "We had a terrible contract," Bob Sanders said. "I think what had happened is that our predecessors bought their way into that one by offering coal at too low a price. The long-term contract at Vesta was just sucking any profits from the other mines right down the tubes. We were getting nowhere."

The result of the 1976 negotiations was a situation that worked out well for both parties. Alberta Power purchased Vesta Mine's substantial reserves for an excellent price, around $10 million, thus gaining an assured coal supply for the 30-year life of the new 375-MW unit to be added to Battle River. Alberta Power also agreed to

1975 ▶

Muhammad Ali retains the world heavyweight boxing title by knocking out former champ Joe Frazier in the "thrilla in Manila."

1976 ▶

In a major expansion into exploration, Pembina Pipe Line Ltd. acquires controlling interest in Western Decalta Petroleum Co. Ltd.

A Little Prayer for Mr. Klimax

In the late 1960s, SaskPower embarked on a 450-MW expansion of the 132-MW Boundary Dam generating station. Two 150-MW units were scheduled to be put into operation by 1970 and a third 150-MW unit in 1973. To gear up for this additional tonnage, Alberta Coal decided to move the 1,700-ton (1,500-tonne) Marion 7800 dragline from the Klimax Mine to Utility. In travelling the eight miles (13 kilometres) to Utility, the 7800 had to cross two highways, three sets of railway track, both the Souris and Long Creek rivers and numerous smaller roads and power lines.

The walk, which started in October 1968, was intense. "We moved 16 hours a day," recalled Utility's mine manager, Louis Carriere. "We hardly ever stopped working." The walk went smoothly until the dragline had to cross the Souris River. "When we got to the river, we filled it in with Cats so we didn't hold up the dragline," Carriere explained. "The river was quite low at that time of year. There was probably three or

four feet of water in the bottom. But the Cats didn't do that much compaction. When we got halfway across, the machine started sinking."

"Thousands of people were watching," added Millard Holmgren, Klimax master mechanic, "but Louis Carriere was with us and he had a lot of experience with draglines. When we came level and moved across, everybody breathed a sigh of relief, and the crowd hollered."

For Archie Hawkes, the mine manager at Klimax, there was no question that the safe river crossing was accomplished only through the grace of God. "Mr. Hawkes came up to me," Holmgren recalled, "and he said, 'You know what did it, Millard? See those two nuns in the crowd? I've been watching them. They were saying a little prayer for you all the way across the river.'"

purchase Manalta's new Bucyrus-Erie 1570-W dragline to put into their rate base as it was more valuable to Alberta Power than to Manalta. This freed up another $15 million or so. In return, Manalta gained a 31-year contract to supply half the coal to be used by the generating station after its expansion in 1979. As it turned out, the fact that the dragline was already being built gave Manalta a crucial bargaining chip. "We negotiated very hard with Alberta Power, using the 1570," Ron Mannix said. "We told Alberta Power, 'We're losing our shirt on the old contract. You can either renegotiate and get this contract straightened out, or we're going to can the dragline and you're going to have a big problem supplying your generator with coal.' That was part of the negotiations on Vesta where we turned everything around."

Now that the matter of the three draglines had been taken care of, Ron Mannix and his management team began modernizing the management structure and operations at Manalta mines and in the head office. "As you normally find when you get new bosses, things don't always work out well with the old employees," Paul Christensen recalled. "And there was some disarray in the company because there were some people who had been around there 30, 40 years. So there was some housecleaning done, which probably needed to be done."

In 1976, Don Kingdon, who had been manager at Loram's largest mine, Highvale, since 1970, became the new manager of operations. He replaced Mac Summersgill, who left the company. At the same time, Ron Mannix and Bob Sanders decided to move all the mine managers to different mines. The idea was to start developing operations management depth by making mine managers familiar with more than one mine. Another reason was simply to shake up operations and bring in new blood and new

1976 ▶

A little body language helps a tee shot at the Loram Group golf tournament.

1976 ▶

Chairman Mao Zedong, leader of the People's Republic of China since 1949, dies of Parkinson's disease.

perspectives. In 1976, the mine managers at all mines except Vesta were changed. Louis Carriere, who had been manager at Utility since 1964, moved to Highvale to fill the vacancy caused by Kingdon's promotion. Carriere's place at Utility was taken by Wayne Kelly, previously mine engineer for Utility and Klimax. George Korsa, manager at Roselyn since 1975, moved to Whitewood. Don Meads, the assistant mine manager at Whitewood, replaced Korsa at Roselyn. Lee Wagar, who had been manager at Whitewood since 1974, moved to Klimax, replacing Cap Jenish, who became area manager for the Saskatchewan mines. In 1977, Roy McBride moved from Vesta into head office to take charge of a new training program. His place as mine manager was taken by Irvine Wiens, formerly assistant mine manager at Highvale.

"We actually changed every single mine manager," Ron Mannix said. "Our feeling was that we had a lot of good guys, it was time for a change, and even just moving one mine manager to another mine would be valuable and beneficial and would get things to work. So we ended up with new mine managers everywhere and were off on a whole new adventure." Directing this next phase in Manalta's history would be a task assigned to a new man. In June 1977, the senior directors of Loram felt that Ron Mannix was ready to take on the next step in his accelerated training program, the move up into the holding company, Loram Co. Ltd., as executive vice president. With Ron Mannix's move to Loram, Bob Sanders, after two and a half years in the business, became president of Manalta.

Bob Sanders found himself leading a company that was remarkably stable for all the changes in top management. This was because one of the great strengths that the Loram structure had developed over the years was that they could change people and not lose continuity. Indeed, between 1967 and 1977, Manalta mines expanded their operating capacity, calmly tripling production as if no changes in upper management had occurred. In 1977, Manalta's mines produced about 10.6 million tons

PACING IN PAKISTAN

In 1977, a Bucyrus-Erie 190-B shovel was purchased for the Klimax Mine. The shovel came from Pakistan, where it was used on the construction of Tarbella Dam, an earthmoving project that the Canadian government had partially funded through the Canadian International Development Agency. Mike Mears, manager of administration for Manalta Coal, went to Pakistan with Dick Wilsey, Manalta's electrical engineer. "The shovel hadn't worked that much because there were so many local people who needed work, the contractor had utilized them rather than the machine," said Mears. "Because of the shovel's excellent condition, we bought it. Then the trick was to get it out of Pakistan."

This job was assigned to John Morgan, who came to Manalta in 1976. By the end of the year, he was

in Pakistan. "I was over there for a period of about 10 weeks," he recalled. "It's not very far from the dam site to Karachi, where the port was, but when that shovel left on the train, it disappeared. I phoned the railways eight, ten times a day. There was an election coming and there was civil unrest. A lot of railway traffic was being used to transport military equipment, so I think the shovel got ran onto sidings and just left there. But one day, there it was, it just showed up."

Morgan would encounter further frustrations getting the 190-B loaded on a ship, but finally the shovel made the trip to Vancouver. There, Morgan got it on rail cars for the trip to Estevan. And it was just in time. Because of drought conditions in Manitoba in 1976 and 1977, Manitoba Hydro's Brandon and Selkirk stations set records for electrical generation. In 1977, production at Klimax reached an all-time high of 1.7 million tons (1.5 million tonnes). Every piece of spare stripping equipment was used to uncover coal, right down to a 1948 5-W dragline.

1976 ▶

The Loram subsidiary, la Compagnie Loram (Québec) Ltée., joint ventures with Komo in the five-year construction of the LG-2 West powerhouse, the third underground powerhouse built by Loram crews. The project generates $91 million in revenue.

1976 ▶

Montreal hosts the Summer Olympic Games.

"A Chance of a Lifetime"

"As soon as I got back from Pakistan, I was asked by Geoff Corry — then president of Cenlor Services — if I would be interested in a secondment to the federal government to join the Canadian Foreign Service," recalled Mike Mears. "We have in Canada a program called the Executive Interchange Program, whereby executives from the business sector will go into the government, and people from the government will come into the private sector. Anyway, Geoff asked me if I would be interested and I said, 'Yes, I would be.' It was a marvellous opportunity for the family. A chance of a lifetime. So I went to meet with the people in Ottawa to be vetted. The person who interviewed me was Ken Taylor, who subsequently became ambassador in Iran at the time of the hostage crisis."

"In May of 1977, my wife and my two children and I went to Ottawa for a couple of weeks and then down to Sao Paulo, Brazil, which probably ranked among the top five cities in the world in terms of population," Mears said. "It had somewhere between 14 and 15 million people. We couldn't speak a word of Portuguese, and we arrived in this incredibly noisy and polluted city. My first assignment was obviously to learn the language. For six weeks, I went to school every day for six hours to learn Portuguese. If you didn't learn it in six weeks, well, that was too bad, as that was all the government was prepared to pay for.

"My duties were to promote Canadian trade from Canada into Brazil and to assist Canadian businessmen coming to Brazil with licensing arrangements or joint ventures or setting up new corporations and so on. We spent two years there — just a wonderful experience for all of us."

(9.6 million tonnes) of coal, nearly 40 per cent of Canada's total production.

Manalta maintained its position as Canada's leading coal producer during a period that saw not only tremendous internal change but the completion of the restructuring of the nation's coal mining industry that had begun in the early 1960s. In 1967, Canada's total coal production was a mere 11.4 million tons (10.3 million tonnes). About one-third of that amount, 3.7 million tons (3.4 million tonnes), came from Nova Scotia, the nation's leading coal-producing province. Another third came from Alberta, with 3.6 million tons (3.3 million tonnes). In 1977, national coal production nearly tripled to 28.7 million tons (26 million tonnes), and the centre of the nation's coal mining industry moved west. Alberta, British Columbia and Saskatchewan, which produced 12.2 million tons (11.1 million tonnes), 8.6 million tons (7.8 million tonnes), and 5.5 million tons (5.0 million tonnes) respectively, were Canada's leading coal-producing provinces. Nova Scotia's production dropped to 2.3 million tons (2.1 million tonnes).

During the same 10-year period, trade with Japanese steel manufacturers developed from virtually nothing to about half of the entire Canadian coal market. In 1967, when Coleman Collieries won the first long-term contract with Japanese customers, Canada exported about one million tons (910,000 tonnes) of coking coal to Japan. By 1977, that figure climbed to 10.6 million tons (9.6 million tonnes).

While the rapid development of the metallurgical coal segment of the industry was the primary development in the 1970s, the thermal coal business continued to grow at a healthy rate. Manalta was a major reason for this growth. In 1977, Manalta's thermal coal production equalled the amount of metallurgical coal exported to Japan by all western Canadian coal producers.

1976 ▶

Canadian Susan Nattrass is the first woman to compete in Olympic trapshooting. During the 1970s, she compiles the longest winning streak of any Canadian athlete and is the most consistent performer of any athlete, in any sport, in the world.

1976 ▶

In Quebec, separatist René Lévesque, centre, leads the Parti Québécois to power.

Mannix International Becomes Maintenance of Way
"I want you guys to make a rail grinder out of this."

The future for Mannix International could be summed up in one word — diversification. Because of the advances in track maintenance equipment, the railways resurfaced major portions of their lines, replacing low-quality gravel and cinder ballast with crushed stone. With many thousands of miles of track on new stone ballast, the need for sleds, plows and autotracks was certain to decline.

The implications were clear. Mannix International had to develop new machines for other markets. The undercutter cleaner — also known as "the Monster" — was a step in one direction. But the company's experience there showed that it had bitten off far more engineering than it could chew. Despite repeated overhauls, the Monster continued to be a disappointment, breaking down as frequently as before. There was simply no getting around the fact that the machine's overall design was an engineering nightmare.

"When the undercutter cleaner worked, it was one of the most fabulous things you ever saw," said Ray Wahl, who joined Mannix International in 1966. "But it would work an hour and a half and then you'd spend a day and a half fixing it. Then it might run for two days, and then you'd spend a week fixing it again. It was something all the time but not necessarily a big thing. There were instances where you'd lose a $2 part, but it'd take you half a day just to get to it because of the way it was all put together."

The overly complex design of the undercutter machine was primarily a consequence of Mannix International's lack of experience in manufacturing powered equipment. The jump from the autotrack to the undercutter cleaner was an attempt to skip several steps in the evolutionary process. But Mannix International was not alone in making this mistake. A frequent complaint of the railways in the late 1960s was that equipment manufacturers, caught up in the rush to

THE DEMISE OF "THE MONSTER"

Late in the 1960s, Mannix International decided to give the undercutter cleaner a third and final chance. That year, the undercutter cleaner, a.k.a. "the Monster," was rebuilt one last time. Ron Mauch, who was hired as a machine operator in 1968, drew the Monster as one of his first assignments. Mauch, who eventually became the company's general manager, recalled that this third prototype was not much of an improvement over the other two versions.

By this time, Mannix International had decided to use a winch cart to pull the machine while it was working because of all the problems in the past with blown transmissions. This resulted in a marginal improvement in productivity, but the undercutter cleaner still remained a losing proposition. "That was the only year that the machine broke even, as far as the bottom line goes," Mauch

said. "That was because we had a winch cart. We broke records with the machine that year. It ran for 48 minutes once without downtime. The crew was very proud of this!"

The Western Pacific job Mauch worked on proved to be the Monster's last. "They finally hauled it back and set it in the yard," said Glenn Shannon. "That machine sat there for two years. I tried to sell it to the junkyard for so much a pound for the iron, but the scrap dealer offered to cut it up for us for $15,000 and haul it away. Instead of us getting money for the machine, he wanted money to haul it away! We finally ended up doing the labour on it. They hauled it away in three or four gondola cars. We salvaged the engines and sold it off that way."

Although a failure, the Monster was a major turning point in the evolution of Mannix International. It supplied the basic idea for the company's next major line of equipment — the shoulder ballast cleaner.

1976 ▶

In a leading environmental initiative, ring-necked pheasants raised by MHL Holdings Ltd. are released by Manalta Coal. The 97 birds quickly adapt to their new, reclaimed surroundings at the Vesta and Roselyn mines.

1976 ▶

The 18-month Lebanese civil war ends with Syrian forces in control of the country, 35,000 people killed and the once-beautiful city of Beirut in ruins. The unrest continues.

HEARTBREAK ON A SPUR TRACK

Familiar with the pitfalls of hasty, trial-and-error development, Dick Peppin allowed plenty of time for the shoulder ballast cleaner to move from idea to prototype to field machine. Preliminary layouts prepared in 1967 led to more than 12,000 hours of design work before the prototype left the production shop for field trials. The first shoulder ballast cleaner was completed in 1968. "When the shoulder ballast cleaner came out, it was a good piece of equipment," recalled Ray Wahl. "It had bugs to work out of it, like anything else, but it could do the job right away."

The early history of the shoulder ballast cleaner was not, however, without its share of heartaches. "Just when we had it to the point where we were very proud of it, we took it up to work on the Duluth, Mesabi & Iron Ore Range Railroad," Dick Peppin said. "They parked us on a spur track that night. We had about four people who had just finished working on the machine, and one guy was still finishing up. Suddenly, they ran an empty ore train into the siding and completely demolished our machine. It was very fortunate that we didn't get anybody killed in that accident. That was our biggest and best machine and we had it all smashed up. We had to load it onto trucks and bring it back to Minneapolis to rebuild it. It took us months."

Although this was a tough break, the incident proved to be only a temporary setback for what would become one of Mannix International's most successful pieces of equipment.

automate maintenance of way work, were making their machines far too complicated. These new machines were difficult to maintain and operate, and much too difficult to repair. The railways wanted simpler machines, with easier maintenance and operation, plus greater reliability.

Although a complete and sometimes embarrassing failure — a scrap dealer wanted $15,000 to cut it up and haul it away — the undercutter cleaner taught Dick Peppin and his people several invaluable lessons. One of the most important was to design simpler equipment. It was decided that the next Mannix machine would concentrate on just one area of track maintenance, rather than attempt to do half a dozen tasks.

It sometimes happens that the seeds for future success are hidden in the failures of the past. This was the case with the Monster. Although a failure, it supplied the basic idea for Mannix International's next major line of equipment. Dick Peppin realized that there was no market for a machine that cleaned both the shoulders and the centre of the track. There was, however, a clearly defined market for shoulder ballast cleaners. Railways had been sold on the idea of mechanized shoulder ballast cleaning for some time. Breaking up pockets of fouled ballast at the end of the tie to promote better drainage meant increased tie life and better riding track.

There was just one hitch. While there was a market for shoulder ballast cleaners, this market was dominated by Mannix International's primary competitor, Speno Railway Services. Speno's massive shoulder ballast cleaners, which were widely used throughout the United States, had one major drawback, however. They had to be pulled by a work train. Peppin believed that Mannix International could make a dent in Speno's market share with a self-propelled shoulder ballast cleaner. He also felt that the company's odds for success were greater in a market with one other major competitor, not a half dozen, as with other types of track maintenance machinery.

Thanks to the Monster, Mannix International had already begun the development of a self-propelled shoulder ballast cleaner. The ballast-cleaning portion of the Monster was the most successful part of the entire machine. "Because the undercutter cleaner was such a complicated machine, we just split it in two to make our shoulder ballast cleaner," explained Glenn Shannon. "We had one unit, the shoulder cleaner, in front that picked up the ballast material, and then another unit behind, the screen car, that screened the material. So that idea was just a takeoff of the first one. There would have never been a shoulder ballast cleaner, if it wasn't for the undercutter cleaner."

1976 ▶

Taking a break during the 1976 Pembina Pipe Line Jasper golf tournament.

1976 ▶

Loram International Ltd. completes the $3.6-million TransCanada PipeLine project near North Bay, Ontario.

1976 ▶

Exploram Minerals Ltd.'s search for resources occurs in British Columbia, Washington, Montana, Colorado, Nevada and the Mexican states of Durango and Zacatecas.

While Mannix International developed this new market, the company acquired a new name. Loram management in Calgary decided to reincorporate the company in Minnesota to help protect patents for the new machines. As Canada's laws were much weaker than U.S. legislation, reincorporating the company in the United States provided stronger patent protection. On April 28, 1969, Mannix International Inc. merged with Mannix Construction Inc., a Loram subsidiary used for U.S. construction projects. Effective May 1, 1969, the former Mannix International became known as Mannix Construction Inc., Maintenance of Way Division. This cumbersome name was soon shortened. Within the Loram Group, Peppin's operation was usually referred to simply as Maintenance of Way.

The name change had little effect on Maintenance of Way's operations, and the company continued to move forward. Yet it came nowhere near producing the revenue of the other operating companies in the Loram Group. According to F.P. Mannix, in 1969, Brock Montgomery, Everett Costello and F.C. Mannix considering shutting the company down. "They wanted to close Maintenance of Way because the company could not crack the $1-million level," he explained, "even though they had 98 per cent of their market." That discussion proved to be a real turning point in Maintenance of Way's history. "In order to get more money," explained F.P. Mannix, "they had to look for a new market. This led them from working under the rail, to on top of the rail."

Top: Early Mannix Construction Inc., Maintenance of Way Division grinding stones at work.

Above: The first Maintenance of Way rail grinder. Shown in the travelling position, eight of the 16 grinding stones are visible under the raised forward section.

"We had to expand into different areas of the railroad track maintenance field," Peppin said. "So we figured that we might as well start grinding the rail. At that time, it was not very popular with the railroads. But we figured it was something that was going to come about." So one day in 1969, Peppin marched into the engineering department carrying a Black & Decker grinder from the shop. "Dick brought a hand grinder into engineering and laid it on the floor, and said, 'I want you guys to make a rail grinder out of this,'" recalled Glenn Shannon. "We asked him, 'How many wheels do you want?' Nobody knew anything, so then we tried to figure it out." Shannon, who became production manager in 1969, was skeptical of the idea of using the small Black & Decker grinder. "I went in and argued about these hand grinders," he recalled. "I said, 'I've been using them all my life. They're not built for this kind of stuff.' So we put one in a box and let it bounce all over the place. It just went all to pieces! But that's how this thing got started."

During 1970 and 1971, while Maintenance of Way worked on its first prototype rail grinder, the company also developed its first tie inserter. "At that time, railroads were putting in about 25 to 27 million ties a year," said Peppin. "So we figured, 'Why not come up with a piece of equipment that will put the ties in faster and better?' The ones then available were not too reliable and cost a lot to maintain and keep in operation. We figured if we could develop a tie inserter that operated with fewer moving parts, it would be cheaper to operate and simpler to maintain in the field. But we went through about three or four of those before we got one that would work."

1976 ▶

Syncrude Co. of Canada continues the exploration and development of the tar sands region and hires Loram International Ltd. to construct the Syncrude North Starter Dikes.

"He and his gang really turned that company around."

In 1972, Dick Peppin was promoted to president of Mannix Construction Inc. and its Maintenance of Way Division. In one sense, the promotion was a promotion in name only. As executive vice president, he had held the highest position in the company. But giving Peppin the title of president was important to Loram management in Calgary, who were extremely pleased with Peppin's results since he started running the track maintenance operation in 1965. "We're talking revenues of $300,000 a year down there in Minneapolis for years," said Brock Montgomery. "Then Dick took over and, boy, I'll tell you, he and his gang really turned that company around."

Even so, Maintenance of Way found itself at a crossroads. Sales more than tripled since Peppin took over the operation, but Maintenance of Way was still a very small company, compared with its competitors. For Maintenance of Way, an order for four tie inserters, totalling about $200,000, was a huge contract. But this was a small piece of business for a company like Kershaw. Kershaw would not only sell the same railway four tie inserters, but also a few ballast regulators, half a dozen tie removers, and several other pieces of equipment, with a total price tag in the millions.

Peppin felt that Maintenance of Way was on the verge of moving into really big business. The company's small plant in Plymouth made expansion impossible, however, so Peppin went to Calgary to present his case for a new manufacturing facility. The initial reaction to Peppin's plan was a bit like the one he got when he had submitted his first budget. "In 1973, Maintenance of

Top: R.A. (Dick) Peppin becomes president of the Maintenance of Way Division in 1972.

Above: The new Loram Maintenance of Way shop and office at Hamel, Minnesota, opens in 1975.

Way was a company that did maybe $1 million in volume and was having a heck of a struggle," said Alex Cummings, one of the Loram vice presidents Peppin reported to in Calgary. "Dick had the idea that if they moved into a larger facility, they could build their machinery with a lot less agony and maintain it better. That would lead to great and wonderful things. But on the history of any financial analysis, you would say that what Dick wanted to do, which was to develop a $2-million shop, was ludicrous."

Still, Peppin was persistent and persuasive. Gradually, Loram management began to see that his notion was not so farfetched after all. Cummings was the first person in Calgary that Peppin won over. "After visiting Dick two or three times," Cummings said, "I understood what he wanted to do, and I also could capture a little bit of the imagination the guy had. So I went to work, and we got approval for the shop."

Groundbreaking for the new plant at 3900 Arrowhead Drive, in Hamel, Minnesota, occurred on May 9, 1974. The new space, three times the size of the old facilities, housed 50 staff. Shop structures covered some 35,000 square feet (3,250 square metres). This allowed plenty of room for expansion. With its new manufacturing facilities, Maintenance of Way was a revitalized, recharged company. "Building the new plant in Hamel certainly turned out to be the right thing to do," said Alex Cummings. "That outfit just took off after that, and Dick has never looked back since."

Late in 1974, Loram management in Calgary decided the time had come to make Maintenance of Way a subsidiary company. "Up until then, Mr. Peppin's operation was actually a division of the construction

1976 ▶

A new brochure developed for Loram International Ltd. wins "Best Brochure" in the 1976 H.G. Love Media Awards for Excellence in Advertising.

1976 ▶

Ora Burggren and Maureen Mannix at the Loram Social Club Christmas and long-service awards party.

company," explained Earl Zumwalt, one of the chief financial men in Calgary. "So his operating results had always been added to the operating results of the construction company. What we wanted to do was spin off the Maintenance of Way Division into a separate corporation so that it stood on its own two feet and was no longer a part of the construction company. Maintenance of Way would sever its ties with the construction company and file its own tax return from that point." On February 25, 1975, the newly incorporated company, Loram Maintenance of Way, Inc., officially came into existence.

With its new products and growing reputation, Loram Maintenance of Way began to move into territory occupied by industry leaders. Loram was quickly gaining ground on Speno in the shoulder ballast cleaning field. The Loram Tie Inserter was also gaining industry acceptance. Loram continued to do good business with its undertrack equipment, although the demand for this machinery was falling off, as had been predicted. To take up the slack, in 1975, Loram Maintenance of Way introduced its crib skeletonizer, a small, self-propelled machine for removing fouled ballast from cribs between the ties.

While the crib skeletonizer was being perfected, Loram put the bulk of its development efforts into a new rail grinder. This was one area where Peppin felt the company could make its mark. "One reason that we wanted to get into the rail-grinding market was that, as in the shoulder ballast cleaning market, there was only one major competitor, and that was Speno," said Peppin. "Rather than trying to attack 25 competitors, we figured that two in the market, ourselves and Speno, was enough."

Another reason was that after years of obscurity, the rail-grinding field appeared on the verge of truly blossoming. "The railroads had finally begun to realize the tremendous amount of savings that could be had by grinding rail rather than changing it out," Peppin explained. "Also you have to consider that the price of steel and the price of rail was increasing dramatically

"THAT MEANT, 'THIS THING IS NOT WORKING'"

Ray Wahl has vivid memories of the trials and tribulations of developing Mannix International's tie inserter. Shortly after he became operations manager, Wahl went to Australia to put some undertrack equipment into service on a Mannix Co. Ltd. railway construction job. This assignment was supposed to last for three months, but after a month or so, Wahl began receiving telexes from Minneapolis.

"Dick Peppin would send them to our rep over there, and he would pass them on to me," said Wahl. "They started

out, 'How much longer will Mr. Wahl be needed prior to returning to the States?' After a while the next telex came over, and it was a little stronger, like, 'If at all possible, Mr. Wahl should curtail his time in Australia and return. We have a need for additional people here.' When the next one came, I knew things were in bad shape. It said, 'Due to overwhelming acceptance of the tie inserter, it is imperative that Mr. Wahl get back as soon as possible.' That meant, 'This thing is not working.'"

By 1972, most of the design problems had been worked out. The reworked machine was highly automated. An electrical sequencing system using microswitches controlled the tie insertion process. The operator simply used four hand levers to run the machine. With this system, a tie was picked up, positioned and rammed into position in just 12 seconds.

It was not long before the new tie inserter caught the attention of the railways. The Southern Railway, impressed by the rugged construction of the machine, was the first customer. They ordered two tie inserters in 1972. By the end of the year, another six machines had been sold.

1977 ▶

R.N. (Bob) Sanders becomes president of Manalta Coal.

1977 ▶

To improve the Running Bar X Ranch herd of crossbred Simmental, Hereford and Angus cattle, MHL Holdings representatives travel to Italy to inspect the stock at the El Fratta operation. They purchase two Simmental bulls.

during that period. Any dollar that we could save by performing required maintenance was a savings to the railroad in the long run."

At this point, Peppin still hoped to establish a niche for a machine to handle maintenance grinding. He felt the company was unable to compete in the grinding market, going against Speno and its 96-stone grinders. Speno had yet to produce a self-propelled machine, however, and Peppin continued to believe that the basic idea of the 16-stone prototype grinder had been good. "Our original thought was to come out with a smaller, self-propelled machine that we could duck into shorter sidings and industry spurs to let the main line traffic pass," said Peppin. "But the 16-stone was underpowered. We decided that if we were going to stay in the business, we had to go with something bigger and better."

This bigger, better grinder was the 24-stone machine. Built in 1976, it was christened Rail Grinder 1, or RG1, since it was the company's first grinder beyond the prototype stage. This machine was built for the Quebec Cartier Railway, an iron ore railway in Quebec. Like the Quebec North Shore and Labrador Railway, the Quebec Cartier was built by the Mannix company.

Perhaps because of the old association with the Mannix company, Quebec Cartier Mining was willing to take a chance on Loram's newly gained rail-grinding

The first 24-stone rail grinder. Some of the people responsible for its creation are, standing from left to right, Bob Vieau, Glenn Shannon, Nils Lind, Sig Rishovd, Don Neff and Al Jenkins. Kneeling are Joan Lamprech, Randy Cross, Bill Klempke and Tim Bad Heart Bull.

expertise. "I think the name Mannix had some bearing because of the construction that was done on the railroad," said Peppin. "The Mannix construction company was very influential in completing the job on time and within budget. I am sure that had some bearing on them deciding to buy this grinder from Loram in Minneapolis."

If Quebec Cartier Mining was taking a chance on Loram, Loram also gambled in guaranteeing to deliver the machine. "We went up, sold it to the railroad, and got their ideas about what type of machine they wanted," said Peppin. "There were not any specifications written for the machine or drawings. It was strictly from what we thought we could do with the machine. Without any engineering drawings, we did a preliminary estimate and said, 'Okay, here's what it is going to cost, and this is what we can sell it or lease it for.' That was our real entrance into the rail-grinding market. After making that very serious commitment, there was no backing out."

RG1 was completed 30 days ahead of schedule. In the summer of 1976, it set out on shakedown runs on the Santa Fe Railroad and Conrail, en route to Montreal, where it would be shipped by boat to Port Cartier, Quebec. "Those railroads said they'd let us transport the machine over their lines," Peppin explained. "Rather than paying them transportation funds, we paid

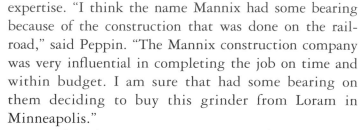

1977 ▶

Quebec enacts the Charter of the French Language, Bill 101, making French the official language of the province.

1977 ▶

Slow-pitch stars at the Manalta summer barbecue.

them by giving them about three or four days of grinding time on each railroad. At the same time, it became known from a sales standpoint that we were in the grinding market. I think that a lot of the railroads stood up and took notice because we were the first self-propelled rail grinder. It was unbelievable for them to see a grinder going down the railroad track under its own power, performing a grinding feat."

Although Loram Maintenance of Way still had a long way to go in learning the science of rail grinding, the company now progressed rapidly, constantly modifying and improving its machinery. As in the old days, the development effort was a group process, with ideas for improvements coming from everyone involved. Peppin gives a lion's share of the credit to the operators of the machinery. "Everyone working at Loram in those early days of the rail grinder really accepted the challenge and looked forward to coming up with the solution because we were the first ones to work under those adverse conditions," said Peppin. "I must admit that the people in the field had more foresight in solving the problems and coming up with the solution than some of the managers did at that time."

The Mannix family celebrating Fred and Margie's 40th wedding anniversary at the Calgary Golf and Country Club. From left to right, F.P., Margie, F.C., Maureen and R.N. Mannix.

"We do the things we do for all Canada."

Despite the challenges of the times, the first step in the transition to the third generation of Mannix family management went smoothly. This was due, in large measure, to the founding principals of the Mannix family. There are a lot of similarities between rearing a family and running a business, where the company founder sets the ground rules very early. If you do it right and maintain those values, growth will be managed so you do not lose the soul of the company. This, indeed, had occurred.

Yet while the founding values remained intact, there was never a desire to cling to the founding company, the construction arm of the group. The desire had been to diversify, thereby ensuring the group's future despite the ups and downs of any one industry. And this, too, had paid off. For example, total Loram Group assets as of December 31, 1974, stood at $175 million. Construction, at $35 million, comprised just under 20 per cent of the total group assets. Oil and gas, at $59 million, comprised 34 per cent. Coal, at $71 million, comprised 40 per cent. U.S. operations, at $8 million, comprised four per cent. Other assets, at $2 million, comprised slightly more than one per cent. By 1977, total Loram Group assets had grown to $340 million.

Obviously, one does not achieve these figures without a lot of hard work and dedication, two of the primary founding principals of the Mannix outfit. "Father tried to instill the work ethic into Freddie and me, and the love of the outfit that he has had," Ron Mannix said. "The outfit is him. He built it and he loves it. He has also given us a sense of responsibility. We have a lot of people in this outfit and we're determining their livelihood every day with the decisions we make. That's a big, big responsibility there, that we must look after. What is important is that this organization, this entity, the outfit, is perpetuated. If it is, it will provide opportunity to people in all of Canada. We do the things we do for all Canada, not just for us and the people in the outfit."

1977 ▶

Charles Chaplin dies December 25.

1977 ▶

The Loram Learjet logs its 5,000th flying hour. At a maximum speed of 500 miles (800 kilometres) per hour, that multiplies out to 2.5 million miles (4 million kilometres) or five trips to the moon.

Chapter 10

IN THE BUSINESS OF BUSINESS

1978 – 1985

It was very prudent for them to separate out the areas of operation. It's my observation that when two guys try to run one thing, it just does not work. I know of only one company, Genstar, where they trade the chairman's and president's job, but that's absolutely unique. The two sides of the company are very different. On one side is an operating company and on the other side is a financial company.

But Ron and Fred are both very much dedicated to survival. It's really very nice to see two young guys working as hard as anybody because they both have enough money; if they never worked another day, it wouldn't matter. That doesn't happen by the third generation. They usually become playboys.

— Fred McNeil, chairman of the board of the Bank of Montreal

I n 1978, the world's population stood at about 4.4 billion, with 200,000 people added daily. And these people, as people have done since time immemorial, daily walked the tightrope between war and peace. Throughout the Seventies, the Middle East continued to be a trouble spot, but in 1978 a "framework for peace" was achieved after 17 days of negotiation between Egypt's President Sadat, Israel's Prime Minister Begin and U.S. President Carter. That same year, Vietnamese troops invaded Cambodia using Soviet-supplied arms to drive out Pol Pot's regime.

Early in 1979, the Shah was driven out of Iran by Islamic fundamentalists who opposed his secular form of oppression. Later that year, the American Embassy in Tehran was seized by militant students who took staff members hostage, most of whom were held for more than 400 days before their release was negotiated. The Canadian ambassador to Iran, Ken Taylor, became a hero when he and his staff hid six American diplomats before spiriting them out of the country. On Christmas Eve 1979, Soviet troops invaded Afghanistan, an event which led to yet another Vietnam-type war. For the next nine years, U.S.-supplied Afghan guerrillas resisted Soviet occupation forces.

Right: Ken Taylor, Canadian ambassador to Iran during the American hostage crisis in 1980. He helps spirit six American diplomats to freedom.

During the late 1970s and into the mid-1980s, separatists proposed to dismantle Canada. Amid bitterness over bilingualism, the twin economic demons of inflation and recession continued to plague the country. To some extent, these troubles persisted in most of the western industrialized nations, but as conditions began to abate throughout the United States and Europe, they lingered in Canada with a crippling tenacity. While Canada's neighbours to the south were applauding the apparent success of "Reaganomics," Canada struggled to keep its financial head above water. In 1982, interest rates approached 20 per cent, 11 per cent of the work force was unemployed and inflation was at 11 per cent — the highest figures since the Great Depression of the 1930s.

The Canadian West was particularly hard hit. A worldwide commodities crisis, brought on by crippling surpluses, kept prices for such products as oil, livestock, grain and mineral resources at extraordinarily low levels. In the oil industry, a traditional bastion of western Canadian economy, prices dropped from $35 US per barrel in 1981 to $28 US in 1985. Simultaneously, an oversupply of grain played havoc with western Canadian farmers. In 1980, grain prices were roughly $222 per ton. By 1985, they had fallen to $186. Farm bankruptcies in the West nearly quadrupled in the first half of the decade. The mining industry was also ravaged. In British Columbia, the hardest hit province, earnings from mining fell from $420 million in 1980 to a loss of $37 million in 1985. Fifteen of the province's 29 major mines closed. Buoyed by a steady market in the Japanese steel industry, only the price of coal remained relatively stable during the first half of the decade.

Ron Mannix becomes president of the Loram Group in 1978.

It was a tough time which would demand tough decisions. It was time for the third generation of the Mannix family to prove, once again, that the family was in the business of business.

The Legacy of a Good Name
"Every man has his time."

In January 1978, management of the operations and staff of the Loram Group's parent holding company, Loram Co. Ltd., transferred to a new company, Mancal Ltd. Despite the name change, the entire corporate entity — the holding company and the operating companies — continued to be referred to as the Loram Group.

At this time, Fred P. Mannix was named chairman of the parent company board and Ron Mannix was named president and chief executive officer of Loram. With these changes, the second generation successfully passed control of the Loram Group to the third generation and F.C. Mannix resigned from all board positions he still held. "He was interested, but he was not going to do anything to lead the troops now — that's up to Freddie and Ronnie," said Paul Christensen, vice president and treasurer for Mancal. "Which makes him kind of big, too. You know, to say, 'Here it is, go with it.' It's not easy for a man to do that, I'm sure. But he's done a great job of it."

At the time that Ron Mannix became president and chief executive officer, he was just 30 years old. To ensure a smooth transition between brothers, Fred P. Mannix left on a year-long National Defence College (NDC) program, designed to give senior military and senior civil service people a course in geopolitics. According to F.P. Mannix, there were several reasons why he left to attend the NDC. "If I stayed at Loram," he

HIGHLANDERS NAME LIEUTENANT-COLONEL

In January 1982, Fred P. Mannix, a graduate of the National Defence College in Kingston, Ontario, was named honorary lieutenant-colonel of the Calgary Highlanders militia infantry unit. F.P. Mannix replaced retiring Lieutenant-Colonel Mark Tennant. Tennant, a former city alderman and a member of the Order of Canada, served with the Calgary Highlanders during the Second World War.

The honorary lieutenant-colonel of a militia regiment assists the commanding officer in ceremonial matters, the maintenance of regimental traditions and the social life of the unit.

1978 ▶

Polish Cardinal Karol Wojtyla becomes Pope John Paul II, the first non-Italian pontiff since 1523.

1978 ▶

A Loram ditcher digs pipeline trench for the Pembina Pipe Line Fort St. John project.

explained, "people would try to end-run around Ron to me, which would not work. Also, we were under pressure by the Canadian government to do things internationally. By going to the NDC, I could learn, as it was 15 per cent military, with the remaining focus on geopolitics." Another reason was intensely personal. "I needed a break," he explained. "I was working from 7:00 a.m. to 7:00 p.m. and it was hurting my marriage. One of the reasons I left for the NDC was to try and save it."

When Ron Mannix became president and chief executive officer, Stan Waters, who had held the position for two years, became president of Lorcan Co. Ltd., a project management, construction and engineering services company initiated by Waters. Upon Fred P. Mannix's return to the business in 1979, in addition to serving as chairman of the parent company's board, he became chairman of Bowfort Services Ltd. and Manalta Holdings Ltd., thereby effectively switching from the operational side of the business to the investment side.

"Freddie Sr. knew their strengths and weaknesses and put Ronnie in charge of the operating companies and Freddie Jr. in charge of the investments," explained Loram board member, Doug Gardiner. "Freddie has got a flair for it. He has got an inquiring mind. He has a very nice personality. People talk to him. He goes all over the place, London, New York, Toronto. Finds out what is going on. Freddie picks people and he picks situations — at any given time he has got a dozen different schemes going. He's backed them with some money and some advice and he has got a good team around him, legal and administration. They listen to some fellow with an invention or somebody with an idea and sift it through, and if they like it, they will give him some money, get him started. I would say, out of the portfolio, there must be eight or ten of them there; two or three casualties, but I think at least six of them are working. For instance, they are in First Choice, they are in CableVision, and they are in salmon farming. A couple of turkeys in there that didn't work out, but you never know. They had reasons to give the job a chance and see how it worked. That's Freddie's forte. He is good at it."

"Ron is extremely painstaking, conscientious, thorough, and because he is all of those things, he has learned a great deal," Gardiner said. "He asks a lot of questions. People like him. He has got a nice appearance and a nice manner. He can walk into any of these offices,

F.C. MANNIX INDUCTED INTO THE BUSINESS HALL OF FAME

In 1979, Junior Achievement of Canada — a national organization of more than 7,000 teenagers in 50 communities — established the Canadian Business Hall of Fame to honour Canadians who made outstanding and enduring contributions to improve the products, processes, efficiencies or the human relations of business. The people selected for this honour were chosen by a group of business editors from major Canadian publications.

Frederick C. Mannix was one of the first six individuals inducted into the Hall of Fame. He and K.C. Irving, an industrialist from New Brunswick, were the only living Canadians inducted. The four other men selected for this honour were: J. Armand Bombardier, who invented the snowmobile and founded Bombardier Inc., a Canadian manufacturing firm; David Dunkelman, founder of the Tip Top Tailors clothing store chain; Hart Massey, who converted his father's foundry into what is known today as Massey-Ferguson Ltd.; and Donald Alexander Smith, Lord Strathcona, best remembered as the man who drove the last spike of the Canadian Pacific Railway.

At a dinner held at the Royal York Hotel in Toronto on April 24, 1979, F.C. Mannix ended his Hall of Fame acceptance speech with these words: "The word I leave you with is COPE. Now if you have C for Concept of your goal, O for Opportunity, P for People and E for Enterprise — private enterprise that is — then you will be able to COPE with any challenge presented to you."

1978 ▶

Varied sports activities are enjoyed at the Pembina/Decalta summer barbecue.

1978 ▶

The Alberta Gas Trunk Line continues to expand its system in the Peace River area of Alberta. Loram pipeliners wrap a section of the Peace River Loop.

and no matter how big the company or how important this fellow Mr. X thinks he is, he gets talking to Ronnie before he realizes what's going on, tells him everything Ronnie wants to know. He has got a wonderful way and Ronnie has learned. He leaves no stone unturned. He does his homework very well. The alterations and changes that Ronnie has made have been a lot of good moves and he has surrounded himself with absolutely topflight people. He gets things done. I give him full marks. He has some darn good ideas."

"Freddie and Ronnie are two completely different personalities," continued Gardiner, "and because of that, they are at each other's throat every once in a while. But they both respect each other's talents and abilities. So they are a good team. They are making a lot of the right moves. Freddie Sr. has got to be a very happy man with what he sees. And, of course, they keep him fully informed, which he loves."

"They both often refer to the past or what their dad did or did not do," added Frederick Harold (Fred) McNeil, president, chief operating officer and director of the Bank of Montreal since 1973, and chairman of the bank's board from 1975, a position he held until his retirement in 1982. "As far as business was concerned, he was their teacher. No question about that. There's nothing soft about Costello or Montomery, either. Those were tough guys, those three, very tough guys. Fred Sr. was a hard rock. Well, you have to be, to build something like he did. You have to be quick and decisive and churned up when things are going wrong. That's a characteristic of anybody who runs a successful business. Different times require different men, too."

"There's a phrase: 'Every man has his time,'" McNeil said. "It's never the same world and what worked in the pioneer period doesn't particularly work in the

From left to right, R.N. Mannix, F.C. Mannix and F.P. Mannix at Fish Creek with family pets Poochie and Travis.

W.H.H. (Howard) Tidswell, secretary and general counsel, Mancal Ltd.

more complicated circumstances. In my opinion, both Fred and Ron adapt very well to this complex world. Very well. It was the family influence, certainly. The upbringing is the main reason. Those boys, from a very early age, were expected to work and they spent most of their summers working. Young guys get to like work. It's more fun than doing something else."

Both sons are deeply conscious of the responsibility, and the legacy, passed to the third generation. "The legacy of F.S. was that he had a record of performance," F.P. Mannix once reflected. "He always got the job done. He had a name. He had integrity. Those were the things that Dad would always say — that his dad left him the legacy of a good name. I think the legacy that F.C. left was one of performance; we always performed. The other thing that F.C. did was seize the opportunity. When the opportunity was there, he'd take a run at it whether it looked like it was too big or too little. It didn't matter. You figured out how to do it and you took a run at it. Seizing the opportunity and the performance once you've got it was, I think, the legacy of F.C."

"What my father gave Freddie and me, despite advice to the contrary from many, many people, was an opportunity to run the outfit," added Ron Mannix. "People said it was like giving a loaded shotgun to 10-year-old kids who did not know anything about shotguns. They felt that Freddie and I were far too young to do it, that we didn't have the judgment or the training that was required, but Father's sentiments were that he didn't give a damn. There's a very significant point and a great asset in that simple statement.

"This came out when Father stood up to the biggest outfits and told them to go fly a kite — that he was going to take a run at them because he figured he was as good as they were. Father always told Freddie and

1978 ▶

Ayatollah Ruhollah Khomeini, after 18 years in exile, leads a popular revolution that topples the Iranian government.

1978 ▶

Celebration by the victorious softball team at the MEGA summer barbecue.

me, 'I'm going to teach you about the business. At some point in time, you're going to have to make a decision: you're either in, or you're out. The only thing that I can do is allow you to make that choice.'"

In December 1980, another major milestone was achieved when Fred P. and Ron Mannix signed a very significant shareholders' agreement and F.C. Mannix transferred voting control to the two of them. The real transfer of the outfit was now complete. In the future, it would be up to Fred P. and Ron Mannix to perpetuate the business however they saw fit.

Two years after the voting control was transferred, Everett Costello and Brock Montgomery once again retired, this time for good. On March 1, 1982, Lorne B. Gordon and W.H.H. (Howard) Tidswell were named directors of all Loram Group companies replacing Montgomery and Costello.

Lorne Gordon joined the Loram Group in 1971 as chief accountant with Alberta Concrete Products in Edmonton. He moved to Calgary in 1972, where he worked as the chief internal auditor for Loram Holdings Ltd. In March of 1973, when the controller of Alberta Concrete Products resigned, Gordon returned to Edmonton until that fall, when he was invited back to Loram as controller. In 1974, he became vice president, oil and gas for Loram Co. Ltd. and in 1977 he was appointed vice president, corporate planning for Pembina Pipe Line Ltd. In 1978, he returned to Loram Co. Ltd., first as assistant general manager, then as vice president and general manager, a position he continued to hold under Mancal Ltd. Gordon was also chairman of the board of Pembina Resources Limited.

Howard Tidswell, a childhood friend of F.P. Mannix, began his association with the Loram Group in 1960, when he worked as a labourer. During subsequent summer months, Tidswell worked as a legal assistant while attending university, earning a bachelor of arts degree (1963) and a bachelor of laws degree (1966) from the University of Alberta. He was admitted to the Law Society in 1967 and in 1970 he joined Loram Co. Ltd. as secretary and general counsel. After three years, he was appointed secretary and general counsel of Loram International Ltd. and in 1980, he became secretary and general counsel of Mancal Ltd. Tidswell became intimately involved at the highest level of the business, becoming president of the shareholders' office, Trison Investments Ltd. He was Fred P. Mannix's closest friend and a superb advisor to the group. Everyone who knew Howard was deeply saddened by his untimely death on October 8, 1983. He had just turned 43 years of age. The Loram

FRED MCNEIL JOINS THE BOARD

Fred McNeil at his ranch in southern Alberta.

Frederick Harold (Fred) McNeil was born in Saskatoon, Saskatchewan, in 1916. The son of a farm implement dealer, he was educated at the University of Manitoba and the University of Saskatchewan. During the Second World War, McNeil served as squadron leader, RCAF Aircrew, earning the Air Force Cross when he rescued a fellow officer from a burning plane.

In the late Forties and early Fifties, McNeil worked as a journalist in Victoria and Vancouver, British Columbia, freelancing for several newspapers and magazines at the going rate of 10 cents a line. From 1954 to 1956, he was a management consultant to Braun & Co., and from 1956 to 1960, served as director of management services for Powell River Co. In 1960, McNeil joined the Ford Motor Company of Canada. When he left in 1965, his position was director, organization, personnel and administration planning. McNeil joined the Bank of Montreal in January 1966 as general manager, personnel planning. After progressing through increasingly senior positions, McNeil was named president, chief operating officer and director in 1973 and chairman of the board in 1975. He remained chairman until his retirement in 1982.

Over the years, McNeil served as a director for many notable companies including Dome Canada Limited, Encor Energy Corporation Ltd., Gendis Inc., Nu-West Group, Telemedia Communications Ltd., The Dominion Life Assurance Company and The Seagram Company Ltd. In 1982, he became a director of companies in the Loram Group, including Bowcal Management Ltd., MHL Holdings Ltd., Mancal Ltd. and Manvest Ltd.

A self-described student of family companies, McNeil said, "The Mannix outfit is very interesting because it's a third generation company. You don't see many of those. Both Fred P. and Ron are pretty energetic. They work. They work hard."

1978 ▶

Loram International constructs earthen cofferdams for the Revelstoke Dam project. The completed upstream cofferdam is shown.

1978 ▶

Loram International also excavates the site for the Revelstoke Dam powerhouse. More than 79,240 linear metres (86,600 yards) of rockbolts and dowels support and stabilize the back slope.

Group, through the Carthy Foundation, organized a memorial scholarship in his name at the Strathcona-Tweedsmuir School, where Tidswell had been an alumnus and an active parent.

David McClement, a chartered accountant who joined the Loram Group in 1960, and who had become the financial architect of the group, had been on the parent company board for many years. President of Bowfort Services Ltd. and a director of virtually all Loram companies at the time, McClement was also named to the boards of directors of all the companies in the Loram Group in 1982. In 1984, after a one-year sabbatical and well-deserved rest, he returned to the group as vice chairman of Mancal Ltd., concentrating his efforts on the operating side of the business.

Another who joined the board in 1982 was Fred McNeil. "Fred Sr. had Montgomery and Costello, who were pretty cranky guys, to fight with him," McNeil said. "I think it was a deliberate policy to get some old crankies to help the boys. So Doug Gardiner and I fulfill that role, particularly since their dad doesn't want to get involved. It's pretty wise you know. I think it's very prudent for a private company, especially a private company, to have outside advisors or directors. It's easy to get your pals around you. Some people can be very cute at being agreeable and they don't serve you well."

David W. McClement, president of Bowfort Services Ltd., and financial architect of the group for many years.

Two Losses that Cut Deep
"A travesty of justice"

While the transition from the second to third generation was being completed, the Mannix family experienced two tremendous blows. The first was the expropriation of the family home at Fish Creek. The second was the death of Margie Mannix. For many, the two events were inextricably intertwined.

Back in 1972, the provincial government set its eyes on one of man's most sacred possessions: his private property. "It became apparent that the City of Calgary had their eyes on Fish Creek Valley as a park," recalled R.J. Burns, legal advisor to the Mannix family and grandnephew of Calgary pioneer Pat Burns. "Mannix had a substantial part of the west end of Fish Creek. Mannix didn't want to sell because it was his home." After Pat Burns' estate, which owned indirectly all the east end of Fish Creek, was acquired by the government, "then they turned the responsibility for acquiring the rest of the park to a deputy minister who had no previous experience in land acquisition," explained Burns. "We tried to leave the Mannix property out of it, but the government wouldn't buy that. They just made up their minds they were going to acquire it. The situation carried on for nearly five years, from 1973 to 1978." For five long years, the threat to Fish Creek loomed like a dark cloud over the family.

Margie Mannix recalled how the family came to Fish Creek. "Fred often spoke of moving to the country — of living on a farm," she said. "Never having lived in the country myself, I really did not give it any serious thought until our daughter Maureen was approaching her eighth birthday. Maureen was 'horse crazy' as many young girls at that age were, and she very much wanted a horse for her birthday. So we broke down and bought 'Hotfoot,' a lovely 12-year-old thoroughbred. To make a long story short, Hotfoot moved us to the country! To Fish Creek, nine miles past the city limits, to the little cottage by the bridge on what is now 37th Street. A little horse stable and a tiny two-bedroom house. Three kids now, six horses, two dogs, and Fred and me, all crowded

Family and friends participate in the annual Fall Hunt at Fish Creek.

◀ 1978

Grande Resources Management prepares railway grade and builds a railway bridge during the Lake Louise project in Banff National Park.

◀ 1978

After 13 days of negotiations, U.S. President Jimmy Carter (centre) leads Egyptian President Anwar Sadat (left) and Israeli Prime Minister Menachem Begin (right) to a framework for peace, the Camp David Accord. The two Middle East countries end 30 years of war.

in like sardines in a can. But we loved living in the country. We were never happier, but we needed to grow. We began to expand by acquiring some land across the road and on the north side of the street.

"In September 1952, our home was started. We had horses, cows, chickens and geese and were becoming quite self-sufficient with our own milk, butter and eggs. Many trees were planted, cared for and watched grow along with our children, who never once asked what to do with their time. We were building a beautiful herd of Hereford cattle and the children joined the 4-H Club and the Pony Club. Over the years, 70-odd cross-country horse jumps had been set up on our property, across fields and trails through the wooded creek area. Our friends and neighbours were always welcome to ride through and enjoy these trails. Even the wild animals knew they were welcome for we never allowed shooting on our property. Before long, we had a large herd of deer along with coyotes, beavers, weasels, squirrels, pheasants, badgers, porcupines and the odd bear that would wander through."

On March 22, 1978, city growth and new planning laws overtook F.C. Mannix's freedom to use his property at Fish Creek as he saw fit. That day, the province expropriated the property for public use in Fish Creek Park. The Mannix home and ranch would be developed as a nature centre and equestrian concession. Fred and Margie Mannix were denied the right to live out the rest of their lives in the home they had built and cherished. "I always felt that was a travesty of justice," David McClement said. "I didn't have a problem with the province taking the property for a park, but to take away the home. It seems to me they should have been able to deal with that on a better basis. Things were pretty offensive to me, offensive from anybody's point of view."

"I have heard Peter Lougheed say strong things about that very type of thing," McClement said, "that

*Margaret (Margie) Mannix,
the guiding light for F.C. Mannix and
the heart and soul of the outfit.*

the federal government coming into the province on the energy issue was like someone moving into your living room, to use an analogy. Peter found that very offensive. But before they even took over the land out there, they had people from the environmental department running through the Mannix family home. I can visualize them standing in the living room, looking at the walls, trying to decide where to hang pictures. This was prior to taking possession, with Mr. Mannix looking on. That, to me, was a travesty of justice."

"When Margie was talking about having to leave their home, she said, 'You know, Doris, it's not the house, it's all the wonderful memories that we cherish so dearly,' " recalled Doris Reilly, whose husband, Al, joined the Mannix outfit in 1941. "I remember one time we went for a walk down along the creek where the children used to swim. They had a little house down there, a little changing house. And Margie said to me, 'If you ever feel like just getting away from it all, Doris, I'll show you where the key is, and just feel free to come.' I thought how wonderful that she would care or know that maybe there would be times that I would feel that I just wanted to be by myself. She was a wonderful person. Just so thoughtful."

"The expropriation was one of the reasons Mother died," Maureen Mannix Eberts said. "Because her home was taken away from her. She couldn't believe that Peter Lougheed, who was the premier of the province, wouldn't just say that private property is private property. You can live there until you die and then go. Which is exactly what should have been done."

Margie Mannix died of a heart attack on December 9, 1979, shortly after she and F.C. had celebrated their 40th wedding anniversary. When Margie's eulogy was being composed, F.C. was asked if there was anything he would like to add. "There's one thing I know for sure," he said, "and that's if it wasn't for Margie, we

1978 ▶

Lortherm Insulation, a new division of Loram International, provides industrial insulation to the petroleum and nuclear industries, including the new Dow Chemical plant at Fort Saskatchewan, Alberta.

1978 ▶

To further diversify the Loram Group, Manvest Ltd. is formed to provide a vehicle for venture capital and other non-core investment activities.

MANVEST LTD

wouldn't be sitting here right now. I owe everything to her."

"Margie was Fred C.'s anchor and his haven," said Doug Gardiner. "Probably the smartest thing Freddie Mannix ever did in his life, when he spotted her, was to never let up until she finally said she would marry him. And you know, it was not easy. She went out in the early days and lived in those construction camps and did it all. She came from a home where, in her wildest dreams, she never figured she would do that. Margie was absolutely marvellous. She was a wonderful homemaker, she loved those kids, she brought them all along, educated them, and created a refined, wonderful atmosphere for them to grow up in. She was just — you've seen her picture — well, she was just as nice as she looked."

"That broke her heart, you know," Gardiner said, "having to move out of the house where they had been for 28 years. Boy, Freddie was bitter about that. And he got no help from Peter Lougheed whatsoever. None. It's just a pity. I think he could have said something with a clear conscience and said, 'Leave the man alone.' When the government did take it, the price they offered was ridiculous. So Freddie got into a four-year lawsuit. Being Irish, he was going to fight."

A VERY SPECIAL LADY

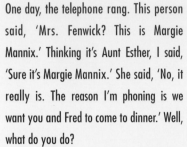

Margie Mannix.

"I've always said that the wives were the haven and comic relief for husbands, to keep them going, survive everything," Mary Fenwick said. "For example, I had an aunt in Calgary who was a real nut; she liked to pull tricks on you. One day, the telephone rang. This person said, 'Mrs. Fenwick? This is Margie Mannix.' Thinking it's Aunt Esther, I said, 'Sure it's Margie Mannix.' She said, 'No, it really is. The reason I'm phoning is we want you and Fred to come to dinner.' Well, what do you do?

"When we went to her place — to show the character of this woman, she was just remarkable — I arrived at the door and said, 'Oh, Margie, I am so embarrassed.' She said, 'Don't be. You know, when Freddie and I were on the Minnewanka Dam, we had such fun with everybody in camp, but every now and then we used to go into Banff and stay the weekend at the Banff Springs Hotel. And we got all cleaned up, and so did the fellows that came in. Quite often I wouldn't recognize them. Fred said to me, 'You really have to be a little more astute because you have coffee with these people and then they see you in Banff and you don't recognize them.' So I made up my mind that I was going to say hello to every familiar face I saw.'"

"They're walking down from the Banff Springs Hotel one day," Mary Fenwick said, "and Margie saw this familiar face. So she stopped and said, 'Isn't it a marvellous day?' And he said, 'Yes, it certainly is.' She said, 'Have you been out yet, have you played golf?' And he said, 'No, I'm going riding.' She said, 'Isn't that grand, have a good day.' And they walked on. Freddie turned to her and said, 'Margie, how long have you known the Prince of Wales?'

"Now, I don't know whether this ever happened, but this was the type of a woman she was, to reveal that to me and make me feel at ease. She was a great role model for us young wives. She was just a very special lady." Margaret Ruth Mannix passed away on December 9, 1979.

Providing the Balance
The Rise and Fall
of Cenlor Services

Not long after becoming president and chief executive officer of Loram in January 1978, Ron Mannix set about choosing his team. "There's a saying that you go from shirtsleeves to shirtsleeves in three generations," he explained. "Most of the time the first generation is the entrepreneur, the second generation is the administrator, and the third one throws it away. Father has had the entrepreneurial instinct, just as his father did, in a different way. You can never really put a finger on that. You can never really analyse or predict it or understand it. It's just part of the man and his makeup. When something happens to hit him that he thinks is important enough, out it comes, and if you happen to be along with him, you hang on and see what happens.

"Everett and Brock were immensely valuable when Father would get to bounding along and get carried away with various ideas. Costello would hammer him on the back and say, 'You can't do that for these reasons,' or 'Don't do it, period, because I don't think you should.' So they were a team that was very significant and valuable because they provided the balance. One of the things that I'm trying to do here is to create a balance between us and our outfit, in the team that's around me."

1978 ▶

The U.S. Congress approves the Panama Canal Treaty, allowing ownership and control of the international waterway to transfer to Panama.

1978 ▶

Edmonton's new rapid transit system is a complete success during the Commonwealth Games held in August. The 14 kilometres (nine miles) of above and underground track are laid by the Railroad Division of Loram International.

One person thought vital to achieving this balance was Alex Cummings, who was brought back into Loram as vice president and general manager. "Ronnie came to me and asked me to come with him," said Cummings. "He told me that he wanted to do away with the four vice president concept that was in effect under Stan Waters. He said I was the guy that had the experience to do the vice president and general manager role, which was my old job under Freddie. What he wanted to do was change the posture of my job to try and accept the fact that it had to have more authority with it, such as approving expenditures and things of that nature." However, within a year, "I had a very difficult health problem show up, a blood pressure problem," explained Cummings. "So I had to advise Ronnie that I had to be moved out of my current assignment."

When Cummings transferred to become president of Pembina, he was succeeded by Lorne Gordon, whom Alex Cummings had brought back to Loram Co. Ltd. as assistant general manager. "Lorne was able to start delegating more authority to the presidents," Cummings said. "I sure as heck made it known that more autonomy had to come when I went down to the oil company. So there were several events that Lorne, as a good administrator, was able to expedite very quickly."

Although the presidents of the operating companies gained more autonomy, the overall issue of control versus management remained. "Ronnie would have long meetings talking about the differences between control and management," explained Gordon. "Ronnie was going to control the companies, but he wasn't going to manage them. Brock and Everett and everybody seemed to agree with those statements, but then nobody could understand what control meant, what management meant."

"It's easy to push authority down, but not so easy to push accountability down," explained Fred McNeil. "That is the challenge. You really can't give up control if

Cenlor Services Ltd. provides centralized administrative services for the entire Loram Group, including corporate security performed by long-time veterans, from left to right, Gordon Tink, Scotty Harper and Harold Hedstrom.

you own the darn thing, can you? But the style of exercising that control is what we're talking about. John L. Weinberg is an investment banker with Goldman Sachs down in New York. He's quite a humorous fellow. He said, 'God damn it, companies should be changed every decade. If they're centralized, decentralize it. If they're decentralized, centralize it.'"

There was already some experience with centralization within the group. Public relations was centralized in the Sixties. Geoff Corry was hired in late 1973 to coordinate the personnel field on a group basis rather than an individual basis. In 1975, Loram Co. Ltd. took over management of the Data Centre from Loram International and began to offer data processing services to other Loram operating companies.

The decision to centralize the Loram Group coincided with corporate thought in the mid-1970s, which had sprung largely out of the need to control the enormous costs of the mainframe computers of the time. Most companies were on a path toward centralization of computing, with many setting up elaborate divisions that provided consolidated services for the entire organization. "Cenlor was created at the time when centralization, and rigorous centralization, was considered to be a good idea," said Lorne Gordon. "The concept of Cenlor was really to collect in one place all of the administrative services that would be needed by any company in the Loram Group."

"The original idea behind Cenlor was that it would be a systems designer and a standard setter," said F.P. Mannix. "The companies would do all the work themselves, but there would be a common system to what we were doing, so that if you were looking for gravel property, for example, you didn't end up with 14 files on the same thing. Cenlor would set the standards and police the standards. There would be two or three people to do the auditing — that the companies were following

1978 ▶

Loram International constructs the three-span Fish Creek Bridge and access road overpass. Both are post-tensioned, cast-in-place concrete decks with cast-in-place piers.

1978 ▶

Celebrants at the Loram Maintenance of Way Christmas party. From left, Dick Peppin, Mary and Jim Gavin, Mary Jeanne and George Farris.

BUILDING A BETTER COUNTRY

F.C. Mannix Appointed to the Order of Canada

On July 1, 1967, the Order of Canada was established as the centrepiece of Canada's system of honours. Its Latin motto — *desiderantes meliorem patriam* — proclaims the aspirations of its members who, in their lives and work, have shown that they "desire a better country."

The granting of honours is a gracious and tangible way for a country to pay tribute to those who exem-

plify the highest qualities of citizenship and whose contributions enrich the lives of their contemporaries. It is appropriate that Canada adopted this practice on the 100th anniversary of Confederation, a time when the achievements of fellow countrymen were uppermost in the thoughts of all Canadians.

Being appointed to the Order of Canada is contingent on achievement and outstanding service to Canada or humanity at large. Appointments are made by the governor general, based on the recommendations of the Advisory Council of the Order, which meets twice a year under the chairmanship of the chief justice of Canada to consider nominations submitted by members of the public. There are three levels of membership in which the number of appoint-

ments is limited: companion (not to exceed 150 in all); officer (46 appointments maximum in any year); and member (92 appointments maximum in any year).

F.C. Mannix was appointed an officer of the Order of Canada in 1985. At an investiture ceremony at Government House in Ottawa on April 10, he was presented with a Badge of the Order by Governor General Jeanne Sauvé. The order's badge is in the form of a stylized snowflake of six points and is worn at the neck by companions and officers, and on the left breast by members.

that standard and so on. That was the original concept of it. Of course, it went totally haywire."

"It really started with the computer centre because back in those days, the construction company was more important than everything else put together," Gordon said. "Because of the nature of their business, they needed to have service promptly when they were bidding and if they had problems on a job, they would take over all the computer services or anything else that was going on. They just had to have service. All the other companies then ended up being second, third or fourth priority depending on where they were in the scheme of things. That resulted in them being pretty unhappy, and it created a lot of animosity in the group because everybody hated the construction company."

In addition to the animosity created by Cenlor, an April 1980 audit revealed that while Cenlor had been created to cut costs, in reality, the reverse had come true. "One of the projects we started looking at was payroll," explained Greg D. Sawatzky, Cenlor's manager of internal audit. "Don Cherry actually did the audit. He was looking at the costs in the computer department and tying that in with the payroll audit. We had this payroll system in-house in Cenlor and they had one or two small changes. But what they thought were small changes were going to cost $50,000 to implement. What we did was look at it and say, 'Okay, let's say we use the bank to do our payroll.' For each employee it came out to cost something like $1 or $2 per month. This $50,000 could be used for many, many years to do the whole payroll of the company."

"One of my first thoughts was maybe we should think about Cenlor and what it's costing us if we can do the payroll for the whole company for a few hundred dollars a month versus hundreds of thousands of dollars," said Sawatzky. "I think that was one of the initial points, even though I know the presidents were also questioning how much Cenlor was costing each of the companies. Cenlor was hiring people left and right. It just seemed out of control."

When Cenlor's budget predictions skyrocketed at the onset of a recession, the Loram Group's experiment with centralization came to an end. "Cenlor had to prepare a preliminary

1979 ▶

The Soviet Union invades Afghanistan. Afghan resistance, while primitive compared to the Soviet military, is effective.

1979 ▶

Five levels of excavation are required for the construction of the LG-4 powerhouse in Quebec. Three levels are shown on a winter night.

1979 ▶

Action at the annual employees' curling bonspiel.

budget much in advance of everybody else so we could send out to all the companies notices as to what their share of Cenlor's costs were going to be," explained Gordon. "We recovered all the costs of running Cenlor from its customers and its customers were the Loram Group companies. I was in my office in August. Geoff Corry, who was the president of Cenlor, came to me with his budget and his administrative budget was $8 million. I can't remember the percentage increase over the last year, but it was absolutely enormous. We had over 100 people in Cenlor. I couldn't believe what I was seeing."

"I thanked Geoff Corry and then I went to see Dave McClement, who was a director, because to even think about doing something negative toward Cenlor was pretty risky business because it had such unanimous and vigorous support from the board," Gordon said. "I said, 'This is what Geoff has brought me and I can't deal with this. This is wrong. We have to stop it.' Dave looked at the numbers and said, 'You're right.' We went to talk to Ron Mannix, and I think we didn't have more than a ten-minute conversation, and that was the end of Cenlor. And when it went away, I'm sure there were parties everywhere."

By 1981, it was clear that Cenlor was an unwieldy, costly and essentially unworkable operation. In 1982, Mancal dissolved the company. While the demise of Cenlor was met with jubilation, it also did much for Ron Mannix's credibility. "Unfortunately, during the same period when Ronnie was giving all these speeches, saying we aren't going to manage, but we are going to control — we don't tell you how to do your payroll, but we do it for you," said Gordon. "We tell you what kind of computer you are going to use and we buy them for you. And we charge you for what we think is right. So we talked out of both sides of our mouths there for the first couple of years. Then the central thing went away because, economically, it was a failure. Then the 'control, not manage' speeches had more credibility. By then we had worked on some projects, and they had contributed to the reality of a little less control than had been there before. So it was an evolutionary kind of thing."

G.D. (Geoff) Corry, president of Cenlor Services Ltd.

To Build an Engineering-Procurement-Construction Firm
Mannix Gill — Pioneering the Process Plant Business in Canada

When F.S. Mannix founded the outfit back in 1898, he worked with a number of partners. While some of these partnerships were created for a specific job, others lasted years. In much this same way, over the years the Loram Group experimented, branching out into different fields. Outside its core areas of business — construction, oil and gas, coal and railroad maintenance of way — the group formed, or acquired, literally dozens of businesses. While most of these were ephemeral, coming into existence for a brief period of time in order to take advantage of work, others lingered for years, struggling to make it to the big time.

One avenue in particular, the engineering-procurement-construction (EPC) field, seemed like a pretty logical development. And yet, despite four decades of taking a stab at it through three different companies — Mannix Gill, Mon-Max and Techman — this pretty logical development turned out to be singularly difficult to accomplish.

Back in 1952, one year after the buyback from Morrison-Knudsen, Mannix Ltd. entered into a joint venture agreement with the J.B. Gill Company of Long Beach, California. Founded in 1923, J.B. Gill was an engineering-construction company that had built oil and gas facilities in California and Oklahoma. The company specialized in the design and construction of compressor and pump stations, gas treatment plants and power and steam generating stations.

Mannix Gill Ltd., a 1952 joint venture with the J.B. Gill Company of California, builds pipeline and power generating station facilities. In 1956, Mannix Gill builds a three-plant facility for Canadian Gulf, the most sophisticated process plant built in Canada during this time.

1979 ▶

MHL Holdings Ltd. sells its office building at 320-7th Avenue S.W. MHL then purchases the Atrium II building, shown, and additional land at 7th Street and 7th Avenue S.W. in Calgary. The majority of the Loram Group head offices relocate to the Atrium II facility.

Mannix Gill was specifically formed to construct the three initial pump stations of the Trans Mountain oil pipeline, a 0.6-metre (24-inch), 1,155-kilometre (718-mile) line running from Edmonton to Burnaby Mountain near Vancouver. Mannix Gill completed the Trans Mountain pump stations on schedule in November 1953. On June 1, 1954, the joint venture was incorporated as Mannix Gill Ltd., a wholly owned subsidiary of Mannix Ltd. Glenn Gill, the son of the founder of J.B. Gill, was named president. During the next four years, Mannix Gill won a modest number of contracts in the rapidly expanding area of pipeline work. In 1954, the company built the main pump station at Pembina and undertook two jobs on the Interprovincial pipeline.

While most of Mannix Gill's jobs over the next three years were straight construction, the company also did engineering consulting work for TransCanada PipeLines, Canadian Gulf, Alberta Gas Trunk Line and Western Minerals. The ability to handle engineering also enabled the company to move beyond pipeline-related work. Between 1953 and 1956,

SAYING GOODBYE TO A GOOD IRISH PHILOSOPHER

On March 28, 1985, Everett Costello passed away. During his eulogy, F.P. Mannix reflected: "The Loram Group is a family business. To the Mannixes, Everett was an integral part of our family — just as he treated us and the companies as a part of his family.

"Everett brought to every business problem a great ability to get to the root of the problem, to seize and hold the objectives, and to apply his quiet keen mind, his shrewd analytical approach and his plain common sense. Everett was a good Irish philosopher — wry, sharp and brief. How many times have you heard:

'You don't want enemies,'

'No business after two drinks . . . upsy-do,' and

'Business first,' at any time, day or night?

"It has been an honour to be associated with Everett, to have worked with him and to have been a student to such a great mentor."

in Alberta during this period. The simple fact was that no one really knew what they were doing at this stage because Alberta natural gas was unlike gas being processed anywhere else in the world. This gas was extremely sour, which means it contained a high percentage of foul-smelling and corrosive hydrogen sulphide. It was also wet, which means it had high amounts of liquid hydrocarbons. Because of the exceptionally high sulphur content and the gas liquids, Alberta gas presented a set of design problems that no engineering firm had dealt with before. The extremely cold temperatures of Canadian winters also produced complex hydration problems that were not understood at first.

While none of the gas processing plants built between 1953 and 1956 were really big moneymakers, they fulfilled an important function in giving engineers the opportunity to develop new technologies, thus paving the way for what was to become a major new industry in Canada. By the late 1950s, the process plant construction business was booming. However, all the contracts for these new plants were being awarded to the big American engineering-construction firms, since no

the first seven gas process plants ever built in Canada were completed. Two of these plants were built by Mannix Gill under engineering-construction contracts in 1956. One of these, a small facility of relatively simple design, was built for Western Leasehold Ltd. at Hobbema. The other, a three-plant facility in the Stettler area for Canadian Gulf, was by far the most sophisticated process plant built in Canada during that time. Nevertheless, the job was a big money loser for Mannix Gill and the company was shut down in 1957.

The problems encountered by Mannix Gill on the Canadian Gulf plant were typical of those experienced at the other gas plants built

Canadian company had either the design or construction experience to undertake process plant work. One person who felt this situation should change was J.K.C. (Con) Mulherin, the president of Montreal Engineering. Montreal Engineering's reputation was in civil engineering and the design of large-scale power projects. Since the company had no process plant experience to speak of, Mulherin felt that the only practical way for the company to break into the business was through a joint venture.

Montreal Engineering-Mannix, as the joint venture was named, was formally organized on August 15, 1961. Later that year, Mannix

1979 ▶

Equipment failures and human errors lead to a loss of coolant and partial meltdown at the Three Mile Island nuclear plant in the United States.

1979 ▶

Joe Clark becomes prime minister of Canada.

hired a manager, G. Roy Sorrenti, a man with a chemical engineering degree from McGill and good contacts in the industry. An indication of just how good those contacts were was the man Sorrenti brought on board to be the joint venture's process engineer. This was Thomas E. (Tom) Morimoto, whom many in the business regarded as the best process engineer in Canada at that time.

In 1962, the Montreal Engineering and Mannix joint venture got under way. The first two years of the joint venture were tough ones, according to Morimoto. "Mon-Max was a very difficult thing to start because Roy Sorrenti and I were the only two employees," he said. "It was very difficult to get any of the type of work we were supposed to be doing. Up to that time, process plant design and construction had all been done by American companies. There were no Canadian companies doing that kind of work. Also, most of the oil companies were American companies. They were naturally going to go with the people that they knew, and we were just upstarts. So it was very difficult to get our first job."

Still, Morimoto's reputation was strong enough to give the joint venture credibility. In 1962, the first contracts came in. "Our first job was for Texas Gulf Sulphur, building a little liquid sulphur storage plant down at Okotoks," said Morimoto. "Then we got a job from Imperial Oil in Devon to build an extension to their fabrication plant. They took a chance on us, and we were very grateful to have the opportunity. So that was a pretty good start. Normally, I think it would have taken several years and you would have had to build up a staff to do it, of course."

According to Morimoto, the joint venture did well on its first jobs, basically breaking even right from the start. Since both owners were satisfied with the progress made, the venture was incorporated on July 1, 1963, as Mon-Max Services Ltd. For the rest of the '60s,

Montreal Engineering, a civil engineering firm, joins the group in 1961 to form Mon-Max Services Ltd., the Mannix organization's first true EPC firm.

The Mon-Max project management team includes highly talented process engineer, Thomas E. (Tom) Morimoto.

the company continued to expand, taking on contracts of increasing scope and complexity. In 1963, Mon-Max designed and constructed a 19-million-litre (five-million-gallon) refrigerated propane storage tank for Greater Winnipeg Gas, the first facility of this kind to be built in Canada.

In 1964, Mon-Max began designing compressor stations for Alberta Gas Trunk Line (AGTL), a connection which would provide them with a substantial amount of engineering work for the rest of the decade. The year 1964 also proved to be a turning point for another reason. That year, Texas Gulf awarded Mon-Max a $2-million contract for a 454-tonne-per-day (500-ton) sulphur recovery unit for its Windfall process plant. This facility, which was completed on schedule in January 1965, was the largest single unit of its kind in North America at that time.

The Windfall job, which Morimoto termed "a breakthrough," firmly established Mon-Max's credentials as an EPC firm. It also put the company on a solid financial footing. As the volume of work and the size of contracts grew, Mon-Max assembled a first-rate team with a pioneering approach to process design computer programs and an innovative eye toward obtaining licensing agreements for new technologies being developed in the industry.

Pete Swityk, who came to Mon-Max from Mannix Co. Ltd. as controller, felt that Mon-Max's greatest innovation was simply that it was the first company of its kind in Canada to compete with the big process plant engineering-construction firms. "Here we were, two Canadian companies, breaking into a field which was dominated by American companies," said Swityk. "We were involved with the same kind of work being undertaken by Fluor and by Bechtel. We were in the big leagues. We were pretty small potatoes in relation to what they

1979 ▶

Well-trained barbecue officials ensure the Turner Valley summer event runs smoothly.

1979 ▶

Margaret Thatcher becomes England's first female prime minister.

were doing, no question about that. But every once in a while they'd go after some of the jobs that we were after, and you felt you were rubbing elbows with them. We felt we had a good opportunity to break into the market, particularly since we were working here in Alberta where most of that type of work was, and secondly, because we were in a good political climate, being a Canadian company."

With topflight personnel and innovative methods, Mon-Max was able to expand its volume of work substantially, taking on a number of large-scale projects. While Mon-Max's biggest contracts were for EPC work, the company was also winning a fair amount of straight engineering work. By 1969, Mon-Max was in negotiations for a joint venture with a consortium called Canatom to redesign and reconstruct the Glace Bay heavy water plant. Canatom was made up of the three largest engineering firms in Canada: Montreal Engineering, Shawinigan Engineering and Surveyer, Nenninger and Chenevert (SNC). At stake would be a contract worth $125 million, the largest chemical plant EPC contract ever awarded to an all-Canadian company.

The year 1969 was a turning point in the history of Mon-Max. The Canatom-Mon-Max joint venture did in fact come into existence and was awarded the contract for Glace Bay. The plant was successfully rebuilt and is now regarded as the best heavy water facility in the Atomic Energy of Canada Ltd.'s system. Although this joint venture would be a major factor in the company's future success, it was also one of the factors that led the Mannix organization to decide to get out of Mon-Max. "Fred C. Mannix never did like the idea of us taking on that heavy water plant," explained Matt Roach, who had been appointed to a task force with the Mon-Max joint venture, "because we were doing it with three other companies and he didn't have control over it. It was a two-thirds type of thing and he didn't like that."

Aerial view of what was then Canada's largest refrigerated propane storage and shipment facility, located in British Columbia. Mon-Max engineered and built the facility for Trans Mountain Oil Pipe Line Company.

Mannix wanted one company, preferably his own, to have control of the Mon-Max joint venture. Montreal Engineering was equally adamant that they would accept nothing less than a 50 per cent interest in Mon-Max. Finally, when it became obvious that no compromise could be worked out, Mannix decided to exercise the "shotgun" buy-sell option that was part of the 1963 joint venture agreement. On August 22, 1972, Mannix offered to buy Montreal Engineering's share of Mon-Max for $300,000. Under the terms of the buy-sell option, Montreal then had 90 days to decide whether to accept or reject the offer. If Montreal rejected it, Mannix would be obligated to sell its interest in Mon-Max to Montreal for the same amount it had offered as a purchase price. On September 20, 1972, Montreal sent a letter saying that they would buy out the Mannix interest. The deal was closed ten days later.

Technologies of Mannix
Chasing the Illusionary Mackenzie Valley Pipeline

In 1969, when it became apparent that the Mon-Max partnership was not working out, the Loram Group decided to form its own engineering company. The basic idea of Techman was to sell the group's collective engineering expertise. Mannix Co. Ltd., the construction company, had developed a first-rate engineering staff, well-known for its ability to find innovative solutions to construction problems. The coal company and the oil and gas company also had engineering divisions. Loram management believed that the group's combined engineering staffs and its broad range of experience in natural resource operations could provide the basis for a major engineering company.

1979 ▶

This D-10 Cat is one of the first three brought into Canada. Loram International uses it on the $11.3-million Gibraltar Mines Limited stripping project near McLeese Lake, British Columbia. The project exposes a copper ore body.

1979 ▶

Loram pipeline crews complete the Regina split casings work for TransCanada PipeLines.

Andy Seraphim, then vice president of construction operations for Loram, was given the responsibility of preparing a study with recommendations for the formation of a Mannix engineering company. "I originally wanted to call it Mannix Engineering," he said. "Fred C. liked the idea okay, but for the sake of privacy, he wanted a different name. So we changed the name to Techman, which stood for Technologies of Mannix."

Mannix Engineering Ltd. was incorporated in Alberta on June 13, 1969. The name change to Techman was made on November 7. At first, Techman was not regarded as a successor to Mon-Max, in which Mannix Co. Ltd. was still a partner. Starting out with a staff of three people — Seraphim and fellow engineers Lou Pozzi and Jack Bruce — and $20,000 in working capital, Seraphim's first priority was to market the new company. Although he essentially had no staff, Seraphim was a talented promoter. Just how talented quickly became apparent. In 1970, Techman's first full year of operation, Seraphim managed to position the company to participate in the engineering for a huge pipeline project which was just entering the conceptual design and feasibility study stage — the Mackenzie Valley, or Arctic, pipeline. Initial cost estimates indicated that this project would be, by far, the biggest construction job ever undertaken in the history of Canada.

While Techman had no pipeline engineers on staff and no track record as an engineering company, it did have access to ideas. One of the main ideas that Seraphim was able to offer to one of the consortia of oil companies planning the Arctic pipeline came from Walter Kosten. Strangely enough, Kosten had found the time to develop this idea because he had been fired from his position as manager of Mannix Co. Ltd.'s Pipeline Division. In 1968, Kosten had the

A.F. (Andy) Seraphim becomes president of Techman in 1969.

Left: An early Techman brochure.

Below: The Canadian Arctic Gas Study Limited consortium is formed to build a pipeline from the Prudhoe Bay, Alaska, field to link with the Alberta Gas Trunk Line.

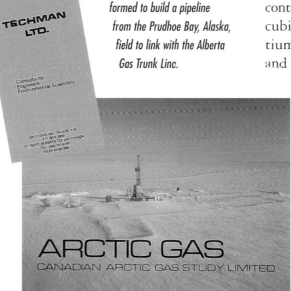

misfortune of being the man ultimately responsible for the disastrous Lakehead pipeline project, the job which is said to have caused Brock Montgomery's heart attack.

"That one caught me," Kosten explained, "so I got lifted out of the Pipeline Division, and I became special projects manager. That, translated, means you get run off, but they didn't know quite what to do with you. For the first little while, I was licking the wounds and not doing very much of anything. However, it was during that period that I offered Mannix a proposal I wrote called, 'Proposed Concept of a Northwest Corridor Transportation System.' This was the introduction if you want, or the entrance or the gateway, into the northern pipeline game for Mannix and Alberta Gas Trunk Line."

In 1969, when Kosten was developing the idea for his proposal, an organization known as the Northwest Study Group was being formed to examine the idea of building a gas pipeline through Canada from the Prudhoe Bay oil field in Alaska. In addition to huge oil reserves, which were to be moved by the Alaska pipeline, this field contained an estimated 676 billion cubic metres (24 trillion cubic feet) of gas. Northwest Study Group was a consortium initially made up of six big U.S. and Canadian oil and gas companies, although it quickly picked up additional investors including Esso, Exxon, Shell and Gulf. The group's engineers were Williams Brothers, one of the largest American design-construct firms in the pipeline business. Northwest Study envisioned a 1.22-metre (48-inch), 4,000-kilometre (2,500-mile) gas pipeline which would cross from Alaska into Canada in the High Arctic and continue down into the United States. The line was projected to cost $35.5 billion.

The Northwest Study Group consisted primarily of American companies. One person who thought that this pipeline through Canada should be designed and built by Canadian firms was Bob Blair, president of Alberta Gas Trunk Line. Well-known in the industry for his pro-Canada and

1979 ▶

A speed swing positions rail on Loram International's section of Calgary's light rail transit system. This $3.3-million project will run into 1981.

1979 ▶

Vietnam invades Cambodia (Kampuchea) to overthrow the murderous Khmer Rouge regime led by Pol Pot. The Pol Pot government has killed almost 1.7 million Cambodian civilians and many have fled to refugee camps in neighbouring Thailand.

pro-Alberta promoting, Blair had started talks with Canadian National Railways and four major U.S. gas networks to form a second consortium to compete with the Northwest Study Group. At this time, Andy Seraphim approached Blair with Kosten's proposal for a northwest corridor transportation system. Blair immediately recognized the value of the idea.

While Kosten's contribution to the concept of the Arctic pipeline was simple and quite obvious, like many good ideas, it was something no one else had given any thought to. "My basic idea was that if you were going to build this pipeline, put in the access first, because you're going to end up paying the cost of transporting materials anyway," Kosten explained. "You were going to spend more money transporting the materials than you would spend on a highway, and you still wouldn't have the highway. Also, you've got gas and oil to move, so you're eventually looking at two pipelines. If you put two alongside the road, then you've written off half the cost of the highway against each pipeline. That's really what that was all about. The idea was sold and Blair picked it up and formed the Arctic Gas Systems Study Group in Alberta Gas Trunk Line."

Seraphim then proposed to Blair that Techman would sponsor a joint venture of engineering firms to design the Arctic pipeline for Arctic Gas Systems. This joint venture, which was put together on September 24, 1970, consisted of Techman, Mon-Max, Shawinigan Engineering and Templeton Engineering, although Templeton withdrew in 1971. This group, which was named Pemcan Services Ltd., would provide the engineering support for Arctic Gas Systems. Kosten, who had left the Loram Group in 1969 after writing his

The Gas Arctic project, shown in this map, proposes to collect the energy assets of the Far North and deliver them to the rest of the continent. This huge project is sponsored by Techman.

Mackenzie Valley proposal, was asked to come back to the organization to handle Techman's participation. In addition to being Pemcan's first manager, Kosten was also the person who thought up its name, which stood for Pipeline Engineering and Management of Canada.

The formation of Pemcan in 1970 is a tribute to Andy Seraphim's ability to promote Loram's pipeline expertise. Montreal Engineering, which was involved in the group through Mon-Max, and Shawinigan were then the two largest engineering firms in Canada. Nevertheless, Seraphim was able to get Techman, a company that had never designed anything, the controlling interest in Pemcan. The venture was split up with Techman getting 25 per cent, Mon-Max 33 per cent, Shawinigan 25 per cent and Templeton seven per cent. What Seraphim was able to sell its two bigger partners was Loram's pipeline expertise, which both firms lacked.

In addition to the Mackenzie Valley corridor concept, Techman engineers were working on a number of other studies for Arctic Gas Systems. One project was location, design and cost estimate studies for a gas pipeline from King Christian Island in the Arctic Ocean to Norman Wells. Another task was providing engineering support for a pipeline test facility at Norman Wells. A third major project was a feasibility study for a molten sulphur pipeline at Ram River. Although this work would send Techman's revenues well over the $1-million mark in 1972, events that year signalled the end of Pemcan. Pipelines in Canada tend to turn into political footballs and the Mackenzie Valley line, which was to be the largest line ever constructed in the country, was no exception to the general rule.

1979 ▶

Blue Ridge Pipeline Constructors Ltd., a new Mannix-owned, Alberta-based pipeline company, begins work. Here a toboggan is used to help move light equipment on a winter job.

1979 ▶

Clowns and balloons provide endless fascination and entertainment for the children at the annual MEGA family barbecue.

In 1972, it became apparent that Ottawa was going to step in to referee the contest between Northwest Study Group and Arctic Gas Systems and their rival engineering groups. "What happened was the government didn't know how they would choose between these two major consortia of owners," Lionel Narraway, Techman's chief engineer, explained. "They said, 'There's no damn way that we are qualified to sort this out, so what we are going to do is have you two conglomerates get together to form one.'"

In September 1972, Northwest Study Group and Arctic Gas Systems combined to form a single study group. After a period of reorganization, the result was an entity called Canadian Arctic Gas Study Limited (Cangas). Pembina was one of the companies in this group, which was a consortium of 26 U.S. and Canadian firms. This forced merger immediately produced all sorts of problems, not the least of which was the question of Pemcan's, and ultimately, Techman's, share of the project.

While Techman had grown to a $3-million-a-year operation in just three years, the future of the company was basically tied to one huge project, and it was anyone's guess when the Mackenzie Valley project would come into existence. Before the pipeline could be built, approvals for permits had to be obtained from both the U.S. and Canadian governments. By the time Seraphim quit in frustration in 1973, 14 different environmental groups on both sides of the border were starting to register complaints. Furthermore, Cangas was no longer the only group trying to obtain the right to build a pipeline from Prudhoe Bay.

Techman Takes a Downturn

With Andy Seraphim gone, Techman immediately lost all the industry contacts he had built up during the previous three years. By mid-1974, nearly all the top engineers in the pipeline group, which had provided most of Techman's revenues, had departed. While Techman still

David Morgan becomes president of Techman in 1974.

A Techman brochure from the mid-1970s showing the transition of the company toward mineral extraction under David Morgan's stewardship.

had a few key administrative people like Jack Bruce on board, the company was back to square one.

Techman's main challenge then became finding a president who could restart the company. After a year's search, David Morgan, a man with an extensive background in mining operations, but almost no experience as a consulting engineer, was hired in July 1974. To get Techman running again, Morgan decided to look for projects in his expertise, which was mining. Morgan's decision to concentrate on mining was not dictated by his background alone. Techman's staff had peaked at 224 people in 1972 during Andy Seraphim's tenure. By the time Morgan was hired, that number had been halved. Because the pipeline engineering staff had been decimated, the prospect of continuing to pursue work in the oil and gas industry was exceedingly dim. The handful of engineers left continued to provide services to Pemcan throughout 1974 and provided Techman with a fair amount of revenue. But with the Arctic pipeline game growing more complicated by the month, it was obvious that Techman could not expect Pemcan to carry the company much longer.

By 1977, Techman had established a fairly solid reputation as a consulting firm for the design of open-pit mines. Starting the year with 46 people, the company had increased to 64 by May to keep up with the work required for the Coleman, Elco and Gregg River projects. Then, in May, Techman was selected with Fluor to perform an engineering audit on Bechtel's cost estimate for the Syncrude project, a huge tar sands project owned by the Province of Alberta through Alberta Energy Co. Ltd. This was a totally unexpected job with a tight deadline, calling for a massive influx of personnel from other Loram Group companies. A joint

1979 ▶

One bolt is tightened by one of the 90-man work force that labours more than 165,000 hours to erect the huge Bucyrus-Erie 2570-W dragline for Utility Coal, a Manalta Coal subsidiary.

1980 ▶

The U.S. Olympic hockey team celebrates its Winter Olympics gold medal victory over the heavily favoured Soviet team.

1980 ▶

Mount St. Helens, located in the state of Washington, erupts on May 18.

venture was formed between Techman and Fluor, with Fluor checking the refinery design and Techman and Loram people examining the tar sands extraction engineering.

To manage this project, Newt Yeomans, who was then vice president of coal for Loram Co. Ltd., was brought in. "F.C. Mannix had told the Alberta government that he'd do a check on the Syncrude estimate," Yeomans said. "At that time, they'd suddenly discovered that instead of costing $400 million or $500 million, Syncrude was going to cost $2.2 billion. So I took a group of people from Mannix and a group from some of the other Mannix companies and also from Fluor and from SNC. We put them in a separate building in Calgary and then within a period of about 35 days, we checked the whole of the Bechtel estimate. When we finished, we gave a presentation to the government. We found that Bechtel's estimate of $2.2 billion was accurate, aside from a few irregularities. Alberta and the federal government used that information to make their agreement to go ahead with Syncrude. That was quite an achievement, and it involved all kinds of people."

While Techman personnel had all the work they could handle and more, it became apparent in the summer of 1977 that the company could be in serious trouble as early as the following year. Canada, along with the rest of the world, was mired in recession. Furthermore, the world market for both metallurgical and thermal coal was weakening, and new coal mining projects were being shelved. With only small jobs coming in and no new coal projects in sight, the outlook for Techman was bleak. In 1979, Techman's volume sank to $1.5 million and its staff had been reduced to 39. With proposal costs alone of $526,000, the company recorded a loss of about half a million dollars. As the fortunes of Techman continued to sink in 1980, Morgan decided to take an early retirement. In July, on his sixtieth birthday, he left the firm.

"To build a world-scale engineering-construction company"

After nearly three decades of trying to get an engineering company running, Loram decided to start all over again with a concept similar to the one behind Mannix Gill, the very first attempt. Techman was going to try to break into the petrochemical process plant business as an EPC contractor. Once again, the company would be going into the market cold, but this time the idea was to do it in a big way.

In previous attempts, Loram's policy was not to hire staff until it had the contracts to put those people to work. It was pretty tough, however, to sell yourself as a company capable of designing major projects with no history as an engineering company and no real design engineers on the payroll. While quite often the reputation of the senior technical personnel in the organization, as in the case of Tom Morimoto, could be a factor that the client would take into consideration, this could be an extremely long and not particularly profitable process, as Mannix had discovered with Mon-Max. In some ways, it was the case of which comes first, the chicken or the egg.

By 1980, Ron Mannix decided in his own pragmatic way that enough was enough. The company had been fooling around with the idea of setting up an EPC firm for more than 30 years. If the concept was ever going to fly, he felt it was time to put some money into the idea, quit dawdling around and build a world-class EPC firm.

In the summer of 1980, Ron Mannix found a man he felt was capable of building Techman into the big EPC firm that he envisioned. This was Sid Jaycock, formerly a senior vice president for Associated Kellogg, the highly successful Canadian subsidiary of Pullman Kellogg, the big U.S. process plant design-construct firm. When Jaycock came in for an interview over lunch with Ron Mannix and Lorne Gordon, he was told that "they were looking to build a world-scale engineering-construction company," he recalled. "At that time, Techman was a small consulting company, but the business that I was asked to build was not a consulting company. I was asked to build an engineering-contracting version of the construction industry, if you will, a Bechtel or Fluor kind of organization."

Sid Jaycock becomes president of Techman in 1980.

1980 ▶

Terry Fox begins his run across Canada to raise awareness and funds for the battle against cancer. His "Marathon of Hope" is a success on both counts, although the disease claims him before he completes the crossing.

1980 ▶

In Poland, striking workers sit under a sign. They form the independent trade union Solidarity (Solidarność). This labour activity begins the collapse of Communist rule in Poland.

1980 ▶

A "pig" used to clean the interior of a pipeline.

"They really wanted to have an engineering-contracting arm like Bechtel and Fluor because, as I read the scene, when the means of delivering industrial projects had shifted from pure construction to an integrated engineering-construction operation, they hadn't been able to achieve that shift," Jaycock said. "In the company's history, there were a number of tries with joint venture-type approaches to get into that field which had not succeeded. The attempts to grow an EPC firm out of the construction company — which had been the historic development plan — just would never have succeeded, and never has succeeded. There have been very, very few, Bechtel being, I think, the one exception and they started in 1939 or something like that, to make the shift. They are the only really successful total service company that has developed out of a heavy-duty construction company. So it's not surprising that attempts to develop a full service company out of Loram International weren't successful. I wouldn't have expected them to be very successful. But they still wanted to be in that business because they saw the future of the industrial construction marketplace being in that area. That was a pretty valid viewpoint in 1980, so they said let's get going and let's get going in a fairly crash way to try and do it — separate it from the traditional construction operation."

"The message that I received when I was interviewed was that they had decided to get somebody from the EPC industry to import that background to build a viable world-scale EPC organization," said Jaycock. "So, late in the development program as companies go, 20 years after those kinds of companies started developing, the Fluors, the Bechtels, the Kelloggs and so on, the Mannixes decided to develop theirs. In those initial interviews, we talked about needing five years of boom times to make our entry, to take a

In 1981, Techman changes its name to Techman Engineering Ltd. and increases the use of cutting edge technology for project development.

Techman adds Calma computer-assisted design and drafting (CADD) capability to improve design functions. This early use of CADD technology underscores the commitment to develop Techman into an industry leader.

piece of the growth chunk of the marketplace and get ourselves established and equipped more efficiently. Then we could compete with anybody." Without five years of an expanding market, of course, the outcome of the venture became highly questionable. Techman was going to be a big gamble.

It was agreed that the new EPC version of Techman would have to be put into place quickly. Jaycock, who liked the idea of this challenge, decided to accept the job and immediately began to look at the alternatives for building Techman up. "Our first pieces of work were studies we did with the people I brought in from the industry shortly thereafter," Jaycock said. "The question was whether we should buy or build. We did some reviews of buying existing companies and that helped the owners make the decision that we were a very late entry into the EPC business."

What Jaycock found was that since the market was booming, the values of most engineering companies were inflated. Mancal could expect to pay top dollar and then have to spend more money modifying the acquisition to fit the new plans. Jaycock also felt that most of the companies that would be available for purchase had technology that was rapidly becoming obsolete. The mini-computer revolution was under way. To be competitive, a start-up company would have to offer the latest in computer-assisted design and drafting (CADD) systems and other computer-based programs for scheduling, forecasting and the like.

Jaycock's recommendation was to install a system built around state-of-the-art engineering tools, to make the company one that could offer the most advanced design and procurement systems then available. This, he felt, would give Techman its marketing edge over its already established competitors. "If you are going to enter

1980 ▶

Canada joins 56 countries and boycotts the Moscow Summer Olympics to protest Soviet military activity in Afghanistan.

1980 ▶

Hockey playing brothers Brennan and Scott Olson found Rollerblade, Inc. and begin the manufacture of in-line skates.

THE WAY WE WERE

Serious thoughts of forming a Loram Group History Centre had been in the minds of many for a long time. However, it was not until April 1985 that the project was launched. The purpose of establishing such a centre was to recognize the many thousands of people who helped build the Loram Group.

Space was retained on the second floor of the Atrium II building at 849–6th Avenue S.W., Calgary, and a full-time staff began sorting and organizing material contained in the many boxes, packages and loose articles stockpiled in the area. There were framed and unframed pictures, photo albums, tapes, slides, films, scrapbooks, reports and pamphlets, artifacts, mem-

orabilia, small tools, technical instruments, office equipment and furniture — mostly from years past, some more recent, but all destined for a future home in the History Centre.

One person who was brought back to the Loram Group after a ten-year absence to help with the History Centre was Mary Perks. Back in 1953, Mary Perks joined the Mannix outfit as secretary to Eric Connelly. "You worked for a family company, and you felt part of it," she said. "You didn't just work with them, they were friends, too. This is why today I remember so many names, many of whom I haven't seen for years and some who I never saw after that. But I know these men and women, they really made an imprint in my mind. It was a people company and a hard-working company. Everybody worked hard. When something had to be done it had to be done now!" Mary Perks' ability to work hard and her memory for names would come in quite handy as the History Centre grew.

late into the market," Jaycock said, "you had better enter in a much more sophisticated way, tooled up with a lot more efficiency and that kind of thing."

Jaycock was also given the option of using the existing Techman as a base or eliminating it and starting over from scratch. He decided to stay with the old Techman for two reasons. First, he felt that the team Morgan had built in the 1970s offered services that many other EPC firms lacked and usually had to seek from outside consulting groups. "I really felt that the kind of skills that were in there added to the traditional EPC package," he said. "They gave us a bigger integration, some product uniqueness, which we needed in a mature marketplace." Jaycock was especially impressed with the environmental group, particularly with Dr. Dwight R. Mudry, whom he regarded as one of the best in the business.

Jaycock's second reason for wanting to keep the old Techman was that it was already up and running, even if it was not particularly successful. "It provided an operating, working home in which to build," he explained. "You had real things happening. I think you miss something if you are just sort of developing theory. When you have to run an operation, there's a sense of discipline that's important as you grow and develop."

While Techman had done poorly in 1978 and 1979, work was starting to come in around the time Morgan left. In April, Techman obtained a mining and oil sands study for Mobil Oil of Canada Ltd. worth $620,000. The next month, the company was hired to do more studies for Baymag on the magnesite property Techman had previously studied. When Jaycock took over in June, Techman's staff was up to 50, which was actually too small to handle the work in geology and mine planning the company had picked up in the second quarter. Jaycock felt that the company needed to hire people immediately.

Toward the end of the summer, Jaycock hired 28 new employees, his first step to turn Techman into an EPC company. Gregg River was slated to be Techman's first big project management contract. Negotiations with the Japanese investors were successfully concluded in September, and construction was scheduled to begin in December. Late in the year, Manalta Coal sent more business Techman's way, giving it contracts for the Mercoal and McLeod River developments. Techman ended 1980 with revenues of $2.4 million, an increase of almost $1 million over 1979. As expected with the start-up expenses, the company recorded a net loss of $706,000.

Techman began 1981 with a new name, Techman Engineering Ltd., and a new structure. In keeping with practices of many big EPC

1980 ▶

Anne Spicer, John Spicer, Liza Saks (Chupik) and Sharon Hardy at the MEGA spring fling.

1980 ▶

Following the successful erection of the dragline at the Utility Mine, a new Bucyrus-Erie 1570-W dragline is commissioned for the Klimax Mine. It is completed under budget, named Prairie Queen and becomes the largest dragline owned by Manalta Coal.

firms, Jaycock divided the company into profit and cost centres. In February, construction got under way on the $180-million Gregg River project, which was being run as a Loram International-Techman joint venture. By April, Techman had 86 people on staff and a $2.9-million backlog of work on hand. Most of this dollar amount was coming from Manalta Coal, for the Gregg River, Mercoal and McLeod projects. Techman also obtained another contract from American Electric Power for a study of that company's Gilbert mine.

By midyear, Jaycock had increased Techman's staff to 111. He had also purchased the Calma computer design graphics system, which was to be delivered that fall. Techman's volume continued to increase at a tremendous rate. New mine studies work from Columbis and Southern Ohio and Fording Coal came in during the summer. Around this time, the new minicomputer equipment came in. In addition to CADD capability, Techman acquired a management information system and project control systems software.

By the end of the year, Techman's staff had been built up to 166. With this much bigger revenue-generating base and several new jobs on the books, volume for the year climbed to $7 million, nearly triple the 1980 figure. Almost overnight, Techman had taken on a new look. Not only was the new computer equipment state-of-the-art, the staff Jaycock had assembled was topnotch and enthusiastic. "We were quite successful in acquiring people in a time when people were very difficult to acquire," he said. "These were people I knew from my 25 years of industrial engineering in Alberta, people I had worked with previously, who wanted to come and join an exciting development. And it was an exciting development."

Early in 1982, Techman entered into a joint venture agreement with Canadian Badger Company

Techman Badger

Techman joint ventures with Canadian Badger Company Limited, another process plant EPC company and a subsidiary of Raytheon, the U.S. firm, to form Techman Badger. This new association focuses on the hydrocarbon processing industries.

Limited, a subsidiary of the Badger Company, Inc. of Cambridge, Massachusetts, a big American EPC firm in the process plant business. Badger was seeking an entree into the booming Alberta petrochemical industry. Techman, in turn, received access to Badger's considerable process plant technologies. "We impressed Badger," Jaycock said, "because we had embarked on a program with our systems and procedures that they would have liked to have done, with our automated design and construction capability. They felt we were going to emerge as a very successful Canadian firm a couple of years down the road, and they wanted to be part of that. As a matter of fact, they pointedly expressed their envy in not being able to start new and do those things. They also recognized that the people we had on our staff were extremely competent and capable. We indeed had some first-rate people from the industry."

Although Techman had drastically redesigned and rebuilt itself in just one year's time, like Techman under Seraphim, Jaycock's Techman was pinning a great deal of its hopes for the future on one megaproject. This was the Alsands project, a mining and oil extraction facility to be built in the heart of Alberta's huge Athabasca Wabasca-McMurray oil sands deposit. It almost goes without saying that this job, like the Arctic pipeline, was not just big; it was going to be the biggest construction job in the history of Canada. Anticipated to cost $6.7 billion, Alsands was sponsored by a consortium which included Hudson's Bay Oil & Gas, Dome Petroleum, Petro-Canada Explorations and the Canadian subsidiaries of Shell, Gulf, Amoco and Chevron Standard.

As with the Arctic pipeline, the engineering and construction for the Alsands project were going to be handled through a joint venture, this time with Monenco and Bechtel Canada. Loram International Ltd. was able to

1980 ▶

Bull riding at the Mancal barbecue.

1980 ▶

Loram Construction Inc. builds the Greater Cleveland Regional Transit Authority railway system in Ohio. Crews set welding production records during the project.

obtain 15 per cent of the partnership because of its extensive tar sands mining work for Sun Oil and Syncrude and the studies Techman had conducted over the years.

And yet, just when it looked like the future was bright, the window of opportunity closed. Back in 1980, when Sid Jaycock and Ron Mannix were discussing Techman over lunch, Pierre Trudeau's National Energy Program (NEP) was being put into place. At the time, many executives in the Canadian oil and gas business predicted that the NEP would have disastrous consequences. By 1982, those predictions were coming true — the NEP's new tax regime severely cut into oil companies' operating revenues. By year-end 1981, short-term loans to the industry had soared to more than $60 billion, triple the figure just four years earlier. The industry also incurred substantial long-term debts in trying to implement Trudeau's policy of repatriating oil company ownership. By mid-1982, $7.8 billion had been sunk into takeovers of foreign-owned companies. This high price tag brought an increase in Canadian ownership of a mere 6.7 per cent. At the same time, it drove out of the country $8.3 billion in direct investment in the industry.

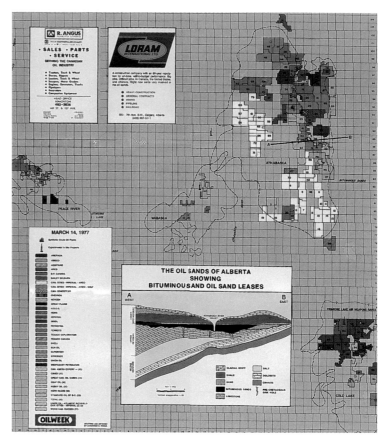

To go with the drastic cut in revenues and the huge increase in debt, the industry was also hit by a worldwide drop in oil prices and a crippling recession. In the summer of 1982, the Canadian dollar fell to an all-time low of 79 cents against the U.S. dollar, the prime interest rate went over the 20 per cent mark, and inflation was staying up around 11 per cent. Between June 1981 and June 1982, oil stocks on the Toronto Stock Exchange dropped an amazing 43 per cent in value.

By the summer of 1982, the oil and gas boom in Canada was most definitely over, and it was clear that Techman was in serious trouble. With the staff now up to 196, the company's manpower utilization rate was running at 46 per cent, versus 61 per cent projected. On June 1, the company went on a four-day work week to reduce overhead without having to cut staff. On June 30, the Alsands project, whose cost had risen to $13 billion, was cancelled because the sponsors could not arrange financing. Techman had invested $1.3 million in the project and had 61 people committed to it. All of these people had to be either reassigned or laid off.

By the end of June, Techman's books showed a $1.7-million loss for the first six months of the year, which was about $1.4 million more than had been forecast. The outlook for the remainder of the year was grim. Gregg River, which had been Techman's biggest source of revenue since 1980, was still using about two-thirds of the engineering staff, but the project was beginning to wind down.

Map showing leases of the Athabasca oil sands.

In September, the picture momentarily brightened when Techman was awarded the first phase of a three-part, $3.5-million alternate tar sands development study. The proposal for the Fording Coal study, which was worth $950,000, was also successful and work got under way. Techman then obtained a conceptual design job for a coal property owned by McIntyre Mines.

But these jobs only postponed the inevitable. With the Gregg River project scheduled to be completed in June 1983, Techman began to lay off staff, cutting back to 175 people by the end of October. The work for both McIntyre and Fording was completed near the end of the year, as was the first phase of the tar sands study. In 1983, with the Canadian economy still in a slump and no new projects in sight, it was obvious Techman had no future.

1980 ▶

The U.S. spacecraft, Voyager 1, explores Saturn, its 14 moons and more than 1,000 rings.

1980 ▶

Paul Christensen hopes for miracles at the MEGA golf tournament.

Loram International Ltd. — The Price of Survival

During this time, the Loram Group's construction arm, Loram International Ltd., was also coming face to face with Canada's struggling economy. Simply put, "the economy went all to hell," said Loram International's vice president and general manager, Dale Anderson. "Work was pretty tough to get. We had the best kind of people working on bidding and estimating new jobs. They were thorough and competent as hell. In fact, we came up with estimates that were as good as or better than 95 per cent of the major contractors in North America. But you have to pay a price for that degree of excellence. You have to carry a pretty competent overhead to provide that. To support that kind of overhead, you have to maintain a fairly big volume, and you've also got to extract a pretty good margin from that volume."

"Our overhead was running around $8 million a year," Anderson said. "That equates to eight per cent on a volume of $100 million, and that's a lot of money. So to stay in business, we had to know that we could profitably complete $100 million worth of work a year. That way we could generate the eight per cent to cover overhead, and only then would we get to any profit. As work dropped off, we ended up paying for a lot of machinery that was parked idle, just sitting in the back lot. You can't make money if you have iron sitting around doing nothing. So we had million-dollar pieces of equipment sitting there for 12 months and never turning a wheel. At that time, interest rates were 15, 16, 17 per cent. That's a lot of carrying charges on a piece of iron that's just rusting out in your backyard."

In 1981, the Heavy Construction Division suffered a major setback. That year, work began on a job for Saskatchewan Power Corporation. The project called for the construction of deep wells, shafts and a 1,430-metre (1,564-yard) drainage tunnel system on the Nipawin hydroelectric power station in east-central Saskatchewan.

Top: Dale Anderson, vice president and general manager of Loram International Ltd.

Above: Early construction on the Nipawin hydroelectric wells, shafts and tunnel project.

While the work itself was simple enough, the correct bidding procedures were not followed, so the normal checks and balances went haywire. "Nipawin turned out to be a disaster," said Anderson. "It was pretty high-risk work. We really didn't have anyone knowledgeable enough to properly bid the work, so that got us into trouble. But it was at a time when there was less work, with less margin, so we felt we had to take the job."

Loram's total revenue from the Nipawin job was $11.7 million. The loss on the job totalled $11.8 million. "That is probably the worst job in the company's history, dollar for dollar," recalled Paul Christensen, who became executive vice president of Loram International in 1982. While the loss was obviously financially traumatic, it served as yet another example of the integrity of the organization and the perpetuation of the principle of completing the job no matter what the cost. Only this time, it was the third generation's time to learn that lesson and perform appropriately.

There were some bright moments in the early Eighties, however. Working with Techman Engineering Ltd., the General Contracts Division helped build the coal preparation plant and related facilities at the massive Gregg River Mine site, 40 kilometres (25 miles) southwest of Hinton, Alberta. Commissioned by Gregg River Resources Ltd., the work also called for the erection of an administration office, a shop complex and a wash plant. In 1982, Loram crews constructed two kilometres (1.2 miles) of railway trackage, a permanent mine office, a maintenance and warehouse plant and two clean-coal storage silos. In erecting these silos, the crews set a Canadian construction record by placing 24,000 cubic metres (31,000 cubic yards) of concrete and 230 tonnes (250 short tons) of reinforcing steel in six and a half days. This intense effort enabled the plant to be opened on schedule in May 1983.

1980 ▶

Archbishop Oscar Romero, a Nobel Peace Prize nominee and El Salvador's leading human rights advocate, is assassinated while saying mass for his recently deceased mother.

1980 ▶

Touring the Vesta Mine during the summer barbecue.

"He was Dil"

Dil Robertson's departure from Loram International Ltd. in 1982 marked the end of a rather colourful era. During his nine-year tenure as the Loram Group's construction company president, stories about Robertson were the stuff of legend.

"Dil was a character," recalled Robertson's executive assistant, Ann Clipstone, who began her career with the Loram Group in 1976. "He really was. It always amazed me that he was a Mormon bishop. He was head of the church in Calgary. You'd never have known it from a work point of view. He was really into it, but when it came to work, he was as tough as any of them.

"I loved working for him because you never knew what the day would bring. He'd breeze in and say, 'Good morning, Sunshine,' and then he'd be slamming doors. If he came in in the morning and his desk drawer wasn't unlocked, he wouldn't bother using a key. He'd just pull the drawer off. He threw more phones and broke more stuff and yelled and screamed. So he yelled and screamed, so what. I really liked the guy. He was Dil."

Vic Lemecha led this record-breaking project. "In January of 1981, I asked to be replaced as manager of the General Contracts Division and be put on as project manager of Gregg River," he said. "At that time, things were winding down in the construction industry in Canada. We were suffering from a shortage of work and a shortage of volume. I knew all of the construction people who were available and who the good ones were, so I was able to pick the best people that we had within the organization. We ended up with probably the best construction management crew that you could find in the country at that time. As a result, the job went very well."

"We started clearing on February 14, 1981," Lemecha said, "about a month after I had been named project manager. That was one of the fastest mobilizations of any project I had been on. Because we were short of volume in other areas, we had the total resources of the company to draw on for people and equipment. We had a lot of equipment available at that time. We ran a very tightly controlled project. As we were the prime contractor, the project manager and the designer, we had total control over all the subcontractors involved. A lot of people at Gregg River had been on the Mount Wright project, and they had all learned the same hard lessons. They knew what had to be done to control a project of that size, which employed about 850 people at its peak. As a result, the job was constructed on schedule and under budget."

In 1982, Paul Christensen replaced outgoing Loram International Ltd. president, Dil Robertson. Christensen, an expert in the financial complexities of the construction business and a capable administrator, brought to the role more than 26 years of experience with the Loram Group. Shortly after assuming the presidency, Christensen faced a crippling blow to Loram International's future when Shell Oil's proposed Alsands oil extraction plant in the Fort McMurray area was cancelled in May of 1982.

"In the early Eighties, we joined forces with Bechtel and Monenco, an engineering firm out of Montreal," explained Anderson. "We were successful in landing a $2-billion to $3-billion project for Shell Oil. The Loram Group had 15 per cent of that venture, which was a pretty major undertaking. When the economy turned around, the oil sands project collapsed and the people had to be dispersed. I was sure sad to see that happen,

Paul Christensen is named president of Loram International Ltd. in 1982. Two years later, he will be named president and chief executive officer of Trison Investments Ltd.

A.W. (Art) Wirth becomes president of Techman in 1983 and president of Loram International Ltd. in 1984.

◄ **1980**

Calgary Deputy Mayor Pat Donnelly and F.C. Mannix break ground for the new MHL Holdings office building at 7th Street and 7th Avenue S.W. in Calgary. The 18-storey structure is scheduled for completion in late 1981.

◄ **1980**

During the Village of Wabamun summer Sportorama Parade, Manalta Coal's Whitewood Mine float wins Best Overall Float and Best in the Commercial Class.

because we had a lot of bright young people coming up through the ranks on that one. They would have been the backbone of a tremendous organization."

"We had great expectations since it was our first project where we would be in the EPC business," Christensen said. "Things were very tough then in '83 and '84. We bid a lot of work but could not be successful if we wanted to be realistic on costs. We shaved some markups, but competitors' prices seemed to ignore true cost. Many times the jobs we bid on would go for a lot less than we thought they would cost." By the beginning of 1984, the flow of new projects came to a near halt. That year, the construction company acquired just one significant project, a contract for the Heavy Construction Division to drill, blast and haul rock overburden at the Quintette Tumbler Ridge coal site in British Columbia.

In 1984, Paul Christensen was named president and chief executive officer of Trison Investments Ltd. and a director of all the companies in the Loram Group. He was succeeded by A.W. (Art) Wirth, a man with 30 plus years' experience in the oil, gas, pipeline and oil sands industries. "In 1980, I joined the Alsands project as vice president and project director, and spent the next two years with the Alsands project," Wirth said. "When that project folded in the summer of 1982, a few months later I became part of the Mannix family operations. I spent about a year as vice president and project director for Techman, then in the later part of 1983, I became president of Techman. Additionally, in the summer of 1984, I became president of Loram International Ltd."

Within months of Wirth's appointment as president, the decision was made to mothball both Techman and Loram International. "In late October, we made the decision to wind down those two operations and put them in a state of limbo until the economic environment improved, market conditions were better and the engineering-construction environment was less competitive," explained Wirth.

"The economic environment and outlook for the foreseeable future were poor for the type of engineering and construction services that we provided," said Lee Morrison, manager of finance and administration. "Of course, the economy of this part of Canada was there for everybody to see. These have not been good years. It was also determined that our chances of making any money were certainly

"THERE IS WISDOM IN KNOWING WHEN TO MOVE ON"

"One of the most significant days in the group, in my experience, was when the far-reaching decision was made for the group to exit the construction industry," said David L. Gjøsünd, who joined Loram in 1978 as a special projects accountant and became Mancal's controller one year later. "The construction industry is what launched this group in 1898, so to acknowledge that we had to exit was not an easy decision. I'm sure for the Mannix brothers, it must have been a difficult decision. However, one of the characteristics of the brothers that really has impressed me all these years that I've been here, is their dogged determination to listen to the advice of other counsellors no matter how challenging to their own preference.

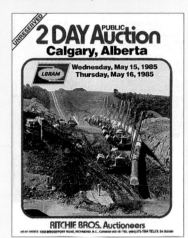

"On November 8, 1984, we were all sitting in the boardroom. The issue on the table was whether we stay in the construction industry. Loram International certainly had not had sterling results for quite a while. Nor had we had good results from the U.S. construction company, Loram Construction Inc. One by one they listened to everybody around the table expressing their views as to whether we should stay or whether we should exit the construction industry. By far the majority gave them the counsel that they should exit.

"A feeling I took away from that meeting was that there is wisdom in knowing when to move on and when to exit. It is not a sign of failure to leave when the writing is on the wall, in fact quite to the contrary. It is a sign of wisdom and strength. The strength of experience in which management can freely draw on the financial wealth accumulated by the construction business for the past 86 years at that stage was best respected by plowing all that into the success of the oil and gas and coal company rather than continuing in an industry that you felt was no longer for us. It was important to recognize that the future success of both the coal and the oil and gas companies was largely possible because of that foundation that the construction company had laid."

1980 ▶

John Lennon, the former Beatle, is murdered in New York City.

1980 ▶

Wives of the executives of Loram International enjoy the annual ladies luncheon during the Managers' Conference. The luncheon tradition was begun in the early 1950s by Margie Mannix.

THE PATH NOT TAKEN

"As construction work was rapidly evaporating, the major decision was made to bite the bullet and get out," said David McClement. "It was made after many heated and tough discussions, but I think a rational decision was made. Certainly, it was not easy, because the construction company had been the whole history of the Mannix family. Of course, it's not written in stone that they will be out of the construction game forever, but it certainly was a major decision even to go out on a short-term basis. I viewed the construction company as a sort of cancerous limb. If you have a cancerous limb, then it is smart to cut it off before it kills the rest of you. So that was done, neat and clean."

In facing this decision, there was some comfort to be found in the precedent set by F.S. Mannix. During tough economic times, he shut down his construction operations, turning to other areas of revenue, such as farming, to provide an income. In so doing, he stopped the drain on his capital, an act which enabled him to have the cash required to reenter the business when times improved. And yet, as simple as this act sounds, some people never have the courage to take it. They hang on until their operating capital — and their future in business —drains away, forcing them to take drastic action.

Consider, for example, the story of ChapStick. Back in the early 1880s, about the time F.S. Mannix was born, a certain C.D. Fleet, M.D., of Lynchburg, Virginia, formulated a waxy lip balm. In 1912, Fleet, strapped for cash, sold the company. The price he got for the entire company — which included the formula for ChapStick — was $5, about the price of four tubes today.

questionable. After all, we were a large contractor with a large investment in equipment. It's like any company. You have a balance sheet to administer, debts to pay and service, and equity to protect. So it was fairly simple. We projected down the road a few years and saw that we might not get the work that we needed to support the effort we had in place. By effort, I mean capital, equipment and people. After making such a projection, we could see that if we continued on our present course we would be heading down a water slide."

Looking ahead, it was clear that by the end of 1985, there would be only one major hydroelectric project being built in all of Canada. For the construction company this was particularly difficult as, at one time, nearly 50 per cent of the company's total revenues were generated from this type of work. In October 1994, the decision was made to wind down all construction company activities, so they stopped bidding new work.

"On Ronnie's side of the house, we faced the tough decision for a family company that had made its stake out of heavy construction," said Fred McNeil. "We had to decide to shut the construction company down because there was no market. And, before that, we had to make the decision to shut down the engineering company [Techman] on which they had spent about $8 million."

"There was a lot of history in the people who were there," Sid Jaycock said. "You could say that Techman had a three-year burst, but in fact, it was a very, very successful three years. We were destroyed, of course, by the disappearance of the marketplace which was one of the basic criteria for starting Techman in the first place — that we had a growth marketplace to develop in. I think the fact that we chose to accept the defeat early in the game, and get out of the business, was a fairly successful decision as well, before we spent any more money that was going nowhere. A few years later, virtually all of our competitors were gone too, and much more painfully."

While the decision to shut down Techman was a difficult one, the decision to mothball the construction company was even more wrenching. "In the Mannixes' case, you can imagine an emotional attachment would have been to the construction business," said McNeil. "But when it had to be killed, they killed it. Otherwise, it would have kept draining and draining money. That's the price of survival. Now, those were all very definitely family decisions. Certainly as far as Doug Gardiner and I were concerned, there were no doubts in our minds. The price of survival often is to face up to those tough decisions."

"Ronnie could see it happening; we could all see it happening," agreed Doug Gardiner. "There were far too many big contractors for far too few jobs. It was degenerating into governments building power production, other hydro production, or other things, and they were thinning out. Finally, it got to the stage where it just didn't make any sense anymore. It was a very traumatic thing for them because of their whole history. They were known all over the world as a construction company. However, when the time

1980 ►

Pembina Resources honours employees with 25 years' service.

1980 ►

Thirty-year veterans are honoured. They include from left to right, Gene Labrosse, Ben Kessler, Gordon Coates, Harvey Boles and Clarence Jahn.

came, it was a nonevent. All they got were compliments for realizing what the world was like and forgetting it. Let the Bechtels and the others carry on, they have got the resources. Bechtels really were bankers as much as they were contractors, at that stage of the game."

"The sad part of it was that it was hard on a lot of people," said Lee Morrison. "On an emotional level, it was difficult for a lot of people to accept. It was particularly hard for a lot of us who have been here a long time. To see the equipment being sold was difficult to accept. We had an auction of all our Canadian equipment in May 1985. We sold off our tremendously large fleet of tractors, heavy off-highway trucks, pipeline equipment, and some railroad equipment and cranes. You name it and we sold it. Seeing all that go, it really made it seem like the construction company was gone forever."

The two major sales of all the equipment and supplies in the business, which both took place in 1985, one in Canada and the other in Texas, went very well. It still took another five years, however, to truly wind up all of the activities of the business including final claims, insurance activities, and the like. Ben Kessler, the longest continuously serving employee and long-term administrator, put all the files and records into storage in Loram's History Centre to record the group's nearly 90 years of construction activity.

In choosing to wind up their construction activities, the family and senior managers opted to manage the business on their terms and conditions versus being forced into a much more difficult situation with the further deterioration of the construction business in the late 1980s and on into the '90s. Effectively, this critical change in direction preserved not only the outfit's reputation, but the relationship with people that the outfit was known for. "The announcement was made," recalled David L. Gjøsūnd. "Employees and business communities at large were told about it. They were all informed. All contracts on hand were fully honoured and all employees were very well treated through generous severance packages. A significant effort was directed toward making the break a clean and responsible one. Outplacement counselling was provided for all the employees who couldn't be relocated in the group. By and large, the feedback I received from the business community was that not many breaks like that had been so well-handled. It was certainly something worth being proud of."

In 1985, Loram International gathers its equipment for a huge auction at the Calgary shops.

"Loram dealt first with all the people in the outfit fairly and decisively with the severance packages, counselling and advice provided to them," added Ron Mannix. "The equity of the company was preserved and then redeployed into the energy business where it was successfully used. Then the relationships with all Loram's customers, suppliers, financial institutions, partners and the community at large were maintained and honoured in the very best manner possible. A number of key employees were absorbed into the business of coal, oil and gas and railway activities, which also helped to reinforce the values that had been so long established in the construction industry."

Yet while tough decisions had been made, there were no assurances that these decisions would guarantee a rosy future. "The decisions made by the Loram Group in 1985 resulted in the group becoming much more energy-focused," Ron Mannix said, "but even that area of business would be no bed of roses with the price of oil down and coal prices in the international market also dropping."

1980 ▶

At Techman's Christmas party, the Royal Court of Techman presides over the assembled employees and guests.

1980 ▶

Later in the evening at the Techman party, mercy is shown to the pilloried.

Pembina and Western Decalta
The Politics of Petroleum

The year 1978 was a milestone in Pembina Pipe Line's history. In May, coincidentally matching the 25th anniversary of the Pembina field's discovery, the company pumped the billionth barrel of oil through its system.

In other areas, Pembina and Western Decalta began constructing gas plants and related facilities which permitted the marketing of shut-in gas reserves in the Brazeau River, Crossfield, Hotchkiss, Leduc and Okotoks areas of Alberta. While continuing its $1-million expansion of the Turner Valley gas plant, the company also began investigating the use of secondary and tertiary crude oil recovery methods in the Turner Valley field. Less than 13 per cent of the Turner Valley oil was yet recovered, leaving some 870 million barrels untapped. Preliminary studies looked into the feasibility of CO_2 injection, which would loosen the viscous oil and allow it to flow to the well bore. Meanwhile, Western Decalta continued its offshore gas production at the Tilbury field off Port Alma, northwest Lake Erie, Ontario, and participated in several wells drilled offshore Texas. In addition, the company's Decalta International Corporation subsidiary held exploration interests in Bolivia and offshore Italy in the Adriatic Sea.

Amid these myriad developments at the close of the decade, after two and a half years as president of Pembina, Al Ross opted to leave. "Decalta was a small company, and when you run a small company, as Charles Lee and I did, you run the company, period," he explained. "When you get into a bigger group, you don't make the same decisions anymore. I think that's very right and I don't have any problem with that, but I had operated for too long under a different mode. When you move over to a bigger group like the

Alex Cummings,
former vice president and general
manager of Mancal, becomes president
of Pembina Pipe Line in 1979.

Pembina Pipe Line continues
to improve the aging Turner Valley
gas plant with a $1-million expansion.

Loram Group, they've got all the manuals that you do on operations and so on. That type of thing is fine and necessary for big companies, but if you're not used to it, working out of a manual is not really your idea of a good time. So I decided it was time to move on and leave. They had lots of good people."

Following Ross' resignation, Alex Cummings, former vice president and general manager of Mancal, was moved into Pembina's top slot. "Alex Cummings was put into the oil company to bring to the oil company the discipline of the construction company," explained F.P. Mannix, who originally brought Cummings in from the field. "It was a deliberate policy of changing people over."

"While I didn't have much experience in oil and gas, I guess I had proved that I could lead the troops okay, so I was asked if I would take over," said Cummings. The year that Ross and Cummings split management, 1979, produced record results. Net earnings for the year were a whopping $6.8 million, up $2.3 million or 51.6 per cent from 1978. Gross revenues increased 28.6 per cent, to a record high of $30 million. Although the company spent more than $15 million on exploratory and operating costs, higher product prices and pipeline throughput made 1979 an exceptional year.

Of course, oil companies worldwide were riding high that year. Energy demand had just peaked. Supplies were tight enough to enable OPEC to write its own ticket on prices. A gasoline shortage, much more acute than in 1974, plagued motorists in North America and Europe. Still, industry conditions were becoming reminiscent of those existing in 1974 and 1975. Confrontations between the Canadian federal and provincial governments over sharing resource revenues were again jeopardizing the level of certainty essential to exploration and development investment.

1980 ▶

The Canadian House of Commons officially adopts "O Canada" as the Canadian national anthem.

1981 ▶

In the Yukon, south of Carcross, Loram International crews work through the winter to meet the April deadline for the construction of the new mill complex for United Keno Hills Mine Limited.

An oversupply of natural gas existed in Canada. While the National Energy Board approved the export of 9.6 billion cubic metres (340 billion cubic feet) of gas to the United States, the volumes were allocated so that several exporters could not finance the construction of transportation facilities. Conversely, the Canadian shortage of crude oil was covered by expensive imports. This put Canada at risk and created onerous deficits in the balance of trade for fuels. Although prices paid to Canadian oil producers had increased steadily for several years, Pembina received less than $14 a barrel in 1979. At the time, world spot market prices were at least double that amount.

In Canada, the decade-long oil price increases shifted the power balance from the federal government and eastern Canadian consumers to Alberta. In the summer of 1980, Alberta's Premier Peter Lougheed, with the province's producers and many citizens, claimed Alberta was "subsidizing" the rest of Canada by not receiving the full world price of oil. It seemed clearly unfair that Canadian oil producers received much less than other oil producers outside Canada. To find and produce more Canadian oil, companies required a stronger financial incentive than the federal government allowed. Paying full price to Canadians seemed more reasonable than paying it to foreign governments.

Predicting these political vagaries of the oil and gas business now fell to Pembina's new president, Alex Cummings. In this, he relied heavily on Lorne Gordon. "When it became apparent that I was going to go down to the oil company, I really got involved in trying to study and analyse the oil business, so I put full time into that," he said. "When I got to the oil company, I found that Lorne Gordon knew all the frailties of the organization. He had been involved in the oil company much more than I had over the years and had been vice president of oil and gas under Stan Waters. He had been very much involved in the acquisition of Western Decalta and had helped set up the structure for Ross to come in as president of the oil and gas companies.

SOME VERY, VERY FINE PEOPLE

Late in 1983, Fred Webb, who received his undergraduate degree in mineral engineering and his graduate degree in business from the University of British Columbia, was working as a project manager with Techman. When offered a transfer to Pembina Pipe Line in Drayton Valley, he had mixed feelings. "The opportunity to get into an operating company after a couple of years in research seemed like a good thing," he said, "and yet I didn't know diddly about oil pipelines. So it was with a certain degree of trepidation that I moved my family to Drayton Valley.

"The real reason for getting the confidence to go was the contact I'd had with the main people in Drayton Valley — Al Horne, the district manager and Reg Samis, the maintenance supervisor — who were running the local operation. They were just excellent folks. I felt that if they'd been working there since 1954, and if they were still there, how bad could it be? I went to Pembina with the idea that they were not under any delusions that I knew anything about oil pipelines and it was going to be a mutual learning experience."

"I was in Drayton Valley for three years and they were probably the best three years of my working career," Webb said. "I learned a lot and there were some very, very fine people. Drayton Valley, at the time, was about 5,000 people, and still is about that size. The Drayton area had really never seen a bad day or a bad year. It started as an oil boomtown in 1954-1955, and had boom years and flat years, but never had a bust. It was just an excellent town for a young family. There were 5,000 people, but there were probably 25 good restaurants. At 5:00 p.m., people would look out in their backyard and say to the kids, 'You're supposed to be home.' The first week there, my wife left her Visa card at the drugstore and they called me at the office to tell me. It was just a fine, fine town."

1981 ▶

Britain's Prince Charles marries Lady Diana Spencer.

1981 ▶

Fred McNeil (left) and David McClement at the Bowfort Services long-service awards dinner.

So we knew where I was going to start, although we didn't know how tough it was going to be."

"Alistair Ross had run Western Decalta ever since its inception back in the 1950s, and he had a lot of old pals in there," continued Cummings. "When he left, those pals left with him, or a goodly number at least. It was mostly loyalties, you might say, and certainly a difficulty in accepting a different style of management. The great difference between Alistair and me was that he was a really experienced oil man. He was professionally trained in the business, in the first place. In the second place, he had worked in the intricacies of an oil and gas outfit all his life, while I hadn't. The only oil and gas experience I had was as a director. When I was vice president and general manager of Loram, I was a director of all the operating companies. Then, of course, I had my old oil experience back when I started my career.

"But at any rate, I started right in with a plan to restructure the company. I did what I thought was necessary to run the organization, which was completely different than what they had been used to, but which was along the lines of other oil companies of similar size. I hired the appropriate people, and we started building the various departments. The overhead went from 90 people to close to 200. It was a most difficult time to find good executives here because the oil business was so heated up back in 1980 and '81 when I was hiring. That was the period when the oil companies were taking off into oblivion. But we had remarkably good success in acquiring good people. We made it into very much of an oil and gas exploration and production company."

The Anschutz Acquisition and the National Energy Program
"We were a foreigner in our own land."

Pembina began the decade with a major, and initially unsettling, purchase. In 1980, it acquired all outstanding shares of Anschutz (Canada) Exploration Ltd. and Anschutz Barge Co. Ltd. These companies were then renamed Pembina Exploration Co. Ltd. and Pembina Drilling Co. Ltd. Although Anschutz (Canada) was a U.S.-registered subsidiary of the Anschutz family corporations of Denver, the company's assets — including land and oil and gas reserves in Western Canada, with the largest asset being the Lake Erie land position — were all in Canada. With the acquisition, Pembina also acquired two floater-type drilling barges and other craft for offshore drilling operations.

Above: In 1980, Pembina acquires Anschutz (Canada) Exploration Ltd. and its drilling subsidiary to move into Ontario natural gas exploration and production.

The drilling barge, Mr. Chris, located on Lake Erie, is part of the Anschutz acquisition.

"During 1980, we made an acquisition which was our first important manoeuvre outside the day-to-day operations of the company," said Cummings. "That was Anschutz (Canada) Ltd. At that time, it was very fashionable for companies to enlarge their holdings by acquisitions. Almost immediately upon my arrival in Pembina, there was great interest in acquisitions expressed by our shareholders. I guess all of us were caught up in the euphoria of the business and seeing that as a possibility of expanding. We looked at quite a few companies and rejected a few. Then we got involved with Anschutz, mostly because we were already operating in Lake Erie as a gas producer. We were one of the only companies in Western Canada that had any interests in Ontario at all. Ultimately, we made an acceptable deal with Anschutz after about six months of negotiation."

The deal closed effective August 1, 1980, for a cash consideration of $71.7 million and the assumption of Anschutz's debt, which totalled nearly $12 million — $5 million in long-term debt, $1.6 million in deferred income taxes and $5 million in working capital deficiency. "We didn't know at the time what the implications of that deal were," said Cummings. "The National Energy Program came along about four months later. Our biggest concern over that issue, or one of the big ones that showed up immediately, was that to expedite the Anschutz deal,

1981 ▶

The central oil battery and gas conservation system is completed by Pembina at the Medicine River field, west of Sylvan Lake in central Alberta. Development of this combined oil and gas field has taken a decade, but production from the area is anticipated for the next quarter century.

1981 ▶

After more than 400 days, Iran releases U.S. diplomats held hostage in Tehran.

we had formed a U.S. company since we were purchasing the shares of a U.S. company. It turned out that, in the eyes of the National Energy Program, we were a foreigner in our own land. The story that follows is a long history of working with the federal government to get the rules of the National Energy Program changed, so that we could at least operate on our Canadian lands as a Canadian operator. Ultimately, we did get the company Canadianized, but it was with a tremendous amount of agony."

During October 1980, the federal government announced its new National Energy Program which imposed a new tax on oil and gas revenues and a schedule of new prices for oil and gas, inadequate in the short term and uncertain in the longer term. Included in the program were the withdrawal of the earned depletion allowance and measures designed to increase the Canadian private sector ownership of the industry. The introduction of these drastic changes aggravated the already strained relations between the federal and provincial governments and resulted in a retaliatory three-stage oil production cutback by the Government of Alberta.

In 1981, one year after the NEP was announced, for the first time since its formation in 1954, Pembina lost money, a substantial $7.8 million. While the loss was large, it was mainly attributable to the skyrocketing interest costs on the debt financing the Anschutz purchase. "We got ourselves into great difficulty with that acquisition because it was the period of time when interest rates went right out of sight," said Cummings. "I remember that the feasibility study on Anschutz was based on an 11 per cent interest rate with 100 per cent financing, but before the first year was out, we were paying 23 per cent. Of course, that had a tremendous impact on the success of that venture."

Unfortunately for Pembina, skyrocketing interest rates were not the only problem encountered in this acquisition. In some ways, the Anschutz acquisition was unnervingly similar to Pandora's box which, when opened in curiosity, unleashed a swarm of evils upon

UNANSWERED PRAYERS

Country and western singer Garth Brooks once recorded a song entitled *Unanswered Prayers*. For Pembina, the title of this song could easily have referred to Obed, a large sour gas field in the Rocky Mountain foothills near Hinton, Alberta, named after Lieutenant-Colonel John Obed Smith, a commissioner of immigration around the turn of the century. Initially discovered in 1964, the Obed field was considered uneconomical until a major discovery of significant reserves occurred in 1984. Interest was further enhanced by a rise in the price of sulphur at about the same time.

While Obed looked like the answer to an oil and gas company's prayers, it was also a high-risk development project. "One of the uncomfortable things I did in 1985, was we had a substantial interest, about a one-third interest in a natural gas field called Obed," recalled Lorne Gordon. "When Obed was discovered, it was one of the top ten discoveries of the decade; it was that large. It was a high-risk development project because it was heavy, deep sour gas. When I went to Pembina and I looked at our financial situation — which wasn't weak, but it wasn't strong — to carry our share of the Obed development would have been a huge cost, about $25 million." Because the financial risk could endanger Pembina's economic health, Gordon prevailed on Mancal to farm out — to give up part of the company's interest in the property in exchange for somebody else making financial contributions to the project — to Esso, who was the operator. These negotiations, which occurred before oil prices crashed, were not unanimously supported.

"Because this discovery was so spectacular and because Western Decalta had been technically responsible for the discovery, the managers who were involved in that discovery were very unhappy with my decision," Gordon said. "Anyway, after the negotiations were completed, Esso started into the development of the project. Fortunately for us, we didn't have to put up any money, so we sat on the sidelines. The project went into tremendous, tremendous overruns. Production rates never did come up to what was expected and the project was an economic disaster."

1981 ▶

Saskatchewan Power Corporation awards Loram International the contract to build deep wells, shafts and a drainage tunnel system to support the Nipawin hydroelectric power station. This giant auger is used on the project.

mankind. "We found a lot of surprises in that acquisition," Cummings said. "For example, there was a drawer full of bills that we didn't know were there that weren't paid. The important lesson was that we made the acquisition before we were ready to do the kind of analytical work necessary."

True to Pembina style, however, the company not only learned from, but capitalized on its mistakes. "We started right in to make the best of developing that deal," said Cummings. "We found that we had to change almost every procedure that they had been using, and go back to some of the things that we had learned on our own. In fact, we had to spend a great deal more capital than we had anticipated to bring the Lake Erie project along. It never did come anywhere close to reaching the operating plan we had perceived at the time of the acquisition. On the other side of the coin, the Anschutz deal formed the basis of a long string of asset developments that wouldn't have happened otherwise, so the company is stronger by that acquisition. We were carrying more debt than we should have, but that's all history."

At the time, however, the Anschutz acquisition put a real strain not only on Pembina's finances, but on the company's administration as well. "When Pembina acquired Anschutz in August 1980, that was the beginning of a very tough time in Pembina's history," explained R.B. (Bob) Michaleski, who joined Loram in 1978 as manager of internal audit. "Anschutz was really an exploration play, didn't have a lot of cash flow and we had assigned a lot of value to an underdeveloped acreage which, in hindsight, turned out not to have as much value as we thought. So it placed quite a significant financial burden on Pembina. It also placed a significant administrative burden on us because the

Offshore drilling requires compact and complex floating platforms.

assets were Canadian assets. It was an operation that was run out of Denver, so we had to Canadianize the company, which was an historic event, to bring it back to Canada. We also had to bring all the records and effectively start processing the financial affairs of the company in Calgary. Given that what we acquired was really a messy operation, not well run at all, and it was placing financial burdens on us, the pressure was on to say, 'Well, what's really going on here?' We had to go through a fairly significant period of time where we were trying to understand what we bought."

"We had gone from a small department to an accounting department of over 40 people," Michaleski said. "We were managing all those 27 subsidiaries for Western Decalta. We were a public company so we had to report to our public and private shareholders, then we had to try to digest and integrate Anschutz. It didn't really stabilize because we were in tough times with the Anschutz acquisition and we had to look at doing something else to find money."

In 1982, Pembina Pipe Line Ltd. was renamed Pembina Resources Limited. In its search for capital, the newly renamed company sold some of its assets. Early in the year, Pembina sold its interest in the oil and gas assets in the Medicine Hat area for $30 million, which yielded an after-tax profit of $13.9 million. Pembina made good use of the sale proceeds, applying most of them to the prepayment of floating-rate debt taken the previous year, thereby reducing Pembina's exposure to future interest rate fluctuations. While the company could no longer count on revenue from this area, gas production in Western Canada was undergoing a general decline. At the same time, the company also sold its 50 per cent interest in South Alberta Pipe Lines Ltd., receiving $1.76 million.

1981 ▶

Lortherm insulates 38,000 metres (41,560 yards) of pipe and 9,500 square metres (11,362 square yards) of machinery at the Turbo Resources Refinery at Balzac, Alberta.

1981 ▶

France's TGV high-speed train begins service. The electrically powered train attains speeds of 380 kilometres (236 miles) per hour.

As a result of the sales, Pembina enjoyed a stunning fiscal reversal in 1982. After the prior year's $7.8-million loss, Pembina's net income totalled a record $18.1 million. Reduced interest costs, reduced royalty rates and gas production from Lake Erie properties contributed to the profits. However, "real" profits were only about $1.4 million. Two "extraordinary items" — the sale of the company's oil and gas assets in the Medicine Hat area and Pembina's 50 per cent interest in South Alberta Pipe Lines Ltd. — led to the big tally.

Pembina also sold its shares of the Western Decalta subsidiary, Petrol Oil and Gas Company Ltd., further easing Pembina's debt burden. "We sold it in a very difficult time," said Cummings, "and it was a difficult company to sell. The sale relieved the financial burden that Western Decalta was carrying. The result was that, with the restructuring of the financial side and the sales of Medicine Hat and Petrol — all of which were applied to the reduction of debt — the financial health of both Pembina and Decalta came back into being manageable."

While the sale of Petrol relieved some of the financial burden that Western Decalta was carrying, it also turned out to be an expensive lesson in gaining a healthier respect for cold, hard cash. Petrol was sold on September 1, 1981, to Universal Explorations Ltd., a Calgary-based oil, gas and mining company. Universal purchased Western Decalta's 65.1 per cent interest in Petrol for $16 million in cash,

Pembina pipeline crews string pipe across the North Saskatchewan River in Alberta.

$6 million in redeemable convertible debentures and three million shares of Universal common stock, which was worth $2.80 a share on the closing date of the deal. The total sale price came to slightly over $30 million, or about $12 per share of Petrol stock. It was not too long, however, before it became clear that the only place the transaction would ever be worth $30 million was on paper.

In 1983, two years after the sale, Universal and Petrol were amalgamated and Petrol Oil and Gas officially disappeared. The Petrol minority shareholders took a big loss since the amalgamation offer was based on a trade of four Universal shares for each share of Petrol. The minority shareholders traded in what had once been a solid stock for shares in a bankrupt company. Loram ended up with $15 million worth of securities, which the company tried to collect for several years. In the end they were worth only $4 million in cash. In the final analysis, the sale price of Petrol worked out to be less than $8 a share.

As Pembina was struggling to right itself financially, the company was also working to upgrade its field facilities. "During that time," Cummings explained, "we also went through a very intensive period of improving the facilities all over the operations of both Pembina and Western Decalta. We put a program together that we knew would take about three or four years to replace and completely redo a lot of those facilities. I think if you look at them now, they're about as high in standards as anybody's in the area."

1981 ▶

Roger Fuller (left) and Howard Tidswell at the inaugural MEGA Stampede breakfast.

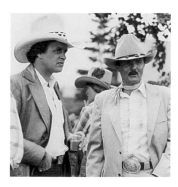

1981 ▶

"Experienced Stampede Chefs" — it says so on the hats — F.P. Mannix, David McClement and Stan Waters about to start cooking at the annual MEGA barbecue.

The Western Accord
New Freedom, New Challenges

In January 1985, Alex Cummings moved to become senior vice president of Mancal and a director of Pembina Resources. His mentor in the oil and gas business, Lorne Gordon, succeeded him as Pembina's president. That same year, the company increased its throughput capacity, replaced the pipeline crossing over the North Saskatchewan River, had net increases in oil and gas reserves from successful exploration and started an experiment with steam injection recovery at Seal, Alberta. Pembina also commissioned Western Decalta's Diamond Valley gas plant, a $25-million sour gas processing facility that would replace the ancient Turner Valley plant.

Nineteen eighty-five was also an historic year for the Canadian oil and gas industry. That year, Canadian energy policy was drastically overhauled, with the five-year-old National Energy Program dismantled in the process. In February, the governments of Canada and Newfoundland signed the Atlantic Accord resolving a decade-long dispute. This accord established the principle that offshore revenue sharing would be similar to that existing between the Government of Canada and the provinces with land-based petroleum activities. The Western Accord between the federal government and the three western provinces, which among other things, laid the foundation for oil price deregulation, came six weeks later.

The Western Accord was a new energy pricing and taxation agreement that, explained Alberta Energy Minister John Zaozirny, gave oil and gas companies "the same treatment for taxation purposes as other Canadian industries. It's going to be taxed on its profits, not on revenues." In late October, a natural gas pricing and marketing policy and a new Canada Lands Policy followed. The agreement on natural gas market and prices provided for a one-year transition period. During this year, the Alberta border and Toronto wholesale prices were frozen at existing levels. The next year, effective November 1, 1986, all gas sales would be freely negotiated between producers and distributors.

The Western Accord deregulated crude oil for the first time since 1973. For more than a decade, essentially all the crude produced in Alberta had been sold to the Alberta Petroleum Marketing Commission at prices determined through agreements between the federal and provincial governments. In fact, since market forces created their own form of regulation prior to that, this marked the first time Canadian oil was truly free. But freedom had its liabilities. Energy producers now had to find buyers for their product. With the incentive of world prices — and a temporary Alberta Petroleum Incentive Program that reimbursed 30 per cent of conventional exploration costs in the province — the oil and gas industry responded to the new energy policies with a surge of activity. And yet, anyone with more than a few years' experience in the petroleum business knows this is a boom and bust industry. At the end of 1985, the biggest oil drilling year in Canadian history, jubilation turned into depression. As some prices tumbled below $10 per barrel in December, oil towns received economic jolts not felt since the 1930s. The likelihood of a severe and sustained downturn in industry activity appeared inevitable.

The new Diamond Valley gas plant is built to replace the old Turner Valley facility.

1981 ▶

It is truly hard to go hungry at the summer barbecues.

1981 ▶

Yes, that is fresh snow on the hill above the course at the annual Pembina Resources Jasper golf tournament.

Gregg River
"All of a sudden, it would be completely thrown into chaos."

For Manalta Coal, Bob Sanders' presidency saw a major transition in the history of the company. Sanders continued the revision of Manalta's management and operations structure initiated by Ron Mannix in 1976 and by the end of 1978, the revamping of Manalta's senior management was complete. Manalta's mines also began whole new adventures. At all mines, new equipment was acquired and mining operations were modernized as long-term coal contracts were renegotiated.

While the central focus of Manalta management in the late 1970s was on placing existing mining operations on solid footing, the Gregg River project, which seemed to have more lives than a cat, once again came back from the dead. In 1979, not long after the second Gregg River project team had been disbanded, the Japanese steel companies again began to show some interest as the steel markets improved. Manalta then assembled a third project team. Since Alex Cummings had moved into Mancal to work with Ron Mannix as vice president and general manager, another person was selected to head the project. This was Roger Poole, formerly vice president, acquisitions, in Mancal. Poole, who joined the Loram Group in 1973, was previously Pembina's controller, vice president of administration of Loram Co. Ltd. and president of Loram Services Ltd. Although Poole proved an excellent project manager, he had no experience in dealing with Japan. Consequently, Bob Sanders soon began devoting a considerable amount of time to Gregg River.

For Sanders, the frequent trips to Japan produced the usual frustrations that by now were a familiar story to all people in Manalta and Mancal who previously worked on Gregg River. "I don't think I have ever undergone the depressions that would result from unfavourable meetings over there," Sanders said. "It's very difficult to describe just how bad you could feel. You'd see what you thought was a negotiation proceeding smoothly, and then all of a sudden, it would be completely thrown into chaos for some obscure reason."

One problem with the negotiations involved the partnership arrangement among the Japanese steel companies. Nippon Steel, Nippon Kokan (NKK), Kawasaki Steel, Sumitomo Metal Industries, Kobe Steel and Nisshin Steel all had different agendas. "All of this time, unbelievable politics had been going on behind the scenes with regard to which coal properties the different mills were pushing and promoting," Ron Mannix explained. To make matters worse, NKK and Kobe Steel, the two coordinators for Canada, were fighting about which Canadian property should receive top priority. NKK favoured Gregg River. Kobe Steel was promoting the Bullmoose project in British Columbia.

In addition, the 1974 and 1978 failures to develop Gregg River caused Manalta to lose credibility with many of the newer executives in some of the mills. "One of the really tough things was that we had been through the same politics before and most of the people in the steel mills were saying, 'Look, those guys are no good,'" explained Ron Mannix. "So politics and events that we had no control over were going against us, and

DON'T LEAVE HOME WITHOUT IT

In 1980, D.J. (Jim) Watkinson, a young Calgary lawyer, was recruited to join Manalta Coal. "After Howard Tidswell hired me, he brought me in to introduce me to Bob Sanders, who was the president of the coal company," recalled Watkinson. "I sat down in the chair in his office and he said, 'Jim, what do you know about coal?' I said, 'The only thing I know about coal is that I remember helping my dad shovel it in the furnace to keep warm during the winter.' He said something like, 'Well, that's a good start.' He then gave me a bunch of material to read on the status of the Gregg River negotiations. Within two weeks, I was on a plane flying to Tokyo to negotiate coal contracts.

"We were supposed to be in Tokyo for six days and not being experienced over there, I just brought a couple hundred dollars along. The airport ride into Tokyo cost $80. Fortunately, I had an American Express card. At that time, I think you could pull out $200 per day, so every day I was making the trek to American Express to pull some money out. We ended up staying for 23 days instead of six days. The hotel room was up in the $20,000 range. The prices were absolutely incredible.

"While I was there, I did get a call from American Express. My charge card had never been up over $2,000 if I was doing a business trip, but I was running up over $30,000 worth of expenses. They phoned up and said, 'Are you Jim Watkinson?' I said, 'Yes, I'm really the Jim Watkinson.' I think they thought maybe someone else was in Tokyo using my card."

1981 ▶

Bob Gruszecki, centre, at the annual Loram International Managers' Conference.

1981 ▶

First Christmas, first Santa Claus, MEGA children's Christmas party.

they were going against us because they didn't believe we'd make the deal." If all this were not enough, problems developed with Mitsui Coal Development (Canada) Ltd., the trading company that was required to be used by the steel mills.

While it often seemed during 1980 that Manalta had no friends in Japan, one extremely powerful supporter backed the Gregg River project. This was the young purchasing agent F.C. Mannix befriended in 1961, Hisao Makita, now the chairman of NKK. Makita was influential in thwarting attempts by Sumitomo and Kawasaki to scuttle the Gregg River negotiations in favour of Australian projects. "NKK had a passion and love for Canada, a great part of which was due to Makita," Ron Mannix said. "Mr. Nimoto was one of Makita's chosen few, but there were numerous meetings on Nimoto's level where we bumped heads and had lots of arguments and discussions. But ultimately Makita went over and talked to some of the more senior people and said, 'Look, in terms of long-term strategy and politically, we've got to be moving to Canada to diversify our supply.'"

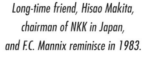

Neither Makita nor Nimoto was successful in completely controlling Sumitomo and Kawasaki, however. In August 1980, negotiations in Japan reached a critical juncture. Although a contract price of $74 a ton was supposedly agreed on, it turned out that this was not exactly the case. "What had been going on behind the scenes was that Mr. Nimoto had been having great difficulty and arguments with Sumitomo and Kawasaki because those two steel mills had not in fact agreed to, and were not willing to agree to, the $74-a-ton price," Ron Mannix explained. Unless a firm agreement on price was reached immediately, the Gregg River project was headed back into the limbo in which it existed since 1956.

When word of this development reached Ron Mannix in Calgary, he decided to go to Japan to have a first-hand look at what was happening. "First of all, I wanted to check things out and find out as much as I could about the markets and what was going on with all of the competition, totally independently," he said. "So I went and talked to other people and asked them to remain quiet, because the Japanese didn't know I was in Tokyo. The second reason was that, to make the deal, somebody had to make a decision on price, and I couldn't get a real feel for what was going on if I was in Calgary on the telephone. To be able to get answers quickly and effectively, Bob Sanders needed somebody right there. He was in charge, and I supported him totally in what he was doing, but he needed to be able to get an objective opinion of what was happening and a yes or no answer to do something or not. The third thing was when we came back to negotiate in 1980 for the third time, my sentiments were that we weren't going to get a fourth chance. Most people in Japan did not believe we would ever make a deal, and neither did most people in our own outfit. It had gotten to the point that if you got assigned to Gregg River, that meant you were on your way out of the outfit because that's what happened to a lot of people."

"Gregg River was the kind of job that nobody ever thought was going to proceed," agreed Vic Lemecha, Loram International's manager of the General Contracts Division. "In the summer of 1980, when we resurrected the project again, I said, 'God, if I have to be involved in another Gregg River estimate, I'm going to be sick.' People were just sick of hearing about this project, especially suppliers and subcontractors. You'd go back to them and they'd say, 'Not again! Are you guys doing another estimate? What do you guys get paid for, estimates or building?'"

However, the summer of 1980 proved to be Gregg River's line in the sand. "I felt strongly that we would not get another chance, so we either made the deal this time around, or we could forget Gregg River forever," Ron Mannix said.

Long-time friend, Hisao Makita, chairman of NKK in Japan, and F.C. Mannix reminisce in 1983.

1982 ▶

SaskTel, the Saskatchewan telephone network, creates the first fibre optics telecommunications network. A fibre optics bundle is shown.

1982 ▶

Argentine forces invade Britain's Falkland Islands. Britain responds with force and defeats Argentina.

"You've got to make a deal."

After a week in Tokyo, Ron Mannix made a decision on price. Nori Kobayama and other people he had talked with assured him that the $74-a-ton price was going to hold up and there was a good possibility that the steel mills would settle for slightly more. Mannix's gut feeling, however, was that this was not going to happen. Right before he was to leave for the airport for his flight back to Calgary, Mannix gave Bob Sanders his final instructions on the cutoff price. "I told Bobby, 'Make the deal,'" Mannix recalled. "'You can go down to the lowest price of $73 a ton.' Nori was saying, and all of the intelligence we had was telling us, that we were going to get at least $74 and maybe $74.25 or $74.50. But I said, 'You've got to make a deal, and Bobby, you've got authority to make the cotton-picking deal down to this level.'"

Sanders was not happy with these instructions, however. "In my mind, I felt that $73 was too low a price to accept," Sanders said. "I really doubted that we could make the thing fly on that low a price. We negotiated all that afternoon and got to the point where we said we wanted $73.50 and the Japanese were offering $73. Ronnie had left, so we came to a stalemate. I wouldn't go down to $73, and they wouldn't come up to $73.50. So we cut off the negotiations at about five o'clock in the evening."

The Manalta group then headed back to the hotel. To their amazement, they found Ron Mannix sitting there waiting for them in the lobby of the hotel. "Ronnie had no suitcase, no room, no money, no coat," Sanders said. "He was with his wife that trip, and she had gone home. But he had turned around when he got to the airport." What had

Manalta Coal president, Bob Sanders, left, during the Gregg River Mine celebrations in Japan.

THE WIZARD OF LORAM

Lorne Gordon visiting a Japanese steel mill.

In most businesses, management thinks rather narrowly, putting round pegs in round holes and square pegs in square holes. Not so at Loram. One of the great strengths of the Loram Group is that when management recognizes potential in a person, they do not hesitate to give that person ample opportunity for growth. A prime example of this principle in action is Lorne B. Gordon.

Gordon, who joined the Loram Group in 1971 as chief accountant with Alberta Concrete Products, proved remarkably adept at fulfilling a number of key roles in the Loram Group — chief internal auditor for Loram Holdings Ltd.; controller of Alberta Concrete Products; controller for Loram; vice president, oil and gas for Loram; vice president, corporate planning for Pembina Pipe Line Ltd.; assistant general manager for Loram Co. Ltd.; vice president and general manager of Loram; president of Pembina and member of the boards of all the companies in the Loram Group.

Throughout the years, Gordon played a pivotal role in many of the turning points in Loram's history. "Lorne is a topnotch financial guy, but he could hang out a shingle as a lawyer tomorrow and no one would know he's not a lawyer," admired Jim Watkinson, a pretty topnotch lawyer himself. "Lorne's really good on agreements and insightful in terms of finding ways to get around and through issues." For example, when the Gregg River agreement "was getting very close to being finalized," Watkinson said, "we would report to Ron Mannix at the end of the day. Then we'd phone back to Lorne Gordon and Lorne would set out positions for us. I didn't know who Lorne was, so it was a real surprise when I found out that Lorne Gordon was just this little kid like me. Actually, not like me, even a little younger than I am. I thought he was some sort of grey-haired wizard they kept up in some private office."

1982 ▶

The egg toss during the Loram Social Club summer barbecue.

1982 ▶

Loram Construction Ltd. wins the Blaine Haul Road and Eagle Access Road contracts from Fording Coal at Elkford, British Columbia. Japanese steel company cutbacks force the cancellation of the Blaine project, but Loram finishes the $14.4-million Eagle project by year-end.

happened was that Mannix had started thinking about worst-case scenarios at the airport. After checking his bags and putting his wife on the plane, he cancelled his reservations and took a cab back to the hotel. "I was worried about what would happen if something really went haywire," Mannix explained. "While I was at the airport, I was thinking, 'If the Japanese say $72 or $71 or something like that, then we'll get into a whole new ball game, but Bob can't get an answer if I leave.' I knew if we couldn't get an answer for something like that, we were going to have a disaster, so that's why I went back to the hotel."

After a quick discussion about what had happened in the afternoon session, Mannix decided to accept the Japanese offer. "So we tracked down the Japanese negotiating team, who were having dinner at another hotel not too far away," Sanders said. "We got them back that night and closed the deal at $73, as they requested. We made the deal that night in my hotel room around ten thirty or eleven. But that could have been the end of the negotiations, I suppose. It would seem, after all the work that had gone on at that time, that the deal would crater over 50 cents. We were down to the last 50 cents, and the arguments had gone as far as they were going to go. If Ronnie had not chosen to come back, I don't think I would have come down to the $73 because I was not satisfied that it was enough money to make the deal fly. I would probably have talked to Ronnie the next day on the phone, and perhaps we could have salvaged the deal then, but it was no doubt easier to salvage it that night than it would have been the next day."

"Bob believed in his own mind that he could get that last little extra bit," Mannix said. "But he wasn't thinking of all the other complications and everything that was going on. He was focused in on that meeting and the negotiations and trying to get everything he could out of it. Ultimately, if you see the situation the way that I saw it, you've got to give up or you've got to make a deal. From that standpoint, I'm convinced in my own mind we got virtually every last cent that we were going to get, because of Bob's toughness and the way he did it. I thought, 'That's all you're going to get, so you had better be realistic.'"

Les Duncan, the legal counsel who was in Japan at the time, then went to work to draft a letter of understanding between all the parties, feverishly working until six on Saturday morning to complete it. By ten that morning, the negotiators were back at it, and by 2:30 that afternoon, the initial Gregg River project agreement was virtually complete. Everyone headed home except Roger Poole, who stayed until Monday morning to get the few remaining Japanese steel mill signatures.

With the contract price finally settled, and the memorandum of understanding signed, then came the arduous process of negotiating all the details of the contract and working out financing plans for the mine development. Financing would be handled in partnership by Manalta and the Japanese companies. Manalta's choice for a lawyer was Don Mawhinney. Mawhinney, who previously worked with the Loram Group on the Empire Mine, was familiar with the peculiarities of dealing with Japanese customers. "Don had our management's respect insofar as legal talents go," said Sanders. "Ronnie and Lorne Gordon trusted what he said, and they trusted him to look out for their interests properly as a lawyer. But Don would also bend over backwards to ensure that the Japanese weren't put off by what he required from a legal standpoint. In other words, he had the flexibility and imagination to word these things in such a way that we had the protection we needed

At the Gregg River signing ceremonies in Japan, some of the Mannix team pose for a group photograph. From left to right, F.P. Mannix, Jim Watkinson, Howard Tidswell, Don Mawhinney, Ron Mannix and F.C. Mannix.

1982 ▶

U.S. space shuttle Columbia deploys two communications satellites during its first operational mission.

1982 ▶

The Canadian-made mechanical manipulator, Canadarm, performs flawlessly while deploying the two satellites launched from Columbia.

without upsetting our customers. I think that between Don and Roger Poole we had an absolutely super pair of brains working on the contract with us."

One key to the Gregg River deal was a first-of-a-kind unincorporated joint venture partnership arrangement between Manalta and the Japanese. While the fundamentals of the joint venture agreement came from Lorne Gordon and his oil and gas and tar sands experience, the partnership idea originated with Cres Oates back in the 1950s. Because of the Empire Mine experience, Oates recommended that in any future dealings with Japan, Manalta should make the Japanese partners in the project. It took until the 1980s, however, for this idea to become a reality.

"Gregg River was like a fairy tale," said Doug Gardiner. "On again, off again, on again, off again. I give Ronnie full marks. He finally said, 'Look, we'll offer these people 40 per cent of this company,' and that did the deal. They said, 'Sure, we like it, we like everything about it, we'll take the 40 per cent.' This locked in the steel companies, and away they went. Had it not been for this 40 per cent, I don't know what would have happened to Gregg River. We would have been a pretty sad story. Ronnie can see — whether he inherited it, or whether it comes by instinct or inclination — he can tell when something is not going well. And then he has to make up his mind: 'Can it be rescued?' or, 'We better get out of here.'"

Ownership of the mine would be through Gregg River Coal Ltd. A Manalta subsidiary incorporated in 1979, this company would be owned 60 per cent by Manalta and 40 per cent by Japanese interests. Manalta also convinced the Japanese that mine development should be an unincorporated joint venture, with the project financing split 60-40.

In 1980, Sanders left the operations end of Manalta and became totally involved in Gregg River and other new mine developments. Lawrie Portigal, executive vice president, became the operating head of Manalta.

R.N. (Ron) Dalby becomes president of Manalta Coal in 1981.

This arrangement of having an executive vice president head the organization while the president was devoting his full attention to the Gregg River project ended January 1981. That month, Mancal selected Ron Dalby, a former executive with one of the largest utility companies in North America, to become the next president of Manalta Coal.

Dalby brought to his new position extensive experience in the energy resources industry. After receiving his engineering degree with honours from the University of Alberta in 1952, he then hired on with Imperial Oil, where he worked for several years in marketing and displayed an ability for handling complicated financial affairs. Next, Dalby joined Northwest Utilities Corporation, a large U.S. utility company with widely diversified interests in North America and Europe. Dalby started out as a distribution systems engineer, but quickly moved up through the organization into the ranks of senior management. By 1967, his abilities had drawn the attention of the senior management of the parent company, International Utilities (IU), in Philadelphia. That year, Dalby joined IU, where he initially worked on corporate development at the vice president level. After earning the reputation of being a first-rate troubleshooter, he served as president of a number of IU subsidiaries.

Dalby left IU to become an independent consultant to businesses in the natural resources development industries. His consulting career was briefly interrupted when he returned to IU as executive vice president of IU subsidiary, Canadian Utilities, the owner of Northwest Utilities, Canadian Western Natural Gas and Alberta Power. There, his assignment was to handle rate increase submissions to the Energy Resources Conservation Board (ERCB). When his work with IU was completed in 1975, Dalby became a principal in an Edmonton-based consulting firm with a clientele of Canadian and international companies with natural resources development interests

1982 ▶

Based in part on prior Techman research, the Norman Wells project begins for Esso Resources Ltd. in the Northwest Territories. Here a Loram pipeline crew lays pipe to the artificial island built in the Mackenzie River. The island protects Esso Resources' well.

1982 ▶

B.C. Hydro & Power Authority awards Loram a $53-million contract to supply and install the mechanical and electrical equipment for the Revelstoke Dam powerhouse, spillway and switchgear building. Shown is the bus tunnel from the switchgear building.

A Great Success Story

On March 18, 1981, the Gregg River contract and the joint venture agreement for the mine development project were signed. "Freddie, typical F.C. Mannix, started that deal with Makita of NKK," Doug Gardiner said. "And he was patient. He said to Makita, 'Someday, we'll mine one of our projects, and you will take the coal.' And Makita said, 'Well, someday.' It was really heart-warming. Makita, at this stage of the game, was in his seventies. There was this marvellous ceremony where they knocked the bung out of a gigantic keg of sake and made some very nice speeches. Makita recalled this in front of all these people, how he and F.C. had been talking, and

how they obviously became very close friends. Anyway, this is typical F.C. It took 20 years, but it happened." With the signing ceremonies for Gregg River completed, an absolutely remarkable era in the history of Manalta Coal came to its conclusion.

"Ronnie achieved something that neither Dad, nor I, nor anybody else could do," said F.P. Mannix. "He managed to negotiate with the top men there and put the deal on stream, and I think that's just fantastic to be able to do that. I think he's done a tremendous job, and I don't think there's anybody else who could have put that deal together. I think it's partly Ronnie's intuition that made the deal go. If there's going to be a great success story, it's Ronnie selling that deal. Certainly it's a great success story to build it on time and on cost, too. That's been under his aegis. Not too many guys have done that in Canada. There are few deals which have turned on one player in such a key way."

in Western Canada. Dalby, who had been a member of the Alberta government's trade mission to Japan in 1963 and 1972, was particularly interested in working with Japanese companies. During the 1970s, Dalby also served a four-year term as chancellor of the University of Alberta, from which he received an honorary doctor of laws degree in 1979.

Shortly after hiring Dalby, the negotiations in Tokyo reached the final stages. On January 27, 1981, Manalta, the six Japanese steel mills and Mitsui signed the master agreement for Gregg River. This event meant the project, after ten years of on-again, off-again negotiations, was finally a go.

For Bob Sanders, Manalta's chief negotiator on Gregg River, the signing of the master agreement was the crowning achievement of his career with the Loram Group. On February 2, 1981, shortly after he returned to Calgary from Tokyo, Sanders resigned as president of Manalta and Gregg River Resources. Ron Dalby assumed the presidency of Gregg River Resources that same day. Early in March, the process of making the transition from Sanders to Dalby was completed and the Gregg River negotiations reached their completion. On March 4, Ron Dalby was officially named president of Manalta and appointed to the company's board of directors. At the same time, virtually all the senior executives of Mancal, including Fred C. Mannix, Fred P. Mannix and Ron Mannix, flew to Japan to oversee the final steps in the contract negotiations and to arrange for the signing ceremonies. On Wednesday, March 18, 1981, the Gregg River contract and the joint venture agreement for the mine development project were signed.

Manalta Coal
Teams Building on the Foundation

Dalby began his Manalta presidency with basically the same senior management in place under Bob Sanders. His two immediate changes involved promoting George Chapel from assistant operations manager to vice president, project development, one of the top tiers of senior management, and bringing in Randall G. (Randy) Provost as the new controller. A chartered accountant, Provost brought a variety of experience to the position, having been with Norcen Energy Resources Limited prior to joining Manalta.

1982 ▶

Canada severs her last legislative link with Britain when she is granted the power to amend the British North America Act of 1867 (renamed the Constitution Act in 1981). The BNA, an act of Britain's parliament, allowed Canadian Confederation. Shown is an entrance to Britain's parliament building.

1982 ▶

Pembina completes its new plant at the Ferrier oil field near Rocky Mountain House. The main battery and two satellite test facilities support wellheads and water injectors for oil and gas extraction.

While not performing a massive senior management housecleaning, Dalby immediately established the policy guidelines he intended to implement. His first act was to assign a large share of responsibility for company management to the operations people. His theory was that the head office was at the coal face, and that the Calgary office supported the head office. He promised that projects would be accomplished by team effort and that people from the inside would make the company work.

Dalby's first major item of business was site development at Gregg River. He selected Gerry Scraba as project manager to handle Manalta's side of the mine development work. Scraba, who had previously worked for Loram International Ltd., the contractor for the mine development work, was quite familiar with the organization and the people. He was also a good friend of Vic Lemecha, the construction manager. After bringing Scraba in as vice president, operations, for Gregg River Resources, Dalby began setting up Manalta's side of the project. The person selected to be the first mine manager at Gregg River was Henning Jensen, the mine manager at Whitewood since 1978. "It was quite an honour to get the job as mine manager, to build an organization from scratch," he said. "I knew that in dollar volume, it would be bigger than

The completed Gregg River metallurgical mine near Hinton, Alberta.

A REAL VISIONARY

In 1978, while in Germany with F.P. Mannix and executives from Calgary Power, Ed Panchysyn suffered a heart attack on a bus. Cradled in F.P. Mannix's arms, he was rushed to the hospital, where he died on February 19. His death was a severe blow to Manalta and a great personal loss to all the people who knew him.

Panchysyn, one of Canada's leading authorities on coal mining and exploration, directed the exploration efforts that enabled Manalta to become one of the largest private coal leaseholders in Canada. When Panchysyn began directing these exploration efforts in the early 1960s, virtually no other company in Canada was actively exploring for coal. By the time of his death, the coal leases for nearly every economically significant property in Western Canada had been picked up.

Coal reserves capable of being mined are estimated to total more than 12 billion tonnes (13 billion tons) in Saskatchewan, Alberta and British Columbia. Largely through Panchysyn's efforts, an extraordinary percentage of this total ended up controlled by Manalta Coal. In F.C. Mannix's opinion, Panchysyn's contribution to the development of Manalta Coal put him in a class by himself. "Mr. Panchysyn was a great man, who got us involved in new mines," he said. "He was a real visionary in seeing where the greatest amount of coal was."

Widely known throughout the industry, Panchysyn held advisory positions at numerous agencies and educational institutions including the Coal Association of Canada, the Alberta Research Council, the University of Alberta, the University of Calgary, Canada West Foundation, the Environment and Energy Development Foundation and the Energy Resources Conservation Board. He was chairman of the Coal Division, Canadian Institute of Mining and Metallurgy (CIMM), co-chairman of the Canadian Coal Conference and a recipient of the CIMM's Distinguished Lecturer Award.

1982 ▶

Her Royal Highness Princess Anne (wearing red hat) tours the Utility Mine near Estevan, Saskatchewan. Ron Mannix (back to camera) explains the operation.

1982 ▶

Dancing the night away at the Turner Valley employees' Christmas party.

anything Manalta had ever done, and I knew we would have more people than in any of the other mines." Meanwhile, Vic Lemecha assembled construction management for Loram International's side of the project.

Dalby, Scraba, and Lemecha proved to be adept at managing the intracompany complexities of the project. "Gregg River was the first time that the Loram Group had undertaken the design, project management and construction," said Lemecha. "Of course, we were the designer and the builder, and most times a builder blames the engineer, while the engineer blames the builder. I tried that a couple of times when we had design problems. I said, 'Well, it's the God damned engineering guys not getting this stuff out on time.' The guy I reported to said, 'Who's in charge of engi-

neering?' I said, 'The manager of engineering.' Then he said, 'Who does he report to?' When I said, 'He reports to me,' he said, 'Well, it seems to me it's your problem, isn't it?' It didn't take too long until I got the message."

The Gregg River project total cost was less than $180 million, or about $84 per tonne of the annual production capacity of 2.1 million tonnes (2.3 million tons). This made Gregg River one of the lowest-cost and most efficient metallurgical coal mines ever built in Canada. By way of comparison, the capital cost of the Quintette Mine, which opened in 1982, was close to $130 per tonne.

In April 1983, Gregg River began producing coal. Work on the preparation plant was completed the following month. That spring, Garry Dirk transferred from the Whitewood Mine to Gregg River to work with Henning Jensen as the mine's operations manager. By the fall of 1983, Gregg River was operating at full capacity. On September 30, the mine was officially opened. In 1984, the first full year of production, Gregg River easily reached its contracted production level of 2.1 million tonnes. The mine was equipped with an international array of machines: Demag shovels from West Germany; LeTourneau, Caterpillar, and Euclid front-end

The official opening ceremonies at the Gregg River Mine in September 1983. The mine is completed on time and under budget.

loaders and trucks from the United States; and Komatsu dozers from Japan made up the equipment fleet. Gregg River also established a first for Manalta mines by using a VAX computer to generate pit designs and mining plans.

While Manalta had ample reason to celebrate the successful conclusion of the Gregg River project in the 1980s, work on Mercoal, McLeod River and Onakawana came to a disappointing end. In 1980, Manalta entered into tentative agreements for thermal coal contracts with the Electric Power Development Company (EPDC) of Japan, a large utility company, for the McLeod River project and with Idemitsu Kosan, a major petroleum and energy company, for the Mercoal project. This business development effort was an offshoot of Bob Sanders' work in Japan on the third round of Gregg River negotiations. "While we negotiated the Gregg River deal, we made two preliminary agreements for the opening of two thermal coal mines, almost in our spare time," Sanders recalled. "We made a deal with Idemitsu as well as with EPDC. We made those deals with no fuss, no muss. We had tentative contracts set up for almost five million tonnes per year of thermal coal." In 1980, in anticipation of these deals, Manalta incorporated two companies, McLeod River Coal Limited for the EPDC contract, and Mercoal Minerals Ltd. for the Idemitsu Kosan contract.

George Chapel, the new vice president of project development, assumed responsibility for the work on Mercoal and McLeod River in 1981. "Everyone was forecasting $100 a barrel for oil, and coal was going to go up there too," Chapel recalled. "It was quite a hectic time because everybody who had a coal property was talking about developing it. At one time while the McLeod project was under way, there must have been about six other proposals on the board."

1982 ▶

Israeli tanks during the invasion of Lebanon.

1983 ▶

Jeanne Sauvé is the first woman to serve as Governor General of Canada.

Chapel assembled project teams for each property. Roger Shaneman was in charge of Mercoal, with projected production around two million tonnes (2.2 million tons) per year. John Morgan headed the team for McLeod River, which was to be about twice the size of Mercoal.

In the spring of 1982, Chapel's two project teams began making their presentations to the ERCB for mining permits for Mercoal and McLeod River. In 1983, the board granted permits to both, citing Manalta's submissions as models other coal companies should follow in the future. Unfortunately, shortly after receiving these two mining permits, EPDC and Idemitsu Kosan informed Manalta that they were putting both projects on hold indefinitely due to the worldwide recession.

Also in 1982, Manalta received more bad news about another potential mine. Back in 1980, Manalta, Ontario Hydro and the federal government had entered into a joint venture agreement to study again the feasibility of developing a coal-fired generating station at Onakawana in northern Ontario. In 1982, the consensus of this $5-million effort was that the project should be shelved. Although the mining plan Manalta developed was sound and environmentally acceptable, the project was simply too expensive. Lifetime costs for a coal-fired 375-MW generating station at Onakawana were estimated at $12 billion, a figure which contrasted with $5.2 billion for a nuclear station of the same capacity and $3.6 billion for hydroelectric. "We were trying to talk Ontario Hydro into developing that property, but it's a very low-grade lignite, and it's in tough conditions," said John Morgan, who worked with George Chapel on this study. "But you never know, it might proceed one day. We still hold the leases there, and that's the key, holding the leases."

While the Gregg River Mine was beginning production, Manalta began expanding the Roselyn Mine, which was renamed the Montgomery Mine in 1982 to honour Brock Montgomery. With the first unit of the 750-MW Sheerness generating station scheduled to be commissioned in 1985, Manalta began work in 1982 on the mine expansion plan. They also entered negotiations with Alberta Power and TransAlta Utilities for the contract to supply the first unit of the new power plant. George Chapel, who coordinated this work, once again assembled a team with John Morgan and Roger Shaneman as key members. In 1983, Tim Jenish joined the team as project manager for the mine expansion work.

In 1984, the two utilities awarded Manalta a 31-year contract, which included an agreement for the sale of the Montgomery Mine reserves in increments of five years' tonnage. The sale of these reserves

"CNR DUE WEST"

Louis Carriere, involved in coal mining since the 1940s, helped develop the methods that enabled Manalta to become Canada's leading coal mining company. For Louis Carriere, who retired in 1980, managing a mine was a bit like flying his private plane. He knew how to get to the required destination, but with his seat-of-the-pants style, there was usually some excitement along the way.

"You'd hear all kinds of stories about Louis flying that airplane," George Chapel recalled. "Louis is a Frenchman and he's got quite an accent. He was flying into Edmonton once, and the control tower told him to get into the circuit to the left. Louis just kept on going, and again the guy from the control room told him to get into the circuit to the left. Louis kept on going, so two minutes later, this guy gets on the radio again and says, 'To the left, to the left. A la gauche, you idiot!' Louis laughs about that one.

"Another time, Louis and Cap Jenish had to go to Winnipeg to pick up parts. They get down there, and the tower gets on the radio and asks Louis what his heading is. The terminology they used at that time was 'track,' so they said, 'What is your track?' Louis didn't respond. So the guy came on the radio again. Louis turns to Cap and asks, 'What railroad is that over there?' Cap tells him that it's the CNR. So Louis picks up the microphone and says, 'CNR due west!' You hear all kinds of stories like that about Louis."

1983 ▶

Maintenance of Way improves on its technologically superior shoulder ballast cleaners. The new high performance version completes the work in less time and travels between jobs at higher speeds.

1983 ▶

A CN coal train is loaded at the Gregg River Mine. Construction of the two concrete silos sets Canadian construction records.

BREAKFAST OF CHAMPIONS

After one and a half years of negotiations on the acquisition of the Poplar River Mine, "The one thing that stands out is the closing," recalled Ross Melrose, who joined Manalta Coal in 1980 as corporate solicitor. "I remember starting at 8:00 a.m. thinking we could sign off the deal at noon. We'd be done and we could go home. That closing went from 8:00 a.m. to 6:00 a.m. the following Saturday morning. There were a lot of details that had not been resolved that had to get resolved. Instead of breaking off, everybody thought, 'Just stay until it's done. Another hour or so, it won't take long.' The sun went down, the sun went up, but we got it done."

"We were at the Hotel Saskatchewan," Melrose said. "We went back to one guy's room at 6:00 a.m. and we were thirsty. One guy had bailed out at 3:00 a.m. He just couldn't hack it anymore and went to bed. We phoned him and said, 'We're in room so and so and we're having some beers for breakfast, so empty your minibar and bring it up.' He swore at us for waking him up, but he joined us."

was the one major problem in the negotiations. "At one point, it appeared that we were at a deadlock," George Chapel recalled. "Our policy at that time was that we would not sell our reserves, no way, but the utilities wanted to own the reserves. Ron Dalby had worked for Alberta Power prior to that, and he could understand their position. Ron was able to convince Mancal that, yes, it's not unreasonable for the utilities to own the reserves because they've got a $1-billion investment in the power plant. It's not unfair for them to want to own the coal, and that's what we did. Ron and I went up and talked to Alberta Power and said we'd do it. So that made the deal viable."

The Montgomery Mine expansion project required about as much work as starting a new mine from scratch. "We were taking a mine that was really stuck in place and time," Tim Jenish explained. "It was sitting in the early 1950s technology. So we had to totally re-equip the mine from the ground up. We had to build a new shop and office complex, we had to buy a new dragline, new loading equipment and new haulers. We had to design the pit and we had to go through all of the necessary steps of getting a new mine licence. So it was quite extensive."

The Acquisition of Poplar River Mine
"We went all night and finally got some ink put on paper."

As work on the Montgomery Mine expansion project got under way, another Manalta team was hard at work on two major projects in Saskatchewan. One project was negotiating with Saskatchewan Power Corporation (SaskPower) to purchase their dragline at Utility Mine. The other was developing a bid for what was to be the largest acquisition in the company's history. The property for sale was SaskPower's Poplar River Mine. As with previous developments in Saskatchewan, the opportunity to purchase Poplar River was based on political developments. In 1982, the Progressive Conservative party gained control of the provincial legislature and put a new premier, Grant Devine, into office. The new administration opposed the growth of Crown corporations in the province's natural resources industries. Shortly after this change in administration, SaskPower decided to sell its big Bucyrus-Erie 2570-W dragline at Utility to Manalta. At the same time, SaskPower announced that it was going to turn over operation of Poplar River to a private company.

1983 ▶

Loram Construction builds the Little Fort Highway to link Highway No. 5 with the Cariboo Highway in British Columbia.

1983 ▶

In Lebanon, international peacekeeping forces compounds are attacked by suicide truck bombers. Fifty-eight French paratroopers and 241 U.S. marines are killed. Lebanon plunges into civil war.

In its proposal to purchase and operate Poplar River, Manalta faced stiff competition from three large companies, all familiar names to Mannix veterans. The first of these competitors was Luscar, Manalta's main competitor in Saskatchewan. The second was Peter Kiewit Sons' Company, an Omaha-based engineering-construction company with one of the largest contract coal mining operations in the United States. Kiewit was the company called in to review Alberta Coal's first contract at Whitewood. The company had also been involved in construction joint ventures with Loram International. The third company was a Morrison Knudsen subsidiary, Northern Construction, a Vancouver-based company M-K purchased after it acquired control of Fred Mannix & Company, Ltd. back in 1943.

SaskPower was pleased with the proposal put together by Manalta's Poplar River team. Manalta offered $102 million for Poplar River and also offered to assume $31 million in lease obligations for the mine's large equipment. The key element in SaskPower's decision, however, was not so much price as it was Manalta's extensive reserves in the area near the mine. An important part of Manalta's proposal was a section detailing plans for relocating the mine to these better properties. By moving onto Manalta-held leases, SaskPower would realize a savings of more than $250 million over the life of the contract, resulting in less expensive energy costs for the people of Saskatchewan.

In 1984, Manalta Coal purchases SaskPower's Poplar River Mine located near Coronach, Saskatchewan. The Bucyrus-Erie dragline is part of the $133-million acquisition.

The negotiations were completed on November 30, 1984. "The last meeting lasted from about 8:00 in the morning to about 7:30 the next morning," recalled Cap Jenish, who joined the company at Roche Percee, Saskatchewan, in 1950 as an electrician. After serving as electrical foreman at Klimax Mine and electrical superintendent at both Utility Coals Ltd. and Klimax Mine, Jenish was named Klimax's mine manager. In 1976, he was appointed area manager for Saskatchewan. "We went all night and finally got some ink put on paper and it was great. It was just wonderful to think that we had accomplished that because, if you look at Poplar River, it was a big operating mine. It was just as big as anything we had except Highvale, and Highvale was a contract mine. Poplar River was putting out about four million tonnes a year, and we just went in and took over."

Another key aspect of this $130-million deal was that Manalta, unlike its competitors, was a wholly Canadian-owned corporation. Canadian ownership of natural resources industries was becoming increasingly important in both national and provincial politics. Manalta strengthened its position as an all-Canadian company by proposing to establish a new Saskatchewan-based subsidiary. This entity would own and operate all Manalta coal mining operations in the province. This subsidiary, originally incorporated on December 29, 1983, in anticipation of a successful bid on Poplar River, was reorganized and renamed Prairie Coal Ltd. on

1983

Lortherm provides insulation services for Shell's Scotford facility. Insulation for the piping includes the 76.2-metre (250-foot) styrene tower.

LEADERS IN RECLAMATION

Top: The XDE-80.
Above: Farming on reclaimed land.

Manalta Coal has long been an innovator in the realm of reclamation. For example, back in 1964, Chuck Doerr and Dick Wilsey built the XDE-80. A huge dozer built out of two Euclid TC-12s — then the largest tractors made — the XDE-80 carried a blade 6.5 metres (21 feet) wide and two metres (six feet) high. "To get the extra power, we took two tractors and joined them end to end, so that we had twice as much pushing power on the blade," Wilsey explained. "We also used what was at that time a quite sophisticated control. Instead of the usual sticks and pedals, we had a simple wheel, like a steering wheel on an automobile, mounted on a stick which would move forward and backward. The first time we took it down to Taber, the driver said, 'Well, we'll see how it does.' So we headed for one of the spoil banks, and he went straight up it. It was an unbelievable performance for a tractor."

In its continuing quest for improved reclamation methods, in June 1980, Manalta Coal, in cooperation with the Alberta Department of the Environment and Alberta Power, undertook an experimental program in reclamation. "Vesta was chosen as one of the test sites for government and industry to try to determine what was best in terms of reclamation," explained Tim Jenish, who became Vesta's assistant mine manager in 1980. The experimental program, designed by Manalta's Roger Shaneman, used ash from the Battle River generating station and various layers of subsoils.

By 1983, when the project was nearly complete, Vesta became a model for reclamation for the entire western Canadian coal mining industry. "I think Vesta was probably one of our first properties to start salvaging topsoil and subsoil," Tim Jenish said. "And I know we were one of the first properties to do the whole process, from the soil salvaging to working the land and putting the land back into crop, and then harvesting and monitoring the results."

December 4, 1984. In August 1985, Manalta named Mike Mears president of Prairie Coal. Shortly thereafter, he went to Estevan to establish the company's corporate headquarters.

On the mine operations level, the change in ownership at Poplar River went extremely smoothly. "The transition from SaskPower owning it to Prairie Coal owning it occurred on the 30th of November, almost like clockwork," commented Bruce Campbell, president and chief executive officer of SaskPower. "One day, 140 employees were working for us, and the next day, they became employees of the coal company. There was no serious disruption at all, except for a breakdown on one of the walking shoes of the big dragline the day after the mine was transferred. There had been a lot of work done between our people and the Manalta people, and a lot of effort had been put into talking to employees and making sure they understood what was going on. The biggest risk was that there would be some labour unrest as a result of the changeover, but it turned out that there literally wasn't any. We gave our former employees the

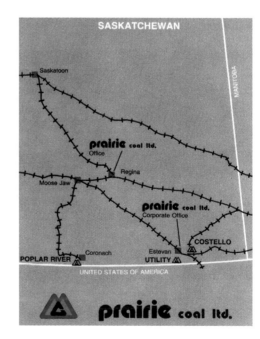

Manalta Coal forms Prairie Coal Ltd. to operate the three Saskatchewan mines, Poplar River, Utility and Costello.

1983 ▶

Loram Construction builds the Greenbelt Tunnel, a part of the overall light rail development in the U.S. capitol, Washington, D.C.

1983 ▶

Philippine opposition leader, Benigno Aquino, is murdered when he returns to the Philippines from exile. His widow, Corazón, mourns him, but she will soon replace the corrupt rule of Ferdinand Marcos when she is elected Philippine president.

opportunity to apply for any vacancies in our corporation that they were qualified for, for an 18-month period. A few of them have come back to us via that route, but not very many."

As the change in ownership at Poplar River was being completed, the strike at Montgomery was finally settled. Back in 1979, when the contract with the Queen Elizabeth generating station came to an end, the small crew of mine workers decided to go on strike for higher wages. Starting in 1980, production at Montgomery (then Roselyn) dropped to well under 90,000 tonnes (100,000 tons) per year, where it remained until the mid-1980s. With the mine workers on strike and only domestic orders for coal, mine manager Don Meads, along with his foreman, Rex Christensen, and a handful of other management personnel ran the mine by themselves.

This strike, which had a strange beginning, came to a strange end. "The workers used to have an association in there amongst themselves," Rex Christensen explained. "Then some of them got dissatisfied and they got to talking to United Mine Workers. Before we knew it, everybody was signed up to it. The United Mine Workers weren't in there long enough to hardly even collect any union dues off the guys, but in January 1979, there were 33 hourly people that went out on strike. There were seven of them that came back in March '79. The company never could get an agreement with United Mine Workers, so those seven guys went to the Operating Engineers, who got in there and decertified the United Mine Workers. They claim that's the first time that's ever happened in Alberta, that a union got decertified. Then the

R.M.P. (Mike) Mears is named the first president of Prairie Coal Ltd.

Management and employee teamwork form the backbone of the success of Manalta Coal.

Operating Engineers finally settled the strike in the spring of 1985. So that went on for a little over six years. That was the longest strike in the history of Alberta."

By 1985, Manalta was a very different organization from just four years earlier. In 1981, when Ron Dalby became president, Manalta's annual production was 13.5 million tonnes (14.9 million tons). By 1985, production had climbed to 23.9 million tonnes (26.4 million tons), an increase of 77 per cent. By 1985, Manalta produced more than 40 per cent of Canada's coal, with less than 15 per cent of Canada's total coal mine employees. Obviously, the shift to technology and larger, more productive equipment was paying off. In 1985, TransAlta awarded the five-year contract for Highvale to Manalta. Together, the acquisition of Poplar River and the Highvale contract ensured that Manalta would remain Canada's largest coal producer.

The key to Manalta's early 1980s successes was the teamwork that rapidly became a hallmark of the company's style. The results of this approach are striking. In just two years, Manalta opened Gregg River, its first metallurgical coal mine. It successfully negotiated a large new contract for Montgomery Mine and restarted the mine from scratch. Manalta purchased and began operating Poplar River Mine and set up a new Saskatchewan coal subsidiary. Each of these projects required major operational and financial planning. And each entailed a considerable degree of risk. That Manalta's management team successfully dealt with all three projects testifies not only to the strength of the company's team approach, but to the fact that the underlying principles were firmly in place.

1984 ▶

Marc Garneau of Quebec City is the first Canadian in space.

1984 ▶

Canadian speed skater Gaetan Boucher wins two golds and a bronze at the Sarajevo Winter Olympics. He is Canada's most decorated Olympian.

Loram Maintenance of Way, Inc.
Sharpening Their Teeth on
New Products and New Ventures

During the 1970s, Loram Maintenance of Way made tremendous strides in its quest to manufacture new technologies and enhance its manufacturing capabilities. As in the past, the company believed innovation was the key to success. Since the days of undertrack leasing, the company was disinterested in doing what was already being done just a little better. Like all truly innovative companies, Maintenance of Way's approach was to view existing technology in an entirely new way. This approach was particularly evident in the development of the company's rail grinders.

By 1978, Loram Maintenance of Way had captured about 10 per cent of the rail grinding market from its competitor Speno. But Dick Peppin was not satisfied with the progress in developing new machinery. His solution was to create a separate Research and Development Department. "There was a problem in that we had an engineering department that was always putting out the fires," Peppin said. "By fires, I mean that if we had a plow or a sled that had a hydraulic problem, everybody dropped what they were doing and solved the problem. So our new development was not coming along like it should have. I determined that we should have one department that did nothing but develop new products and another engineering department that did nothing but solve the problems that we were encountering in the field. Eventually, we'd be able to keep our development program on schedule."

Concurrently, Peppin sought other ways to diversify. An opportunity soon presented itself: Palm

In 1978, Loram Maintenance of Way acquires Palm Industries, a Minnesota manufacturer of cabs and rollover bars for heavy construction equipment.

The newly redesigned tie inserter is a significant improvement over the previous successful machine.

Industries, a Minnesota manufacturer of cabs and rollover bars for heavy construction machinery. Palm was owned by Rauenhorst Corporation, the company that built Loram's plant in Hamel. Rauenhorst decided to sell the business as they came to feel that a manufacturing concern was not compatible with their construction operations. Since Rauenhorst knew that Loram Maintenance of Way was a steel fabricator, they asked Peppin if he might be interested in buying Palm. Peppin felt that Palm might be a good way to diversify the company's manufacturing operations. "We were both fabricators," said Peppin. "Palm just manufactured the cabs, whereas we manufactured the whole machine. So we decided to diversify and go into a manufacturing business that was not related to railroads. We thought that it would be married to us because we were fabricators like Palm, although they were on a lesser scale." Peppin also felt that the little company might prove useful in one other way. "I thought it would make a good training ground for our executives," said Peppin. "We could send them out there, let them operate that company, then bring them back."

Loram Maintenance of Way purchased Palm in 1978 for $900,000. "When we bought Palm, it was in its infancy, similar to Loram 20 years ago," said Peppin. "We found that the markup that we had to place on their equipment didn't lend itself to a very profitable bottom line. We wondered if there was any way that we could take Palm, put some inventive ideas into the manufacture of the cab, and cut costs so we could sell the cabs and rollover bars at a profit, rather than more or less break even. So we acquired new tools and new production facilities, and redesigned the production lines."

1984 ▶

After four months as prime minister, Liberal John Turner, left, shown with his wife Geills, is defeated by Conservative Brian Mulroney, right.

1984 ▶

Canadian entrepreneurs Scott Allott and Chris Haney invent the board game, Trivial Pursuit.

Peppin's main focus remained on the railway business, however. An initial product the new Research and Development Department worked on was an improved tie inserter, as Peppin and his crew were not satisfied with the existing model, though it had sold well. The customers' main complaint was that the machine simply required too much maintenance. "The biggest problem was that they were automated," said operations manager Ron Mauch. "Basically, there were just two buttons and a foot pedal for propelling. It was a beautiful machine to watch. It was very fast and easy to operate. But when it broke down, it was so complicated that the railroad didn't have qualified people to repair it. As a result, they were on the phone talking to us all the time."

Like the first version of the crib skeletonizer, the tie inserter used an electrical system to control the hydraulics. This consisted of a sequencing system controlled by limit switches. The redesigned tie inserter eliminated most of the automated system and replaced it with easy-to-use manual controls. The pantograph boom assembly was retained but considerably redesigned with fewer moving parts. The redesigned machine had the new company look — simple, uncluttered lines and powerful construction. The machine was dependable and extremely easy to maintain. "It's the one we have in the fleet now," said Peppin. "Railroad people have told us that it's the best on the market for the simple reason that it's very reliable."

While the redesign of the tie inserter occurred, Peppin was forced to decide what direction to move rail grinding development. The market for maintenance rail grinders he originally wanted to tap did not seem to exist. Although RG2 performed well on contracts with both the Canadian Pacific and Canadian National, railway officials

RG3, Loram's first 72-stone rail grinder at work near Kamloops, British Columbia.

From left to right, Ron Mauch, Cliff Monnie and Lenny Lawrence, part of the team that created RG3.

advised they needed a machine that removed more metal per pass. Peppin chose to enter the high-production grinding market. Although this meant going head-to-head with Speno, Peppin felt the company's self-propelled grinders, with their Kinecheck system, gave Loram Maintenance of Way an edge. Peppin believed that his people could continue to discover more ways to make their machines even better while continuing to learn more about the science of rail grinding.

Loram Maintenance of Way entered the high-production grinding market by building another 36-stone grinder and coupling it to RG2. This 72-stone machine was called RG3. Doubling the number of grinding stones was only the first step in yet another extensive development process. The company decided to go with even larger motors to power the grinding stones, stepping up from 15-horsepower to 20-horsepower units. This meant a new cycle of research and development to discover a grinding stone capable of withstanding the much greater torque of the 20-horsepower motors. Company engineers worked with their supplier, Norton, one of the world's leading manufacturers of abrasives, to help solve this problem.

The result of this research and development was a huge self-propelled machine that ground rail more efficiently using fewer stones than the Speno grinders. RG3 contained many refinements, including a propulsion system that increased the grinder's top speed for travel between jobs to 96 kilometres (60 miles) per hour. In 1979, Loram Maintenance of Way got a terrific break when RG3 was awarded a small contract by the Union Pacific, a railroad that traditionally used Speno rail grinders. Paul Armstrong, engineer of track for the Union Pacific's

1984 ▶

The Union Carbide pesticide plant near Bhopal, India, leaks lethal methyl isocyanate, killing more than 2,000 and injuring 200,000.

1984 ▶

Manalta Coal acquires Saskatchewan Power's Poplar River Mine near Coronach, Saskatchewan, including this Bucyrus-Erie 2570 dragline. Note the operator's cab on the lower right of the dragline.

northwestern section, convinced the railroad to try the Loram Maintenance of Way machine on a production grinding job near Pendleton, Oregon.

Ron Mauch was the head man on the crew that took RG3 out on its first journey. "We left on a Sunday and we arrived there on a Thursday. We ran that thing 24 hours a day until we got there. We never stopped. I got about six hours of sleep from Sunday to Thursday." RG3 passed its first big test with flying colours. Union Pacific, greatly impressed with the machine, signed Loram Maintenance of Way to do a major portion of its grinding program for 1979. This was the company's big break. "That's really where we got our start in the rail grinder business," said Mauch. "When the job on the Union Pacific was finished, the word got around that Loram would be competing for the majority of the U.S. production rail grinding market. All of us can be indebted to Paul Armstrong from the UP for accepting us into the rail grinding business. That's where we really sharpened our teeth."

Loram Maintenance of Way's impressive progress in rail grinder technology was just one aspect of a decade filled with accomplishments. For instance, the company established itself as a dominant competitor in the shoulder ballast cleaning market. In 1979, the company built its seventh shoulder ballast cleaner, completing the unit two months ahead of schedule. This machine was immediately sent to Wisconsin to work on Burlington Northern track. Four Loram cleaners were then operating 20 hours a day, seven days a week, on Conrail lines in Pennsylvania, while others worked on the Chessie System in Indiana.

The new Research and Development Department creates a machine to electronically read rail imperfections. It is called the rail corrugation analyzer (RCA) and is first used in 1979.

The whole tie extractor is developed in 1979. This revolutionary machine removes an entire tie in one operation allowing the tie to be used for other purposes, such as landscaping, and not wasted along the rail.

Meanwhile, Loram's Research and Development Department was producing at a terrific pace. Besides their work on rail grinders, two new machines were produced in 1979. One was the company's first rail corrugation analyzer (RCA), which used electronic measuring devices to record the height of rail corrugations. The RCA was designed to allow railroads to inspect their track for corrugations to plan future grinding programs more efficiently, an idea which had originated out of conversations between Peppin and Ronald Bailey of the Canadian National Railways back in 1977, when RG2 was first tested in Canada. "Mr. Bailey and I came up with the idea that he needed a tool or some kind of device that would let him know where his problem areas were so that he could concentrate the grinding to solve his problems."

The second new product introduced in 1979 was the Loram Whole Tie Extractor. Unlike earlier tie extractors that cut ties into thirds before removal, Loram's machine pulled the entire tie from under the rail. The whole tie extractor was developed in response to recently enacted environmental regulations prohibiting burning of ties along the right-of-way. Kept whole, the failed ties could be used for construction, landscaping and other structural uses. Loram's tie extractor used a scarifier to break up the ballast around the failed tie, an innovation which made it possible for tie removal without disturbing the surface or line of the track. This was a feature unique to Loram Maintenance of Way's machine.

1984 ▶

Canadian swimmer Alex Baumann exults as he is awarded one of the two gold medals he wins at the Los Angeles Summer Olympics.

1984 ▶

Chilean dictator Augusto Pinochet orders the roundup of suspected Leftists. Some 32,000 persons are detained in a soccer stadium. Many disappear.

Becoming an Industry Leader in a New Age of Deregulation

In 1980, the U.S. Congress passed legislation releasing the nation's railroads from the government's intricate web of regulations. The Staggers Act, which allowed railroads more freedom to set freight rates and abandon unprofitable lines, followed airline deregulation and moves by the Interstate Commerce Commission to loosen its control on highway freight carriers. Along with higher freight rates and increased competition, rail deregulation brought a new uncertainty to the maintenance of way field. Precisely what impact all this new freedom would have on railroad maintenance budgets was difficult to predict. What was certain, however, was that deregulation spawned a wave of railroad mergers and track abandonments.

By the end of 1980, the Interstate Commerce Commission approved three consolidations: the first merged the Frisco and the Burlington Northern to form a railroad stretching from Seattle to Florida; another brought together the Grand Trunk Western and the Detroit, Toledo & Ironton in the Midwest; and the largest united the Chessie System and the Family Lines, together controlling six major lines covering the eastern half of the United States. Industry analysts were predicting a new age of the "megarailroad," where the 30 medium and large-sized carriers would be replaced with just five or six super-railroads.

Railroad track maintenance companies found the impact of these mergers more difficult to assess. While mergers increased the working capital of the railroads, thus providing more money for maintenance of way expenditures, they also resulted in a pooling of track maintenance equipment, a move which could reduce new purchases. And while stopping duplicate rail service would reduce the track miles requiring maintenance work, the increased traffic would speed the rate of deterioration on functioning lines.

However, a few things were certain. In the shuffle of consolidation, decision making shifted from engineering departments to purchasing, making it more difficult for Loram Maintenance of Way to sell its wares based on performance and technical superiority. Deregulation focused the railroads' attention on costs. The less technically minded purchasing agents would likely base their decisions on a price tag rather than arguments of quality or productivity, no matter how sound.

Perhaps the most significant change to track maintenance companies was that they had even less time to work on the track. To compete in a deregulated atmosphere, the railroads hauled heavier loads faster.

"ALL HE SAW WAS ONE BIG BUNDLE OF SMOKE"

As in the past, Loram Maintenance of Way people continued to use problems that occurred in the field as impetus for improvements. One important lesson resulted in the development of improved spark guards on the grinders. This lesson came right when Peppin was showing off one of the new 72-stone grinders to F.C. Mannix, by then retired, and his son, Ron Mannix, head of the Loram Group since 1978.

"This happened out in California," said Peppin. "Ronnie Mannix and crew had come down from Calgary to go on a job inspection, and Mr. Fred C. Mannix happened to be coming out there, too. The grinder was going underneath a highway overpass. Mr. Mannix watched it go by and said, 'You have a good machine there. I have to run now.' Then he jumped in his car and took off."

Peppin and Ron Mannix then got in a car to head off to another job site. As they were driving away, Mannix turned around to get one last look at the big machine. "Ronnie looked back, and all he saw was one big bundle of smoke," said Peppin. "The grinder was on fire. That was caused by a broken hydraulic hose that was squirting oil down where the sparks were coming off the grinding stone. They called the fire department, and they put it out, but we were down for a couple of months trying to get that back in order." Peppin had not forgotten Fred C. Mannix's advice about never making the same mistake twice. Loram's engineering department immediately developed better spark-arresting shields and chain side blankets to reduce the risk of fire.

1984 ▶

Classic cow puck chuck form at the Pembina Turner Valley barbecue.

1984 ▶

President Daniel Ortega and the Sandinista government in Nicaragua are the target of an illegal American CIA mining of harbours throughout the country.

They also ran trains more frequently. Reported *Railway Age* in May 1980: "Railroad chief engineers and their maintenance-of-way officers are in a race against time — track time. They must constantly quicken the pace of track work, because there's less and less time for it. But quality of work must be increasing all the time."

Loram Maintenance of Way accepted this more competitive environment as both an opportunity and a challenge. Dick Peppin was sure that the company was headed in the right direction with higher-speed machines. He continued to lead the company in an aggressive development and marketing effort. "To get our technology, our expertise, and our ability to grind the rail, everybody wanted to try it on for size to begin with," said Peppin. "That's why the small contracts or the small jobs in various parts of the country had to be undertaken. Railroads had to experience our grinder. We had to show them the capabilities of our 72-stone machine." To speed up this process, Loram built a second 72-stone grinder, RG4, in 1980. Because these machines were so innovative, railroads were hesitant to accept Loram Maintenance of Way's new technology. "It took a couple of years to establish ourselves by exposure to all the railroads in the United States and Canada," said Ron Mauch. "During that period, the return on investment was marginal, due to having to take small jobs."

Meanwhile, the company completed its fifth rail grinder, RG5, a 36-stone grinder. This machine was built for the Quebec North Shore and Labrador Railway (QNS&L), the line the Mannix company constructed in

RG5 is the first rail grinder sold to a railway. In 1982, the Quebec North Shore and Labrador Railway enters into a lease-purchase arrangement to service the same line on which prototype Mannix Sleds were used 26 years earlier.

Dick Peppin presents a plaque to QNS&L officials in commemoration of the railway's purchase of RG5.

the 1950s. RG5 was delivered in 1980 on a lease-purchase arrangement. Historically, the QNS&L was the first trial site of Lou Franco's Mannix Sled prototype in 1952. During 1980 and 1981, the railway became a major test site for Loram Maintenance of Way's rapidly evolving rail grinding technology.

RG5 turned out to be exactly what the QNS&L was looking for — and considerably more. "The rate of metal removal surprised us because we only had experience with a competitor's machine," reported Tom McElroy, the railway's maintenance of way superintendent. "With the amount of metal removed and the availability of the machine, we have been able to control corrugation and, in turn, save a lot of rail. We also save money with the Loram Rail Grinder because we don't have to tie up an SD-40 — a rail-mounted camp — with boarding cars and cooks."

When the QNS&L purchased the RG5 in 1982, it immediately sent ripples through the industry. "The 36-stone grinder we sold to the QNS&L probably did more to put our mark on the industry than anything else in the early days," said Bruce Tubbs, superintendent on RG5 in 1981. "People were really looking to that railroad because of the innovations that they were bringing out — the track equipment they had and their track technology. Then the word started getting around that this Loram grinder with 36 stones would remove more metal than Speno's 96-stone machine. Our machine was self-propelled so they didn't have to have a train crew, and we

1984 ▶

Britain and China agree that the British colony of Hong Kong will revert to Chinese sovereignty in 1997.

1984 ▶

Famine kills 300,000 Ethiopians as drought conditions worsen in sub-Sahara Africa. Some 800,000 will die before foreign grain reaches the suffering.

also had a very good speed control system. Plus, RG5 was a machine that performed flawlessly. We had zero downtime on it, and to this day, that machine runs flawlessly."

In 1981, the company introduced its next major innovation. This was RG6, an 88-stone grinder designed to perform what Loram termed "profile" grinding. Up to this point, all rail grinders removed metal from only the top of the rail. Loram Maintenance of Way's idea was that a grinder that addressed the entire running surface of the rail would not only eliminate corrugations, but slow their recurrence. It would reshape the running surface to ensure a better match between the contour of the wheels and the rail. This would extend rail life. To accomplish all this, Loram Maintenance of Way developed a new carriage for the grinding stones. This carriage angled some grinding modules up to 45 degrees to either the field (outside) or gauge (inside) edge of the rail's running surface. Different modules would grind different facets of the rail head. In this way, not only would corrugations be removed but the rail profile would also be corrected.

The Loram Maintenance of Way Shoulder Ballast Cleaner.

Profile grinding was a revolutionary concept. Like all innovative ideas, this new concept did not gain instant acceptance. The decision to develop an 88-stone machine with profile grinding capability was a calculated risk. The 36-stone and 72-stone machines proved that Loram's technology was at least a step ahead of the competition. The two 72-stone grinders in Loram's lease fleet were gaining wide acceptance in the United States. In 1982, for instance, the Union Pacific leased RG4 to do most of its annual grinding program. RG4 ground more than 1,930 kilometres (1,200 miles) of track in Kansas, Nebraska, Wyoming, Utah, Oregon, Washington, Nevada and California. R.M. Brown, the Union Pacific's chief engineer, praised the Loram grinder for doing what he termed "an exceptional job."

Dick Peppin felt, however, that profile grinding was a significant technological advance the railroads would appreciate once they saw the results. The problem was that Loram Maintenance of Way would have to educate the railroads before it could develop a market. This was no easy task, especially with all the personnel changes due to railroad mergers. "The railroads were very reluctant to jump off the deep end," said Peppin. "You have to appreciate the fact, too, that Speno was grinding rail 20 years beforehand. Then a new kid comes on the block with a new toy, so there was a bit of hesitation there."

Gaining industry acceptance for the new profile grinding system took several years. The Family Lines was one of the first big railroads to use the 88-stone machine extensively. They leased RG6 to grind more than 1,000 kilometres (625 miles) of track in Georgia, Tennessee, Kentucky and Indiana in 1982. In 1983, Burlington Northern, one of Loram Maintenance of Way's best customers since the Mannix days, also leased RG6 for major work. As a result, the company's grinding reputation continued to grow.

During the early 1980s, Loram Maintenance of Way also put considerable effort into refining its shoulder ballast cleaner. Dick Peppin was not satisfied with the efficiency of these machines, although U.S. railroads used them widely. The redesign effort actually began in the 1970s. The high performance shoulder ballast cleaner, introduced in 1983, was the end result. This new cleaner was 41.2 metres (135 feet) long and 4.7 metres (15.5 feet) high, and powered by a Cummins 1,150-horsepower diesel engine. The number of buckets on the ditching wheels was increased from 12 to 18, coupled with increased wheel revolution speed. To process the increased flow of fouled ballast, the cleaner section was redesigned with bigger vibratory screens. The improved cleaner could clean more than three kilometres (two miles) of track, or 1,814 tonnes (2,000 tons) of ballast, in one hour. Travel speed

1984 ▶

In India, Sikh extremists occupy the Golden Temple at Amritsar. Prime Minister Indira Gandhi sends in troops who kill between 600 and 1,200 Sikhs. Later in the year, Gandhi is assassinated by two Sikh members of her personal guard. Anti-Sikh riots follow.

1984 ▶

George Chapel and Ron Dalby share a moment at the Manalta Coal Christmas party.

"WE MADE THE THING WORK"

Loram Maintenance of Way built a second 72-stone grinder, RG4, in 1980. This machine's first contract was with the Santa Fe Railroad on a section of track near Denver, Colorado. One operator on RG4's maiden voyage was Bruce Tubbs, who would become operations manager for the Grinding Service Department. Tubbs joined Loram in 1980 as a shoulder ballast cleaner operator. A nuclear-certified welder, he then left Loram to take a job as an underwater welder in the North Sea oil fields. When an injury to his inner ear forced him to quit this job a few months later, he returned to Loram, just in time to help take RG4 out on its first job.

"When we took RG4 out the door, they were still stringing wires on the walkway," said Tubbs. "We didn't just take it out and test it out in front of the shop. We took it out the door and travelled that thing all the way to Denver, Colorado. We did it straight. I had about 105 hours that first week after I came back to work for the company in the grinder division. We put both feet in the water at one time, instead of one foot on shore and one foot in the water, but we made the thing work. That's the way Loram always does it."

between jobs was also doubled over previous machines, increasing top speed to 80 kilometres (50 miles) per hour, while average working speeds increased to approximately two kilometres (1.25 miles) per hour.

In 1983, Loram Maintenance of Way introduced the bantam shoulder ballast cleaner, a scaled-down version of its basic cleaner, with smaller ditching wheels having just nine buckets. The bantam shoulder ballast cleaner was designed for spot maintenance work rather than big out-of-face jobs. Missouri Pacific in Illinois first used this machine on a tie renewal project. The cleaner worked ahead of a tie renewal gang, scarifying and cleaning fouled sections of ballast for easier tie replacement.

During the early 1980s, Loram Maintenance of Way made tremendous strides in both the shoulder ballast cleaning and rail grinding markets. The company developed and refined equipment rapidly, and the business was growing at a terrific rate. However, the future of Palm Industries increasingly troubled Dick Peppin. Despite bringing in new equipment and redesigning the assembly line, the small cab manufacturing company continued to struggle. Peppin finally sent Earl Miller, one of his best managers, to run the little operation. Miller succeeded in turning the company around in a very short period. Although Palm was finally on the road to profitability, Peppin felt the company was ultimately not compatible. "Eventually, what really woke me up, and woke up our people in Hamel, was that it started to affect our production," said Peppin. "We were spending too much time with Palm, and not enough with the area that we were experts in. Consequently, it started to show on our operations."

On April 16, 1984, Loram Maintenance of Way sold Palm at a break-even position. The timing of the sale seemed right. "When we bought Palm, there was a lot of construction activity going on, and a lot of new equipment was purchased," Peppin said. "The type of equipment that lent itself to Palm products was continuously growing. But I think you can say we had a little bit of foresight when we sold because the Japanese had started to invade the U.S. market. Komatsu and various other Japanese companies were coming over with their earthmoving equipment, which came with the cab already on them. Our market was gradually diminishing. So I think that the time that we sold Palm was the right time."

The sale of Palm was well-timed also because Maintenance of Way was entering another major phase in rail grinding development technology. One of the most important developments was in grinding-stone technology. Because its grinders used high-horsepower motors to power the grinding stones, Loram had worked closely with Norton to develop a heavy-duty stone with the proper grit and strength. The result was a new grinding stone, specially made for Loram Maintenance of Way, with considerably longer life. It also removed more metal than any other stone. Another Loram innovation, which the company patented, was a new backing plate to simplify stone mounting.

1985 ▶

An earthquake centred near Mexico City kills 5,000.

1985 ▶

Live Aid, marathon rock concerts organized by Irish singer Bob Geldof, raises millions for relief projects to feed starving Africans.

The earlier mounting system used a steel holder with three chucks and Allen screws that were tightened to grip the stone. Loram Maintenance of Way grew dissatisfied with this system. One problem was that if the chucks were over tightened, the mechanical structure of the stone was affected, leading to excessive breakage. Also, too much time and effort was required to replace stones.

Loram Maintenance of Way's ability to continually refine its rail grinding technology was not going unnoticed by the industry. In 1984, Conrail decided to have a look at Loram's 88-stone machine. The first tryout was on a small job near Pittsburgh, Pennsylvania, on a 32-kilometre (20-mile) section of double track. This track annually carried about 20 million tonnes (22 million tons) of freight, mainly coal and steel. Like other railroads, Conrail was at first extremely skeptical about Loram's radical new approach to rail grinding, but they were won over. Although Conrail would eventually use Loram for about 85 per cent of its rail grinding work, winning the confidence of this railroad was no easy task. "Boy, I'll tell you, it was a hard sell out there," said Bruce Tubbs. "We started out with a small contract. That way you could actually show them what the machine could do. So you were starting to gain that credibility in little bites. It took us several years on Conrail, little bites at a time."

Loram Maintenance of Way also applied its new ideas to smaller rail grinders. In 1983, a 44-stone machine, RG7, was assembled in Australia for the Mt. Newman Railroad, the iron ore railway the Mannix company helped build in the 1960s. This machine was constructed for a three-year grinding contract that was handled by Loram Maintenance of Way's Australian subsidiary, Loram Maintenance of Way (Australia) Pty. Ltd., formed in 1982 to break into the Australian track maintenance market. RG7 was equipped with all the latest innovations, including profile grinding carriages and the new stone backing plate.

In 1984, Loram Maintenance of Way produced a small grinder specially designed for urban rapid transit systems and their light rail vehicles. This first light rail transit (LRT) grinder was a 24-stone machine, consisting of a small locomotive and three grinding cars. Each grinding car carried eight grinding stones, each powered by a 15-horsepower motor. Washington Metro Area Transit Authority in Washington, D.C., bought Loram's first LRT grinder for use on its 64-kilometre (40-mile) light rail transit system.

Since producing their first computerized machine, the rail corrugation analyzer, in 1979, company engineers worked on computerizing rail grinder controls. In 1985, the company introduced its first computerized rail grinder, RG8, an 88-stone machine. Initially, they installed the computer system in only one of the two 44-stone units.

RG7, the 44-stone rail grinder assembled in Australia for the Mt. Newman Railroad.

1985 ▶

Mine reclamation efforts continue at all mines. This reclaimed prairie grassland near the Vesta Mine is part of a multi-year government and industry sponsored study.

1985 ▶

Maintenance of Way introduces a new rail corrugation analyzer, left, that quickly records surface irregularities and determines the amount of grinding required. It is shown with RG9.

"UNTIL AS LONG AS YOU COULD STAY AWAKE AT NIGHT"

In 1981, Loram Maintenance of Way introduced RG6, an 88-stone grinder. Once again, the development process was a learning experience for everyone involved. "We started out working for the Burlington Northern in Minneapolis," said Bruce Tubbs. "The first time we put the profile carriages down, we saw that the engineers had not figured some configuration in the geometry of the modules correctly. So we got new cylinders out there and we welded pieces on. It was about 30 below zero, lying out in the snow on your back, from four in the morning until as long as you could stay awake at night."

After the Loram crew got the modules reconfigured, they took the machine out for its first test run. Tubbs recalled this first trial just about gave Steve Heinen, the Burlington Northern track supervisor, a heart attack. "The first pass down the rail, we ground a single facet with 88 stones that was about one-quarter-inch wide," said Tubbs. "Steve Heinen was brand-new at the job and was going to impress his bosses, and here we were, with an 88-stone machine, covering only one-quarter inch of the rail head. Steve was tearing his hair out. To this day, I can still see him. 'You can't do this!' he kept saying. It took us the rest of the day to finally get the machine to where it would cover the whole rail head."

It took about six months to develop the proper grinding patterns with this machine, but the final results were extremely impressive. Later in 1981, RG6 was field-tested on the Canadian National's mountain region, near Kamloops, British Columbia, on a 200-kilometre (125-mile) section of track. Canadian National officials reported that RG6 had the highest rate of metal removal of any grinder they ever used.

"We wanted to assure ourselves that we were proceeding in the right direction with the computer," Dick Peppin explained. "That was our first experience with a computer on a mobile piece of equipment. We were putting a computer that was developed for a clean office environment on a rail grinder where the environment is dirty. While the machine was grinding, there were metal objects flying through the air, and the temperature ranged from 125 above to 40 below zero." Development of the computer system proceeded rapidly. When the system was perfected, Loram Maintenance of Way computerized both 44-stone units on RG8. Two other computerized rail grinders, RG9 and RG10, were manufactured in 1985. RG9, built specifically for the Canadian market, was Loram's first grinder with onboard living facilities.

Also in 1985, Loram produced a new version of its rail corrugation analyzer. Unlike the first RCA, which was a small unit without self-propulsion, the new RCA was built into a truck equipped with high-rail wheels. This meant that it could drive on the highway to jobs and then go onto the railroad track and propel itself down the track. The unit's electronic measuring devices and onboard computer also enabled the machine to measure the depth and frequency of rail corrugations to the thousandth of an inch, while travelling 48 kilometres (30 miles) per hour.

The different parameters in the design of Loram Maintenance of Way's evolving fleet of equipment all added up to one thing: high-quality machines. "You have to perform quality work," explained Peppin. "You can go five miles per hour and turn out a bunch of junk, and the railroad is not going to be satisfied. That's why we spend so much time designing machines. I guess you could say our first consideration is the bottom line, to make money, but our second one is to make sure the railroads are satisfied, otherwise we're not going to be in business."

1985 ▶

Mikhail Sergeyevich Gorbachev becomes general secretary of the Soviet Communist party.

1985 ▶

In a major marketing blunder, Coca-Cola announces the replacement of its 99-year-old formula with a sweeter Coke for younger tastes. Protests force the reintroduction of the traditional blend under the name Classic.

The Power of Three

As Ron Mannix so aptly stated, there is a saying "from shirtsleeves to shirtsleeves in three generations"— from the entrepreneur, to the administrator, to the one who throws it all away. However, for every rule there is an exception.

"If Freddie and I can't be successful there's something wrong with us," said Ron Mannix, "because we've had all this background and training and we should know something. All of our training historically has taught us to figure out what we're going to do. One of Father's traits was his ability to always ask one more question than anybody could answer. Because you know you're going to get asked the questions, it helps to keep you on your toes. At the same time, it forces you — as far as I am concerned, and I think it's true of Freddie, too — to look at the big picture.

"Now comparing the second to the third generation, Father's focus was much more on the operations, much more on the pure numbers side to the outfit. What we're handling is changing from his generation to ours, because there are so many more things that are having a big impact on the outfit. It's my job to have some feel and understanding of those things, because I can get other people in here to handle those operations. Not that we can ever lose the sensitivity toward the operations side. I continue to look at it, but nonetheless, there's a big change that's going on in the business world that is forcing the top executives of any outfit in the whole industry to look at much more."

From left to right, R.N. Mannix, F.C. Mannix and F.P. Mannix.

"I've had the easiest time of anybody in the whole outfit," Ron Mannix said. "Grandfather started it. The first $5,000 is the most difficult to earn. Father had to buy it back in his time from M-K, and then he expanded it significantly. Freddie, being the oldest son, had the toughest time with the older generation. By the time they figured out how to handle him I came along, so it was a piece of cake for me. Besides, I've got all the good people already around me. What have we done? We haven't done anything in reality in our time and generation in a whole new field and area other than Freddie trying to launch out and create a financial entity."

In typical Mannix style, Ron Mannix is being a bit modest in assessing the third generation's accomplishments. While Fred P. Mannix was building the investment side of the business, Ron Mannix did remarkably well on the operations side. When he was named president and chief executive officer in 1978, the Loram Group's divisions — construction, oil and gas, mining, railroad maintenance — employed 2,400 people. The Loram Group's gross revenue for 1978 was $170 million. Of this total, gross revenue from construction comprised 47 per cent; oil and gas, 30 per cent; mining, 17 per cent; U.S. railway maintenance, six per cent.

During Ron Mannix's first eight years as president and chief executive officer of the Loram Group, gross revenue nearly tripled to $494 million. In addition, the operating companies' piece of the revenue pie radically shifted. In 1985, mining contributed 58 per cent of total Loram Group revenue; oil and gas, 31 per cent; railroad maintenance nearly seven per cent; construction a little more than four per cent. Employees totalled 1,900 people.

The crisis faced by the founding construction business in the early 1980s would have brought many businesses to their knees. But this is not the Mannix heritage. F.S. Mannix responded to the Great Depression by shutting down operations, selling his horses, planting wheat and waiting for better times. In F.S. Mannix's case, better times came when he had an opportunity to branch out into coal stripping. More than 50 years later, his grandsons also adjusted to the reality of a changing marketplace. After mothballing the construction company, they balanced their operations by strengthening their investment in natural resources. Once again, the Mannix family beat the odds.

1985 ▶

After 21 years of military dictatorship, Brazil elects a civilian government.

1985 ▶

Terrorist attacks by Arab, French guerrilla, Islamic and Palestinian groups kill 107, wound more than 428 and, in part, cause the fall of the Italian government because of a crisis over the hijacking of the cruise ship Achille Lauro. Shown are returning hostages from a TWA hijacking by Shiite Muslim extremists.

THE GLOBAL FRONTIER

1986 – 1996

No company that isn't alert to the environment ever survives. Businesses exist to identify needs and fulfill them and these needs change. Economic conditions change. Competition changes. Technology changes. You have to keep up. This is a highly interactive world right now. In the last 25 years it has been transformed. Everything in the business and economic atmosphere is much more interdependent than it used to be.

Both Fred and Ron are showing broad interests, which is quite consequential; they try to keep alert to those trends. Fred is a great reader and Ronnie moves about, so both have that quality of looking around, cogitating on what's happening in our fast-moving world.

— Fred McNeil, retired chairman of the board of the Bank of Montreal and Loram board member

Left: Earth and sun from space.

Right: In 1989, enterprising West Berlin citizens begin chopping through the Berlin Wall. By year-end, East and West Berlin are reunited.

In Ireland, it is easy to understand why the Irish-Gaelic word for "green" — *glas* — also means "blue." It is not only the sea, seldom far away, that brings this ambiguity sublimely to life. The land does, too, as intense Irish greenness mixes with bluish pools of fir or beech, and every tone changes constantly under the play of light. These gentle transformations help to explain the spiritual and poetic qualities for which the landscape of the island is celebrated.

Today, one could say that the magic of light has transformed not only the landscape of Ireland, but the world, as dawn in any part of the world is almost instantaneously reported around the globe. More than any time in history, we are experiencing the interaction of political and economic forces and policy actions on a global basis and as part of an increasingly integrated system. It is not just that we are affected as never before by what happens in the rest of the world, it is much deeper than that. We are all increasingly part of a single system. It is global in its scope and it integrates politics, economics and policy in a continuous and more and more instantaneous fashion.

FORTY YEARS WITH PEMBINA

"In 1994, four of our field staff in Drayton Valley reached 40 years of service with the company," said Fred Webb, Pembina's vice president and general manager. "These were the first people to get 40 years with Pembina. Two of them started on just about the first day of the company. There was Al Horne, John Poloway, Frank Cheple and Ron Howatt. Mr. Poloway was the more senior of the four. He got off the bus before Al Horne.

From left, Al Horne, John Poloway, Frank Cheple and Ron Howatt.

"We had a retirement party in Drayton Valley for these four, as we decided to do all four rather than one at a time. The problem we got into was getting a hall that was big enough. We got the biggest hall, then we had to start restricting attendance. The mayor of the town wanted to attend and the MLA [member of the legislative assembly] wanted to attend. We thanked them very much and said, 'Well, it's going to be company employees and, as with all our retirement parties, the family members of the retirees.'"

"We had the hall full and it was just a tremendous night," Webb said. "We had all kinds of retirees, all the family members of the retirees and the Mannix family. The local office staff and some of the spouses in Drayton spent a lot of time and effort putting together a collection of songs. They made up parodies of popular songs with the words changed to talk about the life and times of the people who were retiring. It was great. It was one of those really remarkable evenings."

We have witnessed the liberation of India and other colonial countries and the unification and stabilization of China. We have seen the rise and fall of the Japanese economy, from Japan's emergence as the world's second largest financial and economic power, to the dubious honour of hosting the longest recession — ten years — of any industrial country. We have watched the collapse of communism, the breakup of the Soviet Union and the unification of Germany.

Against most all expectations, in 1990, the Berlin Wall quite simply came down. Today, one can say that walls are coming down all over the world. The cumulative effect of all the economic, political, intellectual and social changes has created a new world. Canada's great cultural critic, Northrop Frye, has said language is the home of the soul and that all culture is local. That these global trends and local matters can readily conflict, we are now seeing.

There has been nothing like it before in history. It is a world of both danger and opportunity, as there are no precedents to follow. Business firms are no longer considered as solid and permanent as they used to be. To say one owns a business today is to say one owns both an opportunity and a vulnerability. When one person can carry around the computing power that a medium-sized company had a decade ago, then the rules of the game have changed. The Internet, electronic communication and wireless technology are as extraordinary as the invention of the telephone.

Most people manage the results of what has already happened. Great leaders lead into the future. However, it is not much use being right about the future unless you have the skills to get there, usually through the actions of other people. The object is to take the brilliance of the ideas of the people who work with you and focus them to affect the direction of the business. Of course, that it is a lot easier to say than to do. In actuality, the odds of effecting positive, strategic change are slim. Yet here again, at this crucial crossroads in the history of the company, the Mannix family in business was about to beat the odds.

Pembina and Western Decalta Adjust to the New World
"We were first off the mark."

Perhaps nowhere can the benefit of having the right people at the right time be seen more clearly than in the Loram Group's oil and gas subsidiary. In the first quarter of 1985, Loram management had moved Lorne Gordon, then vice president and general manager of Loram Co. Ltd., into Pembina as president of Pembina Resources Limited and Western Decalta Petroleum (1977) Limited. Gordon succeeded Alex Cummings whom Loram appointed chairman of the board of both companies. Randy Provost, most recently Manalta Coal's vice president, finance and corporate planning, filled Gordon's post.

When Canada deregulated oil prices in June 1985, Gordon found himself among the other participants in the oil and gas industry who were facing the challenges

1986 ▶

In January, the U.S. space shuttle Challenger lifts off. An explosion seconds later will kill all seven astronauts onboard.

1986 ▶

Expo 86, the world's fair, opens in Vancouver, British Columbia. Between May 2 and October 13, 22 million people visit the exposition, nine million more than forecast.

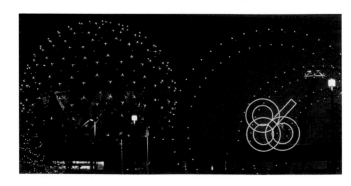

of deregulation in the post-National Energy Program era. The very real risks associated with deregulated prices were illustrated by U.S. spot prices which fell from a November 1985 peak of $31.73 per barrel to less than $8 a barrel in the first quarter of 1986. These decreased prices appeared to be largely explained by increased supply working against steady demand. While Saudi Arabia had previously reduced its market share to support prices, its strategy had changed in the fall of 1985. In 1980, Saudi Arabia's production had reached 10 million barrels per day. By August of 1985, output was reduced to 2.3 million barrels per day. In the next four months, however, output was raised to 6.0 million barrels per day. As these new supplies reached the market, prices fell. While wild swings in spot prices had occurred in the past, the concern was that this new trend might be permanent. Fortunately for Loram, Lorne Gordon not only faced the challenge head on, but in true Gordon style, he had prepared for it in advance.

"Ronnie Mannix has surrounded himself with some absolutely topflight people," commented Loram board member Doug Gardiner. "What he did was pick some brains. He has got Lorne Gordon, who has all the attributes that Ronnie wants. The last job he gave him, he said, 'Go over there, and adjust Western Decalta and Pembina to the real world as it is today, when oil is selling at less than $10 a barrel,' and Lorne Gordon went over and did it. He streamlined the operations, got the cost down so he never lost a cent and the company was making money. A lot of companies did not have enough brains to do that."

Lorne Gordon not only had the brains, he had excellent timing. On an international basis, after peaking in about 1981, oil prices began drifting downward. In

The Diamond Valley gas plant
at Hartell, Alberta.

Canada, the dollar drifted downward faster than the price of oil, so the price of oil in Calgary stayed essentially flat. Consequently, the early 1980s was a very buoyant time for the oil business in Canada. "Strange as it sounds, it seemed to mask the fact that maybe there was a coming problem with the oil prices," explained Gordon, "so the level of activity was extremely high. The activity in Pembina was very high and we were quite concerned about the economic results from that activity. After I ended up as president of Pembina, I spent many months formulating in my own mind what we needed to do and trying to find the courage to then take action. During that time, I consulted with Dave McClement, vice chairman of Mancal Ltd., Ron Mannix and Randy Provost on what direction I thought we should be going."

"Then, in the spring of 1986, we had the price crash in the oil business," Gordon said. "Because I had been doing that work even before the price of oil crashed, we had a pretty definitive game plan. In fact, the oil price crash was the perfect springboard to launch that plan on. In terms of the oil industry in Calgary, by fortuitous timing then, we were first off the mark to get our rightsizing done and we did a very, very substantial rightsizing. We reduced our staff about one-third overall. In the construction, exploration and development parts of the company, there was very substantial downsizing, up to 60 per cent. We sized the company to reinvest our existing cash flow instead of the mode we had been on before. As I say, it was more good luck than good management, but it turned out to be good from two points. From Pembina's point of view, it got Pembina focused very quickly in what was the new world. For the employees who had to look for new jobs, it put them ahead of other people who would be looking

1986 ▶

Maintenance of Way develops a switch and crossing grinder (SX-16). The grinder supplants hand grinding previously necessary at these specialized rail areas. One of these machines is shown in Calgary, Alberta.

1986 ▶

South African prelate and Nobel laureate, Desmond Tutu, calls for international sanctions against South Africa to force an end to apartheid.

"A Special Thing"

"The employees at Drayton Valley have grown up with each other," said Bob Michaleski, Pembina's vice president, finance. "Their families have grown up together so there is a real bond. They relate to all the good and the bad things that went on with their lives — the hard times and the good times. You sure can see that when you have a retirement party for guys who have worked for the company for 40 years. It makes you have an appreciation for what the company has meant to those people. They see the Loram Group as an extension of their family and they feel treated as part of a family as well.

Pembina officers and 35-year inductees. Back row, from left: William Stedman, Arnold McDonald, Ken Hausherr, Frank Cheple and Earl Zumwalt. Front row, left to right: Lorne Gordon, Ernest Ellert, James Streit, Donald Greiner and Alfred Hicks.

"The people out in the field certainly appreciate that. When we bring in people for our Christmas parties, we include their spouses in the day. And if they have to travel from Ontario to Calgary, we pay their airfare and accommodations. They think it's royal treatment. Then to stand in front of their peers and receive a reward for long service, is a very special thing. To be recognized with the owners being present is particularly important to people. Because it doesn't matter what they do, whether they are a labourer in the field or whether they are a president in Calgary, they're recognized."

"We've found that since we've been acquiring companies, when we bring those people into Calgary for the first time, they take that message back to their coworkers in the field," Michaleski said. "Then you find that when you go visit the field people that they're just waiting to come to Calgary to be treated special. That's something that is unique. People feel like they're treated like people. That really is a special thing."

for jobs in the next few years, because as companies became resigned to the fact that oil prices weren't going to bounce back, they started their own restructuring efforts. In the meantime, Pembina had already done it."

The economic problems accompanying the National Energy Program were of Canadian origin and required a Canadian solution. The problems following the precipitous drop in world oil prices in January 1986 stemmed from global forces and the solution lay beyond the Canadian establishment. Yet while Canadian oil and gas companies could not solve the problem, they could and did cut costs in response to the drastic downturn of the industry. Pembina, along with other stakeholders in the oil and gas industry, had to make serious readjustments.

One result of the cost cutting was that, for the first time in 25 years, Pembina cancelled its annual golf tournament. For most companies, the cancellation of a golf tournament would be inconsequential; not so for Pembina. "To the field staff, the Jasper golf tournament made them different from the other people they worked with," explained Fred Webb, who transferred from Techman to Pembina in 1984. "The Jasper golf tournament was something that separated Pembina from the other companies. Pembina staff would be dealing on a day-to-day basis with the production companies in the area, companies like Esso, Chevron, Amoco and Mobil. These were very big companies with lots of benefits and lots of prestige, and we were a very little company. The one thing that Pembina had different was that once a year, the employees got to go to Jasper and do it up proud. It was a way for the Calgary directors and owners to express their thanks to the pipeline staff. Except the cart rentals, the company paid for everything. It was a really first-class affair. This became a very, very significant thing."

"The most difficult decision I had in 1986, when the layoffs occurred, came when I was given a dollar target of how much to reduce operating expenses — G and A expenses," Webb said. "I looked at where I could reduce this amount of money and said, 'The thing to do is cancel the Jasper golf tournament. We laid off one-third of the office staff in Calgary. The most bloodless thing is to do away with this golf tournament.' The answer I got back from the district manager, Larry Gano was, 'No. Find another place.' I said, 'Larry, there is no other place. All we have got in the G and A budget is wages, vehicle expenses, gas, electricity for the building and Jasper. The golf tournament sort of sticks right out.' He said, 'No. There has to be another way.' I said, 'Well, we could take away the cars, but I don't see how we can operate without vehicles.'

1986 ▶

Canada, with five other Commonwealth nations, breaks with Britain and imposes economic sanctions against South Africa as a measure against apartheid.

1986 ▶

Willie Shoemaker, age 54, caps off his 37-year racing career by riding a 17-to-1 underdog, Ferdinand, to win the Kentucky Derby.

"It took three tries, but finally I got approval to cancel the Jasper golf tournament. It was really a difficult decision as Jasper had become part of the folklore. When we cancelled the golf tournament, it had quite an effect on the town of Drayton Valley. There was a concern that Pembina was going under, that this was the beginning of the end. The following year, we had our golf tournament."

Following Pembina's rightsizing, Lorne Gordon embarked upon an ambitious program to revitalize Pembina's management team. "There were a very substantial number of management changes," he explained. "In fact, over the next three years, all the officers of Pembina changed except myself. We did this because the officers who were there before were in tune with the oil business the way it was before the price of oil came down. They just could not get themselves lined up with running the oil business like a business. It took us a number of years to get the company turned around toward having a goal of profitability as opposed to having a goal of cash flow growth or reserve growth. All those things were important, but they needed to follow profitability. We needed to get a management team in place that had that focus. That took until 1988. It was certainly the most difficult thing I have ever done."

One member of the new management team who kept profitability in focus was William (Bill) Stedman, who joined Pembina in 1982 as manager of planning. Following the restructuring, he was named vice president and general manager in 1986. "It was tough times in the oil business," Stedman explained. "We were not making any money in those days. The priority was just to make the company simpler to manage. We had a zillion small working interests all over the place. We tried to simplify the company and end up with a higher concentration of assets to make it easier to manage. That is what we concentrated on for four or five years, simplifying the company, getting better reporting structures, getting people to focus on what really made a difference rather than just shuffling paper around."

When crude oil prices fell in 1986, Pembina also immediately launched its property rationalization program. "Our objective was to reduce the number of marginal properties that we had," explained Ron Pacholko, Pembina's manager evaluations and acquisitions. "The intent was to dispose of the non-strategic properties and add to the working interests held in strategic properties, with no reduction in reserves, production or cash flow." Pembina took a two-pronged approach to its property rationalization program — property swaps and property sales. Property swaps are those in which a percentage ownership in a property is exchanged for a percentage ownership in a property considered strategically advantageous. In property swaps, almost no cash changes hands. Pembina's property rationalization program was yet another strategic move that gave Pembina an edge over others in the industry.

Pembina Resources continues to actively explore for oil and gas throughout much of Western Canada.

Take or Pay Litigation
"Just give us the money."

While Pembina was getting in tune with the new world, the company was also bringing to a close two major legal actions. The first occurred when Pembina settled two take or pay contracts, successfully ending a long-standing lawsuit.

Back in the late 1970s, industry gospel was that the demand for, and price of, oil and gas would continue to rise. Fearing a shortage of oil and gas, many U.S. pipeline companies entered long-term contracts with gas producers to lock in prices. These contracts,

1986 ▶

Highvale Mine coal is delivered to the TransAlta Utilities electrical generating station near the mine. Annual mine production approaches 12 million tonnes (13.2 million tons).

1986 ▶

Libyan-backed terrorists bomb a German disco causing 232 casualties. U.S. warplanes attack various targets in Libya, including the headquarters of dictator Muammar al-Qaddafi. Qaddafi escapes.

called take or pay contracts, included a clause guaranteeing that the pipeline companies would purchase (take) a certain amount of gas each year; if they did not, they agreed to pay for it anyway. Western Decalta Petroleum (1977) Limited's subsidiary, Denver-based Decalta International, was one of several companies active in the Gulf of Mexico during this time. Decalta International signed take or pay contracts with Transcontinental Gas Pipeline Corporation (Transco) and United Pipe Line Company (United) for gas produced in the Gulf and transported primarily to the northeastern United States.

By 1981, the predicted shortages of natural gas had not materialized, leaving the U.S. pipeline companies with several take or pay contracts at higher prices than the current market price. Because of the improved market conditions, Transco and United decided to neither take, nor pay for, the gas to which they had committed. As a result, Decalta International was left holding binding, though through the actions of the pipeline companies, worthless contracts. Boxed into a financial corner, Decalta International commenced litigation against United and Transco. It would be a long and rocky seven years, however, before they reached a settlement.

A key person in this litigation was Jim Watkinson, Pembina's vice president, general counsel and secretary. Watkinson, who joined the Loram Group in 1980 as secretary and general counsel for Manalta Coal Ltd., went on to hold senior legal positions with Manalta, Gregg River Resources and Loram. Not long after joining Pembina, Watkinson went to work on the take or pay litigation. "My experience had been in litigation before I joined the group," he said. "You would not expect when you are in a corporate setting that the most exciting thing you do would be litigation, but we had,

This unusual view looking down a drilling rig shows a Pembina Resources crew completing another well.

within a couple of years of my joining the oil company, some really major litigation cases."

"One was down in Texas on what we call take or pay contracts," Watkinson said. "The amount involved was $25 million US, which was a big sum of money. This was when the gas market had collapsed in the United States. All the pipeline transmission companies that had signed these contracts thinking the price of gas was going to hit $5 per mcf (million cubic feet) were now finding that gas was at $1.20 per mcf, but they had locked in prices for the next five years. It was a major, major issue facing both the producers, who were saying, 'We have contracts,' and the pipeline companies who knew they were paying three to five times the price of the product than if they just went out and bought it on the open market."

Not long after becoming involved in the case, Watkinson began to question the dedication of the Texas law firm representing Pembina. "At the first part of that litigation in the United States, the junior in my office was handling the case," he recalled. "Phil Ladouceur, who was vice president finance, was going down to Texas on other matters. He asked me to come along to meet with the lawyers handling the court case in the United States and see how it was going. So I went down with Phil and met with the lawyers. It is hard to explain, but when I met with them, there was just not the enthusiasm that you would expect for a lawsuit involving $25 million US. When I was litigating, especially back in Thunder Bay, you got all excited about $25,000 claims. Here, you were talking $25 million. Moreover, you had a client prepared to pay good legal fees for good legal advice."

"We were involved in that litigation with a group of about a half dozen partners, but we were running the litigation," Watkinson said. "After I came back, I set out

1987 ▶

During the year, Manalta Coal Ltd. mines supply more than 22 million tonnes (24.3 million tons) of coal with an energy equivalent of 63 million barrels of crude oil.

1987 ▶

A toxin is discovered in Prince Edward Island mussels. It threatens the entire Atlantic shellfish industry. National Research Council scientists isolate the toxin, domoic acid, in only 104 hours, saving lives and the fishery. The organism thought to cause the toxin is shown through an electron microscope.

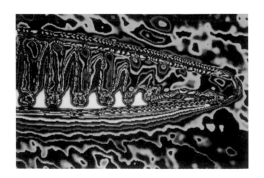

a timetable for the lawyers in the United States — the firm was Butler, Binion — to start working on. Then I took over the file from the junior to push it on and get it moving. I had several meetings with the lawyers in Houston and it was getting to the point where I personally had lost faith in the firm. It was a tough decision because Butler, Binion was a large firm in Texas and we were not familiar with Texas litigation, but I just had a feeling. They had assigned what I would call a more administrative contract-type guy to do the litigation and it was not working. I wrote a memo to Lysle Gust, the Denver vice president of operations, and to Lorne Gordon saying that in my opinion, we should dump the lawyers. We had been with them for some 16 months at this point in time. They had a trial date arranged four or five months in advance, but to get to trial you have to do a number of steps and they were just not completing those steps."

Even as Watkinson was recommending changing law firms, he was getting pressure from Pembina's partners in the lawsuit to accept settlement offers. "At the same time, settlement negotiations had been going on," he said. "The settlement offers started at $750,000 US from the pipeline companies to get us off their backs. It was tough times in the oil industry. Prices had fallen. As the settlements progressed up to $1.5 million, our partners in the lawsuit were saying, 'Just give us the money because we do not want to sit here and fight. We need money right now.'"

Despite this pressure, Watkinson decided to follow his instincts and fire Butler, Binion. In hindsight, while he does not regret that decision, he does feel that he could have better handled the situation with the partners. "We made one big mistake on that one I think, after I look back on it," he said. "We were operating this project, so we took it upon ourselves to fire the lawyers in Texas. I remember Fred P. Mannix gave me a piece of paper later about when you make decisions how you have to inform other people of your decisions. Anyway, I went down and interviewed three different law firms in Texas and moved the file over. Then we had a meeting with all the partners to tell them what had happened. That was the toughest meeting I have ever been to. The partners were saying that we had spent all this money on litigation and now we were bringing in new lawyers and it was going to cost them all this money. We were at about $1,750,000 settlement on the table and they were saying, 'We want to take that settlement.'"

"I remember Lysle and I were sent out of the room after we explained our position," Watkinson said. "They were going to have a vote of no confidence to throw us out of the lawsuit. So it was really tough. I got them at least to agree to hold off the no confidence vote until they met our new lawyers. The new lawyers came in and were so obviously superior to what we had before, the committee did vote to keep us on and to accept the change but very, very reluctantly. They continued to be thorns in our side as we went forward."

THE QUARTER CENTURY CLUB
The Greatest Honour of Them All

Although F.C. Mannix never sought publicity or recognition, he was the recipient of numerous honours recognizing his distinguished career as a builder and businessman. In addition to being one of only two living recipients inducted into the Canadian Business Hall of Fame at its inception in 1979, in 1985 he was named an officer of the Order of Canada, the country's most prestigious civilian honour. F.C. Mannix also held honorary memberships in the Engineering Institute of Canada and in the Association of Professional Engineers, Geologists and Geophysicists of Alberta. Additionally, he was an honorary chairman of the Canadian Institute of Mining and Metallurgy and an honorary associate of the Conference Board of Canada.

While F.C. Mannix was pleased to receive these honours, one of his most rewarding experiences in the later years of his life came in 1988, when the Loram Group celebrated its 90th anniversary. That year, the Quarter Century Club, an organization for Loram employees with 25 or more years of service, was established. F.C. Mannix was extremely proud to join 176 Loram Group employees as one of the charter members of the Quarter Century Club, along with his son, Fred P. Mannix. Ron N. Mannix was inducted four years later, in 1992.

1987 ▶

Manvest Ltd. provides venture capital to First Choice Canadian Communications Corporation to assist in the development of The Family Channel which First Choice hopes to have on the air by the end of 1987.

1987 ▶

Canada continues to explore space and joins with France and Hawaii in the operation of this telescope located in the Hawaiian Islands.

"You want to come outside in the back alley and say that to me?"

Pembina found itself in the unenviable position of fighting not only the defendants, but their partners as well. "Our partners in the negotiations were very unsupportive of our actions," Lorne Gordon said. "We got offers from time to time from the pipeline companies that our partners wanted to accept but we didn't want to accept because we were confident we could do better. In one case, our partners actually started to sue us while we were negotiating with the pipeline companies. So we had people coming at us from every direction."

To make matters worse, the action took place in Texas, the state where 200 brave souls defended the Alamo against General Santa Anna's advancing army of 3,000 Mexicans. In short, while Texans are known for many things, they are not known for backing down. "It is really interesting doing litigation in Texas," marvelled Watkinson. "It is so completely different from anywhere else. The lawyers really like to display their egos in court. By the time we changed lawyers, Transco had also changed lawyers. I will always remember the first meeting we had with Transco's new lawyers. This fellow, a well-known lawyer in Texas, came in and said, 'All right, this lawsuit is changing because Transco is now bringing in the A Team.' That was their team. So they had new lawyers from the other side and, of course, we were much more aggressive as we now had the Vinson and Elkins law firm."

The first court battle was over production of documents. "The lawyer for Transco, who was a very outgoing, flashy lawyer, one you would expect from Texas, was up against Thad Dameris," Watkinson said. "Dameris was a really young lawyer at the time, maybe one year out of the bar. But he is a pretty imposing guy, about six foot two. At one point, the Transco lawyer said something that overstepped the bounds; it was insulting both to our position and to Dameris. Dameris stood up and said, 'You want to come outside in the back alley and say that to me?' And this is right in court! I think that worked for us because from then on, there was not the insult. The older lawyer said, 'This guy's got a little spunk to him.'"

"We worked on that for a year and a half and each month we were sending $150,000 US down there for legal fees," Watkinson said. "Our partners were getting very nervous. When it all broke, we got up to about $6 million. Thad Dameris did a really great job and came up with a seldom used legal principle we were able to invoke

THE CARTHY FOUNDATION

William McCarthy Mannix.

"What goes around, comes around," the old saying goes. The benevolence of the Mannix family can be traced back to a kind deed done by a stranger for a young F.S. Mannix nearly 100 years ago. While still a teenager, F.S. Mannix was trying to buy a team of horses at an auction. When the bidding price went past what F.S. had in his hip pocket, a bystander — noticing the young man's disappointment — is said to have lent him what he needed.

Today, the Mannixes have a separate philanthropic organization, the Carthy Foundation. The Carthy Foundation, named in honour of the McCarthy side of the family, handles the family's and Loram Group's charitable donations. "It was incorporated back in 1965," explained Fred Fenwick, general manager and secretary/treasurer of the foundation until 1989. "At that time, F.C. Mannix was chairman of the board and the family

was the board. It was the intention that through this foundation the philanthropic efforts of the group of companies and the family would be conducted. From the very beginning it was policy that those donations would be made on an anonymous basis. Mr. Mannix did not believe that any public recognition of his philanthropy was necessary."

To this day, the Mannix family still does not believe that any public recognition of their philanthropy is necessary. To a large extent, little is known of their donations. "The family's penchant for charting its own course is legendary, but its generosity is less well-known," proclaimed the *Calgary Herald* on June 18, 1997. "Even in the highly public world of philanthropy, the Mannix name never accompanied its extensive donations. For instance, a magnificent $700,000 Carthy organ in the Jack Singer Concert Hall owes its Calgary presence to the charity of the Mannix family."

1987 ▶

Canada begins to replace its paper one-dollar bill with a coin. The new coin is quickly nicknamed the "loonie" for the loon embossed on the back.

1987 ▶

Rhys T. Eyton, chairman of the Conference Board of Canada, right, presents F.C. Mannix with an Honorary Associate Award in recognition of his distinguished career and contributions to Canada.

and we ended up with a settlement. Lorne flew down for it and we arranged a meeting with the senior person at Transco. It was late in the day in Texas and there had been negotiations all morning. Finally at 4:00 p.m. they said Lorne could meet with the senior person. We were all sitting in the Four Seasons having drinks when Lorne came back from the meeting. He walked in and said that it had been $9 million. Lorne went there and came out with $9 million US! We were just ecstatic. Lorne bought dinner that night and we had an expensive bottle of wine and we flew back on the jet the next morning. That was a good court case that turned out really well."

Overall, it was not a bad settlement for Pembina and the company's partners in the lawsuit, who had wanted to settle for $1.5 million. For Pembina alone, the out-of-court settlement with Transco netted $2.9 million after royalties, which included a market response gas price contract amendment. Pembina's settlement with United, which netted $3.3 million after royalties, was also amended to provide for market response prices. By 1988, it was all over but the celebrating.

Soon after the successful conclusion of the take or pay litigation, Pembina decided to close down the Denver office, which was the office of Decalta International, and sell the company. "At that time, we were in the pack of companies that realized we had about 15 per cent of our operation in the United States," Gordon explained. "It was not an economically sized unit so we decided to sell the assets. That was an important transaction because from that time forward, we have been very focused in Canada. We have not found ourselves globetrotting and not knowing whether we were here or there. The Canadian oil business is pretty huge. We are a small part of it. There is a big enough market for us to pursue right here."

The Norcen-Luscar-Pembina Lawsuit
"Everybody in town knew about it."

The decision to concentrate on the Canadian oil business and the successful conclusion of Pembina's take or pay litigation did not mean the end of Pembina's legal battles, however. Not long after putting the take or pay litigation behind them, Pembina Resources Limited was served with a Statement of Claim issued by Norcen Energy Resources Ltd. and Luscar Ltd., who claimed an interest in certain oil and gas properties Pembina purchased at an Alberta land sale back in 1971. The allegation was that Pembina failed to offer a participating interest — one-third each — which an existing operating agreement required it to do. While Pembina was unable to find any written evidence that it complied with the agreement, the company did obtain oral evidence that the land manager in 1971, who had since died, said he had verbally offered the lands to Norcen and Luscar and both had declined.

Norcen and Luscar alleged breach of trust and breach of fiduciary duty, relying on the principle that Pembina was unjustly enriched due to the breach of the joint operating

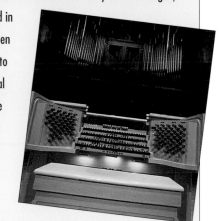

THE GIFT OF MUSIC

The Carthy Organ (Casavant Frères Opus 3623) is the crowning jewel of the acoustically superior Jack Singer Concert Hall. It was designed, engineered and built by Casavant Frères of St-Hyacinthe, Quebec, one of Canada's preeminent organ builders for more than 100 years. The organ, which took 15 months to build in the Casavant factory, was then dismantled and shipped to Calgary. It took an additional five months to install, voice and tune the instrument once it was reassembled in its permanent home in the organ loft of the concert hall. When installed, the combination of organ and 1,800-seat concert hall was considered one of the best organ/concert hall combinations in North America.

The organ was donated to the citizens of Calgary, and the world, by the Carthy Foundation in 1986, and is named in its honour. Dedicated in loving memory of Margaret Ruth Mannix, its inaugural concert was May 6, 1987. The sold-out gala featured Simon Preston, renowned organist and current artistic director of the Royal Bank Calgary International Organ Festival, and the Calgary Philharmonic Orchestra with Mario Bernardi conducting.

In recognition of Hal and Marnie Wyatt, a second Carthy Organ was built by Orgues Létourneau. Donated by the Calgary Universal Foundation for the Organ, it was installed in The Mount Royal College Conservatory Calgary Organ Academy in 1996.

1988 ▶

World figure skating champion Brian Orser leads the Canadian Olympic team into Calgary's McMahon Stadium. Calgary successfully hosts the XV Winter Olympic Games.

1988 ▶

The Calgary Winter Olympic exploits of the Jamaican four-man bobsled team form the basis of the successful movie Cool Runnings.

THE CALGARY INTERNATIONAL ORGAN FESTIVAL

As part of a vision to share the Carthy Organ within the community and with the world, the first Calgary International Organ Festival was held in October 1990. The organ competition and music festival, a showcase of the world's organ virtuosos, was the first International Organ Festival to be held in Canada.

The competition began in July 1990 with two selection rounds. The North American/Pacific Rim round was held at the Cleveland Museum of Art. The European round took place in Lübeck, West Germany, at two of the city's oldest cathedrals. To compete in these selection rounds, 42 organists were chosen from 108 applications representing 19 countries. The organists, who ranged in age from 20 to 34 years old, included past winners of most of Europe and America's top organ competitions, Fulbright scholars, musicians with several commercial recordings to their credit and organists at such prestigious churches as the Karlskirche in Vienna and the Notre Dame Cathedral in Paris.

The top eight performers from these two selection rounds competed at the Calgary International Organ Festival. Six of the world's finest organists and teachers constituted the competition jury. They were: Hans Fagius, Sweden; Martin Haselbock, Austria; Bernard Lagacé, Canada; Simon Preston, England; Russel Saunders, United States and Gillian Weir, England. In addition to their responsibilities as jurors, these world-renowned organists opened the festival, performing in concert with the Calgary Philharmonic Orchestra under the direction of maestro Mario Bernardi.

The festival winner, Kevin Bowyer (United Kingdom), received the 1990 Gold Medal, $12,000, an international concert tour and a recording engagement. The 1990 Silver Medal and $8,000 was awarded to Matthew Dirst (United States). Heidi Emmert (Germany) was awarded the Bronze Medal and $4,000. The 1990 Concerto Prize and $3,000 was awarded to Jonathan Biggers (United States).

---

agreement in 1971. They contended that equity demanded the entire value of the properties be turned over to them. While the properties in question had little value in 1971, the amount in the dispute would ultimately total millions.

For Pembina, the core of the matter was not money, but the fundamental principles upon which the oil business was based and the honour and integrity of everyone involved. "Because the matter dealt with fiduciary duties and trust, it was important to our reputation," explained Lorne Gordon. "We pride ourselves on being a good partner. To claim that we had not met our fiduciary duties and had breached trust — those were very hurtful things."

"The land we bought in 1971 — and I remind you that they brought this claim forward in about 1990 — turned out to be quite productive," Gordon said. "It was a successful oil play. The interest they were claiming by backing into what, in their view, they should have had, with interest on their money from the date the cash flow started coming in, amounted to about $10 million. We were unable to negotiate a settlement with Norcen, although we tried. Luscar was our prime competitor in the coal business, so they were not interested in negotiating anything. They took the position that their legal fees were quite small and the prize was big. It was a very mercenary approach. They basically said, 'Why not? For a few hundred thousand dollars in legal fees, maybe we will make $10 million.'" After a lengthy discovery period, Pembina went to trial. "As I say, we had a very persuasive case that made it pretty clear that we had given these people much more than all the notice they ever deserved," Gordon said. "So we went to trial with quite a bit of confidence. Justice Egbert was the trial judge." Unfortunately for Pembina, they grossly misplaced that confidence.

On November 22, 1991, Justice Egbert ruled that breaches of trust and fiduciary duty had indeed occurred and that Pembina had been unjustly enriched. He awarded judgment to Norcen and Luscar for an amount even greater than what both companies originally requested. "When the judgment came down, that was one of the lowest points in my business career," Gordon said. "They had claimed $10 million in damages from us. Justice Egbert not only found for them, but he awarded them $20 million in damages. It was just overwhelming."

Gordon was not the only one stunned by the judgment. "I remember Len Sali phoning me when the judgment was released. It so struck him his voice was breaking," Watkinson recalled. "We could not

---

1988 ▶

More than 130 Loram Group employees volunteer, as members of Team Petroleum, to support the Calgary Winter Olympic Games.

1988 ▶

Canadian scientists also assist the Olympic effort. The National Research Council uses their nine-metre (29.5-foot) wind tunnel to evaluate the form of Canadian skiers.

believe it. Even when we read the judgment, we could not believe it was happening. Norcen and Luscar had not sued for as much money as the judge was giving them. It was an absolute low point in the times I have worked here. I remember having to go to Ron Mannix's Christmas party on the Saturday night about three days after the judgment came down. Everybody was stunned. The judgment was so important to the oil and gas industry that within weeks, everybody in town knew about it. Every lawyer in town was talking about the Norcen-Luscar-Pembina lawsuit."

After the devastating decision, Pembina increased its legal team, bringing in Les Duncan, who had been involved in the Gregg River negotiations. "Les is a very intellectual-type lawyer," explained Watkinson. "He looks through the problem and easily finds the really finite legal argument that can be used on it. We sort of forced the marriage of Len Sali, who is the pugnacious boxer who keeps working on you until you collapse, with Les Duncan who is more of the intellectual-type legal person. It was tough, but in the end, we came up with a good factum that went to the Alberta Court of Appeal."

"They were arguing that a trust had been created between Pembina, Norcen and Luscar," Watkinson said. "Now, trust is a very difficult area of law to understand unless you spend years and years studying it. I asked Len Sali, 'Who is the number one guy on trusts in Canada?' Len said that Donovan Waters, a professor out at the University of Victoria, had written the definitive textbook on trust law in Canada. So I said 'Len, would you call him up? Send him the decision that was rendered against us at trial' — this is before we went to the Court of Appeal — 'and let's meet with him and go through all the issues of this trust.' We had the feeling for what the arguments were, but when we got into the issue of trust, it was very difficult.

"So Len Sali, Les Duncan and Leslie O'Donoghue, who was working for Les Duncan, flew out to meet the god of trusts, Donovan Waters. He looks like what you would expect a professor to look like — English fellow, white hair, speaks very well and is a really interesting fellow. Anyway, he sits down and goes through everything. For the first 40 minutes, he just did not have any sort of enthusiasm for our position. He made one comment and I said, 'Well, Professor Waters, maybe there has been some sort of little error here. We're Pembina, we're not Norcen-Luscar, they're on the other side of the case.' He said, 'Oh! You're Pembina! I thought you were Norcen-Luscar.' Then he said, 'Well, Pembina, I think you have got a good position. This is not a trust. This thing will not last at the Court of Appeal.'"

Due to the interest in the lawsuit, the case took eight days to argue at the Court of Appeal, about six days longer than normal. "As we got to the trust issue, I knew Les Duncan's argument, the cases he was relying on and the quotes from Donovan Waters' book he was going to use," Watkinson said. "So I said to Lorne Gordon, 'You know what we should do? Why don't we fly Donovan Waters from Victoria into Calgary and have him sit on our side while they're arguing trusts?'"

"I remember that morning because in comes Donovan Waters," Watkinson said. "He didn't sit at the counsel table because that might be a little bit too much, but he sat right behind Les Duncan, who was doing the arguing.

The Pembina legal team that wins the Norcen-Luscar-Pembina lawsuit. Back row, from left to right: John Amundrud; Dalton McGrath; Len Sali, Q.C.; James Watkinson, Q.C. and Alex MacWilliam. Front row, from left to right: Daryl Samuelson; Leslie O'Donoghue; Cathy Good; Les Duncan, Q.C. and Dallas Droppo.

1988 ▶

The National Research Council also improves the Olympic torch and provides a special fuel to ensure the flame keeps burning.

You could see the other side look over at us and go, 'Oh no! It's Donovan Waters!' Les did it really well, too. He started into his argument and then he said, 'And by the way, I trust you realize that this gentleman behind me is Donovan Waters.' Of course, the judges all knew him, especially John Coté. Coté had been a professor of intellectual property and trust law at University of Alberta, so he would have known Waters and he would not have argued with Waters. Waters thought this was just one of the greatest things in which he had ever been involved. After the argument that day, he and I and a couple of the lawyers had a few beers. Waters said, 'I will never forget this — being picked up, driven to the airport and having this private jet fly me from Victoria to Calgary for a five-hour argument and then flown back the same day.'"

Donovan was not the only one who would long remember the case. "The transaction was watched by everybody," Lorne Gordon said. "The principles of law were obviously very important to us, but they were extremely fundamental to the very fundamentals of how the oil industry operates in terms of land transactions. It was a difficult time. There we were, suddenly having a $20-million liability that we had to post a letter of credit from the bank and be prepared to honour at any moment. Anyway, we went through the appeal process. Not only did we win the appeal, but the judgment of the Alberta Appeal Court was scathing." After deliberating for 18 months, in a rare reversal, the Alberta Court of Appeal rejected the findings of Justice Egbert and dismissed the action, with Norcen and Luscar having to pay costs to Pembina.

In the early years of the oil and gas industry, a person's word was their bond. The Alberta Court of Appeal recognized this and stated if Pembina's land manager was alive to testify, he would presumably have cleared up the whole matter. Within weeks of the decision, Norcen settled with Loram, but Luscar appealed to the Supreme Court of Canada. In 1995, Luscar was denied leave to argue and the case was closed.

"It is nice that you come out on the winning side of these things," concluded Watkinson. "Every major litigation that we have had, we have always been on the right side. That is because we always honour our contracts, we do not try to get around things."

Taking Pembina Private
Merging the Past with the Present

During 1988, the Loram Group undertook a corporate reorganization to rationalize the oil and gas operations into a more logical structure. This reorganization was a long-term goal that the differing ownership structures of Pembina, a public company, and Western Decalta, a private one, had previously frustrated. The achievement of this goal can be traced to Black Monday, October 19, 1987.

In the corporate world, Mondays are a tough day at the office. This Monday, however, dawned downright ugly. The Friday before, the Dow Jones industrial average lost 108 points, the first time the bellwether blue-chip index had ever dropped 100 points or more in a day. Brokers brooded over the weekend, sweating over market watchers' predictions that the precipitous drop tolled the end of a five-year bull market. Monday's opening was a sorry sight. Confronted with a bloated book of sell orders in the wake of Friday's rout, and a dearth of buyers at any price, the market buckled at the opening

An exhausted trader at the Toronto Stock Exchange on Black Monday, October 19, 1987.

1988 ▶

Canadian Kurt Browning, who will go on to win five world championships, lands the first quadruple jump in competition.

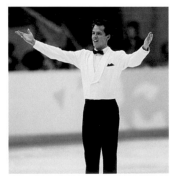

1988 ▶

In May, Pembina pipeline system cumulative throughputs total 1.5 billion barrels. The original estimate for the entire field was 500,000 barrels.

bell. By 11:00 a.m., the Dow had dropped 200 points. No one had ever seen anything like it.

By noon, the market had staged a modest recovery that cut the loss on the Dow to about 130 points. The market then got clobbered by a second wave of selling after reports that the Exchange Commission was flirting with the idea of briefly shutting the market down. Investors capitulated as the session drew to a close, the Dow shedding more than 200 points in the last hour. By the time the dust had settled, the Dow Jones industrial average had plunged 508.32 points to 1,738.41, a decline of 22.62 per cent, nearly double the 12.9 per cent drop in the crash of October 28, 1929. In just one day, Black Monday had wiped about $500 billion off the value of U.S. stocks. The Toronto Stock Exchange 300-stock composite index fared better than New York's, slumping 407.20 points to 3,191.38, only an 11.3 per cent decline. Nevertheless, this drop erased $37 billion off the value of shares listed on the TSE. Overall, Black Monday was a memorable day.

"I will never forget October 1987, when the stock market took its great crash," recalled William M. (Bill) Bone. Bone, who received his bachelor of arts degree from Bishop's University in 1968, followed by a bachelor of laws degree from Queen's University in 1974, joined the Loram Group as secretary and general counsel of Mancal Ltd. in 1986. "We had regular quarterly meetings," he said, "and Pembina's budget meeting was the day after the market dropped so precipitously. There was a tremendous concern of what was happening in the marketplace. At one point in the meeting, there was some paper falling from a building across the street. I remember the joke was made

Top: Roy Grier, left, and Rick Kozak attach the new Pembina Corporation sign at a Diamond Valley oil well. Pembina Corporation is formed when Western Decalta Petroleum (1977) merges with Pembina Resources Limited.

Above: With the merging of Western Decalta and Pembina, a complete corporate restructuring occurs. The team that accomplishes the reorganization includes, back row, from left to right, James Watkinson, Jack Murray, Earl Zumwalt, Linda Dixon and Gary McNamara. In front, from left to right, are Robert Michaleski, Margaret Donaldson and John Amundrud.

that these were share certificates, presumably worthless at this point, that were being torn up and thrown away. In any event, because of that precipitous fall in the market, a decision was made, I think originally recommended by Lorne Gordon as president of Pembina, that we should buy out the minority of Pembina Resources' stock, which was publicly traded at that time."

Without a doubt, the single most important event to occur in the Loram Group in 1987 was the privatization of Pembina Resources Limited. Gordon's speed of action, not to mention timing, was again impeccable. Before the end of October, Gordon had made an official recommendation to the board to take Pembina private. Within a month, all the work had been done on the offer and financing had been arranged. Pembina then made a "substantial issuer bid" to all public shareholders (46 per cent), on November 30, 1987, at a price of $22 per share. A total of 3.6 million shares were tendered for $79.3 million, exclusive of associated costs. Two months later, on January 31, 1988, the second phase of the privatization was completed when Pembina redeemed 253,548 shares for $5.6 million. The total cost of the privatization, including costs, was $86.3 million and financed entirely through the Royal Bank. At long last, a goal that had eluded the Loram Group since their first attempt to take Pembina private in 1975, were finally achieved.

The privatization of Pembina, which was completed on February 1, 1988, brought immediate benefits to the company. "It gave us the opportunity to maximize efficiencies, to consolidate our operations and to amalgamate Pembina Resources with Western Decalta," said Pembina's controller, Bob Michaleski. "We then reorganized into a structure that was designed to be tax-effective

1988 ▶

Wayne Gretzky, whose nickname is "The Great One," is traded to the Los Angeles Kings. The National Hockey League career leader in goals, assists and points, he led the Edmonton Oilers to four Stanley Cup Championships: 1984, 1985, 1987 and 1988.

1988 ▶

At Seoul, Korea, Canadian synchronized swimmer, Carolyn Waldo, wins an individual Olympic gold medal and shares a gold with her partner, Michelle Cameron, in the duet competition. Waldo is the first Canadian woman to win two gold medals in one Summer Olympics.

and more efficient as to the way we were set up. This was a project that I was in charge of, and it was pretty complicated overall. Not only was it complicated from the perspective of having all the legal, accounting and reporting issues, but there was a cultural issue as well. There were the Western Decalta people, the people we had acquired back in the late '70s, and they always thought of themselves as Western Decalta. The Pembina people thought of themselves as Pembina. Well, when we merged the two groups, we combined the past. Now we are trying to get a start for the future where we all see ourselves as being one unit in the same boat rowing the same direction."

Pembina's long-term objective — to establish separate reporting entities for western Canadian oil and gas assets, pipeline operations and Ontario oil and gas assets and to create a management company to oversee all operations — was essentially completed by the end of 1988. In 1989, Pembina Resources Limited and Western Decalta Petroleum (1977) Limited were amalgamated. The resulting company was named Pembina Corporation. Following another major reorganization that same year, Pembina Corporation became the parent company of Pembina Resources Limited, which operated the western Canadian properties, Pembina Pipeline, the owner of the pipeline system, and Pembina Exploration Limited, the operator of the Ontario facilities. Pembina Resources absorbed all remaining Western Decalta operations.

The Acquisition of Peace Pipe Line
"It was the most incredible closing."

What has been incredible about the Nineties is not just the process of ongoing change and its scale and pace, but that so many events have occurred in the most emotionally moving form on the television news. This has been both uniquely revealing and uniquely distorting. For example, as Pembina executives embarked on the single largest acquisition ever undertaken by any Loram Group company, they were upstaged by events taking place on the other side of the globe. War, in real time, marched into the boardroom.

On January 12, 1991, the U.S. Congress approved legislation permitting President George Bush to make war on Iraq if Iraq did not withdraw from Kuwait by January 15. On January 17, at 3:00 a.m., the United States and Allied missiles and planes hit targets in Iraq and Kuwait. In what was history's heaviest bombing, pilots flew more than 1,000 missions per day, dropping thousands of pounds of explosives with computer-guided accuracy. Millions sat mesmerized in front of their television sets, hypnotized by the eerie phosphorescent glow of missiles arching through the dawn.

Noted war photographer Francoise de Mulder snapped this shot of the night bombing of Baghdad, Iraq, just as a bomb exploded, jarring the camera.

The day of the bombing, Pembina president, Lorne Gordon, and Pembina's vice president and general manager, Bill Stedman, made their presentation to the Mancal board for approval to bid $200 million for Peace Pipe Line. "Bill Stedman and I went to Toronto to make the presentation to the Mancal board to get approval to make this $200-million bid," recalled Gordon. "Just as we were making our presentation, the Americans started their offensive strikes in response to Saddam Hussein's occupation of Kuwait. Most of the board members went to watch television and see what was going on as the whole world was expecting oil prices to skyrocket when the guns started firing. Of course, instead of skyrocketing, prices collapsed. Nevertheless, when President Bush launched the troops, everybody on the board was

1988 ▶

The Loram Group commissions five bronzes that reflect dirt-moving equipment at the beginning of the 20th century. Rich Roenisch, an artist from Longview, Alberta, is commissioned to create them.

Mormon board.

Wheeled Fresno.

watching CNN. They said, 'Fine, go ahead.' So there we were with the biggest deal we had ever done in our history and it was given some consideration, but not the focus that you might normally expect."

According to F.P. Mannix, the board did not need to spend an extensive amount of time reviewing the deal because of the preliminary work done by Gordon. "I thought it amazing that the board spent the time it did and decided to go with the deal despite the uncertainty the war created," he said. "This was because Lorne had done his usual thorough job. The material was excellent and the preliminary work by Lorne to the shareholders made it a done deal. Without that preliminary work, where most of the questions had been asked and answered, we would not have decided to go ahead."

Peace pipeline — the system that runs north of Pembina pipeline and covers a very large service area — clearly was a most attractive pipeline to buy. Originally constructed in 1955 to transport crude oil from the Sturgeon Lake area in Alberta to the Edson pump station on the Trans Mountain pipeline, Peace pipeline had experienced several expansions over the years. The result was that, by the fall of 1991, Peace was one of the largest feed sources of oil, condensate and natural gas liquids in Alberta. The company owned and operated more than 2,200 kilometres (1,370 miles) of pipeline with connections to 49 oil fields and 17 gas plants; six truck terminals served remote production areas. Through two wholly owned subsidiaries, Peace also transported condensate from the Brassey field in British Columbia to Alberta. Acquiring Peace Pipe Line would make Pembina a very significant player in the Alberta pipeline industry. Perhaps because of this fact, Pembina was not invited to the bidding table.

"Peace Pipe Line came to us in a strange way in that Dallas Droppo, who is one of our outside counsel, phoned to say that Peace Pipe Line was up for sale," explained Jim Watkinson. "We had not been consulted in the sale. I think maybe some industry players were a little nervous about selling Peace to Pembina, which already had a big pipeline system. But for whatever reason, we were not invited. Lorne Gordon, then, was able to get us into the bidding. Unfortunately, when we started into the bidding, one of the other bidders for the property had already tied up some shares. He had a few weeks' advance on us and had done some lock-up agreements on the shares with a few of the companies. We just could not get in there and get control of it. It was a very difficult transaction in that the party that had outmanoeuvred us at the initial onset of the bidding process had negotiated all these agreements."

"THE LONG ARM OF THE MANNIXES"

Back in the 1940s, a Mannix employee hiked into Lake O'Hara with his young bride to get away for a honeymoon. "Perfect," he figured. "They can never find me here." However, as anyone who has ever worked for the Mannixes knows, they thrive on just this sort of challenge. After the young couple hiked to Lake O'Hara, they found a float plane waiting for them. The pilot informed them that Mannix had instructed him to fly the groom back for "just a few more days' work." Some things never change.

"In August 1991, I was down visiting my sister-in-law in Santa Barbara," recalled Jim Watkinson, a key player in the on-again, off-again Peace Pipe Line acquisition. "I had just been down there a couple of days. Before I'd left, there had been some rumours about Peace Pipe Line coming back. I was downtown shopping and I walked into a Gap store. There was this young woman working at the till and I started looking around. She said, 'Are you from Canada?' I went, 'Yes.' She looks at a little piece of paper and said,

'Is your name Jim Watkinson?' I said, 'Yes.' She said, 'There's a message here for you. You're to phone Lorne Gordon right away.'"

"This is about 11:00 a.m. and I was just starting my vacation," Watkinson said. "I thought, 'Well, I'll phone him, but first I'm going to go and have a couple of margaritas so at least I can say I had some Mexican food down here.' Then I phoned Lorne. The Peace Pipe Line acquisition was back on. I had to fly back that day. The long arm of the Mannixes and how they can get a hold of you is really something."

Fresno.

Water wagon.

Dump wagon.

For Pembina, these pre-existing agreements meant that the logistics behind the deal fell just short of an oil executive's nightmare. "About 14 companies owned Peace Pipe Line," explained Gordon. "These were mostly the major companies, and they all had pieces and various interests in Peace. A condition of their sale was they wanted the buyer to enter what was called a transportation agreement with the sellers. This transportation agreement would set out how tariffs were going to be calculated so that they could protect themselves against somebody just buying it and then increasing the tariff. In fact, all it was going to do was enshrine the tariff methodology that Peace had used for about 25 years. Beyond that, and as part of the transportation agreement, they wanted to receive financial statements so they could audit and see that things were being done according to the agreement."

Pembina decided not to meet these conditions. "We made a cash tender but unconditional, that is to say we would not accept any of those conditions," Gordon said. "It was interesting that in the final cash tender we made, Mancal directed us to pay more than the management of Pembina was willing to recommend, which is a little different. The management of Mancal was quite confident that the amount of our cash bid would impress the owners and we would not have to bother with these transportation agreements. Well, in fact, the owners of Peace Pipe Line did not accept that idea. Our bid was the highest bid, but it did not come with the transportation agreement and access to audited financial statements, so they did not accept our bid. A fellow named Ed Odishaw from Regina, his bid was accepted. He was going to provide a transportation agreement, financial statements, and so on."

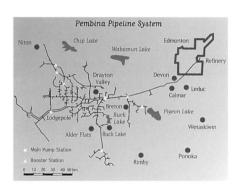

These maps show the combined territories that make up the Pembina and Peace pipeline systems. Pembina's 1991 acquisition of Peace Pipe Line Ltd. adds another 1,800 kilometres (1,120 miles) of feeder pipeline carrying an average of 190,000 barrels per day.

In August of 1991, Pembina got word that Odishaw had been unable to get his financing together and that there had been problems between the various owners of Peace Pipe Line. The result was that the deal had not closed. Pembina was then asked to reconsider the requirement for a transportation agreement, setting off a furious round of negotiations. "The long and short of it was that Pembina agreed to enter into a transportation agreement, and offered a very slight premium over what Odishaw was prepared to offer," Gordon said. "Pembina then picked up the agreements that had been partially negotiated by Odishaw and finished them off. Then we went through very difficult negotiations with all these parties who all wanted something else. They were all very suspicious of one another. No one would agree to sell their shares unless they knew everybody was selling theirs at the same moment. The term we used to describe the problem is that we had to get everybody to jump into the pool at the same time."

"You had the people who had been negotiating these agreements for six to eight months and now their purchaser had disappeared and they had all these agreements," said Watkinson. "There were a dozen or so shareholders and many of them had different private deals. It was a mess. Over the next three weeks, we went through the agreements with a fine-toothed comb. We were able to say at the end of it that they looked fine. The commercial part of the deal was there and we closed the deal within about eight weeks. If you see the Peace closing books, there are maybe 4,000 to 5,000 pages of agreements to finalize this transaction."

"It was the most incredible closing I have ever been involved in," Gordon said. "It took about five hours. The boardroom had to be kept locked. Nobody could leave the room. None of the agreements could leave the room until they were all signed by everybody. Because there were so many agreements, they all had to be signed and everybody had to see that they had all been signed so that everybody knew their positions were safe. Then

1988 ▶

Joe Mastracchio, far left, Dick Peppin, centre, and Bruce Tubbs, far right, prepare to take author Sharon Mercer, second from left, and Roberta Ross, manager of historical development, on a field tour of Maintenance of Way equipment.

1988 ▶

The Loram Group of Companies celebrates the 90th anniversary of the Mannix family in business.

everybody could take their copies of the agreement and leave. It was a dramatic closing. That happened on Halloween 1991."

With the acquisition of Peace, Pembina nearly doubled in size. "Peace Pipe Line was a big bite for us," said Bill Stedman. "Two hundred people worked for Peace, so we almost doubled the size of Pembina Corporation with that acquisition. We realized that we were transporting all the oil that was available to us in Pembina, but the amount was just going down year after year. Peace accessed the area around Grande Prairie which we knew was going to be an active part of the industry. In addition, it seemed like a good fit to take Pembina's blue-collar approach and put it with the advanced white-collar engineering that Peace was doing. It has been a good mix. We brought some cost focus to Peace, but Peace brought a lot of neat technology to Pembina. So we have upgraded both systems by merging approaches to business."

One person who came to Pembina from Peace was Fred Kuipers, who joined Peace in 1982 after spending nearly 18 years with the forest service. "Certainly we were apprehensive when Pembina bought Peace, but we were quite relieved to get it all resolved," said Kuipers, who became Pembina's supervisor of environmental affairs. "I look back now and I am just as pleased as can be that it did happen. The company we currently work for and the management that we currently have are just excellent. In terms of employment, a person could not ask for much better."

There was only one problem, and a significant one at that — it looked like Peace might be headed into bankruptcy. "Peace Pipe Line was completed in October 1991," Lorne Gordon said. "Canadian Hunter led a group of four shippers on Peace Pipe Line's system who were demanding a review of the tolling methodology on Peace pipeline. We negotiated with them from the day we became the owners of Peace Pipe Line until the fall of 1992 when negotiations came to an impasse. Then Canadian Hunter, PanCanadian Petroleum, Rigel Oil and Gas and Crestar filed an application before the Public Utilities Board to have the board review our tariffs under Section 101 of the Public Utilities Board Act. Well, this was a calamity."

"Until that time, there had been no feeder pipelines economically regulated by the Public Utilities Board," Gordon said. "This was an incredibly dangerous thing because the basis on which Canadian Hunter and the group that they led were asking the Public Utilities Board to review the transaction, was they wanted to prevent Peace Pipe

Line from recovering interest on acquisition debt through tariffs. They also did not want Peace Pipe Line to be able to recover any premium they paid in buying the assets of Peace Pipe Line over the book value. Any one of those two things would have meant that Peace Pipe Line was bankrupt, absolutely. So it was a very serious problem.

"The long and short of it is, at the end of the day, we persuaded the Public Utilities Board that they should not regulate Peace Pipe Line or any feeder pipeline. The Public Utilities Board, in their formal decision, decided they had jurisdiction but there was no need to exercise that jurisdiction — that Peace Pipe Line was calculating tariffs consistent with the methodology that had been in place for 30 years. We were able to demonstrate that we had entered into these transportation agreements with people so the shippers had broadly shown support for the tariff methodology and they were not going to change it."

"It is interesting, as a point of history, that we were absolutely adamant that we were not going to have a transportation agreement," Gordon reflected. "We bid a higher price with no transportation agreement and we were not going to show anybody our financial results. Culturally, we do not do that. Absolutely the thing that saved our life in this action was that we had a transportation agreement. If we would not have had the transportation agreement, I believe there would have been a high probability that we would have had a regulated pipeline. So at the end of the day, we ended up accomplishing much more than we would ever have imagined by getting protection for ourselves in the future."

The Story Behind Telesis, Mark and Serenpet
Pembina Comes Face to Face with Income Trusts

With an excellent management team in place and a major reorganization launched at the parent company level, in 1993 Loram appointed Lorne Gordon president and chief operating officer of Loram Corporation. Bill Stedman succeeded him as president and chief executive officer of Pembina. Stedman, who completed a bachelor of science degree at Dalhousie University in 1973 and a bachelor of engineering degree at McGill University in 1975, spent five years in various parts of the world as a design and construction engineer. In 1980, he entered Harvard Business School, graduating with a master of business administration degree two years later. After joining Pembina in 1982, Stedman was employed in various positions of increasing responsibility within the company, becoming vice president and general manager in 1986.

1988 ▶

The first gathering of the Quarter Century Club — employees from all branches with 25 years' service — is held for the 176 initial inductees.

1989 ▶

In March, the metal-and-glass entrance to the Louvre opens. It is designed by I.M. Pei.

Stedman has nothing but praise for Gordon's management style. "It is easy to be intimidated by Lorne because he is really smart," he said. "If you say, 'Lorne, I am thinking about this idea and it looks like this,' he will say, 'Yes, it is a good idea, but if you turn it like this, it is even better.' He can do that in five minutes, but he is really good at not getting in your way. A lot of smart people will say, 'Phone me every morning, and I will tell you what you should do today.' Lorne is good at being supportive and giving you the rope just to go out and do things."

As president of Pembina, Stedman continued Gordon's policy of intelligent management of resources, consolidation of function and focus on growth. In April 1994, Stedman significantly increased Pembina's presence in the Ontario oil and gas industry with the acquisition of 65 per cent of the assets of Telesis Oil and Gas in Ontario for $63 million. As part of this deal, Pembina disposed of 35 per cent of its previously owned assets in Lake Erie for $12 million. The net effect of these transactions left Pembina holding a 65 per cent ownership interest in the offshore Lake Erie assets and a 100 per cent interest in the onshore lands in Ontario. Total reserves acquired by Pembina were 1.3 million barrels of oil and 76 bcf of natural gas. This transaction was the major factor contributing to the increase in Pembina's oil and gas revenues and year-end reserves.

Overall, the acquisition went smoothly. "The Telesis acquisition was very much the Pembina style of business — continuing on, but adding the Telesis assets to what we were already doing," explained Stedman.

The Pembina Corporation management team includes, back row, from left to right, W. Earl Martin, William E. Robinson, Alister R. Lambden, Frederick E. Webb and James Watkinson. Front row, from left to right, are Robert B. Michaleski, William R. Stedman and Geoff C. Merritt.

"The properties in Lake Erie are really a boutique type of operation and two companies were doing that, ourselves and Telesis. So when we took them over, we just put the two together and kept going."

Not long after the Telesis acquisition, Pembina set its sights on acquiring Mark Resources Ltd. In so doing, Pembina encountered an investment craze that would ultimately change the future of the Loram Group — income trusts. Trusts ushered in a whole new ball game, turning the competitive bid process literally upside down. Turning something into a trust seems to produce stock market value out of thin air — people are willing to pay more than they would for regular common shares in a similar company because they get a hefty dividend on their units, a return that can go as high as 12 or 15 per cent of their unit value.

The key difference between a traditional corporate entity owned by shareholders and an income trust is how they are taxed and how they deal with their discretionary cash flow. Trusts are managed to return cash flow to investors, while corporations are managed to return profits and build the value of the business. Dividends paid to corporate shareholders represent earnings that have been subject to tax. However, distributions from a trust to its unit holders are paid out of pretax cash flow that is subsequently taxed in the unit holder's hands. Another key difference is that the value of an income trust is extremely sensitive to prevailing interest rates.

Income trust units have been available to investors for many years in varying forms. However, the unprecedented drop in interest rates to 40-year lows triggered a

1989 ▶

Japan's Emperor Hirohito dies after a 62-year reign. His son, Akihito, succeeds him on the "Chrysanthemum Throne."

1989 ▶

A 7.1 earthquake jolts San Francisco. It is North America's most destructive quake since the 1906 San Francisco quake.

demand for income-producing investments, creating what some called a "trust mania." Loram came face to face with income trusts in October 1995, when Pembina Resources launched its $485-million hostile takeover bid for Mark Resources Ltd. When Pembina offered $7 a share for Mark, which had previously traded in the $6-a-share range, Mark went looking for alternatives. What they found was Enerplus Energy Services Ltd., already established in the energy income trust business. Enerplus offered Mark shareholders $2 a share in cash, and trust units that would receive the cash flow generated by Mark's oil and gas assets. Enerplus turned Mark into a $500-million royalty trust, one of the first large-scale trust deals. The market priced the resulting EnerMark Resources units in the $7 range which later moved up to $9 as interest rates declined. From a $6-a-share price, Mark was transformed into a cash value of $9 a share, a whopping increase of 50 per cent. For investors seeking higher yield alternatives to Canada's low interest rate regime, resource trusts were a revelation.

While it may have been a revelation for some investors, it was a tough blow for Pembina to lose Mark Resources. "I think we did everything we wanted to do to get it," commented Jim Watkinson. "We did not want to pay anything more than we were prepared to pay and someone else was prepared to pay $2 more. The lesson we learned from Mark Resources was that we can say, 'Listen, we've got a good price for these assets and we are prepared to buy them at this price, but if somebody out there is prepared to pay more, we are not going to get the assets.'"

After the failed bid for Mark, Pembina set its sights on Serenpet Inc. Serenpet, a public company whose management had put the company up for sale

Top: In 1994, Pembina purchases the Ontario assets and properties of Telesis Oil and Gas Ltd. One of the acquired assets is the drill ship Telesis.

Above: On December 23, 1996, Pembina Resources Limited acquires Serenpet Inc. The Serenpet purchase adds further production of crude oil, natural gas liquids and natural gas from Alberta and Saskatchewan.

in August 1996, was not the type of company normally subject to a royalty trust. Pembina offered more than $110 million for Serenpet, which had proven and probable reserves of 111.6 bcf of gas, 7.7 million barrels of crude oil and natural gas liquids and 373,000 acres of undeveloped lands. Pembina's offer of $4.80 a share was about a 14 per cent premium over the company's average trading price during the prior 20 days. In the previous year, the shares of Serenpet traded between $2.70 and $4.50 on the Toronto Stock Exchange. Serenpet's board of directors endorsed the bid and the directors and officers, who held 30 per cent of the company's outstanding shares, agreed to tender their holdings to Pembina. Pembina also had the right to match any other offer and would receive a $4-million breakup fee if their bid was unsuccessful, thereby effectively raising the price that a rival would have to pay to more than $114 million. Pembina, which successfully concluded the deal in December 1996, effectively absorbed Serenpet's operations and management within the first four months of 1997.

Manalta Coal
"If you have principle, honesty and integrity...you cannot be beat."

As Pembina has shown, while a man's word may still be his bond, the days when deals were concluded with a simple handshake had long faded into history. Yet Pembina was not the only company in the Loram Group having to deal with complex legal transactions. Manalta Coal also found itself having to adapt to this new world as well.

While the mid-1980s brought significant changes to the Gregg River Mine, unfortunately, the overall tone of these developments was not encouraging. From a purely operational standpoint,

1989 ▶

The property rationalization team continues to improve Pembina's land position. Members are, from left to right, Paul Nazarchuk, Karen Butrenchuk, Lois Kaake and Steve Schneider.

1989 ▶

Boris Yeltsin wins a landslide victory as an opposition candidate to the presidium of the supreme soviet. He predicts a revolt in the USSR within the year if Mikhail Gorbachev fails to institute further reforms.

Gregg River was a tremendous success. The mine had started up smoothly and the first years of operations had gone well. The same could not be said, however, of the world metallurgical coal market. With the Japanese steel industry in a recession and a world oversupply of metallurgical coal, the market declined dramatically throughout the mid-1980s. By way of example, back in 1981, Bob Sanders had been reluctant to make the deal for Gregg River at a price of $73 a tonne. By the late 1980s, the world metallurgical coal price had dropped to around $50 a tonne, a fact which had a significant impact on the Gregg River Mine's future.

"The original deal was based on expectations by both sides that the boom times of the late '70s and early '80s would continue," explained Lorne Repka, whom Manalta Coal named the general manager of the Gregg River Mine in 1989. "So this property, which

This 1991 aerial view of the Gregg River Mine near Hinton, Alberta, shows active mining and reclamation.

is not the easiest or simplest or richest mining property in the world, got developed. As we all know, the upward spiral came to an abrupt end and the world price for met coal failed, quite literally. The Japanese were able to manipulate most of the other suppliers in the world to dance to their tune and reduce their prices, but not us. So we were operating under some duress since the mid-'80s. The feeling was that Gregg River operated on a borrowed life."

The pressure to renegotiate the price downward began building up for the first formal price review — one of three as defined by the long-term contract — which was scheduled for 1986. "To exert some pressure on us, they would not send the ships," recalled George Chapel, who had become Manalta Coal's vice president of operations in 1985. "We had to shut the mine down for 33 days once because there was no place to put the coal. The port was full, the

mine site was full and we had to lay everybody off. The ships showed up in Vancouver but they took somebody else's coal. There were three instances where we shut the mine down. When that happened, we went on record saying that this was in violation of the contract, which it was because they had no right to do that. The contract was very specific. Price review is one thing, but the ships were supposed to be scheduled on an even basis. They were using that as a tool in their negotiations. It was just blackmail, and you are talking big bucks here."

The 1986 price review negotiations ended in a stalemate. "We agreed to an interim or provisional price for one year," Chapel said. "That gave us another year to negotiate. Theoretically, that meant we should have had a new price in '87." However, by 1990, the 1986 price review was still not resolved, a fact that greatly troubled Manalta Coal's president, Ron Dalby. For Dalby, while the complexities of the modern world may require multi-thousand-page contracts, for a man of honour, your word is still your bond. From his point of view, the Gregg River contract had been based upon an agreement on certain principles. In the 1986 price review, he had secured a further agreement based on these principles and had then struck a deal for a new contract price. After shaking hands on this agreement, the Japanese partners decided to seek a further reduction in price. At that point, Dalby decided he was not going to budge on price because to do so would be a violation of the original principles of the deal. The joint venture obviously could not work if one party was allowed to go back and change the rules.

"One thing I do not think the Japanese understand is that if you have principle, honesty and integrity,

1989 ▶

Hurricane Hugo slams into the British Virgin Islands causing death and mass destruction.

1989 ▶

Hungary proclaims itself a democratic republic on October 23, making the future seem bright for this young couple in Budapest.

and if you stay with it, you cannot be beat," Dalby said. "We had the principle in the contract that Lorne Gordon originally handled so effectively, and we had honesty, integrity and consistency in what we did afterward on Gregg River, and that is tough to beat. But where they think they can beat you is that North Americans are always ready to compromise if things are not going their way. If you drew a graph and said, 'Here is our position and here is your position, the North Americans would say, 'We have to compromise.' The Japanese say, 'Well, you make the first move.' The North Americans say, 'Well, since we are that far apart, the best place to go is here in the middle.' The Japanese say, 'You have made a very good move, very good, we appreciate that, but we are prepared to move down here.' And the North Americans wake up one day, and they are way down there. But me, I say, 'Okay, a fair price is here.' So we give them a fair price. We commit ourselves and then we stay there."

In taking this approach, Dalby created new legends in Tokyo for his negotiating tactics. "Once he just sat there for 45 minutes," Chapel related. "He said whatever it was he was going to say, which took him five minutes, and then he just sat there. When he realized that nobody was going to say anything back, he took out his notebook and he started doing other stuff. You see, they know us. Most North Americans, when they are negotiating, do not like a silent pause. But Ron said that when he realized that nobody was going to say anything, he just took out his notebook and started writing. It was like, 'You wanted me over here, I came over here. You wanted to hear something, I told you what I told you before.' So they couldn't accuse him of not going over there. That would indicate that we were not serious. So whenever they called a meeting,

Top: Gregg River coal is exported to Japan from a port near Vancouver, British Columbia. A latex emulsion is sprayed on each full railcar to suppress coal dust during the trip to the West Coast.

Above: The Gregg River Mine received this 1,250-horsepower Caterpillar 994 loader in 1994. The first one in Canada, the Cat 994 is the world's largest mechanical-drive wheel loader.

we went. They could never say we were negotiating in bad faith."

"He took a page out of their book," continued Chapel. "He acted like they did in many ways. He would just keep repeating the same story over and over. Some of the guys who were with him at the table felt embarrassed — reading the minutes from those meetings, you're actually embarrassed. They would ask Dalby a question and he would not answer it. He would talk about his point, and he kept on repeating and repeating and repeating it. That really frustrated them. He had his own focus and he stayed with it. The Japanese may not have liked it, but they respected him for it."

Dalby also made sure that the world metallurgical coal mining community knew about Manalta's situation. "I gave a lot of speeches, principally on Gregg River, to let the world know, and the Japanese know, that we believe that if you enter a contract that is profit-based, then you have a right to pursue that profit," Dalby said. "I gave speeches in various parts of the world and focused attention on the fact that the Japanese were reneging on their contractual commitments. They printed part of one of those speeches in a World Coal Institute publication. I had guys come up and say, 'Hallelujah! I couldn't believe anyone would say this.' Another guy said, 'The Japanese will get you anyway.' But those speeches were on the record and they were good for us."

In the spring of 1990, Manalta made an absolutely unprecedented move — they sued the Japanese investors. The company's position was that in seeking the new price levels, the Japanese investors were not living up to the principles of the contract; that they had, in effect, denied that they were bound to the original principles by reneging on the 1986 price review agreement. That this price

1989 ▶

John Cleghorn, president of the Royal Bank of Canada, joins the Loram board.

1989 ▶

Canada cuts passenger rail service from 405 trains per day to 191. The move is designed to help ease the national debt that is 50 per cent higher, per capita, than in the United States. It costs the government up to $400 each time a passenger boards a VIA Rail train.

review still was not settled after nearly four years was also an indication that the Japanese were negotiating in bad faith. Manalta laid out these facts in a $66-million statement of claim filed against the Japanese investors in the Court of Queen's Bench in Canada on April 4, 1990.

"We were like the mouse and the elephant," explained Ross Melrose, who joined Manalta Coal as corporate solicitor in 1980. "Those steel companies were huge. They were quite amazed that we actually did it. You never sue your customers, that's not a great marketing play. But we explained to them that we were backed in a corner and had no other choice. Their negotiations had been going on for years and we did not want to lose whatever power we had because they were the customer. They had all the power and we were the contractor, so we didn't have much. We wanted to preserve whatever we had. We had a reasonable case, no doubt about it. It was not a frivolous action at all."

While the action was not frivolous, it had a ring of history to it. Back in the early 1900s, when F.S. Mannix and Claude Gallinger shook hands on an agreement, they used to joke, "Whoever says it first has to write the contract." In some ways, the contract with the Japanese was an echo from the past. "If we initiated arbitration, then we would have to go under Japanese law," explained Melrose. "If they initiated it, then we would have to go under Canadian law. Whoever goes first has to do it in the other guy's backyard. That was a really interesting concept. It was a pretty ingenious little plan. You better think twice before you complain."

To keep the matter in their own backyard, Manalta came up with an inspired strategy. "We said, 'Well, it's such a fundamental breach of contract, it isn't an arbitrational issue at all, it is a court issue,'" said Melrose. "So instead of arbitrating, we sued for fundamental breach of contract in the Alberta courts. It was a good way to do it. It never went to trial. It never went to any court applications. We settled it amicably. We still deal with them constantly, obviously, and we get along with them. We're just a little guy compared to them; we're just a small supplier in the total picture of things for them. One of the concerns was any long-term effect, but I think we showed that we do what we promise. Maybe they do respect us."

"Certainly in the minds of Manalta Coal management, the Gregg River final settlements placed the company in the unique position of having mutual respect and understanding between the Japanese steel mills and their supplier, which is the best possible position we could ever be in," concluded Ron Mannix.

Modernization of equipment is evident in the comparison of the modern dragline with the team of horses pulling the wheeled scraper. The dragline removes 23 cubic metres (30 cubic yards) of overburden per bucket load while the scraper removes only 0.27 cubic metres (0.35 cubic yards) per pass.

Continuing to Modernize Operations
"I do take pride in talking about our company."

Although negotiations on Gregg River were a continual headache, they also proved to have unexpected dividends. "Dealing with the Japanese has just been an absolutely fascinating experience," Glenn Woodford said. Woodford, who joined Gregg River Resources as an accountant in 1980, became Ron Dalby's chief financial person on the price review negotiations. "A tremendous amount of discipline has also come out of that. Dealing with the Japanese is an exercise in exactness. One of the things it's taught us is to do things right, to do them properly, and to have our story straight in dealing with anyone. I think that has done a tremendous amount for us in the company."

One way in which the discipline acquired through Gregg River flowed out to Manalta's other mines was through technology transfer. One

1989 ▶

Pro-democracy demonstrations are crushed in Tiananmen Square in Beijing, People's Republic of China. Thousands are believed killed by Mongolian soldiers firing into the crowds of students. Leaders of the democracy movement are executed.

1989 ▶

Stalinist dictator of Romania, Nicolae Ceausescu, praises China for quashing the Tiananmen Square democracy protesters. After Romanian secret police slaughter thousands of civilians, the people and army overthrow the government, convict Ceausescu of genocide and execute him.

peculiarity of the surface coal mining business was that during the 20th century there were no truly revolutionary changes in the big mining equipment used in all mine operations. "Manalta's equipment technology overall hasn't changed significantly," Lorne Repka said. "The big new draglines, of course, are vastly superior to the ones that we were operating when I joined the company in '75. The tonnage of iron it takes now to move a cubic metre of dirt with a dragline, relative to the old ones, is less. So the design is much more refined. But outwardly, to look at a dragline from a distance, one just looks bigger than the other one."

While surface mining hardware had not greatly changed, there were major changes in the engineering of mine operations. One great change was in the introduction of computers with mining software systems for developing mine plans and designing pits, producing schedules, monitoring equipment maintenance and running mine accounting programs. Although the first personal computer (PC) at any Manalta mine was a small Apple computer at Whitewood in 1981, Gregg River became the pilot operation for developing sophisticated computer usage, starting in 1982 when a VAX computer and mining software were installed. From Gregg River, computer hardware and software gradually began to spread to the other mines. "We started that process in '86," explained Tim Jenish, Vesta's mine manager. "We took a system that had been developed at the Gregg River Mine and modified it to meet the needs of a small mine. That worked out really well."

"The first PCs that were brought onto the mine site were pretty simple," recalled Highvale mine manager, Garry Dirk. "The major benefit we saw in the initial PCs was in having the capability to do some spreadsheet programs where we could gather statistics and use that as part of our overall reporting system." Computer programs for spreadsheets not only saved a tremendous amount of time in gathering data but also helped in financial analysis. "We used to keep all our records on big

The two Poplar River draglines at work as night falls.

A dragline operator's view at a prairie coal mine.

spreadsheets, and that was done manually," added Poplar River mine manager, Wayne Kelly. "Now all the spreadsheets are in your computers, and there's a lot more time spent analyzing the information. In the old days, we started compiling the information but once we had it, we didn't know what we wanted to do with it anyway!"

The main benefit of computerization was in mine planning and design, which had undergone a total transformation since the days when Mac Summersgill refused to okay Lorne Repka's purchase of an electronic calculator. "The ability to generate numerous mine plans and mine schedules and truck hauling comparisons and all those things, it's incredible," Lorne Repka said. "It gives us a large degree of refinement capability. In 1975, the stuff was still basically done on a slide rule. On a mine like Gregg River, to do what we do now, we would have had to have probably two or three times the engineering staff. And then their goal would have been finding a mining solution that worked and making only minor revisions to it, because that's all they'd have the time and ability to do. But now one or two guys can hammer out 30, 40, 50 different mine schedules in a week. What if we do this, what if we do that? The computer spits it out. That's been the real difference."

Equipment utilization and maintenance were two other areas where computerization helped make subtle changes that would produce huge results by the end of a year. "You start talking seconds on draglines now," Wayne Kelly said. "As big and bulky as they are, you get it down to the seconds. With a 90-yard dragline, each bucket is the equivalent of uncovering about 700 tonnes of coal. So if you miss one swing in a shift, you miss getting 700 tonnes of coal. The next step is to computerize draglines to the point of getting your operating time, your consumption of electricity, and your wear and tear off your computer automatically. If you can control all that and save yourself a couple dollars in grease at the end of the day, there's that much more money that you have to work with. Maintenance is another area where there's been a lot

1989 ▶

In October, Utility Mine loads and delivers the 50 millionth tonne (55 millionth ton) of coal to the Boundary Dam power station.

of changes. You're getting more and more into computerized preventive maintenance. You have people watching the equipment as opposed to years ago when you just kept on running it until it broke down."

Manalta Coal continued to modernize its operations in the area of reclamation as well. From the late 1970s into the 1980s, reclamation regulations became more sophisticated. Manalta was one of the companies that influenced these regulations by working with governmental agencies to write the new guidelines. And these guidelines worked, even to the point of turning skeptics into believers. "I remember when I first started at Manalta, I read a *Loram Story* that said we reclaimed land to its original, or better, condition and I thought, 'Oh, sure,' being cynical," Ross Melrose recalled. "But when I went out the following summer to some prairie mines and I saw where they reclaimed them, they amazed me it was so good. At Poplar River where I was so heavily involved, I knew where those pits were and to go back now, you wouldn't even know that they had been there. I remember a huge mess. When I went back after it was reclaimed, it was a crop and it was green. I became a believer then."

While Manalta was helping to shape the new regulatory environment, the company was also integrating reclamation work into its mine planning and operations work. "Reclamation is certainly an integral part of the overall mining operation," Garry Dirk said. "In fact, it's one of the very, very early stages of the whole process of mining and it's the last stage as well. The removal of vegetation and soils has to occur in advance of mining. After you remove the coal, the subsequent cut replaces material into the mined-out area. The spoils then have to be levelled and the topsoil replaced and revegetated. From that

Top: Manalta Coal's continuing effort to reclaim mined land includes the government and other coal companies in scientific, long-term studies to ensure the best possible results.

Above: Bighorn sheep graze on reclaimed land at the Gregg River Mine.

point, reclamation becomes a farming operation. You do various things to enhance the productivity of the soil and optimize the yield of the various crops. Once the land is firmly reestablished, then it's turned back to the original owners or other users. So reclamation is certainly a major consideration in all of our mining operations. It's evolved over a period of time to where it has now become a very major component of the overall mine operation."

Manalta's approach to reclamation was to look at this aspect of mining operations as an opportunity to excel. "Reclamation is something, certainly since I've been here in the '80s, where we've done a good job," said Manalta's manager of engineering, Paul Scott. "I'm not ashamed to say that. We've done an excellent job, and we continue to do an excellent job. I've not heard anything except praise for the reclamation efforts we've put in." Because of this effort, Manalta was able to showcase its reclamation efforts. "When reclamation first came in, if you were going for a tour of the mine, reclamation was something that you might go see at the end, if you had time," explained John Morgan, Manalta's manager of Saskatchewan operations. "Now, and this is true in all of our operations, the mine manager will take you to see the reclamation as one of the focal points of a tour. Reclamation has come up from being sort of an add-on to an integral part of the operation."

"I feel good about the industry in general, but I do take pride in talking about our company," said Manalta's manager of environmental services, Bernd Martens, a Techman veteran who joined Manalta in 1986. "Manalta Coal is an industry leader. We had one of our people, Trent Enzsol, who is a biologist by training, find out how the spoil properties were being used.

1989 ▶

W.P. Robinson becomes president of both MHL Holdings companies and vice president and general manager of Bowcal Management Ltd. and Bowfort Services Ltd.

1989 ▶

Former Loram executive Stan Waters becomes Canada's first elected senator.

He found out that they hosted a mule deer population that wouldn't have been in that area if it hadn't been for the spoil piles. The layout of the spoil piles provided cover for deer and a protective environment from the chilling winds that sweep across the prairie. They also fostered plant growth which is important for deer on the winter range. We inventoried some old pits as well in terms of water quality and we developed some stocking programs with the fisheries people. Our company has stocked some old water bodies and the Saskatchewan government is now using them for a brood-type nursery for fish."

John Morgan's father, David Morgan, a former president of Techman, assessed Manalta's historical importance in the development of reclamation practices in this way. "Manalta Coal is one of the leaders in reclamation work," he said. "Generally speaking, they were pioneers in reclamation even before there were government regulations enforcing it. In many, many cases, land that has been mined can be more valuable than the land before it was mined. It is a good idea to enforce reclamation, and as I said, Manalta Coal has certainly been a leader in this respect."

"We invest an awful lot in our people."

Another area where Manalta continued to excel was in industrial relations. The only significant strike ever to occur at any Manalta mine was the one at the Montgomery Mine in central Alberta during the period in the late 1970s and early 1980s. In Saskatchewan, with its long history of troubled industrial relations at coal mines, Prairie Coal continued to maintain an outstanding reputation as a fair employer. "We've had very good relationships with the unions," John Morgan said. "We've had tough negotiations with them, but if you look at the strike record we've had, it's extraordinary really.

Top: Brian Mckinnon, left, and Doug Lamson measure the depth of topsoil to be removed and saved prior to overburden removal at the Montgomery Mine in eastern Alberta.

Above: After the coal from this area at Vesta Mine is removed, subsoil and topsoil are replaced. Crops are then planted and the land returns to its former use.

I'd describe the relationship as very businesslike. The unions realize that even though the coal mines are captive to the power plants, the utility is not the goose that laid the golden egg. They understand they have to be reasonable in their demands because if we're forced to increase our prices for coal due to higher than acceptable labour costs, then we'll see tonnage move to other places."

The standards set by the company's training and development program also place Manalta Coal at the head of the industry. "The senior management here at Manalta Coal certainly sees safety, training, environment and quality as all very key to the future success of the operation," credited Bruce Basaraba, Manalta Coal's manager of training and development services. "We are one of the few mining companies in Canada that actually has a training and development department. I have yet to meet a manager of training and development in the mining industry other than myself. Our competitors in this region do not have somebody like me, or a department like ours."

"We're showing commitment to our people," continued Basaraba. "We're investing in their future. A lot of companies haven't figured that one out, or they're not prepared to take it on. Training has often been seen as a cost in organizations. Often when economic times get difficult, training gets cut immediately, where in our company, we've actually increased the training. The last I saw the industry average, each employee in the mining industry received approximately 14 hours of training a year. At Manalta Coal it's actually just over 30 hours per employee."

One area in which training has paid off is the area of lost-time accidents. "We certainly are at the top of the heap as far as high performance in Alberta," Basaraba said. "In Saskatchewan, we're right up there with the

1990 ▶

C.L. (Chuck) Borsos is named president of Loram Maintenance of Way.

1990 ▶

South African black nationalist leader Nelson Mandela is freed after more than 27 years in prison. He will become president of South Africa in 1994.

mining industries. Our WCB (Worker's Compensation Board) rates in Saskatchewan are lower than office workers; there is a higher incidence of accidents in some offices with office workers. The statistics show that we have done very well. We invest an awful lot in our people. What we are doing ensures that our people are in top shape and trained to take on the next phase of the company. That is what we are looking at for our future."

The continuing process of modernizing mining operations led to great changes in mine management in the 1980s. "The mine manager's job evolved from where you spent 80 per cent of your time in the pit to 80 per cent of your time in the office," Wayne Kelly explained. "You introduced reclaim, you introduced industrial relations, and then computers came along so everybody had to make a few changes there." For Manalta, the key management concept at the mines, as in Calgary, remained teamwork. "We've seen the company go from a very autocratic style of management to a more participatory style where you're getting more people involved in the decision-making process," Tim Jenish said. "More people are dealing with problems rather than just one person. A mine manager years ago was like God. He knew everything about everything, and you never questioned anything he did. That is not the case today."

"A mine manager's position has changed drastically," continued Jenish. "He has got to have a general knowledge of everything, but he's got to get his expertise from the people below him. And he's got to make sure that they are given the responsibility to do the job and the accountability. People in the work force in the mining industry are much better educated than what they were even 10, 15 years ago. It's not unusual to see people come through the door looking for work who have their grade 12 and maybe a bachelor's in administration. So it's a very highly

The Vesta Mine dragline operates near harvested, reclaimed land.

educated work force, and it's up to us, as management, to utilize that expertise even at the frontline level. We have to take full advantage of that and make everyone feel a part of the team."

Through the mid-1980s, Manalta made significant changes in its approach to dealing with its utility company customers. "One of the challenges that was put to us at Vesta was to develop better lines of communication with the owner," Tim Jenish explained. "For a number of years, I think our company took our business for granted, and I don't think we were alone in that respect. But over the years, we've seen that the utility companies were starting to accumulate more knowledge in the area of mining, and they weren't taking everything at face value. So we had to shift gears, work with them, make them feel a part of the process, but still maintain control over what we were doing and how we were doing it."

"When we started this process, I was reporting to Garry Dirk, and we sat down and developed a format that he had seen used at some other properties," Jenish said. "We refined it to implement it in the quarterly meeting with the power companies. We would explain what we proposed to do and how we did in the previous quarter, and we discussed our problems. We told them what we were up against, took their suggestions into consideration, and it worked out very well. The relationship improved tenfold once we started that process. We were quite pleased with the outcome of that."

Another example of Manalta's efforts to improve customer relations was Montgomery Mine, which was officially opened on June 7, 1986. With a new Page 736 dragline, a P&H 1900 coal-loading shovel, and 100-tonne Kress coal haulers, Montgomery's production capacity was expanded to 1.5 million tonnes (1.65 million tons) per year. In 1986, Montgomery's production, which had

1990 ▶

In March, following months of turmoil, Lithuania formerly declares itself independent from the Soviet Union.

1990 ▶

Lech Walesa becomes president of Poland and other Solidarity-endorsed candidates for parliament are swept into office following the 1989 elections, the first free elections in more than 40 years.

been well under 100,000 tonnes during the early 1980s, easily went over the one-million-tonne (1.1-million-ton) mark. Don Meads, the mine manager at Montgomery since 1976, began establishing good relations with Alberta Power and TransAlta personnel from the moment the mine expansion project got under way back in 1984. "We pay a lot more attention to our customers than we did in the past," Meads said. "We have got some good long-term contracts and the company wants to look after those customers and give them the best product we can for the money."

Relocating the Poplar River Mine
"We ventured into unknown territory."

For Prairie Coal's mines in Saskatchewan, the most high-profile event of the late 1980s was the relocation of the Poplar River Mine. The mine was moved from the original mine site SaskPower had developed, called the west block, to the south block of Manalta's reserves in the Willow Bunch field, an event planned since Manalta's acquisition of the mine from SaskPower. Project manager for the mine relocation was Lorne Repka, who worked closely with Manalta's special projects manager, Henry Neufeld, Poplar River Mine manager Wayne Kelly, and a team of engineers and mine operations people. Another key member of the Poplar River Mine relocation team was Manalta's environmental coordinator, Bernd Martens. "It broke new ground in Saskatchewan because it was the first project to go through an environmental assessment under the new laws and process," Martens said. "It's a small

Poplar River Mine manager Wayne Kelly, left, and chief engineer Al Klesse plan for the 1989 dragline walk to the new south block.

The two giant Bucyrus-Erie 2570-W draglines pass the southern Saskatchewan town of Coronach during their walk from the west block to the south block of the Poplar River Mine.

community and the people on the regulatory side are really good people. We've maintained a high-quality level of work, so we've developed trust with the people in Saskatchewan."

For Neufeld, one of the more interesting aspects of the move was an archeological dig. "As it turned out, we had to do some extensive archeological survey and mitigation, meaning we recovered a lot of Indian artifacts," he said. "We had some large crews out there sifting the dirt. Recovering artifacts, or determining if there were any artifacts there in the first place, required that the crews go through the soil layer by layer, and we were dealing with large areas. For some reason, the best coal deposits seem to be in the same place as the Indian campsites. The consultants recovered something like 40,000 artifacts, mostly rock chips. Indirectly, the project helped to develop a better understanding of the Aboriginal use of the area."

For Martens and the other members of the mine relocation team, one of the first major decisions concerned the method chosen to haul the coal from the new mine site to the Poplar River generating station. The team came up with a solution that made the new Poplar River Mine totally different from any other Manalta mine. The idea was to build a nine-kilometre (5.5-mile) railway to cover most of the distance to the generating station, with a one-kilometre (0.6-mile) conveyer system to haul the coal to the railway.

"At the new mine site, we had to build a new road, power lines and a railway extension because at this generating station, the coal is delivered by railcars from the

1990 ▶

Manvest Ltd., with Kenrick, Thornmark Capital Funding Inc. and CIBC Wood Gundy, purchases Simmons Canada, the largest mattress and box spring manufacturer in Canada.

1990 ▶

Iraq invades and annexes Kuwait. The UN votes to sanction Iraq and authorizes the use of force to expel Iraqi forces if they remain in Kuwait after January 15, 1991.

A STROLL IN THE PARK

Like moving Mr. Klimax back in 1968, walking the two huge Bucyrus-Erie 2570-Ws to the north block of the Poplar River Mine in 1994 was primarily notable for being so well planned and executed that nothing untoward happened. "It was uneventful," recalled Wayne Kelly. "It was actually

quite boring after a while except for the tourists along the path. There were a couple of retired guys who spent the whole 13 days out there. They showed up at daylight and didn't go home until dark. Halfway through the walk, we shut everything down and let the school kids and everybody come out and walk around the machines and get their pictures taken. We had about 1,500 people tour the machine in the two days that we shut down."

While there was no adventure in the walk, moving two big draglines 15 kilometres (nine miles) turned out to be a first and caught the attention of coal miners around the world. "This was the first time that anybody had ever tried that long a walk," Kelly said. "It was unique within our company and we found out that it was unique for a lot of companies. Not too many mine sites get an opportunity to do that. Since then, we've had visits from guys in South Africa and Australia who are going through the same thing. So we've been acting as consultants, giving a little bit of advice to them."

mining area to the generating station," Neufeld explained. "The distance from the new mine, the Poplar River South Mine, was similar to the distance from the original mine, and the plant was set up to receive coal by railcars as opposed to delivering directly by truck or conveyer into the plant. During the process of evaluation, we looked at delivering coal by conveyer from the mine area all the way to the plant and then loading the coal into the railway and delivering it that way. The final throes of that project evaluation was it was determined that it would be beneficial to install an overland conveyer for about two kilometres of the distance from the mining area toward the plant. The difficulty there was that although it's flat prairie land, there were hills and a small river valley that we could not take the railway across because of the grades and various other considerations."

"We ventured into unknown territory for us, as far as designing and installing an overland conveyer system," Neufeld said. "We didn't have any experience with long conveyers, although we did have experience with short conveyers in plants such as Gregg River. However, we did have one individual in our group, Al Landerputton, who had worked at Syncrude and had learned a fair amount about the operating characteristics of long conveyers. Lorne Repka was the project manager and he recruited myself and Al Landerputton. Together, the three of us dreamed up these weird and wonderful schemes of using an overland conveyer."

"We already had a number of railway cars and the locomotives, so all we had to do was lay the tracks and we had a railway," Lorne Repka said. "Then we estimated that the conveyer would operate for about a third or a quarter of the cost of haul trucks. The project team felt that it was a good idea from a technical advancement standpoint for us to get into the conveyer technology and see what it was all about. So we went around and visited places in the States and all over, trying to find out what it cost to operate these things and how troublesome or trouble-free they were."

By 1986, the project was well under way. The last step in the process was moving the mine's two Bucyrus-Erie 2570-W draglines. Initially, it appeared that this might be quite an adventure. The last time anyone had moved a large dragline in Western Canada was in 1968, when Alberta Coal's Marion 7800 at the Klimax Mine was moved to Utility. "All the guys who moved that were long gone, so it was a new challenge to us," recalled Wayne Kelly. "Then when we started looking to see who we could get help from, we found out that there was really nobody else who had ever done it before. So we were on our own. We had to develop all our own procedures and develop our own theory, if you will, for the move. Basically, we just relied on everybody's experience. Initially, we had planned to build a roadway for the walk. But between myself and Cap Jenish and a couple of the old pit supervisors at Utility, we could still remember the days when

1991 ▶

At 3:00 a.m. on January 17, coalition forces begin their assault on Iraqi-held Kuwait. Allied firepower devastates the Iraqi forces.

1991 ▶

Following the defeat in Kuwait, Iraqi President Hussein unleashes killing squads against Kurdish minorities in Iraq. Thousands flee to Turkey and Iran.

draglines operated right from the top of the prairie. So we decided, 'Well, let's give it a try right across the topsoil.'"

In 1987, the crew at Poplar River tried a short walk to test out this idea. "We planted a fall rye crop, and then we just walked right over top of the crops," Kelly said. "That proved to everybody that, yes, it can still be done. We had planned for about 42 days for the walk. Then we reevaluated and decided we could do it in 30. About a month before we walked, we said, 'Hey, guys, we should be able to do this in two weeks!'" In the spring of 1989, Henry Neufeld oversaw the final stages of construction of the new mine site buildings, the railway, and conveyer system. On June 1, 1989, the final step in the relocation got under way, as the two big draglines started to walk to the south block. The trip was completed on schedule in two weeks, and by June 23, the two big draglines were stripping overburden at the new mine location.

Overall, the Poplar River Mine relocation project was a tremendous success. "Lorne Repka, Henry Neufeld, Wayne Kelly and their team just did a superb job in making this very major move of a complete mine to its new location," credited Mike Mears, president of Prairie Coal Ltd. "It was a three-year project and, frankly, went off without a hitch. It was extremely well done."

For Wayne Kelly, there was not much time to enjoy the moment. He immediately began to look forward to the next relocation, to the north block. The mine plan prepared for Poplar River back in 1983 entailed first mining the west block for five years, then the south block for five years and finally, in 1994, moving to the north block. This latest move also went off without a hitch, being completed on time and within budget.

The Transition into the Nineties and The Acquisition of Line Creek Mine

As Ron Dalby's tenure as president of Manalta came to an end, Manalta found itself concluding a remarkable period in its history. The 1980s brought a string of accomplishments, including the start-up of the Gregg River Mine and the successful negotiations on the 1990 price review, the purchase and relocation of the Poplar River Mine, the acquisition of the new contract for the Montgomery Mine and the subsequent mine expansion work, and the winning of the bid for the Highvale Mine and contract extension. All this growth occurred during a period of difficult economic conditions for the western Canadian coal mining industry as a whole, in a busy environment that grew increasingly competitive and complicated.

COMING FULL CIRCLE

"By 1992, we started in earnest designing our facilities for the next move from Poplar River South further north," Henry Neufeld said. "By now, we had a total of 30 kilometres of railway from the mining area down to the generating station. This is an interesting little deal because Manalta Coal, or Prairie Coal as it's known in Saskatchewan, is not only a coal mining company, but is the largest private railway operator in Canada, and

maybe even beyond that. That status comes from the fact that the Poplar River Mine produces about four million tonnes of coal per year and transports it over a length of 30 kilometres. That's 120 million tonne-kilometre units per year which, in comparison to CN or CP of course is nothing. In terms of private rail operators, it's quite significant because we own and operate the railway. We're not just shipping our product by rail on somebody else's equipment. I'm sure few people in our company realize that or think of it that way."

"Although we are the biggest single railway operator, it's really not foreign to us in the history of the Loram Group," Neufeld said, "because the history of the construction company is rooted in the construction of railways back at the turn of the century when CP was coming west across Canada. That's really where the company started. In a way, it's kind of ironic that we've come full circle. One hundred years later, we're still in the railway business, except we own it."

1991 ▶

Paul Christensen, a 35-year veteran with the Loram Group, retires as president of Trison Investments Ltd., but continues as president of the Carthy Foundation.

1991 ▶

Jane Goodall continues her groundbreaking research with chimpanzees.

While all these events were taking place, Manalta also succeeded in completely reshaping its management style, with an increased emphasis on customer service and a more team-oriented approach to operations management. On December 31, 1990, when Dalby stepped down after 10 years as president, Manalta was a much different company than ten years before. "Ron was like a breath of fresh air," George Chapel said. "He brought in a different style. He never lost his cool, never raised his voice. I've never heard him swear except once, and when he retired, we gave him a certificate for that! A real class guy, with real good experience, very sophisticated. He'd worked for some major companies, so he'd been through it all before. He was the sort of guy that if he had a job to do, he'd do it, and he helped you. You could always come in and see him. He always had an idea or two, and he always listened to your recommendation. He was very straightforward and very focused. Nobody else could have done what he did with the Japanese. He always tried to stay focused, to put things in the right perspective. He was just a super guy in that respect."

Dalby's last goal in his final months as Manalta's president was to ensure that there would be a smooth transition to the next generation of company management. By the end of the decade, an excellent management team was in place, with an exceptionally strong set of managers both in the head office and at the mines. In Dalby's opinion, Manalta's management was already nicely established and well prepared for the future. His recommendation to Mancal for Manalta's next president was the person who was already the company's second highest ranking executive, George Chapel, the senior vice president and general manager. Chapel was highly flattered by this recommendation, but would not have minded being passed over for promotion, with certain conditions. "I don't mind working for somebody," Chapel said. "I don't have to be top dog, I don't have that ego. But the guy that I have to work for, I have to respect. If they had found another Dalby, I would have had no problem with that. It's that simple. Had they gone out in the street and gotten another Ron Dalby, I would have said fine."

Mancal did not feel, however, that there was any need to look outside the company for executive talent. In addition to being a talented executive, Chapel was known for his extraordinary dedication to the job. He was also legendary for setting an example for his team to follow. "Chapel would spend the first hour of a day on Gregg River matters," recalled Darc' Clarkson, a chartered accountant who joined Manalta Coal in 1977, and worked extensively with Chapel on Gregg River. "So I had that hour with him to talk through whatever was going on at the mine, whatever was going on with the Japanese, and get instructions on whatever he wanted me to do. We developed a pretty good relationship. George took a lot of pride in being there early. Generally speaking, I was in the office about 7:30 in the morning. George would get there about 7:15. I'd walk in the door and right away we'd start. I needed a little bit of start-up time, so I'd come in a little earlier. But George would come in even earlier. Finally, I was coming in at 6:00 and he was coming in at 5:45 and I gave up. He wanted to be there first and that was that. We eventually settled in to around 7:00 a.m. I'd get ready the night before so I didn't come in unprepared."

The management team of Manalta Coal Ltd. in 1995 are, standing, from left to right, Ross M. Melrose, John A. Taylor, Garry G. Dirk and Kevin L. Beingessner. Seated, from left to right, are Glenn W. Woodford, Brent D. Young, George D. Chapel and John R. Morgan.

1991 ▶

In Russia, a coup attempt in August fails when Muscovites en masse oppose the military. The Communist party is suspended, ending 74 years of rule.

1991 ▶

Pembina Corporation acquires Peace Pipe Line Ltd., effectively doubling the pipeline operations. The La Glace facility is shown.

When George Chapel was named the new president and chief executive officer on January 1, 1991, Manalta Coal was once again off on a whole new adventure. The start of the George Chapel era began not quietly as George wished, but with a flourish. "When I took over as president in 1991, it was going to be a quiet year," Chapel recalled. "That lasted about six weeks. Then Shell announced that they were going to put Line Creek up for sale. It was a corporate decision. They were going to focus on their core businesses, and coal wasn't one of them. That took us pretty much until July. We submitted a bid, there was a non-binding offer that was subject to due diligence, we were shortlisted and then we consummated the deal in July. We took over August 1, 1991."

Manalta Coal purchased the Line Creek Mine from Crows Nest Resources Ltd., a Shell Canada subsidiary, for $72.7 million. Originally put into operation in 1982, Line Creek gave Manalta a metallurgical and thermal coal property, a two-million-tonne-per-year (2.2-million-ton) operation with contracts for both metallurgical and thermal coal with Japanese and South Korean customers. The acquisition put Manalta Coal into the international thermal coal market for the first time and more than doubled its metallurgical coal production. Gary Hodges, formerly mine manager at Vesta, became Manalta's first manager at Line Creek.

"Line Creek was critical for us because at the time we thought Gregg River would be pretty well mined out by 1998 and we wanted to be in the international

In August 1991, Manalta Coal Ltd. purchases the Line Creek Mine from Shell Canada Limited. Located near Sparwood, British Columbia, the mine produces bituminous thermal and metallurgical coal for export.

business," Chapel said. "Line Creek was a way of doing it and it wasn't a major stretch for us. Shell had spent anywhere from $300 million to $350 million developing Line Creek Mine, which was the same size as Gregg River; Gregg River cost us $180 million. We had people on board who had been with Gregg River, so they knew that type of operation. We also had the same Japanese customers for about half the production there. That helped us. We thought that the Japanese might not be all that enthused about us taking over Line Creek in view of our difficulties on Gregg River with them, but that was not an issue."

"Line Creek had good people," continued Chapel. "When we took over in August, we made two changes, the mine manager and the office manager. Gradually, we have moved people from Line Creek into other operations and we've moved people from other operations into Line Creek, so we're getting a good blend there." One of the people who came to Manalta with the acquisition of Line Creek was Andrew S. (Andy) Dudzinski, vice president of marketing. "The synergy was a happy circumstance for a number of us for the good reason that we all knew that Manalta was an extremely long-standing and well-known company in the coal business," Dudzinski said.

"More importantly, in one sense, was that they were recognized as being the largest coal mining company in Canada and obviously, one that knew what it was doing in the area of operations and mining of coal," continued Dudzinski. "We ended up with what we called a seamless transition. This was assisted very much by people like

1991 ▶

William M. (Bill) Bone becomes president of Trison Investments Ltd.

1991 ▶

Croatia, Macedonia and Slovenia declare themselves independent from Yugoslavia. Conflicts between the multiple parties begin.

LINE CREEK ACHIEVES ISO 9000

"We were the first."

"Line Creek achieved ISO 9000 in 1992," said Bruce Basaraba, Manalta Coal's manager of training and development services. "We were the first coal mining company in the world to achieve ISO 9000 standards. ISO 9000 standards aren't easy to come by. ISO is the International Standards Organization based in Geneva, Switzerland. They've developed thousands of standards over the years since the '40s on anything and everything. The film you use in a camera is an ISO standard. Threads, bolts, shipping requirements, the standardized metric system we use today, all come under ISO. ISO 9000 is the number they use for the quality assurance standards."

"In Canada, there are probably half a dozen mining companies now that have achieved the ISO standards," Basaraba said. "Our competitors here have just recently achieved the standards, which means we are two to four years ahead of them. I think a lot of people don't understand how important having the ISO certification is. It gives the assurance to the people inside the corporation that we're doing what we say we're doing. It also assures our external customers that this company has got a professional, well-recognized management system in place."

George Chapel and Glenn Woodford, with great encouragement and assistance in making sure that we felt at home in being able to move forward so that the customers wouldn't perceive any change at all. Yes, the ownership of the operation had changed, but in terms of their dealings, deliveries and response to any concerns they may have, all of these things would be handled in a way that, to them, was totally transparent. They would not even dream that they were seeing anything different to what they had seen over the past few years. The happiest aspect for me was exactly that."

While the change in ownership went flawlessly, Chapel felt that the mining operations themselves needed a slight change in direction. "We knew there was potential there so shortly after we took over, we started preparing a long-range plan to see what we were going to do," Chapel said. "Based on that, we started adding and upgrading equipment. The ultimate decision-makers at Shell were not mining people. They were oil and gas people, so they understood a preparation plant, they went first class on that. But when it came down to mining equipment, they had small equipment and everything was just not done right. We went in there and we took a mining perspective and a long-term perspective."

One area where Manalta brought a mining perspective to Line Creek was in determining how best to move the coal. "Ever since the acquisition, it had been studied and evaluated with the intent of improving the existing operations," Henry Neufeld explained. "They had always known that the truck haul from the existing mine area down through the Line Creek Canyon and down in the Elk River Valley was a long and expensive process. This was because the coal had to be hauled in 120-tonne trucks about halfway, dumped on the ground in a stockpile area, then reloaded into smaller 40-tonne trucks to be hauled down through the canyon. The necessity for that was based on the fact that the road and the bridges through the canyon had only been designed for the 40-tonne trucks. When the mine was constructed in the early '80s, it was deemed to be too expensive to build a wide road capable of supporting the heavier trucks through the canyon. There were environmental reasons as well, because to build such a wide road would have destroyed the creek."

"It took quite a while to complete the selection process of the various transportation systems, but ultimately it came back to a conveyer system," Neufeld said. "We had long negotiations with the vendor, Cable Belt, a British manufacturer of conveyer systems, as to what they

1991 ▶

George Chapel becomes president and chief executive officer of Manalta Coal Ltd.

1992 ▶

Canada's Kerrin Lee-Gartner wins gold in the Olympic downhill.

could provide and what warranties they could provide because the system they proposed was a conveyer that could navigate curves. At the time, it was controversial and uncertain as to whether it would work because it had never been done before. Although there are curved conveyers in the world, to our understanding, there were none that were this length with the type and severity of curves that we needed to navigate through the system."

As the decision-making process had eaten up so much time, the actual work schedule was a bit tight. "Because of our schedule being so short, we ended up with a lot of overlap whereby we were already building before the design was really totally complete and analyzed," Neufeld said. "It was quite challenging in order to not have our costs go totally out of hand and, at the same time, continue with the work and get the facility built. The silver lining in the cloud was the fact that our senior management was very understanding of the circumstances. They fully supported all the project efforts insofar as recognizing that we had extra costs that were not budgeted and that were really to be expected. A different viewpoint from management could have been, 'Shoot the messenger!'"

Line Creek started delivering coal on the conveyer on March 15, 1996. While cost of the conveyer project exceeded $30 million, Manalta expected to see a return on their investment through increased efficiency and productivity. The high-tech, 10.6-kilometre (6.6-mile) conveyer system eliminated about 100,000 return trips made annually by trucks hauling coal at the mine. This not only reduced dust from the coal hauling, but improved the safety of the mine by reducing traffic in the narrow canyon area. It also enabled the movement of more raw coal, thereby allowing the mine to increase its clean-coal production.

Manalta's acquisition of Line Creek was both a sign of the new times and a reflection of the old. As in the past, Manalta continued to hold its long-range view despite industry ups and downs. "The time to be moving into coal mining is not when everybody thinks it's the hottest ticket in town," said Manalta's manager of Saskatchewan operations, John Morgan, who was named vice president and general manager of Prairie Coal Ltd. in 1989. He was promoted to vice president and general manager of Manalta Coal Ltd. and president of Prairie Coal Ltd. in 1996. "The oil companies all thundered into the coal business a few years ago and bought leases all over the place and developed mines and now they're all thundering out," Morgan said. "Through our acquisition of Line Creek, we're showing that our philosophy of having confidence in the industry through optimistic times and pessimistic times has served us well."

To lessen the environmental impact of transporting coal down the narrow Line Creek Canyon, Line Creek Mine builds a 10.6-kilometre (6.6-mile) conveyer to carry up to 7.0 million tonnes (7.7 million tons) of coal each year. The new conveyer emerges from underground on the left.

◄ 1992

R.A. (Dick) Peppin retires after 36 years of service. Under his stewardship, Maintenance of Way sets a Loram Group record of 27 consecutive profitable years. His retirement gala is staged at the fantasy western town, Peppinville. Caught entering town are, from left to right, Dick and Mary Peppin, Sig Rishovd and Jerry Thomas, a John Wayne look-alike.

"You Have to Recognize the Individuals"

Gary Hodges, Line Creek Mine general manager, left, congratulates Henry Neufeld on the first load of coal delivered to the Line Creek conveyer.

"One could say the Line Creek cable belt conveyer project was a tough project — high-risk, expensive, a short production schedule," said Manalta's special projects manager, Henry Neufeld. "Just about anything you could think of, we had going against us. It seems like whenever you're doing something that's unique or different, you have the 100-year flood. In 1995, when we were building the conveyer, we had the 100-year flood in British Columbia.

"It was a very difficult construction period with a lot of rain in '95, severe flooding and a severely cold winter. On December 1, it turned cold and it never really warmed up until spring. There was just no relief. There was literally no chinook during this construction period. The field construction entailed a lot of manual labour, so it's not like equipment operators sitting in a nice, warm cab. It was tradesmen on the ground working with their hands, bolting line strands together and conveyer covers under very difficult circumstances."

"You have to recognize the individuals who contributed to the project when they could have said, 'It's too cold and we're not working. We're going home. See you in the spring,'" Neufeld said. "Temperatures were 30 below and these guys were out there working with their gloves off because they were holding small screws, nuts and bolts. We started delivering coal on the conveyer on March 15, 1996. It was a prototype, the first of its kind ever to be built."

Another tradition that has been maintained is the careful evaluation of business opportunities. "The company has always taken a fairly structured but cautious approach to evaluating new endeavours while still maintaining the desire to expand," Garry Dirk said. "We've been able to see a fairly constant growth but we haven't made any bad acquisitions that would have stifled our growth or caused us to have to step back. It seems that all of the expansion opportunities that have come our way have been well engineered and well evaluated. Almost without exception they have been positive opportunities."

Losing Luscar to an Income Trust
"We just couldn't compete."

Manalta Coal continued taking advantage of expansion opportunities by acquiring the Telkwa property in east central British Columbia and the Pickardville-legal property in central Alberta in 1992. Continuing to improve operations, in 1994 the company developed the Manalta Mine System UNIX, which enabled all Manalta mines to communicate electronically, and developed an Environmental Management System for improved environmental protection at mines. Gregg River Mine also introduced a Global Positioning System satellite survey for improved site surveys, which was ultimately adopted at all mines.

In 1995, Manalta Coal responded to another positive opportunity when the company bought out the 40 per cent interest in the Gregg River Mine previously held by its joint venture partners — the Japanese steel companies and Mitsui — for $10 million. "It was near the end of the contract, there were only a couple more years to go, and we figured

The new conveyer route leads to the development of special overpasses that allow animals to safely cross the moving conveyer.

1992 ▶

Bosnia and Herzegovina become independent in what formerly was Yugoslavia. The bloodshed and atrocities in the Balkans intensify.

1992 ▶

A Los Angeles jury acquits police officers in the videotaped beating of motorist Rodney King. South central Los Angeles erupts in riots to protest the verdict. At least 44 people are killed and property damage exceeds $1 billion.

it would be better for us to own 100 per cent of it," explained Ross Melrose. "This was something we had talked about very informally the last few years. Then we started thinking more about it and said, 'Well, let's give them a formal proposal.' We did and they flew it up the flagpole. We reached an agreement in December so we took over 100 per cent of the mine. That gave us freedom to operate it. It was good for the Japanese because then they didn't have to worry about the reclamation liability and all those continual liabilities. So it was advantageous to us and to them."

In the midst of all these positive moves, came an opportunity that Manalta had long dreamed of — in the spring of 1996, Luscar Ltd., a privately owned competitor of Manalta, was offered for sale. This was great news to Manalta, who had wanted to bring Luscar into its fold for more than 40 years. "Luscar was a company that we had gone head-to-head with for the last umpteen years," George Chapel said. "They have been around quite a bit longer than we have and we have been around a long time. They

"I REMEMBER BEING SO IMPRESSED WITH CANADIANS"

Canada is rich in the heritage of its immigrants. For 100 years, Loram has been graced with the breadth of experience these new Canadians bring to their chosen country.

"In 1939 my mom and dad went from Norway to Swaziland as missionaries," recalled David Gjøsünd. "I grew up on the mission station with my twin brother. We could only speak Norwegian and Swazi. One of the few professions I could get into without having financial backing was accountancy. I articled to a friend's father and they took me into their home. I boarded with them because my earnings were very, very meagre. I had to pay my university and board and so on. It's amazing that it could be done." Upon graduation from the University of Natal, Gjøsünd articled in Durban, South Africa, with A.N. Munro and Partners from 1965 to 1969, receiving his South African chartered accountant designation in 1970. That year, he joined Peat, Marwick, Mitchell, joining Protea Holdings Ltd. Group as financial director of five subsidiary companies two years later.

In August 1978, Gjøsünd emigrated to Canada. "There was a hostess onboard Air Canada who helped me," he recalled. "I needed a couple of Canadian dollars, which I didn't have, to rent earphones for our three children and she offered them to me. I got her card and I wrote as soon as I could pay her back and just thanked her so much. I still have that card. I remember being so impressed with Canadians, even in Toronto when they welcomed us as new immigrants to Canada." On September 13, 1978, Gjøsünd joined the Loram Group as special projects accountant for Mancal Ltd. He was named vice president and treasurer of Loram Corporation in 1988.

We knew exactly what they were doing. We had a good feel for how profitable they were, let's put it that way."

Despite an intimate knowledge of Luscar's value, Manalta was unable to make a deal. "When Luscar came up for sale, naturally we were anxious to get involved," Chapel said, "but the Mitchell family had decided that they would look at an income trust approach. In parallel, they would also solicit offers. If the private offers matched what they thought they could obtain under an income trust, then they would go with whatever provided the most money. As I say, we were quite anxious, but once we got into it and realized how the income trust worked, we saw there was no way that we were going to compete. We just couldn't compete. We did a fair amount of due diligence based on what we had, the information we had gathered over the last umpteen years, so we had a good idea of what it was worth. We also had a good idea of how we could rationalize it, how we could bring the two companies together. There was a significant amount

were competitors in all of our operations. Wherever we operated a mine, Luscar was across the road. They were privately owned just like we are. There were several attempts to buy it from the owners. I know F.C. Mannix had attempted to buy them out a few times back in the '50s and '60s. We knew Luscar. It is amazing how well we knew each other.

of money that could be saved, benefits that could be realized."

"We looked at all that very carefully and we still could not come up anywhere near the value that they were expecting to get and indeed did get," Chapel said. "It all boiled down to dollars. The value that we had put on it was significantly less than what the Mitchell family

1992 ▶

Representatives of Mexico, the United States and Canada sign the North American Free Trade Agreement (NAFTA).

1992 ▶

Canadian scullers, Marnie McBean and Kathleen Heddle, win gold in the women's pairs rowing competition at the Summer Olympics. They will repeat this accomplishment in 1996.

received. It wasn't because we underestimated it, it was just that there is so much money out there — people wanting to invest." Ross Melrose agreed, adding, "The Mitchells went to an income fund to raise more money. There is a lot of money out there waiting to be parked on the market, so companies are valued at more than they are worth."

The Mitchell family spun its coal holdings into the Luscar Coal Income Fund for $480 million. The issue price for the Luscar units, including the final installment, was $10 per unit. In August 1997, Luscar units hit their peak at $12.65 per unit. The appearance of income trusts on the Canadian scene had now cost not just Pembina a key acquisition, but Manalta, as well.

Loram Maintenance of Way
"There's individual pride
in each machine."

For Loram Maintenance of Way, the era following the deregulation of the American railroads by the Staggers Act in 1980, was full of bright promise. "That was an exciting time to be at Loram," recalled Jim Perkins, who joined Maintenance of Way in 1979 as an inventory analyst. "In the early '80s we weren't growing that fast, frankly, because we were kind of skin and bones here. We had some real good people but we didn't have a whole lot of them, so you got to do all kinds of interesting things. For example, you might spend your day doing something in the office on the verge of modern management. Then at 5:00 p.m. you'd find out that a machine broke down and you were now a truck driver for the next 12 hours. And then, who knows? But everybody was in the same boat and it was great fun. It was a pretty exciting time because it was just at the beginning of the growth in our rail grinding business."

For a company like Loram Maintenance of Way, the post-deregulation era presented nothing but opportunity.

Maintenance of Way employees proudly display a plaque, engraved with their names, signifying work excellence.

"When the railways moved to become profit-driven rather than a regulated cost-plus kind of industry, that opened up tremendous opportunities for contracting companies," explained Rob Matthews, who joined Maintenance of Way as marketing manager in 1989. "It was almost devastating to the people who sold equipment. It was really lean times for them because with all the line reductions and rationalizations, in many cases, the railways found that they had far too much equipment. Yet the opposite was true with the contracting side. As the railways pruned, and really tried to rationalize what they did and didn't do, there was a tremendous opportunity for a company like Loram that did ballast cleaning and rail grinding."

As Dick Peppin explained, the reason railroads were increasingly hiring contractors for track maintenance work was simple economics. "If the railroad owns the equipment and it is broken down, they still have to pay their labour and take their depreciation on the equipment, so the return on their investment is zero," he said. "If they were to buy a grinder, it was going to cost them about $7 million. They can't leave $7 million sitting on the siding because it's broken down. To prevent that, they get a contractor to bring a new machine out, put it to work on the railroad. If it doesn't perform, the contractor doesn't get paid. So we've got the burden on our backs."

The post-deregulation era also brought an increased appreciation of the benefits of rail grinding. "A lot of knowledge was coming to light on the benefits of rail grinding and what kind of financial payback it had for the railroad," Matthews said. "The railroads were learning that profile rail grinding could really extend the rail life. Again, because the railways were now profit-driven, extending that rail life meant a big payback. So the

1992 ▶

November 1, France bans smoking in most public places. The majority of French smokers ignore the ban.

1992 ▶

Queen Elizabeth agrees to begin paying taxes on her private income and to pay $1.3 million of the Royal Family's expenses, but British taxpayers must pay close to $90 million to repair fire damage to Windsor Castle.

grinding market just exploded and Loram was the key benefactor of that. The company grew by leaps and bounds as the rail grinding market took off. So it was a good time to be in the railway contracting business and an especially good time to be in the contracting business that provided rail grinding services."

Along with being at the right place at the right time, Loram Maintenance of Way had one other key asset — people. Loram people are keenly aware of their reputation in the industry and have a tremendous sense of pride in the work they do and in their accomplishments. "I think that's what makes a Loram individual," Peppin said. "He takes pride in that he had something to do with this piece of equipment that we invented. Time after time, we take a prototype piece of equipment out of the shop and everybody goes and looks at it and they say, 'This is my area,' 'That's my area,' and so on. There's individual pride in each machine."

"I can walk down a machine and see everything my signature's on," concurred Bruce Tubbs, operations manager, grinding services. "I can also see the signature on the machine of the assistants and superintendents, right down to guys who have only been working here a short time. A guy as new as that has got some engineering changes that are a major part of making that machine do its job better or more productively."

Because of this group effort, Loram people are always looking for new and better ways to do things. "We're always asking, 'What if we did it this way?' or 'What if we did it that way?'" said Joe Mastracchio, operations manager, ballast and grade. "Everybody's doing that, even the newest operator on the machine. He comes out and sees something and says, 'Well, what if we did it this way?' All kinds of suggestions come from the guys running the machines. That's how the company got to where it's at today."

The company also puts a premium on professionalism, which means careful attention to detail, even down to such simple things as keeping the machinery clean. "We never let a machine get dirty," said Peppin. "Cleanliness is next to godliness, as they told me in school! I've had a lot of railroad people come over to me and say, 'Coming on a Loram machine is just like going into my wife's kitchen after she's washed the dishes. Very clean and everything's orderly and in its place.' Well, that's what makes a man. If a guy comes to work every morning and he's got grubby clothes on and he gets onto a grubby machine, his attitude is totally different."

THE JOYS OF BUSINESS TRAVEL

"I'm quitting as soon as I get back home."

"India is a truly fascinating place," recalled Rob Matthews, Maintenance of Way's vice president of marketing, who spent time in India helping the company establish a foothold. "Not always fun, but always fiercely interesting. I remember one time, I decided to take the train from

Delhi to Calcutta rather than fly, for a couple of reasons. One, I wanted to take the train and two, flying in India on those airlines is kind of a frightening experience.

"I booked a first-class sleeper. I got on the train and found out the first-class sleeper was a compartment and I was in there with three Indian chaps whom I didn't know from Adam. We started out in the late afternoon and we were cruising right along in the train, looking out at the panorama of India through the window. We were all talking. Some of them spoke very good English and others were tough to understand; still, we were having a good chat and really a fascinating conversation. The Indian music was being piped in over the loudspeaker on the train, and I thought, 'This is the greatest job in the world, what a wonderful experience.' Then dinner came."

"I ate dinner and I just got sick as a dog," Matthews said. "In the compartment that night, I was up and down to the bathroom. I was in and out of the top bunk and these guys were all smoking some kind of very strong Indian cigarette that was just killing me. You know, my attitude changed 180 degrees. I went from thinking I had the best job in the world to, 'I have to be out of my mind. I'm not doing this anymore. I'm quitting as soon as I get back home.'"

1992 ▶

In famine-plagued Somalia, Doctors Without Borders attempt to aid the needy, but the nation descends into anarchy while gangs of armed thugs prevent world aid from reaching those most needy. A UN-approved, U.S.-led military rescue mission enters the country in December and turns into a political disaster for Canada and the U.S.

1992 ▶

On December 31, restrictions on the movement of goods, services, capital and labour are removed within the borders of the European Economic Community (EEC). Passport controls remain in effect. The EEC flag is shown.

It was exactly this personal pride that enabled Loram Maintenance of Way to keep up the remarkable pace at which it was producing new products. In 1986, the company further diversified its shoulder ballast cleaning business by introducing the Loram Ditch Cleaner. Here again, the idea for this product came from observing a problem in the field. Solving problems, coming up with new design concepts and repairing machinery have always been regarded as group projects, where everyone pitches in and everyone's contribution is welcome. "If a machine is broken, there's nobody out there standing by, watching our people work," said Peppin. "Chip in, get the work done. If it takes my labour to get it going, I'm right in there. People enjoy that because a problem is not their individual problem. It's a company problem."

A good example of this principle in action is the Loram Ditch Cleaner, which the company introduced in 1986. The purpose of shoulder ballast cleaning is to promote better drainage so that water flows properly through the ballast off the shoulders of the track bed into the drainage ditches to either side. Loram personnel, however, noticed that in some cases the ditches themselves were clogged so that drainage was poor even after the shoulder ballast had been cleaned. Railroad maintenance of way crews usually cleaned drainage ditches using power shovels mounted on railroad cars or conventional ditching equipment. The excavated material was then dumped off to the side of the right-of-way or loaded into trucks to be hauled away. Loram's Research and Development Department thought that they could develop a more effective method for cleaning ditches by applying the technology for cleaning ballast that they had already developed for their shoulder ballast cleaners.

The ditch cleaner Loram developed used a ditching wheel mounted on a boom that could be swung up to 5.5 metres (18 feet) from either side of the track centre. This wheel was capable of digging up as much as 380 cubic metres (500 cubic yards) of earth per hour, cutting a wide, deep swath below the top of the rail. The earth could then either be wasted to the side of the right-of-way or loaded into a car towed behind the machine. If the railroad chose to save the excavated earth, the Loram Ditch Cleaner introduced additional economies. "The material can be loaded into air-dump trucks, transported to some section of the track that is built on a high fill and then used for bank widening," explained Peppin. "So we solve two problems. We get the ditches cleaned, and we take the muck or the dirt and put it on the high fill areas to stabilize the railroad grade. Plus, our machine loads a 50-cubic-yard air-dump in a matter of minutes, compared to the old clamshell method where they clammed out the material and either cast it to the other side of the track or loaded it into air-dumps. The progress that our ditcher makes, compared to a clamshell or a front-end loader, is about four to one."

Meanwhile, Peppin and his staff had come up with another idea for diversifying Loram's range of services, one that took the company's scope of operations even further toward the edge of the right-of-way. On September 1, 1986, Loram Maintenance of Way acquired Habco, Inc., a company operating a large fleet of equipment for spraying herbicides

Loram Ditch Cleaners improve drainage along the sides of the rail bed. This improves the life of the railway, lessening costs for the owner. Here a ditch cleaner works in eastern Montana on the Burlington Northern Santa Fe line.

1993 ▶

Johanne Johanson, left, coordinator of the Loram Corporation History Centre, and Iris Williams, assistant coordinator, pause in front of part of Loram's 95th anniversary display at the History Centre.

1993 ▶

The Poplar River Mine is the first mine in Saskatchewan to receive final reclamation releases from the provincial government.

along right-of-ways to keep them free from vegetation. With offices in the Minneapolis-St. Paul area and in Kansas City, Missouri, Habco was a major contractor to U.S. railroads, operating six spray trains and 23 high-rail trucks. Habco was one of only five companies in the United States that provided railroads with weed-spraying services. This was one area of work where railroads contracted almost exclusively. The only railroad in the United States that operated its own herbicide-spraying trains was the Santa Fe.

Discussions for the acquisition of Habco had started in 1984 when Habco's president, Donald Horne, approached Dick Peppin and asked him if Maintenance of Way might be interested in acquiring his company. "I've known Donald Horne for the last 30 years," Peppin said. "Mr. Horne is one of the old-time railroaders, old-time equipment developers. He has been around a long time and is an expert in the herbicide area. He started Habco by himself and built it up to a $3-million to $5-million company. When Mr. Horne wanted to retire, he came to me and asked if I would be interested in purchasing Habco. I said we were always looking for something that would maintain our connections with the railroad market and at the same time lend itself to diversification." After Loram purchased Habco, it was then set up as a subsidiary company and renamed Habco Loram, Inc. Ray Wahl was appointed to take over as Habco's chief executive.

All in all, 1986 was an exceptional year for Loram Maintenance of Way. Not only did the company produce a flurry of new products and make refinements to older equipment, it also made a significant acquisition and worked on getting established in foreign markets. In 1986, Maintenance of Way sold a bantam shoulder ballast cleaner and a 24-stone rail grinder for use on a railroad operated by Intercor, a coal mining joint venture between Exxon and the Government of Colombia. That same year,

Computerized control and improved grinding carriages are technological advantages common to all Loram Maintenance of Way rail grinders, including RG10, shown working near Denver, Colorado.

Australasian Railway Services won a contract for a 32-stone rail grinder to be designed and built for the Queensland Railway in Australia.

Meanwhile, Maintenance of Way was continuing to solidify its position as North America's leading supplier of rail grinding machinery. Its new computerized 88-stone machines were receiving enthusiastic acceptance. RG10, built in 1985, went out in 1986 on a renewed three-year contract with the Burlington Northern, while RG11, an 88-stone computerized grinder completed in 1986, was sent off to work on the Union Pacific. In 1986, Maintenance of Way also built RG12, a 44-stone machine, which was sold to the British Columbia Railroad.

In the fall of 1986, Maintenance of Way began a major project to expand and remodel its facilities in Hamel. These plans called for an increase of slightly more than 60 per cent in office, warehouse and manufacturing space. The project was under the overall supervision of Earl Miller, Loram's manager of manufacturing. By the end of 1986, Loram Maintenance of Way's lease fleet had grown to a total of 24 machines, including seven rail grinders, 10 shoulder ballast cleaners, the badger ditch cleaner, the SX-16 switch and crossing grinder and the rail corrugation analyzer, plus tie-handling and undertrack equipment. The company had locked up about 70 per cent of the rail grinding market in North America and controlled a similar percentage of the market for shoulder ballast cleaning.

After the end of such an exceptional year, it was fitting that in 1986 Dick Peppin moved up from president of Loram Maintenance of Way to chief executive officer and chairman of the board. Since he had taken over as head of the organization in 1965, the firm had grown tremendously, both in size and reputation. His leadership was a key factor in the transformation of a little company called Mannix International into the industry leader known as Loram Maintenance of Way.

1993 ▶

The Toronto Blue Jays win baseball's World Series for the second year in a row.

1993 ▶

Buckingham Palace is opened to tourists.

Maintaining the Competitive Edge
"The business needed to have a new focus."

In 1987 and 1988, Loram Maintenance of Way continued to pick up the pace of its activities, developing more new products and increasing its share of the railway track maintenance service contracting marketplace. In 1987, the expansion of its facilities at Hamel was completed. In the new plant, two more 16-stone switch and crossing grinders and a second Loram Ditch Cleaner were under construction. Operations in the field were also growing, as the Burlington Northern signed a new three-year contract for shoulder ballast cleaning services, and CSX, a southeastern U.S. railroad, hired Maintenance of Way to perform an extensive rail grinding program on its lines.

A rail bed also needs the ballast periodically loosened, cleaned and replaced. Loram's Shoulder Ballast Cleaners are designed to achieve all these maintenance requirements.

Maintenance of Way was also putting its engineers to work refining the equipment used by Habco, its weed-spraying subsidiary. In 1987, the plant in Hamel built a custom-designed locomotive to give Habco the first self-propelled spray train in North America. The locomotive was equipped with special electrical controls to allow minute speed adjustments to ensure proper application of the herbicides. This self-propelled train was put into service in 1987 on the Burlington Northern. In 1987, Habco also acquired a new, larger facility in Kansas City, Missouri, for maintaining its fleet of equipment, which had expanded to include seven spray trains and 23 high-rail trucks.

In 1987, in a joint venture with Tamper, a railroad supply company in Australia, Loram designed a 32-stone grinder for the Queensland Railway. Constructed in Brisbane, Australia, this machine had many unique features, including modified grinder modules for the Queensland Railway's narrow-gauge track. The machine also featured a newly developed fire prevention system designed especially for use in the hot, dry brush country the railway passed through.

Meanwhile, Maintenance of Way continued to expand its shoulder ballast cleaning and grade services by adding two more Loram Ditch Cleaners to its lease fleet. Although Maintenance of Way produced only one new rail grinder for the North American market in 1988, the company was busy designing and producing machines for the international market, manufacturing a special 16-stone rail grinder for the West Australian Government Railways. This was a machine which could be converted to operate on narrow-gauge, standard-gauge and broad-gauge track and was also capable of doing both main line and 'switch and crossing' grinding. That same year, Mt. Newman Mining Company asked Maintenance of Way to upgrade the 44-stone machine, which had been grinding rail on its iron ore railroad since 1984. Mt. Newman Mining was exceptionally pleased with the performance of this Loram grinder, which had established a service record of 99.8 per cent availability.

In 1988, Loram further consolidated its position in the Australian track maintenance equipment market by purchasing Tamper Australia's interest in Australasian Railway Services. Formerly a joint venture partnership with Tamper (Australia) Pty. Limited to build and operate a rail grinder for the Mt. Newman mining project, the business was reincorporated as a wholly owned subsidiary of Loram Maintenance of Way and renamed Loram, Pty. Limited. The company's warehouse and office facilities were located in Port Hedland, Australia,

1993 ▶

Bosnian Serbs continue their "ethnic cleansing" against the Muslim minority while peace talks continue and UN peacekeeping forces attempt to impose order.

1993 ▶

The Calgary Highlanders assist UN peacekeeping forces in Bosnia. Honorary Lieutenant-Colonel F.P. Mannix, centre, reviews the militia.

with an additional sales office located in Perth. Maintenance of Way also extended its scope of international operations from its Australian base in 1988, when the company was awarded a contract to build a variable-gauge 16-stone grinder for use on India's broad-gauge track. This was a lightweight machine, specifically designed for the international market and for light rail transit systems.

That same year, continued losses and the prospect of future losses resulted in the sale of Habco Loram, Inc. to its prior owner. "What we had failed to realize with the purchase of Habco was just how important the chemicals purchased were to the business," explained Ron Mannix. "Once the chemical companies got into a market share battle for the railway business, Habco was put in a squeeze position along with other contractors, so we decided to get out of the business."

Meanwhile, the company's Research and Development Department was working on improved technology for future machines. As it had always done in the past, Maintenance of Way continued to seek ways to improve the operation of the equipment already in its grinding fleet, to make an outstanding product even better. "Since the conception of our equipment, we've always been just a pinch of a step up on the competition," said Bruce Tubbs. "Today, it's gone from a pinch to a noticeable difference. Our grinders have a downtime ratio of approximately two per cent and that's looking at about 35,000 miles of grinding. The competition's rate is 25 to 30 per cent."

By 1990, Loram Maintenance of Way had grown tremendously. More than 200 employees had joined the ranks since 1988, mostly in the areas of operations,

Maintenance of Way develops special rail grinders for the variable rail widths of Australian railways. Loram's SX-10 is shown grinding rail through a eucalyptus forest in southeastern Australia.

engineering and support services. These new employees resulted in Maintenance of Way's personnel almost doubling in size in just two short years to 460 employees. As a result of this growth and the company's new global emphasis, major organizational changes were instituted in May 1990, including an event that many thought, or perhaps wished, would never happen. That year, Dick Peppin ceased to be chief executive officer of Loram Maintenance of Way. Even though he retained his position as chairman, and became head of the newly created New Product Development Group, the move meant that Peppin no longer was heading the company. It was a move that many found difficult to accept, as legends, even in their own time, are hard to let go. Even Peppin, though in ill health and at the end of long and illustrious career, found the transition difficult.

"Dick is a fantastic person, but there is a time in life for everything and that was a really hard step for Dick," said Jill Lee, who, after joining Maintenance of Way as receptionist in 1978, went on to work for engineering, payroll, safety and marketing before becoming Peppin's executive secretary in 1988. "I think he literally had to be forced into it or he'd still be with us today. Dick is your fatherly type, your strong mentor. He was just someone always there for you."

"I always had a lot of respect for Peppin," said Don Minge, who joined Maintenance of Way in 1966. "He went through a lot of suits and white shirts. Every time he was out there, he'd intend to stand back, but he'd be in there getting sprayed with mud, oil or something. The thing about Dick being out there and slinging the sledgehammer right with the guys — that

1993 ▶

On September 13, Israeli Prime Minister Yitzhak Rabin, left, shakes hands with Palestine Liberation Organization leader Yasser Arafat, beginning a rapprochement after decades of hostilities.

1993 ▶

Bill Stedman becomes president and chief executive officer of Pembina Corporation.

"I'd Sure Like to Have That Peppin of Yours"

"When Richard came to work in the shop, he would work all day and most nights," recalled his wife, Mary Peppin. "I remember calling and saying, 'Aren't you coming home for dinner?' He'd say, 'I might be home in about two hours.' Two hours would come and I would call again, and he would say, 'I may as well stay now because by the time I get home, I'll have to turn around and come right back again.' I would think to myself that I would tell him he was going to have to give this job up. Then he would come home. He seemed to be enjoying it so much that I would think, 'I'm going to have to let him make that decision. He is going to say one day he can't take it anymore.' Of course, he never did."

In 1992, Dick Peppin retired after 36 years of service. For 25 of those years, he headed Loram Maintenance of Way. From 1965 to 1992, the company never lost money in any year, a 27-year record for the Loram Group of Companies. In many ways, this record can be attributable to Peppin's hands-on dedication to the company.

"Before Peppin came with us, he worked on the railroad as a labourer and he was a good one," said Brock Montgomery. "He sold the company by going out with superintendents of railroads when they were doing maintenance work. Peppin would see somebody struggling to do something, and he'd say, 'Here, I'll help you out.' One time this guy had to lift the rail up to get some piece of iron in. Dick said, 'I'll help you old man. Where's your shovel? Put your shovel down there. Put your pry on here and lift it up and you won't have all this trouble bending over and you can do it twice as fast.' The superintendent was standing there and said, 'Gee, I'd sure like to have that Peppin of yours because he knows more about how to do this work than anybody else we've got in our crew.' Peppin got that company going."

carried through to a lot of the employees. A lot of compliments came back on the calibre of people that Loram had out there. People were amazed at how we could come up with so many good people and hang on to them compared to some of our competition. It was just the way Dick went about things."

Naturally, after more than three decades with Loram Maintenance of Way, with nearly a quarter century of those years spent leading the company, Dick Peppin was a hard man to follow. "I don't think anyone stood a chance because Dick is Maintenance of Way," said Jill Lee. "Without Dick, I don't know where the company would be. Someone else could have done the same job, done it a little differently, but the way history is, Dick is Maintenance of Way. When someone else comes and tries to take his baby after more than 30 years, no one is going to fill those shoes, nor should they try to fill them, which is what Chuck's approach was."

Back in 1987, Peppin, who was beginning to experience health problems, brought in C.L. (Chuck) Borsos as his executive vice president. "Dick Peppin was a classic entrepreneur who loved the company so much he would have died for it, and nearly did," explained Ron Mannix. "We had a difficult time convincing Dick to bring in more people and talent to try and build a stronger team. Chuck Borsos was the man hired by Dick to move to the next stage of development, and he chose well." Borsos, whose last position had been vice president, international business development for American Hoist and Derrick Company, a world leader in locomotive cranes, brought a wealth of engineering, manufacturing and management experience to the company.

In many ways, the transition from Peppin to Borsos represented an evolutionary step in the company's development. "We went from the entrepreneurial phase when Dick was running the company into the more structured organization, which is a necessity at some point in a company's life cycle in order to grow," said Jim Perkins. "Dick was a one of a kind, as many entrepreneurs are, so the transition was not going to be smooth. But then you didn't want to throw the baby out with the bath water, so it was a very, very tricky thing to do."

Borsos, who took all this in stride, was very clear about what changes he wanted to bring to Maintenance of Way. "When you looked at the numbers and what was happening, the company had a remarkable history," he said. "Hard work, dedicated people who would get the job done in spite of the problems, and there were lots of those. Its equipment

1993 ▶

The "Flavr Savr" tomato awaits the approval of its sale to consumers. It is the world's first genetically altered food.

1993 ▶

The Irish Republican Army explodes several bombs in Northern Ireland during the year. While the death toll rises, Sinn Fein leader Gerry Adams is banned from mainland Britain.

was essentially handmade and its technology, at the time, was at least 10 years old. What I saw was that the business needed to have a new focus and it needed skills to meet what the market was going to demand in the future. What I tried to do was to give the people in the company the tools to learn, to grow and to apply new technology."

"When I joined the company, we prided ourselves on having grinders that applied constant horsepower," he said. "The first day or two I sat down with Clyde Hegelund, who was really and truly, in my opinion, the father of this business of grinding at Maintenance of Way. Clyde explained constant horsepower to me and how the railroads really got their money's worth when we applied full horsepower to every grinding motor. I said, 'How can the railroads be getting value if we're not putting that horsepower in the right place? We don't have the flexibility to put it where we want to and in addition to that, we don't know what the rail looks like to know what the right place is.' Coming from a manufacturing background, I looked at our machinery as factories on wheels. So I was applying all my industrial engineering, manufacturing and leasing background to how do we turn these machines into little factories on wheels to be sure we're maximizing the output of that horsepower."

To achieve this goal, Borsos launched the company on what he called a technology renaissance, bringing in outside vendors and experts to further his people's knowledge through training. "You can't make money without spending money," he said. "And you can't make money and become a leader unless you have people who are better

The building housing the Maintenance of Way New Product Development Group and training facility, bottom, and the Hamel, Minnesota, office and manufacturing facility, top left.

skilled and allowed to use those skills more than your competitor. It took anywhere from one to two years to build a new piece of equipment. By giving people the tools and the opportunity to learn how to put systems together, how to use computers, how to reduce costs, how to make machines more reliable, how to make machines that were more flexible, we got those machines built faster and better."

For Borsos, the key to Maintenance of Way's growth was providing support for people. "We launched into a technology renaissance in our company both administratively and technically to design equipment that could get more work done faster, therefore needing higher trained employees," he said. "Our people worked hard, I'm not saying for one second that they didn't work their hearts out and they did, but we needed to give them more tools to do the job either in terms of training, engineering or support. That's what I saw as my mission."

On-the-job training classes, which were first held at the Hamel shops in 1989, increased when Loram completed the renovation of a newly acquired, nearby 31,000-square-foot facility by the end of 1990. Loram quickly realized the benefits in a reduction of production time. "A rail grinder completed early in 1991 was built in the shortest amount of time in company history," said John Hadley, manager of manufacturing. "It was delivered on schedule and, on its first day of operation, it ground 23 miles of track — right out of the shop with minimal debugging." Another rail grinder, which came out of the shop two weeks faster than the previous one, promptly matched this record when it, too, immediately ground an impressive length of track.

1993 ▶

Lorne B. Gordon is named president and chief operating officer of Loram Corporation.

1993 ▶

The Peace Pipe Line Deep Basin team wins the industrial firefighting competition. Team members from left are Dave Ellery, Rob Smith, Dan Doucette, Wayne Tollefson, Lee Tindall and Perry Sorensen.

Along with improving production, Borsos reorganized the company for better efficiency. In September 1990, he merged the engineering and manufacturing departments, and the operations and marketing departments. John Shoenhair, vice president in charge of the newly combined engineering and manufacturing departments, felt that the changes had an immediate impact on the company. "In just a few short weeks, we've seen a tremendous improvement in planning and coordination," he said. "The communication lines between departments are direct and wide open. We've had significant input from our manufacturing and controls people."

Darc¹ Clarkson, vice president in charge of the new Marketing and Operations Services, was equally enthusiastic about the reorganization, as combining the domestic and international operations enhanced Loram's ability to respond to its customers' needs, a move which facilitated the introduction of the company's new European rail grinder. "We're just in the process of putting the finishing touches on our European 32-stone grinder," Clarkson said. "The whole company is excited about our newest international venture and eager for its February '91 setup."

Venturing into the European Marketplace
"It was quite a learning experience."

After pursuing grinding business on a variety of international fronts, including Australia, South America, China and India, Loram Maintenance of Way decided to take on Europe. Although the company's primary competitor, Speno, was firmly established in this market, Maintenance of Way felt that the European market was the company's next logical step.

The management team for Loram Maintenance of Way in the mid-1990s includes, from left to right, Paul V. Wilson, Darc¹ B. Clarkson, Charles L. Borsos, William R. Malmo Jr., Donald A. Powell and Donald D. Cherrey.

"Looking forward, we could see the time coming when, given our position in rail grinding dominance in North America, we would start running out of growth room," explained Don Cherrey, a chartered accountant who joined the Loram Group in 1980. After holding positions at Cenlor Services and Pembina Corporation, Cherrey transferred to Mancal Ltd. in 1988 as controller. In November 1990, he accepted the job as vice president, finance and administration at Maintenance of Way. "If we were to continue to grow, we would have to look elsewhere. We either had to look at other products here in North America, or do what we do somewhere else. The decision was let's stick to our knitting, stick to something we know. We know rail grinding so let's look around and see what's out there. We looked at Europe, and Europe was being serviced by one supplier, Speno International. Plus the European market was good-sized and they were used to the contracting concept that we follow."

For Maintenance of Way, entering the European market took on a degree of urgency as the company's U.S. market began to mature. "We have a situation where we have, for the types of products and services that we provide, a very limited market in North America," said Jim Perkins, who transferred to Loram's marketing department in 1987. "It's really limited and growth opportunities are reducing with every merger. Our product services have not lent themselves very well to the smaller railroads because of the size of the machines and just the mass of the service. You're looking at a crew of anywhere from six to a dozen people on a huge machine that has to go down the tracks to get from point A to point B. There are a lot of railroads out there. There are more railroads than there have probably ever been namewise, short lines and regionals and that type of thing, but they are separated. If we could put our equipment on a truck and

1993 ▶

Randall G. Provost is appointed president of both Bowfort land and investment divisions.

1993 ▶

Defence Minister Kim Campbell becomes Canadian prime minister. She is the first woman to hold this position.

haul it down the highway, pull off and do the work, we would be fine. But we can't do that, so we're really limited for the most part to the larger railroads. So part of our thrust is to look at new money. One area that we're obviously looking at is the international area, offshore."

At first blush, entering the European market appeared easy. "It seemed like a place where you should be able to get 25 per cent of the market by just introducing competition," Cherrey said. "The customers should want to have competition, because it will result in lowering of prices and better quality and more responsiveness. On the surface it seemed like a slam-dunk. Being babes in the woods, we forged onwards and sent a machine over there to do some rail grinding. We spent the first six months travelling around Europe picking up odds and ends of jobs, then we picked up a job in France for three years."

"The biggest complexity in going to Europe was that we viewed Europe as a single market and Europe is not a single market," Cherrey said. "Europe is a collection of individual countries that like to talk about a European Common Market, but is nowhere near that. Each country has its own laws, regulations, safety rules, languages and currency. Moving goods around and paying value-added taxes — when you do it in one country, it's tough enough, but when you try to do it in 10 countries in one year, it becomes an administrative headache. It was quite a learning experience, I guess is probably the way to explain it. It was a somewhat expensive learning lesson on how to do business in Europe."

In 1991, Loram Maintenance of Way acquired the patents and completed negotiations for the remaining assets of Rotrametro S.R.L., an Italian transit rail grinding company known as "Rotra" in the industry. The acquisition of Rotra, which was completed in early 1992,

Top: The modular construction techniques employed by Maintenance of Way allow their SPML series grinders to be easily shipped to the European operation, Loram Rail Limited.

Above: Completed in 1992, Loram Maintenance of Way, Inc. acquires Rotrametro S.R.L., an Italian transit rail grinding company. The Rotra grinders, shown, will help develop the next generation of transit and light rail grinders.

included the assets, patents, machines and business of Rotra. Maintenance of Way renamed its new Italian subsidiary, whose company's office and manufacturing facilities were located near Venice, Loram S.r.l.

The Rotra acquisition brought more challenges to the company's involvement in Europe. One person who experienced these challenges firsthand was P.V. (Paul) Wilson, the son of F.C. Mannix's sister, Luella, and her husband Don. Upon graduation from the University of Alberta in Edmonton with a bachelor of science degree in chemical engineering in 1970, Wilson worked for a year in the oil patch before setting off to see the world. Working periodically to earn money for his adventures, Wilson was gone from Canada for a total of four and a half years. Upon his return to Alberta in 1974, he accepted a position with Alberta Gas Chemicals Ltd., rising through the ranks to be plant manager, methanol facilities in Medicine Hat.

Wilson began his career with the Loram Group in 1989, as manager, special projects. The following year, he served as manager, research and environmental affairs, responsible for preparation and development of research and environmental policies for the group. He joined Loram Maintenance of Way in August 1992 as the manager of business development. Within a week of his arrival, Wilson set off for Europe. "Darc' Clarkson and I got on a plane and flew over there," Wilson said. "That started four years of wild and crazy stuff in terms of trying to get our arms around the European railroad business."

Wilson agrees that part of the problem was the approach that the company took to the market. "We swaggered in like John Wayne coming into a bar — 'I'm here to save you guys,'" he said. "The mistake we made is we didn't stop to realize that even though we were in

1993 ▶

The employee generosity of Loram Group companies earns them Platinum Awards from the United Way. Shown standing, from left, are Chris Courtland, Chris Kramer, Kate MacDonald and Ed Johnston. Seated, from left, are Val Evdokimoff, Sandy Dellenbach and Audry Gulikers.

1993 ▶

In October, the Liberals win a landslide election in Canada and Jean Chrétien becomes prime minister.

a very specialized market segment, rail grinding, so was our competitor. We thought if we knew how to grind here, we knew how to grind anywhere in the world. We underestimated the challenge of grinding on passenger rails, and we just made a series of serious mistakes."

Meanwhile, back in Hamel, Loram Maintenance of Way's shop continued to produce machines. In the fall of 1992, the company introduced Loram's new generation of rail grinders, the 300 series, and the production of the first model of the series, the RG301. RG301, which included the best features of previous rail grinders, as well as some novel innovations, was the most powerful and productive rail grinder ever made by Loram. Manual adjustments required on previous models were replaced by Loram's automated independent module and carriage tilt control, which allowed for maximum metal removal, infinite pattern options and increased capabilities in switch and crossing areas — in other words, more efficient grinding. The highest grinding efficiency yet was achieved with grinding motors of 30 horsepower and new grinding stones.

Integral to this improved technology was Borsos' commitment to training. By the end of 1992, nearly all the company's 550 employees — whether in the office, shop or field — had participated in a variety of training and upgrading programs designed to improve their personal skills and their on-the-job performance. This was a tremendous increase from just three years ago when they held the first on-the-job training classes at the Hamel shop; by August of that year, only 82 operators had attended a total of 11 courses.

On January 1, 1993, Borsos reorganized the company so that the international business was separate from

Top: Loram introduces their next generation of rail grinders, the 300 series, in 1992. RG301 is the most powerful and productive rail grinder ever made.

Above: C21, Loram's new, internationally designed rail grinder.

the domestic business. Darc' Clarkson was put in charge of the domestic and Paul Wilson was put in charge of the international. The next year, the company introduced a new SPML 32-stone grinder for European use, while another machine was undergoing tests for use both in the European market and in North America. This was the C21, for which the company had high hopes. "C21 was designed to be used in North America and also to meet the clearance diagrams of Europe and other parts of the globe which are smaller than over here," explained John Simmons, marketing engineer. "It has higher horsepower and was designed to give us more flexibility than other machines. There are 16 stones on each car and every car is self-supporting." In the spring of 1995, the first pre-production car left Loram's Hamel shop and was tested in grind trains for six months. Then began the fastest start-up of any machine Loram had ever undertaken. By the end of December 1995, C21 was complete.

According to Wilson, the standards set by the C21 were a direct result of the company's European experience. "We swaggered in like John Wayne, but the Europeans taught us to shoot with a much more sophisticated gun," he said. "As a result of our experience there, the Europeans forced us to build a machine to a much higher engineering specification. The C21 is the first manifestation of that. It certainly had a lot of problems, but they're all minor problems that we'll fix. We invested a lot of money in Europe and as a result of that, our engineering effort is much more sophisticated than it has ever been. We're being held to a higher standard and we can meet a higher standard of engineering demands than we ever had before."

1993 ▶

Loram-developed grinding stones are one component that make Loram grinders technologically superior.

1994 ▶

John Durish, Andre Czychun and Lou Goulet, from left to right, plan the Lake Erie drilling season.

1994 ▶

Maintenance of Way introduces the first camp car in Europe. It is a converted passenger car.

"It's a whole new world."

While Maintenance of Way was learning the European market, back in the United States, the railroad industry continued to experience tremendous change. At year-end 1994, there were 531 railroads operating in the United States, but only 12 of these lines ranked as Class I carriers — railroads with revenues exceeding $250 million US. These 12 railroads collectively generated $29.9 billion, or 90 per cent of the industry's total revenues in 1994. On a pro forma basis, the five largest railroads — Union Pacific, Burlington Northern Santa Fe, CSX Transportation, Norfolk Southern and Conrail — collectively accounted for 85 per cent of total industry revenue in 1994.

Such concentration stands in stark contrast to 1974, when the nation's five largest railroads had about a 40 per cent share of revenues. Industry concentration moved to even higher levels in 1995. After a decade-long lull, merger mania once again swept the rail industry. By October 1995, there were only 10 Class I railroads remaining. Following the acquisition of Southern Pacific by Union Pacific, only nine railroads of significant size existed by mid-1996.

In June 1996, Chuck Borsos announced that he would be retiring at the end of the year. "Since I joined Maintenance of Way almost a decade ago," he said, "I have seen many changes. Then, the average speed of our grinding fleet was 2.2 miles (3.5 kilometres) per hour. Now, the average is close to five miles (eight kilometres) per hour and some grinders are routinely working at 10 miles (16 kilometres) per hour. We have not only improved working speed, but productivity has increased. Grinding technology has changed. It is more flexible, more powerful, more accurate than before. The importance of good ballast and ditch cleaning has grown and will continue to grow. I have seen the development of electronic tools — vision systems and control systems — which helped raise our standards of quality and precision even higher. Loram could not have accelerated its growth without computer technology and the innovative applications of technology that will continue to be important in Loram's future."

Chuck Borsos, right, retires at the end of 1996 after 10 years' service. Paul Wilson is selected to replace him and is named president and chief executive officer.

"I am very proud of our accomplishments in the past ten years," Borsos said. "I recognize the contributions everyone at Loram has made to improve what we do and how we do it. The people's can-do attitude and competitive spirit have made Loram the market leader in North America and are helping the company establish successful operations in other parts of the world. It will be interesting to watch us grow. We're not able to grow as fast as coal companies or oil companies that go out and make $100-million acquisitions, so we have to do it the hard way. We do it ourselves, scratch it out and take it away from our competitors on the battlefield rather than through the ranks. It's a great little business."

When Borsos announced that he would be retiring at the end of the year, Loram announced his successor. For some people, the name given came as a bit of a shock. It is also fair to say that no one was more surprised to learn that he would succeed Borsos than the successor himself. While there were several excellent candidates, the person chosen by top management in Calgary was Paul Wilson. Yet while management unanimously thought Wilson was the best person for the job, Wilson did not think he would be considered because of the challenges still needing attention in Europe. "I just assumed they would want me to stay there and keep going to maintain the continuity," he said. "When I heard, I was as stunned as anybody that this was what they had decided to do."

1994 ▶

James Diaz, far left, wins the gold medal and concerto competition at the Calgary International Organ Festival competition. Other finalists shown are Alan Morrison, silver medal, Susanne Rohn, bronze medal, Junko Ito, Catherine Rodland, Anastasia Sidelnikova and Luca Antoniotti.

With the appointment of Wilson to the top spot of the company, Loram Maintenance of Way once again entered a new phase of its development. "Everyone has a job to do," explained Jill Lee, who by now had served as executive secretary to all three of Maintenance of Way's presidents — Peppin, Borsos and Wilson. "Dick did his job by starting from the ground up and building it and developing new equipment. He brought the company to a big success. Chuck took over through a lot of turmoil and a lot of change. He kept the outfit going and did a good job of it. Now we're going into the Paul Wilson era and Paul brings other strengths to the company."

"Paul is a very patient person," Lee said. "He's a very clear, quick thinker. He sits back and looks at the situation first. He is very good at analyzing to see what is going on. He is also very willing to listen to what people have to say, taking their opinions into account. Everything Paul does, he looks at and says, 'Why are we doing this? Is there a better way?' He's looking at everything no matter how minute a detail it is and asking the basic questions. At first people were appalled, then after they started seeing that it was not just them that he was focusing on, they were very enlightened by his interest. He has won a lot of support by doing that."

Another area where Wilson won support was his visits to the field. "In the first three months since the announcement was made, Paul has made four machine visits," Lee said. "The field operations people are just so impressed. One operator was down underneath a rail grinder changing a part. Paul was down under the machine watching and asking him, 'What are you doing? Why are you doing that?' He's down there with the guys in the grease and the dirt. He's right where he needs to be. He has won everyone's respect. People believe in Paul,

A Loram LT-Type II grinder at work on the Portland, Oregon, light rail system. These machines include complete dust suppression systems and are as quiet as a passing automobile.

that he does care what each person is doing. He cares about the bottom line of the company, he cares about safety. He believes in a good, honest, hard day's work from everyone. Everyone is working harder, smarter and just being more objective."

Wilson had just one word he wanted to bring to the company — intensity. "The message I started out with was I'm not happy with the intensity with which the management group was approaching the running of this company," he said. Wilson soon brought his focus to bear on other areas of the company. For one thing, he wanted to finish the job in Europe. "Things are still tough in Europe," he said. "But there will always be this big pot of gold at the end of the rainbow because the market is clamouring for competition. We need to know how to compete in that market. We've paid our dues, let's keep going."

Europe aside, the challenges facing Loram Maintenance of Way are many and complex. This is due, in part, to the fact that the company has to periodically reinvent itself as it continually puts itself out of work. In the earliest days, the company concentrated on under-track work. To support the rails, they replaced inefficient dirt and cinder ballast with long-lasting crushed rock ballast and replaced worn-out ties with tie inserters. They then concentrated on shoulder ballast cleaning and ditch digging to allow the new ballast to drain properly. At this point, the company shifted to the top of the rail, concentrating on rail grinding to improve the riding surface of the rail. After more than a decade, the company had caught up on the backlog of the grinding market in North America, a fact which presented Loram with a whole new set of challenges.

"When I started here in 1979, which is over 17 years ago, we did not even have a rail grinder," Jim Perkins

1994 ▶

The tunnel between France and England opens for rail traffic. Shown are John Kuchler, right, Loram Rail Limited general manager Europe, and Ray Robson, Eurotunnel track group leader, discussing Loram's grinding contract for the tunnel.

1994 ▶

Several hundred thousand people are killed in Rwandan genocide. The UN later admits it failed to act quickly because it could not conceive that the reported atrocities were actually occurring.

recalled. "We had one, but it burnt down. We had undertrack equipment and shoulder ballast cleaners, but no rail grinders at the time. That's totally shifted. There's no undertrack anymore. We were building tie inserters at that time, too, as many as 15 or 20 in a year. That was a good business for us. We certainly don't do that anymore. There's been a shift to the service, and it's good for us. We can handle it."

"If I worked for Procter & Gamble in marketing, I could write you a book about what Procter & Gamble does in marketing," Perkins said. "Loram is a little different. We have three, four services that we provide and we have nine different customers. I have taken a lot of university marketing courses and they are very strongly geared toward selling soap. At Loram, we have no soap. There are relatively few businesses in this situation. It poses some interesting challenges. One interesting challenge is that maybe five years from now our service will be obsolete. Well, we're toast. Without something else coming in the loop, Loram disappears. We need to keep filling those growth curves. The one we have is now reaching maturity, there's no question you could call it mature. There will be some growth, but not enough to make the curve exponentially rise like it did in the mid-'80s through '90. It's flattened out now and we have to bring new things into the curve to give us a boost for volume and new business. It's a challenging time to be in the company right now. It truly is. It's a whole new world."

Fortunately for Loram Maintenance of Way, the company's ability to constantly adapt itself to a changing market has long been the bedrock of the organization. In this, above all else, the company has one utterly magnificent asset — its people. As Perkins said, "We've got good people and we carry on." In this simple statement, which could easily be the company's motto, lies the key to the company's future.

Positioning for the Future
"You have to be prepared for the unexpected."

Meanwhile, on the financial side of the house, F.P. Mannix also found himself dealing with the complexities of operating in a global marketplace. Stan Waters, president of the Bowfort Group until his retirement in 1989, recalled how the financial side of the house came into being. "When F.C. Mannix decided to separate himself from active involvement in the operations, the two sons split the organization," he said. "Ronnie took over the operating companies and Freddie created what could be called the investment companies. The two groups were then the Loram

A ROYAL RELATIONSHIP

For three generations, the Mannix family inspired a remarkable relationship with the Royal Bank of Canada. In the early 1900s, F.S. Mannix earned the respect of Robert Mawhinney, then manager of the Calgary branch. "Mr. Mannix was a man of his word," recalled Mawhinney.

F.S. Mannix's son, F.C. Mannix, never lost sight of his father's central rule that integrity was the key element in business. "Bankers are just as influenced by the calibre of the person as they are with the deal itself," said Doug Gardiner, retired deputy chairman and executive vice president of the bank. "And Fred C. Mannix went far further in that direction than anybody. We backed this man time and time again."

Master of ceremonies, David Gjøsünd, welcomes Royal Bank guests.

Tom Dobson, who handled the Royal Bank's dealings with the Loram Group for years, felt that the integrity of the Mannix family provided the foundation for a relationship that was an exception to a general banking rule. "What we felt with Mannix was that it was a very personal business," he explained. "As a banker, you believed that if you ever got into real trouble, the Mannix family would do their best to extricate you. They would not walk away hiding behind corporate protection. I think that was a major factor in our relationship — the integrity of the family and that type of trust."

"F.S. Mannix trained F.C. Mannix, who trained F.P. and Ron," said David Kitchen, who became manager of the Royal Bank's Calgary branch in 1975. "They believe very strongly in relationships, and it has always been a great relationship between the bank and the Mannix people. I know of no other relationship in the bank like the one with the Mannix people. There is a level of communication that I've rarely, if ever, seen between a client and a bank."

1994 ▶

Exiled author Aleksandr Solzhenitsyn and his wife return to Russia.

1994 ▶

This poster in France welcomes those who have come to commemorate the 50th anniversary of the World War II Allied invasion of Europe, D-Day.

Group, the operating companies, and the Bowfort Group, the investment companies. F.P. was a 50 per cent shareholder in all the operating companies and Ronnie was a shareholder in all the investment companies."

"The Bowfort Group was primarily equity investment, investment banking (venture capital) and real estate," Waters said. "In fact, Bowfort specifically tried to stay away from anything that had an operational flavour. We did not want to run things, we wanted to invest in things. That's not totally true, since we did run operations in the real estate sense; we managed ranches and office buildings and so on. However, Bowfort's main thrust was to balance our exposure, diversify. Manalta Coal is Canada's largest coal miner. The other major operating company is Pembina with all its oil and gas. So the coal and oil and gas is a very major investment but in the natural resources, with all the exposure and sensitivity of natural resources to cycles."

"Some monies generated from those two sources were funnelled into these investment sources, so we were in venture capital," Waters said. "That is why we moved into the insurance business, aerospace technology, computers and software, Atlantic salmon and aquaculture. Those were all part of the diversification efforts. One thrust was geographic dispersion between the United States and Canada and the European and Pacific Rim portfolios. But it was also the function, the kind of business activity that

The Calgary Loram Corporation staff in 1993.

Front row, from left to right, Angie Snider, David Gjøsūnd, Lorne Gordon, Ron Mannix, Randy Provost and Gloria Rothery. Second row, from left to right, Johanne Johanson, Peter Huff, Iris Williams, David Halpin, Sandra Brewin, Anne Spicer, Wes Lucash, Frances Rickbeil, Jack Murray and Roberta Ross. Third row, from left to right, Gerry Armstrong, Sandy Dellenbach, Greg Tarnowski, Carole Melnyk and Greg Sawatzky. Fourth row, from left to right, Dawn Porteous, Nancy Halliwell, Bob Gruszecki and Ross Melrose.

we were looking for in diversification. Have you ever heard of Billy Rose, the famous impresario? He wrote a column for the *New York Daily News* for years. He was a very successful investor and a wise old owl. He once gave advice to investors, which I have appreciated, and wish I had followed more frequently. His advice was "never invest in something that has moving parts or eats." That was his guideline for diversification, and we haven't always followed that.

"Anyway, after I joined Freddie, we created a series of companies under the generic heading, the Bowfort Group of Companies. One was Bowcal Management Ltd., which became the administrative and management company of the Bowfort Group. It roughly parallels the Mancal organization, which is the management of the Loram operating companies, but with the very important difference that in Bowcal all the management staff are double- and triple-hatted to run the real estate and investment companies of the Bowfort Group, whereas the Loram Group operating companies have their own autonomous management and staff structure. We also have Bowfort Services Ltd., which is the investment company where we have our equity portfolio with bond and cash management activities. Finally, we have the real estate activities for Canada in MHL Holdings Ltd. and for the United States in MHL Holdings Inc."

"We were having a very successful run on investment managing — managing our own money — and our

1994 ▶

Pembina celebrates its 40th anniversary. The company is a senior Canadian oil and gas producer, Alberta's largest owner/operator of crude oil and liquids feeder pipelines and is the largest oil and gas producer in Ontario.

1994 ▶

German concerns over "mad cow disease" in United Kingdom beef lead to an importation ban of all U.K. beef into Germany.

outside directors said that they felt we had established a track record which could be inviting to people other than the family and insiders," Waters said. "They felt that we should go out and try to market our ability to run investment portfolios. After some consideration and a great deal of debate, in 1986 we decided to launch Lorinco Inc. and in there, The Lorinco Performance Fund. Now, a performance fund is a high-risk fund aimed at the wealthy, wise and well advised. In other words, it's a kind of euphemism for the sophisticated risk taker who has to be prepared to win as well as lose. The fact is, a lot of these things are risky. We're in a risky business. You have to be prepared for the unexpected. Things change so dramatically in our society."

Risky, unexpected and dramatic change would all be prophetic words for Lorinco, which was an acronym for LORam INvestment COmpany. "The wording of the company name was Lorinco Performance Fund because we expected, through the cycles, to outperform other managers," explained J.I. (Josef) Schachter, president of Lorinco. "We weren't talking quarterly or an annual period. We wanted, over the long-term cycles, to outperform. And with our conservative bent and our quality bent, we were only investing in securities that were greater than $500-million market capitalizations. So we had a very thin area that we were looking at rather than the full gamut of securities."

At the time Lorinco was set up, Bowfort management felt that the bull market had a few more years to run. "We didn't expect the bear market to start until 1988 after the elections," Schachter said. "Therefore, we said, 'Let's have another one or two years under our belt on the long side and then we will have the ability to take advantage of the bear side.'

A GENTLE, GENTLEMAN

After serving as vice chairman of Mancal Ltd. for the past seven years and with more than 31 years of dedicated service to the Loram Group, David W. McClement retired effective January 1, 1992.

McClement was the driving force behind many strategic financial decisions of his time. A key advisor to F.C. Mannix, he also served as an extremely important transitional director for the third generation of the Mannix family in business. "Dave, in his quiet way, was able to guide many of the more difficult issues that we faced," credited Bill Bone. "Of course his knowledge of income tax was very helpful, but even more than that, his common sense and calm manner in the heat of the moment were very helpful. Especially his integrity and his way of doing business — not to try to cut corners and not to try to make cute deals, but to be very principled and when money was owing to pay it. To negotiate a fair deal but not to be overly aggressive at the expense of one's reputation. I think that strategy has paid off well for the group."

"David McClement is the financial architect of the group," added David Gjøsünd. "He is very highly thought of and a prince of a man, really. He is so understanding and helpful and yet a really strong leader in a quiet way."

We talked to people right across the country and the fund was set up. We closed the fund with 29 initial partners and $20 million of assets. Then, surprise of all surprises."

The surprise, of course, was Black Monday, October 19, 1987. "That tested all of our judgments," Schachter said. "We had an interesting experience with the markets and it was detrimental to everyone's financial health. It showed that volatility can be quickly and directly affected on a short-term basis and that crises can happen in a couple weeks; they don't need months to unfold. The precipitous fall happened in a period shorter than even the collapse of 1929. In three weeks, you knocked out about one-third to 40 per cent of the valuations. That has never happened in history. When you knock off more than one trillion dollars of value, that's a lot of money. If you're worth a certain amount of money and your net assets are there, you have no problem spending because you feel rich. When part of that wealth is suddenly gone, it changes your view. All of a sudden you come to the prudence of your forefathers — maybe that's not the appropriate way for a while."

While Lorinco got caught in a market debacle, taking risks was simply the nature of the game. "Risk and the ability to take risk is important," Schachter said. "The ability to define the risks and to harness your energies and make commitments and take advantage of them, I would say the Loram Group has a history of that. We have taken risks throughout our history, in building roads and building the coal operation and building the oil operation. To do those kinds of

1994 ▶

A technician at the Royal Tyrrell Museum of Palaeontology near Drumheller, Alberta, puts the finishing touches on a dinosaur skeleton display.

1994 ▶

In December, Bowfort Capital Ltd. invests in Danier Leather, a Canadian manufacturer and retailer of leather fashions and outerwear.

things took entrepreneurs who did their homework, who were prepared to analyze the opportunities, the risks and returns. And they had dedicated people who were prepared to work. This organization is people, money and opportunity. It's entrepreneurialism. All those facets are part of the history. They're part of today and part of each organization in the Loram Group, including this one. Though the economy may have some problems, there is always going to be some opportunity. The question is reacting and acting."

Reacting, acting and long-term planning took on a renewed priority for both the operating and financial sides of the Loram Group in the 1990s. Primary to this thrust was Vision 2000, a strategic planning initiative launched in 1989. The fundamental objective of Vision 2000 was to ensure the Loram Group's long-term growth and profitability. The ultimate goal was to decide the strategic direction for the group over the next decade. Senior vice president of Mancal Ltd., Jack Wood, was responsible for the organization and chair of the program. Vision 2000 participants consisted of 11 senior directors and management personnel including the president of Manalta Coal Ltd., Pembina Corporation and Loram Maintenance of Way, Inc. Bowcal management participated in real estate and venture capital discussions.

In 1990, after 16 months of study, it was decided that, based on the principle "building on what we know best," the Loram Group would focus on its existing core and related businesses — coal mining, oil and gas production, oil pipelining, railroad maintenance, venture capital and real estate. In other words, in looking to the future, the group decided to stick to their knitting.

Top: Some of the people who contribute to the success of the 1993 reorganization are, from left to right, Lorne Gordon, Don Mawhinney, Ron Mannix, Fred McNeil, F.C. Mannix, seated, Fred P. Mannix and Bob Young.

Above: At the successful conclusion of the 1993 corporate reorganization, F.P. and Ron Mannix shake hands. Standing, from left to right, Maurice Cullity, Richard Shaw, Bill Bone, Craig Jones, Don Mawhinney and Lorne Gordon enjoy the moment.

While the decision was made to build on what the group knew best, nevertheless, the beginning of the decade brought significant changes, as several long-term advisors to the Loram Group retired. Effective December 31, 1990, Fred McNeil and Doug Gardiner retired as directors of the Loram Group after serving 14 and nine years respectively. On September 1, 1991, Paul Christensen retired from his position as president of Trison Investments Ltd., the shareholders' office, after serving more than 35 years with the Loram Group. While he also resigned from his positions on the boards of the various companies in the Loram Group, he continued to serve as chairman of Trison Investments Ltd., president of the Carthy Foundation, as a member of the board of directors of Mancal Ltd. and Bowcal Management Ltd. and as executive consultant to the Loram Group. At this time, William M. Bone, secretary and general counsel of Mancal Ltd. since 1986, was appointed president of Trison Investments Ltd., replacing Christensen.

Effective January 1, 1992, after serving as vice chairman of Mancal Ltd. for the past seven years, and with more than 31 years of dedicated service to the Loram Group, David McClement retired as vice chairman. While he also retired as director of various other companies within the Loram Group, he continued to serve as a member of the board of directors of Mancal Ltd. and Bowcal Management Ltd., and continued as an executive consultant, working on special projects.

While the retirement of these valued advisors meant that the group would sorely miss their sage advice, the most significant change occurred when F.P. Mannix retired from active management in 1993. Although he remained a shareholder, after more than 35 years, he would no longer be

1995 ▶

An earthquake near Kobe, Japan, kills more than 6,000.

1995 ▶

Loram Maintenance of Way wins a five-year contract to grind Canadian National Railways' main line. The complex rail grinder technology would not be possible without each person's individual efforts. Ben Johnsen at work.

involved in the day-to-day activities of the company. From his first job as a water boy on the Iron Ore Company of Canada's railroad at the age of 12, F.P. grew up with the business, blazing the trail for the third generation of the Mannix family in business. "Freddie had the toughest job," credited Ron Mannix. "He was the lead member of the third generation. He was pushed harder and faster than I was, as I am six years younger than he is. Freddie went through turbulent times. His mission was to bring the third generation on board. He helped train me and supported me in building the operation side of the business. As a shareholder, he has been supportive of that growth and we have been united."

On September 1, 1993, the most significant restructuring in the modern era's history occurred. Following nearly three years of planning, a complete reorganization of every component of Loram's business activities took place. With the reorganization, two new corporate entities, Loram Corporation and Interman Holdings Ltd., were created to consolidate the ownership and management of senior member companies. Loram Corporation was established to provide the services and management functions previously provided by Mancal Ltd. The remaining operations of the Bowfort Group, Manvest Ltd. and MHL Holdings Ltd. (renamed Bowfort Capital Ltd. and Bowfort Land Ltd., respectively) were then integrated into the Loram Corporation. The Canadian operating companies, Manalta Coal Ltd., Pembina Corporation, Bowfort Capital Ltd. and Bowfort Land Ltd., would also be directed by Loram Corporation. Interman Holdings Ltd., which was established in recognition of the ever expanding international nature of the operation, would control activities internationally, including the U.S. operation, Loram Maintenance of Way, Inc.

F.P. Mannix and R.N. Mannix remained directors of the principal operating companies and were named directors of Loram Corporation and Interman Holdings Ltd. R.N. Mannix was named chairman and chief executive officer of Loram Corporation. Lorne B. Gordon, formerly president of Pembina Corporation, was appointed president and chief operating officer of Loram Corporation. Randall G. Provost, formerly vice president and general manager of Mancal Ltd., was named president and chief executive officer of Interman Holdings Ltd. and president of Bowfort Land Ltd. and Bowfort Capital Ltd.

The 1993 reorganization provided Loram the opportunity to redesign the board, reflecting an increase in corporate governance. Three new outside directors with a wealth of experience were added to the

A PASSION FOR CANADA

In his dealings with the nation's business leaders, F.C. Mannix established the reputation of being a champion of Western Canada. "I believe we have as much integrity in Alberta as anyone in Ottawa," F.C. Mannix once wrote. "We can find people who will be dedicated and as industrious as easterners. Everyone seems to think by having centralized and remote control that this solves problems. I disagree. Self-discipline is the only salvation for operation of any business or arm of government and we should have it."

Ron N. Mannix has furthered his father's interest in public policy issues. "Recently I have become aware of Ron's role in national affairs through such organizations as the Business Council on National Issues," said Professor John Jennings, Department of History, Trent University and vice chair, Canadian Canoe Museum. "I have had a number of discussions with Ron on current national problems and what has hit me strongest is his uncomplicated passion for Canada and his determination to do something about it. There is a general perception, I'm afraid, that business leaders are essentially self-serving and care little beyond profit. Ron is a great Canadian patriot, who wants nothing for himself or Loram. I find it enormously encouraging that there are people like Ron in positions of influence who are determined to shake Canada out of its pessimism and ingrained dependency on the old social welfare system. I think he will be influential in the new era that is emerging as the old centrist welfare state is fundamentally altered."

1995 ▶

J.R. (John) Morgan is appointed president of Prairie Coal Ltd. and vice president and general manager of Manalta Coal Ltd.

1995 ▶

Ron Mannix, left, presents retiring Royal Bank chairman, Allan Taylor, with a water wagon bronze from Loram's historical collection.

boards of Loram Corporation and Interman at this time: R.A.M. (Bob) Young, senior vice president law and chief compliance officer of TransCanada PipeLines; J. Peter Gordon, former chairman, president and chief executive officer of Stelco; and D.F. (Don) Coonan, former president, Caterpillar World Trading Co. and Caterpillar's vice president, Asia Pacific-Latin America.

At the end of 1994, John Cleghorn retired from the Loram board of directors, following six years of service. When Cleghorn was appointed to the Loram board in 1989, he was president and a director of the Royal Bank of Canada. Prior to his assuming the role of Royal Bank's chairman and chief executive officer in January 1995, a position which would demand major commitments of time and travel, he decided to retire from the Loram and Interman boards. Dr. Michael A. Walker, executive director of the Fraser Institute, an independent Canadian economic, social research and educational organization based in Vancouver, British Columbia, was then appointed to both boards.

To reflect the growing and dynamic nature of the group and to help global thinking and long-range planning, the international activities of the Loram Group were again reorganized in 1995. That year, Loram Corporation acquired Interman Holdings Ltd. for $60 million. Following the acquisition, all Loram Group companies outside Canada were owned by Loram International Ltd., headquartered in Bermuda.

In October 1996, another outside expert joined the board. This was Dr. John L. Ward, the Ralph Marotta Professor of Private Enterprise, Graduate School of Business at Loyola University in Chicago.

Top: In the fall of 1995, Loram's international businesses are reorganized. Those involved in the reorganization include, back row, from left to right, Justin Ferrara, Richard Shaw, Don Mawhinney, Tim Bezeredi, Maurice Cullity, Lorne Gordon and Dallas Droppo. Front row, from left to right, Don Walker, Fred P. Mannix, Ron Mannix and Bill Bone.

Above: The 1998 board of directors of the Loram Companies are, back row, from left to right, Don Coonan, Bob Young, John Ward, Peter Gordon and Michael Walker. Front row, from left to right, Lorne Gordon, Ron Mannix and Fred P. Mannix.

A former dean of Loyola's Undergraduate Business School and former senior associate with the Strategic Planning Institute in Cambridge, Massachusetts, Ward was the president and cofounder of the American Association of Private Enterprise and cofounder of the Loyola Centre for Family Business.

The Loss of a Great Man

The day July 29, 1995, marked the end of an era at Loram. On that Saturday, as the sun was warming the morning air, Frederick Charles Mannix passed away peacefully at home in Calgary, Alberta. He was 81 years old. The real sadness of mourning was mingled with the recognition and celebration of a remarkable life.

A charismatic leader, F.C. Mannix was remarkably reticent about his own accomplishments. "The only time I remember those things is when I reminisce with the old fellows," he once said. "I have always listened rather than talked, so I never did get very well organized in telling stories." While he never got organized telling stories, stories about F.C. Mannix live on in the hearts of all who knew him, as much a part of today's Loram as yesterday's.

One such story arose out of one of F.C. Mannix's visits to the Alberta Resources Railway project in the late 1960s. "F.C. flew in one day, which he used to do quite often," recalled Bill Lee, the office manager on the job. "It was mid-afternoon, and he was kind of tired and wanted to lie down for a while. So the project manager told me to take him down to the visitors' bunkhouse. We always had one bunkhouse for the visitors that was kept nice. On the way there, there was a door open to one of the other bunkhouses, and F.C. said, 'Oh, I'll go in there.'

1995 ▶

A peasant revolt erupts in the Mexican state of Chiapas.

1995 ▶

Manalta Coal's Highvale Mine achieves ISO-9002 status.

I said, 'Oh no, that's not the one. I'll take you down to the other one.' He said, 'Oh, heavens, no,' and went in. There were no sheets or blankets on the beds because the bunkhouse was in the process of being fixed up, but F.C. said, 'This is good enough for me if it's good enough for the men.' And there he flopped, right onto the mattress with no blankets or anything. He was just one of the guys. That really impressed me, the owner of the company sleeping on a bare mattress. That was good enough for him."

F.C. Mannix's unpretentious manner and innate charm inspired deep loyalty. One whose tremendous loyalty and dedication would rise above the call of duty was Ruth Jones. Her exposure to the Loram Group dates from when she was just three years old. "My mom and dad packed up in Vancouver in 1953 and came east to help my grandfather farm," Jones recalled. "On the way east, they stopped in Kamloops, where Dad found out there was a big pipeline job. It turned out to be a Mannix construction job, Trans Mountain pipeline, and Dad got a job working for Mannix. The only house

THE LOSS OF A GREAT CANADIAN

"That's what heroes are made of."

Frederick Charles Mannix passed away on July 29, 1995, at the age of 81. F.C. Mannix was widely regarded as one of the most extraordinary entrepreneurs to have been born in Canada in this century. While his role in the building of modern Canada is impressive, his single most remarkable accomplishment was his work in building the family of companies that today is known as the Loram Group.

"Everybody who worked for Fred knew him, and he knew his men by name," recalled Brock Montgomery. "Not only did Fred know his men, he knew the families of a large number of the people who worked for him and he always inquired how they were. He had the workers' families at heart and helped a tremendous number of them —paying doctors, sending people to the Mayo Clinic, helping them get a home, loaning money at a very low rate and quite often forgetting about it — that sort of thing. There was no doubt about the family feeling. I don't think anybody called it that, but certainly it was the same idea as a family being looked after by its head."

"He had marvellous, innate charm," added Doug Gardiner. "Men liked him because they recognized that he was a man's man. And the women liked him because he was charming, a good conversationalist and a wonderful dancer. He and Margaret were an absolutely marvellous pair. They had, obviously, a very happy life. You've heard some of the stories of him as a boy. Good God, that's what heroes are made of. He was a great Canadian."

they could find to rent was this huge log house. It was two storeys and it had five bedrooms upstairs and two or three downstairs. We never used the upstairs because fireplaces were the only heating; it was really cold up there. Then it turned out that the construction camp was overcrowded and they needed rooms for men, so my mom ended up working for Mannix, too. She took in boarders — the guys were Bechtel men because it was a Bechtel-Mannix job. Those were the earliest memories of my life."

Jones' father, who worked as a foreman on the pipe-stringing crew, often brought his young children with him to the work site. "He'd take my brother and me with him, because we weren't in school yet," Jones recalled, "and we'd ride around in the truck. I remember going to the pipe yard where all the pipe was stored. It was this great, big pipe. We could run right through it; it was just like tunnels. Years later, Brock Montgomery said, 'You know, when you're talking about this, I can remember two little towheaded kids running around, having a good time in the pipe.'"

1995 ▶

In September, Bowfort Capital Ltd. participates in the purchase of the assets of A&W Food Services from Unilever Canada. A&W owns and/or franchises more than 450 restaurants in Canada.

1996 ▶

Paul Wilson is appointed president and chief executive officer of Loram Maintenance of Way, Inc.

THE MUSEUM OF THE REGIMENTS

Her Majesty Queen Elizabeth II officially opens the Museum of the Regiments. Calgary Highlanders' Honorary Lieutenant-Colonel Fred P. Mannix is seated to the Queen's right.

Fred P. Mannix has done much to benefit Canada's military. "Something that has impressed me greatly is the role that Fred has played in the Canadian militia," John Jennings said. "I admire enormously his passion for Canada's military tradition — so much of it is based on the militia's role when called to service in time of war. Most people have become cynical about Canada's military. I find it most impressive that Fred is using his position to try to influence national policy toward the army, instead of just sitting back and lamenting as most of us do."

One way Fred P. Mannix has supported the Canadian military, was the pivotal role he played in the establishment of the Museum of the Regiments in Calgary, Alberta. After meeting with Fred P. Mannix, Her Majesty Queen Elizabeth II decided to personally open the museum. Fred P.'s meeting with the Queen, which lasted longer than scheduled due to the Queen's interest in the subject, caused an aide to remark to the Queen, "My Lady, you are late." According to Fred P., the Queen turned to the aide with a steely stare and said, "Sir, may I remind you that We" — the royal We, of course — "are never late."

Years later, after completing a university degree, a year of work experience and a year of European travel, Fred P. Mannix interviewed Jones for possible employment. Soon after, she was offered a job as F.C. Mannix's assistant. Yet while Mannix thought Ruth would be a valuable member of their group, so too did IBM, who also wanted to hire her. "I phoned my dad and said, 'What do you think?'" Jones recalled. "My dad said, 'Well, I just know that the time I worked for Mannix was great. They were a great company and I think you should work for them. IBM is so big and impersonal, try Mannix.'"

So in 1977, Ruth Jones went to work for F.C. Mannix. "Oh, he was a dynamo," she recalled. "He was an incredible man of 64. I can remember walking down the street with him. I had to run to keep up with the guy and I was only 28." Four years later, on March 31, 1981, one week after the Gregg River signing ceremonies in Japan, F.C. Mannix suffered his first stroke. "It was hard for him because he had always delegated just about everything that he had to do," Jones said. "Suddenly, he was faced with something that only he could do, the therapy. I will never forget this. He couldn't come to the office, so I went out to his home and we would work there. The speech therapist had him doing these writing exercises. She would say, 'Okay Fred, I want you to practise.' Then she'd leave and I'd come in with the mail. We'd do our thing and then he'd say, 'Can you do my exercises?' I said, 'No. I'll do everything else, all this work, but I can't do that.'"

Six years later, in the fall of 1987, Ruth Jones and the love of her life, Dirck Van Audenhove, who had served as a driver for F.C. Mannix, began devoting their lives to caring for him. "After F.C.'s speech got so bad, I went with him everywhere," Jones said. "I became his eyes, ears and voice. My own life went away somewhere. Fortunately, Dirck was involved too. He was involved and loved Mr. Mannix dearly. I could not have done my job without Dirck."

After their years of great personal devotion, F.C. Mannix's passing left a tremendous void in their lives. Not long after, "Ron Mannix, being the generous person he is, wanted me to have a job that I wanted," Jones recalled. "I could see that where they needed some help was organizing a program for the kids because they were all just looming on the horizon and nothing really had been done. So I said, 'I can't think of a job I really want, but I'd like to continue looking after Manfam — the support organization for members of the Mannix family — and, along

1996 ▶

France announces the end of its Pacific nuclear testing.

1996 ▶

The improved ditch cleaners made by Maintenance of Way control the depth of their cut by lasers allowing tolerances as low as 0.6 centimetres over 0.4 kilometres (one-quarter inch over one-quarter mile).

with that, what about if I helped the kids get on board?' So he said I could be the manager of the fourth generation activities. This led to developing programs where the kids would come in and work in each company during their summers and school breaks. That way, every kid would get the same experience, instead of everybody getting a different experience as they came along, depending on what was available."

Ruth Jones set up a remarkably planned and well organized program to bring the fourth generation of the Mannix family into the business in the future. Yet, when the future dawned, it did not look at all like what anyone had planned.

The Future is Going to Look Different from the Present

The year 1996 saw the Loram Group well positioned for the future. Not only was the fourth generation being prepared to come on board, but the companies within the group were in tremendous fiscal shape. During the 10-year period between 1986 and 1996, the Loram Group had experienced responsible, steady growth, with gross revenues climbing from $413.5 million to $780 million. Yet while the Loram Group nearly doubled gross revenues during this ten-year period — setting company net income records along the way — these impressive financial results were achieved with only a slight increase in employees. In 1986, the Loram Group provided employment for 1,800 people. By year-end 1996, the group employed 2,281.

By 1996, Manalta Coal Ltd., the largest coal producer in Canada, operated seven coal mines — two in Saskatchewan, four in Alberta and one in British Columbia. Five of the seven mines produced and sold coal to electrical utilities in Saskatchewan and Alberta and two sold coal exclusively to the metallurgical and thermal export markets with 16 international

Ruth Jones, left, with F.C. Mannix in the mountains above Palm Springs, California.

customers in seven countries. Pembina Corporation was approximately the 30th largest oil and gas producing company in Canada. Its oil and gas operations were situated mainly in Alberta, British Columbia and Ontario. The corporation owned three pipeline systems in central and northwest Alberta, which transported approximately 27 per cent of Alberta's production of conventional crude oil, condensate and natural gas liquids. Bowfort Capital Ltd. was an investment banking company that made equity investments in promising companies that require capital. It also invested in real estate, holding three properties in the Calgary area.

One reason for the Loram Group's success was the company's emphasis on long-range planning. Yet as anyone who has ever participated in long-range planning can tell you, what you plan for does not always turn into reality. "I have been interested, when we have done strategic planning in the Loram Companies, to look back at the past," Lorne Gordon remarked at the end of 1996. "If we were doing strategic planning 20 years ago, we would have had no idea what Loram would look like today. We would have envisioned ourselves as a Bechtel-type worldwide engineering company and building things everywhere. Oil and gas would have been a little side business and so would have been coal. I suspect the same is true today."

"My own view is that looking a decade or so down the road, the principal business in the group will probably be different from somebody who is in the business of owning oil and gas reserves," Gordon said. "I really see that the future — without knowing exactly what the future is going to be — will look different from the present." The world was just about to learn just how prophetic Lorne Gordon's words would be.

1996 ▶

The Irish Republican Army ends its voluntary cease-fire and renews bomb attacks in Northern Ireland. The first-ever visit to England by an Irish head of state occurs when Mary Robinson, prime minister of Ireland, arrives in June. Peace talks begin in Belfast.

1996 ▶

Highvale Mine and TransAlta Utilities sign a new coal supply agreement that extends to the year 2000. To maintain production, Manalta purchases seven new Caterpillar dozers, one of which is shown with Wayne Anderson, Jim Braden, Mike Trommelen, Ray Reipas, Garry Dirk and John Morgan, left to right.

COMMENTARY

Secretive Mannixes in spotlight

Mannix family

Mathew Ingram
Business West

The Mannix empire

WEDNESDAY, JUNE 18, 1997

Mannix empire

The Financial Post

Wednesday, June 18, 1997

Canada's Business Voice

Loram eyes energy spinoffs

Privately owned Calgary holding company considers $1B sale of two major assets,

Loram selling $1.65-billion of holdings

Secretive Mannix family's private firm hires RBC Dominion to unload Manalta Coal and Pembina

Chapter 12

HOW THE FUTURE BEGAN

1997–1998

What has been must go.

What has gone will rise again....

Get ready to live.

— Gustav Mahler, Austrian composer and conductor

othing is permanent except change. The Great Famine of 1845 drove nearly a million Irish from their country, starting a trend that went on for many years. With the Irish economy now thriving and an agreement for peace in the long-bloody North, the motherland's pull on its exiles is powerful. In rooms across America, Canada, England and Australia, Irish are nurturing dreams of returning home. Stories are being told of opportunities in Ireland, some that sound much like the fantastic tales envious dreamers in the Old World once told about British North America. Nevertheless, many young Irish adults are breaking with earlier generations of Irish immigrants who settled in foreign lands for good.

Right: On October 11, 1998, Mary McAleese, the president of Ireland, centre, and her husband, Dr. Martin McAleese, left, look for the names of relatives who died at Grosse Île during the exodus following the Great Famine of the mid-1800s. With them is Sheila Copps, right, the minister of Canadian heritage.

Ireland's Department of Social Welfare, which earlier published pamphlets entitled "Thinking of Going to London?" and "Thinking of Going to the United States?" recently switched gears and put out "Thinking of Returning to Ireland?" — a guide to housing, pensions and workers' rights. The Irish government reports that over the last few years, 13,000 more Irish moved back to Ireland from America than went the other way. While the turnabout is astonishing for a people long motivated by starvation and political and religious repression to forsake their homeland, revolving-door migrations like this one are nothing new. The Irish exodus is simply unusual in that it seems to involve whole households — as opposed to men without families — making the departure of the Irish cultural vibrancy more noticeable.

Not only individuals, but businesses are subject to the winds of change. Joseph Schumpeter, the Austrian-American economist whose theories emphasized the role of the entrepreneur in stimulating investment and innovation, called these winds creative destruction. Creative destruction occurs when innovation makes old ideas and technologies obsolete. For example, in 1917, Baldwin Locomotive was one of the 100 largest corporations in America. Its executives insisted there would never be a replacement for the steam locomotive and the business died when diesel came along. Similar fates awaited Colorado Fuel & Iron, Lehigh Coal & Navigation and Studebaker. Giants in their day, these august industries of the World War I era brought on their demise with an unwillingness to change.

Of course, the makeup of industry has changed. In 1917, the year *Forbes* magazine hit the newsstands, if you wanted to be a master of business, it helped if your product weighed a lot. Towering over *Forbes'* list of the 100 largest U.S. corporations was the U.S. Steel Co., with three times the assets of the next largest company. In today's dollars, the firm's assets totalled $31 billion. The company's blast furnaces, rolling mills, coal mines, barges, ships and shipyards kept 268,000 workers busy. Joining U.S. Steel on *Forbes'* first annual Top 100 were other companies that made heavy things in huge, labour-intensive factories — eight other steelmakers and another 33 companies that extracted material from the earth. These resource producers accounted for 45 per cent of the list's assets.

By 1997, steel had vanished from *Forbes'* roster. Microsoft weighed heavier than all but three companies on the list, despite the fact that a program sold by

Lorne B. Gordon, president and chief operating officer of Loram Corporation, left, with Ron N. Mannix, chairman and chief executive officer, at a Loram Corporation board meeting.

Microsoft weighs next to nothing. It can be shipped instantaneously to any point on the globe. While steel had not disappeared from the American economy, USX-U.S. Steel Group's assets were now worth $6.5 billion, about a fifth of their 1917 value. Its payroll had dropped to 20,800. One by one, over a period of many years, the other natural resource companies slipped off the list. Of the largest 100 companies on the 1917 list, only 15 survived to 1997. Besides six oil companies, there were two automakers and seven others: AT&T, Citicorp, Du Pont, General Electric, Kodak, Procter & Gamble and Sears. The other 85 companies went bankrupt, were liquidated, got swallowed by another firm or were left behind in the rush of progress. Once dominated by huge steel and mining industrials, by 1997, companies that dealt in software, computers and mortgage securities dominated many high places on the Top 100. In essence, what these products have in common is that they are products of the human mind, rather than of the earth.

Yet within this category has been much turmoil. Andy Grove set the tone for this exciting, frightening era when he called his 1996 book *Only the Paranoid Survive.* Intel, whose 300-megahertz Pentium II chip is worth more than its weight in gold, barely made it into the Top 100 in 1987. Ten years later, Intel had leapt to the number five spot with a market value that exceeded that of Detroit's big three automakers combined. In these same years, Apple Computer made a roundtrip, climbing from a market cap of $1 billion to a peak of $7.5 billion, only to fall to $2 billion in 1997. IBM went from a market cap of $170 million (in 1997 dollars), to $137 billion before dropping to $70 billion in 1997.

1997 ▶

In 1497, John Cabot sails across the Atlantic and discovers Newfoundland, establishing Great Britain's claim to North America. The Matthew, a replica of Cabot's ship, retraces his route to celebrate the 500th anniversary of the discovery.

1997 ▶

One of the natural wonders of South Africa is this limestone formation called the pipe organ. It is located far underground in the Cango Caves in the Little Karoo section of the country.

What these companies demonstrate is that to survive and prosper in today's world, it is not enough to shun stagnant industries and identify growth ones. It is much tougher than that. A mistake, unless quickly corrected, could be fatal. A small edge, expertly exploited, could put a firm way ahead of the game. Perhaps the biggest change is that if you think you are in an industry today, you are going to perish. Why didn't bankers see the AT&T Universal Card coming? Because they were bankers. The notion that a telecommunications company could come out with a credit card never entered their minds. Why didn't Xerox see Canon coming? Because although Canon's core technology was image reproduction, they thought Canon made cameras. Today, one has to understand the core of the business, not be blinded by industry think.

Over the next 20 years, an estimated $15 trillion in assets will be transferred from one generation to the next. While most of this wealth transfer will be in the form of family-owned businesses, the viability of many of these transfers is questionable. The fact is, most will fail. Thousands of family businesses will disappear over the next decade. Whether large or small, high-tech or low-tech, public or private, every family-owned business is different. Nevertheless, for a business to be successfully transferred from one generation to another, the generation in control must care about the future.

Caring about the future reflects the sense that life is not only lived for oneself here and now, but that it is

Fred P. Mannix, director.

Robert A.M. Young, left, with fellow Loram board member J. Peter Gordon.

also a trust for future generations. None of us is replaceable; each of us is a small and singular world. When we die, we leave behind an emptiness, a space to try to fill with memories. For families, this space often gets filled by trying to define the legacy of their ancestors. For families in business, this legacy sometimes defines not only who they are, but what they do. Yet this is not a legacy. One cannot perpetuate buildings or industry, as buildings crumble and industry is subject to the winds of creative destruction. What one can perpetuate, however, are principles — integrity, ingenuity, values and idealism — in other words, the legacy of a good name. Nothing in life has more value.

This book began with the premise that there is an evolutionary flow to history. One stage builds on another; each creates precedence for the next. Yet change does not always evolve as a smooth continuum. History has shown us several periods characterized by sharp breaks with the past and entirely new sets of realities and demands. For the survivor, historical breaks require a leap from the conventional into the untried. The entrepreneur realizes that while one can do a good many things with an informed sense of history, one cannot usefully deny that the past is just that — gone. True leaders realize that what may have been premises for success in the past may not be viable for the future.

The world of today is moving so fast that if we hold on to our experience too long, we will be trapped in the old way of looking at things. In other words, it

1997 ▶

Discussions and study are under way concerning the establishment of a natural corridor from the Yukon to Yellowstone Park in the United States. It is thought that the preservation of this ecosystem will preserve top of the food chain predators such as this Canadian lynx.

1997 ▶

Confederation Bridge links Prince Edward Island with Nova Scotia. On May 30, 2,500 runners race toward P.E.I. on the only day when pedestrian traffic is allowed on the bridge.

is not necessarily what we have been taught that matters. It is how fast we can learn. If we don't have instinctive abilities, we're not going to be as effective decision makers in the future as we were in the past. We have to be extrasensitive to market shifts that to other people may not mean a lot, but could be the dawning of a major thread of opportunity.

Companies fail because they become complacent. The status quo has always been easier than change. Fortunately for the future, however, there are still some, like the third generation of the Mannix family in business, who have the courage to choose their own destiny.

The Family Decision to Sell the Energy Assets
"How are we going to ensure that there's a future?"

In the mid-1990s, an entirely new set of realities commanded the attention of the Mannix family in business. With the 30-year Government of Canada bond hovering at the six per cent level, cash-heavy investors clamoured for income-producing investments. In response, a flood of new royalty trusts and income trusts were brought to market, pushing up the prices paid for resource assets.

In recent years, less than $750 million was invested in income trust units. In 1997, assets managed in trusts exceeded $25 billion, most of which occurred in the last year. These developments focused Loram's attention on the relative cost of capital and the competitive position of a corporate shareholder versus that of a royalty trust or an income trust. Ownership transferred to the public through share offerings and income trusts generates enormous amounts of cash that position

Dr. Michael A. Walker,
Loram board member.

companies for future growth through acquisition. Yet if the Mannix family wanted to realize this new reality, speed was of the essence.

The first months of 1997 were a time when booming markets made almost anything seem possible for Canada's investment bankers. Rising stock prices and investors' willingness to throw their money around meant a record year for mergers, acquisitions and financings. Nevertheless, wary investors thought they saw an ominous cloud on the economic horizon, prophesying a ten-year cyclical crash similar to the one that transpired on Black Monday, October 19, 1987. Other, more optimistic folks thought the window of opportunity yawned wide open. Despite the best arguments from either side, predicting the stock market has never been anything more than a crapshoot. As Canadian-born, former Harvard economics professor John Kenneth Galbraith once said, the only function of economic forecasting is to make astrology respectable. Nevertheless, if the window of opportunity was closing as some predicted, there was no time to waste.

On April 30, 1997, a recommendation was made to the Loram board requesting approval to engage a financial advisor to assist in assessing the value of Loram's investments in Manalta and Pembina. It was further recommended that, if appropriate, offers to purchase these assets be considered. At that meeting, the board authorized the solicitation of proposals from potential financial advisors. Subsequently, Nesbitt Burns, CIBC Wood Gundy and RBC Dominion Securities, Inc. (RBC DS) were provided a package of materials regarding Manalta and Pembina and asked to submit a proposal.

1997 ▶

The British Crown Colony of Hong Kong reverts to Chinese rule following 156 years of British sovereignty. Chris Patten, the last British governor of the colony, accepts the Union Jack as it is lowered for the last time.

1997 ▶

Studies throughout the West show the wooden grain elevator, long a fixture of small prairie towns, is in danger of disappearing forever.

On May 15, 1997, RBC DS made their proposal. "We walked them through a very detailed presentation that many of my colleagues spent a good many days preparing without a lot of sleep," recalled Michael J. Norris, vice president and director of RBC DS. "Tony Fell, our chairman and chief executive officer, headed the presentation for us. We felt it was going to be one of the largest privatizations in Canadian history. It was going to be extremely complex because we were looking at three different businesses with different universes of buyers and potentially different solutions. We also knew that, in our judgment of the market, and corresponding to Ron, Fred and Lorne's view, we had to go quickly."

Upon careful review of the proposals, RBC DS was selected to make a presentation to the board on June 9, 1997. At that meeting, the board authorized Loram to engage RBC DS as Loram's financial advisors for the project and to solicit offers for the shares and/or assets of Manalta and Pembina. "This was obviously a monumental decision which extended beyond Ron and Fred and had a lot of history related to it," Norris said. "For them, it had real implications in that they were very proud of their respective management teams. So there was real angst going on behind the scenes and rightly so. Fred was clearly troubled by the process and kept questioning whether it was the right thing to do. Obviously, that's as you would expect with the history of the family and his involvement and growing up with this business. That's not to say that Ron wasn't experiencing exactly the same emotions, but Ron is the CEO of Loram. As CEO he had to be the leader; he didn't have a choice. He was the driver. That was his job. He was the leader of the process."

Member of the Loram board, Dr. John L. Ward.

Throughout the process, the welfare of Loram's employees was a top priority. "The biggest concern for everybody, including the board and family, was what would happen to the people who had really been very much a part of growing this business," said Loram board member, J. Peter Gordon. "They had gathered together, in my opinion, a great group of management. Fred and Ron were very concerned, as we all were, as to what would happen to them. But they were faced as well with a very serious problem. That was, if either Ron or Fred should die, the capital gains tax that they would face would be a very serious blow. It would necessitate getting rid of at least part of the company under a duress situation."

Prior to February 1995, the Mannix family was not subject to tax on the increase in value of Loram until the death of the last remaining child of Ron and Fred Mannix. However, that month, the Canadian government amended the provisions of the Income Tax Act relating to the taxation of family trusts. Because of this amendment, Loram's shareholders were now taxable on death based on the fair market value of their respective interests in Loram. This circumstance, which had tremendously important long-term negative implications to financial planning and management for Loram, was a major factor in the decision to investigate income trusts.

"During the spring of 1997, I learned of Ron's decision to investigate the possible sale of his energy assets," recalled David G. Ward, vice chairman, investment banking, Nesbitt Burns, Inc. "His desire was in part driven by changes in the Canadian tax laws but, more important, he had a clear and correct perspective that values were at generational highs and that it was a

1997 ▶

Canadian Jacques Villeneuve, of the Rothmans Renault Formula 1 racing team, wins the F1 world championship.

time to act. Whether this value resulted from income trusts or the general euphoria of the market, or both, the market in the late summer of 1997 presented a perfect opportunity for maximizing one's investment in these types of assets."

While the market presented a perfect opportunity, it was not an easy decision to make. "The decision to sell the Manalta and Pembina assets was extremely difficult for Fred and Ron Mannix, notwithstanding that they recognized it to be manifestly the best decision from a purely business perspective," said Don Mawhinney, partner, Fraser & Beatty, and a long-time advisor to the Mannix family. Don's father, Robert Mawhinney, was F.S. Mannix's banker at the Calgary branch of the Royal Bank of Canada back in the 1930s. "The ability of Fred and Ron Mannix to make difficult decisions has been a major factor in the success of the Loram companies. The decision to sell Manalta and Pembina was particularly difficult due to the great sense of responsibility the brothers have to their employees."

On June 17, 1997, after months of intense thought and reflection by the shareholders and directors, Loram announced it was initiating a strategic review of its energy assets — that the company would analyze its options and actively consider selling all or part of those assets. The announcement sent shock waves throughout the business community. "By publicly announcing a new strategy for their historic companies, his [F.S. Mannix's] grandsons may have launched a new era for the family empire as it moves into the next millennium," proclaimed the *Calgary Herald* on June 18, 1997.

"Calgary's powerful Mannix family said yesterday it is considering spinning off two big energy companies

Donald F. Coonan, Loram board member.

in a sale that will certainly fetch more than $1 billion for Loram Corp., the family holding company," the *Financial Post* announced on June 18, 1997. "In a news conference at a Calgary hotel, Fred and Ron Mannix said they had hired RBC Dominion Securities Inc. to review Loram's stake in Pembina Corporation, an oil and gas company, and Manalta Coal Ltd., the country's largest coal-mining firm, and solicit bids for the two companies. Fred Mannix, a director of Loram, said the decision to divest the two companies was part of a strategic development process for Loram Corp. 'We are not selling for the sake of selling,' he said. 'A final decision will depend on our detailed review and the nature of any offers received.' He said a decision on the fate of the two companies, which are both profitable, would be made in August. Manalta produces a third of the coal mined in Canada. Lorne Gordon, president and chief operating officer of Loram, said the company mined 27 million tonnes of coal last year from eight mines in Alberta, Saskatchewan and British Columbia and had revenue of $550 million. Gordon said Pembina had revenue of $300 million last year. Its average daily production was 11,500 barrels of oil and natural gas liquids and 100 million cubic feet of natural gas. Pembina also has one of Alberta's largest pipeline businesses, with nearly 3,200 kilometres of lines carrying 325,000 barrels of oil and natural gas liquids daily. The two companies together have 2,300 employees."

"Loram has been traditionally very private about its affairs," the *Financial Post* continued. "It is not clear what values RBC Dominion will place on the companies by the time it finishes its task in August. But Ron

1997 ▶

Growing dissatisfaction in Russia is evident with the thousands of communist supporters who march in central Moscow to celebrate the 80th anniversary of the Bolshevik Revolution.

1997 ▶

Doug Flutie, quarterback for the Toronto Argonauts, leads his team to their second consecutive Grey Cup.

Mannix said the decision to put them on the block was spurred by the popularity of income and royalty trusts in the market. Pembina learned first-hand about the value given to oil and gas royalty trusts when it lost its takeover battle for Mark Resources Ltd. to Enerplus Energy Services Ltd. last year. Gordon said Loram also paid close attention to the value placed on the coal-mining business of Luscar Ltd. The Mark bid 'got our attention,' Gordon said, 'as did the Luscar transaction.'"

While Mark may have gotten Loram's attention, the Luscar deal revealed the depth of the possibilities. "Lorne Gordon is one of the best businessmen that we see in our community," credited Norris. "He has a very thoughtful mind. He is a student of what is going on and he studies trends. Clearly he was very intrigued by the whole development of the trust market. I suspect if you had to go back to a turning point, it was probably when Manalta was trying to buy out Luscar. Luscar was such a large transaction that it gave them a perspective that, 'Yes. This is a deep and substantial market and large transactions can occur.'"

The Luscar transaction stunned everyone. "Ron Mannix said to me, 'Nobody knows that company better than we do,'" stated former Alberta premier, Donald R. (Don) Getty. "Ron said, 'We do the coal mining all over this province, we're right beside them. We know that company and we can put a value on it. We weren't even in the ballpark.' He just shook his head and said, 'I can't understand it. These crazy trusts. How come these trusts can somehow increase the value of a company to where that's not what we would pay for it and have it as a going concern?' He said, 'I'm going to look into these things because it's really staggering.'"

Officers of Loram Corporation, from left to right: Don W. Walker, vice president; David L. Gjøsünd, vice president and treasurer; John K. Amundrud, vice president, general counsel and secretary; and William M. Bone, senior vice president, listen to a presentation at a Loram board meeting.

Peter Gordon agreed that the Luscar trust was quite a revelation. "I think Manalta and Pembina would still be operating as subsidiaries of Loram had we not decided that we wanted to buy Luscar," he said. "In looking at Luscar, we recognized that the value we placed on it was about 50 per cent of the market value. We realized that the assets we were holding — the energy assets, Manalta Coal and Pembina Corporation — were probably also undervalued by about 50 per cent. This made us realize that we might be better as a company, and as a family, to sell the assets and put them into something else."

"We started talking among ourselves saying, 'What is this vehicle? Should we be monetizing the coal business?'" agreed fellow Loram board member, Robert A. Young. "These questions about trusts were more than a passing thought, but we didn't barrel down into any quick decisions. Lorne Gordon then began thinking about what made sense for the shareholders. Was this the appropriate time because of the economic climate and the existence of these sorts of unique financial vehicles to consider monetizing more than just the coal business?"

Throughout the entire process, the calm, keen and cautious intelligence that Lorne Gordon brought to the table was key. "I have to hand it to them," admired John Cleghorn, chairman and chief executive officer of the Royal Bank of Canada and former member of the Loram board. "They really did their homework. They looked at a lot of options. I think it took a lot of courage. I've known Lorne Gordon for a long time. The group has been extremely fortunate to have the talent of Lorne Gordon. He was given responsibility at a very young age and has grown

1998 ▶

A severe ice storm strikes southeastern Ontario and southwestern Quebec, paralyzing the area. More than a million households are without electricity for several days, some more than three weeks.

1998 ▶

Speed skater Catriona Le May Doan powers her way to a gold medal and new Olympic record in the 500 metres at Nagano, Japan. She will later win a bronze in the 1,000 metres.

with it. Lorne can be disarming. He doesn't play to the audience. He doesn't try to overly impress people, but you can see the thoroughness of the way he approaches something. And he looks at all the angles. He's very open to suggestion. The role he's played is central. Every generation of the Mannix family seems to have that. They have two or three people who have assisted the family in going to the next plateau."

"The family has this incredible level of curiosity and are very open to new thoughts, suggestions, ideas," continued Cleghorn. "They screen that down to how does that affect us and what we're doing in the ongoing health of the family investment? Also there is this view of what happens to family companies and the desire to ensure that they don't follow the road of many others, and that is three generations from clogs to clogs. The road is strewn with them. The Mannix family has this need to look beyond the existing enterprise and say, 'How are we going to ensure that there's a future for the family and it's just not all dissipated?'"

Central to this questioning was the knowledge — provided from nearly a century of the Mannix family being in business — that business runs in cycles. "Ron Mannix felt that it was an interesting time in the business world in terms of the cost of capital that different investors would accept as an acceptable return," Norris said. "He perceived that the public markets appeared to be willing to accept a lower cost of capital and a lower return than Loram would see in terms of managing an acceptable business going forward. Ron said that there are cycles in business and we were at a point in the cycle where it made sense to consider, at acceptable pricing, exiting their businesses. They would then wait for other cycles to redeploy that money in businesses that might be more appropriate for the next century. Ron laid out his vision without saying, 'We're going to do it.' What he said was, 'We want to get some professional help in determining what can be done.'"

"Over the course of the six months leading up to the decision, we had various discussions with Loram, and

Michael J. Norris, vice president and director of RBC Dominion Securities, Inc., who leads Royal Bank's team through the sales process.

Dallas L. Droppo, senior corporate partner in the Calgary office of Blake, Cassels & Graydon, who serves as Pembina's legal and tax counsel during the sales process.

Lorne Gordon in particular, about the whole evolution of the trust market in Canada," continued Norris. "The market had grown from one that people had originally thought was a fairly narrow market to one that could encompass many types of business. Lorne was trying to understand all the angles — what were the key drivers for success, what were the downside risks, the depth of the market. He was trying to understand, as you would expect of someone of his competency, all the risks in the opportunity so that when they made their decision, they had their eyes open."

Once Loram reached the decision to review the sale of energy assets, the company took steps to ensure that the entire process was as open, honest and painless as possible for its employees. Immediately before speaking to the press on June 17, 1997, Loram broke the news to company employees. "Ron wanted to get to them as soon as he could and explain to them why and what it would mean to them and what they were going to do to make sure they were taken care of fairly," recalled Getty. "He said to me, 'Every bloody person who works for us is going to be treated fairly or this whole thing doesn't go.' Then he gave me his finger wag and determined head shake repeating, 'This whole thing doesn't go.' That's what he cared about. Fred Jr. mentioned it to me as well. So did Maureen. So, obviously it was a huge factor with them. Those people built the outfit."

To ease the impact as much as possible, Loram put in place a number of plans for Loram, Manalta and Pembina employees, including severance arrangements, sales incentives for senior management and certain other employees, retention bonuses for all employees and enhanced retirement benefits. Additionally, 1997 incentives were paid assuming a full year of earnings, each employee received a special payment of $100 for each year of service, all retirees received a payment of $1,000 and outplacement counselling was provided to anyone who requested it.

"In many transactions of this type, the fear of loss of employment is a serious blow to the work force and it's

1998 ▶

The U.S. women's Olympic hockey team wins the gold medal by defeating the favoured, world champion Canadian team in the finals.

1998 ▶

A warming of the Pacific Ocean north of the equator leads to the El Niño weather phenomenon. This aberrant weather system causes massive rainfall, flooding and unusual temperature variations in the Northern Hemisphere. Here an Ecuadorian woman is saved from her flood-ravaged home by Civil Defence workers.

difficult to motivate everyone to work carefully and hard at this critical time," said Dallas L. Droppo, senior corporate partner in the Calgary office of Blake, Cassels & Graydon. Droppo, who had frequently served as outside counsel for Loram in the past, was Loram and Pembina's legal and tax counsel for either a public or private sale of Pembina's pipeline and oil and gas divisions. "One of the most difficult issues in the sale of all three business units was solved by the Mannix family's lifelong dedication to treating others fairly and with compassion. In short, they had the trust of their employees. This trust, combined with a compensation plan which ensured that everyone who might lose his or her job as a result of the process would be well taken care of, made what would have been a big problem, a nonissue. Once the decision to sell had been made, the family's concern and compassion for the welfare of the employees and their families was evident, and the employees set aside their fear and went to work."

Project Wild Rose
"It was truly an incredible accomplishment."

Following the announcements, Loram, Manalta and Pembina managements and RBC DS embarked upon a multi-track process by which public and private sales were considered for Manalta and each of the pipeline and oil and gas divisions of Pembina, along with asset sales of portions of the three businesses. The objective of this complex approach was to ensure the shareholders received full value for their assets and ready access to all potential markets. Here again, underlying the complexity of the process was the fundamental need for speed.

"Once we were out of the starting gate, we realized this window of opportunity was not going to be there forever," Bob Young said. "So there was a tremendous amount of effort put in fast tracking this. It was done just about as quickly as any deal of this magnitude has ever been done. No one knew. The window could have closed a month before and we would have gone, 'Aw....' Perhaps depending how badly the window slammed down, the deal might not have been done."

One essential theme of the sales process was that only assets that would attract a significant premium over their going concern value to Loram would be sold. For Mike Norris, team leader for RBC DS, another essential ingredient was the name — Project Wild Rose. "In our business, the success of any transaction is usually a function of a good name, part of the luck that one tries to put on a deal," Norris explained. "We chose Wild Rose as symbolic of several things. One is the history of the Mannix family in Alberta, wild rose being Alberta's provincial flower and the western nature of the assets. The other was looking forward to the future of it."

It would be a very busy summer for the members of Project Wild Rose. "The sales process was extraordinary," Dallas Droppo recalled. "As the decision to sell was largely based on market timing, speed was critical. The sheer size and technical complexity would have prevented completion of the sales but for a high level of organization from the top right down through the outfit. While the decision to sell was made prior to the summer, the nature of the transactions, the purchaser and the price were not known until well into the process. This posed a difficult problem in that the outfit had to be ready to do any one deal, or any combination of deals, to keep the market timing advantage."

1998 ▶

On April 10, British Prime Minister Tony Blair, left, and Irish Prime Minister Bertie Ahern sign the Irish peace accord which they hope will bring peace to Northern Ireland. More than 3,400 have died since 1969 because of sectarian strife.

1998 ▶

Massive student protests, the collapse of the economy and general social unrest force Indonesian President Suharto from office after 32 years in power.

"The three business units — coal, pipeline and oil and gas — were each set up to be sold under alternative sale processes, the sale to the public through the new income trust vehicle or by private sale to a large existing business," Droppo continued. "While the workload could be divided into six teams, a private and a public sale team for each business unit, the separate teams required continuous direction and guidance. Accordingly, Ron and Fred, and their senior management team, were constantly under intense pressure to keep up-to-speed and make each decision correctly."

In July, RBC DS, management of the operating companies and Loram prepared and circulated to interested industry participants a company profile for Manalta and Pembina's pipeline and the oil and gas divisions. Also during July and August, the same group prepared a detailed Confidential Information Memorandum (CIM) for each of the three divisions. This CIM was circulated to interested parties in early August with a request, regarding the coal and pipeline divisions, that interested parties submit non-binding bids indicating their initial assessment of value.

"This was an intense process," said Norris. "People worked incredible hours, in some cases through the night to meet deadlines — certainly through the weekends. People on all sides sacrificed their summer vacations, always trying to finish, driven by the market. Everyone involved on the advisors' side viewed it as an extraordinarily prestigious assignment. Nothing other than exceeding everyone's expectations was acceptable. Everyone worked to that standard. I can't say enough about the quality of the people and the commitment that was made by everyone involved, because this only works if everybody is working together."

"It was a process of intense due diligence because Loram is a private company that really had never had financial statements or information geared toward annual reports or public offerings," Norris said. "And the modus

John Morgan, left, and George Chapel take a break in the action to pitch some loonies.

operandi in a private company is don't stretch too hard on budgets because you want to make sure you make them. But we were trying to retool everybody into having what I would describe as more average assumptions that a public business would make in describing itself to potential investors. Our general view was that all the assumptions within the Loram Group were very conservative. That's just how the business was run. There's nothing wrong with that, it's probably very prudent. But if we were going to keep these values, we were going to significantly impair the value that would, in our view, otherwise be reasonably and honestly available to the market. So you don't go out and try to be extraordinarily conservative. You go out and find a middle road."

"At the end of the day, buyers do their own due diligence, which they did, and make their own assessments," continued Norris. "But if you don't tell them about it, they aren't going to look for it. So selling the upside and the growth were critical. There was a lot of debate and a lot of time spent in getting that done. Ultimately, the documents were first-class. Particularly the oil and gas document; it was an incredibly well done document. Some of the very senior producers in town who looked at it said it was the best document that they had ever seen in the process. As much as we would like to take credit, and we'll certainly take some, it was the Geoff Merritts of the world and the Bill Stedmans because the management team was absolutely critical in writing that document."

Concurrent with this activity, each of the three divisions established data rooms to allow interested parties to review detailed information and to hear presentations from senior management. Manalta's data room was never opened to interested parties, however, as the decision to proceed with an initial public offering for the Manalta Coal Income Trust was made before any bidder reached the stage where data room visits were appropriate.

1998 ▶

During the summer, a get-together of past employees and associates of the Mannix family in business is hosted in Calgary. That weekend, the Loram Corporation History Centre holds an open house for all those attending. Alice Kramer, widow of F.S. Mannix's partner Bob Kramer, chats with Hugh Procter, a Mannix relative who worked with the outfit in the 1920s.

1998 ▶

Reunion '98, as the summer get-together is called, allows old friends to reacquaint. Everett Costello's widow, Florence Costello, is greeted by David McClement as they enter the grounds at Heritage Park.

Pembina's data rooms for the pipeline and oil and gas divisions opened in early August and remained open until mid-September. "All the people in the oil industry had their eyes opened dramatically at the size of the company," Getty recalled. "They never knew because Ron Mannix wasn't a big Petroleum Club guy and he didn't hang around with the presidents of the Calgary oil companies. Since Loram kept it all private, I don't know whether they kept track of its size. Once people were able to go into the confidentiality room, the size of it simply staggered them. Some of them said to me, 'I can't believe it. Our company is looking at Mannix-owned oil and gas assets or the pipeline assets and it's staggering.' Some in the community never realized."

Along with the work investigating potential private sales was the multitude of other tasks relating to public sales, including drafting the preliminary prospectuses. This multi-track process put incredible demands on the management of Manalta and Pembina and their advisors, essentially doubling their workload. It was especially challenging for Pembina, with two divisions under review and one management team. "Ideally, we would have liked to have cloned Bill Stedman, but that was not possible," Norris said. "So they had to, as best they could, and they did it well, separate their management team; there was a core team focused on pipeline and a core team focused on oil and gas. Bill had to swing between."

All the while, the Loram board stayed intimately involved. "There was almost a board meeting a week," said Norris. "So we had to prepare reviews and summaries and recommendations for each of those board meetings. Overlaying all of this, was an excellent governance process that was as exhaustive as we have ever seen in any project in which we've been involved; it was really quite something. It is to the credit of Ron and Fred that they had the quality of the board that they had. By and large, the board is comprised of businessmen who were absolutely supportive of the process and constructive to the process."

Ian Wild, left, David Gjøsund and Brent Young check figures at the Manalta Coal Income Trust closing.

"If you look back in hindsight, that team, which included the management of three businesses, the folks at Loram who were acting as quarterbacks, the various legal advisors and tax advisors and us, it was truly an incredible accomplishment," Norris said. "The working group went on for 20 pages of the various people involved in this process. It was immense. Practically on the original schedule, which was the first of September, we essentially had fully evaluated the companies. We had run a process that allowed all the strategic buyers enough data to make a bid, if they were interested. The credit goes to the people in each organization. And that's not just management, it's throughout."

The Sale of Manalta

From the beginning of the review process, Loram management and RBC DS believed that one of two options would generate the highest value for Manalta. As significant synergies existed between Manalta and Luscar, one option was to sell Manalta to Luscar. Luscar could also access funds for the Manalta acquisition in the same income trust market as a new Manalta Coal Income Trust. The other option was to create a stand-alone Manalta Coal Income Trust.

This opinion, coupled with management's assessment that it was critical to get to the market as soon after Labour Day as possible, dictated that top priority be given to the preparation of a preliminary prospectus for the Manalta Coal Income Trust. Considerable effort by all involved resulted in the filing of a preliminary prospectus on August 15, 1997.

1998 ▶

Brock Montgomery arrives at Reunion '98.

1998 ▶

During the awards presentation at Reunion '98, F.P. Mannix and Maureen Mannix Eberts, left, with Ron Mannix behind the podium, bring old-timers to the stage for a well-deserved round of applause. From left to right, Blondie Garbutt, Hans Olesen, Hugh Procter and Sec Procter.

The various securities commissions in Canada requested only minor changes to the document and Loram received approval in only four weeks, about a week sooner than expected. This fast tracking of the preliminary prospectus proved critical to Loram's ability to price the Manalta initial public offering at the very peak of the market.

While the preliminary prospectus was being completed, the CIM was prepared and the private bidding process was formulated. Due to the competitive sensitivities of the Canadian coal industry, the bidding process for Manalta was a staged process. Companies that executed Confidentiality Agreements received a CIM in early August and, if interested, were asked to submit a preliminary non-binding indication of value.

As this process unfolded, the market for income trusts continued to improve as interest rates dropped. To take advantage of that demand, another $3 billion to $4 billion worth of new royalty or income trusts was scheduled to hit the markets in the fall. The Manalta Coal Income Trust was the biggest new income trust and the first in line by approximately two weeks.

Although it looked like Manalta would be first to market, Loram's concern was that a correction in the markets, due to over-saturation or an increase in interest rates, might occur. As every basis point increase or decrease in the yield at which the Manalta Coal Income Trust was priced would result in about a $1-million corresponding increase or decrease in the size of the offering, timing was crucial.

In late August three non-binding bids were received for Manalta and two additional bids were received for particular mines. Of the three bids for the entire

Just some of the paperwork involved in the Manalta Coal Income Trust closing.

company, two were from Luscar and Enerplus, both of which planned to finance their bid by accessing the public income trust markets. The third bid from a United States company was not competitive. The low number of bidders was a direct response to the perception of corporate bidders that they could not compete with the now popular income trust vehicle.

While price competitive, the Enerplus proposal could not add value over Loram's public offering of the Manalta Coal Income Trust — Enerplus had neither coal mining experience nor synergies with Manalta. In addition, significant market risks accompanied the Enerplus offer as delays to allow Enerplus time to perform due diligence and to file a prospectus would occur.

The Luscar bid was for more money than Loram expected to receive from a public offering of the Manalta Coal Income Trust as Luscar, having significant synergies with Manalta, was willing to share part of the resulting savings. However, acceptance of Luscar's offer also entailed accepting significant market risks through delay and reduced control over the process. Because Luscar was not proactive on this transaction, their time to close would be the second week in October, if not later. In addition, there were risks concerning competition bureau approval and the possibility that their due diligence might cause them to try to grind the purchase price or walk from the deal — all factors which could delay closing. When coupled with the market risk and the only moderate (in percentage terms) increase in net proceeds, Loram judged their offer unattractive. Loram then presented a counteroffer to Luscar with a firm price of $875 million, with Luscar accepting all financing, market and regulatory risk and limiting their due diligence to a ten-day period. Luscar declined the counteroffer.

1998 ▶

The outfit has given Calgary's Heritage Park several examples of historic dirt-moving machinery. To ensure they remain in good shape, a cheque for $60,000 is presented to Rick Smith of Heritage Park for a new building to house the equipment and to help in their restoration.

1998 ▶

Several prizes were drawn for those attending Reunion '98. Michelle Rochon wins the grand prize of $1,998, the symbolic prize for the 100th year of the Mannix family in business. The cheque is presented by F.P. Mannix.

As these bids were being received, market conditions for income trusts continued to improve. However, Loram management was increasingly concerned that these truly remarkable conditions would be short-lived in light of growing supply in the marketing phase and increasing negative press from some analysts with respect to income trust units in general. At the same time, Loram received indications from the securities commissions that the Manalta Coal Income Trust Preliminary Prospectus would receive early clearance. This meant that Loram could initiate the marketing road show process during the week of September 8, at least a week ahead of schedule, with pricing of the issue on September 18, followed by closing on October 1, 1997. When Luscar declined Loram's counteroffer, Loram went full speed ahead with the public offering of the Manalta Coal Income Trust.

The Manalta Coal Income Trust was the first, and the largest, of many income trusts to be offered in the fall of 1997. When it was priced, Loram was quite fortunate as the yields on existing income trusts trading in the market were at all-time lows. Manalta units were initially marketed at a yield of 8.75 per cent to 9.25 per cent. The demand for Manalta units was huge, with the issue being two and a half times oversubscribed. As a result, on September 18, the Manalta Coal Income Trust was priced at a yield of 8.7 per cent. This yield was 300 to 400 basis points lower than Loram expected in April 1997, when the sale process commenced in earnest. It was also five basis points below the low end of the range at which it was originally marketed. After pricing of the Manalta

Top: George Chapel, fourth from left, adds some humour to the closing. His appreciative audience includes, from left to right, Lorne Gordon, Fred P. Mannix, Mike Norris and Ron Mannix.

Above: The closing of the Manalta Coal Income Trust. From left to right, Fred P. Mannix, George D. Chapel, Michael J. Norris, Lorne B. Gordon and Ron N. Mannix.

Coal Income Trust, but before closing on October 1, 1997, the Bank of Canada rate went up 25 basis points.

As part of the review process of Manalta, it was determined that certain undeveloped coal reserves and surface rights owned by Manalta would be of little or no value to the Manalta Coal Income Trust. It was felt that Loram might realize greater value for these assets if it dealt with them separately. As a result, through a series of transactions, these assets were transferred to Alberta Coal Sales Limited, a subsidiary of Manalta. Alberta Coal Sales Limited was then sold to Loram for fair market value prior to the sale of Manalta to the Manalta Coal Income Trust. Manalta agreed to manage the assets for Alberta Coal Sales Limited, but essentially the very large undeveloped reserves were kept by Loram Corporation.

Immediately before the closing of the public offering for the Manalta Coal Income Trust, Loram and Manalta undertook a number of reorganization transactions to ensure Manalta was in a position to operate as a public entity consistent with the forecasts in its final prospectus. These transactions also ensured that Loram had organized its affairs properly to maximize the value it would realize on the sale of Manalta.

Closing of the public offering of the Manalta Coal Income Trust occurred at 6:45 a.m. on Wednesday, October 1, 1997, in McCarthy Tétrault's boardroom in Calgary. Initial demand for Manalta installment receipts was so great that trading commenced in the grey market the day after pricing on September 19, but before closing on October 1.

1998 ▶

Late in the evening Reunion '98 winds down. Peter Walz is surrounded by Loram volunteers who are about to give a special bag of gifts to all those who attend the reunion. The volunteers are, from left to right, Sonja Hustad, Sandra Brewin, Johanne Johanson, Regina Walz and Lynn Arsenault.

The Sale of Pembina

The sale of Pembina's pipeline and oil and gas divisions involved much more complex transactions than the sale of Manalta, and a number of different permutations and combinations of transactions were considered throughout the sales process. Pembina's complicated corporate structure, partnerships and tax pools required extensive review coupled with structural and logistical planning. The separation of the oil and gas division from the pipeline division caused considerable work. Coupled with these complications was the fact that the employees of both the oil and gas and pipeline divisions were employees of Pembina Corporation, the parent company. As all other general and administrative expenses were incurred by Pembina, there was a requirement for considerable reorganization in splitting the two divisions prior to sale.

As expected, there was a great deal of interest in the pipeline division from private purchasers. A number of potential buyers performed extensive due diligence in the data rooms and elsewhere in attempting to present a competitive bid. As an example, at one time Imperial Oil had 75 people reviewing the acquisition of the pipeline division. At the same time, extensive due diligence was undertaken by RBC DS, legal and tax counsel and Pembina's management to determine the best structure to maximize the value realized in the event of an initial public offering of the pipeline division. Limited partnerships and income trusts were all considered. After much analysis, the income trust route was selected over a limited partnership in the event of a public offering.

A last-minute review of the paperwork prior to the closing of the Pembina Pipeline Income Fund.

The closing of the Pembina Pipeline Income Fund. Seated, from left to right, Lorne B. Gordon, Ron N. Mannix, Fred P. Mannix and William R. Stedman. Standing is Dallas Droppo.

Drafting of a preliminary prospectus commenced in late July, about a month behind the Manalta Coal Income Trust. On September 5, 1997, a preliminary prospectus for the Pembina Pipeline Income Fund was filed. This preliminary prospectus was approved by all Canadian securities commissions with few requested changes. As part of the multi-track process, in September RBC DS circulated invitations to bid on the shares of Pembina Corporation to those interested participants who had reviewed the books and records of the pipeline division in the data room. On September 19, 1997, the bid process closed, but surprisingly, no bids were received as all potential bidders felt they could not compete with the proceeds Loram would receive from the Pembina Pipeline Income Fund.

Initially, it was felt that the pipeline assets would be sold to a buyer with strategic interests in northwestern Alberta and northeastern British Columbia. Potential buyers with strategic interests in these areas made aggressive attempts at creating structures that would allow them to compete with a stand-alone Pembina Pipeline Income Fund. But in the end, as with Manalta, the small incremental value Loram might realize compared with the risks of delays in the process and, in particular, the increased market exposure caused Loram to forge ahead with their own income fund rather than pursue these other alternatives.

Loram's concerns with the market risk were heightened in the case of the Pembina Pipeline Income Fund, as the marketing of the pipeline fund was about four weeks after Manalta. Thus, it was caught in the midst of a flood

1998 ▶

Phillipe Kirsch, senior legal advisor to Canada's foreign affairs office, is an architect of the International Criminal Court. Adopted by the UN by the Rome Statute of July 1998, the court is a giant step forward in the march toward universal human rights and the rule of law.

1998 ▶

Loram Maintenance of Way hosts a Heritage Celebration in July. Enjoying the early evening are, from left to right, Hanna Christensen, Dick Peppin, Mary Peppin and Paul Christensen.

of income trusts — including another pipeline income fund — increasingly jittery markets and upward movements in interest rates. Additionally, institutional investors were withdrawing from the income trust market compared to a hefty 30 per cent participation in the Manalta issue. For these reasons, when the Pembina Pipeline Income Fund was priced there was insufficient demand for Pembina Pipeline to sell out the issue, resulting in Loram subscribing for eight million units (12.82 per cent) to complete the issue. One institution that initially had committed to taking 10 per cent of the fund (six million units), declined to participate on the Monday before the Wednesday pricing. The income fund was priced at a yield of 9.5 per cent which was at the top of the 9.0 to 9.5 per cent range at which the fund had been marketed.

Notwithstanding deteriorating market conditions during the pricing of the Pembina Pipeline Income Fund, the pricing at a 9.5 per cent yield and the size of the offering at $624.25 million resulted in net proceeds to Loram of $411.5 million. Loram was incredibly fortunate as the pricing of Manalta was at the absolute peak of the market with the Pembina Pipeline Income Fund not far off the mark. As with Manalta, Loram and Pembina undertook a number of reorganization transactions to set up the sales of the oil and gas division and the closing of the public offering for the Pembina Pipeline Income Fund. Closing occurred Friday, October 24, 1997, at 6:30 a.m. in the Bankers Hall auditorium in Calgary.

Top: Jim Watkinson, Pembina's vice president, general counsel and secretary, left, signs papers with Pembina president Bill Stedman.

Above: Jim Watkinson, Bill Stedman, John Amundrud and Lorne Gordon, left to right, at the Pembina Resources closing.

The review by management and RBC DS of the oil and gas division included an assessment of whether the Ontario assets should be marketed separately from or combined with the western Canadian assets. They also reviewed whether a private sale or creation of a royalty trust for all or portions of the assets would yield the highest return to Loram. After an extensive review of the tax pools, the complications of the two partnerships in the oil and gas division, the tax impact of a sale of shares versus assets, the unwillingness of the royalty trust market to pay for exploration upside and the mix of Pembina Resources' assets — with only Ontario and Turner Valley being suitable for a royalty trust — a decision was reached. Over the summer, it was decided that a royalty trust for all or a portion of Pembina Resources' assets was not the best alternative. It was felt that the most value would be realized by a private sale of Pembina Resources.

In September, RBC DS circulated invitations to bid on the purchase of Loram's oil and gas properties to those interested parties who had reviewed the books and records of Pembina Resources in the data room. Respondents were invited to submit bids on the following alternatives: for the shares of Pembina Resources, including all of the operations of the company; for the Ontario assets as a separate operation, or for the shares of Pembina Resources assuming the Ontario assets were not sold or were sold to a separate party.

1998 ▶

F.P. Mannix, right, thanks the Nitty Gritty Dirt Band for the evening of song and dance they provided at the Maintenance of Way Heritage Celebration.

1998 ▶

Throughout the year, Japan's powerhouse economy stumbles. These traders at the Tokyo Stock Exchange watch helplessly as the Nikkei Average plummets.

On September 19, 1997, the bid process closed. Four bids were received for the entire company and five bids were received for specific asset groups. On September 20, 1997, negotiations were initiated with Talisman Energy Inc. On September 23, 1997, Loram's board and shareholders approved the sale of Pembina Resources to Talisman. A share purchase agreement was signed just before midnight on September 30, 1997, about seven hours before the closing of the Manalta transaction. Talisman agreed to pay $501 million and assumed $130.5 million of Royal Bank debt and severance costs of about $6.5 million for the oil and gas division employees. The closing of the purchase and sale of the Pembina Resources shares to Talisman occurred at 2:00 p.m. on October 21, 1997, in the offices of Blake, Cassels & Graydon.

And Then the Window Slammed Shut
"Their timing could not have been better."

Mark Twain remarked, "History doesn't repeat itself, but it sure does rhyme." The elegiac poetry of economic catastrophe was about to prove this true. On September 19, 1997, bids for the oil and gas division closed. Loram announced that Talisman was the successful bidder on October 1, 1997. The Pembina Pipeline Income Fund closed Friday, October 24, 1997. The next business day, Monday, October 27, 1997, history rhymed when Asia's economic woes brought the market's climb to an abrupt halt.

On Grey Monday, the Dow Jones industrial average plunged 554.26 points to 7,161.15, the worst one-day drop ever. The Toronto Stock Exchange 300-stock composite index dropped 434.25 points to 6,599.24, a single-session record point loss. While the Dow's 7.18 per cent loss was only about a third of the 22.61 per cent loss in the crash of October 19, 1987, and the TSE 300's 6.17 per cent loss was about half the 11.13 per cent drop on Black Monday, the aftershocks were quickly felt in investment circles. From October to November, the Canadian market's appetite for income trusts and royalty trusts shrivelled from the most overheated in history to no market at all. By mid-November 1997, the window of opportunity for new resource-based income trusts or royalty trusts slammed shut.

Dallas Droppo, standing, watches over the signing ceremonies at the conclusion of the sale of Pembina Resources to Talisman Energy Inc. Seated, from left, Dr. J.W. Buckee, president and chief executive officer of Talisman, Ron N. Mannix and Fred P. Mannix.

Key players in the closing of the sale of Pembina Resources Limited to Talisman Energy Inc.

"Their timing was great," admired John Cleghorn. "I only played poker with Ronnie once. He quoted his grandfather saying that 'You can always tell how somebody conducts business by the way they play poker.' I guess the other saying would be, 'You got to know when to hold them and know when to fold them.' I was here at the bank and watching the suffering of others during the last downturn. Then I would go to my meetings at Loram, and it was like they never even saw the downturn. They're very steady, with a step-by-step approach to how they are going to proceed. They're a very private company, but when you learn the thoroughness with which they attack an issue, you see it's not by accident that they have been so successful. So here they pick the top of the market in

1998 ▶

At Peggy's Cove, Nova Scotia, a young girl carries flowers to remember her aunt who was one of the victims of Swissair Flight 111 that crashed just offshore while attempting an emergency landing.

1998 ▶

Unrest continues in the Balkans. In late September, a Kosovo Albanian rebel helps two refugees flee advancing Serbian forces to avoid "ethnic cleansing" in the predominantly Albanian province within Serbia.

a period when commodity prices were jumping up and the market was very receptive. Their timing could not have been better — by a week."

"We hit the market at the very top," agreed Peter Gordon. "That is a difficult problem now for those that remain in the income trusts, but that will be recovered too, because the value hasn't changed, it's the market's perception. As the market drops a little bit, you see the concern expressed by the people who are trying to run the company. But this is not related in any way to the treatment that came from the Mannix family and the market will sort itself out. I admire Fred and Ron very much. They are two very different people, but they're people who care about what's going on. Ronnie was a great sense of inspiration for his organization. He certainly was the cheerleader, the person who put the enthusiasm into it. On the other side, Fred was balance on the basis that he was more concerned about the past. I think that by itself was a great influence on both brothers. It was a great experience. It was the biggest transaction that has occurred in Canada in a long, long time. From a private company point of view, it was probably the biggest that has ever occurred. I don't know of another family anywhere in North America that's done this sort of thing."

"Ron and Fred want to change the focus of what they have been doing," continued Gordon. "They also want to make sure those who helped them succeed are looked after. That, in a nutshell, is what it is all about. The thing that Ronnie stressed and Freddie agreed with was, 'If we make it, we share it.' They made relatively wealthy people out of some of their employees and treated them all as family, which they were. Led by Lorne Gordon,

Top and above: Fred P. Mannix and Ron Mannix celebrate the successful conclusion of the sales process by hosting a "pour" for all employees.

they have probably got the top man who can run a coal company, a pipeline company, or an oil company, as the case may be. They have very fine people. Under this top layer, they have a group of 40 or 50 people that we used to see regularly at conferences. They are a fine example of the outfit's character. It's the Mannix family that put them there."

It is a tribute to the outfit's people that the sales caused no major market disruption. "Each sale of a business unit impacted their respective industry immediately," Dallas Droppo said. "A change of control in Manalta, being the largest coal producer in Canada, had the potential to change the face of that industry. Similarly, the pipeline division owned the largest feeder pipeline system in Canada and its smooth operation was crucial to the oil and gas producers who rely on it to get their product to market. Pembina Resources was one of the largest privately held oil and gas companies in Canada and the largest oil and gas company operating in Ontario. Each of these separate marketplaces were shaken by the Mannix announcement to sell. Senior management in companies whose businesses would be affected by the sale watched carefully to see the impact on their own businesses. Transactions of this magnitude, if not well done, can adversely affect the whole industry, and in this case, three separate industries. Fortunately, all three transactions were well done."

The outcome of the sales process was also favourable to the employees. "It was difficult to find any way of realizing the value of the assets without facing the very serious problem of what do you do with the people," Peter Gordon said. "When it came to deciding whether we would go ahead or not, we went on the basis that we

1998 ▶

On September 27, German voters oust Chancellor Helmut Kohl and the Christian Democrats. Kohl will best be remembered as the German who led the reunification movement between West and East Germany in 1990.

1998 ▶

Ron Mannix breaks ground for Balboa Land Investments' new Hyatt Hotel in downtown Calgary.

AN EXCEPTIONAL YEAR FOR BOWFORT

The year 1997 was a propitious year for Bowfort Capital Ltd., with a high level of activity. Simmons Canada Inc. sold its assets to an income fund in October, realizing proceeds of approximately $69 million. Distributions to Bowfort totalled $7.6 million, of which $2.3 million represented a return on its invested capital with the remaining $5.3 million received as dividends.

During 1997, A&W Food Services of Canada Inc. was successful in completing the sale of the remainder of its corporate stores to new franchise owners. This was the key element in Bowfort's business plan when the company invested in A&W, leading the way to a major refinancing. In January 1998, Bowfort received a dividend of $3 million, bringing its cash penetration in A&W to nil.

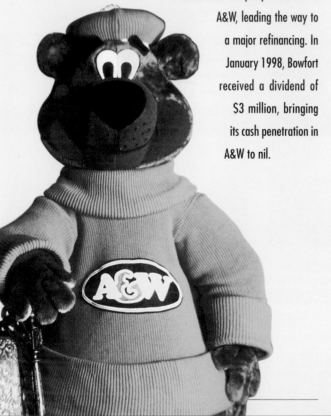

wanted to look at whether we had to sell the properties or whether we could create a number of companies that would include the skills and the people that were already there. The income trusts in both Pembina and Manalta Coal solved that problem almost entirely. In general, it took care of almost all the people and the opportunities for their advancement were there. Talisman's buying of Pembina Resources also opened up opportunities for people. So, if ever it can be a happy separation, or at least a reasonably happy separation, I think that was it."

"They were clearly thinking strategically about the future."

In just a little more than four months after the announcement, Loram completed the sale of its energy assets with the closings of the initial public offerings of the Manalta Coal Income Trust ($870 million), the Pembina Pipeline Income Fund ($624.25 million) and the sale of Pembina Resources Limited to Talisman Energy Inc. for $508 million. The total value of these three transactions, when debt is included, exceeded $2.4 billion and was equivalent in size to the Canadian National Railways' privatization, the largest privatization in Canadian history.

The sheer size of these transactions made Canadian business history. The Manalta Coal Income Trust was the largest income trust/royalty trust in Canadian history. It was also the fourth largest initial public offering in Canada. The Pembina Pipeline Income Fund was the third largest income trust/royalty trust in Canadian history and the ninth largest initial public offering.

"Ron and Fred should take a lot of credit in the leadership and the decision making," Mike Norris said. "From our firm's perspective, it was the most successful process we've ever been involved in and one of the great Canadian business stories, certainly of the decade. It sets the family up now to redeploy those funds and have liquidity to deal with a new set of opportunities."

Fred P. Mannix and Ron Mannix salute Lorne Gordon's vision and dedication to the Loram Group with the formal presentation of a bronze.

1998 ▶

Mark McGuire accomplishes what many thought impossible. In one baseball season, he shatters the record 61 home runs hit by Roger Maris in 1961. McGuire ends the season with 70.

1998 ▶

Late October, passersby look at a stuffed teddy bear that was mysteriously chained to the rear leg of the bull statue near the New York Stock Exchange. The toy bear is apparently a reference to the threat of a bear market.

"The sale of Manalta and Pembina was one of the largest transactions ever undertaken in Canada," said Peter C. Godsoe, chairman and chief executive officer of Scotia Bank and Scotia Bank Group. "It's really quite a watershed. We talk about privatization of railways and airlines. In many ways, this was bigger — just monstrous. It was the largest trust offering in history. It was a great success and I think it speaks to the quality of assets. If you go back to the turn of the century, then through the father, who was a living legend, then the boys and what they have accomplished, it is one of Canada's great success stories. It was so private, very few people knew about it. The Mannixes were always great philanthropists who helped people along the way. You can see it in employees who have been with them 30, 40, 50 years proudly. They are great employers; they were just a well-kept secret."

"As I look at family groups, in what could have been a very awkward situation, Fred and Ron handled everything extremely well," Godsoe said. "They positioned themselves with the next generation so they can do what they will and what they want without the ugliness, the family feud for lack of a better word, that we've seen elsewhere. They both have to be complimented for that. It's a great tribute to both of them, because clearly it could have come out a lot differently, as we've seen all too often, every one of us."

"They were clearly thinking strategically about the future and wished to ensure that their businesses would be assured of strong growth in the 21st century," said Thomas P. d'Aquino, president and chief executive officer of the Business Council on National Issues. "Individuals in the banking and financial community with whom I have spoken, and who were involved in these asset sales, said that working with the Mannixes was a pleasure. They saw in the Mannixes people of great integrity — fair-minded people anxious to ensure that the sales benefited the widest number of employees."

"This is a family that has said, 'We're going to turn back into the community a reasonable proportion of what it is that we make,'" said David Elton, president of the Max Bell Foundation. "They've done that. They've turned it back into the community in a myriad of ways, some of it anonymous. It tends to turn up in the strangest places where you just know that there's been a presence of philanthropy from the Mannix family. They play an important role in the community as a whole. They're one of the few people who do. If you take a look at the city of Calgary, there are a few dozen people who are

"I'M ABSOLUTELY ASTOUNDED"

Al Ries, chairman of Trout & Ries Advertising Inc., once said, "Changing the direction of a large company is like trying to turn an aircraft carrier. It takes a mile before anything happens." Ries obviously never had Loram Corporation for a client.

During the 130-day period between the date of the announcement that Loram was initiating a strategic review of the company's energy assets and the closing of the last transaction, Loram ran seven different processes, completed five major transactions, created more than 1,100 documents, held more than 20 director, family and shareholder meetings and completed $2.4 billion in transactions. An estimated 5,000 people worked to bring the sales process to a successful conclusion.

"To be able to make those kinds of swift moves is unusual, whether you're in a large public company or a private one," admired Richard F. Haskayne, chairman of the board of NOVA Corporation, TransAlta Corporation and MacMillan Bloedel Limited. "Most people can't make such daring moves, so I'm absolutely astounded."

1998 ▶

The collapse of the Russian economy causes the ruble to be devalued. Runs on banks, crackdowns on personal freedoms and empty food counters become a reality.

1998 ▶

F.P. Mannix, left, and Ron Mannix, right, present Pat Gordon with a bouquet of flowers at the final "pour" following the last closing of the 1998 sales. The flowers symbolize the sacrifices made by all Loram spouses during the four-month sales process.

REUNION '98

On Friday, June 5, 1998, Loram hosted what many hailed, "The Party of the Century." Reunion '98 brought together more than 1,400 Loram employees, retirees and others who helped build the outfit. Held at Calgary's Heritage Park grounds, reunion guests enjoyed a variety of historic activities, including riding the rails on a thundering steam locomotive, cruising the Glenmore Reservoir aboard the stern-wheeler *S.S. Moyie,* enjoying a horse-drawn wagon ride and partaking of the thrills of the antique midway.

While all these activities were great fun, by far the most pleasurable activity was finding long-lost friends. All through the park could be heard cries of, "John! I can't believe it! I haven't seen you in 15 years!" and, "Oh, my God, Mary, it is you! Let's not lose touch again!" It was a magical night that will long be remembered by all.

involved in philanthropy to the extent that the Mannix family is, but most of them are not in the same order of magnitude."

"The presence of the Canada West Foundation, the presence of the organ festival, the presence of the kinds of hospitals and universities that we have — these are the kind of things done to build the infrastructure," continued Elton. "It really means the quality of life in the community and they've made a contribution to it. They didn't have to. It wasn't required of them. It started with the grandfather. He inculcated it into his son and his son inculcated it into his children. But it's not simply philanthropy in and of itself, because philanthropy has to be matched with business acumen and a work ethic. That combination of things has been passed down through three generations."

"I have been absolutely amazed and impressed with how the Mannixes have been able to carry the continuity of their sound business judgment through three generations," concurred Richard F. Haskayne, chairman of the board of NOVA Corporation, TransAlta Corporation and MacMillan Bloedel Limited. "In my view, that's unusual because there are many catastrophic examples of how family fortunes have been ruined by the third generation. The Mannixes are probably the best example that I know of who have excellent planning and astute business decisions by all three generations to date."

"The other thing that impresses me about the family is how they've been able to pick the times at which to make major shifts in their business strategy," continued Haskayne. "For example, they were so well-known in the construction business. To collapse it and sell all the equipment and move out of that business was a shock to a lot of people, but deadly accurate in terms of timing. Their early moves into coal, oil and pipelines were also very, very astute in terms of timing. When they reversed that strategy, I was enormously impressed. First of all, that they had the guts to do it. Secondly, I am impressed with the insights they had as to when to do it. Their timing has been impeccable. I have nothing but respect for them."

The respect of the business community is generated by the fact that, unlike companies that bring on their demise by an unwillingness to change, the Mannix family believes that the past is not something to cling to, but a springboard into the future. They are not, nor have they ever been, afraid. "What I find extraordinary about Ron Mannix is his ability to make a decision when it is time to move on," said Larry R. Lunn, director and partner, Connor, Clark & Lunn, Investments Management Ltd. "He demonstrated that back in the 1980s when he moved out of the construction industry and redeployed the capital very well. In the short term, he has been brilliant in his sale of the energy assets. He recognized a unique opportunity and didn't let history stop him from making a bold move."

1998 ▶

On October 5, the U.S. House of Representatives Judiciary Committee votes 21 to 16 to send a recommendation to the U.S. Congress to proceed with an impeachment inquiry against U.S. President William Jefferson Blythe (Bill) Clinton.

1998 ▶

The New York Yankees win the most games of any American League baseball team and cap off the year with a four-game sweep in the World Series. Many believe the 1998 team is the best Yankee team ever.

"A step in the journey"

On September 25, 1997, Loram Corporation and Trison Investments Ltd. amalgamated, with the resulting company continuing under the name Loram Corporation. Prior to the amalgamation, Loram's business was to provide management services to its operating subsidiaries and to provide financial and reporting services to its shareholders, primarily in respect of those subsidiaries. Trison's business was to provide investor relations services to its shareholders, to provide financial services regarding trust and shareholder issues and to provide career planning and guidance for its shareholders' families.

The sale of Loram's investments in Manalta and Pembina materially changed the scope of both businesses and the parent company. Accordingly, it was determined that a single company could adequately provide required services while reducing overhead. W.M. (Bill) Bone became senior vice president of Loram Corporation and D.W. (Don) Walker and R.M.P. (Mike) Mears were appointed as vice presidents.

"I am saddened to see the end of Loram Corporation as I knew it, I'm sure the boys are," Peter Gordon said. "But I think it means perhaps a better opportunity for the family to grow. As the family increased in size, the ownership continued to be 50-50, and there was still a question of how the kids would come into the organization in the long run. That was a difficult problem that we solved. What's been done as a result of the final selling has put more emphasis on, not so much the transfer of assets, but the training of the people who follow the Mannix seniors and obviously can be given an opportunity to enjoy, not only the results of their family's success, but the strengths that the family has. I think it's been a very, very happy arrangement."

"It remains very much an Alberta operation and an Alberta company," said Elton. "The family established a corporate presence that is both national and international. It modified its ownership. It's part of a sense of the times, the changing economy and environment and marketplace in which we live. This isn't just something that happened overnight or was a function of a given change in the demand for a product. This is a family that very carefully and conscientiously built a large multidimensional corporate presence in the community and that's being modified and changed. I see this simply as a step in the journey. It's going to be interesting to watch the next step."

So it is in the end as it was in the beginning. On such beginnings — one man's spirit lifting him above seemingly insurmountable challenges and leading him into the unknown — hangs the future of the world. Let the future begin.

THE FAMILY ENTERPRISE
"Defies all odds"

"To build a large, successful business is a rare accomplishment," said Dr. John L. Ward, Loram board member and the Ralph Marotta Professor of Private Enterprise at Loyola University in Chicago. "To reach the third or fourth generation of family ownership and control defies all odds. It is truly a special economic and family rarity."

"When successful, multi-generational families in business pause to reflect upon the special advantages they have, they almost always conclude that perpetuating the family business tradition is worth substantial extra effort," continued Ward. "This resolve is strengthened by the witness of young, competent, enthusiastic family members making a proud mark. The family business offers tremendous opportunities for individuals. The overriding challenge is how to integrate the need for business continuity and the need for personal independence. Many vehicles help reconcile this contradiction. Leading and governing this process of reconciliation is the central task for the family."

Two pioneers in the field of family business are Philippe and Nan-B de Gaspé Beaubien, founders of the Institute for Family Enterprise in Montreal. The Mannix family has attended the institute's conferences addressing the special issues that arise in a family enterprise. "The association of the Mannix family and the Institute for Family Enterprise has evolved into a true partnership," said the de Gaspé Beaubiens. "We are now at a point where our partnership will endure into the future, because it is based on knowledge, respect, trust and caring."

Above: Descendants of F.S. and Byryid Mannix pose with their families and friends at "Stonewall '98." This Mannix family gathering was held during October in Winnipeg and Stonewall, Manitoba. More than 360 descendants of George Charles and Frances Bunn Mannix met to celebrate the importance of family.

1998 ▶

John Glenn in 1961 becomes the first U.S. astronaut to orbit the Earth. He returns to space October 29 on the U.S. space shuttle Discovery.

1998 ▶

Horses, and the ranch staff that work them, are still vital to the success of the outfit.

Acknowledgments

Written by:

Sharon Christine Mercer

Time Line and Photo Captions by:

Chris Heckman

Researched by:

Kathy E. Anderson, Jay C. Cross, David Finch, Sam Hasegawa, Chris Heckman,
Ruth M. Jones, Margaret-Jean Mannix, Scott Munson, Miriam (Stein) Real and Jay Scott.

Edited by:

Chris Heckman and Linda Rasmussen.

Proofread by:

Linda Rasmussen of Proof Positive Communications.

Review Committee:

William M. Bone, Maureen G. Eberts, Lorne B. Gordon, Robert A. Gruszecki,
Ruth M. Jones, Fred P. Mannix and Ron N. Mannix.

Photographers:

Dozens of photographers, both amateur and professional, have contributed to this book.
Special thanks to: John Bagshaw, Dwayne Brown, David Kitchen, Hilda Onions, Mark Vitaris and
the many Loram employees who donated photos and memorabilia to the Loram History Centre.

Photo Illustration Team:

Headed by Chris Heckman and Iris M. Williams, the photo illustration team included:
Suzanne M. Bourbonnais, David Finch, Sonja Hustad, Ruth M. Jones, Ben A. Kessler,
Grace P. Kneier, Jill A. Lee, Margaret-Jean Mannix and Madge Roach.

Loram's Historical Development:

A number of people worked to preserve Loram's history over the years.
Listed chronologically, they include: Ben A. Kessler, Madge Roach, P.G. Clarke, Mary Perks,
Madeline Barry, Roberta Ross, Maggie Wallis, Johanne Johanson, Jim Tan and Iris M. Williams.
With special thanks to the hundreds of Friends of the History Centre.

Computer Support:

Sathia M. Durai and Patricia E. Rollock.

Design and Production by:

Karo
With special thanks to Michael Dangelmaier, Mark Furlotte, Sandra Hamel and Max LaFontaine.

Printed by:

Sundog Printing Limited, Calgary, Alberta, Canada.
With special thanks to Steve Whitehall.

Loram Oral History Collection

*In 1982, Loram set out to capture and preserve an oral history collection
of some of the individuals important to the outfit. Over the years, first Mimi Real,
then Sharon Mercer, grew this collection to nearly 300 oral histories. Chris Heckman conducted an
additional 14 phone interviews. We wish to thank the following people for opening up their hearts,
their memories and their recollections of times past. Their stories are the soul of this book.*

Don Acres; Marilyn Acteson; Tom Adamcewicz; Bob Aitchison; Vince Allen; John Amundrud; Dale Anderson; J.S. Armstrong; Ron Banister; Bruce Basaraba; Thomas Bell; Harold Benson; Homer Bish; Bill Blackstock; Harvey Boles; Bill Bone; Harry Booth; Chuck Borsos; Bob Bowhay; Gordon Brown; Jack Bruce; Alf Buck; Ora Burggren; R.J. Burns; Mary Cahill; Bruce Campbell; Louis Carriere; Johnny and Louise Carroll; Bob and Melva Carter; George Chapel; Don Cherrey; Arthur Child; Paul Christensen; Rex Christensen; Perry Christian; Jim Christoff; P.G. Clarke; Darc¹ Clarkson; John Cleghorn; Ann Clipstone; Gordon Coates; Leah Collett; A.F. (Chip) Collins; Eric Connelly; Geoff Corry; Everett and Florence Costello; Bill Couch; Shelby Craig; Charlie Crawford; Norris (Buck) Crump; Alex Cummings; Ron Dalby; Thomas d'Aquino; A.M. (Sandy) Day; Joey Dinning; Garry Dirk; Tom Dobson; Chuck Doerr; Herb Donaldson; Gary Donnelly; Dallas Droppo; Harry Duckett; Andy Dudzinski; Earl Dunn; Merv (Red) Dutton; Maureen Eberts; George Eckenfelder; Les Elhatton; Ray, Marg and Norman Ellard; Golda Elliott; David Elton; Ernie and Bette Enarson; Caspar Feist; R.L. (Buz) Fenerty; Fred and Mary Fenwick; Lou and Marney Franco; Katie Fraser; Gordon Fryer; Ron Fyfe; Jack Gallagher; Larry Gano; Blondie Garbutt; Doug Gardiner; Don Getty; David Gjøsūnd; Peter Godsoe; George Goodine; Ron (Ben) Goodman; Lorne Gordon; Peter Gordon; Nony Grainger; Betty Gray; Dan Greger; Dan Hamilton; Marion Hanly; J.R. Hardie; Richard Haskayne; Archie Hawkes; Evelyn Hayward; Tom Henderson; Dick Hermann; Robert Hewitt; Blanche Hilborne; J.B. Hill; Bob Hodgins; Vera Holdsworth; Millard Holmgren; Elmer Holsteine; John Hooper; Al Horne; A.W. (Bert) Howard; Edna Hunt; Hanna Hunter; Sonja Hustad; Roy Inkster; Bill and Mary Jamieson; Sid Jaycock; Cap Jenish; Tim Jenish; John Jennings; Henning Jensen; Kenneth John; J. Robert Jones; Ruth Jones; Carl Kamm; Diane Keith; Wayne Kelly; Ben Kessler; Don Kingdon; David Kitchen; Del Koch; Walter Kosten; Bob and Alice Kramer; Fred Kuipers; Jim Lane; Dorothy Larson; Lenny Lawrence; Bill Lee; Jill Lee; Vic Lemecha; Fred and Olive Livingston; Peter Lougheed; Joe Luco; Larry Lunn; Johnny Lynch; Wally Lynd; Grant MacEwan; Corky Mack; Ernest Manning; Fred C. Mannix; Fred P. Mannix; Ron N. Mannix; George and Ruth Mannix; Elsie Marquess; Bob Marriott; Bernd Martens; Hugh Martin; Joe Mastracchio; Rob Matthews; Ron Mauch; Don Mawhinney; Robert Mawhinney; Roy McBride; Dixie McCall; David McClement; Cecil and Nellie McCormick; Rod McDaniel; Gus McEwan; Henry McKinnon; Syl McKinnon; Fred McNeil; Robert McNeill; Don Meads; Mike Mears; Ross Melrose; Bob Michaleski; Harold Milavsky; Earl Miller; Harold Millican; Don Minge; Brock Montgomery; David Morgan; John Morgan; Tom Morimoto; Lee Morrison; Art Mostowich; Lionel Narraway; Henry Neufeld; Michael Norris; Cres Oates; Titus Oates; Art O'Hanlon; Harry O'Hanlon; Hal O'Keefe; Hans Olesen; Mike Olsen; Bev Ostermann; Alf and Eva Ostgard; Frank and Bess O'Sullivan; Florence Pallcsen; Norman Pallesen; Kathy Parry; Frances Peace; Dave Penner; Dick and Mary Peppin; Jim Perkins; Mary Perks; Pete Peters; Reg Pinchbeck; Graham Pollock; John Poloway; Hugh Procter; Sextus Procter; Randy Provost; George Reid; Doris Reilly; Lorne Repka; Gerry Rinaldi; Matt Roach; Dil Robertson; John Rockingham; Al Ross; Bud Rowland; Jack Saker; Reg Samis; Bob and Florence Sanders; Jack Saucier; Gregg Sawatzky; Joe Scarbo; Josef Schachter; Mike Schoger; Edward Scobey; Paul Scott; Andy and Lou Seraphim; Glenn Shannon; Bill and Mary Sharon; Fred Sheffer; Phil Shirley; Igors Silgailis; Frank Smart; Frank Smith; Renie Spears; Anna Speers; Walter Sprague; Peggy Stack; Bill Stedman; Sam Steffen; Yvonne Stevens; Pansy Strange; Mac Summersgill; Vera Swanson; Peter Swityk; Charlie Thalheimer; L.A. (Chick) Thorssen; Howard Tidswell; Joe Tonelli; Bruce Tubbs; Peter Van Egmond; Ray and Christine Vennard; Lee Wagar; Ray Wahl; Gordon Walker; Neil and Margie Walsh; David G. Ward; Stan Waters; Jim Watkinson; Fred Webb; James and Rita Welch; John Wetsch; W.J. Weymark; Irvine Wiens; Charles and Hazel Wilbanks; Evelyn Wilkinson; Marsh Williams; Richard Wilsey; Luella Wilson; Paul Wilson; Art Wirth; Ron Wolfe; David Wood; R.L. (Woody) Wood; Glenn Woodford; Tom Wozny; Alf and Babe Wright; Newt Yeomans; Robert Young and Earl Zumwalt.

The illustrations in the book are listed by their page number, in italics, with the location on the page identified by a letter, A through F, left to right, top to bottom. Illustrations not identified are provided courtesy of the Loram Corporation History Centre. All others are used with the permission of the following:

Air Canada Archives *125A*
Alberta Government *273B, 264C*
All Sport/Tony Duffy *343D*
American Museum of Natural History
  18B #32950 photo by Dossetter, courtesy of Department of Library Services
Apple Computer Inc. *293A*
Arruza, Tony/Corbis *402B*
Baci/Corbis *430C*
Bank of Montreal Historical
  Art Collection *59D*
  Mechanization of the Lumber Industry by George Menendez Rae
Bartruff, Dave/Corbis *356C*
Bell Canada Historical Collection *21C*
Boulton, Dr. James J. *56D*
Braasch, Gary/Corbis *384C*
British Columbia Archives
  117D #C-07861; *210D* Call # I-26791
British Columbia Archives
  and Record Services *12C* A-00350;
  14C A-03787; *132C* Call # G-02845
Bryn, Colton;Assignments
  Photographers/Corbis *360C, 418C*
Bureau of Reclamation,
  U.S. Department of the Interior
  281A CN-1222-142-11784
Canada's Sports Hall of Fame
  *35C, 35D, 71B, 189E, 235A, 276C,
  316B, 342B*
Canadian Football Hall of Fame *151D*
Canadian Olympic Association *374C,
  394B, 414C, 417C, 395D* Ted Grant
Canadian Pacific Archives
  55C copyright NS.2053;
  55D copyright A.6199
Canadian Sports Images Department
  371E, 445C
Canadian War Museum *49D* 8432
  *Canadians Repairing a Track Under
  Shell Fire,* Innes Meo; *138C; 138D*
  199500-74-035
Canapress *229C* Ball; *234B; 274A;
  274B; 298B; 325A* Cooper; *316C;
  336C; 366C* Mitchell; *372C; 391B*
  Chiasson; *391C* Lamount; *394A* Clark;
  421B; 426C Hanson; *427D; 441A;
  442B; 442C; 443D; 444B; 446B;
  447B; 447C; 448C; 448D* Andino;
  449B Pool; *449C; 454C; 455D; 456C;*

456D Lauro; *457C; 458C* Jenkins;
  458D; 459B; 460B Applewhite; *460C*
Caterpillar Inc. Corporation Archives
  63B, 64B, 67A
CBC Design Library *170D*
  Robert Ragsdale
CBC Still Photo Collection *97B*
Chenet, Jacques M./Corbis *378C*
Chiquita Brands International *131C*
Communication Research Centre,
  Industry Canada *229B, 293C*
Comstock *372D* John Jacquemain
Conger, Dean/Corbis *298C*
Conway, W. Perry/Corbis *443C*
Cooke, Jerry/Corbis *239B*
© AFF / AFS Amsterdam –
  the Netherlands *130C*
Corbis *311B*
CP Rail Corporate Archives
  198A 13396; *251A* 13306; *442C*
de Mulder, Francoise/Corbis
  309C, 317C, 366B, 369B, 396A
Department of Energy, Mines and
  Resources, Ottawa, Canada *4C*
Department of Irish Folklore –
  University College Dublin *2A*
Doody, Norma J. *211C*
Dwayne Brown Studio Inc.
  *Opening Mannix family portrait,
  442A, 443A, 443B, 444A, 445A,
  446A, 447A*
Famous 5 Foundation *49B*
  "Women are Persons..."
  (statue maquette), Barbara Paterson
Fenwick, Fred and Mary
  149A, 199A, 203A
Folio Inc. *Opening image chapter 1*
  Michael Ventura; *1A* Everett C.
  Johnson; *4A* Richard Quataert;
  292C Michael Ventura; *308C* Walter
  Bibikon; *312B* Matthew McVay; *322B*
  Jeff Greenberg; *336B* Bruce Hoertel;
  341E Devon Jacklin; *354D* Bruce
  Hoertel; *360B* Jim Pickerell; *364B*
  Art Stein; *385C* Michael Patrick;
  407D Michael Patrick; *408B* Jeff
  Greenberg; *419C* Jim Pickerell;
  421C Everett C. Johnson
Franken, Owen/Corbis
  337D, 383A, 399B, 405C, 431C

Frederic Remington Art Museum,
  Ogdensburg, New York *4D*
"Galen Rowell/Mountain Light" *3A*
Garanger, Marc/Corbis *207C, 270B*
Garrett, John/Corbis *268D*
Georgia, Lowell/Corbis *323B*
Getty, Hulton/Tony Stone Images *4B*
Gipstein, Todd/Corbis *380C*
Glenbow Archives, Calgary, Alberta,
  Canada *10C* NA-1406-58; *11D*
  NA-293-2; *13A* NA-1847-5; *15A*
  NA-1406-20; *15B* NA-1406-69; *16A*
  NA-5201-1; *16D* NA-2426-11; *17B*
  NA-23-3; *17C* NA-249-27; *17D*
  NA-1406-133; *18A* NA-550-11;
  19A NA-1406-19; *20A* NA-2928-3
  (detail of); *23B* NA-235-2a; *25A*
  NA-1406-33; *26C* NA-2450-1; *27C*
  NA-428-1; *29A* NA-3544-28; *29B*
  NA-1241-10; *29C* NA-2883-33; *30C*
  NA-1702-7; *31A* NA-1375-3; *32D*
  NA-1494-11; *33D* NA-3396-2; *34A*
  NA-218-2; *34C* NA-659-100; *34D*
  NA-3437-5; *36C* NA-303-20; *36D*
  NA-548-2; *36E* NA-86-17; *36F*
  NA-789-21; *37C* NA-1529-10; *39B*
  NA-5315-1; *39C* ND-3-2207; *41B*
  NA-407-10; *41C* NA-2685-101; *42A*
  NA-3641-1; *43C* NA-240-1; *45C*
  NA-698-3; *45D* NA-2156-1; *46A*
  NA-789-161; *46B* NA-952-2; *46C*
  NA-407-14; *47C* NA-4927-1; *48B*
  NA-2144-4; *48A* M2389 f.96; *48C*
  NA-1639-1; *50B* NA-604-1A; *50C*
  NA-1604-30; *51B* NA-520-1; *51C*
  NA-1111-13; *52* NA-748-36; *57A*
  NA-3182-17; *57B* NA-2575-34; *60A*
  M2389 f.96; *60D* NA-5200-136; *61B*
  NA-5200-88; *61E* NA-1004-24; *62D*
  NA-2365-33; *64D* NA-4714-1; *68C*
  ND-8-445; *68D* NA-781-2; *71A*
  NA-1258-22; *73B* NA-2885-2; *73C*
  NA-1258-79; *74A* NA-1831-1; *76C*
  NA-439-5; *79A* NA-1538-4; *81B*
  NA-2597-59; *81C* NA-1987-1; *83C*
  NA-4179-15; *90D* NC-1-1170(d); *91B*
  NA-2771-2; *93B* NA-2335-3; *96B* NA-2335-3;
  96C NA-2800-12; *97C* NA-4357-1;
  103C NA-4868-211; *106A* NA-2864-
  3431-E; *106B* NA-3965-15; *107A*

NA-1623-2; *107D* NA-2362-4; *108D*
  NA-3277-74; *108D;* *110D* NA-4823-1;
  113D NA-2624-3; *119C; 119D*
  NA-1796-27; *122C* NA-3884-14;
  143B NA-1241-59; *144C* NA-5200-3;
  145C NA-789-80; *146A* NA-5124-22;
  150D NA-2389-1; *164D* NA-3164-391;
  177C NA-1491-2; *208C* NA-5178-1;
  266D NA-4141-2
Glenbow Collection, Calgary, Alberta,
  Canada *2C Ships in Arctic-IV,* Peter
  Rindisbacher; *10B Canoes in a Fog, Lake
  Superior,* Frances Anne Hopkins 55.8.1;
  21D Full Dress Uniform N.W.M.P.
  P-4239-63; *22A* Sword and Scabbard
  P-4239-106; *22B* Memorabilia of
  Lord and Lady Wolseley P-4239-141;
  *26B Near Fort Calgary Looking Towards
  the Rocky Mountains,* Marquis of Lorne;
  28D Buffalo Repose, Paul Kane;
  58B The Poker Players, Emil Janel
Glenbow Library, Calgary, Alberta,
  Canada *2B* British North America
  Map, G3300, 1837, A779; *16B*
  Palliser Expedition Map (detail of),
  G3466, S12, 1865, P168, 1984; *44C;
  47D; 58D; 88D; 93B; 108D; 119C;
  128D; 130D; 139D*
Goldsmith, Lynn/Corbis *349B*
Graetz Bros. Ltd. Royal Bank Archives
  180A
Hockey Hall of Fame *31B*
  Doug MacLellan; *135E; 189C; 233B;
  291* Graphic Artists
Holmes, Robert/Corbis *141B*
Houser, Dave G./Corbis *433B*
Hudson's Bay Company Archives,
  Public Archives of Manitoba *80C*
Hulton-Deutsch/Corbis *53A, 202E, 212C,
  219C, 247E, 261C, 270D, 285B, 328C*
Image Communications, F. Scott Grant
  446C
Intel Corporation *285C*
IOC/Olympic Museum Collections *32C*
Irish Tourist Board *5B, 7D*
Jennings, John *272A*
Jimmy Carter Presidential
  Library/Corbis *330D*
John Deere Corporate Archives *22C*
Kennan Ward Photography/Corbis *411B*